Dear West Customer:

West Academic Publishing has changed the look of its American Casebook Series®.

In keeping with our efforts to promote sustainability, we have replaced our former covers with book covers that are more environmentally friendly. Our casebooks will now be covered in a 100% renewable natural fiber. In addition, we have migrated to an ink supplier that favors vegetable-based materials, such as soy.

Using soy inks and natural fibers to print our textbooks reduces VOC emissions. Moreover, our primary paper supplier is certified by the Forest Stewardship Council, which is testament to our commitment to conservation and responsible business management.

The new cover design has migrated from the long-standing brown cover to a contemporary charcoal fabric cover with silver-stamped lettering and black accents. Please know that inside the cover, our books continue to provide the same trusted content that you've come to expect from West.

We've retained the ample margins that you have told us you appreciate in our texts while moving to a new, larger font, improving readability. We hope that you will find these books a pleasing addition to your bookshelf.

Another visible change is that you will no longer see the brand name Thomson West on our print products. With the recent merger of Thomson and Reuters, I am pleased to announce that books published under the West Academic Publishing imprint will once again display the West brand.

It will likely be several years before all of our casebooks are published with the new cover and interior design. We ask for your patience as the new covers are rolled out on new and revised books knowing that behind both the new and old covers, you will find the finest in legal education materials for teaching and learning.

Thank you for your continued patronage of the West brand, which is both rooted in history and forward looking towards future innovations in legal education. We invite you to be a part of our next evolution.

Best regards,

Heidi M. Hellekson
Publisher, West Academic Publishing

ELECTRONIC DISCOVERY AND DIGITAL EVIDENCE

CASES AND MATERIALS

■ ■ ■

By

Shira A. Scheindlin
United States District Judge
Southern District of New York

Daniel J. Capra
Philip Reed Professor of Law
Fordham Law School

The Sedona Conference®

With an Introduction by Professor Richard L. Marcus

AMERICAN CASEBOOK SERIES®

WEST®

Mat #40736929

© 2009 Thomson/Reuters

    610 Opperman Drive
    St. Paul, MN 55123
    1–800–328–9352

Printed in the United States of America

ISBN: 978-0-314-19131-1

TEXT IS PRINTED ON 10% POST CONSUMER RECYCLED PAPER

PREFACE

Civil litigation is primarily about discovery practice. The information that parties obtain during discovery from each other or from third parties will affect whether a case is tried, settled, or resolved by motion. Today, the vast majority of records are created and maintained electronically. Thus, "paper" discovery is a thing of the past and "e-discovery" is the present and the future. The creation and storage of electronic records, and the almost incomprehensible volume of such records, create new challenges regarding preservation and production. By the same token, the admissibility of electronic records raise new questions regarding authenticity and hearsay. The time is therefore ripe to introduce a course on electronic discovery and digital evidence into the law school curriculum. The best way to do that is to write a comprehensive and challenging casebook that will help students (and their professors) address the many intriguing issues that are arising in this critical and developing area of law.

To accomplish this goal the co-authors of this book worked together to present the most interesting cases, together with commentary, addressing discovery and evidentiary issues, in the order in which they arise in the course of litigation.[1] "We owe our gratitude to Professor Rick Marcus, who gives this book a perfect send-off: a brilliant introduction that stands on its own as an important work of scholarship." To set the stage, we begin with a chapter (I) on the explosion of electronic information and how it is stored and retrieved. We turn then to a chapter (II) on the preservation of electronic information covering such questions as when the duty to preserve attaches and what records must be preserved. We move on to a chapter (III) covering the required meeting between counsel at the outset of litigation, when counsel must address issues surrounding the discovery of electronic information. When the discovery process gets into full swing the parties must collect all relevant and responsive data (Chapter IV), produce the relevant information after conducting a privilege review (Chapter V), and if the parties fail to produce relevant information the court must consider the imposition of sanctions based on the spoliation of evidence (Chapter VI). How attorneys, both in-house and outside counsel, should meet their obligations in a professional and ethical manner is the subject of the

---

1. To make the cases easier to read, we have generally deleted the internal citations and footnotes. When we leave internal citations and footnotes in the cases, we do so in the belief that they make a specific contribution to the understanding of the case. When we retain a footnote in a case, we retain its original number.

next chapter (Chapter VII). When producing the equivalent of millions of documents, attorneys must carefully safeguard the client's privileges and protections (Chapter VIII). Finally, at the end of the discovery process, there will be a motion or a trial and evidentiary issues surrounding the electronic records must be confronted (Chapter IX).

There are three co-authors to this book. Judge Shira A. Scheindlin was a member of the Advisory Committee on Civil Rules and a member of the Discovery Subcommittee that drafted the 2006 amendments addressing the discovery of electronically stored information. She is also the author of the landmark *Zubulake* opinions. Professor Daniel Capra of Fordham Law School is the Reporter to the Advisory Committee on Evidence Rules and the principal draftsman of Rule 502 on waiver of privilege. Finally, The Sedona Conference® ("Sedona") has been the leading voice of the legal profession in addressing all of the concerns surrounding electronic discovery. Sedona has issued the most oft-cited publications in this area including the "The Sedona Principles: Best Practices Recommendations & Principles for Addressing Electronic Document Production" and "The Sedona Conference Guidelines for Managing Information and Records in the Electronic Age." "The Sedona Guidelines: Best Practice Guidelines & Commentary for Managing Information and Records in the Electronic Age." Because Sedona is made up of various sectors of the bench, bar, academy and private industry, we take this opportunity to thank those individual members of Sedona who contributed to the preparation of this casebook. Most importantly, we wish to give special thanks to Kenneth J. Withers, Sedona's Director of Judicial Education and Content, who is the personification of The Sedona Conference®, and one of the most knowledgeable people in the world on the topic of e-discovery. Finally, we wish to thank Rachel Spector and Arie Rubenstein, who served as law clerks to the Hon. Shira Scheindlin, as well as Ryan Sklar, David Snyder, Daniel Richards, and Nicholas Smith, law students at Fordham Law School who served as research assistants to Professor Daniel Capra, for their help in finalizing this manuscript.

And to the individual contributors, who assisted in the preparation of the following chapters we extend our deepest thanks: Chapter I: Jason R. Baron and John H. Jessen; Chapter II: Adam Cohen, William P. Butterfield, Jason R. Baron, William F. Hamilton, John H. Jessen, and Laura E. Ellsworth; Chapter III: Ariana J. Tadler; Chapter IV: William F. Hamilton; Chapter V: Ariana J. Tadler, Jason R. Baron, John H. Jessen, Scott A. Carlson, Jay E. Grenig, William F. Hamilton, William P. Butterfield, and M. James Daley; Chapter VI: Paul E. Burns, Adam Cohen, Ronald J. Hedges, and Jay E. Grenig; Chapter VII: Kevin F. Brady, Robert Levy, Ariana J. Tadler, and Laura E. Ellsworth.

We hope that the students and professors who use this casebook will find it useful, versatile, and well organized. It has been our privilege and pleasure to create what we believe is the first comprehensive casebook in this new and exciting area of the law.

SHIRA A. SCHEINDLIN
NEW YORK, N.Y.

DANIEL J. CAPRA
NEW YORK, N.Y.

THE SEDONA CONFERENCE®
    BY: KENNETH J. WITHERS
PHOENIX, ARIZONA

December 2008

*

Summary of Contents

*

TABLE OF CONTENTS

TABLE OF CASES

The principal cases are in bold type. Cases cited or discussed in the text
are roman type. References are to pages. Cases cited in principal
cases and within other quoted materials are not included.

*

TABLE OF STATUTES

*

ELECTRONIC DISCOVERY AND DIGITAL EVIDENCE

CASES AND MATERIALS

*

INTRODUCTION

THE 2006 AMENDMENTS TO THE FEDERAL RULES OF CIVIL PROCEDURE GOVERNING DISCOVERY OF ELECTRONICALLY STORED INFORMATION: FITTING ELECTRONIC DISCOVERY INTO THE OVERALL DISCOVERY MIX

Richard L. Marcus
Horace O. Coil ('57) Chair in Litigation
University of California, Hastings College of the Law
Special Reporter, Advisory Committee on Civil Rules[1]

Electronic discovery is the hottest topic in litigation today. Some suggest that it might be "considered a specialized substantive expertise in the same vein as, for example, patent law," and argue that mishandling such discovery could become a fertile source of malpractice claims.[2] Partly to address such concerns, an electronic discovery industry has emerged that is anticipated to generate over four billion dollars in revenues in 2009. Within law firms, the advent of electronic discovery has prompted the creation of special departments and staff attorney positions to handle the activity. The costs of this form of discovery have mounted quickly; some lawyers now find that the cost of preparing a privilege log identifying electronically stored information ("ESI") withheld on grounds of privilege routinely exceeds one million dollars. Given the rising centrality of electronic discovery to litigation, it is understandable that you have chosen to study the topics covered in this book. This Introduction sets the scene for what follows.

Although electronic discovery emerged as central only in the 21st century, American discovery has been a source of controversy for decades. Beginning in the mid 1970s, Federal Rule changes sought to contain and constrain American discovery. As electronic discovery appeared, a crucial question was whether additional rule changes were needed to handle its challenges. The eventual conclusion was that rule changes were needed, but it is important to appreciate from the outset

---

1. As Special Reporter to the Advisory Committee, I was a primary drafter of the 2006 amendments to the Federal Rules to deal with the challenges of electronic discovery. In this Introduction, I speak only for myself and not for the Committee or anyone else.

2. Janet H. Kwuon & Karen Wan, *High Stakes for Missteps in EDD*, N.J. L.J., Dec. 31, 2007, at E2.

how those changes fit into the broader framework developed for paper discovery. I begin, therefore, with those background developments.

A. The Discovery "Revolution"

American discovery has long been distinctive. For example, in the 1870s American discovery efforts provoked German protests, and various countries have more recently adopted "blocking" statutes designed to prevent American discovery on their shores.[3] Until the 1930s, however, discovery was available in American courts only on a spotty basis. As late as 1911, for example, the Supreme Court inveighed against a "fishing bill" by which a party sought "to pry into the case of his adversary to learn its strength or weakness."[4]

The adoption of the Federal Rules in 1938 produced a revolution because it vastly expanded discovery:

> If one adds up all of the types of discovery permitted in individual state courts, one finds some precursors to what later became discovery under the Federal Rules, but ... no one state allowed the total panoply of devices. Moreover, the Federal Rules, as they became law in 1938, eliminated features of discovery that in some states had curtailed the scope of discovery and the breadth of its use.[5]

And the courts rapidly came to favor the broad discovery. The Supreme Court—which had denounced "fishing expeditions" in 1911—changed its tune by 1947: "No longer can the time-honored cry of 'fishing expedition' serve to preclude a party from inquiring into the facts underlying his opponent's case. Mutual knowledge of all the relevant facts gathered by both parties is essential to proper litigation."[6]

The rulemakers contributed further to expanding discovery. The 1938 rules had continued some constraints on discovery. In 1946, Rule 26(b)(1) was amended to make clear that information need not be admissible to be discoverable, and Rule 34(a) was amended to clarify that there was no need to specify each document that was sought; categorical requests were valid. In the 1960s, the Civil Rules Advisory Committee conducted a broad empirical study of discovery that led to the conclusion that "[d]iscovery has become an integral part of litigation."[7] On the strength of this conclusion, rule amendments that became effective in 1970 removed some remaining constraints. Most significantly, Rule 34 was amended so that a prior judicial order based on a showing of good cause was no longer needed for a document request; after that, document requests could be made without numerical limitations or prior judicial scrutiny. With the 1970 amendments, American discovery reached its high water mark.

---

3. Gary Born, *International Civil Litigation in United States Courts* 849, 856–71 (3d ed. 1996).

4. *Carpenter v. Winn*, 221 U.S. 533, 540 (1911).

5. Stephen N. Subrin, *Fishing Expeditions Allowed: The Historical Background of the 1938 Federal Discovery Rules*, 39 B.C. L. Rev. 691, 719 (1998).

6. *Hickman v. Taylor*, 329 U.S. 495, 507 (1947).

7. William A. Glaser, *Pretrial Discovery and the Adversary System* 51 (1968).

At this point, American discovery also took its place as a feature of the "litigation boom" that many decried. In part, this controversy resulted from the American reliance on private enforcement of legal norms, which prompted resistance in some quarters. Discovery was central to this growth. As a leading federal judge put it:

> Congress has elected to use the private suit, private attorney-general as an enforcing mechanism for the antitrust laws, the securities laws, environmental laws, civil rights and more. In the main, the plaintiff in these suits must discover his evidence from the defendant. Calibration of discovery is calibration of the level of enforcement of the social policy set by Congress.[8]

Some said that broad discovery itself prompted expansion in several of these substantive areas.[9] "Broad discovery is thus not a mere procedural rule. Rather it has become, at least for our era, a procedural institution perhaps of virtually constitutional foundation."[10] Those who deal with discovery—including electronic discovery—must have this background in mind.

B. The Containment Effort: Rule Amendments to Constrain Overbroad Discovery

Nonetheless, growing clamor about the burdens and intrusiveness of discovery fueled efforts to constrain it. Beginning in the 1970s, many strong voices—some, perhaps, motivated by opposition to private enforcement of public law—urged that American discovery produced too much cost and not enough benefit.[11] Discovery remained a central feature of the Advisory Committee's agenda throughout the last quarter of the 20th century. The importance of this history is that this clamor resulted in adoption of a variety of rule changes that are relevant to the handling of electronic discovery.[12] The recent rule changes for electronic discovery were designed to fit within this broader framework.

One key point to appreciate about this clamor from the 1970s to the 1990s is that it resembled much of the current clamor about electronic discovery, particularly in relation to paper discovery under Rule 34. Thus, lawyers that frequently had to respond to discovery requests (often representing defendants) asserted that their opponents were abusing discovery for tactical purposes. They said that dragnet discovery requests produced huge response costs but little or no actual evidence of

---

8. Patrick Higginbotham, *Foreword*, 49 Ala. L. Rev. 1, 4–5 (1997).

9. *See* Jack H. Friedenthal, *A Divided Supreme Court Adopts Discovery Amendments to the Federal Rules of Civil Procedure*, 69 Cal. L. Rev. 806, 818 (1981) (arguing that discovery itself had fueled growth in the substantive law of products liability, employment discrimination, and consumer protection).

10. Geoffrey C. Hazard, *From Whom No Secrets Are Hid*, 76 Tex. L. Rev. 1665, 1694 (1998).

11. For a contemporary catalogue of these objections, see *Addresses Delivered at the National Conference on the Causes of Popular Dissatisfaction with the Administration of Justice* (Apr. 7–9, 1976), 70 F.R.D. 79–246; *Proceedings of the National Conference on Discovery Reform*, 3 Rev. Litig. 1–221 (1982).

12. For a discussion of many of these amendments, see Richard L. Marcus, *Discovery Containment Redux*, 39 B.C. L. Rev. 747 (1998).

importance; overbroad discovery could become a club to extract nuisance settlements. Lawyers that frequently sought information through discovery (often representing plaintiffs) reported that they had to make broad requests to obtain the information they really needed, and that responding parties often resisted proper discovery unjustifiably and/or resorted to "dump truck" practices, delivering enormous quantities of worthless material through which they had to sift to find the important information.

The quarter century of Federal Rules discovery reform did not change the basic American commitment to access to necessary information, but it did produce rule amendments that went into effect in 1980, 1983, 1993, and 2000. Among these many amendments,[13] several stand out as important to the issues covered in this book:

Conference regarding discovery plan and judicial review of the plan: Rule 26(f) was added in 1993 to require the parties to confer before formal discovery began to develop a discovery plan, and to deliver that plan to the judge before the Rule 16(b) scheduling order was entered. At the time of their conference or soon thereafter, under Rule 26(a)(1) the parties are to exchange basic information about the witnesses and documents they may rely upon in support of their respective cases. These provisions in part build upon the growing commitment of the federal judiciary to manage and supervise the cases before them.[14] As part of that managerial orientation, judges came to expect lawyers to cooperate and act in a more forthcoming way.[15] This orientation has become crucial to handling electronic discovery. (See *infra* Chapters III and VII.B.)

Proportionality in discovery: One of the recurrent concerns about paper discovery was that extremely broad discovery requests were easy to draft, extremely burdensome to satisfy, and often produced little or nothing of importance to the case. In 1983, the "proportionality" provisions now contained in Rule 26(b)(2)(C) were added to address these concerns. According to the Advisory Committee's Reporter at the time, the addition of the proportionality provisions represented a "180 degree shift" in attitude toward overbroad discovery.[16] But a decade later, it was reported that the addition of these provisions "seems to have created only a ripple in the caselaw."[17] With the emergence of

---

13. Others included a slight modification of the scope of discovery under Rule 26(b)(1); setting numerical limits on interrogatories and depositions; setting a time limit on depositions; and adding Rule 26(a)(1) requirements of disclosure without the need for a formal discovery request.

14. *See* Richard L. Marcus, *Reining in the American Lawyer: The New Role of American Judges*, 27 Hast. Int'l & Compar. L. Rev. 3 (2003); Judith Resnik, *Managerial Judges*, 96 Harv. L. Rev. 374 (1982).

15. *See generally* Robert Peckham, *The Federal Judge as Case Manager: The New Role in Guiding a Case from Filing to Disposition*, 69 Cal. L. Rev. 770 (1981) (describing the expectations of the judge).

16. Arthur R. Miller, *The August 1983 Amendments to the Federal Rules of Civil Procedure: Promoting Effective Case Management and Lawyer Responsibility*, Federal Judicial Center, 32–33 (1984).

17. 8 Charles A. Wright, Arthur R. Miller & Richard L. Marcus, *Federal Practice & Procedure* § 2008.1 at 121 (2d ed. 1994).

electronic discovery, this proportionality provision may gain added importance. (See *infra* Chapter V.H.)

Certification of compliance with discovery obligations: In 1983, Rule 26(g) was added, directing that an attorney signing a discovery request or response thereby certified that it was proper and justified under the rules. This certification requirement was adopted at the same time Rule 11's certification requirements were strengthened, and the drafters thought that the changes to Rule 26 would have equal importance. But as any first-year civil procedure student learns, the two provisions did not initially pack a similar wallop. The 1983 amendments to Rule 11 caused widespread effects and concern, eventually leading to amendments in 1993 to reformulate that certification requirement. The Rule 26(g) provisions, in contrast, attracted little attention until the advent of electronic discovery, which heightened attention to the responsibilities of counsel. (See *infra* Chapters II.B, IV.B, VI.E and VII.A.)

Supplementation of disclosures and discovery responses, and sanctions including exclusion of materials not disclosed: Until 1993, Rule 26(e) was fairly lax regarding the need to supplement or correct incomplete or incorrect discovery responses. Now it is quite demanding. Rule 26(e)(1)(A) requires timely supplementation whenever a discovery response or disclosure "is incomplete or incorrect." Rule 37(c)(1) directs that a party may not use any information not provided initially or by supplementation, creating a relatively routine bar to presentation of evidence unless it is promptly revealed and raising the possibility of further sanctions.

C. The Rulemaking Response to Electronic Discovery

In a sense, electronic discovery came to the rule amendment process late in the game. To be sure, something of the sort had been there for some time. The far-sighted rulemakers of the 1960s foresaw the need to deal with discovery of computerized materials, and Rule 34 was amended then to permit discovery of "data compilations from which information can be obtained." In 1985, a district judge wrote that "[c]omputers have become so commonplace that most court battles now involve discovery of some type of computer-stored information."[18] The third edition of the Manual for Complex Litigation, in 1995, said that "[c]omputerized data have become commonplace in litigation."[19]

But what we now know as electronic discovery really did not emerge until later. In 1996, the Advisory Committee embarked on its Discovery Project, which was designed to survey the entire array of discovery issues and determine whether further rule revisions were needed to control discovery. Many lawyers told the Committee that it was "fighting the last war" because the real issues regarding discovery had to do with e-mail and the like. The headlines soon confirmed these reports; the government's antitrust suit against Microsoft, featuring Bill

---

18. *Bills v. Kennecott Corp.*, 108 F.R.D. 459, 462 (D. Utah 1985).

19. *Manual for Complex Litigation (Third)* § 21.446 (1995).

Gates' e-mail statements, was "the first major E-mail trial."[20] Since then we have become familiar with the idea that "[c]orporate investigations used to mean following the paper trail, but these days many follow an electronic one."[21] Discovery seeking such materials was clearly a growing field.

The problems generated by electronic discovery sounded very familiar, however—volume, burden, and intrusiveness. By the time electronic discovery emerged, the Advisory Committee had spent two decades dealing with these very problems and developed a variety of rule amendments to address them. Moreover, it seemed that—in contrast to paper discovery—using computers might actually reduce the burden of responding to discovery. In 1978, the Supreme Court had recognized that

> although it may be expensive to retrieve information stored in computers when no program yet exists for the particular job, there is no reason to think that the same information could be extracted any less expensively if the records were kept in less modern forms. Indeed, one would expect the reverse to be true, for otherwise computers would not have gained such widespread use in the storing and handling of information.[22]

By the mid 1990s, others had recognized that the use of computers might make discovery manageable where it would have been too burdensome with paper materials.[23] And creating a new set of rules due to a technological development seemed dubious; although the photocopier dramatically increased the amount of material subject to discovery no rule changes were made as a result.

With the passage of time, however, it became clear that electronic discovery involved issues not presented by paper discovery that justified attention in the rules. A detailed description of the magnitude and nature of ESI is found in Chapter I. But the nature of those distinctive issues serves as the backdrop for a number of specific topics addressed by rule amendment in 2006.[24]

Recognizing "ESI" as a separate object of discovery: Rule 34(a)(1)(A) now confirms that a party may seek discovery of documents or ESI. As the Committee Note emphasizes, this term is defined broadly to encompass all sorts of information stored in any medium including future developments in computer technology. The Rule also specifically authorizes testing or sampling of such materials. As the Committee Note recog-

20.   Steve Lohr, *Antitrust Case Is Highlighting Role of E-mail*, N.Y. Times, Nov. 2, 1998, at C1.

21.   Ellen Byron, *Computer Forensics Sleuths Help Find Fraud*, Wall St. J., Mar. 18, 2003, at B1.

22.   *Oppenheimer Fund, Inc. v. Sanders*, 437 U.S. 340, 362 (1978).

23.   *See* William W. Schwarzer *et al.*, *Civil Discovery and Mandatory Disclosure: A Guide to Effective Practice* I–23 (2d ed. 1994) (noting that "[d]iscovery that otherwise might be impermissibly burdensome, such as requiring detailed identification of all known documents referring to relevant issues, may not be burdensome if the computerized system is able to generate the identifications.").

24.   For further discussion of these issues, see Richard L. Marcus, *E-Discovery and Beyond: Toward Brave New World or 1984?*, 236 F.R.D. 598, 610–17 (2006).

nizes, this additional opportunity may be important for electronic discovery, but it is "not meant to create a routine right of direct access to a party's electronic information system," and therefore "[c]ourts should guard against undue intrusiveness resulting from inspecting or testing such systems." Past experience showed that direct access to another party's computer system could do harm,[25] and the proper handling of such access presents challenges. (See *infra* Chapter V.E.)

Directing the parties to discuss issues relating to electronic discovery: A recurrent phenomenon in the early days of electronic discovery seemed to be that problems arose well into the litigation because the parties had not thought about these issues in advance. One sort of problem could arise when production of ESI proceeded before the parties had discussed the format to be used; the receiving party might report that it was unable to use what it got, while the producing party might object to providing the information in a substitute format. Another sort of problem involved loss of ESI that was available when the suit was filed but was not preserved.[26] Rule 26(f) addresses these issues by directing that during their initial conference the parties discuss preservation of discoverable evidence (of whatever sort) and discuss any issues about electronic discovery, including specifically the form for production of ESI.

Although preservation and form of production are required topics of the Rule 26(f) conference, it is expected that a range of other issues will be discussed. As you cover the topics in this book, reflect on how counsel should approach them in the discovery conference. In order to discuss such issues intelligently, as the Committee Note recognizes, counsel will often need to become well acquainted with the client's electronic information systems, for only with that knowledge can counsel make meaningful commitments. The parties are to report to the court on their discovery plan, and Rule 16(b)(3)(B)(iii) provides for including provisions regarding electronic discovery in the court's scheduling order. Courts engaged in this judicial management activity are likely to expect counsel to be cooperative in developing the electronic discovery plan, and to regard the provisions of the resulting order as binding. This means that much is at stake for lawyers approaching this conference. Those who make commitments they cannot meet will likely suffer later on. (See *infra* Chapter III.)

Addressing form of production: Form of production is normally not an issue with paper information, but with ESI there is a range of possible forms for production, as anyone who has ever received an electronic file that cannot be opened understands. Obviously, a file that won't open is not usable. And equally obviously, different kinds of ESI come in

---

25. *See, e.g., Gates Rubber Co. v. Bando Chem. Indus.*, 167 F.R.D. 90, 111–12 (D. Colo. 1996) (discovering party's "expert" loaded software onto the responding party's drives that overwrote the existing data).

26. *See, e.g., GTFM, Inc. v. Wal–Mart Stores, Inc.*, No. 98 Civ. 7724, 2000 WL 335558 (S.D.N.Y. Mar. 30, 2000) (deposition of an IT representative of defendant revealed that information defendant had initially failed to produce during discovery on the ground it no longer existed had existed at the time of the discovery but had been deleted since then).

different forms—a word processing file and a video can't easily be compared. The problems are easy to imagine. (See *infra* Chapter V.A.)

The problems are not easy to solve in a global way by rulemaking. A rule could direct that a specific form of production be used, but that would not work for all kinds of ESI, and would likely become outdated rapidly given the evolution of technology. The rules therefore don't attempt to provide a specific template for litigants, but to provide a process for tailoring the form of production to the given case. Form of production is one of those things that the parties should discuss during their Rule 26(f) conference, and it may be possible then to adopt a protocol for the case and include that protocol in the court's Rule 16(b) order. Beyond that, they can exchange information during that conference that would assist them in making sensible decisions about form of production later on. The spirit of reasonable cooperation should prevail.

The same attitude explains Rule 34's provisions on form of production. Rule 34(b)(1)(C) permits the party requesting discovery to specify the form for production. If the requesting party does so, the responding party may object under Rule 34(b)(2)(D). If the requesting party does not specify a form, under Rule 34(b)(2)(E)(ii) the responding party must produce in a form in which the information is ordinarily maintained or in a reasonably usable form. The possible use of a form in which the information is ordinarily maintained is often said to refer to "native format." A given party might have the same information in more than one native format; choice of any one of those formats would satisfy the Rule. In any event, the responding party need not produce the ESI in more than one form providing that it gave sufficient notice of the form it intended to use.[27]

One consideration in choosing a form of production is whether it is important to obtain "metadata" or "embedded data." These terms will be defined later in this book (see Chapter V.D); the point here is that there is no transcendental answer to this question. In many cases neither metadata nor embedded data may matter. Indeed, sometimes the parties may prefer to have ESI produced in paper. But in other cases it is important that the information be delivered in a form that permits the requesting party to analyze or otherwise manipulate it. For this purpose some electronic formats—possibly including TIFF or PDF—may not suffice.

Rather than prescribe a specific form, the Rules' goal is to provide a process that minimizes disputes about form. The worst sort of dispute arises when production has already occurred and the receiving party says that the form used does not work but the producing party responds "That's too bad, but you've had your one chance and I won't give the

---

27. As noted below, the Rule also requires the producing party to notify its adversary as to what form it will use before production. The Committee Note observes: "A party that responds to a discovery request by simply producing electronically stored information in a form of its choice, without identifying that form in advance of the production . . . runs a risk that the requesting party can show that the produced form is not reasonably usable and that it is entitled to production of some or all of the information in an additional form."

material to you in another form." To guard against this eventuality, Rule 34(b)(2)(D) directs that—whether or not the request specified a form for production—the responding party must state the form it intends to use before it produces the information. The goal throughout is to identify and crystalize the dispute before the costs of solving it spiral out of control. Ultimately, if the parties cannot agree on form the court must decide what form should be used.

The Rules don't tell the judge how to choose a form when the parties cannot agree. Presumably the judge is not limited to the forms preferred by the parties. (The judge's latitude might sometimes provide the parties with an incentive to agree on a form.) One concern would focus on how the requesting party intends to use the information it obtains. Another might focus on how the producing party uses the information in its business; if it regularly provides information in a given form to others in that business it may be difficult to refuse to provide information in that form through discovery.[28]

Problems of accessibility: Almost by definition, discovery requests seek to compel a party to retrieve and assemble materials that it would not otherwise retrieve and assemble. With paper materials, that gathering process can be very cumbersome. For decades, parties have dealt with this problem by rough-and-ready "proportionality" measures like refusing to search all offices worldwide when relatively complete documentation should be located in certain offices.

With ESI, these accessibility problems can be compounded. This information is so portable that it may be located in myriad places including such diverse items as hand-held devices and home computers of employees. Some may be on hard drives in space not used for purposes listed on the directory. The "delete" key does not delete information, but only releases the space for further use; until that space is overwritten the information remains where it was, albeit often in fragmentary form and no longer easy to locate. Another source of information is the collection of "backup tapes" that almost every organization acquires as part of its disaster-recovery system. These records are made on a regular basis and include an undifferentiated collection of all

---

28. The Freedom of Information Act provides an analogy. Its regulations regarding form for production by governmental agencies call for a "business as usual" attitude focusing on what format the agency uses in its ordinary business activities. Notwithstanding, the Department of Defense once refused to provide materials in a "zip" drive format in response to an FOIA request despite evidence that it would provide information in zip format to its contractors. The Department argued that the "business as usual" approach should be limited to its usual practice in responding to FOIA requests. In *TPS, Inc. v. United States Department of Defense*, 330 F.3d 1191, 1195 (9th Cir. 2003), the court rejected this argument:

> The language of the FOIA does not support a reading that distinguishes between "business as usual" for FOIA requests and "business as usual" for activities that are part of the agency's business.... When an agency already creates or converts documents in a certain format—be it for FOIA requestors, under a contract, or in the ordinary course of business—requiring that it provide documents in that format to others does not impose an unnecessarily harsh burden.

Similarly with form of production in electronic discovery, one presumably should not accept the argument that the only referent is what form the party ordinarily uses to respond to discovery. Of course, there may be confidentiality issues that affect the analogy, but this case does provide a starting point.

data on the captured system at the moment the backup was made. They may be usable only after being "restored," a process that can be costly and take considerable time. Finally, many organizations continue to possess data that were generated by computer systems they no longer use, often called "legacy data." The organizations may have no present way to access the data.

Early on, it appeared that nobody really expected that the initial response to a discovery request would include searching out or unearthing all these kinds of data. The question is now addressed in Rule 26(b)(2)(B), which builds on the proportionality provisions already in the rules and specifies that a party need not produce information from "sources" it identifies as "not reasonably accessible." (See *infra* Chapter V.G.) One premise of this exemption from initial production of responsive data is that "accessible" data will be voluminous and sufficient; ordinarily one would press for more only after first examining what has been produced. But if a party seeking discovery presses for more, the burden remains on the producing party to show that the sources not searched are genuinely not reasonably accessible, and it must do so in terms of the "undue burden or cost" that gathering the data would entail in comparison to its likely value to the litigation. One method for determining whether that cost is undue is sampling. (See *infra* Chapter V.C.) Even if the producing party shows that the sources are not reasonably accessible, the court may order production for good cause, but it may also shift some or all of the cost of retrieving the data to the party insisting that it be retrieved. (See *infra* Chapters V.G and H.)

Preservation and sanctions: As with the problem of form of production, Rule 26(f) now directs the parties to confer at the outset about preserving all types of discoverable information, including ESI. This will hopefully often yield agreements about what should be preserved, a great improvement over a dispute years after the litigation began about things that were not preserved. The value of such agreements is one reason why lawyers must become acquainted with their clients' computer systems; only an informed lawyer can negotiate an appropriate agreement. In the same vein, if the preservation issues cannot be resolved by agreement, a well-prepared lawyer will be able to present the client's position to the judge in connection with the Rule 16(b) report should the adversary seek an early order regarding preservation. And if the adversary does not seek an order and the party does what the lawyer proposed, it will probably be difficult for the adversary to persuade the judge later that a reasonable preservation regime is inadequate.

But the Rules themselves contain no provisions regarding preservation, and special problems attend preservation of ESI. For one thing, the operation of computers can alter information without intentional intervention by the person using the computer. For another, many computer systems are set up—for good reasons—to remove certain information after the passage of specified periods of time. And some storage media—such as backup tapes—are regularly reused, thereby removing information that was on them. Finally, in many companies an employee's computer hard drive is wiped clean when the employee leaves the company, and whatever discoverable data was on that drive is lost (unless recoverable through expensive forensic methods). (See *infra* Chapter I.B.)

Although the Rules do not contain preservation provisions, they do contain sanction provisions, and one goal of some urging electronic discovery rule changes was to create a "safe harbor" for those who comply with reasonable procedures in preserving ESI. Rule 37(e) provides limited protections against sanctions "under these rules."[29] The protections apply only to data lost due to "routine" "operation of an electronic information system."[30] And the routine operation must be in "good faith." This requirement introduces the possible need for a litigation hold, as the Committee Note recognizes:

> The good faith requirement . . . means that a party is not permitted to exploit the routine operation of an information system to thwart discovery obligations by allowing that operation to continue in order to destroy specific stored information that it is required to preserve. When a party is under a duty to preserve information because of pending or reasonably anticipated litigation, intervention in the routine operation of an information system is one aspect of what is often called a "litigation hold."

One recurrent question may be whether there is any duty to preserve sources of ESI that are not reasonably accessible. The key point is that Rule 26(b)(2)(B) does not place such sources entirely off limits for discovery, but only exempts the responding party from searching them in completing its initial discovery response. Given that the court could later order discovery from those sources even if they are shown not to be reasonably accessible, good faith may require that they be retained, as the Committee Note confirms.[31] (See *infra* Chapters II.D and VI.)

Privilege waiver: "The inadvertent production of a privileged documents is a specter that haunts every document intensive case."[32] As a consequence, the Advisory Committee has long sought solutions to the problems created by inadvertent production of privileged material, and the costly and time-consuming review process necessary to minimize that risk.

---

29. Other adverse consequences, not based on the Federal Rules, might result. For example, the rules do not purport to limit the authority of regulators such as the SEC to impose sanctions for failure to preserve materials.

30. This is not limited to a party's system; if the party has retained vendors or outsiders to store the party's ESI losses of information on the vendor's system could be covered.

31. The Committee Note to Rule 37(e) explains: "Whether good faith would call for steps to prevent the loss of information on sources that the party believes are not reasonably accessible under Rule 26(b)(2) depends on the circumstances of each case. One factor is whether the party reasonably believes that the information on such sources is likely to be discoverable and not available from reasonably accessible sources."

32. *FDIC v. Marine Midland Realty Credit Corp.*, 138 F.R.D. 479, 479–80 (E.D. Va. 1991). *See also* Richard L. Marcus, *The Perils of Privilege: Waiver and the Litigator*, 84 Mich. L. Rev. 1605 (1986).

Volume and search issues can compound these concerns when discovery of ESI is sought. Identifying privileged materials is always a challenge, and the possibility that embedded data eligible for protection may be hard to review exacerbates the problems, particularly in a world where the amount of electronic data to be reviewed is enormous. But there is a statutory obstacle to solving this problem by rule.[33] However, Federal Rule of Evidence 502 now addresses these issues. (See *infra* Chapter VIII.D.)

Rule 26(b)(5)(B) does not directly address privilege waiver, but it does provide a process for preserving the issue for a court ruling for all forms of discovery material. Rule 26(f), beyond that, permits the parties to discuss additional arrangements for dealing with problems of privilege waiver, and Rule 16(v)(3)(B)(iv) authorizes the court to embody such agreements in a court order. (See *infra* Chapters III and VIII.)

Discovery from nonparties: Rule 45, dealing with discovery from nonparties, has been amended to include electronic discovery provisions parallel to those added to Rules 26–37 for party discovery. In particular, Rule 45 now addresses not reasonably accessible sources of ESI, sanctions for loss of discoverable information, and privilege waiver. (See *infra* Chapter V.I.)

Admissibility: This Introduction has focused on the electronic *discovery* rules; as noted above, from an early date federal discovery included materials not admissible in evidence. Once obtained, such items may lead to the discovery of admissible evidence, which is what Rule 26(b)(1) contemplates in making inadmissible material discoverable. But parties will, with some frequency, have to grapple with hearsay, authentication, and original document requirements to have the fruits of electronic discovery admitted into evidence. (See *infra* Chapter IX.)

Judicial interpretation and application: Many (maybe all) of these rule provisions call for interpretation and application by judges; they depend on the circumstances of the given case and not on absolute imperatives about what form of production, for example, is appropriate in all cases. The Rules are written in a way that should enable judges applying them to take account of technological change. For example, the determination whether a given source of ESI is "reasonably accessible" could change as new technology facilitates accessing the information. As you work through the materials in this book, therefore, keep in mind that judges tailoring the procedures to specific cases are doing what the rules intended, and that lawyers must therefore tailor their arguments to the specifics of their cases. As an attorney writing about the amended Federal Rules put it shortly before the amendments came into effect: "I wish I could say take two aspirin and call me in the morning, but solving the technological headaches attorneys will undoubtedly grapple with under the framework of the new Federal Rules of Civil Procedure will

---

33. *See* 28 U.S.C.A. § 2074(b) (providing that a rule "creating, abolishing, or modifying an evidentiary privilege" is ineffective unless approved by act of Congress).

require a much stronger dose of medicine, not to mention a dose of reality."[34]

D. The Future of Electronic Discovery

The future of electronic discovery is largely in your hands, as you are the lawyers and judges of tomorrow, and you will be making the arguments and decisions about interpreting the rules in the courts of tomorrow. A few parting observations may be useful, however, before you launch into the body of this book:

Electronic discovery in state court: This Introduction has focused almost entirely on the rules that apply in federal court, and so does this book. But most cases are in state court, and there is no reason to think that electronic discovery will not occur in state courts. What rules will apply there? Obviously that varies from state to state. But there may be considerable reason to expect that the state courts will generally adhere to the sorts of solutions the Federal Rules have adopted. For one thing, the amendments to the Federal Rules generally preceded adoption of parallel provisions for state courts.[35] The Federal Rules apply in the federal courts in every state, so the lawyers in your state will have to know about them to go to federal court and may carry that experience over to their state court cases. For another, the Federal Rules provisions are prominently followed in two sets of proposed rules for state court that have been developed.[36] Thus, you are likely to find that state courts follow rules very much like the ones that apply in federal court.[37]

More knowledgeable lawyers and judges: As the lawyers and judges of tomorrow, you who are products of the first digital generation are likely to be more familiar with the computer issues covered in the book and thus better able than those in my generation to deal with them.

Electronic discovery issues affect plaintiffs as well as defendants: Consider the extent to which defendants in personal injury cases may want discovery of any e-mail messages the plaintiff sent after the injury (*e.g.*, "Don't worry Mom, I wasn't really hurt"). Thus, a plaintiff's lawyer has made the following recommendations:

> To effectively represent a client now, you need to be well aware of the types of evidence that he or she—or family members, friends, and so on—has posted on the Internet. More and more, defendants request production of the client's personal computer, giving rise to

---

34. Matthew D. Nelson, *Easing the Pain of E–Discovery: New Discovery Rules Giving You a Headache? Follow These Tips to Keep Costs Down and Make the Process Smooth and Efficient*, S.F. Recorder, Aug. 23, 2006, at 5.

35. That's not entirely true. Texas adopted a rule dealing with electronic discovery in 1998. *See* Tex. R. Civ. P. 196.4.

36. *See* Guidelines for State Trial Courts Regarding Discovery of Electronically–Stored Information of the Conference of Chief Justices and Uniform Rules Relating to the Discovery of Electronically Stored Information of the National Conference of Commissioners of Uniform State Laws, in Appendices III and II to this book.

37. *See also* Richard L. Marcus, *E-Discovery Beyond the Federal Rules*, 37 U. Balt. L. Rev. 321, 333–37 (2008).

legal issues such as relevance, the client's privacy, and third-party privacy. If the computer was used to post information online, protecting that information will be difficult. Moreover, if it was posted publicly on an OSN site or blog, it may already be in defense counsel's hands before you even get to the fight.

Accordingly, you need to ask your client—at intake or shortly after—for any information about him or her that exists online. Ask about both quantity and content. Of course, you can conduct your own Internet search, but keep in mind that many people use pseudonyms on the Web.[38]

Preservation, accessibility, and form of production issues will likely affect plaintiffs in a way similar to the way in which they affect defendants.

The role of vendors: I began this Introduction by citing the projected revenues for electronic discovery vendors during 2009, and noting that some say mishandling such discovery may lead to malpractice claims. The vendor phenomenon results from understandable worries that lawyers may be unable to handle this process without expert help.

> E-discovery has brought about a kind of role reversal in the legal profession: Now it's the lawyers who find themselves surrounded by circling sharks. Once an e-discovery vendor identifies an attorney or law firm as a potential client, there's often no end to the sales pitches, product demos, complimentary mouse pads, and follow-up emails from perky PR reps.[39]

As you cover the materials in this book, think about when (and whether) you will need the assistance of a vendor in handling the many problems presented.

International constraints: I have stressed the broad American attitude toward discovery. The reality is, however, that the rest of the world looks at American discovery and has a response something like "Are we nuts?"[40] The Continental attitude toward electronic discovery is similar; data confidentiality laws in many countries may be important to application of American electronic discovery.[41] (See *infra* Chapter V.J.)

Enduring importance of electronic discovery: Whatever the constraints, electronic discovery is not going away. Three decades ago, an American judge noted that "the heart of any American antitrust case is the discovery of business documents. Without them, there is virtually no case."[42] That is true of most suits, not just antitrust cases; as investigators have learned to "follow the e-mail trail," lawyers will continue to pursue

---

38. Karen Barth Menzies, *Perils and Possibilities of Online Social Networks*, Trial, July, 2008, at 58.

39. Tom McNichol, *The E–Vendors Cometh*, Cal. Law., Feb. 2008, at 37.

40. *See* Stephen N. Subrin, *Discovery in Global Perspective: Are We Nuts?*, 52 DePaul L. Rev. 299 (2002).

41. *See* Richard L. Marcus, *E-Discovery Beyond the Federal Rules*, 37 U. Balt. L. Rev. 321, 339–40 (2008).

42. *In re Uranium Antitrust Lit.*, 480 F. Supp. 1138, 1155 (N.D. Ill. 1979).

ESI to prove their cases. As one lawyer put it: "What I've found is that when you've got the e-mails, people remember lots and lots of things."[43] I began by stressing the American "revolution" in discovery. Although more recent rule amendments have constrained the most aggressive forms of discovery and stressed the proportionality principle, the basic American commitment to finding the crucial evidence has endured. The rest of the world rejects "fishing expeditions" and tolerates decisions based on limited information in a way we do not.[44] Armed with the information in this book, you will be prepared to continue this American tradition in the Brave New World of electronic discovery.

43. Peter Geier, *A Defense Win in "Enron Country,"* Nat. L.J., Jan. 23, 2006, at 6.

44. *See, e.g.,* Mirjan Damaska, *The Uncertain Fate of Evidentiary Transplants: Anglo–American and Continental Experiments,* 45 Am. J. Comp. L. 839, 843 (1997) (noting that Continental civil procedure exhibits "a considerable degree of tolerance—almost an insouciance, to common law eyes—for the incompleteness of evidentiary material").

FEDERAL DISCOVERY RULES
RULE 16. PRETRIAL CONFERENCES; SCHEDULING; MANAGEMENT

(a) Purposes of a Pretrial Conference.

In any action, the court may order the attorneys and any unrepresented parties to appear for one or more pretrial conferences for such purposes as:

(1) expediting disposition of the action;

(2) establishing early and continuing control so that the case will not be protracted because of lack of management;

(3) discouraging wasteful pretrial activities;

(4) improving the quality of the trial through more thorough preparation, and;

(5) facilitating settlement.

(b) Scheduling.

(1) Scheduling Order.

Except in categories of actions exempted by local rule, the district judge—or a magistrate judge when authorized by local rule—must issue a scheduling order:

(A) after receiving the parties' report under Rule 26(f); or

(B) after consulting with the parties' attorneys and any unrepresented parties at a scheduling conference or by telephone, mail, or other means.

(2) Time to Issue.

The judge must issue the scheduling order as soon as practicable, but in any event within the earlier of 120 days after any defendant has been served with the complaint or 90 days after any defendant has appeared.

(3) Contents of the Order.

(A) *Required Contents.* The scheduling order must limit the time to join other parties, amend the pleadings, complete discovery, and file motions.

(B) *Permitted Contents.* The scheduling order may:

(i) modify the timing of disclosures under Rules 26(a) and 26(e)(1);

(ii) modify the extent of discovery;

(iii) provide for disclosure or discovery of electronically stored information;

(iv) include any agreements the parties reach for asserting claims of privilege or of protection as trial-preparation material after information is produced;

(v) set dates for pretrial conferences and for trial; and

(vi) include other appropriate matters.

(4) Modifying a Schedule.

A schedule may be modified only for good cause and with the judge's consent.

(c) Attendance and Matters for Consideration at a Pretrial Conference.

(1) Attendance.

A represented party must authorize at least one of its attorneys to make stipulations and admissions about all matters that can reasonably be anticipated for discussion at a pretrial conference. If appropriate, the court may require that a party or its representative be present or reasonably available by other means to consider possible settlement.

(2) Matters for Consideration.

At any pretrial conference, the court may consider and take appropriate action on the following matters:

* * *

(C) obtaining admissions and stipulations about facts and documents to avoid unnecessary proof, and ruling in advance on the admissibility of evidence;

(D) avoiding unnecessary proof and cumulative evidence, and limiting the use of testimony under Federal Rule of Evidence 702;

* * *

(F) controlling and scheduling discovery, including orders affecting disclosures and discovery under Rule 26 and Rules 29 through 37;

(G) identifying witnesses and documents, scheduling the filing and exchange of any pretrial briefs, and setting dates for further conferences and for trial;

* * *

(d) Pretrial Orders.

After any conference under this rule, the court should issue an order reciting the action taken. This order controls the course of the action unless the court modifies it.

* * *

(f) Sanctions.

(1) In General.

On motion or on its own, the court may issue any just orders, including those authorized by Rule 37(b)(2)(A)(ii)-(vii), if a party or its attorney:

(A) fails to appear at a scheduling or other pretrial conference;

(B) is substantially unprepared to participate—or does not participate in good faith—in the conference; or

(C) fails to obey a scheduling or other pretrial order.

(2) Imposing Fees and Costs.

Instead of or in addition to any other sanction, the court must order the party, its attorney, or both to pay the reasonable expenses—including attorney's fees—incurred because of any noncompliance with this rule, unless the noncompliance was substantially justified or other circumstances make an award of expenses unjust.

RULE 26.   DUTY TO DISCLOSE; GENERAL PROVISIONS GOVERNING DISCOVERY

(a) Required Disclosures.

(1) Initial Disclosures.

(A) *In General.* Except as exempted by Rule 26(a)(1)(B) or as otherwise stipulated or ordered by the court, a party must, without awaiting a discovery request, provide to the other parties:

(i) the name and, if known, the address and telephone number of each individual likely to have discoverable information—along with the subjects of that information—that the disclosing party may use to support its claims or defenses, unless the use would be solely for impeachment;

(ii) a copy—or a description by category and location—of all documents, electronically stored information, and tangible things that the disclosing party has in its possession, custody, or control and may use to support its claims or defenses, unless the use would be solely for impeachment;

(iii) a computation of each category of damages claimed by the disclosing party—who must also make available for inspection and copying as under Rule 34 the documents or other evidentiary material, unless privileged or protected from disclosure, on which each computation is based, including materials bearing on the nature and extent of injuries suffered; and

(iv) for inspection and copying as under Rule 34, any insurance agreement under which an insurance business may be liable to satisfy all or part of a possible judgment in the action or to indemnify or reimburse for payments made to satisfy the judgment.

* * *

(C) *Time for Initial Disclosures*—In General. A party must make the initial disclosures at or within 14 days after the parties' Rule 26(f) conference unless a different time is set by stipulation or court order, or unless a party objects during the conference that initial disclosures are not appropriate in this action and states the objection in the proposed discovery plan. In ruling on the objection, the court must determine what disclosures, if any, are to be made and must set the time for disclosure.

(D) *Time for Initial Disclosures*—For Parties Served or Joined Later. A party that is first served or otherwise joined after the Rule 26(f) conference must make the initial disclosures within 30 days after being served or joined, unless a different time is set by stipulation or court order.

(E) *Basis for Initial Disclosure; Unacceptable Excuses.* A party must make its initial disclosures based on the information then reasonably available to it. A party is not excused from making its disclosures because it has not fully investigated the case or because it challenges the sufficiency of another party's disclosures or because another party has not made its disclosures.

* * *

(b) Discovery Scope and Limits.

(1) Scope in General.

Unless otherwise limited by court order, the scope of discovery is as follows: Parties may obtain discovery regarding any nonprivileged matter that is relevant to any party's claim or defense—including the existence, description, nature, custody, condition, and location of any documents or other tangible things and the identity and location of persons who know of any discoverable matter. For good cause, the court may order discovery of any matter relevant to the subject matter involved in the action. Relevant information need not be admissible at the trial if the discovery appears reasonably calculated to lead to the discovery of admissible evidence. All discovery is subject to the limitations imposed by Rule 26(b)(2)(C).

(2) Limitations on Frequency and Extent.

(A) *When Permitted.* By order, the court may alter the limits in these rules on the number of depositions and interrogatories or on the length of depositions under Rule 30. By order or local rule, the court may also limit the number of requests under Rule 36.

(B) *Specific Limitations on Electronically Stored Information.* A party need not provide discovery of electronically stored information from sources that the party identifies as not reasonably accessible because of undue burden or cost. On motion to compel discovery or for a protective order, the party from whom discovery is sought must show that the information is not reasonably accessible because of undue burden or cost. If that showing is made, the court may nonetheless order discovery from such sources if the requesting party shows good cause, considering the limitations of Rule 26(b)(2)(C). The court may specify conditions for the discovery.

(C) *When Required.* On motion or on its own, the court must limit the frequency or extent of discovery otherwise allowed by these rules or by local rule if it determines that:

(i) the discovery sought is unreasonably cumulative or duplicative, or can be obtained from some other source that is more convenient, less burdensome, or less expensive;

(ii) the party seeking discovery has had ample opportunity to obtain the information by discovery in the action; or

(iii) the burden or expense of the proposed discovery outweighs its likely benefit, considering the needs of the case, the amount in controversy, the parties' resources, the importance of the issues at stake in the action, and the importance of the discovery in resolving the issues.

(3) Trial Preparation: Materials.

(A) *Documents and Tangible Things.* Ordinarily, a party may not discover documents and tangible things that are prepared in anticipation of litigation or for trial by or for another party or its representative (including the other party's attorney, consultant, surety, indemnitor, insurer, or agent). But, subject to Rule 26(b)(4), those materials may be discovered if:

(i) they are otherwise discoverable under Rule 26(b)(1); and

(ii) the party shows that it has substantial need for the materials to prepare its case and cannot, without undue hardship, obtain their substantial equivalent by other means.

(B) *Protection Against Disclosure.* If the court orders discovery of those materials, it must protect against disclosure of the mental impressions, conclusions, opinions, or legal theories of a party's attorney or other representative concerning the litigation.

(C) *Previous Statement.* Any party or other person may, on request and without the required showing, obtain the person's own previous statement about the action or its subject matter. If the request is refused, the person may move for a court order, and Rule 37(a)(5) applies to the award of expenses. A previous statement is either:

(i) a written statement that the person has signed or otherwise adopted or approved; or

(ii) a contemporaneous stenographic, mechanical, electrical, or other recording—or a transcription of it—that recites substantially verbatim the person's oral statement.

* * *

(5) Claiming Privilege or Protecting Trial-Preparation Materials.

(A) *Information Withheld.* When a party withholds information otherwise discoverable by claiming that the information is privileged or subject to protection as trial-preparation material, the party must:

(i) expressly make the claim; and

(ii) describe the nature of the documents, communications, or tangible things not produced or disclosed—and do so in a manner that, without revealing information itself privileged or protected, will enable other parties to assess the claim.

(B) *Information Produced.* If information produced in discovery is subject to a claim of privilege or of protection as trial-preparation material, the party making the claim may notify any party that received the information of the claim and the basis for it. After being notified, a party must promptly return, sequester, or destroy the specified information and any copies it has; must not use or disclose the information until the claim is resolved; must take reasonable steps to retrieve the information if the party disclosed it before being notified; and may promptly present the information to the court under seal for a determination of the claim. The producing party must preserve the information until the claim is resolved.

(c) Protective Orders.

(1) In General.

A party or any person from whom discovery is sought may move for a protective order in the court where the action is pending—or as an alternative on matters relating to a deposition, in the court for the district where the deposition will be taken. The motion must include a certification that the movant has in good faith conferred or attempted to confer with other affected parties in an effort to resolve the dispute without court action. The court may, for good cause, issue an order to protect a party or person from annoyance, embarrassment, oppression, or undue burden or expense, including one or more of the following:

(A) forbidding the disclosure or discovery;

(B) specifying terms, including time and place, for the disclosure or discovery;

(C) prescribing a discovery method other than the one selected by the party seeking discovery;

(D) forbidding inquiry into certain matters, or limiting the scope of disclosure or discovery to certain matters;

(E) designating the persons who may be present while the discovery is conducted;

(F) requiring that a deposition be sealed and opened only on court order;

(G) requiring that a trade secret or other confidential research, development, or commercial information not be revealed or be revealed only in a specified way; and

(H) requiring that the parties simultaneously file specified documents or information in sealed envelopes, to be opened as the court directs.

(2) Ordering Discovery.

If a motion for a protective order is wholly or partly denied, the court may, on just terms, order that any party or person provide or permit discovery.

(3) Awarding Expenses.

Rule 37(a)(5) applies to the award of expenses.

(d) Timing and Sequence of Discovery.

(1) Timing.

A party may not seek discovery from any source before the parties have conferred as required by Rule 26(f), except in a proceeding exempted from initial disclosure under Rule 26(a)(1)(B), or when authorized by these rules, by stipulation, or by court order.

(2) Sequence.

Unless, on motion, the court orders otherwise for the parties' and witnesses' convenience and in the interests of justice:

(A) methods of discovery may be used in any sequence; and

(B) discovery by one party does not require any other party to delay its discovery.

(e) Supplementation of Disclosures and Responses.

(1) In General.

A party who has made a disclosure under Rule 26(a)—or who has responded to an interrogatory, request for production, or request for admission—must supplement or correct its disclosure or response:

> (A) in a timely manner if the party learns that in some material respect the disclosure or response is incomplete or incorrect, and if the additional or corrective information has not otherwise been made known to the other parties during the discovery process or in writing; or

> (B) as ordered by the court.

* * *

(f) Conference of the Parties; Planning for Discovery.

(1) Conference Timing.

Except in a proceeding exempted from initial disclosure under Rule 26(a)(1)(B) or when the court orders otherwise, the parties must confer as soon as practicable—and in any event at least 21 days before a scheduling conference is to be held or a scheduling order is due under Rule 16(b).

(2) Conference Content; Parties' Responsibilities.

In conferring, the parties must consider the nature and basis of their claims and defenses and the possibilities for promptly settling or resolving the case; make or arrange for the disclosures required by Rule 26(a)(1); discuss any issues about preserving discoverable information; and develop a proposed discovery plan. The attorneys of record and all unrepresented parties that have appeared in the case are jointly responsible for arranging the conference, for attempting in good faith to agree on the proposed discovery plan, and for submitting to the court within 14 days after the conference a written report outlining the plan. The court may order the parties or attorneys to attend the conference in person.

(3) Discovery Plan.

A discovery plan must state the parties' views and proposals on:

> (A) what changes should be made in the timing, form, or requirement for disclosures under Rule 26(a), including a statement of when initial disclosures were made or will be made;

> (B) the subjects on which discovery may be needed, when discovery should be completed, and whether discovery should be conducted in phases or be limited to or focused on particular issues;

> (C) any issues about disclosure or discovery of electronically stored information, including the form or forms in which it should be produced;

(D) any issues about claims of privilege or of protection as trial-preparation materials, including—if the parties agree on a procedure to assert these claims after production—whether to ask the court to include their agreement in an order;

(E) what changes should be made in the limitations on discovery imposed under these rules or by local rule, and what other limitations should be imposed; and

(F) any other orders that the court should issue under Rule 26(c) or under Rule 16(b) and (c).

(4) *Expedited Schedule.*

If necessary to comply with its expedited schedule for Rule 16(b) conferences, a court may by local rule:

(A) require the parties' conference to occur less than 21 days before the scheduling conference is held or a scheduling order is due under Rule 16(b); and

(B) require the written report outlining the discovery plan to be filed less than 14 days after the parties' conference, or excuse the parties from submitting a written report and permit them to report orally on their discovery plan at the Rule 16(b) conference.

(g) Signing Disclosures and Discovery Requests, Responses, and Objections.

(1) *Signature Required; Effect of Signature.*

Every disclosure under Rule 26(a)(1) or (a)(3) and every discovery request, response, or objection must be signed by at least one attorney of record in the attorney's own name—or by the party personally, if unrepresented—and must state the signer's address, e-mail address, and telephone number. By signing, an attorney or party certifies that to the best of the person's knowledge, information, and belief formed after a reasonable inquiry:

(A) with respect to a disclosure, it is complete and correct as of the time it is made; and

(B) with respect to a discovery request, response, or objection, it is:

(i) consistent with these rules and warranted by existing law or by a nonfrivolous argument for extending, modifying, or reversing existing law, or for establishing new law;

(ii) not interposed for any improper purpose, such as to harass, cause unnecessary delay, or needlessly increase the cost of litigation; and

(iii) neither unreasonable nor unduly burdensome or expensive, considering the needs of the case, prior discovery in the case, the amount in controversy, and the importance of the issues at stake in the action.

(2) Failure to Sign.

Other parties have no duty to act on an unsigned disclosure, request, response, or objection until it is signed, and the court must strike it unless a signature is promptly supplied after the omission is called to the attorney's or party's attention.

(3) Sanction for Improper Certification.

If a certification violates this rule without substantial justification, the court, on motion or on its own, must impose an appropriate sanction on the signer, the party on whose behalf the signer was acting, or both. The sanction may include an order to pay the reasonable expenses, including attorney's fees, caused by the violation.

RULE 30. DEPOSITION BY ORAL EXAMINATION

(a) When a Deposition May Be Taken.

(1) *Without Leave.* A party may, by oral questions, depose any person, including a party, without leave of court except as provided in Rule 30(a)(2). The deponent's attendance may be compelled by subpoena under Rule 45.

(2) *With Leave.* A party must obtain leave of court, and the court must grant leave to the extent consistent with Rule 26(b)(2):

(A) if the parties have not stipulated to the deposition and:

(i) the deposition would result in more than 10 depositions being taken under this rule or Rule 31 by the plaintiffs, or by the defendants, or by the third-party defendants;

(ii) the deponent has already been deposed in the case; or

(iii) the party seeks to take the deposition before the time specified in Rule 26(d), unless the party certifies in the notice, with supporting facts, that the deponent is expected to leave the United States and be unavailable for examination in this country after that time; or

(B) if the deponent is confined in prison.

(b) Notice of the Deposition; Other Formal Requirements.

(1) Notice in General.

A party who wants to depose a person by oral questions must ive reasonable written notice to every other party. The notice must state the time and place of the deposition and, if known, the deponent's name and address. If the name is unknown, the notice must provide a general description sufficient to identify the person or the particular class or group to which the person belongs.

(2) Producing Documents.

If a subpoena duces tecum is to be served on the deponent, the materials designated for production, as set out in the subpoena, must be listed in the notice or in an attachment. The notice to a party deponent may be accompanied by a request under Rule 34 to produce documents and tangible things at the deposition.

* * *

(6) Notice or Subpoena Directed to an Organization.

In its notice or subpoena, a party may name as the deponent a public or private corporation, a partnership, an association, a governmental agency, or other entity and must describe with reasonable particularity the matters for examination. The named organization must then designate one or more officers, directors, or managing agents, or designate other persons who consent to testify on its behalf; and it may set out the matters on which each person designated will testify. A subpoena must advise a nonparty organization of its duty to make this designation. The persons designated must testify about information known or reasonably available to the organization. This paragraph (6) does not preclude a deposition by any other procedure allowed by these rules.

* * *

(f) Certification and Delivery; Exhibits; Copies of the Transcript or Recording; Filing.

* * *

(2) Documents and Tangible Things.

(A) Originals and Copies. Documents and tangible things produced for inspection during a deposition must, on a party's request, be marked for identification and attached to the deposition. Any party may inspect and copy them. But if the person who produced them wants to keep the originals, the person may:

(i) offer copies to be marked, attached to the deposition, and then used as originals—after giving all parties a fair opportunity to verify the copies by comparing them with the originals; or

(ii) give all parties a fair opportunity to inspect and copy the originals after they are marked—in which event the originals may be used as if attached to the deposition.

(B) Order Regarding the Originals. Any party may move for an order that the originals be attached to the deposition pending final disposition of the case.

* * *

RULE 33. INTERROGATORIES TO PARTIES

(a) In General.

(1) Number.

Unless otherwise stipulated or ordered by the court, a party may serve on any other party no more than 25 written interrogatories, including all discrete subparts. Leave to serve additional interrogatories may be granted to the extent consistent with Rule 26(b)(2).

(2) Scope.

An interrogatory may relate to any matter that may be inquired into under Rule 26(b). An interrogatory is not objectionable merely because it asks for an opinion or contention that relates to fact or the application of law to fact, but the court may order that the interrogatory need not be answered until designated discovery is complete, or until a pretrial conference or some other time.

(b) Answers and Objections.

(1) Responding Party.

The interrogatories must be answered:

(A) by the party to whom they are directed; or

(B) if that party is a public or private corporation, a partnership, an association, or a governmental agency, by any officer or agent, who must furnish the information available to the party.

(2) Time to Respond.

The responding party must serve its answers and any objections within 30 days after being served with the interrogatories. A shorter or longer time may be stipulated to under *Rule 29* or be ordered by the court.

(3) Answering Each Interrogatory.

Each interrogatory must, to the extent it is not objected to, be answered separately and fully in writing under oath.

(4) Objections.

The grounds for objecting to an interrogatory must be stated with specificity. Any ground not stated in a timely objection is waived unless the court, for good cause, excuses the failure.

(5) Signature.

The person who makes the answers must sign them, and the attorney who objects must sign any objections.

(c) Use.

An answer to an interrogatory may be used to the extent allowed by the Federal Rules of Evidence.

(d) Option to Produce Business Records.

If the answer to an interrogatory may be determined by examining, auditing, compiling, abstracting, or summarizing a party's business records (including electronically stored information), and if the burden of deriving or ascertaining the answer will be substantially the same for either party, the responding party may answer by:

(1) specifying the records that must be reviewed, in sufficient detail to enable the interrogating party to locate and identify them as readily as the responding party could; and

(2) giving the interrogating party a reasonable opportunity to examine and audit the records and to make copies, compilations, abstracts, or summaries.

RULE 34.   PRODUCING DOCUMENTS, ELECTRONICALLY STORED INFORMATION, AND TANGIBLE THINGS, OR ENTERING ONTO LAND, FOR INSPECTIONAND OTHER PURPOSES

(a) In General.

A party may serve on any other party a request within the scope of Rule 26(b):

(1) to produce and permit the requesting party or its representative to inspect, copy, test, or sample the following items in the responding party's possession, custody, or control:

(A) any designated documents or electronically stored information—including writings, drawings, graphs, charts, photographs, sound recordings, images, and other data or data compilations—stored in any medium from which information can be obtained either directly or, if necessary, after translation by the responding party into a reasonably usable form; or

(B) any designated tangible things; or

(2) to permit entry onto designated land or other property possessed or controlled by the responding party, so that the requesting party may inspect, measure, survey, photograph, test, or sample the property or any designated object or operation on it.

(b) Procedure.

(1) Contents of the Request.

The request:

(A) must describe with reasonable particularity each item or category of items to be inspected;

(B) must specify a reasonable time, place, and manner for the inspection and for performing the related acts; and

(C) may specify the form or forms in which electronically stored information is to be produced.

(2) Responses and Objections.

(A) *Time to Respond.* The party to whom the request is directed must respond in writing within 30 days after being served. A shorter or longer time may be stipulated to under Rule 29 or be ordered by the court.

(B) *Responding to Each Item.* For each item or category, the response must either state that inspection and related activities will be permitted as requested or state an objection to the request, including the reasons.

(C) *Objections.* An objection to part of a request must specify the part and permit inspection of the rest.

(D) *Responding to a Request for Production of Electronically Stored Information.* The response may state an objection to a requested form for producing electronically stored information. If the responding party objects to a requested form—or if no form was specified in the request—the party must state the form or forms it intends to use.

(E) *Producing the Documents or Electronically Stored Information.* Unless otherwise stipulated or ordered by the court, these procedures apply to producing documents or electronically stored information:

(i) A party must produce documents as they are kept in the usual course of business or must organize and label them to correspond to the categories in the request;

(ii) If a request does not specify a form for producing electronically stored information, a party must produce it in a form or forms in which it is ordinarily maintained or in a reasonably usable form or forms; and

(iii) A party need not produce the same electronically stored information in more than one form.

(c) Nonparties.

As provided in Rule 45, a nonparty may be compelled to produce documents and tangible things or to permit an inspection.

RULE 37. FAILURE TO MAKE DISCLOSURES OR TO COOPERATE IN DISCOVERY; SANCTIONS

(a) Motion for an Order Compelling Disclosure or Discovery.

(1) In General.

On notice to other parties and all affected persons, a party may move for an order compelling disclosure or discovery. The motion must include a certification that the movant has in good faith conferred or attempted to confer with the person or party failing to make disclosure or discovery in an effort to obtain it without court action.

(2) Appropriate Court.

A motion for an order to a party must be made in the court where the action is pending. A motion for an order to a nonparty must be made in the court where the discovery is or will be taken.

(3) Specific Motions.

(A) *To Compel Disclosure*. If a party fails to make a disclosure required by Rule 26(a), any other party may move to compel disclosure and for appropriate sanctions.

(B) *To Compel a Discovery Response*. A party seeking discovery may move for an order compelling an answer, designation, production, or inspection. This motion may be made if:

(i) a deponent fails to answer a question asked under Rules 30 or 31;

(ii) a corporation or other entity fails to make a designation under Rule 30(b)(6) or 31(a)(4);

(iii) a party fails to answer an interrogatory submitted under Rule 33, or

(iv) a party fails to respond that inspection will be permitted—or fails to permit inspection—as requested under Rule 34.

* * *

(5) Payment of Expenses; Protective Orders.

(A) *If the Motion Is Granted (or Disclosure or Discovery Is Provided After Filing)*. If the motion is granted—or if the disclosure or requested discovery is provided after the motion was filed—the court must, after giving an opportunity to be heard, require the party or deponent whose conduct necessitated the motion, the party or attorney advising that conduct, or both to pay the movant's reasonable expenses incurred in making the motion, including attorney's fees. But the court must not order this payment if:

(i) the movant filed the motion before attempting in good faith to obtain the disclosure or discovery without court action;

(ii) the opposing party's nondisclosure, response, or objection was substantially justified; or

(iii) other circumstances make an award of expenses unjust.

(B) *If the Motion Is Denied.* If the motion is denied, the court may issue any protective order authorized under Rule 26(c) and must, after giving an opportunity to be heard, require the movant, the attorney filing the motion, or both to pay the party or deponent who opposed the motion its reasonable expenses incurred in opposing the motion, including attorney's fees. But the court must not order this payment if the motion was substantially justified or other circumstances make an award of expenses unjust.

(C) *If the Motion Is Granted in Part and Denied in Part.* If the motion is granted in part and denied in part, the court may issue any protective order authorized under Rule 26(c) and may, after giving an opportunity to be heard, apportion the reasonable expenses for the motion.

(b) Failure to Comply with a Court Order.

(1) Sanctions in the District Where the Deposition Is Taken.

If the court where the discovery is taken orders a deponent to be sworn or to answer a question and the deponent fails to obey, the failure may be treated as contempt of court.

(2) Sanctions in the District Where the Action Is Pending.

(A) *For Not Obeying a Discovery Order.* If a party or a party's officer, director, or managing agent—or a witness designated under Rule 30(b)(6) or 31(a)(4)—fails to obey an order to provide or permit discovery, including an order under Rule 26(f), 35, or 37(a), the court where the action is pending may issue further just orders. They may include the following:

(i) directing that the matters embraced in the order or other designated facts be taken as established for purposes of the action, as the prevailing party claims;

(ii) prohibiting the disobedient party from supporting or opposing designated claims or defenses, or from introducing designated matters in evidence;

(iii) striking pleadings in whole or in part;

(iv) staying further proceedings until the order is obeyed;

(v) dismissing the action or proceeding in whole or in part;

(vi) rendering a default judgment against the disobedient party; or

(vii) treating as contempt of court the failure to obey any order except an order to submit to a physical or mental examination.

(B) *For Not Producing a Person for Examination.* If a party fails to comply with an order under Rule 35(a) requiring it to produce another person for examination, the court may issue any of the orders listed in Rule 37(b)(2)(A)(i)-(vi), unless the disobedient party shows that it cannot produce the other person.

(C) *Payment of Expenses.* Instead of or in addition to the orders above, the court must order the disobedient party, the attorney advising that party, or both to pay the reasonable expenses, including attorney's fees, caused by the failure, unless the failure was substantially justified or other circumstances make an award of expenses unjust.

(c) Failure to Disclose; to Supplement an Earlier Response, or to Admit.

(1) Failure to Disclose or Supplement.

If a party fails to provide information or identify a witness as required by Rule 26(a) or 26(e), the party is not allowed to use that information or witness to supply evidence on a motion, at a hearing, or at a trial, unless the failure was substantially justified or is harmless. In addition to or instead of this sanction, the court, on motion and after giving an opportunity to be heard:

(A) may order payment of the reasonable expenses, including attorney's fees, caused by the failure;

(B) may inform the jury of the party's failure; and

(C) may impose other appropriate sanctions, including any of the orders listed

* * *

(e) Failure to Provide Electronically Stored Information.

Absent exceptional circumstances, a court may not impose sanctions under these rules on a party for failing to provide electronically stored information lost as a result of the routine, good-faith operation of an electronic information system.

(f) Failure to Participate in Framing a Discovery Plan.

If a party or its attorney fails to participate in good faith in developing and submitting a proposed discovery plan as required by Rule 26(f), the court may, after giving an opportunity to be heard, require that party or attorney to pay to any other party the reasonable expenses, including attorney's fees, caused by the failure.

RULE 45.   SUBPOENA

(a) In General.

(1) Form and Contents.

(A) *Requirements—In General.* Every subpoena must:

(i) state the court from which it issued;

(ii) state the title of the action, the court in which it is pending, and its civil-action number;

(iii) command each person to whom it is directed to do the following at a specified time and place: attend and testify; produce designated documents, electronically stored information, or tangible things in that person's possession, custody, or control; or permit the inspection of premises; and

(iv) set out the text of Rule 45(c) and (d).

(B) *Command to Attend a Deposition—Notice of the Recording Method.* A subpoena commanding attendance at a deposition must state the method for recording the testimony.

(C) *Combining or Separating a Command to Produce or to Permit Inspection; Specifying the Form for Electronically Stored Information.* A command to produce documents, electronically stored information, or tangible things or to permit the inspection of premises may be included in a subpoena commanding attendance at a deposition, hearing, or trial, or may be set out in a separate subpoena. A subpoena may specify the form or forms in which electronically stored information is to be produced.

(D) *Command to Produce; Included Obligations.* A command in a subpoena to produce documents, electronically stored information, or tangible things requires the responding party to permit inspection, copying, testing, or sampling of the materials.

* * *

(c) Protecting a Person Subject to a Subpoena.

(1) Avoiding Undue Burden or Expense; Sanctions.

A party or attorney responsible for issuing and serving a subpoena must take reasonable steps to avoid imposing undue burden or expense on a person subject to the subpoena. The issuing court must enforce this duty and impose an appropriate sanction—which may include lost earnings and reasonable attorney's fees—on a party or attorney who fails to comply.

(2) Command to Produce Materials or Permit Inspection.

(A) *Appearance Not Required.* A person commanded to produce documents, electronically stored information, or tangible things, or to permit the inspection of premises, need not appear in person at the place of production or inspection unless also commanded to appear for a deposition, hearing, or trial.

(B) *Objections.* A person commanded to produce documents or tangible things or to permit inspection may serve on the party or attorney designated in the subpoena a written objection to inspecting, copying, testing or sampling any or all of the materials or to inspecting the premises—or to producing electronically stored information in the form or forms requested. The objection must be served before the earlier of the time specified for compliance or 14 days after the subpoena is served. If an objection is made, the following rules apply:

(i) At any time, on notice to the commanded person, the serving party may move the issuing court for an order compelling production or inspection.

(ii) These acts may be required only as directed in the order, and the order must protect a person who is neither a party nor a party's officer from significant expense resulting from compliance.

(3) Quashing or Modifying a Subpoena.

(A) *When Required.* On timely motion, the issuing court must quash or modify a subpoena that:

(i) fails to allow a reasonable time to comply;

(ii) requires a person who is neither a party nor a party's officer to travel more than 100 miles from where that person resides, is employed, or regularly transacts business in person—except that, subject to Rule 45(c)(3)(B)(iii), the person may be commanded to attend a trial by traveling from any such place within the state where the trial is held;

(iii) requires disclosure of privileged or other protected matter, if no exception or waiver applies; or

(iv) subjects a person to undue burden.

(B) *When Permitted.* To protect a person subject to or affected by a subpoena, the issuing court may, on motion, quash or modify the subpoena if it requires:

(i) disclosing a trade secret or other confidential research, development, or commercial information;

(ii) disclosing an unretained expert's opinion or information that does not describe specific occurrences in dispute and results from the expert's study that was not requested by a party; or

(iii) a person who is neither a party nor a party's officer to incur substantial expense to travel more than 100 miles to attend trial.

(C) *Specifying Conditions as an Alternative.* In the circumstances described in Rule 45(c)(3)(B), the court may, instead of quashing or modifying a subpoena, order appearance or production under specified conditions if the serving party:

(i) shows a substantial need for the testimony or material that cannot be otherwise met without undue hardship; and

(ii) ensures that the subpoenaed person will be reasonably compensated.

(d) Duties in Responding to Subpoena.

(1) Producing Documents or Electronically Stored Information.

These procedures apply to producing documents or electronically stored information:

(A) *Documents.* A person responding to a subpoena to produce documents must produce them as they are kept in the ordinary course of business or must organize and label them to correspond to the categories in the demand.

(B) *Form for Producing Electronically Stored Information Not Specified.* If a subpoena does not specify a form for producing electronically stored information, the person responding must produce it in a form or forms in which it is ordinarily maintained or in a reasonably usable form or forms.

(C) *Electronically Stored Information Produced in Only One Form.* The person responding need not produce the same electronically stored information in more than one form.

(D) *Inaccessible Electronically Stored Information.* The person responding need not provide discovery of electronically stored information from sources that the person identifies as not reasonably accessible because of undue burden or cost. On motion to compel discovery or for a protective order, the person responding must show that the information is not reasonably accessible because of undue burden or cost. If that showing is made, the court may nonetheless order discovery from such sources if the requesting party shows good cause, considering the limitations of Rule 26(b)(2)(C). The court may specify conditions for the discovery.

(2) Claiming Privilege or Protection.

(A) *Information Withheld.* A person withholding subpoenaed information under a claim that it is privileged or subject to protection as trial-preparation material must:

(i) expressly make the claim; and

(ii) describe the nature of the withheld documents, communications, or tangible things in a manner that, without revealing information itself privileged or protected, will enable the parties to assess the claim.

(B) *Information Produced.* If information produced in response to a subpoena is subject to a claim of privilege or of protection as trial-preparation material, the person making the claim may notify any party that received the information of the claim and the basis for it. After being notified, a party must promptly return, sequester, or destroy the specified information and any copies it has; must not use or disclose the information until the claim is resolved; must take reasonable steps to retrieve the information if the party disclosed it before being notified; and may promptly present the information to the court under seal for a determination of the claim. The person who produced the information must preserve the information until the claim is resolved.

(e) Contempt.

The issuing court may hold in contempt a person who, having been served, fails without adequate excuse to obey the subpoena. A nonparty's failure to obey must be excused if the subpoena purports to require the nonparty to attend or produce at a place outside the limits of Rule 45(c)(3)(A)(ii).

RULE 11.   SIGNING PLEADINGS, MOTIONS, AND OTHER PAPERS; REPRESENTATIONS TO THE COURT; SANCTIONS

(a) Signature.

Every pleading, written motion, and other paper must be signed by at least one attorney of record in the attorney's name—or by a party personally if the party is unrepresented. The paper must state the signer's address, e-mail address, and telephone number. Unless a rule or statute specifically states otherwise, a pleading need not be verified or accompanied by an affidavit. The court must strike an unsigned paper unless the omission is promptly corrected after being called to the attorney's or party's attention.

(b) Representations to the Court.

By presenting to the court a pleading, written motion, or other paper—whether by signing, filing, submitting, or later advocating it—an attorney or unrepresented party certifies that to the best of the person's knowledge, information, and belief, formed after an inquiry reasonable under the circumstances:

(1) it is not being presented for any improper purpose, such as to harass, cause unnecessary delay, or needlessly increase the cost of litigation;

(2) the claims, defenses, and other legal contentions are warranted by existing law or by a nonfrivolous argument for extending, modifying, or reversing existing law or for establishing new law;

(3) the factual contentions have evidentiary support or, if specifically so identified, will likely have evidentiary support after a reasonable opportunity for further investigation or discovery; and

(4) the denials of factual contentions are warranted on the evidence or, if specifically so identified, are reasonably based on belief or a lack of information.

(c) Sanctions.

(1) In General.

If, after notice and a reasonable opportunity to respond, the court determines that Rule 11(b) has been violated, the court may impose an appropriate sanction on any attorney, law firm, or party that violated the rule or is responsible for the violation. Absent exceptional circumstances, a law firm must be held jointly responsible for a violation committed by its partner, associate, or employee.

(2) Motion for Sanctions.

A motion for sanctions must be made separately from any other motion and must describe the specific conduct that allegedly violates Rule 11(b). The motion must be served under Rule 5, but it must not be filed or be presented to the court if the challenged paper, claim, defense, contention, or denial is withdrawn or appropriately corrected within 21 days after service or within another time the court sets. If warranted, the court may award to the prevailing party the reasonable expenses, including attorney's fees, incurred for the motion.

(3) On the Court's Initiative.

On its own, the court may order an attorney, law firm, or party to show cause why conduct specifically described in the order has not violated Rule 11(b).

(4) Nature of a Sanction.

A sanction imposed under this rule must be limited to what suffices to deter repetition of the conduct or comparable conduct by others similarly situated.

The sanction may include nonmonetary directives; an order to pay a penalty into court; or, if imposed on motion and warranted for effective deterrence, an order directing payment to the movant of part or all of the reasonable attorney's fees and other expenses directly resulting from the violation.

(5) Limitations on Monetary Sanctions.

The court must not impose a monetary sanction:

(A) against a represented party for violating Rule 11(b)(2); or

(B) on its own, unless it issued the show-cause order under Rule 11(c)(3) before voluntary dismissal or settlement of the claims made by or against the party that is, or whose attorneys are, to be sanctioned.

(6) Requirements for an Order.

An order imposing a sanction must describe the sanctioned conduct and explain the basis for the sanction.

(d) Inapplicability to Discovery.

This rule does not apply to disclosures and discovery requests, responses, objections, and motions under Rules 26 through 37.

I

THE EFFECT OF ELECTRONIC INFORMATION ON DISCOVERY PRACTICE

■ ■ ■

A. EXPLOSION OF INFORMATION AND INCREASED SOURCES OF INFORMATION

What makes "e-discovery" different from traditional discovery practice? In what ways has the world changed since 1938, when the Federal Rules of Civil Procedure took effect?

EXCERPT FROM James N. Dertouzos, *et al.*, *The Legal and Economic Implications of E–Discovery: Options for Future Research*, RAND Institute for Civil Justice 1–2 (2008), available at http://www.rand.org/pubs/occasional_papers/OP183.

Discovery is at the very heart of the civil process in America. Access to relevant evidence is central to the "search for truth." The discovery process is performed ostensibly in preparation for trial, but in fact the information obtained is a key factor in driving negotiated resolutions of disputes. In addition, discovery can be a major cost driver. Given the importance of discovery, it is not surprising that litigants and the lawyers who represent them are struggling in their efforts to cope with the changes in the legal landscape due to the evolution of information technologies.

Today, virtually all information is in electronic form. Electronically stored information grew at the rate of 30 percent annually from 1999 through 2002. * * * The sheer volume is astounding. A data processing center for a major corporation can contain 10,000 tapes or more. One tape can store as much as a 1 trillion bytes (1 terabyte) of information or even more. If converted to hard copies, information contained on a single tape would be the equivalent of a 200–mile-high stack of paper. The types of "discoverable" data in electronic form are also proliferating. Many are similar to previous hard-copy documents such as might be found in the printed output of Microsoft Word files and Excel spreadsheets. But discovery also includes more transitory forms that were never found in the pre-electronic world, with the primary example being email messages.

A 2002 estimate put the number of emails sent worldwide at over 30 billion and predicted that that number would double by 2006. In addition, companies retain vast relational databases that are continuously updated. These systems contain payroll, sales, manufacturing, and supplier transactions and provide a snapshot of an entire enterprise, something not possible with hard-copy ledgers. A vast amount of information is stored on data recovery systems or "backup" tapes. Historical information is retained on decades-old legacy systems that are now difficult to access and read. Data that have supposedly been deleted from computers may still in fact exist in "slack memory" and the various nooks and crannies of hard drives. Most application and system files maintain a myriad of bookmark files, activity logs, and temporary files, potentially leaving a detailed audit trail of internal corporate processes that was never imaginable before. Additionally, many application files (such as a Microsoft Word document) also have embedded "metadata" that provide details about the author or the history of edits or other activities. And to complicate matters even more, the stand-alone desktop computer is now only one source of data, given the explosion of various platforms capable of holding electronically stored information. These include personal digital assistants (PDAs), laptops, thumb drives, telephone calls that are placed through the internet (via voice over Internet Protocol, [VoIP]), smart cards, and cell phones.

What are the implications of this proliferation of electronic data on the legal discovery process? What are the costs and benefits of these trends? What are their likely impacts on litigation outcomes? How are business practices changing in response to these developments? Do the Federal Rules of Civil Procedure that were enacted in December 2006 help litigants address the issues raised by e-discovery? How can policies be improved regarding e-discovery? These are some of the questions yet to be addressed by the research community.

EXCERPT FROM George L. Paul & Jason R. Baron, *Information Inflation: Can the Legal System Adapt?*, 13 Rich. J.L. & Tech. 10 (2007).

A. THE LEGAL PROFESSION CONFRONTS AN INFLATIONARY EPOCH

In the original writing technology, the rate of flow of information was limited because it depended on distribution of information artifacts. With the plastic and networked nature of new age writing, we are no longer wedded to original records. We can distribute thousands or even millions of identical records in an instant. These can be read in real time, affecting other people, who are also imbedded in the system. Recipients modify the system further by sending out their own writings, often editing messages they receive. All this leaves multitudinous records of thought, word, and action as evidence. We can edit; change formats; respond; converse with twenty people at once; and even move, speak, and write in virtual worlds as an avatar.

* * *

Probably close to 100 billion e-mails are sent daily, with approximately 30 billion e-mails created or received by federal government agencies each year. The amount of stored information continues to grow exponentially.

Perhaps more easily grasped, the amount of information in business has increased by thousands, if not tens of thousands of times in the last few years. In a small business, whereas formerly there was usually one four-drawer file cabinet full of paper records, now there is the equivalent of two thousand four-drawer file cabinets full of such records, all contained in a cubic foot or so in the form of electronically stored information. This is a sea change.

* * *

Take then, for example, litigation in which the universe subject to search stands at one billion e-mail records, at least 25% of which have one or more attachments of varying length (1 to 300 pages). Generously assume further that a model "reviewer" (junior lawyer, legal assistant, or contract professional) is able to review an average of fifty e-mails, including attachments, per hour. Without employing *any* automated computer process to generate potentially responsive documents, the review effort for this litigation would take 100 people, working ten hours a day, seven days a week, fifty-two weeks a year, over fifty-four *years* to complete. And the cost of such a review, at an assumed average billing of $100/hour, would be $2 billion. Even, however, if present-day search methods (such as in the tobacco litigation example) are used to initially reduce the e-mail universe to 1% of its size (i.e., 10 million documents out of 1 billion), the case would still cost $20 million for a first pass review conducted by 100 people over 28 weeks, without accounting for any additional privilege review.

When one considers all of the ESI that a given organization may have in its possession, the types and quantities can be staggering. In the three year period from 2004 to 2007, the average amount of data in a Fortune 1000 corporation grew from 190 terabytes to one thousand terabytes (one petabyte). Over the same time period, the average data sets at 9,000 American, midsize companies grew from two terabytes to 100 terabytes. Overall, the global data set grew from five exabytes (five billion gigabytes) in 2003 to 161 exabytes in 2006. It is estimated that in 2007 the amount of information created and replicated globally surpassed 255 exabytes.

Given the amount of ESI that exists within the average organization, the ability to quickly and efficiently identify, locate, retrieve, and preserve the targeted set of ESI most likely to be responsive to the matter at hand becomes essential. Understanding what types of data are likely to play a role in e-discovery, the possible storage locations of such data, and the likely ways in which the targeted data may be organized have all become important factors in designing a discovery effort that will be focused and productive.

1. How Much New Information Is Created Each Year?

EXCERPT FROM Peter Lyman & Hal R. Varian, *How Much Information? 2003*, available at http://www2.sims.berkeley.edu/research/projects/how-much-info–2003/execsum.htm.

1. **Print, film, magnetic, and optical storage media produced about 5 exabytes of new information in 2002. Ninety-two percent of the new information was stored on magnetic media, mostly in hard disks.**

- *How big is five exabytes?* If digitized with full formatting, the seventeen million books in the Library of Congress contain about 136 terabytes of information; five exabytes of information is equivalent in size to the information contained in 37,000 new libraries the size of the Library of Congress book collections.

- *Hard disks store most new information.* Ninety-two percent of new information is stored on magnetic media, primarily hard disks. Film represents 7% of the total, paper 0.01%, and optical media 0.002%.

- *The United States produces about 40% of the world's new stored information,* including 33% of the world's new printed information, 30% of the world's new film titles, 40% of the world's information stored on optical media, and about 50% of the information stored on magnetic media.

- *How much new information per person?* According to the Population Reference Bureau, the world population is 6.3 billion, thus almost 800 MB of recorded information is produced per person each year. It would take about 30 feet of books to store the equivalent of 800 MB of information on paper.

2. **We estimate that the amount of new information stored on paper, film, magnetic, and optical media has about doubled in the last three years.**

- *Information explosion?* We estimate that new stored information grew about 30% a year between 1999 and 2002.

- *Paperless society?* The amount of information printed on paper is still increasing, but the vast majority of original information on paper is produced by individuals in office documents and postal mail, not in formally published titles such as books, newspapers and journals.

The Lyman & Varian report includes the following useful table:

Table 1.1: How Big Is an Exabyte?	
Kilobyte (KB)	1,000 bytes OR 10^3 bytes 2 Kilobytes: A Typewritten page. 100 Kilobytes: A low-resolution photograph.
Megabyte (MB)	1,000,000 bytes OR 10^6 bytes 1 Megabyte: A small novel OR a 3.5 inch floppy disk. 2 Megabytes: A high-resolution photograph. 5 Megabytes: The complete works of Shakespeare. 10 Megabytes: A minute of high-fidelity sound. 100 Megabytes: 1 meter of shelved books. 500 Megabytes: A CD–ROM.
Gigabyte (GB)	1,000,000,000 bytes OR 10^9 bytes 1 Gigabyte: a pickup truck filled with books. 20 Gigabytes: A good collection of the works of Beethoven. 100 Gigabytes: A library floor of academic journals.
Terabyte (TB)	1,000,000,000,000 bytes OR 10^{12} bytes 1 Terabyte: 50000 trees made into paper and printed. 2 Terabytes: An academic research library. 10 Terabytes: The print collections of the U.S. Library of Congress. 400 Terabytes: National Climactic Data Center (NOAA) database.
Petabyte (PB)	1,000,000,000,000,000 bytes OR 10^{15} bytes 1 Petabyte: 3 years of [NASA Earth Observation System] data (2001). 2 Petabytes: All U.S. academic research libraries. 20 Petabytes: Production of hard-disk drives in 1995. 200 Petabytes: All printed material.
Exabyte (EB)	1,000,000,000,000,000,000 bytes OR 10^{18} bytes 2 Exabytes: Total volume of information generated in 1999. 5 Exabytes: All words ever spoken by human beings.

2. What Makes "E-Discovery" Different From Traditional Discovery?

"Broad discovery is a cornerstone of the litigation process contemplated by the Federal Rules of Civil Procedure."[1] Arguably, how lawyers propounded and responded to discovery requests did not materially change between the 1930s and the 1990s, until the advent of office automation and the growth of the Internet. Document requests were propounded with the expectation that the receiving party, at counsel's direction, would devote sufficient resources to perform a reasonably diligent search for records found in hard-copy repositories including central file room areas and among work papers stored in offices.

Recognition that the volume of ESI presented different challenges for the practitioner occurred years before the 2006 amendments to the Federal Rules of Civil Procedure.

EXCERPT FROM Kenneth J. Withers, *Computer-Based Discovery in Federal Civil Litigation*, 2000 Fed. Cts. L. Rev. 2, 3–4 (2000) (footnotes omitted).

In the days of conventional paper-based discovery, most organizations had centrally-located files or a limited number of physical file locations. In the PC-based world, each employee may have a desktop computer, plus disks or other removable data storage media, a laptop computer, a home computer, and a hand-held

---

1. *Jones v. Goord*, No. 95 Civ. 8026, 2002 WL 1007614, at *1 (S.D.N.Y. May 16, 2002).

personal organizer, all containing potentially relevant data. Larger organizations will have network servers connecting and storing data for many PCs, plus backup and archival data storage (discussed below). Offsite and even offshore data storage facilities, Internet service providers, and other third parties may also hold data subject to discovery. The cost and complication of conducting discovery in a modern, distributed business computing environment can be enormous.

In paper-based record-keeping systems, outdated records, papers with no business significance, and superfluous copies are destroyed routinely. Records managers maintain paper files in "business-record order." In computerized business environments, equivalent electronic records management systems seldom exist. Copies of documents are made routinely, distributed widely, and seldom purged when outdated. Potentially discoverable records are stored according to computer logic, as opposed to "business-record" logic, and can be difficult to locate and untangle from irrelevant and privileged records.

The combination of multiple locations, tremendous volume, and arcane or non-existent records management practices is potentially explosive for defending counsel. In *Linnen v. A.H. Robins Co.*, 1999 WL 462015 (Mass. Super. Ct.), the defendant faced sanctions in the form of costs and a spoliation inference stemming from counsel's failure to completely investigate stored computer backup tapes, while representing to the court that all relevant computer files had been produced. *Linnen* was one of the various state product liability actions stemming from the marketing and distribution of a diet drug combination popularly known as "Phen-fen," which was linked with primary pulmonary hypertension. After counsel for defendant Wyeth–Ayerst Laboratories denied the existence of e-mail backup tapes early in discovery, deposition testimony of Wyeth staff revealed that nearly 1,000 backup tapes had been set aside for unrelated litigation. But by the time of the disclosure, tapes covering a relevant four-month period had been destroyed in the routine course of business.

The attorneys have an obligation to investigate their clients' information management system thoroughly to locate potentially relevant and discoverable material, no matter how technically opaque that information system may appear. Such an investigation goes well beyond simply asking the client for the relevant files and trusting that the client itself has a complete understanding of its own information technology infrastructure.

* * *

Computer-based discovery offers substantive advantages, as well. Evidence that would have been impossible or extremely difficult to obtain can now become part of the truth-seeking process.

Drafts of documents that were routinely lost or destroyed in the conventional paper-based world are now retrievable. Nearly all of the modern panoply of computer-mediated communications, from e-mail messages to digital telephony to virtual conferences, are recorded and saved as digital "documents." Vast amounts of data that would have been impossible to collect and manipulate in the conventional paper-based business world can be assembled, transmitted, manipulated, and analyzed by computer.

3. How Electronic Information Is Stored and Retrieved

When considering the discovery of ESI, it is useful to review the various types of ESI that can be created, the physical ways in which such ESI can be stored, and the typical organizational schemas under which it can be organized. These various metrics can be used to target that ESI most likely to provide useful information.

a. Types of ESI

There are potentially thousands of different types of data that could exist within an enterprise data set. Typically, however, most organizations have a limited set of potential data types on a limited number of applications that create ESI. Thus, an important component of an ESI discovery plan is to identify the types of data that may yield responsive information. Interviews with key players and with an organization's computer staff are two ways to determine which data types are worth focusing on.

From the perspective of creating a discovery plan, there are two fundamental categories, or types, of ESI: (1) data created by individual custodians using local applications; and, (2) data created by individual custodians using an enterprise application and/or which is automatically created and/or captured by an enterprise application.

i. Custodian–Based ESI

Custodian-based ESI is familiar to anyone who uses a computer, as it is the data that is created when using application programs on personal computers or through the use of personal digital devices such as cell phones and personal digital assistants. The key to custodian-based ESI from the discovery perspective is not necessarily what the application is or where the application is based, but rather that the custodian controls the creation, content, storage, and disposition of the data file created.

ii. Application Data

An application program, often referred to simply as an application, is any program that is designed to perform a specific function directly for a custodian or, in some cases, for another application program. For the purposes of discovery, key features of application programs are that they are initiated by the custodian, the custodian creates the content (data) by directly interacting with the application (whether personal-computer-based, a network application, or even an internet-based application,) and the custodian determines where the resulting application data file will be stored, what it is going to be named, its usage, and how long it will remain in existence.

Examples of application programs include:

* Word processors

* Spreadsheet programs

* Database programs

* Web browsers

* Software development tools

* Graphical presentation programs

* Document publishing programs

* Sales and personal contact management programs

* Document scanning and storage programs

* Voice-to-text conversion programs

* Printed-text-to-digital-text conversion programs

* Draw, paint, and image editing programs

* Financial management programs

* Music management programs

* Text and other instant messaging-type communication programs

iii. *Personal Digital Devices*

A personal digital device is an electronic device operated by a custodian that is capable of creating ESI. These devices can be very specific in the types of data they hold, such as a photograph in a camera, or multi-purpose in the sense that they can hold specific types of ESI and act as a storage device for non-device-specific types of data. For example, an iPod is fundamentally a hard drive that has a music-playing application program (iTunes) on it. It can hold digitized music that is used by the application and/or it can be used to hold virtually any other type of data file.

Examples of common personal digital devices include:

* Cell phones

* Blackberry

* PDA's (personal digital assistant)

* Cameras

* iPods or other similar device

iv. Messaging Systems

Messaging systems are a special form of application in that they share characteristics of both custodian-based applications and enterprise applications. Most messaging systems, especially those within organizations, are enterprise-wide and enterprise-hosted applications, meaning that the messaging program itself is maintained in a central location and is available for use by all those with an authorized account. Furthermore, the messaging system typically stores some custodian-specific messaging data at this central location. Like a custodian-based application, however, most messaging systems also allow the individual custodian to maintain some portion of her messaging data locally on her personal computer or at some other location she may designate.

When targeting ESI in a messaging system during discovery, one must consider both the enterprise and the individual nature of the system. Inquiry must be made to both the enterprise staff charged with the housing and operation of the messaging system and the individual custodian using the system in order to determine the location, quantity, scope and usage characteristics of the ESI sought.

Examples of common messaging systems include:

* Electronic Mail

  ● Messages

  ● Calendar entries

* Voice Mail

* Instant Messaging

v. Enterprise–Based ESI

Enterprise-based ESI is data that has been created by individual custodians using an enterprise application and/or which has been automatically created and/or captured by an enterprise application. An enterprise application is typically a system where the application and its associated data reside in a central location within the organization. The application is generally one that is used by many custodians across various units within the organization, all of whom need access to all or part of the application data set.

For purposes of discovery, the key aspect of an enterprise application is that the custodian using the application does not have control over the application, its general interface, or where or how the associated data is stored or managed. Accordingly, when considering enterprise data, it is important to involve the organization's computer management staff responsible for the operation of the targeted enterprise application.

vi. Organization–Specific Applications

Most large organizations have teams of software developers that write special-purpose, company-specific application programs designed to automate part of the company's business function. For example, an agricultural products company may develop an application designed specifically for tracking their crops. These applications are typically enterprise in nature and are managed by the company's information technology ("IT") department.

For purposes of discovery, organization-specific applications often require more effort to identify, locate, assess and review. Because these applications are unique, it is difficult to find information about them or their corresponding data sets in the vendor market. A special effort must be made to identify the existence of these applications and the identity of those individuals who have knowledge about them.

vii. Databases

Most organizations utilize database applications to organize their products and business workflow. Databases often serve as the "back-room" for other application programs, holding the information that is created in an organized fashion. Enterprise databases tend to be central stores of large volumes of structured data relating to a particular business activity or business function (i.e. product inventory). As with organization-specific applications, it is important to identify their structure and their content.

viii. Generic Enterprise Applications

In addition to customized organization-specific applications, many organizations employ standardized enterprise applications that have been designed and built to solve a particular business need. Because these applications are generally available in the marketplace, it is relatively easy to find information about the application and about the data files that the application supports.

Common examples of generic enterprise applications include:

* Accounting

> Automated accounting is the grandfather of all enterprise applications. Automated accounting systems record and process the accounting transactions of an organization. Most automated accounting systems are modular in nature, allowing the organization to choose those modules that it needs at the time, while also allowing it to add more functions as needed.

* CRM—Customer Relationship Management

> CRM is a term applied to the systems and processes implemented by a company to facilitate their contact with their customers. CRM software is used to support these systems and processes, typically by storing information on current and past customers, prospective customers, and often sales leads. The information in the CRM application is typically accessed by employees in departments such as sales, marketing, product development, and customer service.

* EDRM—Electronic Document and Records Management

The purpose of an EDRM system is to enable an organization to manage its documents throughout the document life cycle, from creation to destruction. EDRM applications typically follow a document from its inception as a work-in-progress until it has passed through a series of defined steps to become a formal record within the organization. EDRM applications often associate a retention code with each record, thereby enabling the organization to destroy records once they have reached the end of their economic, regulatory, legal, or otherwise defined life cycle.

* ERP—Enterprise Resource Planning

An ERP system is an organizational support system based on a common database that integrates the data needed for a variety of business functions such as Manufacturing, Supply Chain Management, Accounting, Human Resources, and Customer Relationship Management. Most ERP systems are modular in nature, allowing the organization to choose those modules that it needs at the time, while allowing it to add more functions as needed. The ultimate goal of the ERM system is to integrate all of the data in the organization into a single database that can then be used to optimize business workflows.

* PLM—Product Lifecycle Management

A PLM system provides an organization an automated platform to manage the entire life cycle of a product, from its conception, through design and manufacture, to service and disposal. It provides the organization with a single source of all product-related information necessary for collaborating with business partners, for supporting product lines, and for developing new or enhanced product lines.

* SCM—Supply Chain Management

An SCM system provides an organization with an automated platform to plan, implement, and control all aspects of its supply chain by tracking the movement and storage of raw materials, work-in-process inventory, and finished goods from start to completion. A comprehensive SCM system encompasses all aspects of sourcing, procurement, logistics, and collaboration with partners, such as suppliers, intermediaries, third-party service providers, and customers.

* SDLC–Systems Development Life Cycle

An SDLC system provides an organization an automated platform to manage the models and methodologies that the organization uses to develop systems, generally computer systems. Most SDLC systems are modular in nature, allowing the organization to choose those modules that it needs at the time, while allowing it to add more functions as needed.

* SRM—Supplier Relationship Management

An SRM system provides an organization with an automated platform for managing its organizational buying processes, including the purchase of in-house supplies, raw materials for manufacturing, and goods for inventory. With the goal of reducing costs and ensuring that the organization has the materials it needs, a comprehensive SRM system measures and manages supplier performance, defines and enforces purchasing requirements, and coordinates the purchasing process with the real-time needs of the organization.

ix. Internet

From a discovery perspective, the information presented by an organization's web pages, and the information gathered from visitors to those web pages, comprises a set of ESI that can be investigated. Increasingly, organizations are connecting their internet access points to databases and other application systems in an attempt to provide a low cost, single point of access to customers and prospective customers.

x. Intranet

An intranet is a private computer network established by an organization that uses Internet protocols and network connectivity to create a private, in-house version of the Internet. Intranets are typically used to provide a secure forum for the organization to share information with its employees. Utilizing a familiar web browser interface, employees can access employee manuals, corporate calendars, updates on corporate events and milestones, records management policies, employee blogs, sales and marketing materials, stock quotations, and the like. Increasingly, intranets are being tied into corporate applications, legacy systems, and databases in an attempt to provide a single-source interface to the company.

xi. Extranet

An extranet is a private network established by an organization that uses Internet protocols, and network connectivity to create a private, in-house version of the Internet that is then shared with selected extra-organizational parties, such as vendors, suppliers, clients, and business partners. Utilizing a familiar web browser interface, those granted access to the organization's extranet can gain access to sales materials, catalogs, production updates, account information, electronic mail, instant messaging, and blogs. Increasingly, extranets are being used to create virtual business communities where business partners come together to share information.

b. How ESI Is Stored

i. Online Storage of ESI

When ESI is stored online, the information is available to a user, on a computer system, in virtually real-time. The definition of online as established by the United States General Services Administration calls for an online system to be available for immediate use on demand without human intervention, in operation, functional and ready for service.

ESI stored online is the most familiar form of data to users of computer systems. When a computer user sits at her computer or workstation, creates a data file using an application program, and then stores that file on the computer or on the corporate network, she has created ESI stored online. When a computer user sits at her computer or workstation and retrieves a file from the local hard drive or from a networked drive, she is retrieving ESI stored online.

Online storage devices are primarily hard drives, whether singly in a personal computer or connected together in an array in a networked system. Hard drives allow fast access to data without any form of human intervention. As online storage provides the fastest retrieval time for ESI, it is typically used for those files that need to be immediately available at all times, which includes virtually all enterprise applications. Given the relatively low cost of online storage, most custodians choose to store their personal data files online as well.

From a discovery perspective, online data is relatively easy to identify, locate, search, retrieve and preserve.

ii.   Near–Line Storage of ESI

Near-line storage is the storage of data on direct access removable media. When a near-line storage device is re-attached to a computer system, the ESI stored thereon becomes available to the user online. Near-line storage provides inexpensive, reliable, and virtually unlimited data storage, but with less accessibility than with online storage, as it requires the step of reintegrating the storage device with the computer system.

Near-line storage is often used for the portability of, and/or to make a backup copy of, ESI. Near-line storage is a convenient way to store ESI that is used periodically, such as music on a CD disk, or to transport ESI from one location to another.

The major categories of near-line storage include:

* Magnetic disks
  * 3.5–inch diskettes
  * Iomega Zip Disk and Syquest-type removeable disks
* Compact disks (CD)
  * CD recordable disks (CD–R)
  * CD rewriteable disks (CD–RW)
  * Digital versatile disk rewriteable disks (DVD–RW)
* Solid state storage (flash memory data storage device)

- Memory card
- Memory stick (USB flash drive)

* Removeable DASD (Direct Access Storage Device) (Hard Drive) Devices

- iPods
- Portable hard drives

Other devices that can serve as near-line storage devices include:

* Remote online backups

* Disk-based backups

* Printers with storage capability

* Fax machines with storage capability

* Copy machines with storage capability

From a discovery perspective, the portability of near-line storage can create identification and location problems. Additionally, while retrieval of ESI from a given near-line source is rarely an issue, retrieval from numerous near-line sources can create logistical and cost issues associated with the requirement for re-integrating the near-line storage device with the computer system before information can be retrieved.

iii. Offline Storage of ESI

Off-line storage maintains ESI on a medium or a device that is not under the control of a processing unit and which is not available for immediate use on demand by the system without human intervention. Compared with online and near-line storage, off-line storage is very slow. The advantage of off-line storage is that it is relatively inexpensive, easily transported, and protects the data from alteration and/or infection. Because of the benefits provided by off-line storage, it is often integral to an organization's backup, or disaster recovery, program. The primary form of off-line storage is magnetic tape. When used as a backup medium, online ESI is written to (stored on) a magnetic tape. The recorded magnetic tape is typically then taken off-site from the organization and stored in a secure and controlled environment to protect it from natural disaster. If all or part of the ESI recorded on the magnetic tape is lost or damaged on the online system, the magnetic tape can be used to return a copy of the ESI to the online system. The time and cost associated with restoring ESI from a magnetic tape is substantial compared with the cost of online or near-line access, and backup tapes are therefore used as a last resort.

From a discovery perspective, backup tapes are a difficult and expensive environment in which to search for ESI. They must be retrieved, mounted and restored to the online system before any of the ESI on those tapes can be accessed. Given that backup tapes are used for backup, however, magnetic tape may be the only location that particular data exists if it has been removed from all other online and near-line sources.

4. Has the Increasingly Computer–Based World of Discovery Increased or Decreased the Cost of Litigation?

Compare Kenneth J. Withers, *Computer-Based Discovery*, 2000 Fed. Cts. L. Rev. at 1–2:

> A tremendous body of professional and academic literature is developing around the issue of computer-based disclosure, discovery, and evidence. Most of this literature is premised on the notion that computer-based discovery increases the cost and complexity of civil litigation. But no empirical research directly compares computer-based discovery to analogous conventional discovery, and there is a strong argument for the opposite premise, that the exchange of computer data, as opposed to paper, will reduce cost and delay. The costs of photocopying and transport can be reduced dramatically or eliminated altogether.[9]

> * * *

> The time involved in reviewing and organizing evidence can be reduced by using word-searching, sorting, and other forms of computer manipulation. The cost of using a litigation support system is reduced dramatically if the documents are in electronic form from the start and do not need to be scanned. Finally, electronic discovery leads logically to electronic evidence. It stands to reason that many of the media conversion costs associated with electronic courtroom presentations can be reduced or eliminated if the documents are in electronic form from the start.

with 2008 Rand Study, *The Legal and Economic Implications of Electronic Discovery*, at 2–3:

> Despite the potential of computer technology to make storage, search, and exchange of information less expensive and less time-consuming, the most frequent issue raised by those we interviewed was the enormous costs—in time and money—to review information that is produced. This is because the sheer volume of records that are identifiable and producible is greater with electronic processes, potentially relevant information that might never have been recorded previously is now being routinely retained, and because the requesting attorneys are aggressive in seeking out such information. Despite the technical advantages of modern IT systems, electronic documents still have to be individually examined by producing attorneys for relevance and privilege concerns before they are delivered to the requesting side. Interviewees indicated that as much as 75 to 90 percent of additional costs attributable to e-

---

9. In the nationwide breast implant litigation, MDL–926, conversion of just one-third of the discovery documents and court papers to computer form resulted in an estimated savings of $1,146,500 in copying costs per party requesting a complete set of the documents.

discovery are due to increases in attorney billings for this "eyes-on" review of electronic documents.

Many of these concerns focused on email, although it is our perception that issues related to transactional databases (orders, production, sales, pricing) are also potentially significant because these files are complex, idiosyncratic, and designed primarily to specific business, as opposed to legal, purposes. In addition, these files are not always in a form that is easy to interpret. In such cases, the burden of transforming the format of information can be significant.

Corporate litigants also voiced concern over their inability to provide convincing documentation about the magnitude of costs associated with broad e-discovery requests. Some of these litigants asserted that many judges do not have an adequate grasp of the technical and cost issues raised by e-discovery and continue to apply paper-based thinking when ruling on discovery disputes. In their view, the potential relevance of requested information was generally outweighed by the imposed burdens. These burdens are likely to increase exponentially with the size, complexity, and scope of the business enterprise. On the other hand, many firms cited a more routinized and efficient e-discovery production process as a competitive advantage in business-versus-business litigation.

As a result of these increased costs of discovery, the legal process may have become more expensive. In small-value cases, these costs could dominate the underlying stakes in dispute. Depending on the legal and factual questions and the discovery issues at play, plaintiffs may have a higher probability of suing and defendants may be more likely to settle in some types of litigation. In addition, e-discovery also affects the flow of information and changes expectations about likely case outcomes. In all kinds of cases, changes in the magnitude and structure of litigation costs, as well as changed perceptions about case value, will alter litigant incentives to file suits, settle cases, and go to trial.

5. Records Management as a Solution

A report from a leading private records consulting firm, Cohasset Associates, supports the view that electronic records management policies are still not well understood and are otherwise underutilized.[2] How would implementing electronic records management solutions help solve or reduce the problem of information overload?

Are there ways to employ filtering and de-duplication techniques so as to significantly reduce the volume of data that must be culled and collected as part of the e-discovery process, prior to the later, more labor-intensive review stage (which still necessarily requires manual review, at least in part)?

---

2. *See* Electronic Records Management Survey—2007: A Call for Collaboration, *available at* http://www.cohasset.com/survey_research.html.

6. Recommendations for Changes in Legal Culture and Practice

Paul & Baron provide four recommendations functioning as at least partial solutions to grappling with the challenge of information inflation:

EXCERPT FROM George L. Paul & Jason R. Baron, *Information Inflation: Can the Legal System Adapt?*, 13 Rich. J.L. & Tech. 10 (2007) (selected footnotes omitted).

First, there must be a change in culture among litigation lawyers. The last 30 years have seen truculence, gamesmanship, and a supreme rule of "volunteer nothing." Because of the new complexity and volume of information, however, the game theory underlying much of litigation has changed. Litigators must collaborate far more than they have in the past, particularly concerning the discovery of information systems. If they do not, they act against their own self-interest. The new "e-discovery" Federal Rules of Civil Procedure explicitly provide for this collaborative process * * *. This iterative collaboration signifies a needed revolution in discovery practice.

Next, a family of computer technology employing new types of search methods and techniques beyond the use of mere keywords should now be considered for use in litigation.[3] In particular, lawyers and judges should be far more tolerant of using statistical techniques, like sampling, as part of a reasonable search process. Litigators can no longer depend on manual review alone. It is too time-consuming and expensive—with costs often exceeding the amount in dispute. Yet the use of machines to search written records continues to pose a challenge, as language is an ever-evolving, elastic form which has proved notoriously hard to search.[4]

In addition, there is the issue of the necessary skill, or technique, to use such computer search tools. How many in the profession have such skill? Have such tools been adequately tested or proven? No. But there is no choice but to shape new tools, and new processes for using them.

Third, there must be innovation in the law, particularly governing inadvertent disclosure of privileged information. New rules on inadvertent disclosure should be given effect, which limit or elimi-

---

3. Generically called "search and retrieval" technology, such methods create a database of all candidate files, including their text and metadata, and then use computer processors to identify documents with a designated word, or combination of words, or probability of appearance of words. *Keyword* searching, *Boolean* searching, *fuzzy logic*, *Bayesean* belief networks, *vector space models*, and the use of *taxonomies* and *ontologies* are all examples of such search and retrieval technology....

4. *See, e.g.*, David Blair, *Wittgenstein, Language and Information: "Back to the Rough Ground!"* 302 (2006) (summarizing prior 1985 Blair & Maron study in which retrieval effectiveness was measured for 40,000 documents captured in a large corporate litigation, where results of the study showed a large amount of indeterminacy of meaning in natural language in light of the fact that "while [the] lawyers and paralegals were convinced that they were retrieving over seventy-five percent of the desired documents, they were, in actuality retrieving only twenty percent!").

nate the waiver of privilege, or the system will become impossibly expensive through continued need for meticulous review.

Finally, from this point forward lawyers must embrace creative, technological approaches to grappling with knowledge management as information inflation continues apace. Failure to do so will severely hamper the legal profession's ability to meaningfully retrieve and process evidence. All this equates to perhaps the biggest new skill set ever thrust upon the profession—a revolution for the practice. What it means to be a lawyer will change rapidly in the years to come.

How realistic is it to expect that lawyers will move towards universal cooperation on matters involving e-discovery, as part of the pre-trial process? What additional procedural reforms might be suggested, beyond the 2006 rules amendments, to deal with the problem of information inflation?

7. How Well Do Lawyers Understand the Technical Aspects of ESI?

In *Alexander v. Federal Bureau of Investigation,*[5] otherwise known as the "Filegate" case, plaintiffs filed a claim under the Privacy Act alleging that White House officials in the Clinton Administration violated the privacy rights of individuals by continuing to possess and access certain FBI files containing highly sensitive reports of interviews taken in connection with those individuals being nominated to positions requiring security clearances. Filed in 1996, the case bogged down in evidentiary proceedings related to the alleged loss of White House e-mail due to technical defects in the operation of the White House e-mail archiving system. A White House technician submitted a declaration stating that "all" e-mail had been preserved on the "ARMS" system (Automated Records Management System). Plaintiffs alleged that this technician knew or should have known that glitches had occurred resulting in the failure of the ARMS system to capture a significant portion of e-mail. Two million e-mails were eventually restored from backup tapes as a result of the lawsuit. After holding over fifty days of hearings on the subject of missing White House e-mail, the judge eventually concluded that there had been misunderstandings on the part of high level officials and counsel, but no deliberate misconduct or wrongdoing in the filing of declarations or in making representations to the court.

> The Court has concluded that the essential errors made by the White House Counsel's Office were caused by a lack of familiarity with computer terminology and language and workings by the lawyers involved. Mr. Barry, the computer expert, simply talked a different language, and the lawyers he dealt with did not fully appreciate the significance of some of the information that he gave them, and the information he didn't give them. All of this occurred long before development of current sophisticated ways that lawyers

---

5.   541 F. Supp. 2d 274 (D.D.C. 2008).

have had to learn to deal with computer experts. It calls to the Court's mind its own experience in dealing with intelligence officials, *i.e.*, if you don't use the right words in your question, you won't get the right answer. You have to learn to ask the question in a number of ways, and probe and examine and get into the nitty-gritty to understand what the truth is. None of the White House lawyers involved in this matter did that. But plaintiffs produced no evidence whatsoever that any of those lawyers deliberately obstructed justice, or deliberately provided what turned out to be false information to the Court. Not only is the evidence not "clear and convincing," as would be required for this Court to rule for plaintiffs on their contempt motion, but there is simply no evidence of any deliberate effort to conceal the truth. Plaintiffs would have the Court infer that some grand conspiracy existed to deprive them of necessary information. Plaintiffs simply have no such evidence.[6]

Writing in 2008 about events of many years earlier, the court noted that "[a]ll of this occurred long before development of current sophisticated ways that lawyers have had to learn to deal with computer experts."[7] How confident are you that this type of misunderstanding couldn't happen again?

B. RETRIEVING BACKUP INFORMATION

1. Backups

Organizations typically make backups for three reasons:

First, a backup protects the organization from losing its valuable data in case of a disaster (natural or manmade) or in case of a computer system failure that results in data loss. *Second*, a backup can be used to restore specific data files that have been accidentally deleted, modified, or corrupted. *Third*, many organizations use backups as a generic form of long-term data archiving. In this capacity, backups are made and are held by the organization as a central repository of data over time.

2. Typical Categories of Backups

While a backup is technically any process that moves a file from its on-line storage location to another on-line, near-line or off-line storage location, there are some typical ways in which backups are created by custodians and within organizations. In terms of discovery, it is important to understand the various ways in which both the client and the adversary conduct and organize their backup systems. This involves discussions with both individual custodians to determine how they back up data, as well as with the organization's computer staff to determine how organizational backups are conducted.

There are two different types of backups, unstructured and structured.

---

6. *Id.* at 277–78.

7. *Id.* at 277.

a. Unstructured Backups

An unstructured backup is typically an ad-hoc copying of a small number of custodian-selected files to some form of on-line, near-line, or off-line repository. Unstructured backups are typically placed onto near-line stores like CD–R, DVD–R, or USB thumb-drive-type media. Unstructured backups typically have little or no information about what was backed up or when the backup took place, and there is typically little consistency to the frequency and/or content of such backups. Unstructured backups are probably the easiest to implement by the custodian, but they are the least managed and are prone to dispersal and loss.

From a discovery perspective, unstructured backups are usually very difficult to deal with. They require in-depth inquiry to identify, locate, and retrieve and, once retrieved, are costly to integrate into the discovery process due to the resources needed to identify the backup method, the types and quantities of data, and the inefficiencies associated with loading a relatively small amount of data.

b. Structured Backups

A structured backup is a backup of a predictable target set of data that occurs on a set timetable. Structured backups occur most frequently within organizations and they account for the vast majority of data stored within backups. Structured backups, and especially those conducted systematically by an organization's computer services department, typically have detailed descriptions about what was backed up, when it was backed up, and how it was backed up. From a discovery perspective, structured backups are generally easier to identify, locate, and retrieve, and a greater level of analysis can generally be conducted as to the types and quantities of data contained thereon.

c. Local Backup

Local backups are typically backups of data files conducted by custodians through the use of devices contained within, or attached directly to, their personal computer workstation. From a discovery perspective, local backups are usually sporadic in nature, stored in various locations, inconsistent in terms of types and quantities of data stored, and difficult to restore.

Typical local backup schemas include:

- Backing up data files to magnetic disks such as floppy diskettes, Iomega Zip disks, or Syquest-type removable disks.

- Backing up data files to compact disks (CD's) such as CD recordable disks (CD–R), CD rewriteable disks (CD–RW), or Digital versatile disk rewriteable disks (DVD–RW)

- Backing up data files to solid state storage (flash memory data storage devices) such as memory cards or memory sticks (USB flash drives)

• Backing up data files to removable DASD (Direct Access Storage
Device) (Hard Drive) devices such as iPods or other portable hard
drives

d.   Internet Backup

As high-speed Internet service has become more widely available
and more robust, backup methodologies utilizing the Internet to create
remote backup stores is growing in popularity. These remote sites can
simply be other personal or organizational sites that the custodian can
access, or they can be sites created by companies providing backup and
storage services.

As remote Internet backup sites are organizationally and, typically,
geographically removed, backing data up to the Internet can provide
protection against geographically clustered disasters that could affect
backup data stored in the same region as the host data. Even with high-
speed Internet capability, Internet backups are substantially slower than
backups to local disk storage or to backup tape. This speed issue
generally limits the amount of data that a custodian chooses to send to a
remote Internet site. Some organizations also feel uncomfortable placing
their data into the hands of third-parties to hold and manage, fearing
that sensitive data may be compromised.

From a discovery perspective, it is important to understand that the
custodian typically determines the frequency of, and the composition of,
the backup set that is sent over the Internet. Care must be taken to fully
understand the extent to which a given custodian uses Internet backup,
the frequency of such backups, the manner in which data is selected for
backup, and the details of the remote site at which the data is stored.

e.   Enterprise Backup

Perhaps the most common form of backup in a corporation or
other organization is the enterprise backup. An enterprise backup is
conducted by an organization's computer services staff involving business unit-level or organization-wide computer systems. A backup of an
organization's e-mail system on a daily basis is an example of an
enterprise backup. Because they are conducted by the organization's
computer services staff for the purpose of providing a disaster recovery
copy of the organization's data, enterprise backups tend to be the most
structured in terms of the scope of the data targeted, the frequency of
the backup, the consistency of the media onto which the backup is
made, the recoverability of the backed up data, and the length of time
the backup is maintained before disposal.

From a discovery perspective, enterprise backups are often the
easiest to identify, locate, and retrieve, although the volume of backup
sets that often exist within an organization can make the logistics of the
discovery very difficult. It is also important to keep in mind that
magnetic tapes can fail, thereby compromising the entire backup set to
which that tape belonged. There may also be difficulties associated with

interpreting the many types of data files that are often co-mingled on enterprise backups.

3. Types of Backup Schemas

Within categories of backups there are different backup schemas that can be employed. Understanding the schema chosen for a given backup is an important component in developing a proper model for restoring a backed up set of data, especially when restoring multiple backups to obtain data from a targeted time period.

Typical backup schemas include:

a. Full Backup

A full backup is a backup of every file on the targeted computer system, whether or not that file has changed since the previous backup. Because a full backup copies every file on the targeted system to the backup media, it takes the longest to accomplish and requires the most storage space on the backup media. In terms of restoration, however, a full backup provides the fastest restoration time when restoring the full data set.

Due to the time and tape space required, full backups are generally conducted on a periodic basis as part of a hybrid backup schema. For example, a full backup may be conducted every Sunday night, while an incremental backup is conducted on the days in between. Full backups are also typically performed on systems that are about to undergo hardware and/or software changes as a means to protect against data loss in case the changes do not work or damage the file storage systems.

b. Incremental Backup

An incremental backup is a backup of every file on the targeted computer system that has changed since the last backup took place, regardless of whether the last backup was a full backup or an incremental backup. Because an incremental backup only targets those files that have changed since the last backup, which is typically a fraction of the total data set, it is usually the fastest type of backup and the one that requires the least storage space on the backup media. However, incremental backups also require the longest time and the most tapes to restore.

Due to the inefficiencies associated with restoring an incremental-only backup schema, it is rare to see an incremental-only backup schema. In most organizations, an incremental backup schema is used in conjunction with a full backup.

c. Differential Backup

A differential backup is a backup of every file on the targeted computer system that has changed since the last full backup. While a differential backup is not as fast as an incremental backup, it is faster than a full backup as it does not copy every file. Correspondingly, a differential backup requires more storage space than an incremental backup, but less than a full backup. When used in combination with a full backup, differential backups can provide an effective and efficient backup process.

d.   Continuous Data Backup

A continuous backup is a real-time backup that immediately logs every change on the targeted computer system to a secondary system. This is often done by saving byte or block-level differences rather than file-level differences, which fully utilizes the real-time nature of the system. Effectively, pieces of files are saved as they are changed. If restoration is needed, the management system knows how to piece everything back together in proper form. With a continuing decrease in hard disk storage costs, continuous backup, sometimes referred to as mirroring, may become more popular.

Examples of the differing backup schemas

- *Full Backup:* If you perform a full backup every day of the week and the system crashes on Friday, you would need to restore the full backup set from Thursday to restore the data.

- *Full Plus Incremental Backup:* If you perform a full backup each Sunday and incremental backups every night and the system crashes on Friday, you would need to restore the full backup from Sunday along with the incremental backups from Monday, Tuesday, Wednesday, and Thursday to restore the data.

- *Full Plus Differential Backup:* If you perform a full backup each Sunday and differential backups every night and the system crashes on Friday, you would need to restore the full backup from Sunday and the differential backup from Thursday.

- *Continuous Backup:* If the system crashes on Friday, you simply restore the files from backup.

4.   Backup Rotation

A backup rotation schema is the method chosen for managing backup sets when multiple media are used in the backup process. The rotation schema determines how and when each magnetic tape is used in a backup and for how long it is retained once it has backup data stored on it. The most common backup rotation schema is referred to as the Grandfather–Father–Son model, which defines three sets of backups—daily, weekly and monthly. The daily (Son) backups are rotated on a daily basis with one set graduating to Weekly (Father) status each week. The weekly backups are rotated on a weekly basis with one graduating to Monthly (Grandfather) status each month. Many organizations add to this model by removing one or more monthly tapes to an annual or multi-year storage.

Another common rotation schema is to use a rolling set of magnetic tapes over and over again. This incremental model defines a pool of backup media and, once the entire pool has been used, re-writes to the oldest set. For example, with a daily backup onto a set of ten tape sets, you would have ten days worth of individual daily backups. When all of the tape sets are used, the oldest one is inserted and re-used.

Tape rotation schemas can get very complicated based upon the needs of the organization. In terms of discovery, it is important to determine what tape rotation model is used and how it is implemented. With any rotation model there will be gaps in the tape sets due to human, machine, or tape failures. There may also be other models that have been created for a special purpose.

5. How ESI Is Stored From a Custodian/Records Management Point of View

From a technology standpoint, ESI can be stored on a variety of magnetic, optical, and solid-state media. The manner in which ESI is stored by the custodian onto these media can vary greatly, however, and has to do with both the organization's records management plan and the custodian's own desires regarding the naming and storage location of his or her data.

When considering what ESI may relate to a given discovery matter, it is important to consider where such data may have been placed by a custodian or, indeed, whether such data was ever under the direct control of the custodian.

There are five typical ways in which ESI can be stored:

a. Custodian–Centric Data Storage: Much of the ESI used by a custodian on a day-to-day basis, especially application data, is under the direct control of the custodian. It is the custodian who creates the content associated with a given data file, names it, and determines where the file will be saved. The custodian is also the default "records manager" for her data in the sense that she determines how long data will survive before being deleted. In terms of discovery, the custodian is often the best source of information about her data set, including:

- Types of data created (*i.e.*, what applications were used, including enterprise applications)
- Quantities of data created
- File naming conventions used
- Data storage locations
- Whether custodian-based backups were created
- Others with whom the custodian corresponded and/or shared files
- Use of electronic mail and attachments[8]

---

8. E-mail is a unique application in the sense that it has both enterprise and local characteristics. Technically e-mail is an enterprise software platform, but users use and often store e-mail messages and attachments locally. Accordingly, it makes sense in discovery to investigate e-mail from both the

b. Virtual Workgroup–Centric Data Storage: A virtual workgroup is a group of individuals who work on a common project using digital technologies such as e-mail, instant messaging, shared application programs and databases, calendaring, and file management. Many virtual workgroups share a common data file through the use of applications that support such use. While the custodian creates some of the content for the application data file, she may have little or no say in how the data file is named, where it is stored, how it is ultimately used, or how long it remains in existence. Many times these issues are handled either by organization rules or by a custodian named as the workgroup leader.

As networking and the Internet become more pervasive, and as application software providers enable workgroup features into their software, the concept of virtual workgroups is likely to grow. Rather than sending a file to a number of individuals and then integrating their suggestions and changes, the data file remains in a central location and the users modify it directly, with each person's edits and/or notations identified by name.

In terms of discovery, the custodian is often the best source of information about his or her participation in a virtual workgroup.

c. Business Unit–Centric Data Storage: Many organizations are structured like holding companies, made up of many business units that maintain their own computer operations but that share some overall application platforms, such as e-mail. A single organization may also have different operating divisions that it treats as business units. Custodians working in one business unit within a larger organization may spend most of their time working on the business unit's computer system, but at least part of their time on platforms owned and managed by the parent organization. From the custodians' viewpoint, they are working on a single system. Behind the scenes, however, many different operating and data storage environments may be involved. While a custodian may create the content associated with a given data file and name it, in some business-unit environments the custodian may have little or no choice as to where the data file is saved. This is especially true when enterprise applications are used.

In terms of discovery, both the custodian and organizational computer services staff need to be considered as sources of information about the underlying computer system being used and the location(s) of related data stores.

d. Enterprise–Centric Data Storage: Virtually every organization utilizes enterprise applications in its business model. E-mail is the best example of an enterprise application. One of the key characteristics of an enterprise application is that the data file(s) associated with the application are stored and managed at a central location within the organization, typically by professional computer services staff. Custodi-

---

enterprise level through discussions with organizational computer services personnel and locally through discussions with individual custodians as to how they use their e-mail system.

ans using the enterprise application may have desktop applications that belong to and/or interact with the enterprise application, or they may simply "log on" to the enterprise application and use it directly at its central location. While the custodian may create new data using the enterprise application and/or modify existing information, the custodian typically has no say in how the data file is named, where it is stored, or how it is managed.

In terms of discovery, both the custodian and organizational computer services staff are considered sources of information about the enterprise applications being used and the location(s) of related data stores.

e.   Third Party–Centric Data Storage: With the increased use of outsourced computer operations and the use of Internet-based applications, more and more organizational data is being stored and managed by third-parties. Outsourcing means that a third-party manages the hardware and software infrastructure for an organization for a fee. In effect, the third-party is serving as the computer services department for the organization. An Internet-based application is one in which a user using the Internet goes to a third-party site and logs onto an application program provided by the third-party. The user then uses the application as if it resided on her desktop or on the enterprise computers. In both situations, the data created by the user remains with the third-party provider. In terms of discovery, the custodian, the organizational computer services staff, and the third-party's computer staff are considered sources of information about the applications being used and the location(s) of related data stores.

6.   Fundamental Computer Forensic Issues

a.   Forensic Disk Images

When used in conjunction with discovery, the term forensics relates to the use of specialized techniques for the recovery, authentication, and analysis of specific ESI. Forensic examinations are typically used when a matter involves issues that require the reconstruction of computer usage patterns; the examination of residual data left after deletion; technical analysis of computer usage patterns; and/or other testing of the data that may de destructive in nature. In order to conduct a forensic examination, the ESI, and the storage device on which the ESI resides, must be collected in a manner that requires specialized expertise.

The most common form of forensic collection is to make an image of the storage media on which the targeted ESI resides. This image, sometimes called a bit image, is an exact copy of the storage device—such as a hard drive, a CD, or any other disk format—including all areas that contain data and all areas that appear to be empty (but which may actually contain remnants of data). The image is a single file containing the complete contents and structure of the storage device. A disk image file is created by making a sector-by-sector copy of the source media, thereby completely copying the entire structure and contents of the storage media.

Forensic images are acquired with the use of specialized software tools. When used properly, these images contain a copy of everything that is on the target media, including live and deleted data. Forensic images are also sometimes referred to as a bitstream image, a bit image, or a cloned image. This image can be used to re-create an exact copy of the storage device on which a forensic examination can be conducted. The forensic examination can then be conducted on the re-created drive in exactly the same way in which it could have been done on the original device. Because forensic examinations often involve destructive testing, and because they require the ability to replicate their findings, this ability to work on re-created drives is critical.

The primary question when considering a forensic collection is whether or not the facts surrounding the matter at hand suggest that a forensic examination is needed. Was unique, important data deleted? Is it likely that deleted data can be recovered? Is it important to show usage activity and usage patterns? Is it important to authenticate a particular file in order to show that the represented data and/or time of creation is accurate? Do you need to confirm that all of the text in a document is original or that a critical e-mail was really sent when it appears to have been?

Because imaging software is commonly available, and because the vast majority of training programs in the field of electronic discovery revolve around forensics, there is a growing tendency to want to "image everything." But unless an argument can be made that the matter at hand will benefit from a forensic collection and additional examination, there is no reason to do a forensic collection just because the technology exists to do it.

If the matter allows a non-forensic acquisition and analysis of ESI, then a data collection is what is required. A data collection, as opposed to a forensic collection, collects files at the file level, not at the disk level, basically by copying the desired information and processing it into a review system. Data collection is faster and cheaper than a forensic collection and is the type of collection that is warranted if a forensic collection is not required.

b.   File Deletion

A computer's file system determines how the computer stores and manages files on its attached storage media. There are several file systems in use today, and all offer some form of file recovery once a file is deleted. Consider the FAT file system, one of the most commonly used file systems today, as an example. When a file is deleted on a File Allocation Table (FAT) file system, its directory entry[9] in the FAT remains stored on the disk, although the file name is altered in a way

---

9.   A file's directory entry is much like a person's listing in a telephone book. It holds the file's name and its storage location on a piece of storage media, such as a hard drive, a CD, or a DVD. The directory entry tells the computer where to find the data file.

that lets the system know that the storage space occupied by the (now deleted) file is again available for use by a new file or by an expanded version of an existing file. The majority of the deleted file's information, such as its name, time stamp, file length and location on the disk, remain unchanged in its directory entry in the FAT. The deleted file's content will remain on the storage media until it is overwritten by another file. The more file activity there is on a particular computer system, the more unlikely it is that a file can be recovered, as the likelihood that the storage areas where the file had resided will be overwritten is greater.

Specialized software tools, some provided with, or built into, the operating system, allow for the recovery of a deleted file provided that a new file or data set has not overwritten the areas of the storage device holding the deleted file in question. At the simplest level, these tools allow the modified file name of the deleted file to be changed back into a name format that does not indicate a deleted file. The file then becomes a "live" file again, and available for use by an application program. In some cases a greater level of reconstruction is required to retrieve some or all of a deleted file. If the directory entry for the deleted file has been overwritten, or if some of the data storage areas for the deleted file have been overwritten, it will be more difficult to recover the file.

Some computer operating systems provide a layered approach to data deletion. Microsoft's Windows platform, for example, does not really delete a file when a deletion request is made. The file is placed in a "recycle bin" where it awaits final deletion. Until the file is removed from the recycle bin, it can be easily recovered as it had not really been deleted in a technical sense. When the file is "dumped" from the recycle bin for deletion, it can often still be recovered if the space has not been reutilized.

As with forensic collection, the key question in discovery regarding the recovery of deleted data is whether or not the facts surrounding the matter at hand suggest that data recovery is needed. Was unique, important data deleted? Is it likely that deleted data can be recovered? Was the file located on a system where file activity was such that recovery is likely? Is the matter at hand one where file deletion is suspected or traditionally part of the pattern of activity for such matters, such as in trade secret theft? If the matter is one where deleted data recovery may be important, then attempts should be made to identify and recover appropriate files. If not, then deleted data recovery is not warranted and is ultimately a waste of time and resources.

As with imaging, data recovery software is commonly available, and because many of the training programs in the field of electronic discovery revolve around forensics (which is often targeted towards data recovery), there is a bias to target deleted data. But unless an argument can be made that the matter at hand will benefit from the recovery of deleted data, there is no reason to attempt such recovery just because the technology exists to do it.

II

PRESERVATION OF ELECTRONIC INFORMATION

■ ■ ■

A. RECORDS RETENTION POLICIES

ARTHUR ANDERSEN LLP v. UNITED STATES

544 U.S. 696 (2005)

CHIEF JUSTICE REHNQUIST delivered the opinion of the Court

As Enron Corporation's financial difficulties became public in 2001, petitioner Arthur Andersen LLP, Enron's auditor, instructed its employees to destroy documents pursuant to its document retention policy. A jury found that this action made petitioner guilty of violating 18 U.S.C. §§ 1512(b)(2)(A) and (B). These sections make it a crime to "knowingly use intimidation or physical force, threaten, or corruptly persuade another person . . . with intent to . . . cause" that person to "withhold" documents from, or "alter" documents for use in, an "official proceeding."[1] The Court of Appeals for the Fifth Circuit affirmed. We hold that the jury instructions failed to convey properly the elements of a "corrup[t] persua[sion]" conviction under § 1512(b), and therefore reverse.

Enron Corporation, during the 1990's, switched its business from operation of natural gas pipelines to an energy conglomerate, a move that was accompanied by aggressive accounting practices and rapid growth. Petitioner audited Enron's publicly filed financial statements and provided internal audit and consulting services to it. Petitioner's "engagement team" for Enron was headed by David Duncan. Beginning in 2000, Enron's financial performance began to suffer, and, as 2001 wore on, worsened. On August 14, 2001, Jeffrey Skilling, Enron's Chief Executive Officer (CEO), unexpectedly resigned. Within days, Sherron Watkins, a senior accountant at Enron, warned Kenneth Lay, Enron's newly reappointed CEO, that Enron could "implode in a wave of accounting scandals." She likewise informed Duncan and Michael Odom, one of petitioner's partners who had supervisory responsibility over Duncan, of the looming problems.

---

1. We refer to the 2000 version of the statute, which has since been amended by Congress. [See the amendment discussed below.]

On August 28, an article in the Wall Street Journal suggested improprieties at Enron, and the SEC opened an informal investigation. By early September, petitioner had formed an Enron "crisis-response" team, which included Nancy Temple, an in-house counsel.[3] On October 8, petitioner retained outside counsel to represent it in any litigation that might arise from the Enron matter. The next day, Temple discussed Enron with other in-house counsel. Her notes from that meeting reflect that "some SEC investigation" is "highly probable."

On October 10, Odom spoke at a general training meeting attended by 89 employees, including 10 from the Enron engagement team. Odom urged everyone to comply with the firm's document retention policy. He added: "If it's destroyed in the course of [the] normal policy and litigation is filed the next day, that's great.... We've followed our own policy, and whatever there was that might have been of interest to somebody is gone and irretrievable."[4] On October 12, Temple entered the Enron matter into her computer, designating the "Type of Potential Claim" as "Professional Practice—Government/Regulatory Investigation." Temple also e-mailed Odom, suggesting that he "remind the engagement team of our documentation and retention policy."

On October 16, Enron announced its third quarter results. That release disclosed a $1.01 billion charge to earnings.[5] The following day, the SEC notified Enron by letter that it had opened an investigation in August and requested certain information and documents. On October 19, Enron forwarded a copy of that letter to petitioner.

On the same day, Temple also sent an e-mail to a member of petitioner's internal team of accounting experts and attached a copy of the document policy. On October 20, the Enron crisis-response team held a conference call, during which Temple instructed everyone to "make sure to follow the [document] policy." On October 23, Enron CEO Lay declined to answer questions during a call with analysts because of "potential lawsuits, as well as the SEC inquiry." After the call, Duncan met with other Andersen partners on the Enron engagement team and told them that they should ensure team members were

---

3. A key accounting problem involved Enron's use of "Raptors," which were special purpose entities used to engage in "off-balance-sheet" activities. Petitioner's engagement team had allowed Enron to "aggregate" the Raptors for accounting purposes so that they reflected a positive return. This was, in the words of petitioner's experts, a "black-and-white" violation of Generally Accepted Accounting Principles.

4. The firm's policy called for a single central engagement file, which "should contain only that information which is relevant to supporting our work." The policy stated that, "[i]n cases of threatened litigation, ... no related information will be destroyed." It also separately provided that, if petitioner is "advised of litigation or subpoenas regarding a particular engagement, the related information should not be destroyed." Policy Statement No. 780 set forth "notification" procedures for whenever professional practice litigation against [petitioner] or any of its personnel has been commenced, has been threatened or is judged likely to occur, or when governmental or professional investigations that may involve [petitioner] or any of its personnel have been commenced or are judged likely.

5. The release characterized the charge to earnings as "non-recurring." Petitioner had expressed doubts about this characterization to Enron, but Enron refused to alter the release. Temple wrote an e-mail to Duncan that "suggested deleting some language that might suggest we have concluded the release is misleading."

complying with the document policy. Another meeting for all team members followed, during which Duncan distributed the policy and told everyone to comply. These, and other smaller meetings, were followed by substantial destruction of paper and electronic documents.

On October 26, one of petitioner's senior partners circulated a New York Times article discussing the SEC's response to Enron. His e-mail commented that "the problems are just beginning and we will be in the cross hairs. The marketplace is going to keep the pressure on this and is going to force the SEC to be tough." On October 30, the SEC opened a formal investigation and sent Enron a letter that requested accounting documents.

Throughout this time period, the document destruction continued, despite reservations by some of petitioner's managers.[6] On November 8, Enron announced that it would issue a comprehensive restatement of its earnings and assets. Also on November 8, the SEC served Enron and petitioner with subpoenas for records. On November 9, Duncan's secretary sent an e-mail that stated: "Per Dave—No more shredding. . . . We have been officially served for our documents." Enron filed for bankruptcy less than a month later. Duncan was fired and later pleaded guilty to witness tampering.

In March 2002, petitioner was indicted in the Southern District of Texas on one count of violating §§ 1512(b)(2)(A) and (B). The indictment alleged that, between October 10 and November 9, 2001, petitioner "did knowingly, intentionally and corruptly persuade ... other persons, to wit: [petitioner's] employees, with intent to cause" them to withhold documents from, and alter documents for use in, "official proceedings, namely: regulatory and criminal proceedings and investigations." * * * [T]he jury returned a guilty verdict. The District Court denied petitioner's motion for a judgment of acquittal.

The Court of Appeals for the Fifth Circuit affirmed. It held that the jury instructions properly conveyed the meaning of "corruptly persuades" and "official proceeding"; that the jury need not find any consciousness of wrongdoing; and that there was no reversible error.
* * *

Chapter 73 of Title 18 of the United States Code provides criminal sanctions for those who obstruct justice. Sections 1512(b)(2)(A) and (B), part of the witness tampering provisions, provide in relevant part:

"Whoever knowingly uses intimidation or physical force, threatens, or corruptly persuades another person, or attempts to do so, or engages in misleading conduct toward another person, with intent

---

6. For example, on October 26, John Riley, another partner with petitioner, saw Duncan shredding documents and told him "this wouldn't be the best time in the world for you guys to be shredding a bunch of stuff." On October 31, David Stulb, a forensics investigator for petitioner, met with Duncan. During the meeting, Duncan picked up a document with the words "smoking gun" written on it and began to destroy it, adding "we don't need this." Stulb cautioned Duncan on the need to maintain documents and later informed Temple that Duncan needed advice on the document retention policy.

to ... cause or induce any person to ... withhold testimony, or withhold a record, document, or other object, from an official proceeding [or] alter, destroy, mutilate, or conceal an object with intent to impair the object's integrity or availability for use in an official proceeding ... shall be fined under this title or imprisoned not more than ten years, or both."

In this case, our attention is focused on what it means to "knowingly ... corruptly persuade" another person "with intent to ... cause" that person to "withhold" documents from, or "alter" documents for use in, an "official proceeding."

We have traditionally exercised restraint in assessing the reach of a federal criminal statute, both out of deference to the prerogatives of Congress, * * * and out of concern that a fair warning should be given to the world in language that the common world will understand, of what the law intends to do if a certain line is passed * * *.

Such restraint is particularly appropriate here, where the act underlying the conviction—"persuasion"—is by itself innocuous. Indeed, "persuading" a person "with intent to ... cause" that person to "withhold" testimony or documents from a Government proceeding or Government official is not inherently malign. Consider, for instance, a mother who suggests to her son that he invoke his right against compelled self-incrimination, or a wife who persuades her husband not to disclose marital confidences.

Nor is it necessarily corrupt for an attorney to "persuade" a client "with intent to ... cause" that client to "withhold" documents from the Government. In *Upjohn Co.* v. *United States*, 449 U.S. 383 (1981), for example, we held that Upjohn was justified in withholding documents that were covered by the attorney-client privilege from the Internal Revenue Service (IRS). No one would suggest that an attorney who "persuaded" Upjohn to take that step acted wrongfully, even though he surely intended that his client keep those documents out of the IRS' hands.

"Document retention policies," which are created in part to keep certain information from getting into the hands of others, including the Government, are common in business. * * * It is, of course, not wrongful for a manager to instruct his employees to comply with a valid document retention policy under ordinary circumstances.

Acknowledging this point, the parties have largely focused their attention on the word "corruptly" as the key to what may or may not lawfully be done in the situation presented here. Section 1512(b) punishes not just "corruptly persuading" another, but "*knowingly* ... corruptly persuading" another. The Government suggests that "knowingly" does not modify "corruptly persuades," but that is not how the statute most naturally reads. It provides the *mens rea*—"knowingly"—and then a list of acts—"uses intimidation or physical force, threatens, or corruptly persuades." * * *

The parties have not pointed us to another interpretation of "knowingly . . . corruptly" to guide us here. In any event, the natural meaning of these terms provides a clear answer. * * * Only persons conscious of wrongdoing can be said to "knowingly . . . corruptly persuade." * * *

The outer limits of this element need not be explored here because the jury instructions at issue simply failed to convey the requisite consciousness of wrongdoing. Indeed, it is striking how little culpability the instructions required. For example, the jury was told that, "even if [petitioner] honestly and sincerely believed that its conduct was lawful, you may find [petitioner] guilty." The instructions also diluted the meaning of "corruptly" so that it covered innocent conduct.

* * * The District Court based its instruction on the definition of that term found in the Fifth Circuit Pattern Jury Instruction for § 1503. This pattern instruction defined "corruptly" as "knowingly and dishonestly, with the specific intent to subvert or undermine the integrity" of a proceeding. The Government, however, insisted on excluding "dishonestly" and adding the term "impede" to the phrase "subvert or undermine." The District Court agreed over petitioner's objections, and the jury was told to convict if it found petitioner intended to "subvert, undermine, or impede" governmental factfinding by suggesting to its employees that they enforce the document retention policy.

These changes were significant. No longer was any type of "dishonest[y]" necessary to a finding of guilt, and it was enough for petitioner to have simply "impede[d]" the Government's factfinding ability. * * * By definition, anyone who innocently persuades another to withhold information from the Government "get[s] in the way of the progress of" the Government. With regard to such innocent conduct, the "corruptly" instructions did no limiting work whatsoever.

The instructions also were infirm for another reason. They led the jury to believe that it did not have to find *any* nexus between the "persuasion" to destroy documents and any particular proceeding. In resisting any type of nexus element, the Government relies heavily on § 1512(e)(1), which states that an official proceeding "need not be pending or about to be instituted at the time of the offense." It is, however, one thing to say that a proceeding "need not be pending or about to be instituted at the time of the offense," and quite another to say a proceeding need not even be foreseen. A "knowingly . . . corrupt persuader" cannot be someone who persuades others to shred documents under a document retention policy when he does not have in contemplation any particular official proceeding in which those documents might be material.

* * *

For these reasons, the jury instructions here were flawed in important respects. The judgment of the Court of Appeals is reversed, and the case is remanded for further proceedings consistent with this opinion.

Editor's Note:

The statutes covering destruction of records have been broadened to cover destruction in circumstances like *Arthur Andersen*. The Sarbanes–Oxley Act amended 18 U.S.C. § 1512 to provide as follows:

(c) Whoever corruptly—

(1) alters, destroys, mutilates, or conceals a record, document, or other object, or attempts to do so, with the intent to impair the object's integrity or availability for use in an official proceeding; or

(2) otherwise obstructs, influences, or impedes any official proceeding, or attempts to do so,

shall be fined under this title or imprisoned not more than 20 years, or both.

Does this amendment cover the activity at issue in *Arthur Andersen*?

RAMBUS, INC. v. INFINEON TECHNOLOGIES AG

222 F.R.D. 280 (E.D. Va. 2004)

PAYNE, DISTRICT JUDGE

[This is a patent case, in which the court found (in what it refers to as the March 17 Opinion) that Rambus destroyed a significant amount of electronic information that was subject to discovery. The instant opinion concerns whether certain sanctions for spoliation are warranted. Rambus argues that a spoliation finding is not warranted because the documents were destroyed pursuant to a standard policy.]

Through depositions, Infineon has established that Rambus' document purging program resulted in the destruction of evidence relevant to this action * * *. Thus, it is established that Rambus intentionally destroyed evidence and that at least some of this evidence was relevant to this action.

Furthermore, it is also settled that some destruction occurred at a point in time when Rambus anticipated litigation and therefore had a duty to preserve the evidence. * * * On the basis of what was known as of the March 17 Opinion, Infineon had shown that Rambus formulated and instituted a document retention and destruction policy in early 1998. Beginning in March of that year, Joel Karp ("Karp"), a non-lawyer who serves as Rambus' Vice President of Intellectual Property, drafted a document retention policy based on information supplied by a law firm, Cooley Godward, LLP ("Cooley Godward"). * * *

As of the March 17 Opinion, it also had been shown that, in the summer of 1998, Karp and outside counsel gave presentations on the document retention policy, presenting several slide shows to employees to inform about the system. Then, Karp kicked-off the document retention program on September 3, 1998 with "Shred Day," an event at which each employee at Rambus' corporate headquarters in Mountain View, California was provided with a burlap bag with the instructions to bag all documents slated for the shredder. Infineon, of course, described Shred Day in a rather sinister fashion, pointing to internal Rambus emails that reflect that Shred Day culminated in a 5:00 p.m. beer, pizza, and champagne "celebration." Rambus, in contrast, framed this beer, pizza, and champagne treat not as a "celebration," but rather as corporate incentive and morale boosting after a day of heavy sack lifting and laborious document review. Whatever Rambus' motivations may have been, it was uncontested as of the March 17 Opinion that, all told, Rambus employees shredded approximately 20,000 pounds of documents on Shred Day—some 2 million pages of documents. In addition, it was known that on several additional days in the fall of 1998, the shredder trucks returned to Rambus, resulting in the destruction of additional documents.

As of the March 17 Opinion, it was also known that Lester Vincent ("Vincent"), Rambus' former outside patent prosecution counsel who drafted many of the Rambus claims had, pursuant to instructions from Rambus, destroyed some documents just before Rambus instituted this litigation in 2000 but before Rambus sent a letter to Infineon accusing it of infringement. And, it was known that, thereafter, Rambus instructed its other outside counsel to follow suit.

* * *

Infineon also pointed to depositions of various Rambus employees and executives. For instance, Allen Roberts, Rambus' Vice President of Engineering, testified under oath that Karp directed him to purge his files at least in part because "such materials are discoverable in subsequent litigations." Furthermore, Tony Diepenbrock ("Diepenbrock"), a lawyer in Rambus' in-house legal department, testified that one of the understood reasons behind Shred Day was that "some of that stuff is discoverable."

* * * Thus, by the March 17 Opinion, Infineon had presented evidence that, taken together, rather strongly indicated that Rambus had explicitly linked development of its document retention policy and the shredding of documents with the company's preparations for patent litigation.

* * *

E. Rambus' Position on Spoliation

Rambus correctly notes that today virtually all companies have document retention policies. Rambus contends that its document retention policy is fairly typical, is in accordance with the general standards applicable to such programs, and was adopted for legitimate business reasons, not in anticipation of litigation.

In support of these contentions, Rambus quotes from a slide presentation that Karp gave to Rambus employees immediately before

Shred Day. These slides instruct employees that, *inter alia,* documents designated as containing trade secret information should be retained for the life of the trade secret, that personnel records should be kept for a period of three years, and that employees should "LOOK FOR THINGS TO KEEP" and to "LOOK FOR REASONS TO KEEP IT."

In addition, although Rambus does not dispute the fact that it destroyed documents because of their "discoverability," it suggests that Infineon has misunderstood the true nature of Rambus' concerns. Rambus argues that, in the late 1990s, Karp and other Rambus executives became concerned that Rambus was keeping far too many documents and back-up tapes and that, if Rambus was ever asked to produce documents in discovery or as the result of a third-party subpoena, it would require vast resources to sift through the materials. For instance, Karp testified under oath that:

> "My concern was that if I was ever asked to produce these thousands of back-up tapes, regardless of what they concerned—they did not just contain e-mail, they contained everything—that it would be a task that would be beyond the human endurance to try to figure out what was on those things."

In addition, Richard Barth ("Barth"), a former Rambus employee who testified at deposition regarding the document retention policy and Shred Day, stated:

> "I don't recall [Karp] being so much worried about documents that were harmful to Rambus in that it would reveal you know, some dastardly secret. What I do remember is that, yeah, we are pack rats and the amount of stuff that we had was enormous. And the concern was that if we had to go and grind through all that and produce it, it would just kill us. We'd get no engineering done. All our resources would be consumed by plowing through old stuff."

Thus, although Rambus admits that it instituted its document retention policy out of discovery-related concerns, it contends that these concerns were related to the legitimate purpose of reducing search and review costs, not for the purpose of eliminating potentially-damaging documents that a future adversary might discover.

The position of Rambus is significantly undermined by the fact that Rambus has not shown that it was exposed to litigation other than the patent litigation which it was itself formulating in 1998, 1999, and 2000. Nor did the *in camera* document review reveal that Rambus considered itself threatened by litigation instituted by others. And, considering Rambus' assessment that its intellectual property was not respected by others, it is unlikely that the need to defend litigation brought by others was on the company's mind at the time. Indeed, the only litigation mentioned in Rambus' documents is that which it intended to bring.

In sum, although Rambus has presented evidence that, in concept, it structured its document retention program like a lawful program and that some of its articulated reasons for adopting the policy were conceptually valid, these arguments ignore the rather convincing evidence that Rambus intentionally destroyed potentially relevant documents notwithstanding that, when it did so, it anticipated litigation. In any event, even if Rambus had been instituting a valid purging program, it disregarded the principle that even valid purging programs need to be put on hold so as to avoid the destruction of relevant materials when litigation is "reasonably foreseeable."

F. Analysis of the Spoliation Issue in Perspective of the Entire Record as Described Above

* * *

In sum, the record to date shows that, from early 1998 through 2000, Rambus had in effect a document retention program that was conceived and implemented as an integral part of its licensing and litigation strategy. That strategy, including the document retention program portion thereof, was devised and implemented with the aid and advice of lawyers, both in house and outside. The company's plan was to destroy discoverable documents as part of its litigation strategy and the allegedly privileged documents evince that plan. Other evidence shows that the document destruction plan continued to be implemented throughout 1999 and 2000 while the litigation strategy of which it was a constituent element was also in final preparation and implementation.

By any measure, on this record, Infineon has made a prima facie showing that Rambus intentionally has engaged in the spoliation of evidence * * *. Rambus' defense to this proof is that it established a legitimate document retention program for legitimate reasons. That defense simply does not square with the record as it currently stands. There is nothing legitimate about devising and implementing a plan to destroy documents as a core part of a patent licensing and litigation strategy. * * *

Where, as here, Rambus intended to engage in a specified kind of litigation, with specified, carefully selected litigation targets in specified venues and, as part of its plan to do so, set about to destroy documents relevant to those litigations, the courts cannot sanction a document retention program as legitimate. Here, the program was set up for what, on the record to date, rather clearly appears to have been an impermissible purpose—the destruction of relevant, discoverable documents at a time when Rambus anticipated initiating litigation to enforce its patent rights against already identified adversaries. Indeed, that purpose runs contrary to the rule that there is a duty not to destroy documents when litigation to which they are relevant is anticipated.

* * *

Document retention programs, lawfully implemented, are certainly permissible. But, even lawful programs must be suspended or adjusted when litigation is reasonably anticipated and the in-place program runs the risk of destroying potentially relevant materials. As the record now stands, Rambus' conduct here defies that precept in that Rambus actually started a program because it anticipated that it would soon begin litigation. The fact that the litigation commencement date was deferred by Rambus does not alter that fact. Instead, it permits the inference that Rambus deliberately destroyed documents while it improved (in its view) its litigation posture and while it refined its litigation strategy and slightly altered its litigation targets. Research has disclosed no precedent for finding that such conduct is legitimate or that document destruction under those circumstances can be clothed with propriety merely by calling it a "document retention program."

* * *

[The court, after finding spoliation, reserves the question of sanctions for a later opinion.]

COMMENTARY

A "records retention policy" is generally understood to mean a set of official guidelines or rules governing storage and destruction of documents or ESI. Such policies typically define different types of records, how they are to be treated generally under the policies for retention purposes, and often provide retention schedules defining specific time periods for retention of certain records. Depending on the nature of the entity promulgating the policy, the retention periods applied to specific categories of records may be driven by regulatory or other legal requirements, practical business, or technical needs.

As the Supreme Court notes in the *Arthur Andersen* opinion, there is nothing wrong with having a policy that requires the destruction of documents—as long as this destruction does not occur at a time when a legal preservation duty has already arisen with respect to the documents to be destroyed under the policy. This is consistent with prior case law, which to some degree is codified in Rule 37(e) of the Federal Rules of Civil Procedure, providing that certain sanctions will not apply under ordinary circumstances where information is lost as a result of routine destruction before a preservation duty has arisen.

Moreover, there are significant legal benefits to actively managing records retention. Consistent adherence to records retention policies enables an enterprise to explain why certain records are available for production in discovery and why others are not. The availability of the "safe harbor" of Rule 37(e) is predicated, *inter alia*, on the ability to show some "routine" in the retention and destruction of records. Avoiding the cost of searching and reviewing millions of e-mails that have outlived their business utility and were under no regulatory or other legal retention requirement is another potential major benefit.

Dealing with records retention issues became more complicated with the explosion in volume and variety of ESI. As the retention of greater volumes of ESI becomes easier and less expensive due to advances in storage technology, the difficulty of selectively identifying what should be retained and what should be destroyed in compliance with records retention policies can increase. Suspending systems put in place to implement such policies, such as regular purges of e-mail from servers or recycling of backup media, in order to comply with preservation obligations, can raise significant challenges for legal and IT personnel. Not surprisingly, the issue of when and how records retention policies need to be suspended in the face of the duty to preserve has been the focus of much recent case law.

The *Arthur Andersen* case shows that the decision to comply with a retention policy by destroying records in the face of a legal preservation duty is a bad one. For a records retention policy to act as a shield against spoliation allegations, it must be shown to have been implemented consistently. Where exhortations to comply with a policy's destruction requirements come at the time a legal duty to preserve has already been triggered, compliance with the policy not only fails as a shield, but provides the very basis for a spoliation claim.

Most of the case law examining the issue of whether records were destroyed legitimately pursuant to routine records retention policies addresses situations where the defendant's actions are in question. Accordingly, it is easy to forget that plaintiffs also have a duty (as seen in *Rambus*) to suspend regular destruction under records retention policies when they reasonably anticipate litigation. Generally, plaintiffs are the parties with the earliest opportunity to anticipate litigation given that they are the ones planning it and therefore controlling the timing of its initiation.

Since the Federal Rules of Civil Procedure were amended in 2006, including the addition of Rule 37(e), courts have continued to punish failures to suspend routine document destruction pursuant to records retention policies in the face of a preservation duty. It is important to note that, in the spirit of the *Arthur Andersen* case, these cases do not fault the policies themselves—but merely the failure to suspend such policies when faced with the need to apply a litigation hold. Examination of these cases shows the variety of types of retention policies applied to electronic information and demonstrates the fundamental truth that there is no one-size-fits-all records retention policy; instead, in the language of the Advisory Committee Note to Rule 37(e), these policies should be designed to meet the "business and technical" needs of the party in question.

PROBLEMS

1. Can destruction of records under a records retention policy before those records can be reasonably anticipated to be relevant to a

particular future litigation constitute spoliation? Under what circumstances?

2.   Should a very short retention period for e-mail give rise to a presumption of spoliation? Why? What steps can a party with such a short retention period take to defend its policy?

B.   IMPLEMENTING THE DUTY TO PRESERVE

ZUBULAKE v. UBS WARBURG LLC
"Zubulake V"

229 F.R.D. 422 (S.D.N.Y. 2004)

SCHEINDLIN, DISTRICT JUDGE

Commenting on the importance of speaking clearly and listening closely, Phillip Roth memorably quipped, "The English language is a form of communication! ... Words aren't only bombs and bullets—no, they're little gifts, containing meanings!" What is true in love is equally true at law: Lawyers and their clients need to communicate clearly and effectively with one another to ensure that litigation proceeds efficiently. * * *

I.   INTRODUCTION

This is the fifth written opinion in this case, a relatively routine employment discrimination dispute in which discovery has now lasted over two years. Laura Zubulake is once again moving to sanction UBS for its failure to produce relevant information and for its tardy production of such material. In order to decide whether sanctions are warranted, the following question must be answered: Did UBS fail to preserve and timely produce relevant information and, if so, did it act negligently, recklessly, or willfully?

This decision addresses counsel's obligation to ensure that relevant information is preserved by giving clear instructions to the client to preserve such information and, perhaps more importantly, a client's obligation to heed those instructions. Early on in this litigation, UBS's counsel—both in-house and outside—instructed UBS personnel to retain relevant electronic information. Notwithstanding these instructions, certain UBS employees deleted relevant emails. Other employees never produced relevant information to counsel. As a result, many discoverable e-mails were not produced to Zubulake until recently, even though they were responsive to a document request propounded on June 3, 2002. In addition, a number of e-mails responsive to that document request were deleted and have been lost altogether.

Counsel, in turn, failed to request retained information from one key employee and to give the litigation hold instructions to another.

They also failed to adequately communicate with another employee about how she maintained her computer files. Counsel also failed to safeguard backup tapes that might have contained some of the deleted e-mails, and which would have mitigated the damage done by UBS's destruction of those e-mails.

The conduct of both counsel and client thus calls to mind the now-famous words of the prison captain in *Cool Hand Luke*: "What we've got here is a failure to communicate." Because of this failure by *both* UBS and its counsel, Zubulake has been prejudiced. As a result, sanctions are warranted.

II. FACTS

The allegations at the heart of this lawsuit and the history of the parties' discovery disputes have been well-documented in the Court's prior decisions[5] * * * . In short, Zubulake is an equities trader specializing in Asian securities who is suing her former employer for gender discrimination, failure to promote, and retaliation under federal, state, and city law.

A. Background

Zubulake filed an initial charge of gender discrimination with the EEOC on August 16, 2001. Well before that, however—as early as April 2001—UBS employees were on notice of Zubulake's impending court action. After she received a right-to-sue letter from the EEOC, Zubulake filed this lawsuit on February 15, 2002.

Fully aware of their common law duty to preserve relevant evidence, UBS's in-house attorneys gave oral instructions in August 2001— immediately after Zubulake filed her EEOC charge—instructing employees not to destroy or delete material potentially relevant to Zubulake's claims, and in fact to segregate such material into separate files for the lawyers' eventual review. This warning pertained to both electronic and hard-copy files, but did *not* specifically pertain to so-called "backup tapes," maintained by UBS's information technology personnel. In particular, UBS's in-house counsel, Robert L. Salzberg, "advised relevant UBS employees to preserve and turn over to counsel all files, records or other written memoranda or documents concerning the allegations raised in the [EEOC] charge or any aspect of [Zubulake's] employment." Subsequently—but still in August 2001—UBS's outside counsel met with a number of the key players in the litigation and reiterated Mr. Salzberg's instructions, reminding them to preserve relevant documents, "including e-mails." Salzberg reduced these instruc-

---

5. *See Zubulake I*, 217 F.R.D. 309 (addressing the legal standard for determining the cost allocation for producing e-mails contained on backup tapes); *Zubulake v. UBS Warburg LLC*, 2003 WL 21087136 (S.D.N.Y. May 13, 2003) ("*Zubulake II*") (addressing Zubulake's reporting obligations); *Zubulake v. UBS Warburg LLC*, 216 F.R.D. 280 (S.D.N.Y. 2003) ("*Zubulake III*") (allocating backup tape restoration costs between Zubulake and UBS); *Zubulake v. UBS Warburg LLC*, 220 F.R.D. 212 (S.D.N.Y. 2003) ("*Zubulake IV*") (ordering sanctions against UBS for violating its duty to preserve evidence).

tions to writing in e-mails dated February 22, 2002—immediately after Zubulake filed her complaint—and September 25, 2002. Finally, in August 2002, after Zubulake propounded a document request that specifically called for e-mails stored on backup tapes, UBS's outside counsel instructed UBS information technology personnel to stop recycling backup tapes. *Every* UBS employee mentioned in this Opinion (with the exception of Mike Davies) either personally spoke to UBS's outside counsel about the duty to preserve e-mails, or was a recipient of one of Salzberg's e-mails.

B. Procedural History

In *Zubulake I,* I addressed Zubulake's claim that relevant e-mails had been deleted from UBS's active servers and existed only on "inaccessible" archival media (*i.e.,* backup tapes). Arguing that e-mail correspondence that she needed to prove her case existed only on those backup tapes, Zubulake called for their production. UBS moved for a protective order shielding it from discovery altogether or, in the alternative, shifting the cost of backup tape restoration onto Zubulake. Because the evidentiary record was sparse, I ordered UBS to bear the costs of restoring a sample of the backup tapes.

After the sample tapes were restored, UBS continued to press for cost shifting with respect to any further restoration of backup tapes. In *Zubulake III,* I ordered UBS to bear the lion's share of restoring certain backup tapes because Zubulake was able to demonstrate that those tapes were likely to contain relevant information. Specifically, Zubulake had demonstrated that UBS had failed to maintain all relevant information (principally e-mails) in its active files. After *Zubulake III,* Zubulake chose to restore sixteen backup tapes. In the restoration effort, the parties discovered that certain backup tapes were missing. They also discovered a number of e-mails on the backup tapes that were missing from UBS's active files, confirming Zubulake's suspicion that relevant e-mails were being deleted or otherwise lost.

Zubulake III begat *Zubulake IV,* where Zubulake moved for sanctions as a result of UBS's failure to preserve all relevant backup tapes, and UBS's deletion of relevant e-mails. Finding fault in UBS's document preservation strategy but lacking evidence that the lost tapes and deleted e-mails were particularly favorable to Zubulake, I ordered UBS to pay for the re-deposition of several key UBS employees—Varsano, Chapin, Hardisty, Kim, and Tong—so that Zubulake could inquire about the newly-restored e-mails.

C. The Instant Dispute

The essence of the current dispute is that during the re-depositions required by *Zubulake IV,* Zubulake learned about more deleted e-mails and about the existence of e-mails preserved on UBS's active servers that were, to that point, never produced. In sum, Zubulake has now presented evidence that UBS personnel deleted relevant e-mails, some of which were subsequently recovered from backup tapes (or elsewhere) and thus produced to Zubulake long after her initial document requests, and some of which were lost altogether. Zubulake has also presented evidence that some UBS personnel did not produce responsive documents to counsel until recently, depriving Zubulake of the documents for almost two years.

1. Deleted E–Mails

Notwithstanding the clear and repeated warnings of counsel, Zubulake has proffered evidence that a number of key UBS employees— Orgill, Hardisty, Holland, Chapin, Varsano, and Amone—failed to retain e-mails germane to Zubulake's claims. Some of the deleted e-mails were restored from backup tapes (or other sources) and have been produced to Zubulake, others have been altogether lost, though there is strong evidence that they once existed. Although I have long been aware that certain e-mails were deleted, the redepositions demonstrate the scope and importance of those documents.

a. At Least One E–Mail Has Never Been Produced

At least one e-mail has been irretrievably lost; the existence of that e-mail is known only because of oblique references to it in other correspondence. It has already been shown that Chapin—the alleged primary discriminator—deleted relevant e-mails. In addition to those e-mails, Zubulake has evidence suggesting that Chapin deleted at least one other e-mail that has been lost *entirely*. An e-mail from Chapin sent at 10:47 AM on September 21, 2001, asks Kim to send him a "document" recounting a conversation between Zubulake and a co-worker. Approximately 45 minutes later, Chapin sent an e-mail complaining about Zubulake to his boss and to the human resources employees handling Zubulake's case purporting to contain a verbatim recitation of a conversation between Zubulake and her co-worker, as overheard by Kim. This conversation allegedly took place on September 18, 2001, at 10:58 AM. There is reason to believe that immediately after that conversation, Kim sent Chapin an e-mail that contained the verbatim quotation that appears in Chapin's September 21 e-mail—the "document" that Chapin sought from Kim just prior to sending that e-mail—and that Chapin deleted it. That e-mail, however, has never been recovered and is apparently lost.

Although Zubulake has only been able to present concrete evidence that this one e-mail was irretrievably lost, there may well be others. Zubulake has presented extensive proof, detailed below, that UBS personnel were deleting relevant e-mails. Many of those e-mails were recovered from backup tapes. The UBS record retention policies called for monthly backup tapes to be retained for three years. The tapes covering the relevant time period (circa August 2001) should have been available to UBS in August 2002, when counsel instructed UBS's information technology personnel that backup tapes were also subject to the litigation hold.

Nonetheless, many backup tapes for the most relevant time periods are missing * * *. Zubulake did not even learn that four of these tapes were missing until after *Zubulake IV*. Thus, it is impossible to know just how many relevant e-mails have been lost in their entirety.[32]

b.   Many E–Mails Were Deleted and Only Later Recovered from Alternate Sources

Other e-mails were deleted in contravention of counsel's "litigation hold" instructions, but were subsequently recovered from alternative sources—such as backup tapes—and thus produced to Zubulake, albeit almost two years after she propounded her initial document requests. For example, an e-mail from Hardisty to Holland (and on which Chapin was copied) reported that Zubulake said "that all she wanted is to be treated like the other 'guys' on the desk." That e-mail was recovered from Hardisty's August 2001 backup tape—and thus it was on his active server as late as August 31, 2001, when the backup was generated—but was not in his active files. That e-mail therefore *must* have been deleted subsequent to counsel's warnings.

Another e-mail, from Varsano to Hardisty dated August 31, 2001— the very day that Hardisty met with outside counsel—forwarded an earlier message from Hardisty dated June 29, 2001, that recounted a conversation in which Hardisty "warned" Chapin about his management of Zubulake, and in which Hardisty reminded Chapin that Zubulake could "be a good broker." This e-mail was absent from UBS's initial production and had to be restored from backup; apparently neither Varsano nor Hardisty had retained it. This deletion is especially surprising because Varsano retained the June 29, 2001 e-mail for over two months before he forwarded it to Hardisty. Indeed, Varsano testified in his deposition that he "definitely" "saved all of the e-mails that [he] received concerning Ms. Zubulake" in 2001, that they were saved in a separate "very specific folder," and that "all of those e-mails" were produced to counsel.

As a final example, an e-mail from Hardisty to Varsano and Orgill, dated September 1, 2001, specifically discussed Zubulake's termination. It read: "LZ—ok once lawyers have been signed off, probably one month, but most easily done in combination with the full Asiapc [downsizing] announcement. We will need to document her performance post her warning HK. Matt [Chapin] is doing that." Thus, Orgill and Hardisty had decided to terminate Zubulake as early as September 1, 2001. Indeed, two days later Orgill replied, "It's a pity we can't act on

---

32. In *Zubulake IV*, I held that UBS's destruction of relevant backup tapes was negligent, rather than willful, because whether the duty to preserve extended to backup tapes was "a grey area." 220 F.R.D. at 221. I further held that "litigants are now on notice, at least in this Court, that backup tapes that can be identified as storing information created by or for 'key players' must be preserved." *Id.* at 221 n.47.

Because UBS lost the backup tapes mentioned in this opinion well before *Zubulake IV* was issued, it was not on notice of the precise contours of its duty to preserve backup tapes. Accordingly, I do not discuss UBS's destruction of relevant backup tapes as proof that UBS acted willfully, but rather to show that Zubulake can no longer prove what was deleted and when, and to demonstrate that the scope of e-mails that have been irrevocably lost is broader than initially thought.

LZ earlier." Neither the authors nor any of the recipients of these e-mails retained any of them, even though these e-mails were sent within days of Hardisty's meeting with outside counsel. They were not even preserved on backup tapes, but were only recovered because Kim happened to have retained copies. Rather, all three people (Hardisty, Orgill and Varsano) deleted these e-mails from their computers by the end of September 2001. Apart from their direct relevance to Zubulake's claims, these e-mails may also serve to rebut Orgill and Hardisty's deposition testimony. Orgill testified that he played no role in the decision to terminate Zubulake. And Hardisty testified that he did not recall discussing Zubulake's termination with Orgill.

These are merely examples. The proof is clear: UBS personnel unquestionably deleted relevant e-mails from their computers after August 2001, even though they had received at least two directions from counsel not to. Some of those e-mails were recovered (Zubulake has pointed to at least 45), but some—and no one can say how many—were not. And even those e-mails that were recovered were produced to Zubulake well after she originally asked for them.

2. Retained, But Unproduced, E–Mails

Separate and apart from the deleted material are a number of e-mails that were absent from UBS's initial production even though they were not deleted. These e-mails existed in the active, on-line files of two UBS employees—Kim and Tong—but were not produced to counsel and thus not turned over to Zubulake until she learned of their existence as a result of her counsel's questions at deposition. Indeed, these e-mails were not produced until after Zubulake had conducted thirteen depositions and four re-depositions.

During her February 19, 2004, deposition, Kim testified that she was *never* asked to produce her files regarding Zubulake to counsel, nor did she ever actually produce them, although she was asked to retain them. One week after Kim's deposition, UBS produced seven new e-mails. The obvious inference to be drawn is that, subsequent to the deposition, counsel for the first time asked Kim to produce her files.

* * *

On March 29, 2004, UBS produced several new e-mails, and three new e-mail retention policies, from Tong's active files. At her deposition two weeks earlier, Tong explained (as she had at her first deposition, a year previous) that she kept a separate "archive" file on her computer with documents pertaining to Zubulake. UBS admits that until the March 2004 deposition, it misunderstood Tong's use of the word "archive" to mean backup tapes; after her March 2004 testimony, it was clear that she meant active data. Again, the inference is that UBS's counsel then, for the first time, asked her to produce her active computer files. [Judge Scheindlin notes that at least one email held by Tong provides circumstantial evidence rebutting deposition statements from a Warburg supervisor that he was not involved in Zubulake's termination.]

Zubulake now moves for sanctions as a result of UBS's purported discovery failings. In particular, she asks—as she did in *Zubulake IV*—that an adverse inference instruction be given to the jury that eventually hears this case.

III. LEGAL STANDARD

Spoliation is "the destruction or significant alteration of evidence, or the failure to preserve property for another's use as evidence in pending or reasonably foreseeable litigation." "The determination of an appropriate sanction for spoliation, if any, is confined to the sound discretion of the trial judge, and is assessed on a case-by-case basis." The authority to sanction litigants for spoliation arises jointly under the Federal Rules of Civil Procedure and the court's inherent powers.

The spoliation of evidence germane "to proof of an issue at trial can support an inference that the evidence would have been unfavorable to the party responsible for its destruction." A party seeking an adverse inference instruction (or other sanctions) based on the spoliation of evidence must establish the following three elements: (1) that the party having control over the evidence had an obligation to preserve it at the time it was destroyed; (2) that the records were destroyed with a "culpable state of mind" and (3) that the destroyed evidence was "relevant" to the party's claim or defense such that a reasonable trier of fact could find that it would support that claim or defense.

In this circuit, a "culpable state of mind" for purposes of a spoliation inference includes ordinary negligence. When evidence is destroyed in bad faith (*i.e.*, intentionally or willfully), that fact alone is sufficient to demonstrate relevance. By contrast, when the destruction is negligent, relevance must be proven by the party seeking the sanctions.

In the context of a request for an adverse inference instruction, the concept of "relevance" encompasses not only the ordinary meaning of the term, but also that the destroyed evidence would have been favorable to the movant. "This corroboration requirement is even more necessary where the destruction was merely negligent, since in those cases it cannot be inferred from the conduct of the spoliator that the evidence would even have been harmful to him." This is equally true in cases of gross negligence or recklessness; only in the case of *willful* spoliation does the degree of culpability give rise to a presumption of the relevance of the documents destroyed.

IV. DISCUSSION

In *Zubulake IV,* I held that UBS had a duty to preserve its employees' active files as early as April 2001, and certainly by August 2001, when Zubulake filed her EEOC charge. Zubulake has thus satisfied the first element of the adverse inference test. As noted, the central question implicated by this motion is whether UBS and its counsel took all necessary steps to guarantee that relevant data was both preserved and produced. If the answer is "no," then the next question is whether UBS acted wilfully when it deleted or failed to timely produce relevant information—resulting in either a complete loss or the production of responsive information close to two years after it was initially sought. If UBS acted wilfully, this satisfies the mental culpability prong of the adverse inference test and also demonstrates that the deleted material was relevant. If UBS acted negligently or even recklessly, then Zubulake must show that the missing or late-produced information was relevant.

A. Counsel's Duty to Monitor Compliance

In *Zubulake IV*, I summarized a litigant's preservation obligations:

> Once a party reasonably anticipates litigation, it must suspend its routine document retention/destruction policy and put in place a "litigation hold" to ensure the preservation of relevant documents. As a general rule, that litigation hold does not apply to inaccessible backup tapes (*e.g.*, those typically maintained solely for the purpose of disaster recovery), which may continue to be recycled on the schedule set forth in the company's policy. On the other hand, if backup tapes are accessible (*i.e.*, actively used for information re-trieval), then such tapes *would* likely be subject to the litigation hold.

A party's discovery obligations do not end with the implementation of a "litigation hold"—to the contrary, that's only the beginning. Counsel must oversee compliance with the litigation hold, monitoring the party's efforts to retain and produce the relevant documents. Proper communi-cation between a party and her lawyer will ensure (1) that all relevant information (or at least all sources of relevant information) is discovered, (2) that relevant information is retained on a continuing basis; and (3) that relevant non-privileged material is produced to the opposing party.

1. Counsel's Duty to Locate Relevant Information

Once a "litigation hold" is in place, a party and her counsel must make certain that all sources of potentially relevant information are identified and placed "on hold," to the extent required in *Zubulake IV*. To do this, counsel must become fully familiar with her client's docu-ment retention policies, as well as the client's data retention architecture. This will invariably involve speaking with information technology per-sonnel, who can explain system-wide backup procedures and the actual (as opposed to theoretical) implementation of the firm's recycling policy. It will also involve communicating with the "key players" in the litiga-tion, in order to understand how they stored information. In this case, for example, some UBS employees created separate computer files pertaining to Zubulake, while others printed out relevant e-mails and retained them in hard copy only. Unless counsel interviews each em-ployee, it is impossible to determine whether all potential sources of information have been inspected. A brief conversation with counsel, for example, might have revealed that Tong maintained "archive" copies of e-mails concerning Zubulake, and that "archive" meant a separate on-line computer file, not a backup tape. Had that conversation taken place, Zubulake might have had relevant e-mails from that file two years ago.

To the extent that it may not be feasible for counsel to speak with every key player, given the size of a company or the scope of the lawsuit, counsel must be more creative. It may be possible to run a system-wide keyword search; counsel could then preserve a copy of each "hit." Although this sounds burdensome, it need not be. Counsel does not have to review these documents, only see that they are retained. For example, counsel could create a broad list of search terms, run a search for a limited time frame, and then segregate responsive documents.[75] When the opposing party propounds its document requests, the parties could negotiate a list of search terms to be used in identifying responsive documents, and counsel would only be obliged to review documents that came up as "hits" on the second, more restrictive search. The initial broad cut merely guarantees that relevant documents are not lost.

In short, it is *not* sufficient to notify all employees of a litigation hold and expect that the party will then retain and produce all relevant information. Counsel must take affirmative steps to monitor compliance so that all sources of discoverable information are identified and searched. This is not to say that counsel will necessarily succeed in locating all such sources, or that the later discovery of new sources is evidence of a lack of effort. But counsel and client must take *some reasonable steps* to see that sources of relevant information are located.

2. Counsel's Continuing Duty to Ensure Preservation

Once a party and her counsel have identified all of the sources of potentially relevant information, they are under a duty to retain that information (as per *Zubulake IV*) and to produce information responsive to the opposing party's requests. Rule 26 creates a "duty to supplement" those responses. Although the Rule 26 duty to supplement is nominally the party's, it really falls on counsel. * * *

The *continuing* duty to supplement disclosures strongly suggests that parties also have a duty to make sure that discoverable information is not lost. Indeed, the notion of a "duty to preserve" connotes an ongoing obligation. Obviously, if information is lost or destroyed, it has not been preserved.

The tricky question is what that continuing duty entails. What must a lawyer do to make certain that relevant information—especially electronic information—is being retained? Is it sufficient if she periodically re-sends her initial "litigation hold" instructions? What if she communi-

---

75. It might be advisable to solicit a list of search terms from the opposing party for this purpose, so that it could not later complain about which terms were used.

cates with the party's information technology personnel? Must she make occasional on-site inspections?

Above all, the requirement must be reasonable. A lawyer cannot be obliged to monitor her client like a parent watching a child. At some point, the client must bear responsibility for a failure to preserve. At the same time, counsel is more conscious of the contours of the preservation obligation; a party cannot reasonably be trusted to receive the "litigation hold" instruction once and to fully comply with it without the active supervision of counsel.

There are thus a number of steps that counsel should take to ensure compliance with the preservation obligation. While these precautions may not be enough (or may be too much) in some cases, they are designed to promote the continued preservation of potentially relevant information in the typical case.

First, counsel must issue a "litigation hold" at the outset of litigation or whenever litigation is reasonably anticipated. The litigation hold should be periodically re-issued so that new employees are aware of it, and so that it is fresh in the minds of all employees.

Second, counsel should communicate directly with the "key players" in the litigation, *i.e.,* the people identified in a party's initial disclosure and any subsequent supplementation thereto. Because these "key players" are the "employees likely to have relevant information," it is particularly important that the preservation duty be communicated clearly to them. As with the litigation hold, the key players should be periodically reminded that the preservation duty is still in place.

Finally, counsel should instruct all employees to produce electronic copies of their relevant active files. Counsel must also make sure that all backup media which the party is required to retain is identified and stored in a safe place. In cases involving a small number of relevant backup tapes, counsel might be advised to take physical possession of backup tapes. In other cases, it might make sense for relevant backup tapes to be segregated and placed in storage. Regardless of what particular arrangement counsel chooses to employ, the point is to separate relevant backup tapes from others. One of the primary reasons that electronic data is lost is ineffective communication with information technology personnel. By taking possession of, or otherwise safeguarding, all potentially relevant backup tapes, counsel eliminates the possibility that such tapes will be inadvertently recycled.

* * *

3. What Happened at UBS After August 2001?

* * *

a. UBS's Discovery Failings

UBS's counsel—both in-house and outside—repeatedly advised UBS of its discovery obligations. In fact, counsel came very close to taking the precautions laid out above. *First,* outside counsel issued a litigation hold in August 2001. The hold order was circulated to many of the key players in this litigation, and reiterated in e-mails in February 2002, when suit was filed, and again in September 2002. Outside counsel made clear that the hold order applied to backup tapes in August 2002, as soon as backup tapes became an issue in this case. *Second,* outside counsel communicated directly with many of the key players in August 2001 and attempted to impress upon them their preservation obligations. *Third,* and finally, counsel instructed UBS employees to produce copies of their active computer files.

To be sure, counsel did not fully comply with the standards set forth above. Nonetheless, under the standards existing at the time, counsel acted reasonably to the extent that they directed UBS to implement a litigation hold. Yet notwithstanding the clear instructions of counsel, UBS personnel failed to preserve plainly relevant e-mails.

b. Counsel's Failings

On the other hand, UBS's counsel are not entirely blameless. * * * In this case, counsel failed to properly oversee UBS in a number of important ways, both in terms of its duty to locate relevant information and its duty to preserve and timely produce that information.

With respect to locating relevant information, counsel failed to adequately communicate with Tong about how she stored data. Although counsel determined that Tong kept her files on Zubulake in an "archive," they apparently made no effort to learn what that meant. A few simple questions—like the ones that Zubulake's counsel asked at Tong's re-deposition—would have revealed that she kept those files in a separate *active* file on her computer.

With respect to making sure that relevant data was retained, counsel failed in a number of important respects. *First,* neither in-house nor outside counsel communicated the litigation hold instructions to Mike Davies, a senior human resources employee who was intimately involved in Zubulake's termination. *Second,* even though the litigation hold instructions were communicated to Kim, no one ever asked her to produce her files. And *third,* counsel failed to protect relevant backup tapes; had they done so, Zubulake might have been able to recover some of the e-mails that UBS employees deleted.

In addition, if Varsano's deposition testimony is to be credited, he turned over "all of the e-mails that [he] received concerning Ms. Zubulake." If Varsano turned over these e-mails, then counsel must have failed to produce some of them.

In sum, while UBS personnel deleted e-mails, copies of many of these e-mails were lost or belatedly produced as a result of counsel's failures.

c. Summary

Counsel failed to communicate the litigation hold order to all key players. They also failed to ascertain each of the key players' document management habits. By the same token, UBS employees—for unknown reasons—ignored many of the instructions that counsel gave. This case represents a failure of communication, and that failure falls on counsel and client alike.

At the end of the day, however, the duty to preserve and produce documents rests on the party. Once that duty is made clear to a party, either by court order or by instructions from counsel, that party is on notice of its obligations and acts at its own peril. Though more diligent action on the part of counsel would have mitigated some of the damage caused by UBS's deletion of emails, UBS deleted the e-mails in defiance of explicit instructions not to.

Because UBS personnel continued to delete relevant e-mails, Zubulake was denied access to e-mails to which she was entitled. Even those e-mails that were deleted but ultimately salvaged from other sources (*e.g.*, backup tapes or Tong and Kim's active files) were produced 22 months after they were initially requested. The effect of losing potentially relevant e-mails is obvious, but the effect of late production cannot be underestimated either. "As a discovery deadline . . . draws near, discovery conduct that might have been considered 'merely' discourteous at an earlier point in the litigation may well breach a party's duties to its opponent and to the court." * * *

I therefore conclude that UBS acted wilfully in destroying potentially relevant information, which resulted either in the absence of such information or its tardy production (because duplicates were recovered from Kim or Tong's active files, or restored from backup tapes). Because UBS's spoliation was willful, the lost information is presumed to be relevant.

B. Remedy

Having concluded that UBS was under a duty to preserve the e-mails and that it deleted presumably relevant e-mails wilfully, I now consider the full panoply of available sanctions. In doing so, I recognize that a major consideration in choosing an appropriate sanction—along with punishing UBS and deterring future misconduct—is to restore Zubulake to the position that she would have been in had UBS faithfully discharged its discovery obligations. That being so, I find that the following sanctions are warranted.

First, the jury empanelled to hear this case will be given an adverse inference instruction with respect to e-mails deleted after August 2001, and in particular, with respect to e-mails that were irretrievably lost when UBS's backup tapes were recycled. No one can ever know precisely what was on those tapes, but the content of e-mails recovered from other sources—along with the fact that UBS employees wilfully deleted e-mails—is sufficiently favorable to Zubulake that I am convinced that the contents of the lost tapes would have been similarly, if not more, favorable.

Second, Zubulake argues that the e-mails that *were* produced, albeit late, "are brand new and very significant to Ms. Zubulake's retaliation claim and would have affected [her] examination of every witness . . . in this case." Likewise, Zubulake claims, with respect to the newly produced e-mails from Kim and Tong's active files, that UBS's "failure to produce these e-mails in a timely fashion precluded [her] from questioning any witness about them." These arguments stand unrebutted and are therefore adopted in full by the Court. Accordingly, UBS is ordered to pay the costs of any depositions or re-depositions required by the late production.

Third, UBS is ordered to pay the costs of this motion.[102]

Finally, I note that UBS's belated production has resulted in a self-executing sanction. Not only was Zubulake unable to question UBS's witnesses using the newly produced e-mails, but UBS was unable to prepare those witnesses with the aid of those e-mails. Some of UBS's witnesses, not having seen these e-mails, have already given deposition testimony that seems to contradict the newly discovered evidence. * * * Zubulake is, of course, free to use this testimony at trial.

These sanctions are designed to compensate Zubulake for the harm done to her by the loss of or extremely delayed access to potentially relevant evidence.[103] They should also stem the need for any further litigation over the backup tapes.

* * *

V. CONCLUSION

In sum, counsel has a duty to effectively communicate to her client its discovery obligations so that all relevant information is discovered, retained, and produced. In particular, once the duty to preserve attaches, counsel must identify sources of discoverable information. This will usually entail speaking directly with the key players in the litigation, as well as the client's information technology personnel. In addition, when the duty to preserve attaches, counsel must put in place a litigation hold and make that known to all relevant employees by communicating with them directly. The litigation hold instructions must be reiterated regularly and compliance must be monitored. Counsel must also call for employees to produce copies of relevant electronic evidence, and must arrange for the segregation and safeguarding of any archival media (*e.g.*, backup tapes) that the party has a duty to preserve.

---

102. Fed. R. Civ. P. 37(b)(2).

103. Another possible remedy would have been to order UBS to pay for the restoration of the remaining backup tapes. Zubulake, however, has conceded that further restoration is unlikely to be fruitful.

Once counsel takes these steps (or once a court order is in place), a party is fully on notice of its discovery obligations. If a party acts contrary to counsel's instructions or to a court's order, it acts at its own peril.

UBS failed to preserve relevant e-mails, even after receiving adequate warnings from counsel, resulting in the production of some relevant e-mails almost two years after they were initially requested, and resulting in the complete destruction of others. For that reason, Zubulake's motion is granted and sanctions are warranted. UBS is ordered to:

1. Pay for the re-deposition of relevant UBS personnel, limited to the subject of the newly-discovered e-mails;

2. Restore and produce relevant documents from Varsano's August 2001 backup tape;

3. Pay for the re-deposition of Varsano and Tong, limited to the new material produced from Varsano's August 2001 backup tape; and

4. Pay all "reasonable expenses, including attorney's fees," incurred by Zubulake in connection with the making of this motion.

In addition, I will give the following instruction to the jury that hears this case:

You have heard that UBS failed to produce some of the e-mails sent or received by UBS personnel in August and September 2001. Plaintiff has argued that this evidence was in defendants' control and would have proven facts material to the matter in controversy.

If you find that UBS could have produced this evidence, and that the evidence was within its control, and that the evidence would have been material in deciding facts in dispute in this case, you are permitted, but not required, to infer that the evidence would have been unfavorable to UBS.

In deciding whether to draw this inference, you should consider whether the evidence not produced would merely have duplicated other evidence already before you. You may also consider whether you are satisfied that UBS's failure to produce this information was reasonable. Again, any inference you decide to draw should be based on all of the facts and circumstances in this case.

* * *

VI. POSTSCRIPT

The subject of the discovery of electronically stored information is rapidly evolving. When this case began more than two years ago, there was little guidance from the judiciary, bar associations or the academy as to the governing standards. Much has changed in that time. There have been a flood of recent opinions—including a number from appellate courts—and there are now several treatises on the subject. In addition, professional groups such as the American Bar Association and the Sedona Conference have provided very useful guidance on thorny issues relating to the discovery of electronically stored information. Many courts have adopted, or are considering adopting, local rules addressing the subject. Most recently, the Standing Committee on Rules and Procedures has approved for publication and public comment a proposal for revisions to the Federal Rules of Civil Procedure designed to address many of the issues raised by the discovery of electronically stored information. [The electronic discovery amendments ultimately adopted are set forth at the beginning of this casebook].

Now that the key issues have been addressed and national standards are developing, parties and their counsel are fully on notice of their responsibility to preserve and produce electronically stored information. The tedious and difficult fact finding encompassed in this opinion and others like it is a great burden on a court's limited resources. The time and effort spent by counsel to litigate these issues has also been time-consuming and distracting. This Court, for one, is optimistic that with the guidance now provided it will not be necessary to spend this amount of time again. It is hoped that counsel will heed the guidance provided by these resources and will work to ensure that preservation, production and spoliation issues are limited, if not eliminated.

COMMENTARY

1. Do Non–Parties Have an Obligation to Preserve?

What if a party knows a non-party holds relevant information but does not itself have direct or constructive control over that information? Does the party have any obligation to ensure its preservation? If it does, how can it fulfill that obligation?

Some courts have held that the party's preservation obligation includes the duty to inform the opposing party of the relevant evidence held by the third-party and the risk of its possible destruction.[1] But what ability do litigants have to ensure the third-party preserves the relevant evidence? Does the notice by a party to the third-party that the information is relevant to potential litigation create a duty for the third party to preserve it? If third-parties independently determine that the ESI they hold will be relevant to pending or future litigation involving others, does that knowledge create a third-party preservation duty?

Generally, the answer to both questions is "no." Preservation of evidence, particularly of ESI, can be costly. Thus, courts have recognized that the obligations of non-parties to preserve evidence are different that those imposed on the parties.[2] Unless the duty arises from

---

1.   See, e.g., Silvestri v. General Motors Corp., 271 F.3d 583, 591 (4th Cir. 2001).

2.   See Sedona Conference Commentary on Non–Party Production & Rule 45 Subpoenas 2 & n.4 (2008) (citing Fletcher v. Dorchester Mut. Ins. Co., 773 N.E.2d 420, 424–25 (Mass. 2002) (noting that non-parties do not have an obligation to preserve evidence for use by others)).

a contractual agreement to preserve information or other special relationship that may give rise to the duty, non-parties generally do not have an obligation to preserve relevant data even when they anticipate it might be relevant.

Some jurisdictions, however, recognize a common law tort for either intentional or negligent third-party spoliation of evidence where the third party had reason to know of the litigation.[3] Even in jurisdictions where no common law preservation duty of third parties is recognized, courts may still impose the duty where the third party has a contractual or other special relationship with the party seeking preservation. An example of a relationship that might give rise to a third-party duty to preserve is that between an insurance company and a policy holder involved in litigation.[4] Where no such relationship exists, courts in jurisdictions not recognizing a common law tort of third-party spoliation may instead place the onus of third-party preservation on the party seeking it.

Although the following case involves the preservation of physical evidence rather than of ESI, it nicely illustrates the point. In *MetLife Auto & Home v. Joe Basil Chevrolet, Inc.*, the New York Court of Appeals refused to recognize a common law tort for spoliation against a third-party auto insurer who had custody of a vehicle involved in a claim by a homeowner against the auto manufacturer.[5] Even though the auto insurer had agreed verbally to preserve the evidence, the court declined to find a third-party duty to preserve because there was no relationship between the home insurer and the auto insurer. The Court noted that the home insurer could have purchased the vehicle from the auto insurer, paid for the costs of preservation, or filed suit and issued a subpoena duces tecum on the non-party auto insurer. Because Metlife was suing for the auto insurer's failure to preserve the vehicle *before* the claim in the primary suit was filed, it could not have issued a production or preservation subpoena on the auto insurance company. Thus, parties informed of the existence of relevant evidence held by third parties before they have the ability to issue third-party subpoenas should consider taking other steps to ensure it is preserved. Courts, however, will not intervene in pre-litigation preservation disputes.[6]

---

3. *See* Robert L. Tucker, *The Flexible Doctrine of Spoliation of Evidence: Cause of Action, Defense, Evidentiary Presumption, and Discovery Sanction*, 27 U. Tol. L. Rev. 67, 67–71 (1995) (discussing cases in which third-parties were held liable for the tort of spoliation, and the elements of the tort).

4. *See, e.g., Fada Indus., Inc. v. Falchi Bldg. Co.*, 730 N.Y.S. 2d 827, 838 (N.Y. Sup. Ct. Queens Co. 2001) ("the obligation of the insurer to defend must carry with it the obligation to preserve key evidence relied upon by its insured").

5. 1 N.Y.3d 478, 483 (2004).

6. *See Texas v. City of Frisco*, No. 07–383, 2008 WL 828055, at *3 (E.D. Tex. Mar. 27, 2008) (finding State's request for protective order excusing it from complying with City's letter demanding that the State preserve electronic data and for a declaratory judgment on the scope of parties' preservation obligations non-justiciable because no suit had been filed and facts regarding potential litigation "not sufficiently immediate to establish an actual controversy" (quotation omitted)).

2. Preservation Obligations and Third–Party Subpoenas

Under Rule 45, if a third-party is served with a subpoena seeking documents or other production after the action has been filed, does the subpoena create an independent duty not only to produce the information, but also to preserve relevant information? Rule 45 is silent on the effect of a subpoena on the third party's preservation obligations. If a subpoena creates both a production *and* a preservation obligation, how long should the third party be required to preserve information, and what information must it maintain?[7] After a recipient has fully complied with a subpoena, most courts hold that any preservation obligation that arose with service of the subpoena terminates.

While Rule 45 allows parties to serve subpoenas on non-parties, it does not require third parties to produce ESI if it is not reasonably accessible unless the issuing party can show good cause.[8] Do *In re Napster* and *Warner Brothers Records*, cited above, suggest that third parties served with a subpoena for ESI that is not reasonably accessible have a duty to suspend their normal document destruction policies to preserve the information until the question of good cause is resolved, regardless of the cost of doing so?

What if parties are unable to serve document subpoenas on non-parties holding relevant ESI even *after* the case is filed? How might they ensure relevant evidence is not destroyed? Under the Private Securities Litigation Reform Act, discovery in private securities fraud actions is stayed until a motion to dismiss has been decided unless discovery is necessary to preserve evidence or prevent undue prejudice to a party. The Act provides that, during the stay, *parties* have the obligation to preserve evidence as though document requests had been issued. But non-parties holding relevant evidence have no such statutory obligation. What can be done to ensure that non-parties holding relevant ESI and other evidence preserve it until the stay is lifted? Courts may permit parties to issue "preservation subpoenas" on non-parties. But most allow them to do so only with the court's permission even where non-parties' document retention and destruction policies may result in imminent destruction of relevant ESI.[9]

3. Privacy and Preservation

Even where a party may be under a preservation obligation, federal privacy laws may prevent preservation and production of relevant ESI

---

7. *See In re Napster Copyright Litig.*, No. 00 MDL 1369, 2006 WL 3050864, at *6 (N.D. Cal. Oct. 25, 2006) (holding subpoena issued to third-party imposes preservation obligation on all information relevant to the subpoena until requested materials are produced and disputes related to the subpoena have been resolved); *Warner Bros. Records v. Does 1–14*, No. 07 Civ. 706, 2008 WL 60297, at *2 (D.D.C. Jan. 4, 2008) (ordering third-party to preserve evidence until resolution of motions to quash third-party subpoena).

8. *See* Fed. R. Civ. P. 45 (d)(1)(D), 1991 Advisory Committee Note.

9. *See, e.g., In re Cree Inc. Sec. Litig.*, 220 F.R.D. 443, 447 (M.D.N.C. 2004) (quashing preservation subpoenas served on non-parties without leave of court despite risk that routine document destruction policy might destroy relevant data); *In re Tyco Int'l, Ltd. Sec. Litig.*, No. 00 MDL 1335, 2000 WL 33654141, at *3, 5 (D.N.H. July 27, 2000) (permitting plaintiff to serve preservation subpoenas on third parties where plaintiff sought leave of court and produced evidence that similar entities "typically overwrite and thereby destroy electronic data").

held by parties and non-parties. For example, the Stored Communications Act, prohibits providers of electronic communications services from disclosing the content of stored customer communications to any person, except the federal government upon a court-issued warrant. The Act has no exceptions for civil actions.[10] If such communications providers cannot produce the content of communications, can they ever have a duty to preserve it? Note that many other federal laws also limit disclosure of private information, but allow entities holding such information to disclose it in response to court-approved discovery requests.[11]

Can contractual obligations regarding the privacy of customers' personal information limit the preservation obligations of a party or non-party? Suppose a website host promises not to collect or store personal information about its users. Can that party be sanctioned for failing to preserve such information after the preservation obligation arose or be ordered to preserve such information going forward? What if the privacy policy is viewed as an integral part of the service offered by the host? In *Columbia Pictures Industries v. Bunnell*, plaintiffs sought the IP addresses of a website's users who they alleged violated copyright law when using the site's file sharing service to trade copyrighted materials.[12] The website's privacy policy prohibited the site operator from collecting personal information about users not knowingly provided by those users. As a result, the website host did not preserve server log data, including the users' IP addresses. In holding that the website owner must preserve such data, including IP addresses, the court never reached the issue of whether a party's privacy policy could trump its preservation obligations or whether preservation obligations could force a party to change its customer privacy policies. Instead, the court merely concluded that IP addresses did not constitute personal information, finding that the addresses identified computers, not users.

4. Preservation Obligations Under Federal Law

An independent obligation to preserve information may arise from federal or state statutes and regulations requiring that certain types of data be preserved, regardless of whether an entity is, or may become, a party to litigation. For example, the Sarbanes–Oxley Act of 2002, passed in the wake of high profile corporate accounting scandals, created new obligations for auditors of publicly traded companies to retain all records, including electronic records, relating to audits for five years after the audit is conducted.[13] The Securities and Exchange Act, and the

---

10. *See* discussion of *In re Subpoena Duces Tecum to AOL, LLC*, 550 F. Supp. 2d 606, 609–10 (E.D. Va. 2008) at Chapter V.I *infra*.

11. *See, e.g.*, 15 U.S.C. §§ 6801(a), 6802, 6802(e)(8) (requiring financial institutions to protect privacy of customers' personal information, but permitting disclosure to respond to judicial process); *id.* § 6502(b) (prohibiting operators of web sites and other online services from disclosing personal information collected from children without parental consent, but providing exception for response to judicial process).

12. No. CV 06–1093, 2007 WL 2080419 (C.D. Cal. May 29, 2007). This case is found at Chapter II.E, *infra*.

13. *See* 18 U.S.C. § 1520(a)(1)-(2).

SEC's regulations implementing it, impose extensive record retention requirements on stock exchanges, members of the exchanges and securities dealers.[14] The Fair Labor Standards Act and the regulations issued pursuant to it require employers to retain payroll, collective bargaining agreements and other employment contract records for three years; business volume records for three years in the form in which they were maintained in the ordinary course of business; and employment and earning records, such as time cards, for two years.[15] Health care providers that participate in the Medicare program are required by the Department of Health and Human Services to retain certain medical records for five years.

Although a party may have an independent duty to retain records under federal or state law, a violation of that obligation may not necessarily result in spoliation sanctions. In *Sarmiento v. Montclair State University*, an unsuccessful job candidate filed an employment discrimination claim against the University and sought sanctions in the form of an adverse inference against the defendant for its failure to retain the selection committee's notes that related to the decision not to hire.[16] The plaintiff alleged, *inter alia*, that sanctions were warranted because the University violated federal regulations that required universities and colleges to retain hiring and other records.

The court held that "[a]lthough a regulation may supply the duty to preserve records, a party seeking to benefit from an inference of spoliation must still make out the other usual elements" of that claim.[17] Those elements included a requirement that the litigation be reasonably foreseeable; in this case, the court held that it was not. What do you think of this result? Should foreseeability matter when an obligation to preserve data existed independent of the risk of litigation? Should independent statutory or regulatory obligations to preserve data be enforceable by parties other than the government's enforcement entity?

C.   TRIGGER DATE

ZUBULAKE v. UBS WARBURG LLC
"Zubulake IV"

220 F.R.D. 212 (S.D.N.Y. 2003)

SCHEINDLIN, DISTRICT JUDGE

"Documents create a paper reality we call proof." The absence of such documentary proof may stymie the search for the truth. If documents are lost or destroyed when they should have been preserved because a litigation was threatened or pending, a party may be preju-

---

14. *See* 15 U.S.C. § 78q(a).

15. *See* 29 U.S.C. § 211(c); 29 C.F.R. § 516.5–6.

16. 513 F. Supp. 2d 72 (D.N.J. 2007).

17. *Id.* at 94.

diced. The questions presented here are how to determine an appropriate penalty for the party that caused the loss and—the flip side—how to determine an appropriate remedy for the party injured by the loss.

Finding a suitable sanction for the destruction of evidence in civil cases has never been easy. Electronic evidence only complicates matters. As documents are increasingly maintained electronically, it has become easier to delete or tamper with evidence (both intentionally and inadvertently) and more difficult for litigants to craft policies that ensure all relevant documents are preserved. This opinion addresses both the scope of a litigant's duty to preserve electronic documents and the consequences of a failure to preserve documents that fall within the scope of that duty.

I. BACKGROUND

This is the fourth opinion resolving discovery disputes in this case. * * * In brief, Laura Zubulake, an equities trader who earned approximately $650,000 a year with UBS, is suing UBS for gender discrimination, failure to promote, and retaliation under federal, state, and city law. She has repeatedly maintained that the evidence she needs to prove her case exists in e-mail correspondence sent among various UBS employees and stored only on UBS's computer systems.

On July 24, 2003, I ordered the parties to share the cost of restoring certain UBS backup tapes that contained e-mails relevant to Zubulake's claims. In the restoration effort, the parties discovered that certain backup tapes are missing. In particular:

	Missing Monthly Backup Tapes
Matthew Chapin (Zubulake's immediate supervisor)	April 2001
Jeremy Hardisty (Chapin's supervisor)	June 2001
Andrew Clarke and Vinay Datta (Zubulake's coworkers)	April 2001
Rose Tong (human resources)	Part of June 2001, July 2001, August 2001, and October 2001

In addition, certain isolated e-mails—created after UBS supposedly began retaining all relevant e-mails—were deleted from UBS's system, although they appear to have been saved on the backup tapes. As I explained in *Zubulake III*, "certain e-mails sent after the initial EEOC charge—and particularly relevant to Zubulake's retaliation claim—were apparently not saved at all. For example, [an] e-mail from Chapin to Joy Kim [another of Zubulake's coworkers] instructing her on how to file a complaint against Zubulake was not saved, and it bears the subject line 'UBS client attorney priviledge [sic] only,' although no attorney is copied on the e-mail. This potentially useful e-mail was deleted and resided only on UBS's backup tapes."

Zubulake filed her EEOC charge on August 16, 2001; the instant action was filed on February 14, 2002. In August 2001, in an oral directive, UBS ordered its employees to retain all relevant documents. In August 2002, after Zubulake specifically requested e-mail stored on backup tapes, UBS's outside counsel orally instructed UBS's information technology personnel to stop recycling backup tapes.

Zubulake now seeks sanctions against UBS for its failure to preserve the missing backup tapes and deleted e-mails. * * *

II. LEGAL STANDARD

Spoliation is "the destruction or significant alteration of evidence, or the failure to preserve property for another's use as evidence in pending or reasonably foreseeable litigation." The spoliation of evidence germane "to proof of an issue at trial can support an inference that the evidence would have been unfavorable to the party responsible for its destruction." However, "the determination of an appropriate sanction for spoliation, if any, is confined to the sound discretion of the trial judge, and is assessed on a case-by-case basis." The authority to sanction litigants for spoliation arises jointly under the Federal Rules of Civil Procedure and the court's own inherent powers.

III. DISCUSSION

It goes without saying that a party can only be sanctioned for destroying evidence if it had a duty to preserve it. If UBS had no such duty, then UBS cannot be faulted. I begin, then, by discussing the extent of a party's duty to preserve evidence.

A. Duty to Preserve

"The obligation to preserve evidence arises when the party has notice that the evidence is relevant to litigation or when a party should have known that the evidence may be relevant to future litigation." Identifying the boundaries of the duty to preserve involves two related inquiries: *when* does the duty to preserve attach, and *what* evidence must be preserved?

1. The Trigger Date

In this case, the duty to preserve evidence arose, at the latest, on August 16, 2001, when Zubulake filed her EEOC charge. At that time, UBS's in-house attorneys cautioned employees to retain all documents, including e-mails and backup tapes, that could potentially be relevant to the litigation. In meetings with Chapin, Clarke, Kim, Hardisty, John Holland (Chapin's supervisor), and Dominic Vail (Zubulake's former supervisor) held on August 29–31, 2001, UBS's outside counsel reiterated the need to preserve documents.

But the duty to preserve may have arisen even before the EEOC complaint was filed. Zubulake argues that UBS "should have known that the evidence [was] relevant to future litigation," as early as April 2001, and thus had a duty to preserve it. She offers two pieces of evidence in support of this argument. *First*, certain UBS employees titled e-mails pertaining to Zubulake "UBS Attorney Client Privilege" starting in April 2001, notwithstanding the fact that no attorney was copied on the e-mail and the substance of the e-mail was not legal in nature. *Second*, Chapin admitted in his deposition that he feared litigation from as early as April 2001 * * *.

Merely because one or two employees contemplate the possibility that a fellow employee might sue does not generally impose a firm-wide duty to preserve. But in this case, it appears that almost everyone associated with Zubulake recognized the possibility that she might sue. For example, an e-mail authored by Zubulake's co-worker Vinnay Datta, concerning Zubulake and labeled "UBS attorney client priviladge [sic]," was distributed to Chapin (Zubulake's supervisor), Holland and Leland Tomblick (Chapin's supervisor), Vail (Zubulake's former supervisor), and Andrew Clarke (Zubulake's co-worker) in late April 2001. That e-mail, replying to one from Hardisty, essentially called for Zubulake's termination: "Our biggest strength as a firm and as a desk is our ability to share information and relationships. Any person who threatens this in any way should be firmly dealt with.... Believe me that a lot of other [similar] instances have occurred earlier."

Thus, the relevant people at UBS anticipated litigation in April 2001. The duty to preserve attached at the time that litigation was reasonably anticipated.

2. Scope

The next question is: What is the scope of the duty to preserve? Must a corporation, upon recognizing the threat of litigation, preserve every shred of paper, every e-mail or electronic document, and every backup tape? The answer is clearly, "no". Such a rule would cripple large corporations, like UBS, that are almost always involved in litigation. As a general rule, then, a party need not preserve all backup tapes even when it reasonably anticipates litigation.[22]

At the same time, anyone who anticipates being a party or is a party to a lawsuit must not destroy unique, relevant evidence that might be useful to an adversary. "While a litigant is under no duty to keep or retain every document in its possession ... it is under a duty to preserve what it knows, or reasonably should know, is relevant in the action, is reasonably calculated to lead to the discovery of admissible evidence, is

---

22. *See, e.g., The Sedona Principles: Best Practices, Recommendations & Principles for Addressing Electronic Document Discovery* cmt 6.h (Sedona Conference Working Group Series 2003) ("Absent specific circumstances, preservation obligations should not extend to disaster recovery backup tapes....").

reasonably likely to be requested during discovery and/or is the subject of a pending discovery request."

i.   Whose Documents Must Be Retained?

The broad contours of the duty to preserve are relatively clear. That duty should certainly extend to any documents or tangible things * * * made by individuals "likely to have discoverable information that the disclosing party may use to support its claims or defenses."[25] The duty also includes documents prepared *for* those individuals, to the extent those documents can be readily identified (*e.g.*, from the "to" field in e-mails). The duty also extends to information that is relevant to the claims or defenses of *any* party, or which is "relevant to the subject matter involved in the action." [26]Thus, the duty to preserve extends to those employees likely to have relevant information—the "key players" in the case. In this case, all of the individuals whose backup tapes were lost (Chapin, Hardisty, Tong, Datta and Clarke) fall into this category.

ii.   What Must Be Retained?

A party or anticipated party must retain all relevant documents (but not multiple identical copies) in existence at the time the duty to preserve attaches, and any relevant documents created thereafter. In recognition of the fact that there are many ways to manage electronic data, litigants are free to choose how this task is accomplished. For example, a litigant could choose to retain all then-existing backup tapes for the relevant personnel (if such tapes store data by individual or the contents can be identified in good faith and through reasonable effort), and to catalog any later-created documents in a separate electronic file. That, along with a mirror-image of the computer system taken at the time the duty to preserve attaches (to preserve documents in the state they existed at that time), creates a complete set of relevant documents. Presumably there are a multitude of other ways to achieve the same result.

iii.   Summary of Preservation Obligations

The scope of a party's preservation obligation can be described as follows: Once a party reasonably anticipates litigation, it must suspend its routine document retention/destruction policy and put in place a "litigation hold" to ensure the preservation of relevant documents. As a general rule, that litigation hold does not apply to inaccessible backup tapes (*e.g.*, those typically maintained solely for the purpose of disaster recovery), which may continue to be recycled on the schedule set forth in the company's policy. On the other hand, if backup tapes are accessible (*i.e.*, actively used for information retrieval), then such tapes *would* likely be subject to the litigation hold.

However, it does make sense to create one exception to this general rule. If a company can identify where particular employee documents

---

25.   Fed. R. Civ. P. 26(a)(1)(A).

26.   Fed. R. Civ. P. 26(b)(1).

are stored on backup tapes, then the tapes storing the documents of "key players" to the existing or threatened litigation should be preserved if the information contained on those tapes is not otherwise available. This exception applies to *all* backup tapes.

iv.   What Happened at UBS After August 2001?

By its attorney's directive in August 2002, UBS endeavored to preserve all backup tapes that existed in August 2001 (when Zubulake filed her EEOC charge) that captured data for employees identified by Zubulake in her document request, and all such monthly backup tapes generated thereafter. These backup tapes existed in August 2002, because of UBS's document retention policy, which required retention for three years. In August 2001, UBS employees were instructed to maintain *active* electronic documents pertaining to Zubulake in separate files. Had these directives been followed, UBS would have met its preservation obligations by preserving one copy of all relevant documents that existed at, or were created after, the time when the duty to preserve attached.

In fact, UBS employees did not comply with these directives. Three backup tapes containing the e-mail files of Chapin, Hardisty, Clarke and Datta created after April 2001 were lost, despite the August 2002 directive to maintain those tapes. According to the UBS document retention policy, these three monthly backup tapes from April and June 2001 should have been retained for three years.

The two remaining lost backup tapes were for the time period *after* Zubulake filed her EEOC complaint (Rose Tong's tapes for August and October 2001). UBS has offered *no* explanation for why these tapes are missing. * * * [I]t appears that UBS did not directly order the preservation of Tong's backup tapes until August 2002, when Zubulake made her discovery request.

In sum, UBS had a duty to preserve the six-plus backup tapes (that is, six complete backup tapes and part of a seventh) at issue here.

B.   Remedies

* * *

Adverse Inference Instruction

Zubulake * * * argues that UBS's spoliation warrants an adverse inference instruction. Zubulake asks that the jury in this case be instructed that it can infer from the fact that UBS destroyed certain evidence that the evidence, if available, would have been favorable to Zubulake and harmful to UBS. In practice, an adverse inference instruction often ends litigation—it is too difficult a hurdle for the spoliator to overcome. The *in terrorem* effect of an adverse inference is obvious. * * * Accordingly, the adverse inference instruction is an extreme sanction and should not be given lightly.

A party seeking an adverse inference instruction (or other sanctions) based on the spoliation of evidence must establish the following three elements: (1) that the party having control over the evidence had an obligation to preserve it at the time it was destroyed; (2) that the records were destroyed with a "culpable state of mind" and (3) that the destroyed evidence was "relevant" to the party's claim or defense such that a reasonable trier of fact could find that it would support that claim or defense. In this circuit, a "culpable state of mind" for purposes of a spoliation inference includes ordinary negligence. When evidence is destroyed in bad faith (*i.e.*, intentionally or willfully), that fact alone is sufficient to demonstrate relevance. By contrast, when the destruction is negligent, relevance must be proven by the party seeking the sanctions.

a.   Duty to Preserve

For the reasons already discussed, UBS had—and breached—a duty to preserve the backup tapes at issue. Zubulake has thus established the first element.

b.   Culpable State of Mind

Zubulake argues that UBS's spoliation was "intentional—or, at a minimum, grossly negligent." Yet, of dozens of relevant backup tapes, only six and part of a seventh are missing. Indeed, UBS argues that the tapes were "inadvertently recycled well before plaintiff requested them and even before she filed her complaint [in February 2002]."

But to accept UBS's argument would ignore the fact that, even though Zubulake had not yet requested the tapes or filed her complaint, UBS had a duty to preserve those tapes. Once the duty to preserve attaches, any destruction of documents is, at a minimum, negligent. (Of course, this would not apply to destruction caused by events outside of the party's control, *e.g.*, a fire in UBS's offices).

Whether a company's duty to preserve extends to backup tapes has been a grey area. As a result, it is not terribly surprising that a company would think that it did *not* have a duty to preserve all of its backup tapes, even when it reasonably anticipated the onset of litigation. Thus, UBS's failure to preserve all potentially relevant backup tapes was merely negligent, as opposed to grossly negligent or reckless.

UBS's destruction or loss of Tong's backup tapes, however, exceeds mere negligence. UBS failed to include these backup tapes in its preservation directive in this case, notwithstanding the fact that Tong was the human resources employee directly responsible for Zubulake and who engaged in continuous correspondence regarding the case. Moreover, the lost tapes covered the time period *after* Zubulake filed her EEOC charge, when UBS was *unquestionably* on notice of its duty to preserve. Indeed, Tong herself took part in much of the correspondence over Zubulake's charge of discrimination. Thus, UBS was grossly negligent, if not reckless, in not preserving those backup tapes.

Because UBS was negligent—and possibly reckless—Zubulake has satisfied her burden with respect to the second prong of the spoliation test.

c. Relevance

Finally, because UBS's spoliation was negligent and possibly reckless, but not willful, Zubulake must demonstrate that a reasonable trier of fact could find that the missing e-mails would support her claims. In order to receive an adverse inference instruction, Zubulake must demonstrate not only that UBS destroyed relevant evidence as that term is ordinarily understood, but also that the destroyed evidence would have been favorable to her. "This corroboration requirement is even more necessary where the destruction was merely negligent, since in those cases it cannot be inferred from the conduct of the spoliator that the evidence would even have been harmful to him." This is equally true in cases of gross negligence or recklessness; only in the case of *willful* spoliation is the spoliator's mental culpability itself evidence of the relevance of the documents destroyed.

On the one hand, I found in *Zubulake I* and *Zubulake III* that the e-mails contained on UBS's backup tapes were, by-and-large, relevant in the sense that they bore on the issues in the litigation. On the other hand, *Zubulake III* specifically held that "nowhere (in the sixty-eight e-mails produced to the Court) is there evidence that Chapin's dislike of Zubulake related to her gender." And those sixty-eight e-mails, it should be emphasized, were the ones selected by Zubulake as being the *most* relevant among all those produced in UBS's sample restoration. There is no reason to believe that the lost e-mails would be any more likely to support her claims.

Furthermore, the likelihood of obtaining relevant information from the six-plus lost backup tapes at issue here is even lower than for the remainder of the tapes, because the majority of the six-plus tapes cover the time prior to the filing of Zubulake's EEOC charge. The tape that is most likely to contain relevant e-mails is Tong's August 2001 tape—the tape for the very month that Zubulake filed her EEOC charges. But the majority of the e-mails on that tape are preserved on the September 2001 tape. Thus, there is no reason to believe that peculiarly unfavorable evidence resides solely on that missing tape. Accordingly, Zubulake has not sufficiently demonstrated that the lost tapes contained relevant information.

d. Summary

In sum, although UBS had a duty to preserve all of the backup tapes at issue, and destroyed them with the requisite culpability, Zubulake cannot demonstrate that the lost evidence would have supported her claims. Under the circumstances, it would be inappropriate to give an adverse inference instruction to the jury.

* * * UBS Must Pay the Costs of Additional Depositions

Even though an adverse inference instruction is not warranted, there is no question that e-mails that UBS should have produced to Zubulake were destroyed by UBS. That being so, UBS must bear Zubulake's costs for re-deposing certain witnesses for the limited purpose of inquiring into issues raised by the destruction of evidence and any newly discovered e-mails. In particular, UBS is ordered to pay the costs of re-deposing Chapin, Hardisty, Tong, and Josh Varsano (a human resources employee in charge of the Asian Equities Sales Desk and known to have been in contact with Tong during August 2001).

* * *

COMMENTARY

1. When Does the Duty to Preserve Arise?

"A preservation obligation may arise from many sources, including common law, statutes, regulations, or a court order in a case."[18] In addition, courts have held that the duty to preserve arises when a party knows, or reasonably should know, that the evidence is relevant to pending or future litigation. The point at which a party had actual knowledge or notice of pending or future litigation is relatively simple to identify. By contrast, determining when a party reasonably should have anticipated litigation—that is, when a party had constructive knowledge of future litigation—is the far more difficult question, and is often a key issue in dispute during court consideration of spoliation motions. Broadly put, a party should preserve evidence when the party is on notice of a potential litigation or investigation. But what is "notice"? And at what point can it be later determined that litigation should have been "reasonably anticipated"?

2. How Should Parties Identify When the Duty to Preserve Has Been Triggered?

The determination of when the duty to preserve has been triggered is inherently fact specific. The Sedona Conference has suggested that in general, "[t]he determination of whether litigation is reasonably anticipated should be based on good faith ... a reasonable investigation and an evaluation of the relevant facts and circumstances."[19] Where a court must evaluate whether a party's decision to preserve evidence, or not to do so, was reasonable, it should ask whether that decision was made in good faith and was reasonable given the facts available to the party at the time the decision was made.

Anticipated litigation must be something more than a mere possibility or general discontent. "The future litigation must be 'probable,'

---

18. Rule 37, 2006 Advisory Committee Note.

19. Sedona Conference, *The Sedona Conference Commentary on Legal Holds: The Trigger and the Process*, 3, 10 (Public Comment Version 2007), *available at* http://www.thesedonaconference.org/content/miscFiles/Legal_holds.pdf ("Sedona Legal Holds").

which has been held to mean 'more than a possibility.' "[20] It is very likely that the duty is triggered when a party provides unequivocal notice of its intent to file a claim, even if it has not yet filed a formal complaint.[21] In general, "[r]easonable anticipation of litigation arises when an organization is on notice of a *credible threat* it will become involved in litigation or anticipates taking action to initiate litigation."[22] But what facts and circumstances might suggest a credible threat? And how "credible" must that threat be?

In *Hynix Semiconductor Inc. v. Rambus, Inc.*,[23] the plaintiff's duty to preserve was not triggered when it contemplated litigation against copyright infringers only if negotiations failed and where the litigation depended upon other contingencies. Litigation became probable only when the plaintiff interviewed litigation counsel. When parties indicate a preference for negotiation, even though litigation is a possible outcome, the duty may not yet be triggered. For other courts, the "possibility" of litigation may be sufficient to trigger the duty. In *Zubulake*, the court found a duty triggered when nearly all employees associated with Zubulake recognized the "possibility" that she might sue. Is this a different standard than the one used in *Hynix Semiconductor*? Does widespread recognition of "possible" litigation increase its probability? What if only one employee believes litigation is likely?

a. Plaintiffs' Duty to Preserve

When considering *plaintiffs'* duty to preserve, courts may be more likely to find the duty triggered before litigation formally commences than for defendants, in large part because plaintiffs control the timing of litigation. In *Cyntegra, Inc. v. Idexx Laboratories, Inc.*,[24] Cyntegra, a competitor to Idexx Labs, alleged that Idexx engaged in anti-competitive agreements with its buyers that severely disadvantaged Cyntegra's ability to generate revenue and profits. In March 2006, after Cyntegra was unable to make payments to an outside service that stored nearly all of Cyntegra's data, the service deleted Cyntegra's files—including information relevant to Idexx's defense. Three months later, Cyntegra filed its claim. The court asserted that because plaintiffs control when litigation begins, they "must necessarily anticipate litigation before the complaint is filed."[25] Because all of Cyntegra's injury resulted from conduct occurring prior to March—the point at which the data were destroyed—

---

20. *In re Napster, Inc. Copyright Litig.*, 462 F. Supp. 2d 1060, 1068 (N.D. Cal. 2006) (quoting *Hynix Semiconductor Inc. v. Rambus*, No. C–00–20905, 2006 WL 565893, at *21 (N.D. Cal. Jan. 5, 2006)). *Accord Treppel v. Biovail Corp.*, 233 F.R.D. 363, 371 (S.D.N.Y. 2006) ("[T]he mere existence of a dispute . . . did not mean that the parties should reasonably have anticipated litigation at that time and taken steps to preserve evidence.").

21. *See Longview Fibre Co. v. CSX Transp., Inc.*, 526 F. Supp. 2d 332, 341 (N.D.N.Y. 2007) (CSX's duty to preserve track maintenance records essential to defense of property damage claim arose "at the very latest" when CSX notified defendant of its intent to sue for damage to tracks).

22. Sedona Legal Holds, at 5 (emphasis added).

23. No. 00–20905, 2006 WL 565893, at *22 (N.D. Cal. Jan. 5, 2006).

24. No. 06–4170, 2007 WL 5193736 (C.D. Cal. Sept. 21, 2007).

25. *Id.* at *3.

the court concluded the plaintiff must have anticipated litigation by that date. Although plaintiff attempted to negotiate with Idexx to mitigate or eliminate the tying arrangements prior to filing suit, the court found that "[p]laintiff should have known that negotiation breakdowns were a distinct possibility, and that legal recourse might be necessary to prevent bankruptcy."[26] How does this result compare with the outcome in *Hynix Semiconductor*, where negotiation was also a precursor to bringing suit and where evidence suggested litigation was explicitly contemplated? Can the two cases be reconciled?

Even when plaintiff does not file a claim until long after the conduct giving rise to the event occurred, the court may find reasonable anticipation of litigation. In *Silvestri v. General Motors Corp.*,[27] the plaintiff claimed his injuries sustained in a car accident were exacerbated when the vehicle's airbag failed to deploy. After the accident, Silvestri nearly immediately retained counsel, who in turn hired experts who inspected the vehicle and the accident site within weeks of the accident. One expert concluded that the airbag should have deployed and that there was therefore a valid case against GM. The experts asserted they understood the inspection was conducted in anticipation of litigation and suggested to plaintiff's counsel the need to preserve the vehicle for GM's inspection. A few months after the accident, the owner of the vehicle sold it and the new owner repaired the damage, preventing GM from inspecting the car in its post-accident/pre-repair condition. On these facts, the court found that Silvestri anticipated litigation shortly after the accident and the duty to preserve was triggered at that time.

b. Pre–Filing Communications Between Counsel

Pre-filing communications between the litigants can also provide constructive notice that litigation is likely. Demand letters stating a claim may be sufficient to trigger an obligation to preserve. But the clarity and content of pre-filing communications can significantly impact whether a party should have reasonably anticipated litigation. While something less than a clear indication of intent to sue may be sufficient to trigger the duty, correspondence that merely presents a basis for the dispute may be inadequate. In *Cache La Poudre Feeds LLC v. Land O'Lakes, Inc.* (set forth in Chapter II.F, *infra*), the court held that the defendant's duty to preserve evidence was *not* triggered at the time of the pre-filing communication, which the court found "equivocal" because it did not threaten litigation, suggested initial interest in avoiding litigation, and did not demand preservation of relevant materials.[28] Under the rationale of *Cyntegra, Hynix Semiconductors, Inc.,* and *Silvestri,* would the plaintiff's duty have been triggered at that time?

When a party receives pre-filing correspondence from opposing counsel that is suggestive of potential litigation, but neither specifies the

---

26. *Id.*

27. 271 F.3d 583 (4th Cir. 2001).

28. 244 F.R.D. 614, 622–23 (D. Colo. 2007).

nature of, or events giving rise to, the claim, nor explicitly threatens litigation, does the duty to preserve impose any obligation on the recipient to further investigate to determine whether a litigation threat exists? In *Stallings v. Bil–Jax*, the court found that although a letter from plaintiff's counsel was vague, it "provided some notice to [defendant] that Stallings might bring a lawsuit against it. . . . [and defendant] had ample time to make a timely request for additional information regarding the nature of the incident referred to in the letter."[29] Thus, the court found that the defendant was at least partially responsible for the destruction of relevant evidence.

c. Pre–Filing Preservation Letters

While post-litigation discovery requests clearly put a party on notice of the relevance of data requested, what of pre-filing preservation letters? Although the common law duty of preservation does not depend on receipt of a preservation letter, "prudent counsel would be wise to ensure that a demand letter ... addresses ... preservation obligations."[30] Properly crafted pre-litigation preservation letters can impose the duty of preservation. For example, a plaintiff's preservation letter sent six days after a fatal accident seeking preservation of the tractor-trailer allegedly at fault, and another request eighteen days after the accident for preservation of driving records and on-board electronic tracking devices were specific as to evidence requested and put defendant on notice that litigation was imminent.[31]

Can broad or overly inclusive preservation letters successfully trigger a pre-litigation duty to preserve all the information requested? In *Frey v. Gainey Transportation Services, Inc.*,[32] the court declined to impose sanctions on the defendant for failing to preserve evidence demanded by plaintiff in a pre-litigation preservation letter sent fifteen days after the incident giving rise to the claim and ten days before the claim was filed. While the fact that the plaintiff retained counsel should have put defendant on notice that litigation was at least a "possibility," the court noted that compliance with the fifteen-page demand letter would have required defendant to preserve virtually all business records and would have exceeded allowable discovery under the Federal Rules of Civil Procedure.

If the preservation request is too narrow, does the receiving party have a duty to preserve relevant evidence not mentioned in the letter by the sender? In *Healthcare Advocates, Inc. v. Harding, Earley, Follmer & Frailey*,[33] the court rejected plaintiff's assertion that defendant had notice of its duty to preserve temporary cached files containing website screen shots when the plaintiff sent a post-filing subpoena seeking production

---

29.   243 F.R.D. 248, 250, 252 (E.D. Va. 2007).

30.   *Cache La Poudre Feeds, LLC v. Land O'Lakes, Inc.*, 244 F.R.D. 614, 623 (D. Colo. 2007).

31.   *See Garrett v. Albright*, No. 06–4137, 2008 WL 681766, at *2 n.5, *3 (W.D. Mo. Mar. 6, 2008).

32.   No. 05–1493, 2006 WL 2443787 (N.D. Ga. Aug. 22, 2006).

33.   497 F. Supp. 2d 627 (E.D. Pa. 2007).

of computers and *copies* of archived screen shots, requesting that nothing be deleted or altered on the computers, and notifying defendant that its actions in accessing archived copies of plaintiff's web pages may have violated federal law. The court noted that the defendant had preserved the copies and was not under a duty to preserve the cached files since the letter said nothing about preserving the temporary cached files on the computers. Moreover, the court noted that defendant could not have reasonably understood the letter to impose such a duty when defendant had never saved the cached files to the computers' hard drives.

What if the recipient of the preservation letter, but not the sender, knows of the existence of other relevant evidence not requested by the letter? Is the duty to preserve triggered? Suppose ABC Corp. receives a pre-suit preservation letter from a putative plaintiff's counsel making clear he will bring a suit under the Age Discrimination in Employment Act, claiming the company's recent implementation of a reduction in force ("RIF") plan was designed to eliminate older and more costly employees from the workforce and replace them with younger employees. The letter specifically demands that ABC Corp. preserve data held or generated by six persons, mentioned by name: the two human resources staff who implemented and managed the RIF and who now manage the hiring process; two top executives who ordered the plan; the outside consultant who designed the plan; and plaintiff's manager who fired him. Plaintiff is unaware, however, that another ABC Corp. employee generated and now maintains a database, model, and results of a statistical analysis of the impact of the RIF by age, gender, and race.

Does the letter, which does not request preservation of that data or mention the employee by name, impose on ABC Corp. a duty to preserve data held by that employee? What if the relevance of the unrequested data was more ambiguous? What result then? Is there, or should there be, a duty to inquire as to what other data not mentioned in a preservation letter might be relevant to the claim?

d. Closely Related Proceedings

Closely related investigations or proceedings involving similar facts and claims can also provide pre-filing constructive notice of future litigation. In *Zubulake*, the court identified the trigger date as the day on which the plaintiff's discrimination complaint was first filed with the Equal Employment Opportunity Commission ("EEOC"). An EEOC complaint at least provides the possibility of a civil suit and clearly puts an employer on notice that either a suit by the federal government or the complainant is likely to follow.

3. Application to a Hypothetical Scenario

Assume the following hypothetical scenario: An employee shouts at the supervisor, "I can't take your abuse any longer! I'm quitting, and I will sue you and the company. You'll be hearing from my lawyer!" The disgruntled employee then marches off the company premises.

a. The Defendant Employer

Is the employer now on notice of a potential litigation? Should the employer now reasonably anticipate litigation? Is litigation pending, imminent or reasonably foreseeable? Has the duty to preserve relevant ESI been triggered? The answer to this question has very serious implications. If the company decides that the above event has in fact given rise to a preservation duty, a series of significant and costly events will occur. The legal department must put into effect a litigation hold to preserve relevant data throughout the company. To do this, the company's lawyers or management will likely meet with retained counsel and then interview the pertinent witnesses about the underlying event to determine the employee's likely claims and the company's defenses. The next step is to determine what data is relevant to the claims and defenses and the multitude of locations where that data may be stored. In short, the determination of whether a triggering event has occurred has huge consequences. A "yes" answer entails significant work and expense. A "no" answer runs the risk of being second guessed years later after data has been lost.

The easy answer would be to preserve data under almost all circumstances. However, counsel cannot play it safe by preserving data every time there is a disagreement or conflict. Almost all disagreements and conflicts are resolved far short of litigation and, from a practical perspective, the cost and effort to preserve all data for every such instance would cripple large corporations that are almost always involved in litigation.

Regarding our disgruntled employee, would these questions be important to know?

1. How long has the employee worked for the company?

2. Has the employee ever brought a claim against the company or a previous employer?

3. Has the employee walked off the job on other occasions?

4. What were the employee's performance reviews?

5. Has the supervisor had other employees walk off the job?

6. Has the company received a letter threatening litigation from an attorney representing the employee?

7. Does the employee have a colorable claim?

8. What additional questions would **you** suggest?

Add at least five more questions that you think would be helpful in reaching a decision as to whether a duty to preserve is triggered.

b. The Plaintiff Employee

At some point prior to the day the lawsuit is filed, the plaintiff had come to a decision that litigation was likely. At what point must he put a litigation hold in place? Suppose that our disgruntled employee heads home after work and proceeds to draft a message to a Facebook group describing the events at work and seeking advice as to whether he should consult an attorney. Has a duty already arisen requiring him to preserve this message and all other e-mails along with postings to wikis, blogs, and other Internet locations, even before meeting with potential counsel?

If so, what is the scope of the preservation duty? Will the disgruntled employee be seeking compensation for his emotional pain and suffering? If so, is there an immediate duty to preserve all ESI reflecting on the quality of the disgruntled employee's daily activities? Additionally, what is the reach of such a preservation duty? Must the disgruntled employee request that his friends preserve their electronic data that may be relevant to his claims?

PROBLEM

Which of the following factors gives rise to a duty to preserve ESI?

A. The company receives a letter demanding preservation of data and enclosing a copy of a draft complaint.

B. The filing of a suit where the company is alleged to be a co-conspirator.

C. The receipt of a form letter from an attorney alleging a client slipped and fell on the company's premises and threatening a class action unless the matter is quickly settled for $10,000.

D. The filing of an employment discrimination charge with the State Human Rights Commission.

E. A letter to the local Better Business Bureau by a consumer alleging poor service and refusal to accept return of a defective product.

F. A computer hacker has hacked into the medical billing department of a hospital and obtained social security, date of birth, home address and credit card information for hospital patients.

G. An accounting firm reads in the paper that one of its clients is being investigated by the SEC for improperly valuing some of its assets in its financial disclosures.

H. An anonymous post on an internet service provider's online message board defames someone.

D. WHAT RECORDS MUST BE PRE-SERVED? ACCESSIBLE AND NOT REASONABLY ACCESSIBLE ESI

ZUBULAKE v. UBS WARBURG LLC
"Zubulake IV"

220 F.R.D. 212 (S.D.N.Y. 2003)

SCHEINDLIN, DISTRICT JUDGE

Editor's Note: This case is set forth in Chapter II.C, *supra*. On the question of accessible and inaccessible data, the court provided the following analysis:

A party or anticipated party must retain all relevant documents (but not multiple identical copies) in existence at the time the duty to preserve attaches, and any relevant documents created thereafter. In recognition of the fact that there are many ways to manage electronic data, litigants are free to choose how this task is accomplished. For example, a litigant could choose to retain all then-existing backup tapes for the relevant personnel (if such tapes store data by individual or the contents can be identified in good faith and through reasonable effort), and to catalog any later-created documents in a separate electronic file. That, along with a mirror-image of the computer system taken at the time the duty to preserve attaches (to preserve documents in the state they existed at that time), creates a complete set of relevant documents. Presumably there are a multitude of other ways to achieve the same result.

* * *

The scope of a party's preservation obligation can be described as follows: Once a party reasonably anticipates litigation, it must suspend its routine document retention/destruction policy and put in place a "litigation hold" to ensure the preservation of relevant documents. As a general rule, that litigation hold does not apply to inaccessible backup tapes (*e.g.*, those typically maintained solely for the purpose of disaster recovery), which may continue to be recycled on the schedule set forth in the company's policy. On the other hand, if backup tapes are accessible (*i.e.*, actively used for information retrieval), then such tapes *would* likely be subject to the litigation hold.

However, it does make sense to create one exception to this general rule. If a company can identify where particular employee documents are stored on backup tapes, then the tapes storing the documents of "key players" to the existing or threatened litigation should be preserved if the information contained on those tapes is not otherwise available. This exception applies to *all* backup tapes.

COMMENTARY

1. What ESI Must Be Preserved?

Zubulake IV makes clear that the duty to preserve applies to *all relevant* information, including ESI, in the possession, custody or control of a party regardless of where it is located. Given that ESI is involved in virtually every aspect of daily communications, a broad interpretation of that duty could require preservation of extensive amounts of data. One court defined the types of relevant data that may be covered by a preservation obligation:

> "Documents, data, and tangible things" shall be interpreted broadly to include writings, records, files, correspondence, reports, memoranda, calendars, diaries, minutes, electronic messages, voice mail, E-mail, telephone message records or logs, computer and network activity logs, hard drives, backup data, removable computer storage media such as tapes, discs and cards, printouts, document image files, Web pages, databases, spreadsheets, software, books, ledgers, journals, orders, invoices, bills, vouchers, check statements, worksheets, summaries, compilations, computations, charts, diagrams, graphic presentations, drawings, films, charts, digital or chemical process photographs, video, phonographic, tape or digital recordings or transcripts thereof, drafts, jottings and notes, studies or drafts of studies or other similar such material. Information that serves to identify, locate, or link such material, such as file inventories, file folders, indices, and metadata, is also included in this definition.[34]

But there are some limitations on the scope of the duty to preserve: it does not include "every shred of paper, every e-mail or electronic document, and every backup tape."[35]

The degree to which ESI is "accessible" bears on the preservation obligation. *Zubulake IV* held that ESI that is "not reasonably accessible" must be preserved only if the ESI is relevant to the litigation and is not available on a more accessible source.

Zubulake IV noted that backup tapes that are routinely used for information retrieval would be considered reasonably accessible; only those used solely for disaster recovery purposes would generally be considered "not reasonably accessible." Why might backup tapes used *only* to restore a system be considered inaccessible? In part, because "by their nature [backup tapes are] indiscriminate.... They capture all information at a given time and from a given server but do not catalogue it by subject matter."[36] Backup tape systems not designed for

---

34. *In re Flash Memory Antitrust Litig.*, No. C–07–00086, 2008 WL 1831668, at *1 (N.D. Cal. Apr. 22, 2008).

35. *Zubulake IV*, 220 F.R.D. at 212.

36. *McPeek v. Ashcroft*, 202 F.R.D. 31, 33 (D.D.C. 2001).

routine retrieval are far less "readily usable." Parties thus need not suspend their normal systems for overwriting disaster recovery tapes even when they are aware the preservation duty has been triggered unless they know, or should know, that the ESI contained on them are potentially relevant to the claim and that those data are non-duplicative of other accessible information.[37]

The Sedona Conference suggests that additional "data-type factors" may be useful in evaluating whether ESI is or is not reasonably accessible after the media storage type has been identified. Data-type factors help identify the technical burden of preservation and production and include the following considerations:

- "transient complexity" associated with ESI that is stored but routinely overwritten to conserve storage space;

- "hidden complexity" associated with recovering deleted files that cannot be viewed without specialized knowledge or tools;

- "extraction complexity" associated with recovering and reassembling data fragments;

- "preservation complexity" associated with preserving cache and temporary files on personal computers;

- "search complexity" associated with scanned documents, such as handwritten letters, that have not been subject to Optical Character Recognition—a technology that makes such documents searchable; and

- "dispersion complexity" of reviewing data stored on multiple personal digital devices.[38]

2. Is Mere Relevance Enough to Trigger the Duty to Preserve Not Reasonably Accessible ESI?

Under *Zubulake IV*, all *relevant* ESI, even if inaccessible, must be preserved regardless of cost, if the information is not available in another accessible form. The Federal Rules of Civil Procedure likewise suggest that the mere fact of inaccessibility does not relieve a party of its preservation obligation.[39] Other courts have taken a contrary view, finding the preservation duty does not cover inaccessible ESI regardless of its relevance to potential litigation.[40]

---

37. *See Zubulake IV*, 220 F.R.D. at 218.

38. *The Sedona Conference Working Group 1 Commentary: Preservation, Management and Identification of Sources of Information that Are Not Reasonably Accessible* fig. 2 (forthcoming 2008).

39. *See* Fed. R. Civ. P. 26(b)(2)(B), 2006 Advisory Committee Note ("[a] party's identification of sources of electronically stored information as not reasonably accessible does not relieve the party of its common-law or statutory duties to preserve evidence"); Fed. R. Civ. P. 37(e), 2006 Advisory Committee Note (parties may not "exploit the routine operation of an information system to thwart discovery obligations by allowing that operation to continue in order to destroy specific stored information that it is required to preserve").

40. *See Oxford House, Inc. v. City of Topeka*, No. 06–4004, 2007 WL 1246200 (D. Kan. Apr. 27, 2007) (noting that even if backup tapes contained relevant e-mails that had been deleted from the server and were unavailable elsewhere, there was no duty to prevent the tapes from being overwritten because they were used only for disaster recovery purposes).

If mere relevance triggers the duty to preserve inaccessible ESI, how do parties determine whether the information is relevant? Evaluating preservation obligations based on relevance poses particular difficulties for parties at the pre-litigation stage before parties have had the opportunity to meet and confer on preservation issues. How should parties assess *ex ante* the potential relevance of ESI before a claim has been filed? How would an *ex ante* assessment of relevance differ from an *ex post* assessment? Pre-litigation assessment necessarily depends on what the party knew or should have known about the potential claim before it was filed.[41]

Should there be a requirement for *heightened* relevance before parties are required to preserve inaccessible ESI? Must the ESI be particularly relevant to the litigation to justify costs and burdens of preserving inaccessible ESI?[42] In *Best Buy Stores L.P. v. Developers Diversified Realty Corp.*,[43] defendants sought sanctions where the plaintiff downgraded a once accessible database into an inaccessible format. The court rejected sanctions in the absence of a showing that the database was of "particular relevance to this litigation," noting that because of the breadth and nature of the information in the database, it would have been "relevant to virtually any litigation involving [the plaintiff]."[44]

3. Should the Costs of Preserving Not Reasonably Accessible ESI Bear on the Duty to Preserve It?

Should potential relevance be weighed against the costs of preserving inaccessible ESI? In *McPeek v. Ashcroft*, the court relied upon the concept of the "marginal utility" of the ESI when considering production obligations for relevant but inaccessible information stored on backup tapes.[45] Noting that it would be impossible to know in advance what information might be on the tapes, the court weighed the "theoretical possibility" that the backup tapes would contain information relevant to the claim against the high financial and human resource costs of restoring the tapes.[46] In *McPeek*, the Department of Justice was the defendant; thus, the court expressed concern that the time and cost of

---

41. *See, e.g., Healthcare Advocates v. Harding, Earley, Follmer & Frailey*, 497 F. Supp. 2d 627, 640–41 (E.D. Pa. 2007) (finding no duty to preserve temporary cache files of web page screenshots when party could not have reasonably known electronic files would be relevant to future litigation and copies of screenshots had been preserved); *In re Kmart Corp.*, 371 B.R. 823, 848–49 (N.D. Ill. 2007) (declining to impose sanctions where plaintiff "failed to establish that [defendant] knew there was relevant, discoverable information among the documents being destroyed pursuant to the company's preexisting document retention/destruction policy"); *Hansen v. Dean Witter Reynolds Inc.*, 887 F. Supp. 669, 676 (S.D.N.Y. 1995) (declining to impose sanctions for failing to preserve information regarding quantity of employee's output in employment discrimination claim where employer was on notice that performance would be relevant to potential litigation but quality, not quantity, was basis for performance assessments).

42. *See* Sedona Principle 9 ("[a]bsent a showing of *special need and relevance* a responding party should not be required to *preserve*, review, or produce deleted, shadowed, fragmented, or residual" ESI).

43. 247 F.R.D. 567, 570 (D. Minn. 2007).

44. *Id.*

45. 202 F.R.D. 31, 34 (D.D.C. 2001).

46. *Id.* at 33.

recovery would detract from the agency's other responsibilities. For courts that consider costs relative to the possible relevance of the information, how much might the limited resources and nature of the parties affect courts' evaluation of whether there was a duty to preserve relevant, non-duplicative, inaccessible ESI? While *McPeek* involved production obligations and who should bear the costs of restoration, what does the court's approach suggest about how parties' might evaluate their preservation obligations?

An approach incorporating the costs of preservation would require parties to first identify potentially relevant ESI and the sources on which it might be located, assess the likelihood that relevant information may actually be stored on those sources, evaluate the degree to which the information is accessible, and determine whether duplicate copies exist. If accessible duplicates are not available, *Zubulake* suggests the party must preserve them even if they are stored on inaccessible sources. If relevance of inaccessible ESI, rather than cost of preservation, were the only consideration, what might be the implications for large corporations that are routinely sued for a range of claims? Would they have an ongoing duty to preserve virtually all inaccessible ESI?[47]

If cost becomes a factor in evaluating the preservation obligation for not reasonably accessible ESI, *what* costs should be considered: The costs of ongoing preservation only, or both preservation costs and recovery costs that would be incurred should the inaccessible ESI later be requested in discovery? If future restoration costs are a permissible consideration in the initial preservation decision, does a decision *not* to preserve based on future restoration costs deprive a requesting party of its ability to later discover relevant ESI even when it is willing to bear recovery costs?

Which is the preferable approach: a preservation duty for inaccessible ESI based on relevance alone or a test balancing preservation costs with the value or relevance of the information? For defendants? For plaintiffs? Who is likely to know more about what information may be relevant before a claim is filed? Who is more likely to know where relevant information is stored?

4. What Impact, If Any, Should the Size of the Claim Have on the Scope of the Preservation Duty for Not Reasonably Accessible ESI?

Consider the following scenario: Assume that Jane sues her employer for wrongful termination, a claim to which e-mail and other ESI are relevant. Jane's salary was $20,000 per year. The cost of preserving active data stores is $500. The cost of preserving backup tapes on which relevant ESI may be stored is $15,000. Shortly after Jane was fired, the

---

47. *See Concord Boat Corp. v. Brunswick Corp.*, No. C–95–781, 1997 WL 33352759, at *1 (E.D. Ark. Aug. 29, 1997) (holding that a corporation was not under a duty to preserve relevant e-mails before the complaint was filed because such a duty would require the party to preserve all e-mails on the theory that most might someday be relevant to litigation).

employer upgraded its database. The cost of preserving the legacy database, which likely contains information relevant to whether Jane received disparate treatment relative to other similarly situated employees, is $50,000. Considering these costs, which of these data stores must the employer preserve to meet its preservation obligations? Does the relatively small amount of damages that Jane might recover mitigate the scope of the preservation duty? If the size of the claim is taken into account, what might be the implications for a claimant who seeks monetary relief that is small in the context of corporate budgets but significant to the claimant in light of his or her income and resources?

5. Does Downgrading ESI From an Accessible to an Inaccessible Format Violate the Preservation Duty?

If information is reasonably accessible at the time the preservation duty was triggered, what obligation do parties have to maintain that information on the accessible storage media?

The court in *Best Buy Stores L.P. v. Developers Diversified Realty Corp.* recently considered this question.[48] Plaintiff had developed a database for use in unrelated litigation. Although at the time discovery in the pending case was underway, the database was intact and searchable, it was later downgraded by storing the original data from which the database was created on difficult-to-search backup tapes—storage media generally considered to be not reasonably accessible. The court held that the plaintiff did not have a duty to maintain the data in an accessible form because, in part, preservation costs would have exceeded $27,000 per month.

A similar question was at issue in *Quinby v. WestLB AG*.[49] There, the court declined to impose sanctions on a defendant that downgraded relevant e-mails from an accessible to inaccessible format well after it had notice of potential litigation because it found the preservation duty does not include "a duty to keep the data in an accessible format."[50] In a later decision, however, the court required defendant to bear the recovery costs since it chose to downgrade ESI it should have known would be relevant to later litigation.[51] The court in *Treppel v. Biovail* reached a contrary conclusion.[52]

Are there other factors that should be considered when determining whether downgrading of accessible, relevant information is a violation of the preservation duty? Should it matter if such downgrading was, or was not, a routine business practice?

---

48.   247 F.R.D. 567, 569–71 (D. Minn. 2007).

49.   No. 04 Civ. 7406, 2005 WL 3453908 (S.D.N.Y. Dec. 15, 2005).

50.   *Id.* at *8 n.10.

51.   *See Quinby v. WestLB AG*, 245 F.R.D. 94, 111 (S.D.N.Y. 2006).

52.   233 F.R.D. 363, 372 n.4 (S.D.N.Y. 2006) (finding that "permitting the downgrading of data to a less accessible form—which systematically hinders future discovery by making the recovery of the information more costly and burdensome—is a violation of the preservation obligation").

6. Does the Duty to Preserve Include Metadata Embedded in ESI?

Metadata is information about a particular data set which describes "how, when and by whom it was collected, created, accessed, modified and how it was formatted."[53] Converting a file from its original, or "native," format—the form in which the file was created—into an image file, such as Adobe Portable Document Format ("PDF") or Tagged Image File Format ("TIFF"), strips the metadata, providing only a static image of the document. In addition, "stripping" technology exists to scrub documents of their metadata without converting them into another format. Some ESI, such as databases and spreadsheets created using formulae and linked data sources, cannot be stripped of metadata without losing substantial information.

Does the duty to preserve relevant ESI include preservation of documents in their native format? Metadata in the production context may provide valuable information. Rule 34 requires that documents be produced "as they are kept in the usual course of business" and, unless otherwise specified by the requesting party, in the "form ... in which [they are] ordinarily maintained or in a reasonably usable form."[54] The 2006 Advisory Committee Note to Rule 34 illustrates the Rule's intent:

> [T]he option to produce in a reasonably usable form does not mean that a responding party is free to convert [ESI] from the form in which it is ordinarily maintained to a different form that makes it more difficult or burdensome for the requesting party to use the information efficiently in the litigation. If the responding party ordinarily maintains the information it is producing in a way that makes it searchable by electronic means, the information should not be produced in a form that removes or significantly degrades this feature.

This commentary suggests that metadata may not be stripped if it makes the documents less useful or less searchable. But the Sedona Principles provide a different interpretation:

> The form in which [ESI] is "ordinarily maintained" is not necessarily synonymous with the form in which it was created. There are occasions when business considerations involve the migration or transfer of [ESI] to other applications or systems.... Absent an attempt to deliberately downgrade capabilities or characteristics for the purposes of avoiding obligations during specific litigation, migration to alternative forms for business purposes is not considered inconsistent with preservation obligations.[55]

Do you agree that Rule 34's wording suggests there is no preservation obligation to *maintain* ESI in the form in which it was originally *created*? Does Rule 34 suggest that metadata can be stripped from the original

---

53. *The Sedona Conference® Glossary: E–Discovery & Digital Information Management* 33 (2d ed. 2007). *See* Appendix VI, *infra*.

54. Fed. R. Civ. P. 34(b)(2)(E)(i).

55. The Sedona Principles at 61, 63.

document format if doing so was consistent with normal preservation practices, even if the metadata were particularly relevant? Should stripping metadata be impermissible only if the purpose of doing so is to avoid discovery obligations? And if Rule 34 *does* imply an obligation to *produce* files in their native format, what does it suggest about the duty to *preserve* files in that format?

Metadata can be valuable because it provides information directly relevant to the claim, may help authenticate a document, and may aid in document management. For example, metadata may be directly relevant to a copyright infringement claim because it can demonstrate who copied, accessed or modified a file. However, one court asserted that "[m]ost metadata is of limited evidentiary value, and reviewing it can waste litigation resources."[56] What if the *only* value of the metadata is its ability to aid in document management during the litigation—that is, it provides no *substantive* information, but the embedded data allow very large quantities of ESI to be easily grouped and searched? Can preserving and producing otherwise irrelevant metadata conserve litigation resources?

In *In re Payment Card Interchange Fee & Merchant Discount Antitrust Litigation*,[57] the defendants objected to plaintiffs' production of relevant e-mails in TIFF format because it degraded their searchability, even though, if subject to optical character recognition, the TIFFs would be searchable. The court required plaintiffs, going forward, to produce e-mails in their native format, finding that the conversion to TIFF ran "afoul of the Advisory Committee's proviso that data ordinarily kept in electronically searchable form should not be produced in a form that removes or significantly degrades this feature."[58] Should metadata that is itself irrelevant to the claim but which aids in document management be preserved? If metadata can be used by the producing party to search for documents, but need not be preserved for the requesting party, what disadvantages might the requesting party face? Given that metadata may have inherent value to searchability and document authenticity, should there be a rebuttable presumption that metadata are relevant even when the metadata itself provide no substantive information that directly relates to the claims or defenses?[59]

Some courts have issued preservation orders that explicitly include metadata among the categories of ESI that parties must preserve, or have required preservation of electronic documents in their native format.[60] In *Hagenbuch v. 3B6 Sistemi Elettronici Industriali S.R.L.*, the

---

56. *Wyeth v. Impax Labs., Inc.*, 248 F.R.D. 169, 171 (D. Del. 2006) (citing *Shirley Williams v. Sprint/United Mgmt. Co.*, 230 F.R.D. 640, 646 (D. Kan. 2005)). This case is found at Chapter V.D, *infra*.

57. No. 05–1720, 2007 WL 121426 (E.D.N.Y. Jan. 12, 2007).

58. *Id*. at *4 (quotation omitted).

59. *See* Mike Breen, Comment, *Nothing to Hide: Why Metadata Should Be Presumed Relevant*, 56 Kan. L. Rev. 439 (2008).

60. *See In re Flash Memory Antitrust Litig.*, No. C–07–00086, 2008 WL 1831668, at *1 (N.D. Cal. Apr. 22, 2008) (reminding parties of obligation to preserve relevant documents, including "information that serves to identify, locate, or link such material . . . such as metadata").

court rejected defendant's argument that TIFF documents provided all the relevant information plaintiff needed, holding the metadata will "allow [plaintiff] to piece together the chronology of events and figure out, among other things, who received what information and when."[61] By contrast, the court in *Wyeth v. Impax Laboratories, Inc.* held that since the requesting party did not specifically ask for metadata to be produced, the producing party could properly produce only static image files.[62]

Do these production decisions and the discovery obligations created under Rule 34 create an inference that the scope of the preservation duty includes preservation of documents in their native format with metadata intact, independent of any court preservation order? If parties have an obligation to produce documents in their native format, do they have an obligation to preserve them in that format?

E.   DOES ESI INCLUDE EPHEMERAL DATA?

COLUMBIA PICTURES INDUSTRIES v. BUNNELL
No. CV 06–1093, 2007 WL 2080419 (C.D. Cal. May 29, 2007)

CHOOLJIAN, MAGISTRATE JUDGE

ORDER * * * GRANTING IN PART AND DENYING IN PART PLAINTIFFS' MOTION TO REQUIRE DEFENDANTS TO PRESERVE AND PRODUCE SERVER LOG DATA AND FOR EVIDENTIARY SANCTIONS * * *.

* * *

II.   PROCEDURAL HISTORY

On February 23, 2006, plaintiffs filed a complaint against defendants for copyright infringement. Plaintiffs allege, *inter alia,* that defendants knowingly enable, encourage, induce, and profit from massive online piracy of plaintiffs' copyrighted works through the operation of their internet website. * * * Defendants filed an Answer on May 24, 2006.

On March 12, 2007, plaintiffs filed a * * * Motion for an Order (1) Requiring Defendants to Preserve and Produce Certain Server Log Data, and (2) for Evidentiary Sanctions' ("Plaintiffs' Motion") * * * . Specifically, plaintiffs seek the preservation and production of the following data: (a) the IP addresses of users of defendants' website who request "dot-torrent" files; (b) the requests for "dot-torrent files"; and (c) the dates and times of such requests (collectively "Server Log Data").

---

61.   No. 04 C 3109, 2006 WL 665005, at *3 (N.D. Ill. Mar. 8, 2006).

62.   248 F.R.D. 169, 171 (D. Del. 2006). This case is found at Chapter V.D, *infra.*

Plaintiffs' Motion also seeks evidentiary sanctions against defendants for their alleged spoliation of the Server Log Data. * * *

* * *

III. FACTS

Defendants operate a website known as "TorrentSpy" which offers dot-torrent files for download by users. The dot-torrent files offered on defendants' website do not contain actual copies of a full-length content item. Rather, they contain data used by a "BitTorrent client" on a user's computer to access the content in issue.

As certain aspects of the technical operation of the website are relevant to the resolution of this matter, the court first sets forth its understanding and findings, based upon the evidence presented, of the operation of the relevant aspects of: (i) websites in general; (ii) defendants' website prior to the filing of Plaintiffs' Motion; and (iii) defendants' website proximate or subsequent to the filing of Plaintiffs' Motion, as the record reflects that the method of operation changed during the pendency of this action.

A. Operation of Websites in General

In general, when a user clicks on a link to a page or a file on a website, the website's web server program receives from the user a request for the page or the file. The request includes the IP address of the user's computer, and the name of the requested page or file, among other things.[7] Such information is copied into and stored in RAM. RAM is a form of temporary storage that every computer uses to process data. Every user request for a page or file is stored by the web server program in RAM in this fashion. The web server interprets and processes that data, while it is stored in RAM, in order to respond to user requests. The web server then satisfies the request by sending the requested file to the user. If the website's logging function is enabled, the web server copies the request into a log file, as well as the fact that the requested file was delivered. If the logging function is not enabled, the request is not retained. While logging such information can be useful to a website operator in many respects, and may be a usual practice of many website operators, such logging is not essential to the functionality of a website. [8]

---

7. An IP address is a standard way of identifying a computer that is connected to the Internet. With an IP address, a party could identify the Internet Service Provider ("ISP") providing internet service to the user of the computer corresponding to such IP address. Only the ISP, however, could link the particular IP address to an individual subscriber. As in the case of a subscriber to a particular telephone number, the identity of the subscriber to an IP address is not necessarily indicative of the person using the service at a given time.

8. As a general matter, logging data can be useful for maintenance and upkeep of a site, to identify and correct technical problems with the site, to examine the website traffic patterns and evaluate the performance of the site, and to audit and evaluate data related to advertising on the site.

B. Operation of Defendants' Website Prior to the Filing of Plaintiffs' Motion

Defendants' web server is located in the Netherlands. A factor in the decision to use a server in the Netherlands was to attract business from those individuals who did not wish their identities to be known, as defendants believe the Netherlands to have stricter privacy laws governing such information. Defendants use the web server Microsoft Internet Information Services (IIS) 6.0 to operate their website. The IIS web server program contains logging functionality—meaning that it has the capacity, if the logging function is not disabled, to retain the Server Log Data.

Since its inception, defendants' website's logging function has not been enabled to retain the Server Log Data. Such logging is not necessary to, or part of defendants' business operations. The decision not to enable the logging function was based, at least in part, on the belief that the failure to log such information would make the site more attractive to users who did not want their identities known for whatever reason. Although defendants did not affirmatively retain the Server Log Data through logging or other means, the data went through and was temporarily stored in the RAM of defendants' website server for approximately six hours.

C. Operation of Defendants' Website Proximate or Subsequent to the Filing of Plaintiffs' Motion

At some point proximate or subsequent to the filing of Plaintiffs' Motion, defendants altered the method through which the website operates. Defendants' server no longer receives all, or all facets of the Server Log Data, or at least not in the same way.[11] Instead, defendants now contract with a third party entity, "Panther," which essentially serves as a middleman in the process. Panther has multiple servers around the world, including approximately 25 servers in the United States. Requests from users who visit defendants' website for a dot-torrent file on defendants' server are now routed from a location not hosted on defendants' server to a Panther server geographically proximate to the users making the requests. Panther's servers in the United States serve United States users. In cases involving an initial request for a specific dot-torrent file, defendants' website now receives such request from Panther. Defendants' website sends the requested dot-torrent file to Panther. Panther then sends the file to the original requesting party. However, once a particular dot-torrent file has been requested from defendants' website by Panther, Panther then caches it and can provide

---

11. Prior to the filing of Plaintiffs' Motion, defendants' website provided links to third-party sites that have torrent files on their sites, as well as links to torrent files on the cache of defendants' website. Once defendants made the recent change in their method of operation, defendants' website no longer does such caching. Instead, a third party under contract to defendants performs that function. However, when a user runs a search on defendants' website, every search is a request on defendants' server. Similarly, when a user gets a list of results back, clicks one of those links, and gets taken to a detailed dot-torrent page hosted by defendants' server, all of those pages—on which the names of dot-torrent files are identified—are hosted on defendants' server.

it in response to subsequent requests for the same dot-torrent file without the need to obtain it from defendants' server. In the latter circumstance, defendants' server no longer receives data reflecting a request to download the particular dot-torrent file. Thus, Panther now receives the Server Log Data in issue in its RAM. Panther, however, does not retain logs of such information. Defendant Parker testified that defendants switched to Panther because it allows for significantly faster processing and delivery of content. Defendants deny that the decision to contract with Panther was motivated by a desire to avoid being in possession of Server Log Data or to bypass a possible court order.[13]

D. Plaintiffs' Preservation Request

On May 15, 2006, [plaintiffs] sent a notice to [defendants'] counsel formally reminding counsel and [defendants] of their obligation to preserve all potentially discoverable evidence in their possession, custody or control related to the litigation, including all logs for the Torrent-Spy website, and records of all communications between defendants and users of the website, including instant-messaging and other chat logs. This notice did not specifically request that defendants preserve Server Log Data temporarily stored only in RAM. Plaintiffs do not point to any other preservation request which specifically addresses data temporarily stored only in RAM. The court further notes that prior to the filing of Plaintiffs' Motion, the docket does not reflect that plaintiffs sought a preservation order.

IV. DISCUSSION

A. The Server Log Data in Issue Is Relevant

Pursuant to Rule 26(b)(1) of the Federal Rules of Civil Procedure, parties may obtain discovery regarding any matter, not privileged, that is relevant to the claim or defense of any party. Plaintiffs argue that the Server Log Data is relevant to numerous claims and defenses, including whether defendants' users have directly infringed plaintiffs' copyrighted works, and to what extent defendants' website is used for purposes of copyright infringement. The court agrees. * * *

B. The Server Log Data in Issue Is Electronically Stored Information

Rule 34(a) of the Federal Rules of Civil Procedure provides for the discovery of documents or electronically stored information—including writings, drawings, graphs, charts, photographs, sound recordings, images, and other data or data compilations stored in any medium from which information can be obtained. "Rule 34(a) applies to information that is fixed in a tangible form and to information that is stored in a medium from which it can be retrieved and examined." Advisory

---

13. In light of the change in the method of operation, and the timing thereof, as well as the other evidence in the record, the court finds that defendants have the ability to manipulate at will how the Server Log Data is routed. Indeed, defendants represent that they could disengage and resume the functions currently performed by Panther if directed to log the Server Log Data in issue.

Comm. Notes to the 2006 Amendment of Rule 34. The Advisory Committee Notes further indicate that Rule 34(a)(1) "is expansive and includes any type of information that is stored electronically," and that it "is intended to be broad enough to cover all current types of computer-based information, and flexible enough to encompass future changes and development."

Defendants argue that the Server Log Data does not constitute electronically stored information under F.R. Civ. P. 34(a) because the data has never been electronically stored on their website or in any medium from which the data can be retrieved or examined, or fixed in any tangible form, such as a hard drive. Plaintiffs assert that the Server Log Data is electronically stored information because such data is copied to the RAM while user requests are processed.

Although the parties point to no cases in which a court has assessed whether data present only in RAM constitutes electronically stored information under Rule 34, the Ninth Circuit has addressed whether data in RAM is electronically stored information in another context. In *MAI Systems Corp. v. Peak Computer, Inc.*, 991 F.2d 511, 518–19 (9th Cir. 1993), the Ninth Circuit determined in the context of the Copyright Act, that software copied into RAM was "fixed" in a tangible medium and was sufficiently permanent or stable to permit it to be perceived, reproduced, or otherwise communicated for a period of more than transitory duration. It defined RAM as "a computer component in which data and computer programs can be temporarily recorded." RAM has elsewhere been described as providing "temporary storage." *See also Apple Computer, Inc. v. Franklin Computer Corp.*, 714 F.2d 1240, 1243 n.3 (3d Cir. 1983) ("RAM . . . is a chip on which volatile internal memory is stored which is erased when the computer's power is turned off.").

In light of the Ninth Circuit's decision in *MAI*, and the similarity between the definitions of electronically stored information in the Advisory Committee Notes to Rule 34 and the Copyright Act, the latter of which was in issue in *MAI*, this court concludes that data in RAM constitutes electronically stored information under Rule 34. Based on the evidence in the record, the court finds that the Server Log Data in this case is transmitted through and temporarily stored in RAM while the requests of defendants' website users for dot-torrent files are processed. Consequently, such data is electronically stored information under Rule 34.

C. The Server Log Data in Issue Is within the Possession, Custody or Control of Defendants

Rule 34(a) is limited in its scope to documents and electronically stored information which are in the possession, custody or control of the party upon whom the request is served. Prior to the filing of Plaintiffs' Motion, the Server Log Data was received, at least in large part, in defendants' website's RAM, and therefore was clearly within defendants' possession, custody and control. As the Server Log Data is now directed to Panther's RAM as opposed to the RAM on defendants' website, the court must also consider whether the Server Log Data routed to Panther is in defendants' possession, custody or control.

Federal courts have consistently held that documents are deemed to be within a party's possession, custody or control for purposes of Rule 34 if the party has actual possession, custody or control, or has the legal right to obtain the documents on demand. * * * The record reflects that defendants have the ability to manipulate at will how the Server Log Data is routed. Consequently, the court concludes that even though the Server Log Data is now routed to Panther and is temporarily stored in Panther's RAM, the data remains in defendants' possession, custody or control.

D. Requiring the Preservation and Production of the Server Log Data Is Not Tantamount to Requiring the Creation of New Data

Rule 34 only requires a party to produce documents that are already in existence. Accordingly, "a party cannot be compelled to create, or cause to be created, new documents solely for their production." *Paramount Pictures Corp. v. Replay TV ("Replay TV")*, 2002 WL 32151632, *2 (C.D. Cal. 2002).

Defendants argue that because their website has never recorded or stored Server Log Data since the commencement of the website's operations, requiring defendants to retain such data would be tantamount to requiring them to create a record of the Server Log Data for its production. Plaintiffs contend that the Server Log Data already exists because such data is generated by the website users, received by a web server operated by, or under contract to defendants, and utilized to respond to user requests. As suggested by the court's analysis above, the court concludes that the Server Log Data in issue exists and, at least until recently, was temporarily stored in defendants' RAM.

As noted above, because the Server Log Data is temporarily stored in Panther's RAM, and is in the possession, custody or control of defendants, defendants would not be required to create new information for its production. * * * [B]ecause the Server Log Data already exists, is temporarily stored in RAM, and is controlled by defendants, an order requiring defendants to preserve and produce such data is not tantamount to ordering the creation of new data.

E. An Order Requiring the Preservation of Server Log Data Is Appropriate

Plaintiffs' Motion requests that the court issue an order requiring defendants to preserve the Server Log Data. Plaintiffs contend, *inter alia,* that defendants are and have been obligated to preserve the Server Log Data, and that activating a logging function to preserve and store the server log data would impose no undue burden or cost on defendants. Defendants object to plaintiffs' request for a preservation order on the grounds that the Server Log Data is not subject to any preservation obligation and that requiring such preservation would be unduly burdensome.

In determining whether to issue a preservation order, courts undertake to balance at least three factors: (1) the level of concern the court has for the continuing existence and maintenance of the integrity of the evidence in the absence of an order directing preservation; (2) any irreparable harm likely to result to the party seeking the preservation of the evidence absent an order directing preservation; and (3) the capability of the party to maintain the evidence sought to be preserved, not only as to the evidence's original form, condition or contents, but also the physical, spatial and financial burdens created by ordering evidence preservation. * * *

As defendants do not currently retain and affirmatively object to retention of the Server Log Data, and in light of the key relevance of such data in this action, the first two factors clearly weigh in favor of requiring preservation of the Server Log Data.

The third factor requires more analysis. The parties offer drastically different views regarding the degree to which defendants may be burdened if they are required to preserve the Server Log Data. As the "burden" issues relative to preservation significantly overlap with the "burden" issues relative to production, the court will address such issues together.

First, the court considers the potential burden attendant to employing a technical mechanism through which retention of the Server Log Data in RAM may be enabled. Plaintiffs contend that employing such a technical mechanism would be a trivial matter involving little more than a setting change on the web server program. Defendants concede that the activation of a logging function to enable the retention of Server Log Data in RAM, in and of itself, would not be difficult. Consequently, the court finds that it would not be an undue burden on defendants to employ a technical mechanism through which retention of Server Log Data in RAM is enabled.

Second, the court considers the potential burden attendant to actually retaining (*i.e.*, recording and storing) and producing the Server Log Data. * * *

(i) Volume of Data/Resulting Costs/Impact on Website Functionality

Defendants represent that the Server Log Data would accumulate 30–40 gigabytes (30,000 to 40,000 megabytes) a day—a volume which defendants' current server does not have the capacity to record, store or copy, and the retention of which would negatively affect the functionality of their website, and require a costly re-design of their system and the installation of new equipment. Defendants further argue that the costs of producing such material would be prohibitive. However, during the hearing in this matter, it became evident that defendants' representation regarding the volume of Server Log Data was significantly overstated.

Rather than estimating the volume of incoming Server Log Data *only*, defendants estimated the volume of *all* requests for data. On cross-examination, defendant Parker conceded that collecting and recording only the subset of Server Log Data would "most likely" result in a volume of data far less than 40 gigabytes (40,000 megabytes) a day. * * * Defendant Parker testified that he had not considered data storage issues if the volume was significantly smaller, *i.e.,* if the Server Log Data in issue had a volume of only one gigabyte (1000 megabytes) a day. He did concede, however, that if the logging was limited to only the Server Log Data (as opposed to *all* incoming data), he would not have the same concerns about, *inter alia,* computer processing unit usage.

Based upon the evidence regarding the estimated volume of data resulting from the logging of solely the Server Log Data in issue (as opposed to all data) and the other evidence presented, the court finds that defendants would not be unduly burdened as a consequence of the volume of Server Log Data if required to preserve and produce such data.

(ii) Privacy/First Amendment/Federal Statutory Issues

Defendants also raise issues concerning the privacy of their website users based upon defendants' privacy policy, the First Amendment and multiple federal statutes. * * * [T]he court does not find defendants' arguments to be persuasive, particularly in light of the fact that this order directs defendants to mask users' IP addresses before the Server Log Data is produced. The court finds that defendants' asserted interest in maintaining the privacy of the users of their website can be adequately protected by the protective order already entered in this action and the masking of the users' IP addresses.

* * *

F. An Order Requiring the Production of Certain Server Log Data Is Appropriate

Defendants contend that they should not be ordered to produce the Server Log Data for the same reasons, discussed above, that cause defendants to believe that a preservation order should not issue. Plaintiffs maintain that such data should be produced, at least in a form that masks the IP addresses.

On a motion to compel discovery, the party from whom electronically stored information is sought must show that the information is not reasonably accessible because of undue burden or cost. F.R. Civ. P. 26(b)(2)(B). If such a showing is made, a court may nonetheless order discovery from such sources if the requesting party shows good cause, considering the limitations of F.R. Civ. P. 26(b)(2)(C). A court may limit discovery of electronic materials under F.R. Civ. P. 26(b)(2)(C) if: (i) the discovery sought is unreasonably cumulative or duplicative, or is obtainable from some other source that is more convenient, less burdensome, or less expensive; (ii) the party seeking discovery has had ample opportunity by discovery in the action to obtain the information sought; or (iii) the burden or expense of the proposed discovery outweighs its likely benefit, taking into account the needs of the case, the amount in controversy, the parties' resources, the importance of the issues at stake in the litigation, and the importance of the proposed discovery in resolving the issues.

Based on the discussion, analysis, and findings above, the court further finds: (1) defendants have failed to demonstrate that the Server Log Data is not reasonably accessible because of undue burden or cost; (2) plaintiffs have shown good cause to order discovery of such data; (3) the discovery sought is not unreasonably cumulative or duplicative or obtainable from some other source that is more convenient, less burdensome, or less expensive; (4) plaintiffs have not otherwise had the opportunity to obtain the data sought; and (5) the burden and expense of the proposed discovery does not outweigh its likely benefit, taking into account the needs of the case, the amount in controversy, the parties' resources, the importance of the issues at stake in the litigation, and the importance of the proposed discovery in resolving the issues. [31]

G. Evidentiary Sanctions

Plaintiffs' Motion also requests evidentiary sanctions against defendants in light of defendants' alleged wilful failure to preserve, and intentional spoliation of, the Server Log Data.

Pursuant to F.R. Civ. P. 37(f), absent exceptional circumstances, a court may not impose sanctions under the discovery rules based on a party's failure to provide electronically stored information lost as a result of the routine, good faith operation of an electronic information system. A "good faith" operation may require a party to modify or suspend certain features of that routine operation to prevent the loss of information, if that information is subject to a preservation obligation. Advisory Comm. Notes to the 2006 Amendment to Rule 37.

A litigant is under a duty to preserve what it knows, or reasonably should know, is relevant in the action, is reasonably calculated to lead to the discovery of admissible evidence, is reasonably likely to be requested during discovery, and/or the subject of a pending discovery request. Therefore, "[o]nce a party reasonably anticipates litigation, it must suspend its routine document retention/destruction policy and put in place a 'litigation hold' to ensure the preservation of relevant documents." *Zubulake v. UBS Warburg LLC,* 220 F.R.D. 212, 218 (S.D.N.Y. 2003). As a general rule, the litigation hold does not apply to inaccessi-

---

31. The court emphasizes that its ruling should *not* be read to require litigants in all cases to preserve and produce electronically stored information that is temporarily stored only in RAM. The court's decision in this case to require the retention and production of data which otherwise would be temporarily stored only in RAM, is based in significant part on the nature of this case, the key and potentially dispositive nature of the Server Log Data which would otherwise be unavailable, and defendants' failure to provide what this court views as credible evidence of undue burden and cost.

ble electronically stored information, such as back-tapes, which may continue to be recycled on the schedule set forth in the company's policy.

As noted above, although this court now finds that defendants have an obligation to preserve the Server Log Data in issue that is temporarily stored only in RAM, in the absence of (1) prior precedent directly on point in the discovery context; (2) a specific request by defendants to preserve Server Log Data present solely in RAM; and (3) a violation of a preservation order, this court finds that defendants' failure to retain the Server Log Data in RAM was based on a good faith belief that preservation of data temporarily stored only in RAM was not legally required. Consequently, the court finds that evidentiary sanctions against defendants for spoliation of evidence are not appropriate.

* * *

V. CONCLUSION

Based upon the foregoing, IT IS HEREBY ORDERED:

1.   Defendants are directed to commence preservation of the Server Log Data in issue within seven (7) days of this order and to preserve the Server Log Data for the duration of this litigation or until further of this court or the assigned District Judge. As the record reflects that there are multiple methods by which defendants can preserve such data, the court does not by this order mandate the particular method by which defendants are to preserve the Server Log Data.

2.   Defendants shall initially produce the Server Log Data * * * by no later than two weeks from the date of this order. Defendants thereafter have a continuing obligation regularly (no less frequently than every two weeks) to update such production. Although defendants are required to preserve the IP addresses of the computers used to request dot-torrent files, defendants are not, at least at this juncture, ordered to produce such IP addresses in an unmasked/unencrypted form. Instead, defendants shall mask, encrypt, or redact IP addresses through a hashing program or other means, provided, however, that if a given IP address appears more than once, such IP address is concealed in a manner which permits one to discern that the same IP address appears on multiple occasions. Plaintiffs are prohibited from using "brute force" or any other means to pierce or reverse any such mask/encryption/ redaction. The court does not by this order either mandate or prohibit notification to the users of defendants' website of the fact that the Server Log Data is being preserved and has been ordered produced with masked/encrypted/redacted IP addresses.

* * *

COMMENTARY

1. Does the Scope of the Duty to Preserve Include Relevant But Ephemeral Data?

Transitory or ephemeral data pose particular difficulties for parties considering the scope of their preservation obligation. Ephemeral data has been defined as "data not to be stored for any length of time beyond their operational use and . . . susceptible to being overwritten at any point during the routine operation of the information system."[63] Temporary cache files of web pages visited present the classic example of ephemeral data: users surf the web, web pages are temporarily cached on their computers to allow the web page to load quickly when it is next accessed, and then overwritten as the cache storage fills up. Many other forms of transitory data exist.

How should parties treat ephemeral data when their preservation duty arises? The Sedona Principles suggest that courts should not require extraordinary efforts to preserve "particularly transitory" electronically stored information.

To date courts have not sanctioned parties for failing to preserve ephemeral data. A key question for courts considering the issue may be whether ephemeral data is actually "stored" in any meaningful sense. Most courts have generally not found a duty to preserve ephemeral data. For example, in *Healthcare Advocates, Inc. v. Harding, Earley, Follmer & Frailey*, the court rejected sanctions on the defendant law firm for failure to preserve temporary cache files of archived web pages accessed through a third-party, public website.[64] Defendant accessed the archived pages in an effort to gather evidence to defend its clients in an unrelated case brought by plaintiffs and preserved copies of the pages accessed relevant to that case. The court noted that cache files were not apparently relevant to the pending claim, were deleted automatically, and may have "been lost the second another website was visited."[65]

In *Convolve, Inc. v. Compaq Computer Corp.*,[66] the court rejected sanctions sought for the defendant's failure to preserve data readings on an electronic device used to "tune" computer hard drives, where the data collected from the device were routinely written-over when the next measurement was taken with the device. The court noted that in contrast to e-mail, "the data at issue here [were] ephemeral" and the defendants had no business reason to maintain them as "[t]hey exist[ed]

---

63. Kenneth J. Withers, *"Ephemeral Data" and the Duty to Preserve Discoverable Electronically Stored Information*, 37 U. Balt. L. Rev. 349, 366 (2008).

64. 497 F. Supp. 2d 627 (E.D. Pa. 2007).

65. *Id.* at 642.

66. *See* 223 F.R.D. 162, 177 (S.D.N.Y. 2004). *See also Malletier v. Dooney & Bourke, Inc.*, No. 04 Civ. 5316, 2006 WL 3851151 (S.D.N.Y. Dec. 22, 2006) (rejecting sanctions for failure to preserve purportedly relevant chatroom conversations with customers on its website where the defendant did not have a means to preserve the transitory online discussions and it was unlikely the conversations would have provided relevant evidence).

only until the tuning engineer [made] the next adjustment, and then the document change[d]."[67]

One commentator has suggested that courts should consider four factors in deciding whether ephemeral data should be preserved: (1) whether the data are uniquely relevant to the litigation; (2) how the data are ordinarily treated by the party "in the ordinary course of business;" (3) whether preservation imposes excessive costs or burdens relative to the value of the data; and (4) whether technologies exist to preserve the data.[68] Just as ESI's accessibility may depend on evolving technologies that make formerly cost-prohibitive restoration economically viable, any obligation to preserve ephemeral data may depend, in part, on whether technologies exist to preserve it in a non-transitory state, and the costs associated with implementing those technologies.

2. How Ephemeral Can ESI Be?

Notwithstanding the Magistrate Judge's remark in a footnote that the *Columbia Pictures* ruling "should not be read to require litigants in all cases to preserve and produce electronically stored information that is temporarily stored only in RAM," the decision in *Bunnell* has been criticized as representing a possible judicial expansion of the concept of what constitutes ESI for purposes of triggering legal preservation obligations under the Federal Rules. A number of other courts have also addressed the question of what constitutes ESI.[69]

EXCERPT FROM Douglas R. Rogers, *A Search for Balance in the Discovery of ESI Since December 1, 2006*, 14 Richmond J.L. & Tech. 8 (2008):

> The court in *Columbia Pictures* made clear that it was not saying the defendant had violated any duty to preserve documents before the issuance of the order. However, if the court had the authority to order production of the information on RAM because the RAM constituted ESI, it could logically follow that the defendants have a duty to preserve that information to the extent it is relevant, at least from the time the litigation starts:
>
> When a "forensic image" is taken of a computer, that image only records data (bits) on the hard drive of the computer, not data on RAM. In order to capture data on RAM, typically one "(1) saves the data to a hard drive or CD ROM, or (2) installs a 'data dump program,' which downloads the data on RAM at any particular time through the hard drive of the computer." In other words, a strong argument can be made that data is not retrieved and examined from RAM, but is retrieved and examined from hard drives and CD ROM's.

---

67. *Convolve, Inc.*, 223 F.R.D. at 177.

68. *See* Kenneth J. Withers, *"Ephemeral Data" and the Duty to Preserve Discoverable Electronically Stored Information*, 37 U. Balt. L. Rev. 349, 374–77 (2008).

69. *See, e.g., Healthcare Advocates, Inc. v. Harding, Earley, Follmer & Frailey*, 497 F. Supp. 2d 627 (E.D. Pa. 2007) (Internet cache); *Malletier v. Dooney & Bourke, Inc.*, No. 04 Civ. 5316, 2006 WL 3851151 (S.D.N.Y. Dec. 22, 2006) (chat room conversation); *Convolve Inc.*, 223 F.R.D. at 177 (oscilloscope readings).

Although not directly on point, the reasoning of a 2005 Florida state court decision on RAM seems to contain better reasoning than the reasoning in *Columbia Pictures*. In *O'Brien v. O'Brien*, 899 So. 2d 1133 (Fla. App. 2005), an appeal of a divorce decision, the court addressed the use at trial of communications intercepted by the wife from the husband's computer. The wife had installed, without the knowledge of the husband, a spyware program on the husband's computer that copied and stored electronic communications between the husband and another woman. That spyware program took snapshots of what appeared on the computer screen, allowing it to capture and record chat conversations, instant messages, and e-mails. The husband learned of the software, removed the software, and obtained a permanent injunction to prevent the wife's disclosure of the intercepted communications in violation of the Florida equivalent of the Federal Wiretap Act. The wife appealed and argued that the communications were retrieved from storage, and therefore, were not intercepted communications in violation of the Florida Act. The court in *O'Brien* rejected the wife's argument that the communications were, in fact, stored once the text image became visible on the screen. The court reasoned:

> We do not believe that this evanescent time period is sufficient to transform acquisition of the communication from a contemporaneous interception to retrieval from electronic storage. We conclude that because the spyware installed by the Wife intercepted the electronic communication contemporaneously with transmission, copied it, and routed the copy to a file on the computer's hard drive, the electronic communications were intercepted in violation of the Florida Act.

> In other words, the Florida court concluded that simply because information was displayed on a computer screen, and thus was on RAM, did not mean it was stored information. Although *O'Brien* involved the Florida equivalent of the Wiretap Act, and not Rule 34, *O'Brien* draws a reasonable distinction between information on RAM and information stored on non-volatile memory.

The Magistrate Judge's opinion was affirmed on appeal.[70] As of late 2008, the *Columbia Pictures* case remains virtually the only case to require the preservation of ephemeral data in the form of RAM. Interestingly, in a later decision in the case, the court granted plaintiffs' motion for terminating sanctions due to defendants' "widespread and systematic efforts to destroy evidence."[71]

EXCERPT FROM Kenneth J. Withers, *"Ephemeral Data" and the Duty to Preserve Discoverable Electronically Stored Information*, 37 U. Balt. L. Rev. 349, 360–68 (2008).

---

70. *See Columbia Pictures, Inc. v. Bunnell*, 245 F.R.D. 443, 445 (C.D. Cal. 2007).

71. *Columbia Pictures, Inc. v. Bunnell*, No. CV06–1093, 2007 WL 4877701, at *8 (C.D. Cal. Dec. 13, 2007).

The American Heritage Dictionary defines ephemeral as: "1. Lasting for a markedly brief time ... 2. Living or lasting only for a day, as certain plants or insects do." Similarly, Merriam–Webster's Dictionary defines ephemera as "something of no lasting significance" and ephemeral as "lasting a very short time."

Outside the context of discovery, ephemeral data can refer to data on "satellite geometry, position, and movement." However, judges and legal commentators in the electronic discovery field use the [term] ephemeral data to refer specifically to data found in RAM, as in the *Columbia Pictures* case, and more broadly to other types of data that are briefly stored on computers.

Paper documents may also be characterized as ephemeral. Telephone messages, meeting notes, desktop calendar entries, drafts, photocopies, Post–It Notes, and a myriad of other documents are created in enormous quantities in government, business, and daily life. Beyond their immediate business purpose, ephemeral paper documents have little or no value and are routinely disposed of with no legal consequence. In professional records management circles, these documents are considered non-records, and employees of well-managed enterprises are instructed to dispose of them in short order. Absent any specific legal, regulatory, or statutory records retention requirement, businesses are free to do so.

However, paper ephemera are not always disposed of immediately or properly, and accumulate in all organizations. If it is relevant and non-privileged, paper ephemera may be subject to discovery as a document within the meaning of Federal Rule of Civil Procedure 34, and therefore may be subject to the common law duty of preservation if litigation is reasonably anticipated. If litigation is anticipated, even a well-intentioned decision to clean up the files of ephemera could constitute spoliation.

Computer-based information systems generate a tremendous volume and variety of electronic communications and documents, many of which have become commonplace in discovery. There is no dispute that email comes within the definition of a document under Rule 34; email has been routinely requested and produced in discovery for many years prior to the December 1, 2006 amendment to Rule 34 that explicitly incorporated electronically stored information within the scope of document discovery. Many organizations depend on email communications as much as they depended on paper correspondence and memoranda for communications in the past, and they may treat email as a record in their records management policies. Other organizations may treat email as ephemeral non-records, with very short retention policies. Email messages may be deleted from the system (or otherwise rendered inaccessible to the user) within days of receipt, if the messages are not moved into designated files or if the user's allocated email storage space is exceeded. As with paper ephemera, the law allows such strict policies. However, "[o]nce a party reasonably anticipates litigation, it must suspend its routine document retention/destruction policy and put in place a 'litigation hold' to ensure the preservation of relevant documents." *Zubulake IV*, 220 F.R.D. 212, 218 (S.D.N.Y. 2003). Because email has become so essential to routine business operation, and therefore highly relevant in litigation, organizations have invested tremendous resources in developing systems to better manage email, reduce email volume, and meet preservation requirements.

Instant Messaging (IM) is another form of computer-mediated communication, common in business and daily life, but rarer in discovery. While similar in some respects to email, IMs are more likely to be considered ephemeral by users and system administrators, and therefore fall outside the records management policy. Email is more analogous to a physical document, in that it is composed, sent by the author (and simultaneously saved on the author's computer), routed via servers and networks to the recipient, and stored until retrieved by the recipient. IM, however, is a virtually simultaneous transmission, during which the author composes a message on one computer that appears on the screen of the recipient's computer, and when the recipient closes the communication, the IM conversation disappears. Unlike email, IM users do not exchange electronic documents, but rather engage in an electronic conversation, analogous to a telephone call. Behind the scenes, however, much more is happening with IM, and that activity is what calls the ephemeral nature of IM into question.

Fundamentally, all computer activity, from simple word processing to Internet communications, is the result of the input of digital code, processing of that code by chips and software following a complex set of mathematical instructions, and the output of resulting digital code in a form we perceive. Using an IM application, for instance, a sender might type "EPHEMERAL DATA" on the keyboard. The action of pressing the keys "E–P–H–E–M–E–R–A–L--D–A–T–A" is translated by the keyboard input software into a binary code, specifically:

01000101 01010000 01001000 01000101 01001101 01000101
01010010 01000001 01001100 00100000 01000100 01000001
01010100 01000001.

The computer's graphics processor, in conjunction with the IM application, quickly transforms this binary code into the words "EPHEMERAL DATA" which appear on the sender's screen in the appropriate place, with the appropriate font and color. In what appears to be a simultaneous action, the IM application sends the same binary code, embedded in a digital packet, via a network, to the recipient's computer. There the recipient's computer, graphics processor, and IM application recreate the same image of the words "EPHEMERAL DATA" on the recipient's screen, where it remains until it is scrolled away by additional words, or the IM session is terminated. But although the image is gone from the screen, the tracks of this communication remain. At each step of the process, the binary code (as well as other data generated by the process) was copied to one or more virtual workbenches where the appropriate software application transformed the code to send to the next step. At the speed of light, these strings of digital code replicate themselves from one place to another, both inside the computer and on the network.

In simple terms, IM is the 21st century version of the 19th century telegraph. At the railway station in Deadwood the sender would have the telegraph operator tap the word "ephemeral" to the recipient in Tombstone in the digital language of the day, Morse code:

. .—. .... .—. .—. .— .—..

* * *

Similarly, we are accustomed to thinking of computer operations, the digital code that we perceive as text, images, and sounds, as a stream of information; although on close inspection the stream is actually a series of pools and eddies. The pools and eddies of the digital stream have various names (memory, RAM, virtual memory, swap or SWP files, file cache, buffer, printer spool, Internet cache), various characteristics, and varying levels of accessibility. Some of these sources, like RAM, are considered "volatile"; they are erased if the power is shut down or the system rebooted. Other sources, such as an Internet cache, reside on the hard drive and are considered both persistent and ephemeral, like quiet pools of data inviting reflection. Still other sources, such as swap files or residual data from deleted files, are old and not likely to be accessed, like stagnant swamps full of debris.

The common feature among all types of ephemeral data is that they are created by the computer system as a temporary byproduct of digital information processing, not consciously created, viewed, or transmitted by the user. While the ephemera are neither apparent nor routinely accessed by the user, they may be essential to the efficient operation of the information system and may be accessible to technicians and system administrators. The data are ephemeral to the extent that they are not intended to be stored for any length of time beyond their operational use and may be susceptible to being overwritten at any point during the routine operation of the information system. However, under the holding of *Columbia Pictures*, ephemeral data may be considered electronically stored information: * * * therefore, they are "within the scope of discoverable information under Federal Rule of Civil Procedure 34."

Law enforcement has long recognized the value of ephemeral data in criminal investigations. Search warrants for ESI routinely request the seizure of whole computer systems, so that volatile computer memory found on the hard drive can be preserved. Forensic analysis of a computer system starts with the creation of a bitstream image of the computer, a process developed to preserve the ephemeral data and non-apparent system files that may be evidence of criminal activity or data that sophisticated cyber criminals have attempted to hide. Developing procedures to preserve ephemeral data in criminal investigations is a priority in law enforcement.

But civil discovery is not conducted as a criminal investigation. Absent a showing that potential evidence is likely to be destroyed, thus prejudicing the requesting party's case, a court will not authorize the requesting party to have direct access to computer hard drives or the seizure of evidence. *In re Ford Motor Co.*, 345 F.3d 1315, 1316 (11th Cir. 2003) (ruling plaintiff was not entitled to direct, unlimited access to defendant's computer database); *Balfour Beatty Rail, Inc. v. Vaccarello*, No. 3:06–cv–551–J–20MCR, 2007 WL 169628, at *3 (M.D. Fla. Jan. 18, 2007) (ruling plaintiff may not inspect the defendant's computer without good cause). The parties are expected to identify and implement the steps necessary to fulfill their data preservation obligations; the standard they must meet is reasonableness, not perfection. As suggested by the magistrate judge in the *Columbia Pictures* case, the duty of preservation is tempered by proportionality considerations, analogous to those in discovery under Rule 26(b)(2)(C).

3. What Unique Issues Are Raised by Various Types of ESI?

The following is a list of miscellaneous potential categories of evidence in the form of ESI. What special issues are raised in terms of preservation, formatting, and access to each ESI application? What questions would you wish to ask the opposing party in a Rule 26 "meet and confer"with respect to particular ESI applications?

- E-mail
- Attachments to e-mail
- Word processing
- Spreadsheets
- Corporate web pages; intraweb pages
- Wikis
- Blogs
- RSS Feed (automatic notification of website updates)
- Instant and Text Messaging
- Voice mail

- Voice Over Internet Protocol (VOIP)
- Encrypted forms of documents
- Data in third-party locations
- Metadata—audit trail information
- Metadata—statistical information
- Metadata—embedded or shadow metadata
- Cookies
- Disaster Recovery Backup tapes
- Backup servers
- PDAs, handheld devices, iPods
- Optical disks
- Home computers; laptops
- Floppy disks
- Flash drives
- Cache
- Slack space data
- Internet browser history files
- Site log files
- Bookmarks
- Avatars (virtual characters on sites in Second Life®)
- Biometric data
- GPS Data
- GIS Data (geographic information system data)

F. LITIGATION HOLDS/MONITORING

CACHE LA POUDRE FEEDS, LLC
v. LAND O'LAKES, INC.

244 F.R.D. 614 (D. Colo. 2007)

SHAFFER, MAGISTRATE JUDGE

This Matter comes before the court on Plaintiff Cache La Poudre Feed[s], LLC's Motion for Relief from Discovery Violations * * * committed by Defendants Land O'Lakes, Inc. and Land O'Lakes Farmland Feed LLC (collectively "Defendants" or "Land O'Lakes"). * * *

BACKGROUND

Plaintiff Cache La Poudre Feeds, LLC manufactures and sells animal feed in Colorado. Cache La Poudre claims that since March 1991, it has used its PROFILE trademark and sold PROFILE products in several states. * * * Plaintiff contends that in 2001, more than ten years after Cache La Poudre established rights in its PROFILE mark, Defendants Land O'Lakes, Inc. and Land O'Lakes Farmland Feeds, LLC began using the same trademark to re-brand over 400 of their products and to consolidate 36 brands of animal feed products into one brand, PROFILE. * * *

* * *

The instant case has spawned numerous discovery disputes and hearings.[3] * * * Cache La Poudre contends that relief is warranted based upon Defendants' failure to satisfy their discovery obligations * * *.

ANALYSIS

* * * Courts now face the challenge of overseeing discovery at a time when potential access to electronically stored information is virtually limitless, and when the costs and burdens associated with full discovery could be more outcome-determinative, as a practical matter, than the facts and substantive law. * * * Commentators have proposed practices and standards for discovery that reflect the explosion in electronic documents and data. See, e.g., *The Sedona Principles: Best Practices, Recommendations & Principles for Addressing Electronic Document Production* (Sedona Conference Working Group Series July 2005) [hereinafter The Sedona Principles]. The instant motion requires the court to grapple with many of these same issues.

I.   Land O'Lakes' Alleged Destruction of Relevant Documents

Plaintiff's motion accuses Defendants of spoliation, based on Land O'Lakes' failure to discontinue its practice after April 2002 of routinely eliminating e-mail and overwriting backup electronic media. Cache La Poudre insists that by allowing these practices to continue, Land O'Lakes destroyed relevant and otherwise discoverable e-mails and other electronic information, thereby insuring that this material would not be available through discovery.

To ensure that the expansive discovery permitted by Rule 26(b)(1) does not become a futile exercise, putative litigants have a duty to preserve documents that may be relevant to pending or imminent litigation. See *Zubulake v. UBS Warburg, LLC*, 220 F.R.D. 212, 216 (S.D.N.Y. 2003) ("the obligation to preserve evidence arises when the party has notice that the evidence is relevant to litigation or when a party should have known that the evidence may be relevant to future litigation"). "Spoliation" has been defined as "the destruction or significant alteration of evidence, or the failure to preserve property for

---

3.   Both sides have engaged in discovery conduct that unnecessarily protracted the litigation and increased its attendant costs for all parties. The unnecessarily rancorous tone of counsels' rhetoric, both in writing and during court hearings, has only exacerbated the situation and hindered the parties' ability to find a reasonable solution to their discovery disputes.

another's use as evidence in pending or reasonably foreseeable litigation."

* * *

In determining whether sanctions are appropriate, the court must first determine whether the missing documents or materials would be relevant to an issue at trial. If not, then the court's analysis stops there. If the missing documents would be relevant, the court must then decide whether Land O'Lakes was under an obligation to preserve the records at issue. Finally, if such a duty existed, the court must consider what sanction, if any, is appropriate given the non-moving party's degree of culpability, the degree of any prejudice to the moving party, and the purposes to be served by exercising the court's power to sanction.

Land O'Lakes began shipping its PROFILE products nationwide by at least January 2002. It is also undisputed that Land O'Lakes adopted an automatic e-mail destruction program in May 2002. Pursuant to this program, any e-mails older than 90 days would be automatically deleted, even if the e-mail was created before the elimination program was established. The relevance of e-mails and electronically stored information created after 2001 that address the development and implementation of Land O'Lakes' PROFILE brand should be self-evident.

The second prong of the court's analysis, that is Land O'Lakes' duty to preserve, poses greater problems for Cache La Poudre. In most cases, the duty to preserve evidence is triggered by the filing of a lawsuit. However, the obligation to preserve evidence may arise even earlier if a party has notice that future litigation is likely. While a party should not be permitted to destroy potential evidence after receiving unequivocal notice of impending litigation, the duty to preserve relevant documents should require more than a mere possibility of litigation. Ultimately, the court's decision must be guided by the facts of each case.

Here, Plaintiff argues that Defendants "should have and did anticipate legal engagement with Cache La Poudre as early as April 4, 2002." Having carefully reviewed all the exhibits proffered by the parties, I conclude that the record does not persuasively support Plaintiff's position.

It is undisputed that counsel for Cache La Poudre contacted Land O'Lakes' General Counsel, Peter Janzen, by telephone on April 4, 2002. During that conversation, Mr. Janzen apparently was told that an individual in Colorado had been using the phrase "Profile Showcase" as a trademark for animal feeds since 1990. Mr. Janzen was also aware in April 2002 that this same "individual filed an intent to use application in 2000 that was abandoned in 2001 for failure to respond."

On June 5, 2002, Cache La Poudre's outside counsel, Cheryl Anderson–Siler, wrote to Mr. Janzen to follow-up on her April telephone call. In her June 5th letter, Ms. Anderson–Siler stated that Cache La Poudre had been using its PROFILE trademark for at least 10 years and expressed her client's concern over the possibility of confusion for "our respective customers." Ms. Anderson–Siler warned that Land O'Lakes' "very active marketing campaign ... may present a situation that may become a very serious problem." In closing, Ms. Anderson–Siler explained that the primary purpose of her letter

> is to clearly put [Land O'Lakes] on notice of our client's trademark rights and clearly establish the opportunities we have given Land O'Lakes to avoid exposure. The second purpose of this letter is to determine whether this situation can be resolved without litigation and media exposure ... We think you will agree that the company's interests are best served by trying to resolve this unfortunate and difficult situation.

Rather than threatening impending litigation, Ms. Anderson–Siler's June 5th letter implied that her client preferred and was willing to explore a negotiated resolution. *Compare Washington Alder LLC v. Weyerhaeuser Co.*, 2004 WL 4076674 (D.Or.2004) (finding that a letter from Washington Alder threatening to sue for antitrust violations put Weyerhaeuser on notice of possible litigation and triggered a duty to preserve documents).

In the wake of these developments, in June 2003, the parties again raised the possibility of a non-litigious resolution. On June 3, 2003, Land O'Lakes' outside counsel contacted Ms. Anderson–Siler to "explore the possibility of obtaining a consent from your client to register" the LAND O'LAKES PROFILE mark for agricultural animal feed. Counsel closed his letter by saying he would "appreciate a call to discuss this possibility and terms." Ms. Anderson–Siler responded by letter on June 17, 2003. Her letter again expressed Cache La Poudre's concern "that Land O'Lakes is continuing to pursue registration of [its] mark as any use of such a mark in the feed industry would be likely to infringe our client's longstanding PROFILE trademark." However, rather than threatening litigation, Ms. Anderson–Siler indicated her client "would be willing to listen to what Land O'Lakes might propose."

Cache La Poudre initiated legal action against Land O'Lakes on February 24, 2004 with the filing of its initial Complaint. As of that date, Defendants clearly had an obligation to preserve relevant evidence. On March 5, 2004, for the first time, counsel for Cache La Poudre sent a letter to Peter Janzen which specifically put Land O'Lakes on notice to "prevent spoliation, destruction, alteration, modification, concealment, loss, secretion, or removal of evidence by any of the defendants." Plaintiff's letter also notified Defendants that they had an affirmative obligation to maintain and preserve evidence.

This court recognizes that under different circumstances, a demand letter alone may be sufficient to trigger an obligation to preserve evidence and support a subsequent motion for spoliation sanctions. However, such a letter must be more explicit and less equivocal than Cache La Poudre's 2002 and 2003 correspondence with Land O'Lakes.

In this case, Land O'Lakes had been selling under its PROFILE brand for several months before Ms. Anderson–Siler sent her first letter to Mr. Janzen. Although Ms. Anderson–Siler noted the potential for customer confusion and alluded to Land O'Lakes' possible "exposure," her letter did not threaten litigation and did not demand that Land O'Lakes preserve potentially relevant materials. Rather, Cache La Poudre hinted at the possibility of a non-litigious resolution. Ms. Anderson–Siler's correspondence with Land O'Lakes' outside counsel in June 2003 was no more emphatic or explicit in raising the prospect of litigation. Ms. Anderson–Siler's correspondence in 2003 also did not include a demand for preservation of evidence. Given the dynamic nature of electronically stored information, prudent counsel would be wise to ensure that a demand letter sent to a putative party also addresses any contemporaneous preservation obligations.

In fact, Cache La Poudre waited nearly two years after Anderson–Siler's April 4, 2002 telephone conference with Peter Janzen to bring the instant lawsuit. That delay, coupled with the less-than adamant tone of Cache La Poudre's letters belies Plaintiff's contention that Land O'Lakes should have anticipated litigation as early as April 4, 2002, and therefore had a duty to preserve evidence as of that date. I acknowledge that the common-law obligation to preserve relevant material is not necessarily dependent upon the tender of a "preservation letter." However, a party's duty to preserve evidence in advance of litigation must be predicated on something more than an equivocal statement of discontent, particularly when that discontent does not crystalize into litigation for nearly two years. Any other conclusion would confront a putative litigant with an intractable dilemma: either preserve voluminous records for a indefinite period at potentially great expense, or continue routine document management practices and risk a spoliation claim at some point in the future.

Plaintiff has described Land O'Lakes as a "$6 Billion dollar conglomerated entity," with no less than 40 local file servers at its main business office, and additional file servers at other business locations. According to Land O'Lakes' current Director of Technology Services, since 2002 Land O'Lakes has managed over 400 servers, each of which is backed up on a daily basis, weekly for five weeks, monthly for a year, and annually forever. Recently enacted amendments to the Federal Rules of Civil Procedure recognize that suspending or interrupting automatic features of electronic information systems can be prohibitively expensive and burdensome.

> [I]t is unrealistic to expect parties to stop such routine operation of their computer systems as soon as they anticipate litigation. It is also undesirable; the result would be even greater accumulation of duplicative and irrelevant data that must be reviewed, making discovery more expensive and time consuming.

See May 27, 2006 Report of the Advisory Committee on the Federal Rules of Civil Procedure, at 71. Under the particular facts of this case, this court finds that Defendants' duty to preserve evidence was triggered by the filing of Plaintiff's Complaint on February 24, 2004. Accordingly, Cache La Poudre's request for spoliation sanctions predicated on actions or omissions that occurred before that date is denied.

II.   Land O'Lakes' Alleged Post–Filing Discovery Misconduct

After February 24, 2004, Defendants unquestionably had an obligation to preserve and produce non-privileged materials responsive to properly framed discovery requests. Land O'Lakes insists that it fully complied with this obligation, by conducting a reasonable inquiry to find responsive documents based upon its understanding of where such documents and information could be located. In response to Cache La Poudre's discovery requests, Defendants claim to have produced over 50,000 pages of documents, including 415 e-mails related to PROFILE, and compact disks containing relevant data regarding PROFILE products.

Land O'Lakes claims to have imposed a litigation hold within a matter of days after Plaintiff filed the instant lawsuit. Defendants insist that this litigation hold prevented the destruction of any electronic documents in existence as of that date, as well as any subsequently produced electronic documents. Land O'Lakes employees "understood that they were to save any document that currently existed on their system, as well as in their files." Land O'Lakes looked for electronic documents in the possession of current employees, and printed versions of electronic documents generated by employees who left the company after February 2004. No attempt was made to find electronic versions of documents prepared by departed employees because attorneys involved in the discovery process were under the impression that those materials no longer existed in electronic form since information systems personnel routinely cleaned an employee's computer hard drive after they left the company.

* * * [W]hen Land O'Lakes received a request for production in this case * * * [current] employees who were involved in creating and marketing the PROFILE brand were asked to check for responsive materials, including paper documents, e-mails and compact disks. These materials were then turned over to outside counsel to be reviewed for relevancy. As additional requests came in, Land O'Lakes expanded its inquiry to include individuals who might have materials responsive to those particular requests. Janzen [General Counsel for the defendant] claims that he confirmed that Land O'Lakes employees understood that they were to produce all materials relating to the PROFILE litigation, and then reconfirmed that employees had produced all the required materials. However, Janzen acknowledged that he relied on the employees' ability to locate responsive documents and gave each employee the discretion to identify documents that "related to the litigation." Mr.

Janzen and outside counsel simply accepted whatever materials employees provided.

Land O'Lakes concedes that it never reviewed information contained on backup tapes in identifying and producing responsive materials. * * * Land O'Lakes has approximately 400 backup tapes for the years 2001–2005. When he was deposed, Mr. Janzen testified that he understood that "backup tape is kept for ten days and then written over" and that Land O'Lakes does not have backup tapes for the computer hard drives used by former employees. Apparently, Mr. Janzen was not aware that Land O'Lakes also has monthly and annual backup tapes. Mr. Janzen concluded that it was unnecessary to review backup tapes because he believed that any documents on the backup tapes relevant to this litigation could also be found in another more readily accessible location. However, Janzen concedes that Land O'Lakes made no attempt to verify his assumption.

Mr. Janzen testified on June 15, 2006, that no efforts were made to contact former Land O'Lakes employees in the course of identifying and collecting responsive materials. Land O'Lakes apparently never contacted former employees to determine how or where they might have backed up information while they were with the company. To the extent that relevant documents had not been lost when hard drives were wiped clean, Janzen simply assumed that they [were] located on hard drives that were shared with current employees and, as such, would be found through the discovery production process.

Against this backdrop, Plaintiff argues that Land O'Lakes failed to properly discharge its obligation to locate, preserve and produce all relevant, non-privileged materials after February 24, 2004. More particularly, Cache La Poudre insists that after February 24, 2004, Defendants and their counsel failed to make certain that all sources of potentially relevant information were identified and placed "on hold." [The court discusses the factors set forth by Judge Scheindlin concerning the duty to preserve information, in *Zubulake V, supra*]

* * *

Plaintiff * * * argues that Land O'Lakes failed to properly monitor compliance with its discovery obligations by not conducting "systemwide keyword searches." Indeed, Plaintiff contends that Defendants had an "obligation" to undertake such keyword searches. I am not convinced that Judge Scheindlin's opinion in *Zubulake V* should be interpreted so inflexibly. Certainly, "once a 'litigation hold' is in place, a party and her counsel must make certain that all sources of potentially relevant information are identified and placed 'on hold.'" *Zubulake v. UBS Warburg LLC*, 229 F.R.D. at 432. In discharging that responsibility, Judge Scheindlin conceded that it might not be possible for counsel to speak with every key player, and suggested as an alternative that it "[may be] possible to run a systemwide keyword search" to identify responsive materials. I do not interpret Judge Scheindlin's suggestion as establishing an immutable "obligation." To the contrary, in the typical case, "[r]esponding parties are best situated to evaluate the procedures, methodologies, and technologies appropriate for preserving and producing their own electronic data and documents." *See The Sedona Principles*, at 31. To the extent that Plaintiff seeks sanctions based on a perceived "obligation" to conduct keyword searches, I will deny that request.

Plaintiff argues that Defendants failed to become familiar with their own computer system and their document retention policies and architecture. As a result of this shortcoming, Plaintiff believes that Land O'Lakes did not know where to look for relevant information. According to Cache La Poudre, Land O'Lakes or its litigation counsel also "had a duty to take possession or otherwise safeguard backup tapes to eliminate the possibility of inadvertent recycling." It appears that Mr. Janzen did not have a full understanding of his company's computer systems or the process for creating computer back-up tapes. However, Plaintiff's request for relief based on these shortcomings sweeps too broadly.

As noted, counsel for Land O'Lakes was required to undertake a reasonable investigation to identify and preserve relevant materials in the course of responding to Plaintiff's discovery requests. Such an investigation would not automatically include information maintained on computer back-up tapes.[12] "As a general rule, [a] litigation hold does not apply to inaccessible back-up tapes ... which may continue to be recycled on the schedule set forth in the company's policy." *Zubulake v. UBS Warburg LLC*, 229 F.R.D. at 431. As of December 2006, a party responding to discovery requests must identify but need not produce electronically stored information that is not reasonably accessible because of undue burden or cost. See Fed.R.Civ.P. 26(b)(2)(B). One such source of information might be backup tapes containing archived data. Land O'Lakes' Director of Technology Services indicates that Land O'Lakes has approximately 400 back-up tapes for the years 2001 through 2005.

In order to recover a document or file from the backup tapes that contains a specific word, such as "PROFILE," each tape would first have to be restored and then the search conducted. The restoration of each tape would take approximately 8 hours per tape, in serial fashion, since there are a limited number of restoration servers. It would therefore take over 3200 man hours just to restore the approximately 400 backup tapes from the last four years. Defendants claim that it would take an additional 800 man hours to search through all restored tapes.

Plaintiff claims that several Land O'Lakes employees involved in the PROFILE project left the company after the lawsuit commenced. * * * According to Plaintiff, Defendants made no attempt to preserve or place

---

12. *Quinby v. WestLB AG*, 2005 WL 3453908, at *7 (S.D.N.Y. 2005) (describing backup computer tapes as " 'snapshots' taken at a particular point in time," and suggesting, for example, that "e-mails that are sent or received and then deleted between snapshots will not be captured on back-up tapes").

a litigation hold on the computer hard drives used by these employees. Mr. Janzen acknowledged that Land O'Lakes continued its practice of expunging the hard drives of former employees even after this litigation commenced. I find that such a procedure, if applied after February 24, 2004 with respect to employees who played a significant or decision-making role in the development and implementation of the PROFILE brand, violated Defendants' obligation to preserve evidence in this case. Cache La Poudre has not established that Defendants intentionally destroyed electronically stored information to deprive Plaintiff of discoverable information. However, the record does demonstrate that Defendants were less than thorough in discharging their duty to implement adequate steps to insure that discoverable information would be preserved.

* * * As Judge Scheindlin acknowledged, "it may not be feasible for counsel to speak with every key player" and unrealistic to presume that counsel will necessarily succeed in identifying and searching all sources of discoverable information. *Zubulake v. UBS Warburg LLC*, 229 F.R.D. at 432. However, counsel cannot turn a blind eye to a procedure that he or she should realize will adversely impact that search. Land O'Lakes directed employees to produce all relevant information, and then relied upon those same employees to exercise their discretion in determining what specific information to save. As Mr. Janzen said repeatedly, he and outside counsel simply accepted whatever documents or information might be produced by Land O'Lakes employees. Yet here, counsel was aware that an accessible source of information (i.e., computer hard drives used by departed employees) was being eliminated as a routine practice, thereby further distancing counsel from the discovery process and his monitoring obligations. By wiping clean the computer hard drives of former employees who worked on the PROFILE project, Land O'Lakes effectively eliminated a readily accessible source of potentially relevant information. This procedure is all the more questionable given Mr. Janzen's understanding that Land O'Lakes did not keep backup tapes for computer hard drives for more than ten days. Once a "litigation hold" has been established, a party cannot continue a routine procedure that effectively ensures that potentially relevant and readily available information is no longer "reasonably accessible" under Rule 26(b)(2)(B).

Finally, Plaintiff insists that Land O'Lakes failed to take affirmative steps to monitor compliance to ensure that all sources of discoverable information were identified and searched. * * *

In this case, Land O'Lakes's General Counsel and retained counsel failed in many respects to discharge their obligations to coordinate and oversee discovery. Admittedly, in-house counsel established a litigation hold shortly after the lawsuit commenced and communicated that fact to Land O'Lakes employees who were believed to possess relevant materials. However, by his own admission, Land O'Lakes' General Counsel took no independent action to verify the completeness of the employees' document production. As Mr. Janzen explained, he simply assumed that the materials he received were complete and the product of a thorough search. While Mr. Janzen presumed that e-mails generated by former employees would be located on shared computer drives utilized by current employees, he made no effort to verify that assumption. Without validating the accuracy and completeness of its discovery production, Land O'Lakes continued its routine practice of wiping clean the computer hard drives for former employees. Under the circumstances and without some showing of a reasonable inquiry, it is difficult to understand how Defendants' retained counsel could legitimately claim on July 7, 2005 [in a letter to the plaintiff] that Land O'Lakes had "made every effort to produce all documentation and provide all relevant information."

While instituting a "litigation hold" may be an important first step in the discovery process, the obligation to conduct a reasonable search for responsive documents continues throughout the litigation. A "litigation hold," without more, will not suffice to satisfy the "reasonable inquiry" requirement in Rule 26(g)(2). Counsel retains an on-going responsibility to take appropriate measures to ensure that the client has provided all available information and documents which are responsive to discovery requests. As the Advisory Committee Notes make clear, "Rule 26(g) imposed an affirmative duty to engage in pretrial discovery in a responsible manner that is consistent with the spirit and purposes of Rules 26 through 37." In this case, I find that Defendants failed to meet this standard.

* * *

IV. Sanctions

* * *

I do not find that Cache La Poudre's ability to litigate its claims has been substantially prejudiced by Defendants' failure to implement and monitor an adequate record preservation program. However, Defendants' failure to preserve potentially relevant and responsive information by wiping clean computer hard drives and counsels' failure to properly monitor the discovery process has interfered with the judicial process. Moreover, Land O'Lakes' failure to fully comply with their discovery obligations has forced Plaintiff to incur additional litigation expenses.

* * *

* * * I conclude that a monetary sanction is appropriate in this case. Cache La Poudre incurred legal expenses in connection with the pending motion that would not have been required had Land O'Lakes and it counsel undertaken a reasonable investigation to identify and preserve relevant materials, and then taken affirmative and effective steps to monitor compliance with discovery obligations. * * * I will require Defendant Land O'Lakes to pay Cache La Poudre the sum of $5,000 to reimburse some of the legal fees and expenses incurred in taking Mr. Janzen's deposition in Minneapolis, Minnesota and preparing the instant Motion for Relief from Discovery Violations. While Plaintiff almost certainly incurred fees and costs of more than $5,000 in having counsel travel to and from Minnesota, attend the Janzen deposition, and prepare a 40–page motion, the court finds that the fees and costs awarded in this Memorandum Order are appropriate under the circumstances of this case and consistent with the objectives under Rule 26(g) and Rule 34. I will also require Defendants to reimburse Plaintiff for court reporter fees and transcript costs associated with the June 15, 2006 deposition of Mark Janzen.

COMMENTARY

ESI presents unique preservation problems because it is a series of electronic impulses that are potentially voluminous and scattered into many storage locations. It is also fragile and easily prone to change and alteration without prompt affirmative preservation. The process to properly preserve this delicate and irreplaceable type of information involves three steps: (1) determining when the duty to preserve arises, discussed in Chapter II.C, *supra*, (2) determining what data must be preserved, discussed in Chapter II.D, *supra*, and (3) determining how to assure preservation.

1. What Should an Organization Do After the Duty to Preserve Arises?

The first step after an event triggering preservation is to convene a "claims and defenses" meeting of the company officials and the legal team to determine the case issues. Why address the issue first? Why not go directly to preservation? Not all data can or should be preserved. Even a significant dispute between a company and an important long-standing customer will likely constitute a small fraction of the data and information maintained by a company. The angry employee may be one of thousands of employees. All the data of an on-going business cannot be maintained based on the needs of a single lawsuit.

The claims and defenses assessment meeting will typically include counsel for the company ("in-house counsel"), retained counsel ("outside counsel") and the company management involved in the dispute. The goal of the assessment meeting is to determine the potential plaintiff's claims and the company defenses. Each claim is then assessed with respect to each element that will be at issue if the claim is litigated. The same process should be followed for the company's defenses.

Once the issues are identified, the assessment team (or "e-discovery team") must determine where information related to the issues resides. Most often, this is best accomplished by first determining which employees (or "custodians") generate, receive or otherwise access potentially relevant information. Each custodian will have numerous potential data locations that must be preserved. This is when representatives of the company's IT Department and Records Management Department must join the e-discovery team. Armed with knowledge of the issues and the potential custodians, counsel, company management, records manager, and IT representatives with knowledge of the company's network can begin the process of locating and securing locations that may contain relevant ESI. In some instances, referring to the company's document retention policy will also assist the team in determining where certain kinds of information are located, or whether those sources of information are no longer available.

Next, the e-discovery team must identify those employees with knowledge of the complainant's performance. For example, the e-mail of a co-worker should be preserved if there is reason to believe the e-mails may reflect the work performance of the work group.

2.   How to Preserve Relevant Data?

Counsel must issue a litigation hold notice once a duty to preserve has been determined. This notice is addressed to those persons within the company who are custodians of data locations where relevant data might lie. Here is an example of a litigation hold notice in a case involving the alleged failure to consummate the purchase of goods.

LITIGATION HOLD NOTICE

DIRECTIVE TO CEASE DESTRUCTION OF PAPER RECORDS AND ELECTRONIC DATA

TO: Distribution List

FROM: General Counsel

DATE:

Defendants have recently been sued in a dispute involving purchase orders and product sold by Plaintiff. We intend to vigorously defend this lawsuit.

The law requires us to take immediate steps to preserve all **paper records** and **electronic data** that is relevant to the litigation. Paper records and electronic data (**including duplicates**) must be preserved at all storage locations including your office computer, home computers, and other portable electronic media such as discs and thumb drives. Failure of preserve all paper records and electronic data may result in legal sanctions.

Please immediately review the following list of **preservation categories** of documents (paper and electronic data) which must be preserved. All electronic data and paper documents including drafts, e-mail negotiations and communications related to or about any of these categories must be preserved.

1. All documents related to any contract, negotiation, or communication with Plaintiff.

2. All documents related to contracts and agreements with Plaintiff, including guarantees.

3. All paper rebates submitted and processed by Defendants related to consumer purchases of Plaintiff's products. All rebate processing data and information stored in any database pertaining to Plaintiff's products.

4. All financial and accounting records pertaining to Plaintiff

5. All notes, memoranda, and spreadsheets related to Plaintiff.

6. All advertisements and promotions of Plaintiff's products.

7. All documents and data about customer service pertaining to Plaintiff's products.

8. All documents and data regarding the receipt of Plaintiff's products.

9. All shipping and receiving documents and data regarding Plaintiff's products.

10. All returns of Plaintiff's products and all consumer complaints about Plaintiff's products or the quality of Plaintiff's products.

11. All information about the flat screen television market and market pricing of flat screen televisions during 2006 and 2007.

12. All consumer inquiries and complaints about Plaintiff-related rebates.

13. All documents and data about any audit or accounting with respect to Plaintiff rebates.

14. All documents and data about the advertising and promotion of Plaintiff's products.

Please determine immediately whether you have in your possession, custody or control **any paper or electronic data about, concerning, or related to** any of the above preservation categories. Such paper documents or electronic data are called responsive paper documents or electronic data.

Please determine whether any responsive data is located on your laptop or office computer, home computer, Blackberry, PDA, discs, CDs, DVD's, memory sticks, or thumb drives, or any other electronic storage location. Please immediately suspend the deletion (manual or automatic) of relevant electronic data from any location where you believe responsive data may be found.

> With respect to paper documents, please check all your office files and home files. Please immediately suspend the destruction of any responsive paper documents.
>
> If you have any doubts about what paper or electronic data to preserve, please contact me. If you have any responsive paper documents please immediately advise your supervisor. If you have any responsive electronic data held or stored at any location or on any media **other than your office desktop computer or company laptop**, please immediately advise your supervisor.
>
> * * *

* * * The structure of a litigation hold notice is to (1) identify the litigation, (2) specify the parties to the litigation, (3) specifically identify the documents to be preserved, (4) provide a contact point within the Company to answer questions, and (5) provide for a formal verification. Most companies prefer the litigation hold notice to come from the Legal Department.

PROBLEM

You are General Counsel for Quick Feet Athletic Shoes and Clothing Company ("Quick Feet"). Complaining Consumer ("CC") has retained an attorney who has brought a class action complaint against Quick Feet. Quick Feet sells athletic products through its website and at thirty retail locations in malls around the state. Its warehouse is located in Chicago, Illinois. All consumer purchases through its website are shipped to the consumer from the Chicago warehouse by commercial ground service. The Chicago warehouse also supplies all thirty Quick Feet retail locations around the state. You have conducted your claims and defenses assessment with the management team and IT Department. You have learned from your investigation that Quick Feet contracted with three United States-based manufacturing companies to make athletic shoes using an experimental technique utilizing one-half the stitching customarily used in the industry. Using this experimental method allows the athletic shoes to be produced much more quickly than using standard methods. However, your investigation has also shown that athletic shoes manufactured under the one-half stitching method become tattered and unusable within two to three months. You have also learned from your claims and defenses assessment that Quick Feet markets its athletic equipment under the slogans "Your Gear for a Lifetime" and "Wear Me Forever." CC seeks to represent a class of national consumers who have been allegedly victimized by this deceptive and unfair marketing practice of selling inferior products in connection with false advertising claims.

Your team has informed you (1) that Quick Feet utilizes athletic shoe manufacturers that have certified that each uses production methods that meet industry standards, (2) that Quick Feet attaches to each garment a tag containing a warning that the athletic shoes are not defect free, and (3) that Quick Feet sells its athletic shoes at dramatically reduced prices compared to other branded athletic shoes.

Quick Feet maintains its own e-mail, accounting, customer service, and Internet web servers in Philadelphia, Pennsylvania and communicates with its manufacturers by e-mailing its purchase orders. First Florida pays its manufacturers by direct deposit to The USA Bank.

All sales employees at the thirty retail locations are provided laptops. Quick Feet has a data backup rotation where the oldest backup tape is one month old. Quick Feet limits the storage of e-mail inboxes and outboxes to one gigabyte of data per user. Regardless of the volume of e-mails in the inboxes and outboxes, all e-mails are automatically deleted after thirty days.

Prepare a litigation hold notice and separate directions to the IT Department regarding the preservation of data.

Once you have issued the litigation hold notice, your work to preserve relevant data is not over because a litigation hold without more will not satisfy the "reasonable inquiry" requirement in Rule 26(g)(2). As a part of the obligation to preserve relevant documents, legal counsel has the continuing duty to ensure that discoverable information is not lost. Counsel might consider taking the following steps:

- suspending the routine document retention/destruction policy;

- becoming fully aware of the client's document retention policies and data retention architecture;

- communicating with the "key players" in the litigation to understand how they stored information;

- taking reasonable steps to monitor compliance with the litigation hold so that all sources of discoverable information are identified and searched; and

- having identified all sources of potentially relevant information, retaining that information and producing information responsive to the opposing party's requests.

Compliance with a litigation hold is not a simple matter. The purpose of the litigation hold is to notify the recipients of the obligation to preserve data. But a litigation hold notice distributed throughout a company is of little value if it is not followed or implemented.

First, how does counsel assure that the litigation notice has been received and will be implemented by the company employees? Some counsel require a signed certification by the employee that the litigation hold notice has been received, understood and implemented. Here is an example of such a certification or acknowledgment.

Acknowledgment

(Please provide to your immediate supervisor)

I acknowledge I have read the above attached Litigation Hold memorandum. I will forthwith conduct a reasonable search for responsive paper documents and electronic data. I will preserve any such electronic data and paper documents. I will not delete any data from any locations that I believe may contain responsive electronic data. I understand that this preservation request is on-going and requires the continuing preservation of data, including data created or received both before and after receipt of this Notice.

_____

(sign and date)

Is this adequate to assure compliance? What is the Company's exposure if the employee fails to implement the litigation hold directive or does so in a shabby and sloppy manner? How can counsel conduct a reasonable investigation to assure the litigation hold is being implemented? No attorney has yet been faulted or sanctioned by the courts for conducting client document interviews and becoming too knowledgeable of the sources of a client's relevant data, but there are many who have been sanctioned for not doing so.[72]

Other problems associated with compliance and implementation of a litigation hold arise when there is negligence or malfeasance. For example, would it be foreseeable that an employee who has received a litigation hold notice instructing her not to destroy any ESI associated with a particular company deletes e-mail in one folder because she knows the e-mail is retained in a second folder in her inbox or because she understands that the sender of the e-mail has created a special folder that contains the e-mail? The notion that duplicative e-mails and near duplicates of e-mail must be retained is something counsel may grasp but is easily misunderstood by employees. What if the employee prints all the relevant e-mails and then deletes the electronic files? The employee might reasonably think all e-mail has been retained, when, in fact, the deletion constitutes spoliation.

With these concerns in mind, after the delivery and receipt of confirmation of the litigation hold notice, an interview should be scheduled with each custodian to review what data the custodian holds and how it must be preserved. Even if the company's IT representative has already given counsel a detailed description of what sources of company data an employee may use that are relevant to the litigation, the IT representative may have no way of knowing that a particular custodian also maintains company data relevant to the case on a personal computer at home or a portable personal USB drive. With the advent of free and unlimited e-mail storage on internet service providers like Yahoo or

---

72. _See, e.g., Metropolitan Opera Assoc. v. Local 100_, 212 F.R.D. 178, 221–24 (S.D.N.Y. 2003). This case is found at Chapter VI.C, _infra_.

AOL, employees may frequently send work e-mails to their personal accounts to get around storage limits imposed on their corporate e-mail accounts. Document collection interviews with key custodians also give counsel the opportunity to confirm that the custodian has understood what is expected, and more importantly, that counsel knows the custodian has taken the time to comply with the litigation hold.

3. Lifting Litigation Holds

Much time and money is spent on properly implementing and maintaining a legal hold, but little attention is given to lifting a legal hold. A legal hold may be lifted once the litigation is finally resolved, assuming that preserved data is not relevant to any other existing or anticipated litigation. This can be a difficult challenge if a company is simultaneously involved in multiple lawsuits, or is a large company that is constantly engaged in litigation. For example, what if an employee transfers to a different department and now her documents are relevant to more than one lawsuit—when can you lift the litigation hold on her data? What if a company settles a securities class action lawsuit, but the Securities and Exchange Commission is still investigating the company over the same disclosures that were the subject of the class action? With regard to a litigation hold implemented in anticipation of litigation that never materializes, how long before the hold can be lifted? The decision to lift a litigation hold must be made only after conducting due diligence to ensure that the preserved data set is not relevant to any claims or defenses for other litigation matters, including audits or investigations.

G. PRESERVATION ORDERS

CAPRICORN POWER CO., INC. v. SIEMENS WESTINGHOUSE POWER CORP.

220 F.R.D. 429 (W.D. Pa. 2004)

GIBSON, DISTRICT JUDGE

Synopsis

Both the Defendant and the Plaintiffs have filed motions requesting orders of court that direct the preservation of documents and things. The current case law does not provide a definitive test to apply when deciding such motions. Upon review of the circumstances, and being guided by present law, a three part test is developed and applied by the Court. Under such a test, both motions for an order of preservation are denied. * * *

Factual/Procedural History

* * *

This matter came to trial before a jury on January 12, 2004 and ended in a mistrial on January 15, 2004. [The case involved a dispute over a purchased generator.] The mistrial was declared because an expert report dated June 23, 2000 was not produced by Plaintiff until January 15, 2004. The expert report was referred to by a witness on January 14, 2004 in the course of a *Daubert* hearing concerning [admissibility of] the expert opinions of Dr. Bagnall and was turned over to counsel for Defendant before the resumption of trial testimony on the morning of January 15, 2004. Prior to beginning testimony on January 15, 2004 the Court heard oral argument from both parties on the Defendant's Motion for Mistrial and subsequently granted the motion, finding that the late production prejudiced the Defendant's case as to the preparation of its expert witnesses, the cross-examination of the Plaintiffs' witnesses, as well as the fact that the expert report "may have a significant impact upon the entire posture and strategy of Defendant's case."

Subsequently, the Defendant moved for the preservation of documents in a motion filed on February 18, 2004 requesting a court order be issued to preserve all relevant material set forth in the subpoena attached to the Defendant's Motion. Based upon the testimony of Dr. Bagnall, the Defendant believes other potential materials exist that would be relevant to its case. Defendant requests an order to "fully secure all of the information gathered by Mr. Bagnall and CTC," and to "properly prepare for filing of dispositive Motions based upon this new evidence." * * *

The Plaintiffs filed their response and a counter-motion on March 9, 2004. Plaintiffs do not object to the Defendant's motion, except to the extent that they believe an order for preservation of material should be issued as to both parties.

* * *

Analysis

The Court notes that orders directing parties to preserve materials or documents are common in circumstances in which evidence is subject to being destroyed or lost in routine and sometimes not-so-routine deletion or destruction of information in various mediums. However, the reported case law concerning standards for deciding such motions is scant.

* * *

Federal Rule of Civil Procedure 34 addresses the production of documents and things and the entry onto land for discovery purposes. Absent from Rule 34 is a procedure to preserve documents, things or land from damage or destruction that could compromise the integrity or the very existence of the evidence requested. Rule 34 does refer the reader to Rule 37, the rule governing the compelling of individuals or entities to produce discovery and accompanying sanctions, when an objection to a request or a failure to respond or permit inspection occurs. Nonetheless, Rule 37 also does not address the situation where potential evidence may be compromised or destroyed.

* * *

While remaining consistent with the Federal Rules of Civil Procedure, but still addressing the need to perform the judicial duty to oversee and decide discovery disputes, this Court believes that a balancing test which considers the following three factors should be used when deciding a motion to preserve documents, things and land: 1) the level of concern the court has for the continuing existence and maintenance of the integrity of the evidence in question in the absence of an order directing preservation of the evidence; 2) any irreparable harm likely to result to the party seeking the preservation of evidence absent an order directing preservation; and 3) the capability of an individual, entity, or party to maintain the evidence sought to be preserved, not only as to the evidence's original form, condition or contents, but also the physical, spacial and financial burdens created by ordering evidence preservation.[2]

At the outset, in implementing this balancing test it is important to stress that the type of evidence will change from case to case and clearly the attendant circumstances of each case will dictate the necessity of the preservation order requested. The issues raised by a request for a preservation order require the trial court to exercise its discretion, and the factors set forth in the balancing test are only intended to assist the court by focusing on important areas which will arise in all such cases. Finally, it is important to note that the Court believes that a motion for a preservation order can be granted with regard to all items of evidence which are *discoverable* in accordance with Federal Rule of Civil Procedure 26(b)(1), without the necessity of establishing that the evidence will necessarily be relevant and admissible at trial.

1. Level of Concern for the Continuing Existence and Integrity of the Evidence

The first prong of the balancing test, namely the court's level of concern for the continuing existence and maintenance of the integrity of the evidence, is clearly a necessary component in the determination whether to grant or deny a preservation order. This is so because in the

---

2. * * * It must * * * be noted that many of the * * * cases reviewed by the Court that concern the granting of an order of preservation have cited to the *Manual for Complex Litigation,* in its second, third, and fourth editions. In the fourth edition, § 11.442 entitled "Preservation" speaks to the need for preservation orders in complex litigation. Sample Order 40.25 in the *Manual* sets forth a model for a preservation order. These sections of the *Manual* do not contradict our analysis and findings. The Court recognizes that it has become routine to order the preservation of evidence prior to the beginning of the discovery period at the initial case management conference and sometimes even before such a conference in complex litigation. *Manual for Complex Litigation, Fourth* § 11.442. The circumstances of the three motions before the Court do not concern "complex" litigation nor are we at the initial stages of discovery with all of the attendant circumstances which are normally present in cases for which the *Manual for Complex Litigation* is intended to provide guidance. *Id.* at §§ 10.1, 11.442. Therefore, the Court does not invoke any of the recommendations of that manual for the present analysis.

absence of any significant past, present or future threat to the continuing integrity or existence of the evidence, such an order is superfluous.

At times evidence may be outside of the possession of all parties and this may create a concern for the continuing existence of the evidence at question. Other circumstances may provide a basis for concern that a party is intentionally damaging or destroying the evidence, or is planning such an action, in order to compromise the case of its opponent. Still other circumstances may arise where the parties disagree as to the correct manner of the handling of the evidence. The reviewing court, as well as the parties, should be focused upon maintaining the integrity of the evidence in a form as close to, if not identical to, the original condition of the evidence. In the presence of a significant threat, if an order of court can prevent the loss, deterioration or destruction of evidence, while also considering all other relevant circumstances, then such an order may be an appropriate remedy. However, if the evidence, no matter where its location, how it is maintained, or who maintains it, will be lost, deteriorated or destroyed an order of preservation may not be necessary if the parties take immediate action to obtain or reproduce from the evidence the information needed; however, if the parties are not cooperative in this situation, then an order directing the preservation of the evidence in question in a manner that will preserve the whole of the evidence for the benefit of all parties may be necessary.

2. Possibility of Irreparable Harm to the Party Seeking Preservation in the Absence of a Preservation Order

Second, the degree of the harm likely to result to the party seeking the preservation order must also be weighed. At times, evidence may be a "one-of-a-kind", an irreplaceable item such as where a key item of evidence is tested through "non-destructive" means. The loss or destruction of certain evidence can result in significant prejudice to the party seeking to use it in proving the party's claims. In appropriate cases it becomes a judicial duty to protect a party from likely harm by acting to prevent the loss or destruction of evidence, thereby ensuring that the party may prosecute or defend its case in a court of law.

Additionally, certain evidence may be so integral and essential to a party's case that an order of preservation or some other manner of preventative maintenance of the evidence may be required, even in the absence of a threat of imminent, significant harm to the integrity or existence of the evidence. While such circumstances may be rare, they may require a preservation order from a court, thus allowing this second factor to overcome the absence of a significant level of concern as required under the first prong of the balancing test.

Clearly, however, a more compelling argument for a preservation order will be made where both factors are present. Considering that the loss of any evidence may damage a claim to some degree, a party could conceivably argue that the loss of any item of evidence intended to be offered at trial will cause harm sufficient to justify an order of preservation. Accordingly, while it could be argued that a court should always enter an order preserving evidence when a question arises as to its continued existence or integrity, such a reflexive, invariable judicial action in response to each motion for preservation of evidence would be impracticable and would trivialize the need for preservation orders in truly justifiable circumstances.

Therefore, where the need expressed by the moving party for a preservation order is based upon an indefinite or unspecified possibility of the loss or destruction of evidence, rather than a specific, significant, imminent threat of loss, a preservation order usually will not be justified. Also, where an imminent, specific threat to the evidence is demonstrated, but the level of harm which will result is not significant, then an order of preservation usually will not be justified. In most cases, the presence of both factor one and factor two to a significant degree will be required in order for a preservation order to be justified. However, it must be remembered that in a balancing test one factor may be so crucial that the presence of just that one factor may provide a sufficient justification for an order of preservation.

3.   Ability to Maintain and Preserve the Evidence

Third, the capability to maintain the evidence sought to be preserved must also be weighed with the other two factors. Evidence can take many forms in the world today. Considerations such as storage space, maintenance and storage fees, and physical deterioration of the evidence are just a few of the considerations to be evaluated when considering this final factor of the three-part balancing test. Certain circumstances may impose burdens upon those parties and non-parties possessing evidence which may be unfair or oppressive to the point that a judicially imposed allocation of the burdens between the parties to the civil action may be required. Preservation of evidence may be particularly burdensome for non-parties, considering that their interest in the pending civil action is minuscule while the restrictions that can be imposed in a motion for preservation may be expensive and voluminous. In such instances, the party seeking preservation, and possibly the opposing party, may be required to ensure the preservation of the evidence, rather than placing that burden upon uninvolved third party possessors of the evidence.

The problems involved in the maintenance of evidence will vary considerably depending upon the medium in which the evidence is contained. If the evidence is stored upon a computer floppy disk or hard drive, finding physical space to store the evidence will not be as much of an issue as it will be in the situation involving an accumulation of paper documentation over a period of many years where a preservation order may have to encompass substantial copying and warehousing. On the other hand, informational evidence stored within a computer hard drive may present a difficulty in that it may be compromised or degraded as new information is added and pieces of old information are "deleted" and subsequently written over by the computer. As a result, the timing of the preservation order may be of the essence, especially if the person possessing the computer is without knowledge that the information contained on the computer hard drive is evidence which needs to be preserved. Such a situation may require immediate action by the court to preserve such electronic evidence at least temporarily in order that the parties may have an opportunity to confirm that such evidence is relevant to the claims before the court. This computer information example is only one hypothetical scenario; the circumstances and considerations to be evaluated in determining the need for a preservation order can be limitless since evidence to be used at trial can be in a myriad of forms and mediums.

Applying this three part balancing test to the circumstances and considerations present in the case *sub judice*, the Court finds no need or justification to enter an order preserving evidence as requested by the Defendant and Plaintiffs.

Defendant requests a preservation order for those materials cited in its subpoena dated January 23, 2004 served upon Concurrent Technologies Corporation (hereinafter "CTC") in Johnstown. Among the materials requested were hard and electronic copies of documents and correspondence sent to and from Dr. Bagnall; all records, written or electronic, photographic or videographic, in CTC's possession obtained from the Colver Power Facility as well as physical pieces (the end box and shroud) from the generator at issue in the case and copies of testing results completed with regard to those pieces in addition to other written and electronic records. The Defendant asserts that a preservation order is required for the following reasons: that Dr. Bagnall during the *Daubert* hearing related the fact that other documents and materials may exist which may be relevant to the case; the need to "fully secure" this information and file "dispositive Motions based upon this new evidence"; the responsibility of a party to preserve evidence under F.R.C.P. 34; and the fact that the "Plaintiffs will not be harmed by such an Order" but that the Defendant would be "further substantially and irreparably harmed by the denial of the request to maintain the critical evidence intact from CTC." Defendant also states that it extended the time for responding to the subpoena by ten business days before filing this motion after CTC failed to comply with the extended deadline.

Under these circumstances there is no demonstration by the Defendant that evidence will be lost or destroyed. The attendant circumstances and reasons for the failure to produce the subject report, in which Dr. Bagnall participated, until the fourth day of trial, which event resulted in a mistrial, are not explained within the motion. The failure to produce that report may have resulted from a sheer oversight, rather than from any intent on the part of the Plaintiffs. The facts currently before the Court do not lead the Court to conclude that the circumstances that lead to the mistrial warrant the granting of a preservation order; indeed the report was produced following Dr. Bagnall's reliance upon it in his testimony. The report was not destroyed by the Plaintiffs but was retained as a litigation related document which was originally considered to be privileged as a consultant's report rather than a report of an expert expected to testify.

* * *

Had there been evidence of attempted damage or destruction of the report or the data compilations used to produce it, the Court's level of concern for protection of the integrity and existence of the evidence would be different. The Plaintiffs indicate in their response that they have continued to preserve the materials referenced in the Defendant's Motion. Without proof of destruction or degradation of the evidence, the Court finds that the circumstances surrounding the non-production of the report are an insufficient basis upon which to conclude that the integrity or existence of the evidence is threatened in the absence of a preservation order.

In consideration of the irreparable harm which allegedly will occur absent a preservation order, an allegation * * * which the Court understands [is] based upon the possible importance of the information which the Defendant believes may be contained in the items for which an order of preservation is requested, at this time a preservation order is found to be insufficiently justified under the second prong of balancing test. The information sought could provide a valid basis for the Defendant to posit an alternative theory of circumstances that resulted in the damage of the generator. The evidence sought includes some pieces of the generator that are suspected will lead the Defendant's experts to formulate this alternative theory. As a result, this factor, namely the importance of the evidence, if more fully developed by the Defendant and supported by the facts, could have favored the granting of the preservation order. However, on the basis of the record before the Court this factor does [not] provide a sufficient basis for a preservation order.

Finally, the information available to the Court does not adequately address the issue of maintenance of the evidence with regard to such relevant considerations as: storage of the physical evidence and whether the evidence can be maintained in a state close to its "original" character which it possessed when first removed from the generator; the maintenance of electronic information, recordings and email existing within the medium of hard drives, floppy disks, or other digital storage formats; and the traditional concerns of ensuring the maintenance of paper documentation which include locating, cataloging and storing such documents for purposes of litigation. These considerations are not meant to be exhaustive, but illustrative of the concerns that need to be addressed when evaluating the burden of maintaining evidence that is ordered to be preserved by a court.

Such maintenance of the evidence considerations were not examined by either party in the case *sub judice*. However, the Court notes that most of the evidence is comprised of physical documentation and electronic documentation, in addition to physical evidence. The Plaintiffs make no claim of inconvenience or inability to maintain the evidence requested from their consultant, CTC. Therefore, the Court finds that the factor regarding the actual continuing physical maintenance and possession of the materials requested does not favor the granting of the preservation order.

In weighing all three of these factors, the Court concludes that a preservation order as requested by the Defendant is not justified or necessary under the present circumstances. While loss of the subpoenaed materials would prejudice the Defendant, the Court's level of concern for the loss or degradation of the evidence in question is not sufficiently elevated based upon the lack of the presence of a specific, imminent threat supported by the record. In addition, the other two factors do not favor the granting of a preservation order. Accordingly, the Defendant's Motion for Order of Court Directing Preservation of Documents, Software and Things is denied.

The Plaintiffs in responding to the Defendant's motion presented their own Motion for Order of Court Directing Preservation of Documents, Software and Things. The Plaintiffs initially state in their motion that they do not object to the granting of the Defendant's motion if the order encompasses information sought to be preserved by both parties and not just the Defendant. The Plaintiff then proceeds to discuss the circumstances of the Defendant filing its motion as well as Defendant's alleged failure to comply fully with requested discovery prior to the January 2004 trial. In noting various documents and things that have not been produced by the Defendant in discovery, the Plaintiffs state:

> Because of Defendant's past failures to produce documents and materials during the course of discovery in this matter and because of Defendant's apparent intent to now change the nature of its defense in this action, it is necessary for Plaintiffs to set forth herein the types of documents and materials within the possession, custody or control of Defendant that require preservation and production.

However, the Plaintiffs' motion reads more like a motion to compel documents and things not previously produced than a motion for a preservation order. There is no indication that those materials sought are in danger of being lost or destroyed. In addition, the absence of these materials apparently has not hampered or delayed the Plaintiffs' prosecution of their case in that in January 2004 this case went to trial.

* * *

* * *

Motions for the preservation of evidence should be restricted to those circumstances which raise significant concern that discovery lawfully sought by a party will be lost indefinitely without immediate court action in the form of an order of preservation. The Plaintiffs' Counter–Motion for Order of Court Directing Preservation of Documents, Software and Things is denied.

* * *

COMMENTARY

Aside from providing that parties should "discuss any issues about preserving discoverable information" early in the proceedings,[73] the Federal Rules do not specify how relevant information should be preserved or how one litigant can ensure that the other will not destroy relevant information before it is produced in the course of litigation. In some cases, one or both parties may ask the court to enter a preservation order that will instruct a party to preserve certain types of information and dictate how it is to be preserved. It is important to remember, however, that a party's obligation to preserve relevant information exists even in the absence of such an order.

1. Seeking a Preservation Order

A litigant requests a preservation order because it anticipates that its opponent may fail to comply with its preservation obligations. For example, a preservation order may be entered against a party who has a history of discovery misconduct or spoliation violations or whose routine operating procedures or document retention practices will likely result in destruction.[74]

The inherently temporary or fleeting nature of certain types of information may also lead a party to seek a preservation order. In *Columbia Pictures Industries v. Bunnell*, discussed in Chapter II.E, *supra*, the plaintiffs claimed that discovery of the defendants' server's RAM was necessary in order to show how often users were downloading copyrighted movies.[75] Because the RAM was overwritten every six hours, the plaintiffs sought a preservation order. After an extensive analysis, the court issued an order directing the defendants to maintain the server logs, which preserved the RAM.[76]

Sometimes, the preserving party may itself have reasons to seek a preservation order. A court order that clearly defines and delimits a litigant's obligations could benefit the preserving party by potentially reducing its administrative and financial burdens. Additionally, if the

---

73. Fed. R. Civ. P. 26(f) *et seq.*

74. *See, e.g., Del Campo v. Kennedy*, No. C–01–21151, 2006 WL 2586633 (N.D. Cal. Sept. 8, 2006).

75. No. CV 06–1093, 2007 WL 2080419 (C.D. Cal. May 29, 2007).

76. *See Columbia Pictures, Inc. v. Bunnell*, 245 F.R.D. 443 (C.D. Cal. 2007) (affirming the magistrate judge's order requiring defendants to preserve and produce server logs).

preserving party faithfully complies with the court's order, the litigant may shield itself from future spoliation claims.

If discoverable information in the hands of a non-party custodian is at risk of being destroyed before production, a preservation notice and subpoena may be issued to the third party. *In re Pacific Gateway Exchange, Inc. Securities Litigation* involved a defendant that had filed for Chapter 11 and was in bankruptcy proceedings. During this process, most of the defendant's employees had left, and there were few personnel remaining to be responsible for preservation and production. Additionally, the court noted that there may be relevant data on former employees' personal computers. Finding a "significant risk that relevant documents, both paper and electronic, could be irretrievably lost, which could result in prejudice to plaintiffs[,]" the court permitted the parties to serve a subpoena and notice to preserve documents to third parties.[77]

Similarly, *In re Tyco International, Ltd. Securities Litigation* was a multidistrict securities fraud litigation, in which the court agreed with plaintiffs that various third-parties, such as accountants, auditors, and consultants, may possess discoverable information about the transactions at issue. The court acknowledged that, unlike the defendants, these non-parties had not necessarily received notice of the lawsuit. Moreover, plaintiffs had produced evidence showing that because these third parties were large corporations, they would likely "overwrite and thereby destroy electronic data in the course of performing routine backup procedures."[78] Accordingly, the court held that it would permit plaintiffs to serve preservation notices and subpoenas on these non-parties, provided that plaintiffs submitted revised, "appropriately tailored" subpoenas that particularized the types of evidence to be preserved.[79]

2. Issuing a Preservation Order

Some courts have taken the approach of issuing a preservation order only where the standard for injunctive relief has been met.[80] Courts applying the injunctive relief standard to a request for a preservation order generally require the requesting party to demonstrate "potential irreparable injury" and also show that there is a "real danger that the acts to be enjoined will occur, that there is no other remedy available, and that, under these circumstances, the court should exercise its discretion to afford the unusual relief provided by its injunction."[81]

Other courts have taken a different approach, recognizing a trial court's inherent power "to control the discovery process and overall case

---

77. No. C 00 1211, 2001 WL 1334747, at *1–2 (N.D. Cal. Oct. 17, 2001).

78. No. 00–MD–1335, 2000 WL 33654141, at *3 (D.N.H. Jul. 27, 2000).

79. *Id.*

80. *See, e.g., Madden v. Wyeth*, No. 3–03–CV–0167, 2003 WL 21443404 (N.D. Tex. Apr. 16, 2003).

81. *Humble Oil & Refining Co. v. Harang*, 262 F. Supp. 39, 43 (E.D. La. 1966). *Accord In re Potash Antitrust Litig.*, No. 3–93–197, 1994 WL 1108312 (D. Minn. Dec. 5, 1994) (declining to issue preservation order where there was no showing that the requesting party would be irreparably harmed without it).

management" as a separate source of authority for issuing preservation orders.[82] In *Pueblo of Laguna v. United States*, the Court of Federal Claims held that "a document preservation order is no more an injunction than an order requiring a party to identify witnesses or to produce documents in discovery."[83] Drawing on its inherent power to manage the litigation before it, the court held that a preservation order should issue if the requesting party demonstrates "that it is necessary and not unduly burdensome."[84]

In *Capricorn Power*, the court devised a third test that does not strictly adhere to the injunctive relief standard, but yet requires a more in-depth analysis than the *Pueblo* court. The *Capricorn Power* balancing test was intended to give particular consideration to the policies and goals of discovery by weighing the following factors: (1) the court's level of concern for the continuing existence of the evidence absent a preservation order; (2) any irreparable harm likely to result to the requesting party absent a preservation order; and (3) the capability of the other party to preserve the evidence, which takes into account "the physical, spatial and financial burdens created by ordering evidence preservation."[85]

In yet another variation, some courts, especially in complex cases, employ a standard, "first day" order at the start of the litigation that contains form language regarding the parties' preservation obligations.[86] For example, in some multidistrict litigation, the first order the court issues may automatically require all parties to "preserve all documents and other records containing information potentially relevant to the subject matter of this litigation."[87]

State courts have also begun to address preservation of ESI. In 2006, the Conference of Chief Justices released "Guidelines for State Trial Courts Regarding Discovery of Electronically–Stored Information."[88] The Guidelines state that a trial court should only issue a preservation order upon "a threshold showing that the continuing existence and integrity of the information is threatened."[89] Following a threshold showing, the Guidelines instruct trial courts to consider four factors—similar to those used in *Capricorn Power*—in fashioning an order: (1) the nature of the threat to the ESI; (2) the potential for irreparable harm without an order; (3) the responding party's ability to

---

82. *Capricorn Power*, 220 F.R.D. at 433.

83. *Pueblo of Laguna v. United States*, 60 Fed. Cl. 133, 138 n.8 (2004).

84. *Id*. at 138.

85. 220 F.R.D. at 434.

86. *See Manual for Complex Litigation* § 11.442 (4th ed. 2004) ("Before discovery starts, and perhaps before the initial conference, the court should consider whether to enter an order requiring the parties to preserve and retain documents, files, data, and records that may be relevant to the litigation.").

87. *In re Prudential Ins. Co. of Am. Sales Practices Litig.*, 169 F.R.D. 598 (D.N.J. 1997).

88. *See* Appendix III.

89. *Id*. § 9.A.

maintain the information sought; and (4) the physical, technological, and financial burdens in preserving the information.

3. Content and Scope of Preservation Orders

A preservation order should be narrowly tailored to the specific risks and needs of the case to avoid imposing unduly burdensome requirements on the parties. Because the litigants know best what information is needed, where it is kept, and how it can most efficiently be preserved, a court may institute a general, temporary preservation order and instruct the litigants to meet and confer to develop a more detailed, customized preservation agreement. Such an order may also be useful if one party refuses to discuss in detail the issue of preservation.[90] When ordered to meet and confer to develop a preservation plan, litigants should evaluate the following considerations:[91]

(a) the extent of the preservation obligation, identifying the types of material to be preserved, the subject matter, time frame, the authors and addressees, and key words to be used in identifying responsive materials;

(b) the identification of persons responsible for carrying out preservation obligations on behalf of each party;

(c) the form and method of providing notice of the duty to preserve to persons identified as custodians of documents, data, and tangible things;

(d) mechanisms for monitoring, certifying, or auditing custodian compliance with preservation obligations;

(e) whether preservation will require suspending or modifying any routine business processes or procedures, with special attention to document management programs and the recycling of computer data storage media;

(f) the methods to preserve any volatile but potentially discoverable material, such as voicemail, active data in databases, or electronic messages;

(g) the anticipated costs of preservation and ways to reduce or share these costs; and

(h) a mechanism to review and modify the preservation obligation as discovery proceeds, eliminating or adding particular categories of documents, data, and tangible things.

PROBLEMS

1. An American Indian tribe has sued the United States seeking an accounting and to recover for monetary loss and damages relating to the

---

90. *See, e.g., Del Campo v. Kennedy*, No. C–01–21151, 2006 WL 2586633 (N.D. Cal. Sept. 8, 2006) (ordering the parties to meet and confer to develop a preservation plan and issuing an interim preservation order). *See also Manual for Complex Litigation* § 40.25 (4th ed. 2004) (sample interim order and direction to meet and confer).

91. These meet and confer "Subjects for Consideration" are taken from the sample preservation order in the *Manual for Complex Litigation* § 40.25 (4th ed. 2004).

Government's alleged mismanagement of the tribe's trust funds and other properties.

A similar case is pending in another jurisdiction. In that case, Government agencies have mishandled Indian records. Documents, including electronic records, containing Indian-related information relevant to the matter have been destroyed. There has been unsatisfactory oversight of administrative procedures, and management has been unable to respond effectively when made aware of violations. Many facilities in which Indian records have been stored are in general disrepair, and there are insufficient systems and methods for ensuring preservation. Regulations regarding Indian-record retention have not been effectively implemented, and on numerous occasions, there have been improper attempts to transfer Indian records.

The plaintiff tribe in the instant case has requested that the court issue an order directing various Government agencies to take steps to ensure the preservation and availability of documents, in various media, potentially relating to its claims against the Government.

Should the court issue the requested order? Would you come to a different conclusion depending on the test used?

2. The plaintiff tribe has made specific proposals with regard to the terms of the requested preservation order. Plaintiff has asked the court to prohibit generally the destruction of records relevant to the case absent plaintiff's prior written concurrence or further order from the court. Plaintiff also requests that the court impose restrictions on the inter- and intra-agency transfer of records, requiring that no transfer of records can occur without plaintiff's concurrence or a court order. In the alternative, plaintiff requests an opportunity to examine such records prior to their movement.

Consider points (a) through (h) listed above. As counsel for plaintiff, what would you add to the proposal? As counsel for the Government, what would you challenge about the proposal? Are there important issues not addressed by plaintiff's proposal?

H. POSSESSION, CUSTODY, OR CONTROL

IN RE NTL, INC. SECURITIES LITIGATION
244 F.R.D. 179 (S.D.N.Y. 2007)

PECK, MAGISTRATE JUDGE

Plaintiffs * * * have moved for discovery sanctions against defendant NTL Europe, Inc. and "nominal non-party NTL, Inc.," claiming that they hindered and delayed document discovery in this case and allowed numerous documents and electronically stored information ("ESI"), including the e-mails of approximately forty-four of NTL's "key players," to be destroyed. * * *

FACTS

The Securities Lawsuits and NTL's Bankruptcy

The * * * plaintiffs filed suit on April 18, 2002 against a company then known as NTL, Inc. ("Old NTL"), alleging federal securities laws violations. Old NTL and several of its subsidiaries entered into Chapter 11 bankruptcy, emerging on September 5, 2002 with a "Second Amended Joint Reorganization Plan of NTL Incorporated and Certain Subsidiaries" (the "Bankruptcy Plan"). Two main companies emerged out of the bankruptcy: NTL Europe, Inc. ("NTL Europe"), the successor company to Old NTL, and NTL, Inc. ("New NTL"), formerly known as NTL Communications Corp. ([e].g., Bankruptcy Plan at 31–32.) NTL Europe was primarily responsible for selling off Old NTL's unprofitable assets, and New NTL became the surviving operational company with control of the company's European telecommunications assets. The Bankruptcy Plan specifically allowed the * * * securities lawsuits to go forward after the bankruptcy, against the individual defendants and NTL Europe (as successor to Old NTL) * * * .

Document Sharing Clauses in The Demerger Agreement and Transitional Services Agreement

Pursuant to the Bankruptcy Plan, defendant NTL Europe and non-party New NTL entered into a "Demerger Agreement" dated January 10, 2003, which specifies that:

4. ACCESS TO INFORMATION

For a period of ten years from the date of this Agreement, each party shall ... allow the other party and its personnel to have access to (during normal business hours and following not less than 48 hours' notice) and (at the expense of the party requesting the information) take copies of all documents, records or other materials containing any information which that party or any of its Group Companies or affiliated joint ventures might reasonably require to be able to comply with their respective legal, regulatory, accounting or filing obligations, or to resist, appeal, dispute, avoid or compromise any tax assessment, provided that nothing in this clause shall permit either party to copy any document, record or other material which is subject to legal privilege. Furthermore, each party shall ... allow reasonable access to such of its duly authorised personnel, at all reasonable times during business hours upon prior written notice, as are required to permit the availability, access or, subject to the above restriction, copying of such information.

* * *

Old NTL's 2002 Document Hold Memoranda

On March 13, 2002, a document "hold" memo was circulated to approximately seventeen employees of Old NTL:

Although, under usual circumstances, destruction of documents/files, in the ordinary course is permitted, under certain circumstances, a company is under a duty to preserve documents that could be relevant to disputes with third parties. Basically, what this means is that you can have a policy that dictates which and when documents can be destroyed in the ordinary course, but once you are on notice that there may be litigation you are required to retain documents that would reasonably constitute evidence even if under your retention policy you would destroy such documents in the ordinary course.

Accordingly, given the obvious possibility that we may encounter a heightened risk of litigious activity in the ongoing restructuring process, it is imperative that all documents that even possibly could be evidence in any such a matter be retained.

Thank you.

On March 14, 2002, the same memorandum was forwarded to approximately twenty-eight more employees at Old NTL with the following instruction: "Please read and note carefully Lauren Blair's (Assistant General Counsel in New York) memorandum on the retention of documents. Please forward to your reports as you consider appropriate. Many thanks."

On or about June 6, 2002, while Old NTL was in bankruptcy, another document hold memorandum about the [securities actions] was circulated to employees. The memo stated in part:

NTL Incorporated and certain of its officers have been named as defendants in a number of purported securities class action lawsuits. The complaints in those cases generally allege that NTL failed to accurately disclose its financial condition, finances and future prospects in press releases and other communications with investors prior to filing for reorganization in federal bankruptcy court.

We presently do not know of any facts that would support these allegations, and we intend to defend the lawsuits vigorously.

In connection with such lawsuits, NTL and its affiliates may be required to produce documents relevant to plaintiffs' claims. Therefore, as we have previously informed you, we are required to take reasonable steps to preserve all potentially relevant material that may exist (whether in paper or electronic format). Relevant materials may include sales data, minutes or notes of meetings or conversations, financial statements, credit facilities and other loan documents, press releases, PowerPoint presentations and any other documents (including drafts) relating to the business, assets, properties, condition (financial or otherwise), and results of operations of NTL or its affiliates at any time after April 1, 1999.

Please ensure that these types of documents are preserved until further notice. When in doubt about possible relevance, you should err on the side of retaining the material.

A Brief History of Discovery in this Case Relevant to this Motion

On May 2, 2005, the * * * plaintiffs served their initial document requests upon defendant NTL Europe and the individual defendants. On June 1, 2005, defendant NTL Europe and the individual defendants filed their objections and responses. Defendant NTL Europe's response to the document requests stated that "NTL will produce documents, if any, responsive to [the] request." Defendant NTL Europe, however, did not produce any responsive documents or e-mails. Defendant NTL Europe's counsel informed plaintiffs' counsel that all corporate records relating to the 1999–2002 pre-bankruptcy period were in non-party New NTL's possession and that defendant NTL Europe did not possess any of these records.

* * *

On August 16, 2005, plaintiffs served a subpoena upon non-party New NTL requesting production of essentially the same documents as plaintiffs had requested from defendant NTL Europe. Approximately two months later, non-party New NTL made seventy boxes of documents available to plaintiffs' counsel for inspection and copying.

On November 21, 2005, plaintiffs' counsel sent a letter to New NTL's counsel noting that New NTL had not produced several requested categories of documents, including financial analyses, subscriber integration and billing issues, and e-mail. On November 30, 2005, New NTL's counsel responded that New NTL does "not believe responsive documents that fall into the categories of documents which you reference in your letter as missing exist and/or can be produced," and concluded that in light of its "limited role" in the litigation, New NTL's production was "full and complete." New NTL's counsel also orally told plaintiffs' counsel that "responsive e-mails did not exist because the company's [computer] servers had been 'upgraded' after the reorganization."

* * *

On December 20, 2005, plaintiffs' counsel took a Rule 30(b)(6) deposition of Jeffrey Brodsky, defendant NTL Europe's CEO. Brodsky testified that NTL Europe does not have physical possession of Old NTL's books and records. Because non-party New NTL retained the operating telecommunications assets after the bankruptcy, New NTL had physical possession of the books and records. This was the reason that defendant NTL Europe did not produce any documents in response to plaintiffs' May 2, 2005 subpoena. * * *

In a letter dated January 24, 2006, New NTL's counsel disclosed to plaintiffs' counsel that New NTL had performed selected, targeted searches of 23,000 boxes of files in storage in four locations in the

United Kingdom and had located no additional responsive documents, and further asserted that reviewing every box in storage to locate documents responsive to plaintiffs' document requests would be "overly burdensome, unreasonable, unrealistic and extraordinarily costly for [non-party] NTL." * * *

At [a] January 25, 2006 New NTL Rule 30(b)(6) deposition, David Bond, a New NTL in-house lawyer testified that New NTL's IT system was outsourced to IBM in late 2002 or early 2003. Bond did not know what the e-mail retention policy was at the time of the outsourcing to IBM; IBM's current e-mail retention policy with respect to a former employee's e-mail account is that New NTL's IT department has access to the account for three months after an employee leaves the company, then it goes to a back-up tape for nine months, after which it may be overwritten. Bond testified that the policy with regard to the e-mail accounts of current New NTL employees is that employees are free to retain e-mails or discard them "to suit their needs." In order to retain an e-mail, an employee must move the e-mail from their inbox to a separate folder, otherwise the e-mails in the inbox will start to be deleted after approximately three months. Bond stated that employees received new computers at the time of the outsourcing to IBM, and he did not know whether e-mails written on the old computers were placed on back-up tapes as part of the outsourcing. Bond was not aware of any communications within New NTL at the time of the outsourcing to IBM regarding retention of e-mail or documents pertinent to ongoing litigation.

* * *

On February 8, 2006, plaintiffs took the deposition of George Bernet, the information technology manager at Old NTL's executive offices in New York starting in 2001. Bernet testified that no one ever asked him to save or preserve information because of threatened or pending litigation. Bernet stated that NTL's New York server was decommissioned in 2004, with all electronic files transferred to the company's UK servers. After that, the old computers from the New York office were donated to charity. Bernet testified that full back-up tapes for the New York office were moved to the company's new Manhattan offices and also to a bank vault.

On March 1, 2006, New NTL produced CD's containing the e-mail files of ten present or former NTL employees, three of which had already been provided to plaintiffs two weeks before. Therefore, as of March 1, 2006, plaintiffs had received e-mail files for only twelve of the fifty-eight employees requested. On March 13, 2006, New NTL produced the New York office back-up tapes to plaintiffs' counsel. At plaintiff[s'] expense, the back-up tapes were restored and converted to readable, searchable files. Plaintiffs' counsel's review of the back-up tapes revealed that they contained e-mails from senior executives who worked in NTL's executive offices in New York, but that the tapes did not contain any e-mail from 2001, the main year in which plaintiffs allege that defendant NTL Europe and its executives committed securities violations.

On March 17, 2006, IBM's attorney advised plaintiffs' counsel that IBM completed the searches of the New NTL electronic files in its possession, and out of a list of fifty-seven current and former NTL employees, IBM found files for thirteen employees, most of whose files New NTL's counsel previously had produced to plaintiffs. In e-mail correspondence between New NTL's counsel and plaintiffs' counsel, New NTL confirmed that it had searched several times for e-mails relating to the remaining current and former employees on the list and did not find anything at all, even though some produced documents indicate that at least three of those employees had e-mail accounts during the time period pertinent to the document request.

* * *

On June 27, 2006, plaintiffs' counsel updated the Court on the progress of discovery. As of that date, the majority of the e-mails from the files of forty-four of the current and former employees on plaintiffs' list of "key players" were still missing from New NTL's document production * * *. Additionally, very few pieces of external correspondence and personal meeting notes were provided, and no NTL communications with securities analysts or investment firms were produced. * * *

On August 14, 2006, the * * * plaintiffs provided their final update to the Court regarding discovery. The * * * plaintiffs confirmed that they had completed the depositions of the individual defendants, that they questioned the individual defendants about specific categories of missing documents and e-mails, and were told that many of the documents and e-mails from those categories previously existed but never were produced, presumably because they were discarded. * * *

ANALYSIS

* * *

II. PLAINTIFF'S MOTION FOR AN ADVERSE INFERENCE IS GRANTED

A. Legal Standard Governing Adverse Inference Instructions

"The spoliation of evidence germane to proof of an issue at trial can support an inference that the evidence would have been unfavorable to the party responsible for its destruction." *Zubulake v. UBS Warburg LLC*, 220 F.R.D. 212, 216 (S.D.N.Y. 2003). * * *

"A party that seeks an adverse inference instruction for destruction or late production of evidence must show that: (i) the party having control over the evidence had an obligation to preserve or timely produce it; (ii) the party that destroyed or failed to timely produce evidence had a 'culpable state of mind'; and (iii) the missing or tardily produced evidence is relevant to the party's claim or defense 'such that a reasonable trier of fact could find that it would support that claim or defense.' "

1. Duty to Preserve Evidence

* * *

c. Defendant NTL Europe Had "Control" Over The Relevant Documents

Defendant NTL Europe contends that, although it was the party designated after bankruptcy to continue as the defendant in this case, it nevertheless did not have "control" over any documents or ESI relevant to plaintiffs' document requests because they were in non-party New NTL's possession; therefore defendant NTL Europe contends that it was not responsible for any spoliation which may have happened since this case was filed.

* * *

Under Rule 34, "control does not require that the party have legal ownership or actual physical possession of the documents at issue; rather, documents are considered to be under a party's control when that party has the right, authority, or practical ability to obtain the documents from a non-party to the action." *Bank of New York v. Meridien BIAO Bank Tanzania Ltd.*, 171 F.R.D. 135, 146–47 (S.D.N.Y.1997); *see also, e.g., Golden Trade, S.r.L. v. Lee Apparel Co.*, 143 F.R.D. 514, 525 (S.D.N.Y.1992) (The courts have "interpreted Rule 34 to require production if the party has the practical ability to obtain the documents from another, irrespective of his legal entitlement to the documents.").

Here, defendant NTL Europe had both the legal "right" and certainly the "practical ability" to obtain the relevant documents from New NTL, and therefore had the necessary "control" of those documents to be able to preserve and produce them in this litigation, for three separate reasons:

First, the document sharing clause in the Demerger Agreement makes it clear that New NTL was to make available to defendant NTL Europe any documents that it needed to be able to comply with its legal obligations, such as this lawsuit. Moreover, defendant NTL Europe's CEO demonstrated that NTL Europe had the simple "practical ability" to obtain the relevant documents from New NTL; he testified that "[w]henever there was a document that we needed [from New NTL] . . . , we would call [New NTL] and ask if they had it, and if they had it, they'd send it." Based on these agreements and testimony, * * * defendant NTL Europe had the legal and/or practical ability to obtain documents (including e-mail) from New NTL. * * * Accordingly, the Court holds that defendant NTL Europe had "control" over documents and ESI at New NTL for the purpose of this litigation.

Second, even if defendant NTL Europe and non-party New NTL had not been parties to the Demerger Agreement * * * this Court finds that defendant NTL Europe still should be held to have "control" over the relevant documents and ESI possessed by New NTL for the purposes of document production in this case, under the reasoning of the decision in *Bank of New York v. Meridien BIAO Bank Tanzania Ltd.*, 171 F.R.D. at 146–49. There, one of the original defendants went through a bankruptcy reorganization and assigned its interests to a new party. The Court in *Bank of New York* found that * * * the "[t]reatment of both assignor and assignee as parties for discovery . . . is proper when to do otherwise would frustrate discovery, regardless of whether this frustration is intentional or not . . . Otherwise a litigant by contracting with a third party could nullify and evade the rules of procedure." The Court ultimately held that "[i]t would be patently unfair if [the assignee party] were able to continue to discover relevant information from [plaintiff] while relegating [plaintiff] to seek information from [the assignor] as a non-party," and thus the Court ordered the assignee party to "produce all documents relevant to the issues in this action" that were in the assignor's possession. In so holding, the Court also noted that the assignee party had demonstrated an ability to retrieve critical documents from the assignor when needed, suggesting that the assignee party defendant had the requisite "practical ability" to obtain documents that satisfies the requirements of Rule 34.

This Court finds the situation in this case analogous to that in *Bank of New York*. Plaintiffs here filed their case against Old NTL prior to its entry into bankruptcy. Upon emergence from bankruptcy, defendant NTL Europe was assigned to be the entity to replace Old NTL in the lawsuit. Defendant NTL Europe's CEO testified that NTL Europe had the practical ability to obtain any documents it needed from New NTL. Therefore, under *Bank of New York*, * * * defendant NTL Europe had "control" over "Old NTL's" documents possessed by New NTL that were relevant to this lawsuit, and in any case, it would be patently unfair for defendant NTL Europe to benefit from the artificial separation of entities that was created after the bankruptcy. * * *

There is, however, a third reason why NTL Europe can be sanctioned for failing to produce relevant documents and electronically stored information, even if (as it claims), it had no legal or practical ability to obtain the documents and ESI from New NTL. Once the duty to preserve material for litigation arises—as it did here * * * before NTL emerged from bankruptcy—the party has a duty to initiate a "litigation hold" and preserve potentially responsive documents and ESI. *See, e.g., Zubulake v. UBS Warburg LLC*, 229 F.R.D. 422, 433–34 (S.D.N.Y. 2004). NTL initiated such a hold (or at least sent some hold memos to that effect). If defendant NTL Europe thereafter turned relevant "held" documents and ESI over to New NTL without itself preserving (or insuring that New NTL would preserve) such information for possible production in this litigation, it failed in its obligation to preserve relevant material, and thus spoliated evidence (assuming the other requirements for spoliation are met). Thus, either the Demerger Agreement gave defendant NTL Europe the ability to obtain relevant documents and ESI from New NTL, in which case it had sufficient "control" to be responsible to produce the material in discovery, or if the Demerger Agreement did not give defendant NTL Europe that right, then defendant NTL Europe failed to have a sufficient litigation hold in place and therefore engaged in spoliation when it transferred documents to New NTL. Counsel for defendant NTL Europe conceded that NTL Europe did not take any action to ensure that New NTL would preserve the documents and ESI that it received from NTL Europe after the bankruptcy.

For the reasons set forth above, defendant NTL Europe had "control" and thus a duty * * * to preserve documents and ESI relevant to this litigation, even though most of those documents and ESI ended up in the physical possession of non-party New NTL.

2. Culpable State of Mind

* * *

Defendant NTL Europe's conduct demonstrates a sufficiently culpable state of mind to warrant spoliation sanctions. While Old NTL circulated two document hold memoranda to certain employees, many NTL employees never received the memoranda. Moreover, there is no evidence that either of the two NTLs ever reminded employees (especially at New NTL) of the need to continue to preserve relevant documents and ESI. The evidence, in fact, is that no adequate litigation hold existed at the NTLs. In late 2002 or early 2003, NTL's IT system was outsourced to IBM, which apparently did not have any document hold in place at all. New NTL employees also received new computers at the time of the outsourcing to IBM, and New NTL does not know whether any e-mails written on the old computers were saved or not. Additionally, New NTL did not convey any litigation hold instructions to IBM at the time of the outsourcing. More generally, defendant NTL Europe's counsel conceded that NTL Europe took no steps after bankruptcy to ensure that New NTL personnel continued the litigation hold.

As a result, NTL Europe (through New NTL) was only able to produce e-mail files for thirteen out of fifty-seven requested current and former NTL employees who are the "key players" involved in plaintiffs' allegations. * * * Consequently, the Court finds that NTL Europe's utter failure to preserve documents and ESI relevant to plaintiffs' allegations in this case * * * to be at least grossly negligent. * * * The second requirement for imposition of an adverse inference instruction therefore is met.

3. Relevance

* * *

"Where a party destroys evidence in bad faith, that bad faith alone is sufficient circumstantial evidence from which a reasonable fact finder could conclude that the missing evidence was unfavorable to that party. Similarly, a showing of gross negligence in the destruction or untimely production of evidence will in some circumstances suffice, standing alone, to support a finding that the evidence was unfavorable to the grossly negligent party." * * *

As discussed above, the * * * plaintiffs have demonstrated that defendant NTL Europe's failure to preserve documents and ESI relevant to plaintiffs' allegations was at a minimum grossly negligent. * * * Thus, no extrinsic proof of relevance is necessary, and the * * * plaintiffs are entitled to an adverse inference spoliation instruction.

* * *

Because the * * * plaintiffs have shown that NTL Europe had the duty to preserve documents and ESI relevant to this litigation * * * , that NTL Europe was at a minimum grossly negligent in allowing documents and ESI including the e-mails of approximately forty-four key players to be destroyed, and that those e-mails were relevant to the * * * plaintiffs' claims, the * * * plaintiffs have demonstrated that an adverse inference instruction spoliation sanction against defendant NTL Europe is warranted in this case.

HATFILL v. THE NEW YORK TIMES COMPANY
242 F.R.D. 353 (E.D. Va. 2006)

O'GRADY, MAGISTRATE JUDGE

* * * Plaintiff has brought this defamation action against Defendant, after Defendant published a series of columns, written by Nicholas Kristof, alleging that Plaintiff was involved in the anthrax attacks which killed five people in 2001. * * * Plaintiff served a request for Production of Documents, under Fed. Rule Civ. P. 34, on Defendant, asking for documents related to published and unpublished reporting on the anthrax attacks involving a number of Defendant's reporters and researchers. However, this motion to compel concerns only the potentially responsive documents in the physical possession of William Broad, a science reporter for Defendant, specifically 6,000 words of interview notes stored on Mr. Broad's personal flash memory drive.[2]

---

2. A flash drive is re-writable storage device integrated with a USB interface. The drive is small and lightweight such that it can [be] attached to key chain or lanyard. To access the data stored on a flash drive, the flash drive must be attached to a computer for power, but the computer can read the files off the flash drive without saving them to the computer's hard drive.

I. Background

On September 15, 2006, Plaintiff deposed Mr. Broad, pursuant to a Rule 45 subpoena. During the deposition, Mr. Broad stated that he stored his unpublished materials, including the 6,000 words of interview notes related to his investigation of the anthrax attacks, on his flash drive. Mr. Broad stated that the notes memorialized approximately thirty interviews with different sources and that the sources provided the information in reliance on Mr. Broad's promise to keep the sources' identities in confidence or to keep the information confidential and use [it only] for Mr. Broad's background knowledge. Mr. Broad does not recall showing the contents of the notes to anyone, including his editors at Defendant's newspaper. The flash drive, containing the notes, is always in the personal possession of Mr. Broad, although he regularly attaches the drive to computers owned by Defendant as part of his work duties.

Plaintiff argues that Defendant has failed to fully respond to its request for production because Defendant has not produced Mr. Broad's 6,000 word notes related to the anthrax investigation. Plaintiff contends that these notes are within Defendant's "possession, custody and control" regardless of whether the employee keeps the notes at home or at work and thus must be produced in response to a production request, pursuant to Rule 34(a). Plaintiff further argues that the notes are discoverable material, pursuant to Rule 26(b)(1), based on depositions of both Mr. Kristof and Mr. Broad as well as e-mail communications between the two reporters. Defendant argues that the notes are in the sole personal possession, custody, and control of Mr. Broad and thus Defendant is not required to produce the notes under Rule 34. * * *

II. Possession, Custody or Control under Rule 34(a)

Under Rule 34, the party responding to a production request must provide responsive documents which are in the possession, custody or control of the party. See Fed.R.Civ.P. 34(a)(1). The U.S. Court of Appeals for the Fourth Circuit has not interpreted the phrase "possession, custody or control." However, a number of district courts within the Fourth Circuit have considered this issue [and hold that] control is defined as actual possession of a document or "the legal right to obtain the document on demand." This two-prong definition comports with the findings of other circuits.

In this case, Defendant does not have physical possession of the flash drive containing Mr. Broad's notes. While Mr. Broad may have used computers owned by Defendant in order to access the flash drive, according to Mr. Broad, the notes themselves have not been stored on Defendant's computers. The only question remaining is whether Defendant has a legal right to obtain the notes from Mr. Broad. Defendant argues that it ceded to its reporters any right to possess or control dissemination of notes and unpublished materials. In relinquishing these rights, Defendant sought to remove uncertainty for reporters regarding dissemination of unpublished material that the reporter generates or obtains. This policy is embodied in both the collective bargaining agreement with its reporters' union requiring Defendant to provide legal representation to reporters who elect not to comply with subpoenas for their confidential work product as well as Defendant's Records Retention Policy. Finally, Defendant allows reporters to take such notes and unpublished materials with them if they leave Defendant's employment * * *. The Court finds that these actions show that Defendant has ceded any legal rights to Mr. Broad's notes, and that its policy also has a clear substantive purpose and is not an artificial wall created for the purpose of avoiding discovery requests.

The Court, therefore, finds that Defendant does not have possession, custody or control under the two-prong definition of control under Rule 34(a); thus, this Court will not compel Defendant to produce Mr. Broad's notes.

* * *

COMMENTARY

1. What Is Control?

It is important to recognize that Rules 26, 34, and 45 all have "possession, custody, or control" requirements. The requirement in Rule 26 is particularly important because it may create a trap. Under Rule 26, a party discloses documents in its "possession, custody, or control" on which it intends to affirmatively rely. Thus, a Rule 26 disclosure could be viewed as an admission that a party has "possession, custody, or control" over certain records, which may affect its responses to Rule 34 discovery demands.

a. The Factual Record

In re NTL, Inc. Securities Litigation highlights the importance of the factual record to a discovery dispute. Even more damaging than the Demerger Agreement itself may have been the testimony about access to information. NTL Europe's CEO testified that "[w]henever there was a document that we needed [from New NTL] ... , we would call [New NTL] and ask if they had it, and if they had it, they'd send it."[92] The court held that the CEO's testimony "demonstrated that NTL Europe had the simple 'practical ability' to obtain the relevant documents from New NTL."[93]

b. Practical Ability

The *In re NTL* court relied, in part, on NTL Europe's "practical ability" to obtain the documents in question. Whether a party's "prac-

---

92. 244 F.R.D. at 195–96.

93. *Id.*

tical ability" to obtain discovery materials means that a party has "control" over those materials has been the subject of some debate. In *Prokosch v. Catalina Lighting, Inc.*, the court wrote: "[t]herefore, 'under Rule 34, 'control' does not require that the party have legal ownership or actual physical possession of the documents at issue; rather, documents are considered to be under a party's control when that party has the right, authority, or practical ability, to obtain the documents from a non-party to the action.' "[94] The court ordered the defendant to produce certain documents that it "may not physically possess, but which it is capable of obtaining upon demand."[95]

The Seventh Circuit rejected the "practical ability" test in *Chaveriat v. Williams Pipe Line Co.*, in overturning a trial court's decision to exclude certain evidence because the plaintiffs failed to turn over chromatograms to the defendant for more than two years. The chromatograms were in the possession of NET, a third party, and the plaintiffs ultimately asked for and received them from NET. After stating the "possession, custody, or control" requirement, the court wrote:

> The plaintiffs could no doubt have asked NET to give it the chromatograms; judging from what happened later, NET would have complied; and maybe if it had balked, the plaintiffs could have bought the chromatograms from it. But the fact that a party could obtain a document if it tried hard enough and maybe if it didn't try hard at all does not mean that the document is in its possession, custody, or control; in fact it means the opposite.[96]

Similarly, in *Bleecker v. Standard Fire Insurance Co.*, the court also rejected the "practical ability test." The issue involved documents in the possession of a third-party insurance adjuster. Plaintiff asserted that the defendant had the ability to "command" the documents. The court wrote:

> Plaintiff's and Defendant's definitions of control differ greatly. Plaintiff asserts that even if a party does not have the right to require a non-party to produce documents, the party's practical *ability* to produce the documents determines whether the defendant has "control" of the document. On the other hand, defendant contends that "control" encompasses the legal *right* to obtain the requested document.[97]

The court agreed with the defendant: "In order for the material to be discoverable, defendant must have some type of legal right to the material plaintiff seeks to discover."[98]

---

94.   193 F.R.D. 633, 636 (D. Minn. 2000) (*quoting Bank of N.Y. v. Meridien BIAO Bank Tanzania, Ltd.*, 171 F.R.D. 135, 146 (S.D.N.Y. 1997)).

95.   *Id.*

96.   11 F.3d 1420, 1426–27 (7th Cir. 1993).

97.   130 F. Supp. 2d 726, 739 (E.D.N.C. 2000).

98.   *Id.*

c. Parties and Third–Party Data Stores

Obviously, the parties to litigation have an obligation to preserve relevant evidence, including ESI, as soon as the duty to preserve arises. Even before being formally named in a complaint, a person or entity that reasonably anticipates *becoming a party* to future litigation has the duty to preserve. Chapter II.C, *supra*, discusses when the duty arises.

But what are the obligations of parties to preserve relevant information they know is held by third parties? This question is particularly important in the context of ESI. Today, many businesses outsource their information technology needs, both maintaining day-to-day electronic data on servers owned and operated by third-party hosts and storing long-term inactive data, such as disaster recovery backup tapes and other archival data with vendors providing off-site storage.

In addition to evidence over which a party has direct care, custody or control, the duty to preserve may extend to evidence over which a party has indirect control. In *Cyntegra, Inc. v. Idexx Laboratories*, for example, the plaintiff filed an antitrust complaint against a competitor, alleging that it engaged in an unlawful tying scheme that harmed plaintiff's business. Plaintiff stored most of its electronic data on third-party servers run by a vendor, Net Nation. Because plaintiff was delinquent on payments to NetNation, the vendor deleted plaintiff's data from its servers. In sanctioning the plaintiff for NetNation's destruction of the evidence, the court held that:

> Plaintiff had sufficient control and legal right over the deleted files to constitute fault. Plaintiff contracted to store business documents on NetNation's computer servers. At least until ... payment was discontinued, Plaintiff could direct the flow of information to and from NetNation's servers. Because [Plaintiff's duty to preserve had already arisen at time payment was discontinued], it had an affirmative duty to make payments and preserve the evidence. Plaintiff cannot bypass this duty by abandoning its documents to a third-party and claiming lack of control. Plaintiff could have saved or printed the information after determining it could no longer make payments.... A contractual relationship with a third-party entity provides, at a minimum, an obligation to make reasonable inquiry of the third-party entity for the data at issue.... Plaintiff had sufficient, albeit indirect, control to preserve evidence, and by failing to do so, violated an affirmative duty.[99]

Similarly, one of the reasons that the NTL court faulted NTL Europe was that it gave documents it controlled and that should have been preserved to New NTL without any requirement that New NTL preserve the documents. Thus, the court was guarding against a litigant evading its preservation obligations by arguing that it no longer controlled the information.

---

99. *Cyntegra, Inc. v. Idexx Laboratories*, No. 06–4170, 2007 WL 5193736, at *5 (C.D. Cal. Sept. 21, 2007).

d. Parent, Subsidiary, and Affiliate Corporations

Courts generally hold that a parent corporation has a sufficient degree of ownership and control over a wholly-owned subsidiary such that the parent is deemed to have control over the subsidiary's documents.[100] This principle has been applied even when the subsidiary is not owned directly but, rather, is owned by an intermediate corporation that is itself a wholly-owned subsidiary of the parent corporation.[101]

In *Alcan International Limited v. S.A. Day Manufacturing Co.*, the court ordered a U.S. corporate defendant to produce documents in the possession of its foreign affiliate. The court stated that the U.S. and foreign companies "are corporate members of a unified worldwide business entity," issue consolidated financial statements, use the same corporate logo, and have regular contact regarding the issues in the case.[102] The court wrote: "It is 'inconceivable' that [the defendant] would not have access to this information and the ability to obtain it, not only for the purpose of proving its claims in this lawsuit but also for the purpose of conducting its business. . . ."[103]

The court reached a different result in *Goh v. Baldor Electric Co.* In that case, a dispute that involved activities in Asia, the plaintiffs sought to compel Ernst & Young LLP to produce documents from Ernst & Young Singapore and Ernst & Young Thailand. The court found that plaintiffs failed to meet their burden of showing control because the three companies, while part of a common association, operated separately. Ernst & Young Singapore and Ernst & Young Thailand "refused to turn over documents to Ernst & Young LLP in Dallas because it has a policy against voluntarily providing documents to be used in litigation."[104] The court ruled: "[W]here Ernst & Young's foreign entities have refused to voluntarily provide the documents in question, it necessarily follows that Ernst & Young LLP in Dallas does not have control over the documents."[105]

e. Control Imposed by Law

Control may be imposed by law. *Tomlinson v. El Paso Corp.* involved claims that the employer's actions relating to a pension plan violated ERISA. Plaintiffs sought discovery of certain data from a third-party benefits administrator, and the employer claimed that it neither pos-

---

100. *See, e.g., United States v. International Union of Petroleum & Indus. Workers*, 870 F.2d 1450, 1452 (9th Cir. 1989) ("A corporation must produce documents possessed by a subsidiary that the parent corporation owns or wholly controls."); *Camden Iron & Metal, Inc. v. Marubeni Am. Corp.*, 138 F.R.D. 438, 441 (D.N.J. 1991) (parent corporation has control over documents in physical control of wholly-owned or-controlled subsidiary); *In re Uranium Antitrust Litig.*, 480 F. Supp. 1138, 1152 (N.D. Ill. 1979) (corporate parent must produce documents of wholly-owned subsidiary but not documents of 43.8%-owned subsidiary that conducted its corporate affairs separately).

101. *See Lethbridge v. British Aerospace PLC*, No. 89 Civ. 1407, 1990 WL 194915, at *1 (S.D.N.Y. Nov. 28, 1990).

102. 176 F.R.D. 75, 79 (W.D.N.Y. 1996).

103. *Id.*

104. No. 3:98–064–T, 1999 WL 20943, at *3 (N.D. Tex. Jan. 13, 1999).

105. *Id.*

sessed nor controlled the data and, therefore, could not produce it. The court rejected the employer's argument. U.S. Department of Labor regulations applying to ERISA plans required that the employer maintain the data that plaintiffs sought. The court wrote:

> ERISA imposes upon the Defendants the duty to ensure that the "recordkeeping system has reasonable controls" such that its employee benefits records are "accessible . . . in such a manner as they may be readily inspected or examined." . . . Defendants cannot delegate their duties to a third party under ERISA. . . . Consequently, Defendants are in possession, custody or control over the requested data . . . such that they have, or should have, the authority and ability to obtain the requested data.[106]

f.   Control Based on Agency

Corporations may have a legal right to obtain documents from their agents. In *City of Seattle v. Professional Basketball Club, LLC*, plaintiff sought the production of documents, including e-mails, from members of the limited liability corporation. The court stated:

> Here, the question is whether the City has met its burden in establishing that PBC has a legal right to obtain documents from its members. That question turns on whether a principal-agent relationship exists between PBC and its members. . . .[107]

Applying Oklahoma law, the court examined the operating agreement applicable to PBC and determined that each member was a "manager" under Oklahoma law. The court concluded: "Because a manager is an agent . . . the requisite principal-agent relationship exists to establish that PBC has the legal right to obtain documents upon demand from its members."[108]

g.   Outside Directors

Most major U.S. corporations have outside directors as part of their boards. These directors may have material responsive to production requests. Do corporations have an obligation to preserve documents in the hands of outside directors, who are deliberately separate from the corporation? In *In re Triton Energy Limited Securities Litigation*, Triton did not inform its outside directors to preserve documents. Triton argued that it only had control over its employees and the documents within the employees' possession, and the outside directors were not employees. The court never answered the question of control, but instead stated: "The Court is of the opinion that it would have been prudent and within the spirit of the law for Triton to instruct is officers and directors to preserve and produce any documents in their possession, custody, or control."[109]

---

106.   245 F.R.D. 474, 477 (D. Colo. 2007).

107.   No. C07–1620, 2008 WL 539809, at *2 (W.D. Wash. Feb. 25, 2008).

108.   *Id.*

109.   No. 5:98CV256, 2002 WL 32114464, at *6 (E.D. Tex. Mar. 7, 2002).

h. Control Over Third Party Service Providers

In *Columbia Pictures v. Bunnell*, discussed in Chapter II.E, *supra*, defendants contracted with Panther, a third-party service provider, to serve as a "middleman" for people trying to access defendants' website. Plaintiffs sought server log data from defendants, and that data was in the hands of Panther. The Magistrate Judge concluded that defendants controlled the server log data:

> The record reflects that defendants have the ability to manipulate at will how the Server Log Data is routed. Consequently, the court concludes that even though the Server Log Data is now routed to Panther and is temporarily stored in Panther's RAM, the data remains in defendants' possession, custody or control.[110]

On appeal, the district court agreed with the Magistrate Judge's conclusion that defendants controlled the server log data: "As the record reflects that Defendants have the ability to reroute the Server Log Data through their own servers ... , the Court finds that the Magistrate Judge's finding that the Defendants' [sic] control the Server Log Data was not clearly erroneous."[111]

In *Keir v. Unumprovident Corp.*, the defendant failed to take the necessary steps to preserve back-up tapes in the possession of a third-party vendor. The plaintiffs sought the production of e-mails, which required the defendant to preserve certain back-up tapes maintained by IBM, a third-party vendor. Various errors and missteps resulted in the loss of certain potentially-relevant e-mails. While the court ultimately ruled that the mistakes were the "fault of no one," the court found that the defendant failed to consult with IBM to ensure that the relevant back-up tapes were preserved.[112]

i. Practice Note: Attorneys as Equals Before the Courts

At a hearing before the Magistrate Judge, counsel for NTL Europe consented to NTL Europe reviewing and producing documents held by New NTL.[113] NTL Europe moved for reconsideration, alleging that the attorney was "too junior to knowingly consent."[114] The Magistrate Judge rejected the argument: "Second-guessing a more junior attorney's representation to the Court is not a basis for a firm to seek reconsideration. It certainly is not a basis for the Court to grant it."[115]

---

110. No. CV 06-1093, 2007 WL 2080419 (C.D. Cal. May 29, 2007).

111. *Columbia Pictures, Inc. v. Bunnell*, 245 F.R.D. 443, 453 (C.D. Cal. 2007).

112. No. 02 Civ. 8781, 2003 WL 21997747, at *13 (S.D.N.Y. Aug. 22, 2003).

113. *See In re NTL, Inc.*, 244 F.R.D. at 189–90.

114. *Id.* at 190.

115. *Id.*

PROBLEMS

1.   Plaintiff sues defendant, a former employee, for violating a non-compete agreement and the Trade Secrets Act. Plaintiff alleges that prior to resigning, and in an effort to obtain employment, defendant repeatedly sent e-mails to one of plaintiff's competitors containing sensitive information. Plaintiff moved to compel defendant to produce the e-mails that he sent to the competitor, who is now defendant's employer. Does defendant control the documents that he sent to his new employer?

2.   Plaintiff sues defendant for employment discrimination. Defendant is a U.S. corporation and its parent corporation is a foreign corporation. Plaintiff seeks to compel the defendant to produce documents in the possession of the defendant's foreign parent corporation. Should defendant be compelled to produce documents in the possession of its foreign parent? What factors should be considered in deciding whether a subsidiary corporation should be compelled to produce documents in the possession of its parent corporation?

2.   What Is Possession?

PHILLIPS v. NETBLUE, INC.

No. C 05–4401, 2007 WL 174459 (N.D. Cal. Jan. 22, 2007)

CONTI, DISTRICT JUDGE

I.   Introduction

Plaintiff Ritchie Phillips, dba R & D Computers, ("Plaintiff") brings this suit against Netblue, Inc., formerly known as YFdirect, et al. ("Defendants") alleging violations of the Controlling the Assault of Non–Solicited Pornographic and Marketing ("CAN–SPAM") Act of 2003, 15 U.S.C. §§ 7701 et seq. and California Business and Professions Code §§ 17529 et seq. Presently before the Court is Defendants' Motion to Dismiss the Complaint for Plaintiff's Failure to Preserve Evidence.

II.   Background

* * *

All or most of the emails which form the basis of this action are not traditional text-based messages. Rather, they consist, in significant part, of hyperlinks. When the recipient opens the email, the recipient's email program reads some of these hyperlinks and displays images which reside on a remote web-server; the images themselves are not contained in the email, rather the email contains instructions which tells the recipient's email program to display the images contained on the server.

Other hyperlinks contained in the email, when clicked by the recipient, direct the recipient's web browser to an advertisement. However, frequently the recipient's web browser is not directly taken to an advertisement, but is first taken to an intermediary website, namely that of the advertiser's "affiliate" which sent the email. This site then automatically redirects the recipient's web browser to [the] advertisement located on the advertiser's server.

Defendants do not claim that Plaintiff destroyed any of the emails containing these hyperlinks. Rather, Defendants fault Plaintiff, first, for not preserving the images which these hyperlinks should display when the email is open, and claim that the hyperlinks contained on these emails can no longer be used to gather these images because "[m]any of the image files no longer exist on the remote web-servers." Defendants do not allege that Plaintiff has ever had possession or control of these remote web-servers.

Defendants also fault Plaintiff for not preserving the URLs from the series of websites to which a recipient's web browser would be directed upon clicking an advertisement link in the email. Defendants state that the advertisement links contained in the emails are no longer active, but make no claim that Plaintiff had any role in their deactivation.

III.   Legal Standard

* * *

Upon finding that a party has spoiled or destroyed evidence, a court may sanction it in one of three ways: by giving an adverse inference instruction to the jury; by excluding certain testimony which is based on the spoiled or destroyed evidence; or, in extreme or "outrageous" cases, dismissing the claim of the responsible party.

Fundamentally, a court's decision whether to sanction a party for allegedly spoiling or destroying evidence depends on a finding that the party had a duty to preserve the evidence in question, which it breached. Only after answering this question in the affirmative, need the court determine what, if any, sanctions are appropriate.

IV.   Discussion

Determining whether a party breached its duty of preservation requires a court to determine: 1) the scope of the accused party's duty of preservation, 2) whether the evidence in question falls within this scope, and 3) whether the actions taken by the accused party violated this duty.

As noted above, Defendants have not alleged that Plaintiff destroyed or spoiled the actual emails which they received, i.e. the email messages containing a combination of text and hyperlinks. Rather, Defendants argue that Plaintiff had the obligation to memorialize the emails as they would have appeared if opened in an email program soon after their receipt, i.e. with the images which the email program would have displayed upon automatically accessing the remote web-server where those images resided. Defendants further argue that Plaintiff had the affirmative obligation "to record the series of URLs ... to get to the final website," to which a recipient would be directed upon clicking the advertisement hyperlink in the email.

In other words, Defendants maintain that Plaintiff should have: 1) opened the emails they received; 2) then captured or recorded the images which Plaintiff's email program would have displayed upon opening the email and automatically following the hyperlinks it contained; 3) clicked on any advertisement hyperlink contained in the email; and 4) recorded the URLs of the websites to which Plaintiff's web browser would have been directed upon clicking the advertising link, including the URLs of websites which did not display any information to Plaintiff, but rather just directed Plaintiff's web browser to another website.

The absurdity of this argument is patent. * * * The fundamental factor is that the document, or other potential objects of evidence, must be in the party's possession, custody, or control for any duty to preserve to attach. * * * One cannot keep what one does not have.

Defendants do not complain that Plaintiff failed to keep safe from harm or destruction what Plaintiff had; they admit that Plaintiff retained the e-mails as they were sent to him. See Motion and Reply. Rather, they complain that Plaintiff did not memorialize other evidence to which the e-mails could have [led] Plaintiff. This is not a complaint regarding Plaintiff's alleged failure to preserve evidence, but rather Plaintiff's alleged failure to gather evidence. The law imposes no obligation upon a party to gather evidence other than the requirement that a party have sufficient evidence to support their claim. The question whether either party in this action has met that requirement is one which will be decided by the jury.

V. Conclusion

For the foregoing reasons, Defendants' Motion to Dismiss the Complaint for Plaintiff's Failure to Preserve Evidence is DENIED. * * *

COMMENTARY

a. Opportunity to Possess/Functional Control

In *In re WRT Energy Securities Litigation*, the court held that a party had a duty to preserve documents which it had been given an opportunity to possess but declined. In that case, as a result of a bankruptcy, Gulfport, a third party, acquired 1,100 boxes of documents that were being preserved as part of ongoing litigation. After the parties in the securities fraud case had reviewed the documents, Gulfport's general counsel notified the parties that it intended to destroy the documents because it would be leasing the warehouse in which they were being stored. None of the parties objected to Gulfport disposing of the documents.

After the documents had been destroyed, plaintiffs disclosed, for the first time, that their expert would be opining on additional topics, and the defendants objected because it no longer had access to the documents to refute plaintiffs' expert's new opinions. The court held that plaintiffs had an obligation to preserve the documents that were relevant to previously undisclosed expert topics despite the fact that plaintiffs neither had custody of the documents nor destroyed them. The court wrote:

> In the instant case, the plaintiffs . . . had functional control of the Gulfport documents since they were advised that the documents would be destroyed and were given the opportunity to take custody of them. Therefore, the preservation obligation attached.[116]

As a result of plaintiffs' failure to preserve the documents, the court ruled that plaintiffs could not contest key issues at trial, that defendants would receive an adverse inference instruction, and that plaintiffs must pay for defendants' attorneys' fees associated with the motion as well as for new analyses that defendants' expert had to perform.

b. Access Alone Does Not Equal Possession

In *In re Kuntz*, the Texas Supreme Court ruled, in a divorce proceeding, that access alone does not equal possession. In an effort to enforce a settlement agreement, the wife sought discovery about royalty payments to which the husband was entitled. The documents belonged to MOXY (an oil company) and were in the possession of CLK, a consulting firm in which the husband was a manager and minority owner. Additionally, the documents contained trade secrets and the consulting agreement between MOXY and CLK obligated CLK to maintain the confidentiality of the documents.

The husband asserted that "in his individual capacity, he does not have physical possession of the requested documents and has no legal right to obtain the documents from either CLK or MOXY."[117] The wife argued the opposite, stating that the "testimony in this case was un-equivocal that the [documents] were in the [husband's] offices and he could get them anytime he wants."[118] The Texas Supreme Court agreed with the husband:

> [Husband], an employee of CLK, lacks both physical possession of MOXY's trade secret [documents] or any "right to possess" MOXY's trade secret [documents]. At best, all [husband] has is access to MOXY's trade secret [documents] and that access is strictly limited to use of the [documents] in furtherance of his employer's services performed for MOXY. Like a bank teller with access to cash in the vault, [husband] has neither possession nor any right to possess MOXY's trade secret [documents].[119]

---

116. *In re WRT Energy Sec. Litig.*, 246 F.R.D. 185, 195 (S.D.N.Y. 2007).

117. *In re Kuntz*, 124 S.W.3d 179, 183 (Tex. 2003).

118. *Id.*

119. *Id.* at 183–84.

c. Possession Does Not Require Ownership

It is actual possession, not ownership, that determines whether a party must produce documents. In *In re Bankers Trust Co.*, a bank claimed that it could not produce documents in its possession because the Federal Reserve had provided the documents to the bank and maintained ownership over the documents. The court rejected the argument, stating that the bank was in "actual possession" of the documents and that "legal ownership ... is not determinative."[120]

The bank also claimed that it could not produce the documents because a federal regulation forbade the bank from doing so. The court also rejected this argument. While recognizing that "federal regulations should be adhered to and given full force ... whenever possible," the court found that the Federal Reserve, which promulgated the regulation in question, did not have "the power to promulgate federal regulations in direct contravention of the Federal Rules of Civil Procedure."[121] The court concluded, "Congress did not empower the Federal Reserve to prescribe regulations that direct a party to deliberately disobey a court order, subpoena, or other judicial mechanism requiring the production of information."[122]

Similarly, in *United States v. National Broadcasting Co.*, a dispute arose over former President Nixon's documents. The court wrote: "It must be noted that any determinations made by this Court regarding the motions before it does not involve the question of 'ownership' of former President Nixon's documents. What is involved here is the 'possession, custody and control' of these documents."[123]

PROBLEM

1. Would the result have been different in *In re Kuntz* had the husband been sued in his capacity as a manager and owner of the consulting firm? Why?

---

120. *In re Bankers Trust Co.*, 61 F.3d 465, 469 (6th Cir. 1995).

121. *Id.* at 469–70.

122. *Id.* at 470.

123. *United States v. National Broad. Co.*, 65 F.R.D. 415, 419–20 (C.D. Cal. 1974).

III

MEET AND CONFER (RULE 26(F)) AND INITIAL SCHEDULING CONFERENCE (RULE 16)

■ ■ ■

IN RE SEROQUEL PRODUCTS LIABILITY LITIGATION

244 F.R.D. 650 (M.D. Fla. 2007)

BAKER, MAGISTRATE JUDGE

In this multidistrict litigation, Plaintiffs have sued Defendants for claims arising for alleged injuries from ingesting AstraZeneca's Seroquel, an atypical anti-psychotic medication that allegedly can cause diabetes and related disorders.

Plaintiffs have moved for sanctions based on AstraZeneca's "failure to timely comply with numerous discovery obligations since the inception of this litigation" based on four categories of conduct. Plaintiffs base their Motion for Sanctions, first, on AZ's failure to produce, in a readable format, key elements of the IND/NDA [Investigational New Drug/New Drug Applications prepared for the FDA] in November 2006 as ordered, [and] not producing a key element until June 2007. Second, Plaintiffs contend that AZ failed to produce organizational charts by January 2006 as ordered and withheld the vast majority of them until May 14, 2007. Third, Plaintiffs argue AZ failed to identify all relevant databases which it was obligated to identify in January 2007, instead identifying only a fraction; to date, Plaintiffs have now identified fifty-nine relevant databases. Fourth, Plaintiffs' strongest contention is that, although AZ was to produce electronic discovery from its self-chosen "custodians"—those employees most knowledgeable about Seroquel and its development—AZ waited until mid-May to begin production of the overwhelming majority of the documents and the documents actually produced have significant errors of omission and were not readable or searchable.

* * *

I. Background

This multidistrict litigation was transferred to the Middle District of Florida by the Judicial Panel on Multidistrict Litigation on July 10, 2006.

Doc. No. 1. On August 15, 2006, Judge Conway entered an order setting the first pretrial status and discovery conference for September 7, 2006. At that hearing there was a substantial discussion as to expectations for the progress of discovery. It was the Court's expectation that the indisputably relevant material would be produced quickly and without difficulty, despite its volume. Counsel for AZ requested 60 days to complete electronic formatting of the NDA and IND. This extra time was deemed necessary to eliminate the possibility of being unable to meet the Court's deadlines. The Court's reliance on experienced counsels' ability to accomplish routine matters routinely and timely was in vain.

During the status conference held on November 20, 2006, the Court requested that the parties meet and confer "to submit either agreed proposals to cover document preservation, production protocol and resolution of this issue about formatting of things already produced by December 5, 2006." However, instead of submitting an agreed proposal for production protocol and formatting, the parties submitted competing proposals apparently without a good faith conference * * *. Three days before the December 8, 2006 status conference, the parties finally began discussions about electronic documents being produced with searchable load files, bates-stamped TIFF's[1] and various metadata fields. Following the status conferences before the Court on December 11—which the Court had to adjourn and carry over to December 12, 2006 because the parties had been unable to agree ahead of time—the parties proposed a Joint Motion to adopt two case management orders [hereafter CMO2].

The Joint Motion stated, "It is the stated policy of AZ counsel, and its client, [ ] commensurate with the goals of these MDL cases[,] get to Plaintiffs' counsel *in a timely manner* and in *a format usable* the necessary production documents that the opposing side will need to help them develop, evaluate, and understand their cases for purposes of ultimate prosecution and/or dismissal of cases." * * * On its face, the proposal did that. Unfortunately, AZ has not lived up to producing discovery in a timely manner or useable format.

The proposed CMO 2 submitted by the parties set forth deadlines for AstraZeneca's production of organizational charts for its corporate structure, the Seroquel team, and the drug safety team for the past ten years; listings of 80 (eighty) custodians from whom it is collecting documents; listing of databases concerning document production and preservation; timing for interviews of knowledgeable AstraZeneca IT persons, and the parties' agreed format of the production of custodial files. As the Court commented at the time, "The failure of the Defen-

---

1. TIFF (Tagged Image File Format) is one of the most widely used and supported graphic file formats for storing bit-mapped images, with many different compression formats and resolutions. A TIFF file is characterized by its "tif" file name extension. The Sedona Conference Glossary for E–Discovery and Digital Information Management (The Sedona Conference Working Group Series, May 2005 Version), available at http://www.thesedonaconference.org; cited in *Williams v. Sprint/United Management Co.* 230 F.R.D. 640. 643 (D. Kan. 2005).

dant to investigate and understand its own records and documents and to prepare them for production has not met the expectations of the Court as discussed at the September 2006 Conference." The Court also commented on its misgivings as to the "proposed CMO 2 regarding production and preservation of Defendant's documents, [which] still seems unduly cumbersome. Nonetheless, if the parties are confident that their agreement will allow them to present issues to the Court for appropriate consideration and disposition without delays engendered by claims of non production of information, the proposal can be approved."

On January 26, 2007, Judge Conway entered CMO 2, portions of which were adopted verbatim from the parties' proposed CMO 2. That order set forth specific undertakings and obligations regarding provision of discovery without the need for separate requests under the rules of procedure. Matters included a schedule for production of organizational charts; identification of AZ's first round of eight chosen witnesses, all of whose documents would be produced earliest; AZ's identification of relevant databases (including informal interviews with AZ's IT staff); the required format for electronic documents (including required metadata fields); and deduplication of documents.

On April 26, 2007, Plaintiffs filed their Motion to Compel Defendants to Provide Complete Certified Production of the First Eight Custodial Files and All Other Custodial Files Produced to Date; * * * The Court denied the Motion to Compel without prejudice to allow the parties time to confer "in good faith and *in extenso*" on the issues described in the Motion to Compel; the Court also set an evidentiary hearing on the matters raised in the Motion for June 13, 2007, alerting the parties:

> ANY PARTY WHOSE CONDUCT NECESSITATES THE EVIDENTIARY HEARING SHOULD EXPECT THE IMPOSITION OF SANCTIONS FOR ANY UNREASONABLE OR INAPPROPRIATE CONDUCT OR POSITION TAKEN WITH RESPECT TO THESE MATTERS.

On June 8, 2007, the evidentiary hearing was canceled based on the parties' Joint Statement of Resolved Issues and Notice that a Hearing is Not Required filed on June 7, 2007. At that time, Plaintiffs accepted the representations made by AZ that corrections would be made to the problems Plaintiffs identified in the Motion to Compel, *e.g.*, load files, metadata, bates numbering, page breaks, excel spreadsheets, and blank documents; the CANDA [Computer Assisted New Drug Application, filed with the FDA] would also be produced; and the parties would continue to confer on the database production.

However, less than one month later, on July 3, 2007, Plaintiffs filed their Motion for Sanctions, one business day before the July 5, 2007 Status Conference. * * *

II. Legal Framework

Standards for Electronic Discovery in Complex Litigation

As businesses increasingly rely on electronic record keeping, the number of potential discoverable documents has skyrocketed and so also has the potential for discovery abuse. Of even more consequence in this complex litigation is the fact that it involves development of a drug that spent many years in development by an international corporation and has been distributed worldwide, with the number of Plaintiffs in this multi-district litigation exceeding 6,500. The Manual for Complex Litigation (Fourth Edition) provides the following guidance for dealing with such vast amounts of data:

> Computerized data have become commonplace in litigation. The sheer volume of such data, when compared with conventional paper documentation, can be staggering. . . . One gigabyte is the equivalent of 500,000 type-written pages. Large corporate computer networks create backup data measured in terabytes, or 1,000,000 megabytes; each terabyte represents the equivalent of 500 billion [sic] typewritten pages of plain text.

> Digital or electronic information can be stored in any of the following: mainframe computers, network servers, personal computers, hand-held devices, automobiles, or household appliances; or it can be accessible via the Internet, from private networks, or from third parties. Any discovery plan must address issues relating to such information, including the search for it and its location, retrieval, form of production, inspection, preservation, and use at trial.

* * *

> The judge should encourage the parties to discuss the scope of proposed computer-based discovery early in the case, particularly any discovery of data beyond that available to the responding parties in the ordinary course of business. The requesting parties should identify the information they require as narrowly and precisely as possible, and the responding parties should be forthcoming and explicit in identifying what data are available from what sources, to allow formulation of a realistic computer-based discovery plan. Rule 26(b)(2)(C)(iii) allows the court to limit or modify the extent of otherwise allowable discovery if the burdens outweigh the likely benefit—the rule should be used to discourage costly, speculative, duplicative, or unduly burdensome discovery of computer data and systems. . . .

* * *

MANUAL FOR COMPLEX LITIGATION § 11.446, *Discovery of Computerized Data* (Fourth Ed. 2004).

Against the backdrop of the heightened demands for usability and searchability of the electronic discovery produced in a multi-district case, is the need for the parties to confer on the format of the production, keeping in mind that the responding party is best situated to evaluate the procedures, and the need to produce the information in a reasonably usable form to enable the receiving party to have the same ability to access, search, and display the information.

Particularly in complex litigation, there is a heightened need for the parties to confer about the format of the electronic discovery being produced. Pursuant to Federal Rule of Civil Procedure 26, the parties are expected to confer, not only on the nature and basis of their claims and defenses, but also to discuss "any issues relating to disclosure or discovery or electronically stored information, including the form or forms in which it should be produced." FED. R. CIV. P. 26(f)(3). Rule 26(f) was amended on December 1, 2006 to direct the parties to discuss discovery of electronically stored information during their discovery-planning conference. FED. R. CIV. P. 26(f) advisory committee notes. * * * According to Rule 26:

> It may be important for the parties to discuss their systems, and accordingly important for counsel to become familiar with those systems before the conference. With that information, the parties can develop a discovery plan that takes into account the capabilities of their computer systems. In appropriate cases identification of, and early discovery from, individuals with special knowledge of a party's computer systems may be helpful.

> * * * For example, the parties may specify the topics for such discovery and the time period for which discovery will be sought. They may identify the various sources of such information within a party's control that should be searched for electronically stored information. They may discuss whether the information is reasonably accessible to the party that has it, including the burden or cost of retrieving and reviewing the information. Rule 26(f)(3) explicitly directs the parties to discuss the form or forms in which electronically stored information might be produced. The parties may be able to reach agreement on the forms of production, making discovery more efficient.* * *

FED. R. CIV. P. 26(f)(3), Committee Note.

A leading resource on dealing with electronic discovery is the Second Edition of the Sedona Principles, on which AZ relied at the July 26, 2007 hearing on the Motion for Sanctions. Principle 3 states, "Parties should confer early in discovery regarding the preservation and production of electronically stored information when these matters are at issue in the litigation and seek to agree on the scope of each party's rights and responsibilities." *The Sedona Principles, Second Edition: Best Practices, Rec-*

ommendations & Principles for Addressing Electronic Document Discovery (The Sedona Conference Working Group Series, 2007).[2]

* * *

III. Contentions and Analysis

* * *

Particular Issues

1. IND/NDA—Plaintiffs contend that AZ failed to produce a key element of the IND/NDA in November 2006 as ordered, not producing it until June 2007, and the materials produced were not in usable form. At the September 7, 2006 hearing, AZ stated that the electronic formatting of the IND/DNA had begun. The Court allowed AZ until November 7, 2006 to produce it even though, as the Court pointed out, much of the material had been produced to the FDA in electronic format and should have been prepared for production earlier. Plaintiffs contend they had to spend "nearly two months of work" to make it suitable for substantive review and the production omitted the CANDA safety database—which was not produced until June 8, 2007.

Plaintiff[s'] expert and fact witness, Jonathan Jaffe, testified that on November 15, 2007, Plaintiffs realized the IND/NDA production was not searchable for several reasons: no metadata was retrieved; there were multi-page TIFF images, some of which consisted of more than 20,000 pages; there was nothing showing bates numbering; 8% of the entire production was in one lengthy document which could only be opened with a very powerful work station; and there were no load files; thus the production was not in a usable or searchable format. At that point, on November 17, 2006, Mr. Jaffe sent to AZ's counsel an email suggesting fixes to the IND/NDA. As of nine months later, or the date of the July 26, 2007 hearing, AZ had not fixed problems according to Mr. Jaffe, whose team attempted to fix problems themselves by splitting apart the documents and redoing the bates numbering. AZ had offered to do it for $26,000 over 6 weeks; it took Mr. Jaffe's team more than a month with a few dedicated team members.

Mr. Jaffe further testified that in November to December 2006, Plaintiffs asked for electronic documents in native or near native format, with metadata, and extracted text and image files, that had page breaks in it. Mr. Jaffe * * * described extensive efforts to resolve technical issues. Mr. Jaffe made multiple requests to speak to technical people, but he was told there was no IT person with whom he could confer regarding the IT issues.[4] * * *

---

2. The Sedona Conference is a nonprofit legal policy research and educational organization which sponsors Working Groups on cutting-edge issues of law. The Working Group on Electronic Document Production is comprised of judges, attorneys, and technologists experienced in electronic discovery and document management matters.

4. AZ's refusal to allow contact between individuals with appropriate technical backgrounds as part of the effort to resolve technical issues is an inexplicable departure from the requirements of Rule 26, the Sedona Principles and this Court's expressed expectations.

* * *

3. Database Production—Plaintiffs argue AZ failed to identify all relevant databases by January 5, 2007, which it was obligated to do pursuant to CMO 2; instead AZ identified only 15 databases. However, to date, Plaintiffs have identified fifty-nine relevant databases through additional interviews, depositions, and meetings. Plaintiffs contend that AZ has produced no information whatsoever from any of these databases, and they are resisting producing databases without Requests for Production. Plaintiffs requested basic information about each database in order to assist with prioritization, formatting and production—information which, by its own admission, AZ refused to provide until July 2, 2007.

AZ responds that it should not be sanctioned because Plaintiffs have "not even served AZ with any discovery requests for wholesale production of the databases," AZ has not violated an order to produce, and it only identified a small number of databases initially because they only had to identify those that correlated to the 14 discrete categories identified by Plaintiffs. In addition, AZ has produced IT witnesses for informal interviews and four days of 30(b)(6) depositions about AZ databases.

CMO 2 required that, by January 5, 2007, AstraZeneca provide Plaintiffs with a list of databases of the following type: 1) adverse event database; 2) sales call tracking database; 3) IMS database; 4) clinical communications database; 5) regulatory database; 6) regulatory contact databases; 7) clinical trial database; 8) medical literature database; 9) research report database; 10) documentum or similar databases (document management systems used by many pharmacy companies); 11) visitor speakers bureau and/or thought leader databases; 12) clinical payments database; 13) field force rosters; and 14) instant message, voicemail, discussion forum and prior website page databases, transcripts and recovery.

By January 25, 2007, AstraZeneca was required to allow Plaintiffs to conduct informal interviews, in person or by telephone, of a knowledgeable AstraZeneca-employed IT person or persons who can adequately address plaintiffs' questions about said databases and how information can potentially be produced or extracted from them. "If, after any such interview, Plaintiffs determine that the individual cannot adequately answer their questions or does not have the requisite knowledge about the database in question, plaintiffs shall identify the issues for which they seek additional information, and AstraZeneca shall promptly identify an IT employee with knowledge of such issues and present that person for interview." AZ's identification of the databases would not be construed as an agreement to produce them; the parties were to confer regarding the discoverability and feasibility of any request for production of a database, including the form and scope of any such production.

Testimony from the only two witnesses presented[6] who had any involvement in the discovery process (as well as the exhibits) establishes that, with respect to identification and production of relevant portions of databases, "what we have here is failure to communicate." Worse, the posturing and petulance displayed by both sides on this issue shows a disturbing departure from the expected professionalism necessary to get this case ready for appropriate disposition. Identifying relevant records and working out technical methods for their production is a cooperative undertaking, not part of the adversarial give and take. This is not to say that the parties cannot have reasonable disputes regarding the scope of discovery. But such disputes should not entail endless wrangling about simply identifying what records exist and determining their format. This case includes a myriad of significant legal issues and complexities engendered by the number of plaintiffs. Dealing as effective advocates representing adverse interests on those matters is challenge enough. It is not appropriate to seek an advantage in the litigation by failing to cooperate in the identification of basic evidence. The parties' mode of proceeding here has prevented the presentation of any genuine issues as to the proper scope of production of material from databases. Both parties must bear some of the responsibility for the breakdown, but it is primarily AZ, as the creator and owner of the information, which has failed to make a sincere effort to facilitate an understanding of what records are kept and what their availability might be.

The Court finds sanctions are warranted for AZ's violation of the Court's explicit order in CMO 2 that the Plaintiffs were to interview AZ's IT employees and[,] if [ ] they still had questions after the interview, would identify the issues for which they still needed information, and AstraZeneca was to identify an IT employee with the relevant knowledge. In addition, the parties were to confer regarding the discoverability and feasibility of any request for production of a database. Based on the testimony of Mr. Jaffe, Plaintiffs' interviews of the AZ IT employees left questions about the databases unanswered because they were not clear or specific. Plaintiffs' attempt to get further clarification through the chart was within the bounds of conferring further under CMO 2.

* * * AZ stopped participating in the process to confer on the databases despite its explicit agreement to produce them and to cooperate in providing personnel familiar for Plaintiffs to interview to determine which ones to seek production of. [AZ's representative testified that] AZ never intended to produce databases, it would only produce some subset of information; yet he emailed Plaintiffs' counsel that AZ would work cooperatively with Plaintiffs on production of databases. AZ's failure to cooperate in identification leading to appropriate produc-

---

6. AZ's decision to offer only the testimony of a junior level attorney, only somewhat versed in technical issues and one who came late to the process is puzzling. AZ provided essentially no information as to how it organized its search for relevant material, what steps it took to assure reasonable completeness and quality control. Its efforts at finding solutions to technical problems are likewise unilluminated.

tion of its relevant databases is conduct sanctionable under Rule 37. The relief to be awarded will be dealt with separately.

4. Custodial Production—AZ's biggest failure has been what can properly be characterized as "purposeful sluggishness" in the production from its self-chosen "custodians"—those employees most knowledgeable about Seroquel and its development. Plaintiffs contend AZ waited until mid-May 2007 to begin production of the overwhelming majority of the documents from these "custodians" and the documents produced have significant errors of omission and are not readable or searchable. Plaintiffs contend that the custodial production has a great deal of missing data, *e.g.*, although AstraZeneca has a system to deliver voicemail, faxes, and video into Outlook inboxes, none has been produced; there are few emails from some custodians, and email boxes are missing from alternate email boxes. Plaintiffs also contend that many relevant emails and documents were not identified and produced because AZ performed an unreasonable key word search.[7] Plaintiffs allege that other relevant documents were omitted because the best available de-duplication method was not used; AZ missed deadlines and produced the electronic documents late; a significant portion of the production had blank pages; new load files were not searchable, in part because the date formats in the metadata were inconsistently loaded and email attachments not consistently associated or identified; authors were not identified as custodians for files; transposed metadata recipients/authors; and no page breaks were inserted in 3.75 million pages.

AZ responds that Plaintiffs have not met the standard for imposing sanctions, which is bad faith. AZ argues that Plaintiffs' discovery issues have been a moving target, and that issues raised by Plaintiffs have been resolved or "in the process of being resolved" by July 20, 2007. AZ has produced "massive" amounts of discovery—10 million pages[8]—with few mistakes and by the June 30, 2007 deadline. AZ argues that Plaintiffs were aware that it was using search terms to limit the "custodians" discovery to identify potentially responsive electronic documents, citing the Sedona Principles. AZ contends that it gave Plaintiffs a list of its 60 search terms in April 2007 and if Plaintiffs wanted AZ to use additional terms, Plaintiff could have simply asked for them. * * *

* * *

The record shows a number of specific failings in AZ's chosen efforts to meet its discovery commitments. The key word search was plainly inadequate. Attachments, including non-verbal files, were not provided. Relevant emails were omitted. AZ's deduplication method

---

7. Examples include omitting Seroquel's generic name, acronyms for diabetes, hyperglycaemia spelled the British way; and endocrine. The search method apparently failed to include common misspellings or the singular forms of words and failed to make allowance for spaces or dashes.

8. In argument, AZ has repeatedly relied on the sheer volume of documents produced as an accomplishment somehow justifying its shortcomings. In the context of this case, the Court is not impressed by the large number of relevant documents, especially since vast quantities were produced in a virtually unusable manner.

remains mysterious. Production was tardy. AZ's efforts in preventing and solving technical problems were woefully deficient. These shortcomings were adequately and persuasively described by Plaintiffs' witnesses. * * *

AZ purported to embrace the requirements of Rule 26 and the Sedona Principles. However, the reality was to the contrary. For example, while key word searching is a recognized method to winnow relevant documents from large repositories, use of this technique must be a cooperative and informed process. Rather than working with Plaintiffs from the outset to reach agreement on appropriate and comprehensive search terms and methods, AZ undertook the task in secret. Common sense dictates that sampling and other quality assurance techniques must be employed to meet requirements of completeness. If AZ took such steps, it has not identified or validated them.

Many of the other technical problems * * * likely could have been resolved far sooner and less expensively had AZ cooperated by fostering consultation between the technical staffs responsible for production. Instead, AZ shielded its third party technical contractor from all contact with Plaintiffs. This approach is antithetical to the Sedona Principles and is not an indicium of good faith.

This is not to say that AZ completely ignored its responsibilities. Mr. Dupre [a lawyer representing AZ] and other representatives from his firm did participate in extended efforts to confer with Plaintiffs. However, the lateness and general ineffectuality of these efforts was demonstrated by Mr. Dupre's concessions as to the limitations of his role. Mr. Dupre admitted on cross-examination that he had nothing to do with developing the key word search in this case and had never prepared any other key word search before; he did not know who was the architect of the key word search. Despite this lack of knowledge, he was confident that he knew how the emails were collected. Mr. Dupre also had no knowledge of how the 80 "custodians" were chosen. In response to a query from the Court, Mr. Dupre could not identify with certainty who was responsible from AZ or its counsel or vendor for assuring document production had been sufficient to comply with the Local Rules and the Sedona Principles. In terms of the documentation about how the key word search was developed, Mr. Dupre testified that AZ used [a] stock interview for "custodians"; but he was not privy to any sort of written protocol. He testified that there was no document production quality control or master plan with which he was familiar. He testified that the vendor never discussed the key word list with Plaintiff, and that vendors never participated in a meet and confer, although IT experts from lawyers attended the meet and confer.

* * *

Sanctions may be imposed against AZ under Rule 37(b)(2) based on its noncompliance with a court order, notwithstanding a lack of willfulness or bad faith, although such factors "are relevant . . . to the sanction to be imposed for the failure." 8A Charles Alan Wright, Arthur R. Miller & Richard L. Marcus, FEDERAL PRACTICE & PROCEDURE § 2283, at 608 (2d ed. 1994). * * * "Sanctions proceedings can be disruptive, costly, and may create personal antagonism inimical to an atmosphere of cooperation. Moreover, a resort to sanctions may reflect a breakdown of case management.... On the other hand, *the stakes involved in and the pressures generated by complex litigation may lead some parties to violate the rules.* Although sanctions should not generally be a case management tool, a willingness to resort to sanctions, *sua sponte* if necessary, may ensure compliance with the management program.... Although sanctions should be a last resort, they are sometimes unavoidable and may be imposed for general or specific deterrence, to punish, or to remedy the consequences of misconduct." *Id.*

Based on the testimony at the hearing, the Court is troubled by nature of the parties' efforts to "meet and confer" on specific issues. One of the apparently successful efforts to collaborate on discovery, which led to cancellation of the June hearing, was, to an unacceptable degree, illusory. AZ suspects that Plaintiffs have, to some degree, attempted to manufacture issues and to raise them just prior to scheduled status conferences so as to tarnish AZ in the eyes of the Court. This mistrust undermines the efficacy of the meet and confer requirement. AZ itself, despite what must be considerable expenditures in attempting to comply with discovery, has failed to bring appropriate personnel to the table at appropriate times to resolve non adversarial issues.

In this case, AZ never discussed with Plaintiffs which search terms to use as part of the search. There was no dialogue to discuss the search terms, as required by Rules 26 and 34. AZ eventually disclosed in April 2007 that a key word search had been conducted, not in seeking collaboration on the words to use, but rather as part of the dialogue on certifying the "custodial" production. More astounding is AZ's continued failure to produce single-page TIFF documents that would be "usable" or "reasonably accessible" in accordance with the federal discovery rules and the Sedona Principles. AZ's interpretation of CMO 2, that it did not explicitly require page breaks, is absurd—Mr. Dupre could not explain any other way the documents would be guaranteed to appear as "single pages." Mr. Dupre attributed many of the severe problems with the load files and the metadata to vendor errors. According to the Sedona Principles cited by AZ several times at the hearing, a party is responsible for the errors of its vendors. [Sedona Principle 6d]. Moreover, such problems in fundamental aspects of the production, worked on by different vendors, were inevitable in a 10 million page without the requisite quality control oversight.

CONCLUSION

The Court finds that AZ has been "purposely sluggish" in making effective production to Plaintiffs. Given the Court's mandate of a tight schedule in this case, AZ's various decisions and problems that resulted in this sluggishness appears to have benefitted AZ by limiting the time available to Plaintiffs to review information and to follow up.

* * *

> [A]s a discovery deadline or trial date draws near, discovery conduct that might have been considered "merely" discourteous at an earlier point in the litigation may well breach a party's duties to its opponent and to the court.... [When defendant] had repeatedly missed deadlines to produce the e-mails—[defendant] was under an obligation to be as co-operative as possible. Viewed in that light, [defendant's] "purposefully sluggish" acts—particularly its as-yet-unexplained refusal to answer basic technical questions about the tape until prompted to do so by the District Court—may well have constituted sanctionable misconduct in their own right.

Residential Funding Corp. v. DeGeorge Financial Corp., 306 F.3d 99, 112 (2d Cir. 2002).

Similarly, in this case, AZ has not been as cooperative as possible in resolving the custodial issues. It is undisputed that the production "completed" on June 30, 2007 had load file, metadata, page break and key word search problems, making the 10 million pages of documents unaccessible, unsearchable, and unusable as contemplated under the Rules. It was not clear at the July 26 hearing, or even as of the date of this Order, that these profound technical issues have been resolved by the re-production efforts delivered to Plaintiffs on July 20, 2007. The Court finds that sanctions are warranted for AZ's failure to produce "usable" or "reasonably accessible" documents.

However, the Court is unable to determine the appropriate nature and amount of sanctions at this time. Plaintiffs will be allowed a further opportunity to present evidence and argument as to any prejudice or damages from AZ's failure timely to produce "usable" or "reasonably accessible" documents in this litigation, including motion costs.

COMMENTARY

As demonstrated by *In re Seroquel*, the various volume, formatting, readability, and searchability issues surrounding ESI can present difficult problems for litigants, potentially creating time-consuming and expensive discovery disputes. Consequently, courts increasingly interpret Rule 26 to require the parties to cooperate and communicate to avoid these potential problems. The 2006 Amendments to Rule 26 have impliedly removed the adversarial element from the Rule 26(f) discovery conference or "meet and confer." Recent cases indicate that attorneys, who up until recently often treated discovery as just another phase in the adversarial process, have been slow to recognize that Rule 26 now encourages cooperation and transparency in electronic discovery practices.

The meet and confer(s) called for by Rule 26(f) work in conjunction with the parties' Rule 16 pretrial conference with the court. Specifically,

Rule 26(f)(1) requires the parties to meet and confer to develop a proposed discovery plan prior to the Rule 16 pretrial conference, typically scheduled by the court at the outset of the litigation for the purpose of creating a scheduling order for discovery and other pretrial matters. After the Rule 26(f) meet and confer, the parties must submit a written report to the court outlining a proposed discovery plan for the litigation. At the Rule 16 pretrial conference, the parties meet with the court to discuss, among other matters, the proposed discovery schedule and any anticipated discovery disputes. After the Rule 16 conference, the court issues a scheduling order, generally based in part on the parties' report, containing deadlines that will govern the timing of discovery and, potentially, provisions relating to the retrieval and pro-duction of ESI. The Rule 26(f) discovery conference is not merely a perfunctory exercise. Rather, it is an opportunity for the parties to educate themselves and their adversaries, anticipate and resolve elec-tronic discovery disputes before they escalate, expedite the progress of their case, and assess and manage litigation costs. As a matter of strategy, the Rule 26(f) discovery conference provides the parties an opportunity to prepare themselves for the Rule 16 pretrial conference, so that they can demonstrate to the court that they have made diligent, good faith efforts to comply with the Rules and the court's policies and that they are, therefore, deserving of its confidence.

The obligation to address electronic discovery at the Rule 26(f) meet and confer rests with the litigants. The 2006 Amendments do not *require* judges to address electronic discovery in the Rule 16 scheduling order. Perhaps due to this flexibility, the attention paid by courts to litigants' meet and confer obligations varies widely across jurisdictions and from judge to judge. This may seem surprising given the ubiquity of electron-ic discovery disputes, but a survey of the relevant case law yields opinions that focus on electronic discovery in widely varying degrees. Likewise, some jurisdictions have promulgated local rules containing exhaustive lists of topics to be addressed by the parties at a Rule 26(f) meet and confer, while others limit their treatment of the issue to a simple verbatim recitation of Rule 26(f). Some courts defer heavily to the "best practices" and guidelines published by organizations such as The Sedona Conference and the American Bar Association. The following notes discuss some of the issues courts and litigants are addressing with regard to Rule 26(f).

1. The importance of the Rule 26(f) meet and confer is indirectly underscored by Rule 16(f)(1)(B), which authorizes a court to impose sanctions on a party or its attorney if either "is substantially unprepared to participate—or does not participate in good faith—in the [Rule 16 pretrial] conference." Although this provision was not directly affected by the 2006 Amendments, it incorporates by reference portions of Rule 16 and Rule 26 that were revised to address electronic discovery, effectively holding litigants to a higher standard of preparedness with regard to electronic discovery matters by subjecting them to a risk of

sanctions for failure to sufficiently prepare for the Rule 16 pretrial conference.

The *Seroquel* case provides one example of a party's failure to live up to a court's Rule 16 expectations. Almost a year before writing the *Seroquel* opinion, the Magistrate Judge admonished the parties for failing to resolve their discovery and scheduling issues through the meet and confer process. Significantly, the Magistrate Judge noted that he was "flabbergasted as to how unprepared the parties [were]." Though neither party was sanctioned under Rule 16(f)(1)(B), the parties' pretrial disappointments caused the court to lose confidence in them, and its frustration with their conduct weighed heavily against them at later stages in the litigation.

If your adversary does not place a sufficient level of importance on electronic discovery, how might you nonetheless sufficiently prepare for the Rule 16 pretrial conference? Should you be prepared to discuss your client's systems, even though your adversary has not requested information about them? How might you document your efforts, and your adversary's disinterest, to protect you and your client should electronic discovery problems arise in the future?

2.   The practical purpose of the Rule 26(f) meet and confer requirement is to facilitate the early identification of electronic discovery issues for the purpose of preventing expensive and time-consuming discovery disputes. Once identified, the parties must be prepared to discuss any potentially problematic electronic discovery issues at the Rule 16 pretrial conference. The Advisory Committee Note to Rule 16 discusses the interplay between the two rules:

> The amendment to Rule 16(b) is designed to alert the court to the possible need to address the handling of discovery of electronically stored information early in the litigation if such discovery is expected to occur. Rule 26(f) is amended to direct the parties to discuss discovery of electronically stored information if such discovery is contemplated in the action. * * * In many instances, the court's involvement early in the litigation will help avoid difficulties that might otherwise arise.

If parties fail to adequately address electronic discovery issues during the Rule 26(f) meet and confer, and as a result, fail to identify to the court during the Rule 16 pretrial conference any anticipated electronic discovery issues, should they be precluded from raising any later-identified electronic discovery problems as the basis for a discovery motion? Suppose the later-identified problems could have been addressed inexpensively and efficiently had the parties bothered to discuss them at the Rule 26(f) meet and confer?

3.   In *O'Bar v. Lowe's Home Centers, Inc.*, the court provided the parties lengthy and detailed "guidelines" to follow during and after

their Rule 26(f) meet and confer.[1] For example, the court directed the parties to meet and confer on the following issues, among others:

A. The anticipated scope of requests for, and objections to, production of [ESI], as well as the form of production of ESI and, specifically, but without limitation, whether production will be of the Native File, 3 Static Image, or other searchable or non-searchable formats.

B. Whether Meta–Data is requested for some or all ESI and, if so, the volume and costs of producing and reviewing said ESI.

C. Preservation of ESI during the pendency of the lawsuit, specifically, but without limitation, applicability of the "safe harbor" provision of Fed.R.Civ.P. 37, preservation of Meta–Data, preservation of deleted ESI, back up or archival ESI, ESI contained in dynamic systems, ESI destroyed or overwritten by the routine operation of systems, and, offsite and offline ESI (including ESI stored on home or personal computers). This discussion should include whether the parties can agree on methods of review of ESI by the responding party in a manner that does not unacceptably change Meta–Data.

* * *

E. Identification of ESI that is or is not reasonably accessible without undue burden or cost, specifically, and without limitation, the identity of such sources and the reasons for a contention that the ESI is or is not reasonably accessible without undue burden or cost, the methods of storing and retrieving that ESI, and the anticipated costs and efforts involved in retrieving that ESI. The party asserting that ESI is not reasonably accessible without undue burden or cost should be prepared to discuss in reasonable detail the basis for such assertion.[2]

The guidelines were intended to be followed by the litigants whenever possible and would be "considered by the Court in resolving discovery disputes, including whether sanctions should be awarded pursuant to Fed. R. Civ. P. 37."[3]

The *Lowe's* approach sets forth the court's expectations clearly at the outset of discovery, but does it unduly restrict litigants' ability to independently craft their own discovery plans? In contrast, does the less prescriptive *Seroquel* approach place a greater burden on litigants to anticipate the precise standards to which their meet and confer efforts will later be held?

---

1. No. 04 Civ. 19, 2007 WL 1299180 (W.D.N.C. May 2, 2007).

2. *Id.* at *4–5.

3. *Id.* at *4.

4. **EXCERPT FROM** Judge Lee H. Rosenthal, *A Few Thoughts on Electronic Discovery After December 1, 2006*, 116 Yale L.J. Pocket Part 167, 176–77 (2006).

[J]udges must be simultaneously demanding and patient. Judges should not relax the emerging standard for a meaningful meet-and-confer exchange on electronic discovery issues. But at the same time, judges must understand the difficulties lawyers face in trying to learn their clients' information systems as well as the other disclosure and meet-and-confer subjects early in the case.

To what extent, if at all, should judges provide guidance to parties who lack knowledge regarding issues relating to electronic discovery? Given our adversarial system of justice, is it appropriate for judges to give such parties a "leg up" in observing and implementing the new rules? In considering this issue, is it relevant that electronic discovery practices and standards are currently rapidly evolving and vary across jurisdictions?

5. In *In re Bristol–Myers Squibb Securities Litigation*, the court noted that "lawyers try cases, not judges," and placed on the attorneys' shoulders the burden of cooperatively preparing an electronic discovery plan:

[Rule] 26(f) provides that before a Rule 16 Conference, the parties "confer ... to develop a proposed discovery plan...." In the electronic age, this meet and confer should include a discussion on whether each side possesses information in electronic form, whether they intend to produce such material, whether each other's software is compatible * * * and how to allocate costs involved with each of the foregoing. [Local Rule] 26(b)(2) addresses the requirements of [Federal Rule] 26(f) and, in addition, requires parties to discuss any "special procedure." Moreover, the standard initial scheduling order in this District contains instructions on topics to be discussed in the preparation of a Joint Discovery Plan which include "(3) a description of all discovery problems encountered to date, the efforts undertaken by the parties to remedy these problems, and the parties' suggested resolution of problems; [and] (4) a description of the parties' further discovery needs." Although there may be room for clearer direction in existing rules and orders that explicitly address cost allocation in production of paper and electronic information, counsel should take advantage of the required Rule 26(f) meeting to discuss issues associated with electronic discovery.[4]

6. The 2006 amendments' explicit reference to the importance of discussing electronic discovery issues during the Rule 26(f) meet and confer prompted many courts to revise their local rules. For instance, the United States District Courts for the District of Maryland and the

---

4. 205 F.R.D. 437, 443–44 (D.N.J. 2002).

District of Kansas have implemented detailed local rules governing electronic discovery.[5]

State court judges have also devised electronic discovery guidelines. In 2006, the Conference of Chief Justices recommended that, following an initial discovery hearing or conference, a judge "should inquire whether counsel have reached agreement on [a variety of electronic discovery issues] and address any disputes."[6]

Given the importance of complying with a court's expectations regarding the discovery of ESI, attorneys must familiarize themselves with the electronic discovery local rules in force in each jurisdiction in which the attorney practices? If you were litigating a case in Maryland or Kansas, might you consider associating with a local counsel possessing superior knowledge of the local rules? If you found yourself practicing in a jurisdiction with a dearth of local rules governing electronic discovery, what authorities might you consult to determine what topics you should address during your meet and confer? What are the pros and cons of litigating in a jurisdiction with very specific and prescriptive local rules governing electronic discovery? Do such rules impose an unduly stringent standard on attorneys? Do they create a risk of inconsistent standards across jurisdictions? Do they hinder the natural evolution of the standards by which attorneys engage in electronic discovery?

7.   Because electronic discovery consultants are often hired to assist attorneys in retrieving, preserving, and producing electronic information, is the participation of such consultants in the Rule 26(f) meet and confer necessary for the parties to have meaningful discussions about their electronic discovery activities? Recall that in *Seroquel*, the court, among other things, criticized the defendant for shielding its electronic discovery consultant from contact with the plaintiffs. Significantly, the court argued that this failure to include knowledgeable electronic discovery consultants in the meet and confer is "antithetical to the Sedona Principles and is not an indicium of good faith."

8.   In determining that sanctions were warranted for discovery abuse in *Seroquel*, the court analyzed the whole of the discovery process leading up to the parties' dispute. The parties' efforts to meet and confer made up a very important part of this larger examination. Should attorneys engage in meet and confers and other electronic discovery activities with an expectation that the court may eventually scrutinize these activities? If so, how does this expectation of judicial scrutiny affect the meet and confer process? To what extent should a litigant memorialize the meet and confer process, and in what form?

---

5. *See* United States District for the District of Maryland, *Suggested Protocol for Discovery of Electronically Stored Information*, available at http://www.mdd.uscourts.gov/news/news/ESIProtocol. pdf.; United States District Court for the District of Kansas, *Guidelines for Discovery of Electronically Stored Information*, available at http://www.ksd.uscourts.gov/guidelines/electronicdiscoveryguidelines. pdf.

6. *See infra* Guidelines for State Trial Courts Regarding Discovery of Electronically Stored Information, Appendix III p. 654.

IV

DATA COLLECTION

■ ■ ■

A. SEARCHING ALL APPROPRIATE SOURCES

PESKOFF v. FABER

No. 04–526, 2006 WL 1933483 (D.D.C. July 11, 2006)

FACCIOLA, MAGISTRATE JUDGE

This case was referred to me for the resolution of discovery disputes. Currently pending before me is Plaintiff's Motion to Compel Discovery. * * *

I. BACKGROUND

Plaintiff Jonathan Peskoff ("Peskoff") brought this lawsuit against defendant Michael Faber ("Faber") to recover damages for financial injury resulting from Faber's operation of a venture capital fund, called NextPoint Partners, LP, and the fund's related entities. Peskoff alleges fraud in the inducement, breach of fiduciary duty, breach of contract, conversion, common law fraud and deceit, unjust enrichment, and violations of 10 U.S.C. §§ 1962(c) and 1964(c) (Civil RICO).

NextPoint GP, LLC ("NextPoint GP") is the general partner of the venture capital fund. Both Peskoff and Faber were managing members of NextPoint GP. As of February 13, 2004, Peskoff was no longer a managing member, but he claims the retention of a membership interest. * * *

The NextPoint Management Company, Inc. ("NextPoint Management") was organized as a vehicle for receiving the management fees due from the venture capital fund to NextPoint GP and for fulfilling NextPoint GP's management responsibilities to the fund. Faber's responsibilities included handling routine finances, record keeping, and fundraising activities. Peskoff's responsibilities included oversight of the portfolio companies in which the venture capital fund invested and identification and evaluation of potential new investments.

Plaza Street Holdings, Inc. ("Plaza Street") is a corporation controlled solely by Faber that was paid by NextPoint Management for "consulting services." Among other things, Peskoff alleges that Faber caused NextPoint Management to pay Plaza Street $400,000 for consulting services that were neither needed nor provided and that these payments were for the sole purpose of diverting funds from the Next-Point entities to Faber personally.

Peskoff now moves the Court for * * * an order compelling Faber to produce additional e-mails sent to and authored by Peskoff while he was employed at NextPoint Management.

* * *

E-Mails

Peskoff * * * seeks the production of e-mails that he received or authored while employed at NextPoint Management. Peskoff argues that these e-mails "are highly likely to contain information relating to the ownership issues in this case, the suspect transactions identified in the Complaint and other relevant matters." During the course of discovery, Faber produced computer disks containing documents, including e-mails, that were obtained from Peskoff's computer, but these disks did not include any e-mails that Peskoff received or authored between mid–2001 and mid–2003. In moving to compel, Peskoff argues that Faber has failed to adequately explain why these two-years worth of e-mails have not been produced, where the e-mails might be located within NextPoint's computer system or archives, or what specific steps were taken to locate the emails.

In opposition, Faber contends that "no electronic documents have been withheld" and that, if the sought after e-mails are not on the computer disks provided, then they no longer exist. Faber explains that NextPoint Management subleases space from Mintz, Levin, Cohn, Ferris, Glovsky and Popeo, PC ("Mintz Levin") and its electronic files are stored on Mintz Levin's server. When Peskoff's employment ended, counsel "caused the creation of an archive of all Peskoff electronic files, including documents stored on his computer hard drive, email, and any other Peskoff electronic documents." This entire archive was produced to Peskoff.

As a threshold matter, there does not appear to be any dispute that the e-mails are likely to contain relevant information. Moreover, "[d]uring discovery, the producing party has an obligation to search available electronic systems for the information demanded." *McPeek v. Ashcroft*, 202 F.R.D. 31, 32 (D.D.C. 2001) (citing to Fed.R.Civ.P. 34(a)). The parties' disagreement turns instead on whether the missing e-mails still exist and can be located. The sought after e-mails could fall into three categories: e-mails to Peskoff, e-mails from Peskoff, and e-mails about Peskoff, and could be located in several possible places.

First, the e-mail account that Peskoff used while working at Next-Point Management might still contain the e-mails in his inbox, sent items, trash, or other named folders.

Second, the e-mails may be in the inbox, sent items, trash, and other folders of e-mail accounts of other employees, agents, officers, and representatives of the NextPoint entities, who may have been the author or recipient of the e-mails at issue.

Third, the e-mails may be on the hard drive of Peskoff's computer or within any depository for NextPoint e-mails. The e-mails may be accessible from those locations through simple search technology, such as by conducting a key word search (*i.e.*, a search on "Peskoff" or his e-mail address). Thus, even if the e-mails cannot be located by searching particular files, they yet may be located on the hard drive or other depository by finding all files where a particular word appears.

Fourth, with the help of a computer forensic technologist, the e-mails, even if deleted, may be recoverable from other places within Peskoff's computer, such as its "slack space." *See United States v. Triumph Capital Group, Inc.*, 211 F.R.D. 31, 46 n. 7 (D. Conn. 2002) (" 'Slack space' is the unused space at the logical end of an active file's data and the physical end of the cluster or clusters that are assigned to an active file. Deleted data, or remnants of deleted data can be found in the slack space. . . .").

Finally, the e-mails may even be recoverable from periodic backups tapes or disks made of Mintz Levin's server. *See Zubulake v. UBS Warburg LLC*, 217 F.R.D. 309, 319 (S.D.N.Y.2003).

However, based on the information before the Court, I cannot determine at what level Faber searched for the requested Peskoff e-mails. All I know is that an archive was created "of all Peskoff electronic files, including documents stored on his computer hard drive, e-mail, and any other Peskoff electronic documents." This statement tells me little, if anything about the scope of Faber's search.

Accordingly, within ten business days from the date of this memorandum opinion, Faber shall file a detailed affidavit specifying the nature of the search it conducted. Peskoff shall have ten business days therefrom to respond to the adequacy of the search described in that affidavit. Once I receive Faber's affidavit and Peskoff's response, if any, I will consider whether additional searches are necessary. I should indicate that I may have to hold an evidentiary hearing in which I take testimony from Faber's employees and other witnesses about the effectiveness and cost of any additional searches.

B. THE ROLE OF OUTSIDE COUNSEL

QUALCOMM INC. v. BROADCOM CORP.

No. 05 Civ. 1958, 2008 WL 66932 (S.D. Cal. Jan. 7, 2008)

MAJOR, MAGISTRATE JUDGE

At the conclusion of trial, counsel for Broadcom Corporation ("Broadcom") made an oral motion for sanctions after Qualcomm

Incorporated ("Qualcomm") witness Viji Raveendran testified about emails that were not produced to Broadcom during discovery. The trial judge, United States District Court Judge Rudi M. Brewster, referred the motion to this Court * * *. On May 29, 2007, Broadcom filed a written motion requesting that the Court sanction Qualcomm for its failure to produce tens of thousands of documents that Broadcom had requested in discovery. Qualcomm timely opposed, and Broadcom filed a reply. This Court heard oral argument on Broadcom's motion on July 26, 2007.

[The background of the case is fully discussed in Chapter VI.E–Spoliation and Sanctions. The portion of the opinion dealing with failures in collecting data follows.]

* * *

Qualcomm violated its discovery obligations by failing to produce more than 46,000 emails and documents that were requested in discovery and that Qualcomm agreed to produce. * * * Qualcomm has not established "substantial justification" for its failure to produce the documents. In fact, Qualcomm has not presented any evidence attempting to explain or justify its failure to produce the documents. Despite the fact that it maintains detailed records showing whose computers were searched and which search terms were used * * * Qualcomm has not presented any evidence establishing that it searched for [critical] records or emails on its computer system or email databases. Qualcomm also has not established that it searched the computers or email databases of the individuals who testified on Qualcomm's behalf at trial or in depositions as Qualcomm's most knowledgeable corporate witnesses; in fact, it indicates that it did not conduct any such search. The fact that Qualcomm did not perform these basic searches at any time before the completion of trial indicates that Qualcomm intentionally withheld the documents. * * * The conclusion is * * * supported by the fact that after trial Qualcomm did not conduct an internal investigation to determine if there were additional unproduced documents; but, rather, spent its time opposing Broadcom's efforts to force such a search and insisting, without any factual basis, that Qualcomm's search was reasonable.

Qualcomm's claim that it inadvertently failed to find and produce these documents also is negated by the massive volume and direct relevance of the hidden documents. As Judge Brewster noted, it is inexplicable that Qualcomm was able to locate the * * * documents that either supported, or did not harm, Qualcomm's arguments but were unable to locate the * * * documents that hurt its arguments. * * *

Assuming arguendo, that Qualcomm did not know about the suppressed emails, Qualcomm failed to heed several warning signs that should have alerted it to the fact that its document search and production were inadequate. The first significant concern should have been raised in connection with the Rule 30(b)(6) depositions of Christine

Irvine and Scott Ludwin. Both individuals testified as the Qualcomm employee most knowledgeable about Qualcomm's involvement in the JVT [Qualcomm's assertion that it was not involved in that group was a fact that was critical to its case]. But, Qualcomm did not search either person's computer for JVT documents, did not provide either person with relevant JVT documents to review, and did not make any other efforts to ensure each person was in fact knowledgeable about Qualcomm's JVT involvement. These omissions are especially incriminating because many of the suppressed emails were to or from Irvine. If a witness is testifying as an organization's most knowledgeable person on a specific subject, the organization has an obligation to conduct a reasonable investigation and review to ensure that the witness does possess the organization's knowledge. Fed.R.Civ.P. 30(b)(6).[6] * * * An adequate investigation should include an analysis of the sufficiency of the document search and, when electronic documents are involved, an analysis of the sufficiency of the search terms and locations. In the instant case, a reasonable inquiry should have included using the * * * search terms and searching the computers of Raveendran, Irvine, Ludwin (and other Qualcomm employees identified in the emails discovered on the computers of these witnesses). This minimal inquiry would have revealed the existence of the suppressed documents. Moreover, the fact that Broadcom alleged, and Qualcomm agreed or acquiesced, that Irvine was not sufficiently knowledgeable about Qualcomm's JVT involvement or adequately prepared for her deposition, should also have alerted Qualcomm to the inadequacy of its document search and production.

* * *

Qualcomm had the ability to identify its employees and consultants who were involved in the JVT, to access and review their computers, databases and emails, to talk with the involved employees and to refresh their recollections if necessary, to ensure that those testifying about the corporation's knowledge were sufficiently prepared and testified accurately, and to produce in good faith all relevant and requested discovery. * * * Qualcomm chose not to do so and therefore must be sanctioned.

2. Attorneys' Misconduct

The next question is what, if any, role did Qualcomm's retained lawyers play in withholding the documents? * * * [T]he Court finds it

---

6. Qualcomm's self-serving statements that "outside counsel selects ... the custodians whose documents should be searched" and the paralegal does not decide "what witnesses to designate to testify on behalf of the company" does not relieve Qualcomm of its obligations. Qualcomm has not presented any evidence establishing what actions, if any, it took to ensure it designated the correct employee, performed the correct computer searches, and presented the designated employee with sufficient information to testify as the corporation's most knowledgeable person. Qualcomm also has not presented any evidence that outside counsel knew enough about Qualcomm's organization and operation to identify all of the individuals whose computers should be searched and determine the most knowledgeable witness. And, more importantly, Qualcomm is a large corporation with an extensive legal staff; it clearly had the ability to identify the correct witnesses and determine the correct computers to search and search terms to use. Qualcomm just lacked the desire to do so.

likely that some variation of option four occurred; that is, one or more of the retained lawyers chose not to look in the correct locations for the correct documents, to accept the unsubstantiated assurances of an important client that its search was sufficient, to ignore the warning signs that the document search and production were inadequate, not to press Qualcomm employees for the truth, and/or to encourage employees to provide the information (or lack of information) that Qualcomm needed to assert its non-participation argument and to succeed in this lawsuit. * * * This conduct warrants the imposition of sanctions.

[The court imposed sanctions on both Qualcomm and a number of its lawyers. As to the lawyers, the court stated that had they "insisted on reviewing Qualcomm's records regarding the locations searched and terms utilized, they would have discovered the inadequacy of the search and the suppressed documents. Similarly, Leung's difficulties with the Rule 30(b)(6) witnesses, Irvine and Ludwin, should have alerted him (and the supervising or senior attorneys) to the inadequacy of Qualcomm's document production and to the fact that they needed to review whose computers and databases had been searched and for what." The court concluded that the specified lawyers "did not make a reasonable inquiry into Qualcomm's discovery search and production and their conduct contributed to the discovery violation." For a full discussion of the sanctions imposed, see the discussion of *Qualcomm* in Chapter VI.E, *infra*.]

COMMENTARY

As the cases above illustrate, all sources that may contain responsive information must be identified and searched. It is also important that all counsel work together to be sure that all responsive information is collected. Outside counsel must acquire the necessary skills to understand the technical aspects of its clients' data. This may require the assistance of a technical or forensic computer expert. For example, terms such as "legacy data," "rollover servers" and "partitioned drives" have not been the traditional discovery fare of outside counsel. Nonetheless, a failure to understand these technical concepts has resulted in the imposition of sanctions based on counsel's failure to explain why responsive information was never collected, even though it was available. In short, the problems relating to the collection of data differ from the question of preserving data.

For example, in *Phoenix Four, Inc. v. Strategic Resources Corp.*,[1] the outside counsel was sanctioned when it was discovered on the eve of trial that relevant data residing on a partitioned section of a server had not been located or produced. The court roundly criticized counsel for failing to interrogate the client fully regarding its information systems. The court noted:

---

1. *Phoenix Four, Inc. v. Strategic Resources Corp.*, No. 05 Civ. 4837, 2006 WL 1409413 (S.D.N.Y. May 23, 2006).

Further, [counsel's] obligation under *Zubulake V* extends to an inquiry as to whether information was stored on that server and, had the defendants been unable to answer that question, directing that a technician examine the server.[2]

Thus, there are times when outside counsel must direct in-house counsel and other employees within a company to examine sources of information that they might otherwise overlook. Counsel might also be required to test the accuracy of a client's response to document demands to be sure that all appropriate sources of data have been searched and that responsive information has been collected and eventually reviewed and produced. Suppose an employee's web browsing activities are at issue. Outside counsel advises the client to capture the cached web browsing history of the particular employee. Should outside counsel then monitor the client's collection efforts? Must she interview the person who performed the acquisition or obtain a written certification? Should she document all her instructions regarding collection efforts?

In *Qualcomm,* the court found it likely that one or more of the outside counsel chose not to look in the correct locations in order to collect responsive documents, accepted the unsubstantiated assurances of their client that its search was sufficient, and ignored the warning signs that the document collection efforts were inadequate. Outside counsel, together with in-house counsel, is responsible for performing an adequate data collection, and may be liable for any failure to do so. As a result, it is always wise to document the steps taken to collect responsive ESI.

PROBLEM

A large national company has been served with a lawsuit alleging false consumer advertising. The class representative alleges that she was tricked into purchasing an extended warranty by misleading language in the written sales materials describing the warranty that suggests the warranty will cover product damage from misuse. The class representative seeks to represent a class of all consumers who purchased the product warranties.

You have been retained by the company to defend the litigation. You immediately recognize that one issue in the case will be the company's drafting of warranty language and whether the company tested the warranty language and whether the company received any complaints about the alleged ambiguity in the warranty language that might suggest the product warranty covered misuse.

You advise the company that evidence of confusion over the warranty will be relevant, and alert the company to identify all sources on which responsive information may reside. One source of data may be e-mails received at the company web site that specifically provides for the

---

2. *Id.* at * 6.

submission by e-mail of complaints and questions about the company's products and services. You advise the company that this e-mail data should be retained for later searching of what you anticipate will be a production request for customer confusion regarding the warranty.

You learn from the company's loss prevention manager that the data was preserved last year by another law firm. The manager will not provide you with the name of the other law firm, but assures you that the data is "OK" and "if you need it, you'll have it." What steps should you take to insure that this data is not only preserved but searched for responsive information? Is the information provided by the Loss Prevention Manager sufficient to satisfy your obligation to undertake a reasonable investigation to search for and produce responsive information?

The following excerpt provides a helpful checklist as to how counsel should assist a client with an appropriate effort to locate responsive information during a litigation. While preservation may be the first step in response to a litigation or a threat of litigation, once a litigation begins and a litigation hold is in place, the next important step is to collect the information that has been retained. Many counsel overlook the separate step of collection and it is just as important as preservation, review and eventually production.

EXCERPT FROM Hon. Shira A. Scheindlin & Jonathan M. Redgrave, *Ch. 22: Discovery of Electronic Information*, in *Business and Commercial Litigation in Federal Courts* 2d (Robert L. Haig, ed., rev. ed. 2008).

IX. Practice Aids

A. Checklists

§ 22:71. Checklist: interviews of various organization employees

The following checklist is intended as a guide to assist counsel in identifying the existence and location of potentially relevant electronically stored information when conducting litigation-related due diligence inquiries. The list, by its very nature, is both over-inclusive and under-inclusive. In particular, the facts and circumstances of any given case will dictate the nature and extent of preservation and production obligations, and by extension the necessary level of due diligence. With that caveat, counsel should review these possible topics to determine which matters need to be explored in any particular case.

* Initial steps:
  - identify records likely to be relevant to the claims and defenses in the litigation
  - identify employees likely to have knowledge and information relevant to the subject matter of the litigation

- identify information services personnel (which can be diffi-cult because the organization of information services depart-ments varies among companies, and, given the dynamic nature of both technologies and applications, tends to change frequently)

- identify hardware support group personnel

- identify the group responsible for system maintenance, back-up tapes and tape archives

- identify applications group personnel (*e.g.*, e-mail system administrators and others creating and supporting applica-tions for specific departments or groups within the corpora-tion)

* Inquiries that may be appropriate for employees who may possess relevant information can include:

- Computer hardware used:
  - desktop and/or laptop computers
  - home computers used for business purposes
  - other hand-held devices (*e.g.*, Palm Pilots)

- Applications used:
  - E-mail
  - instant messaging
  - message attachments
  - internet e-mail
  - shared e-mail systems with service providers, etc.
  - voice-mail
  - desktop/laptop applications
  - word processing
  - spreadsheets
  - presentation software (*e.g.*, Power Point)
  - office management software (*e.g.*, calendars, task lists and notes)
  - databases
  - server/mainframe applications
  - report applications (*i.e.*, applications that generate sales reports, quality assurance reports, etc.)
  - report preparation and form applications (*e.g.*, work/pro-ject status reports)
  - shareware
  - Internet and Intranet usage

– web logs (a/k/a "blogs" or "weblogs")

● Computer file storage:

– retention of e-mail and use of e-mail files/folders on desktop/laptop hard drives or servers

– retention of draft and final documents (reports, memoranda, etc.) on desktop/laptop hard drives or servers, particularly documents not otherwise retained in hard copy form[3]

– retention of downloaded files received from employees or other sources

– retention of office management files (*e.g.*, calendars and task lists)

– retention of files or documents by administrative assistants or secretaries[4] and

– use of removable media (*e.g.*, CD–ROMs, DVDs, floppy disks or thumb drives)

* Information services department management may be the best source of the following information:[5]

● overviews of departmental organization

● policies and procedures regarding business retention of data and applications

● overviews of tape archives and policies and procedures for retaining archived data and applications

● retrieval of archived data and applications

● overviews of backup and disaster recovery policies and procedures

● retention procedures pursuant to litigation holds and preservation orders

---

3. If document management systems are used, documents (files) created by system users are likely to reside on a server and possibly on the user's personal computer hard drive. In addition, the user may have dedicated server space where files may be located. In discovery, an opposing party may argue that a computer file is a different document than a hard copy of the document because of additional information archived by the application associated with the stored file. Certain word processing applications, for example, automatically generate information (referred to as "metadata") regarding create dates, edit dates, and so on that do not appear on a printed version of the document (file). Consideration accordingly must be given to the retention of the computer-stored file even if a hard copy version has been made. The same consideration must be given to existing e-mail even if a print version of the e-mail has been retained in hard copy form.

4. Interviews of secretaries and administrative assistants to higher ranked executives and managers is a good policy. More senior personnel are less likely to maintain their own calendars and task lists or create their own documents on computer and are not likely to know the manner in which their secretary or administrative assistant maintains computer files.

5. Developing a working relationship with information services department management and fostering an understanding of litigation demands on the part of management is crucial. The diversion of resources to litigation support is a significant concern because information services is frequently viewed by corporate management as "overhead" and the department's priorities are skewed toward client (user) services and satisfaction. Outside litigation counsel are not clients.

- overviews of applications and databases and identification of any applications portfolios
- overviews of e-mail systems and history of e-mail systems[6]
- overviews of hardware, including its location (*e.g.*, mainframes, servers or personal computers)
- number and location of personal computers (including any provided for home use)
- other supported handheld devices that store data or files

* Information services or information security personnel may be the best source for the following information:
  - backup frequency
  - retention of backup tapes before overwriting
  - overviews of disaster recovery systems and identification of any map or portfolio of disaster recovery[7]
  - overviews of tape archives and identification of archived historical data and applications
  - databases or indices to archived tapes
  - retrievability and capacity to load and read archived historical data and applications
  - retention periods for archived data and applications
  - use of password and encryption technologies
  - retention of archived data and applications for litigation purposes

* E-mail systems administrators are likely the best source of the following information:
  - overviews of system structure (*e.g.*, number of servers, number of post offices and mailboxes)
  - overviews of system capabilities (*e.g.*, attachments or folders)
  - volume of traffic
  - maintenance and retention of message logs
  - retention period for unread messages
  - frequency of overwriting deleted items
  - shared systems with service providers, suppliers or corporate family
  - policies regarding system use

---

6. E-mail systems have developed very rapidly. Larger corporations may have (or have had) multiple systems over time and multiple systems that were (or are) concurrently in use. Generally, e-mail systems that have been taken off-line and replaced will not be pertinent because e-mail associated with the system are unlikely to exist; however, an inquiry should be made to determine if any backup tapes of the system were archived and might contain e-mail and attachments to e-mail.

7. A disaster recovery system map or portfolio might provide a valuable overview of applications and databases.

- retention for litigation purposes

* In addition, the following inquiries may be directed to applications administrators:[8]

- descriptions of pertinent applications

- descriptions of report formats[9]

- identification of databases and descriptions of data sources and data entry

- descriptions of how data is edited (*e.g.*, does new data replace old data in a field and is historical data retained)

- descriptions of how the applications are backed up

- information on whether historical data is archived

- descriptions of whether applications have been significantly modified during the relevant time period and, if so, were prior versions of the applications retained and can they be reinstalled and can data or reports be replicated or generated

§ 22:72.   Checklist: investigating the hardware environment

The client's computer hardware environment should be investigated to determine what devices are available to employees and where the devices are located. The information services department is likely the best source of information. The inquiry should include:

* Availability of desktop and laptop computers

* Use of networks with servers

* Use of mainframe computers

* Use of other, hand-held devices that store information

* Use of home-based or employee-owned personal computers and laptops that have remote access to the client's hardware and may store information or files

* Use of CDs or other digital media to store historical records

* Use of digital voice-mail systems that store messages for extended periods

---

8. The initial step is to identify the databases and applications that may contain relevant information and then identify the current and, if available, former applications administrators. As previously noted, applications administrators may be assigned by department, and the administrators assigned to relevant departments also may need to be interviewed. With respect to databases, interviewers should be aware of so-called "relational databases"—*i.e.*, multiple databases maintained on a corporate-wide basis from which specific information is accessed and processed to prepare reports formatted for particular departments or business purposes. System users likely are aware of only the reports formatted for their business use or the limited number of data fields that they can search.

9. In many applications, the systems administrator and programming staff have the capability of designing a large variety of reports limited only by the fields of data in the underlying database(s). A potentially significant discovery issue is whether the discovering party is entitled only to reports as generated in the ordinary course of business or to the underlying data and the application to formulate their own reports.

* Possible retention of tape recordings, for example, of video teleconferences

The objective of the inquiry is to determine where and how pertinent records might be stored and located. For example, if certain categories of employees are entitled to have remote access to the client's system, home-based personal computers may contain pertinent and discoverable records that either have never been imported to the client's hardware or may not have been retained by the client.[10] In light of the 2006 amendments to Rule 26(b)(2)(B) that address disclosure and discovery of information that is "not reasonably accessible" it is also important to assess the burdens and costs that may be involved in retrieving and producing electronically stored information from hardware, especially older or retired (legacy) systems.

§ 22:73.   Checklist: investigating backup systems and archives

Inquiries should be made of the appropriate information services or data security personnel to determine:

* The frequency with which backup tapes of data and applications are made (*i.e.*, daily, weekly, monthly or at longer intervals)

* Schedules for recycling and overwriting retained backup tapes

* Locations of backup tapes (on-site or off-site)[11]

* The existence of additional sets of data and application disaster recovery tapes

* The existence of archived historical data and related applications

* The types of data and applications archived

* Locations in which archived materials are kept (on-site or off-site)

* Any ability to load and run archived data and related applications

Outside counsel should be aware that corporate management and in-house counsel often are not fully aware of the backup and archived materials maintained by information services personnel. In many instances, the culture of information services departments is to retain historical information whenever possible in order to meet the potential demands of their clients—the users of the system—and such departments may be far more concerned about being unable to retrieve information than they are about storing too much of it that long ago became useless.

§ 22:74.   Checklist: investigating applications

The rapid expansion and use of e-mail has captured the attention of litigators and legal commentators because some users consider e-mail

---

10. Home-based and employee-owned computers may present difficult issues relating to what is (and is not) within the corporation's possession, custody or control. Those issues are outside the scope of this chapter.

11. Generally, off-site backup systems are not relevant to litigation issues because those systems simply replicate the current on-site system.

to be (1) less formal than other forms of business communication and (2) as transitory as a phone conversation. Consequently, they exercise less discretion in creating it. But e-mail is only one type of business application that the litigator must investigate. Other types of applications include, but are not limited to:

* Engineering and computer assisted design ("CAD") applications that may have replaced blueprints

* Product ingredient and formula databases and applications

* Manufacturing quality assurance applications, data collection and data storage

* Financial records data generation, storage and related applications

* Supplier bidding and purchasing applications

* Product distribution and sales databases and applications including payment and accounts receivable data

* Advertising, marketing and product promotion databases and applications

* Customer and consumer information databases and consumer contact and complaint databases and applications

* Accident and incident report databases and applications

* Product testing and research report generation databases and applications

* External and governmental relations databases and applications, including lobbying expenditures and political contributions

* Indices of stored files, records and other document collections such as research or business libraries

* Litigation-related databases and applications[12]

* Corporate Internet websites that might include representations about products or services, product warnings, consumer "hot-lines" or links to other corporate data sets

* Databases and applications shared with service providers and suppliers

* Document management systems such as iManage, PC Docs or DOCS Open[13]

---

12. Corporations involved in substantial litigation may have developed litigation support systems and applications that, although they are used by outside counsel, reside on company computers. Systems of that type create difficult issues that should be discussed when considering the effect of preservation orders.

13. Document management systems may be of particular significance because (a) the system may archive documents not existing in other forms and (b) the file for a document may contain information about the creation, editing and distribution of the document that is not apparent on the face of the document.

* "Shareware" (*i.e.*, applications that allow contemporaneous editing of a document that can be fed back to the author or originator of the document)

* Desktop and laptop applications including word processing, spreadsheet programs, database software, presentation software and office management software

* Corporate "intranets" that contain items such as on-line corporate directories, corporate news and announcements, corporate policies and procedures, and corporate published statements

* Digital voice-mail systems

* Video teleconferencing systems with possible analog or digital storage

* Web logs (a/k/a "blogs" or "weblogs")

Even this list is incomplete, especially for clients who are sophisticated computer users. But if a client has made a substantial investment in hardware and has an information services department or outside service provider, the client likely has developed and implemented a computer application for virtually all regularly conducted business activities. In light of the 2006 amendments to Rule 26(b)(2)(B) that address disclosure and discovery of information that is "not reasonably accessible" it is also important to assess the burdens and costs that may be involved in retrieving and producing electronically stored information contained on data applications, especially older or retired (legacy) systems.

V

PRODUCTION ISSUES

■ ■ ■

A. RULE 34: FORM OF PRODUCTION (PAPER, ELECTRONIC, NATIVE, OR OTHER FORMS)

D'ONOFRIO v. SFX SPORTS GROUP, INC.

247 F.R.D. 43 (D.D.C. 2008)

FACCIOLA, MAGISTRATE JUDGE

* * *

I. Background

This lawsuit involves claims by plaintiff, Audrey (Shebby) D'Onofrio, that she received disparate treatment from her employer, SFX Sports Group, Inc. ("SFX"), based upon her gender. Plaintiff also alleges that she was subjected to a hostile work environment and was terminated in retaliation for her protected activities. She brings this lawsuit under the District of Columbia Human Rights Act ("DCHRA"), the Equal Pay Act, and the District of Columbia Family Medical Leave Act.

* * *

III. Electronically Stored Information

Many of the discovery disputes at issue in the Motion relate to electronically stored information. In particular, plaintiff * * * asks the court to compel the production of the Business Plan in its original electronic format, with accompanying metadata * * *.

A. Business Plan

* * *

Plaintiff argues that Rule 34 permits the production of documents outside of their original format only "if necessary," and, in this case, no such necessity exists. Defendants respond that: (a) plaintiff did not request that the Business Plan or any other documents be produced in a specific format; (b) production in original electronic format with metadata is not required by the Federal Rules of Civil Procedure or in the absence of a clear agreement or court order, neither of which are present here; and (c) plaintiff has not made any attempt to demonstrate the relevance of the metadata.[4]

1. Rule 34—"If Necessary"

As an initial matter, plaintiff argues that Rule 34 of the Federal Rules of Civil Procedure permits the production of documents other than in their original format only "if necessary." Rule 34(a) states, in relevant part:

> (a) In General. A party may serve on any other party a request . . . :

> (1) to produce and permit the requesting party or its representative to inspect, copy, test, or sample the following items in the responding party's possession, custody, or control:

> (A) any designated documents or electronically stored information-including writings, drawings, graphs, charts, photographs, sound recordings, images, and other data or data compilations-stored in any medium from which information can be obtained either directly or, if necessary, after translation by the responding party into a reasonably usable form[.]

Rule 34(a) does not set forth constraints on the manner of production, but instead establishes the permissible scope of a request. ("A party may serve on any other party a request . . ."). Consequently, the "if necessary" clause seized upon by plaintiff is actually a constraint on the requesting party rather than the responding party. In other words, electronic data is subject to discovery if it is stored in a directly obtainable medium. If, however, it is not stored in a directly obtainable medium, a request may be made of the responding party to translate the electronic data into a "reasonably usable form." Because the step of translating this type of electronic data adds an extra burden on the responding party, the request may only seek for it to be done "if [the translation is] necessary." It is not the case that this clause requires the responding party to produce data in its original form unless "necessary" to do otherwise.

2. Request for Specific Form of Production

This does not end the analysis of whether a responding party might be required to produce electronic data in its original form with metadata. To the contrary, Rule 34(b) states that a discovery request "may specify the form or forms in which electronically stored information is to be produced." Fed. R. Civ. P. 34(b)(1)(C). In this case, plaintiff argues

---

4. Metadata has been defined as "information about a particular data set which describes how, when, and by whom it was collected, created, accessed, or modified and how it is formatted." *Williams v. Sprint/United Management Co.*, 230 F.R.D. 640, 646 (D. Kan. 2005) (quoting *The Sedona Guidelines: Best Practice Guidelines and Commentary for Managing Information & Records in the Electronic Age* app. F).

that she so specified in Instruction No. 4 of Plaintiff's Requests for the Production of Documents (the "Instruction"):

> [F]or any documents that are stored or maintained in files in the normal course of business, such documents shall be produced in such files, or in such a manner as to preserve and identify the file from which such documents were taken.

It is apparent that this language, when first written, was not meant to encompass electronic data. Instead it addresses a common concern of paper discovery: the identification of a document's custodian and origination. It is for this reason that the Instruction applies to documents "stored or maintained in files" and why it seeks to "preserve and identify" the identity of that file. Indeed, the Instruction makes perfect sense when one presumes "file" to refer to a physical file cabinet or folder.

Of course, "file" can also mean electronic data stored on an electronic medium. Using this definition, the Instruction can be strained to provide the responding party with two options for producing electronic documents: (a) produce the electronic file containing the document (i.e. a .PDF or .XLS file), or (b) produce the document in such a manner as to "preserve and identify the file from which" it was taken. The inclusion of the word "preserve" makes it very difficult to understand how the Instruction could apply to electronic documents; after all, how can the production of a document without the electronic file encompass the "preserv[ation]" of that electronic file? A more credible reading of the second option is that a document need not be produced as an electronic file if the alternate production "preserve[s the] identi[ty of] the file from which" it was taken. In practice this would likely refer to a "trailer" at the bottom of a printed electronic document containing its location on electronic storage media (*i.e.* an electronic spreadsheet could be printed on a piece of paper with the trailer "c: accounting harry FY07 charts.xls"). I do not know if defendants provided such a trailer because plaintiff did not attach the Business Plan to its Motion or provide any other detail concerning its format, other than to state that it was not in its original form with accompanying metadata. Nevertheless, it is clear that the Instruction, if applicable to electronic files, permits production of the Business Plan in a non-native form without accompanying metadata.

Ultimately, then, it does not matter whether the Instruction referred to paper or electronic files—a plain reading leads to the conclusion that plaintiff did not make a request that the Business Plan be produced solely in its original format with accompanying metadata. A motion to compel is appropriate only where an appropriate request is made of the responding party. *See* Fed. R. Civ. P. 37(a)(1)(B). Because no such request has been made concerning the Business Plan, the Court will not compel the defendant to produce it in its original form with accompanying metadata.[9] *See, e.g., Wyeth v. Impax Labs., Inc.*, No. Civ.A. 06–222, 2006 WL 3091331, at *1–2 (D. Del. Oct. 26, 2006) ("Since the parties have never agreed that electronic documents would be produced in any particular format, [Plaintiff] complied with its discovery obligation by producing image files.").

* * *

COMMENTARY AND PROBLEMS

Notwithstanding the clarity of the 2006 Amendments to Rule 34, the form of production of electronic records is fertile ground for dispute, often resulting from the parties' failure to adequately communicate and reach agreement on this issue. This failure is generally the result of: (1) one or more parties' failure to specify a form of production as allowed by Rule 34; or (2) one or more parties' lack of knowledge of the technological complexities attendant to electronic discovery. As demonstrated by *D'Onofrio* and the cases discussed below, both of these pitfalls can result in costly and time-consuming motion practice, and potentially a court order requiring duplicative productions in multiple formats.

1.   In *D'Onofrio*, the plaintiff's failure to specify the form in which the defendant should produce the business plan prevented the plaintiff from obtaining it in native format with the corresponding metadata, which arguably would have given her the ability to access and analyze the Business Plan both substantively and contextually, on par with her adversary. In denying the plaintiff's motion to compel, the court noted that the plaintiff failed to demonstrate that native production was necessary and warranted. Taking into account the various points made by the court, how might the plaintiff have demonstrated her need for production of the Business Plan in native format? Might the plaintiff have protected herself if, in her requests for production, she requested all documents in hard copy format, but reserved her right to later request specific documents again in native format? Could the plaintiff have reasonably been expected to know, prior to reviewing the Business Plan in hard copy, that a native production was preferable? What steps, if any, might the plaintiff have taken to discern information that would have helped her to realize this preference? Would the plaintiff have benefitted from engaging in a meet and confer with the defendant in which she asked detailed questions about the categories of information for which she intended to seek production, including questions about how that information was created, stored, and/or transmitted? Is it reasonable to expect a requesting party, who has no familiarity with the responding party's information or systems, to know which questions to ask? Had the plaintiff engaged in a meet and confer and *not* received

---

9.   Where the requesting party "does not specify a form for producing electronically stored information, a [responding] party must produce it in a form or forms in which it is ordinarily maintained or in a reasonably usable form or forms." Fed. R. Civ. P. 34(b)(2)(e)(ii).

helpful information, would this factor, if disclosed to the court, have been relevant to the court's analysis? If so, how so?

2.   Suppose a party requests the production of certain e-mails and their corresponding attachments, but the responding party produces the attachments separated from the e-mails, such that the requesting party has no indication of what e-mails and attachments correspond to one another. To what extent does the producing party have an obligation to ensure that attachments are produced with their corresponding parent e-mails? Does producing the e-mails divorced from their attachments comply with Rule 34(b)(2)(E)(i)'s requirement that a party produce ESI as it is "kept in the usual course of business"? Should a requesting party be obligated to expressly request that attachments be produced with their corresponding parent e-mails? Or should this be assumed?

The issue of e-mail attachment linkage was addressed in *PSEG Power New York, Inc. v. Alberici Constructors, Inc.*, where, due to a vendor software problem, the plaintiff produced three thousand e-mails divorced from their attachments.[1] Although all e-mails and attachments were produced, the requesting party was unable to determine which e-mails and attachments corresponded to one another. In considering the defendant's motion to compel a reproduction of the e-mails "in a reasonably usable form," the court considered the following three factors: 1) the relevance of the requested information; 2) whether or not it was reasonably accessible; and 3) if reproduction would be unduly burdensome or costly. After consideration of these factors, the court ordered the plaintiff to reproduce the e-mails together with their attachments. Specifically, the court noted that production of e-mails divorced from their attachments did not comply with Rule 34's requirement that electronic information be produced as it is kept in the usual course of business or in a reasonably usable format.

In *PSEG*, the court noted that the discovery dispute was the result of a vendor software problem. Should the plaintiff request that the vendor reprocess the documents at no charge and reimburse the plaintiff for the costs of defending the motion to compel? Given the uncertainties and unknown expenses inherent in electronic discovery, what contractual protections might be beneficial to a party who seeks to hire an electronic discovery vendor to process and assist with the production of electronic information?

Should a requesting party that complies with Rule 34 and expressly specifies the requested form(s) of production have a reasonable expectation that the responding party will perfectly comply? To what extent should a court have such an expectation? Also consider whether a producing party should be obligated to produce information in a form that is the same as the form in which it intends to use the information in preparing and litigating the case.

---

1. *See PSEG Power N.Y., Inc. v. Alberici Constructors, Inc.*, No. 05–0657, 2007 WL 2687670 (N.D.N.Y. Sept. 7, 2007).

3.   In *Lawson v. Sun Microsystems, Inc.*, the plaintiff sent a letter to the defendant requesting production of all ESI in native format, yet failed to specify the requested form of production in the formal discovery requests the plaintiff later served upon the defendant. In response to the plaintiff's formal discovery requests, the defendant produced paper copies of the responsive documents. The plaintiff moved to compel production of the documents in native format. Defendant objected, arguing that the plaintiff failed to specify the requested form of production in the document requests and noting that Rule 34(b) does not require duplicative productions in multiple formats. The court granted the plaintiff's motion to compel, holding that although the plaintiff's letter was not a formal request, it "should nonetheless have provided Defendant sufficient notice of the form desired by Plaintiff."[2]

Should the defendant's counsel have sought clarification from the plaintiff's counsel regarding the potentially conflicting instructions relating to the specified form of production? Could this problem have been avoided had the parties negotiated a stipulation regarding the form of production to ensure that there were no time-consuming and costly "miscommunications"?

4.   In contrast to *Lawson*, the court in *Autotech Technologies Ltd. Partnership v. Automationdirect.com, Inc.* addressed a defendant's motion to compel production of documents in native format even though the defendant never specified this format in its requests for production and the plaintiff had already produced the same documents in hard copy. The court denied the defendant's motion to compel, explaining that defendant "was the master of its production requests; it must be satisfied with what it asked for."[3] In addition, the court stated that the defendant failed to demonstrate that the hard copy production was not "reasonably usable" within the meaning of Rule 34(b).

Based on the decisions in *Lawson* and *Autotech*, in adjudicating a motion to compel a "re-production" of documents or electronic information in a format alternative to that already produced, are the courts applying a cost-benefit analysis rather than examining whether the parties complied with the black letter law of Rule 34? In other words, is a court more likely to be persuaded by: (1) an argument that the alternative/duplicative form of production is truly necessary to prepare the case for trial; or (2) an argument that the requesting party failed to expressly state the requested form of production in accordance with Rule 34? Would an emphasis on #2 disproportionately weigh form over substance?

5.   Rule 34 does not define what constitutes a "reasonably usable form" of production. Rather, the terminology is broad, allowing the Rule to evolve as technology evolves. Considering how quickly technolo-

---

2. *Lawson v. Sun Microsystems, Inc.*, No. 07–0196, 2007 WL 2572170, at *5 (S.D. Ind. Sept. 4, 2007).

3. *Autotech Techs. Ltd. P'ship v. Automationdirect.com, Inc.*, 248 F.R.D. 556, 560 (N.D. Ill. 2008).

gy continues to evolve, is it reasonable to rely on older cases for guidance on what forms of production are "reasonably usable"?

6.   Sedona Principle 12 suggests that requesting parties consider the following factors in determining what form of production to specify:

a.   the forms most likely to provide the information needed to establish the relevant facts of the case;

b.   the need for metadata to organize and search the information produced;

c.   whether the information sought is reasonably accessible in the forms requested; and

d.   the requesting party's own ability to effectively manage and use the information in the forms requested.[4]

In order to sufficiently consider these factors, should you meet and confer with your adversary to obtain knowledge regarding how the adversary creates and stores electronic information before you make a formal demand for such information? Likewise, should you meet and confer with your adversary in order to learn what software it intends to use to review and manage any electronic information you produce? At what point in the discovery phase of the litigation would such discussions be most effective for the purposes of avoiding disputes and minimizing costs? To what extent is it advisable at the outset of litigation to put your adversary on notice of the categories of electronic information you intend to seek with a corresponding demand to preserve all such information in native format until such time as production issues are resolved?

7.   In *3M Company v. Kanbar*, the defendant moved to compel the plaintiff to "organize" the electronic information it produced in response to the defendant's overly broad requests for production.[5] In an attempt to address the defendant's concerns, the plaintiff disclosed the custodian of each electronic document in its production. Nonetheless, the court ordered the plaintiff to reproduce the requested information in a "reasonably usable" electronic format and required both parties to meet and agree on what is "reasonably usable." Although the court granted the defendant's motion to compel, the court noted that the discovery dispute was, in part, of the defendant's "own making" as a result of the defendant's broad discovery requests.

Did the court do the parties a disservice by directing them to meet and confer rather than ruling on what constitutes a reasonably usable electronic format? Or rather, did the court simply require the parties to cooperate in solving a problem "of their own making"? Suppose you can demonstrate to the court that your client is a disorganized record keeper. Should this allow you to produce the documents or electronic information as kept in the usual course of "disorganized" business? If

---

4.   *The Sedona Principles* at 192.

5.   No. 06–01225, 2007 WL 1725448, at *1 (N.D. Cal. June 14, 2007).

you are the requesting party, how might you narrowly tailor your discovery requests to avoid a "data dump," given the large potential volume of ESI and the time and costs associated with reviewing it? Is it feasible to do so during the initial stages of discovery when you do not yet have any familiarity with your adversary's documents, electronic systems, or record keeping practices?

8.   In contrast to *3M*, in *MGP Ingredients, Inc. v. Mars, Inc.*, the court considered similar arguments but ruled differently. In *MGP*, the defendant produced 48,000 pages of documents and ESI as they were kept in the ordinary course of business. The plaintiff moved for an order directing the defendant to specify by Bates range which documents and ESI corresponded to each of the plaintiff's discovery requests. The defendant objected to the plaintiff's motion, arguing that Rule 34 only requires that "a party who produces documents for inspection shall produce them as they are kept in the usual course of business *or* shall organize and label them to correspond with the categories in the request." The court agreed with the defendant, and in denying the plaintiff's motion, explained that "[t]he Rule is phrased in the disjunctive, and the producing party may choose either of the two methods for producing the documents. If the producing party produces documents in the order in which they are kept in the usual course of business, the Rule imposes no duty to organize and label the documents, provide an index of the documents produced, or correlate the documents to the particular request to which they are responsive."[6]

Under what circumstances might it be preferable to produce documents or ESI to correspond to the discovery requests rather than as kept in the ordinary course of business? Do you think the discovery disputes in *3M* and *MGP* could have been avoided if the parties had conducted a meet and confer regarding the form of production? The *MGP* court thought so.

> While the Court recognizes that Plaintiff now faces the formidable task of having to determine which documents are responsive to each particular request, Plaintiff was the party who formulated the requests in the manner it did and Plaintiff must take responsibility for undertaking the task of determining which documents relate to each set of its twenty-some requests. Plaintiff might have avoided this task by relying on a provision of Rule 34(b) which allows the parties, prior to production, to "otherwise agree" as to the manner in which the documents will be produced. In other words, the parties may, by agreement, deviate from the rule requiring the responding party [to] produce the documents (and any [ESI]) as kept in the usual course of business or to organize and label them to correspond to the requests. Here, however, there apparently was no attempt to reach such an agreement prior to the production.[7]

---

6.   No. 06–2318, 2007 WL 3010343 at *3 (D. Kan. Oct. 15, 2007).

7.   *Id.* at *4.

9. Processing and producing ESI can, in some instances, be significantly more costly than producing hard copy documents. As such, the expense of producing ESI may provide an incentive for litigants to request such information for the improper purpose of obtaining leverage in the litigation by increasing the adversary's litigation costs. If your adversary requests that you produce ESI, how might you demonstrate that producing the documents in electronic form would not provide significantly more information that producing the documents in hard copy form? How would you demonstrate that producing the documents in electronic form is unduly burdensome and costly?

B. SEARCH METHODS

VICTOR STANLEY, INC. v. CREATIVE PIPE, INC.

250 F.R.D. 251 (D. Md. 2008)

GRIMM, MAGISTRATE JUDGE

The plaintiff, Victor Stanley, Inc. ("VSI" or "Plaintiff") filed a motion seeking a ruling that five categories of electronically stored documents produced by defendants Creative Pipe, Inc. ("CPI") and Mark and Stephanie Pappas ("M. Pappas", "S. Pappas" or "The Pappasses") (collectively, "Defendants") in October, 2007, are not exempt from discovery because they are within the protection of the attorney-client privilege and work-product doctrine, as claimed by the Defendants. VSI argues that the electronic records at issue, which total 165 documents, are not privileged because their production by Defendants occurred under circumstances that waived any privilege or protected status. * * * For the reasons that follow, I find that all 165 electronic documents are beyond the scope of the attorney-client privilege and work-product protection because assuming, arguendo, that they qualified as privileged/protected in the first instance * * * the privilege/protection was waived by the voluntary production of the documents to VSI by Defendants.

Background Facts

* * * [T]he court ordered the parties' computer forensic experts to meet and confer in an effort to identify a joint protocol to search and retrieve relevant ESI responsive to Plaintiff's Rule 34 requests. This was done and the joint protocol prepared. The protocol contained detailed search and information retrieval instructions, including nearly five pages of keyword/phrase search terms. * * * Counsel for Defendants had previously notified the court on March 29, 2007, that individualized privilege review of the responsive documents "would delay production unnecessarily and cause undue expense." To address this concern, Defendants gave their computer forensics expert a list of keywords to be used to search and retrieve privileged and protected documents from the population of documents that were to be produced to Plaintiff. * * *

After receiving Defendants' ESI production in September, 2007, Plaintiff's counsel began their review of the materials. They soon discovered documents that potentially were privileged or work-product protected and immediately segregated this information and notified counsel for Defendants of its production, following this same procedure each time they identified potentially privileged/protected information. * * *

* * * Defendants, who bear the burden of proving that their conduct was reasonable for purposes of assessing whether they waived attorney-client privilege by producing the 165 documents to the Plaintiff, have failed to provide the court with information regarding: the keywords used; the rationale for their selection; the qualifications of M. Pappas and his attorneys to design an effective and reliable search and information retrieval method; whether the search was a simple keyword search, or a more sophisticated one, such as one employing Boolean proximity operators;[9] or whether they analyzed the results of the search to assess its reliability, appropriateness for the task, and the quality of its implementation. While keyword searches have long been recognized as appropriate and helpful for ESI search and retrieval, there are well-known limitations and risks associated with them, and proper selection and implementation obviously involves technical, if not scientific knowledge. *See, e.g., The Sedona Conference Best Practices Commentary on the Use of Search & Information Retrieval Methods in E–Discovery*, 8 Sedona Conf. J. 189, 194–95, 201–02 ("[A]lthough basic keyword searching techniques have been widely accepted both by courts and parties as sufficient to define the scope of their obligation to perform a search for responsive documents, the experience of many litigators is that simple keyword searching alone is inadequate in at least some discovery contexts. This is because simple keyword searches end up being both over-and under-inclusive in light of the inherent malleability and ambiguity of spoken and written English (as well as all other languages)."). To address this known deficiency, the Sedona Conference suggests as best practice points, inter alia:

---

9. Keyword searching may be accomplished in many ways. The simplest way is to use a series of individual keywords. Using more advanced search techniques, such as Boolean proximity operators, can enhance the effectiveness of keyword searches. Boolean proximity operators are derived from logical principles, named for mathematician George Boole, and focus on the relationships of a "set" of objects or ideas. Thus, combining a keyword with Boolean operators such as "OR," "AND," "NOT," and using parentheses, proximity limitation instructions, phrase searching instructions, or truncation and stemming instructions to require a logical order to the execution of the search can enhance the accuracy and reliability of the search. *The Sedona Conference Best Practices Commentary on the Use of Search & Information Retrieval Methods in E–Discovery*, 8 Sedona Conf. J. (2007) at 200, 202, 217–18 ("Sedona Conference Best Practices"). In addition to keyword searches, other search and information retrieval methodologies include: probabilistic search models, including "Bayesian classifiers" (which searches by creating a formula based on values assigned to particular words based on their interrelationships, proximity, and frequency to establish a relevancy ranking that is applied to each document searched); "Fuzzy Search Models" (which attempt to refine a search beyond specific words, recognizing that words can have multiple forms. By identifying the "core" for a word the fuzzy search can retrieve documents containing all forms of the target word); "Clustering" searches (searches of documents by grouping them by similarity of content, for example, the presence of a series of same or similar words that are found in multiple documents); and "Concept and Categorization Tools" (search systems that rely on a thesaurus to capture documents which use alternative ways to express the same thought). *See Sedona Conference Best Practices, supra,* at 217–23.

Practice Point 3. The choice of a specific search and retrieval method will be highly dependent on the specific legal context in which it is to be employed.

Practice Point 4. Parties should perform due diligence in choosing a particular information retrieval product or service from a vendor.

Practice Point 5. The use of search and information retrieval tools does not guarantee that all responsive documents will be identified in large data collections, due to characteristics of human language. Moreover, differing search methods may produce differing results, subject to a measure of statistical variation inherent in the science of information retrieval.

Practice Point 6. Parties should make a good faith attempt to collaborate on the use of particular search and information retrieval methods, tools and protocols (including as to keywords, concepts, and other types of search parameters).

Practice Point 7. Parties should expect that their choice of search methodology will need to be explained, either formally or informally, in subsequent legal contexts (including in depositions, evidentiary proceedings, and trials).

* * *

Use of search and information retrieval methodology * * * requires the utmost care in selecting methodology that is appropriate for the task because the consequence of failing to do so, as in this case, may be the disclosure of privileged/protected information to an adverse party, resulting in a determination by the court that the privilege/protection has been waived. Selection of the appropriate search and information retrieval technique requires careful advance planning by persons qualified to design effective search methodology. The implementation of the methodology selected should be tested for quality assurance; and the party selecting the methodology must be prepared to explain the rationale for the method chosen to the court, demonstrate that it is appropriate for the task, and show that it was properly implemented. In this regard, compliance with the Sedona Conference Best Practices for use of search and information retrieval will go a long way towards convincing the court that the method chosen was reasonable and reliable, which * * * may very well prevent a finding that the privilege or work-product protection was waived.

In this case, the Defendants have failed to demonstrate that the keyword search they performed on the text-searchable ESI was reasonable. Defendants neither identified the keywords selected nor the qualifications of the persons who selected them to design a proper search; they failed to demonstrate that there was quality-assurance testing; and when their production was challenged by the Plaintiff, they failed to carry their burden of explaining what they had done and why it was sufficient.

* * *

Conclusion

* * * [T]he court finds that the Defendants waived any privilege or work-product protection for the 165 documents at issue by disclosing them to the Plaintiff. Accordingly, the Plaintiff may use these documents as evidence in this case, provided they are otherwise admissible. * * *

COMMENTARY

1. Strengths and Weaknesses of Keyword Searching

Law students are well versed in using Westlaw, Lexis, and increasingly, their favorite Internet browser and search engine, to search for case law precedent. However, the information retrieval task of searching for "the" case (or select few cases) to support a particular legal proposition made in a brief is a very different one than the task confronting the lawyer in e-discovery, for any number of reasons. In the case of e-discovery, upon receipt of a Rule 34 document request, counsel and client are under a duty to make a reasonable search for "all" relevant, non-privileged documents and ESI within the scope of the particular request (assuming the request is well-framed). The task of finding "all" relevant documents and ESI is increasingly elusive, first because databases of all kinds are growing larger, and second, due to the inherent complexities involved in conducting searches through collections of ESI—both due to a myriad of ESI applications, as well as the broad variety of sources where ESI may be stored (servers, databases, PDAs, backup tapes). Even in the simplest case requiring a search of on-line e-mail, there is no guarantee that using keywords will always prove sufficient.

EXCERPT FROM *The Sedona Conference® Best Practice Commentary on the Use of Search and Information Retrieval Methods in E–Discovery* (2007), 8 Sedona Conf. J, *available at* http://www.thesedonaconference.org:

Issues with Keywords

Keyword searches work best when the legal inquiry is focused on finding particular documents and when the use of language is relatively predictable. For example, keyword searches work well to find all documents that mention a specific individual or date, regardless of context. However, although basic keyword searching techniques have been widely accepted both by courts and parties as sufficient to define the scope of their obligation to perform a search for responsive documents, the experience of many litigators is that simple keyword searching alone is inadequate in at least some discovery contexts. This is because simple keyword searches end up being both over-and under-inclusive in light of the inherent malleability and ambiguity of spoken and written English (as well as all other languages). Keyword searches identify all documents containing a specified term regardless of context, and so they can possibly capture many documents irrelevant to the user's query. For example, the term "strike" could be found in documents relating to a labor union tactic, a military action, options trading, or baseball, to name just a few (illustrating "polysemy," or *ambiguity* in the use of language). The problem of the relative percentage of "false positive" hits or noise in the data is potentially huge, amounting in some cases to huge numbers of files which must be searched to find responsive documents. On the other hand, keyword searches have the potential to miss documents that contain a word that has the same meaning as the term used in the query, but is not specified. For example, a user making queries about labor actions might miss an email referring to a "boycott" if that particular word was not included as a keyword, and a lawyer investigating tax fraud via options trading might miss an email referring to "exercise price" if that term was not specifically searched (illustrating "synonymy" or *variation* in the use of language). And of course, if authors of records are inventing words "on the fly," as they have done through history, and now are doing with increasing frequency in electronic communications, such problems are compounded. Keyword searches can also exclude common or inadvertently misspelled instances of the term (*e.g.*, "Phillip" for "Philip," or "strik" for "strike") or variations on "stems" of words (*e.g.* "striking"). So too, it is well known that even the best of optical character recognition (OCR) scanning processes introduce a certain rate of random error into document texts, potentially transforming would-be keywords into something else. Finally, using keywords alone results in a return set of potentially responsive documents that are not weighted and ranked based upon their potential importance or relevance. In other words, each document is considered to have an equal probability of being responsive upon further manual review.

More advanced keyword searches using "Boolean" operators and techniques borrowed from "fuzzy logic" may increase the number of relevant documents and decrease the number of irrelevant documents retrieved. These searches attempt to emulate the way humans use language to describe concepts. In essence, however, they simply translate ordinary words and phrases into a Boolean search argument. Thus, a natural language search for "all birds that live in Africa" is translated to something like ("bird* + liv* + Africa"). At the present time, it would appear that the majority of automated litigation support providers and software continue to rely on keyword searching. Such methods are limited by their dependence on matching a specific, sometimes arbitrary choice of language to describe the targeted topic of interest. The issue of whether there is room for improvement in the rate of "recall" (as defined in the next section) of relevant documents in a given collection is something lawyers must consider when relying on simple and traditional input of keywords alone.

Use of Alternative Search Tools and Methods

Lawyers are beginning to feel more comfortable using alternative search tools to identify potentially relevant electronically stored information. These more advanced text mining tools include "conceptual search methods" which rely on semantic relations between words, and/or which use "thesauri" to capture documents that would be missed in keyword searching.

* * *

"Concept" search and retrieval technologies attempt to locate information that relates to a desired concept, without the presence of a particular word or phrase. The classic example is the concept search that will recognize that documents about Eskimos and igloos are related to Alaska, even if they do not specifically mention the word "Alaska."

* * *

Other automated tools rely on "taxonomies" and "ontologies" to help find documents conceptually related to the topic being searched, based on commercially available data or on specifically compiled information. This information is provided by attorneys or developed for the business function or specific industry (*e.g.*, the concept of "strike" in labor law *vs.* "strike" in options trading). These tools rely on the information that linguists collect from the lawyers and witnesses about the key factual issues in the case—the people, organization, and key concepts relating to the business as well as the idiosyncratic communications that might be lurking in documents, files, and emails. For example, a linguist would want to know how union organizers or company officials might communicate plans, any special code words used in the industry, the relationships of collective bargaining units, company management structure, and other issues and concepts. Another type of search tool relies on mathematical probabilities that a certain text is associated with a particular conceptual category. These types of machine learning tools, which include "clustering" and "latent semantic indexing," are arguably helpful in addressing cultural biases of taxonomies because they do not depend on linguistic analysis, but on mathematical probabilities. They can also help to find communications in code language and neologisms. For example, if the labor lawyer were searching for evidence that management was targeting neophytes in the union, she might miss the term "n00b" (a neologism for "newbie"). This technology, used in government intelligence, is particularly apt in helping lawyers find information when they do not know exactly what to look for. For example, when a lawyer is looking for evidence that key players conspired to violate the labor union laws, she will usually not know the "code words" or expressions the players may have used to disguise their communications.

* * *

For a more in-depth discussion of alternatives to keyword searching, see the Appendix to the Sedona Search Commentary (discussing various new search technologies).

2. Should Expert Testimony Be Required to Explain to the Trier of Fact How Search Protocols Were Constructed?

UNITED STATES v. O'KEEFE

537 F.Supp.2d 14 (D.D.C. 2008)

FACCIOLA, MAGISTRATE JUDGE

The indictment charges that the defendant, Michael John O'Keefe, Sr., when employed by the Department of State in Canada, received, quid pro quo, gifts and other benefits from his co-defendant, Sunil Agrawal, for expediting visa requests for employees of Agrawal's company, STS Jewels.

By his Order of April 27, 2007, Judge Friedman required the government to conduct a thorough and complete search of both its hard copy and electronic files in "a good faith effort to uncover all responsive information in its possession custody or control."

The first category of "responsive information," as defined by Judge Friedman, was "requests respecting visa applications submitted by or on behalf of STS Jewels employees—including requests for expedited visa interview appointments, decisions granting or denying such interview requests, and the grant or denial of the visas themselves." This search was to be of the files of the consulates in 1) Toronto, Canada, 2) Ottawa, Canada, 3) Matamoros, Mexico, 4) Mexico City, Mexico, 5) Nogales, Mexico, and 6) Nuevo Laredo, Mexico.

The second category of "responsive information" was "all written rules, policies, procedures and guidelines regarding the treatment of expedited visa application appointments and visa application approvals at the above-mentioned posts in Canada and Mexico." The government was also required to "produce any memoranda, letters, e-mails, faxes and other correspondence prepared or received by any consular officers at these posts that reflect either policy or decisions in specific cases with respect to expediting" visa applications.

As to the latter, Judge Friedman emphasized his expected scope of the search and the necessity for it. He stated:

[I]t now appears from discovery produced on March 21, 2007 that employees below the level of consular officers—including even consulate secretaries and non-U.S. citizen employees—may approve requests for and schedule expedited visa interview appointments. The files of any such persons and the consulates themselves therefore also must be searched. Such communications go directly to the defense of showing that the requests made by or on behalf of STS employees are similar to other requests for expedited visa interview appointments that (it is asserted) have routinely been granted without the provision of anything of value.

Defendants, who have received the government's submission in compliance with this Order, have moved to compel, protesting that the government has not fulfilled the responsibilities Judge Friedman imposed.

I. Detailed Information About the Government's Searches

First, for each location searched, defendants demand a comprehensive description of all of the sources that were searched (both paper and electronic), how each source was searched, and who conducted the search.

In its opposition, the government produced the declaration of Peggy L. Petrovich, the Visa Unit Chief at the United States Consulate General in Toronto, Canada. According to Ms. Petrovich, she, along with her five-member staff, did the following in her effort to comply with Judge Friedman's April 27, 2007, Order:

* * *

B. Electronic Record Files

1. Search and Yield: She searched all active servers and backup tapes (retained for two weeks) and that search yielded "responsive e-mails, the [Standard Operating Procedures] previously mentioned, and the NIV (Non–Immigrant Visa) Schedule Calendar located on Toronto's shared public drive."

2. Parameters of the Search Conducted: "[T]he electronic search included all e-mail and stand-alone electronic documents, e.g., documents prepared on our office software applications, regarding expedited appointments located on shared drives, personal drives and hard drives for all consular officers and locally-engaged staff, i.e., secretaries and other employees, who approved or scheduled expedited non-immigrant visa interviews, or who played any role in the process."

3. Search Terms: She used the following search terms: "early or expedite* or appointment or early & interview or expedite* & interview." She had "[t]he Information Management Staff conduct the search of personal and hard drives because they have access to all drives from the network server, not just shared drives."

4. Review of Results: She reviewed the results of the search and "removed only those clearly about wholly unrelated matters, e.g., emails

about staff members' early departures or dentist appointments." She "made sure that all emails residing in the shared email address folders that related to expedited appointments were included in the results ... that were produced in electronic format and provided on cd-rom."

5. Deleted Emails: "According to the Information Management staff, any emails deleted prior to [her] search" in May 2007 are gone. Electronically stored information is backed up for two weeks and then the back up tapes are reused and their previous contents obliterated. "No other back-up server for electronic documents, either on-or off-site, exists."

6. O'Keefe Emails: "All currently existing responsive emails located during the search of Michael O'Keefe's personal drive were included in the cd-rom" that the government gave the defendants. Since the hard drives from the computers O'Keefe used were previously seized by the government, they could not be searched.

7. SOPs: "The only other responsive materials discovered during the electronic search for stand-alone electronic documents were the SOPs [described in paragraph 4, supra] and the NIV Schedule Calendar which was provided in hard copy format."

8. Lack of documents: There were no responsive documents from "Mike Schimmel, the previous visa unit chief; Peggy Petrovich, the current visa unit chief; Pat Haye, the visa assistant who has main responsibility for processing expedited appointment requests; and, Jane Boyd, the visa assistant who has main responsibility for scheduling appointments for diplomatic and official applicants."

II.   Problems with the Government's Production

* * *

B.   Electronic Production

Defendants marshal several objections and concerns about the government's search of the electronically stored information. They take the government to task for 1) not interviewing the employees as to their use of electronic means as a form of communication regarding expedited reviews, 2) not having the employees search their own electronically stored information and 3) not indicating what software it used to conduct the search or how it ascertained what search terms it would use.

Defendants caution that, if forensic searchware was not used, there is a likelihood that stored e-mail folders in .pst files were either not searched or not searched accurately. * * *

* * *

* * * Whether search terms or "keywords" will yield the information sought is a complicated question involving the interplay, at least, of the sciences of computer technology, statistics and linguistics. *See* George L. Paul & Jason R. Baron, *Information Inflation: Can the Legal System*

Adapt?', 13 Rich. J.L. & Tech. 10 (2007). Indeed, a special project team of the Working Group on Electronic Discovery of the Sedona Conference is studying that subject and their work indicates how difficult this question is. *See The Sedona Conference, Best Practices Commentary on the Use of Search and Information Retrieval*, 8 The Sedona Conf. J. 189 (2007), *available at* http://www.thesedonaconference.org/content/miscFiles/Best_Practices_Retrieval_Methods_revised_cover_and_preface.pdf. Given this complexity, for lawyers and judges to dare opine that a certain search term or terms would be more likely to produce information than the terms that were used is truly to go where angels fear to tread. This topic is clearly beyond the ken of a layman and requires that any such conclusion be based on evidence that, for example, meets the criteria of Rule 702 of the Federal Rules of Evidence [governing expert testimony]. Accordingly, if defendants are going to contend that the search terms used by the government were insufficient, they will have to specifically so contend in a motion to compel and their contention must be based on evidence that meets the requirements of Rule 702 of the Federal Rules of Evidence.

* * *

3. Can Search Protocols Be Negotiated?

EXCERPT FROM George L. Paul & Jason R. Baron, *Information Inflation: Can the Legal System Adapt?*, 13 Rich. J.L. & Tech. 10 (2007):

> **Step 1:** The parties meet and confer on the nature of each other's computer hardware and software applications. Proposals are exchanged on the scope of search obligations, in terms of databases and applications to be searched, what active and possibly legacy media are to be made subject to search, and any limitations on scope keyed to particular individuals within an institution, particular time periods, or other ways to limit the scope of the search obligation. Keywords are proposed as a basis for conducting searches, with attention paid to negotiating appropriate Boolean strings of terms, with a full range of proximity operators, wildcard, truncation and stemming terms (to the extent any or all such techniques can be utilized). Alternative concept-based search methodologies are discussed, to the extent either party has experience in using and has found to be efficacious in finding documents. A timetable is agreed upon for conducting initial searches.

> **Step 2:** In the interval between meet and confers, parties conduct searches in accordance with the representations made at the initial meet and confer. Based on sampling techniques or other methods employed, estimates are gathered on the volume of data potentially to be made subject to search in light of the wording of opposing parties' search requests.

> **Step 3:** Returning to the meet and confer table, the parties describe how initial searches were conducted and what are the preliminary

results. Based on a finding that either too few or too many files were retrieved corresponding to particular specific requests, search protocols are adjusted accordingly for a second round of searching. If some form of open discovery measures are agreed to, an exchange of actual documents found as the result of the initial searches takes place at this juncture, so as to provide the opposing party with the opportunity to essentially request "more like this" (or not).[8] Even, however, absent fully open discovery, more limited reporting is made of search results, in order to narrow or expand search requests as appropriate.

Step 4: The process continues in iterative fashion as agreed to by the parties, until a mutually agreed time, or a mutually agreed cap on numbers of responsive documents is reached.

As is well known in the field of economics, the art of war, and elsewhere, cooperative behavior can be encouraged and will rationally arise within an otherwise adversarial paradigm (including outright state of hostility between parties), where a continuing relationship exists and there is a modicum of goodwill existing in the form of trust. No reason exists not to similarly employ models of cooperation in attempting to narrow the search task in light of information inflation.[9]

BOOLEAN NEGOTIATION EXERCISE

Hypothetical Complaint: *The Estate of Virginia Vesta v. Agni Paper Co., et al.*

A Complaint has been filed for compensatory and punitive damages alleging wrongful death, negligence and medical malpractice. Plaintiff Virginia Vesta is a resident of Halema'uma'u City in the State of Vulcan. She was employed at a pilot plant owned and operated by defendant Agni Paper Company. The Complaint alleges that on January 2, 2008, plaintiff drove to the Agni Pilot Plant where she parked her car in the company parking lot, after which she proceeded to her work station where her job was to sample paper prototypes of various types of stationery that Agni produces. Agni is a company known for its fire-resistant stationery. It has developed special patents for certain types of

---

8. The envisioned process is one application of the idea of "relevance feedback," a well-known concept in the information retrieval field. "Traditional relevance feedback methods require that users explicitly give feedback by, for example, specifying keywords, selecting and marking documents, or answering questions about their interests. Such relevance feedback methods force users to engage in additional activities beyond their normal searching behavior." Diane Kelly & Jaime Teevan, *Implicit Feedback for Inferring User Preference: A Bibliography*, Sigir Forum 1 (2003), *available at* http://www.sigir.org/forum/2003F/teevan.pdf.

9. Alternatively, there is always the possible remedy of cost shifting, which has come into vogue regarding searching information that is "not reasonably accessible" because of the complexities of modern information systems. *See* Fed. R. Civ. P. 26(b)(2)(B). *See generally Zubulake v. UBS Warburg LLC (Zubulake I)*, 217 F.R.D. 309, 324 (S.D.N.Y. 2003) (allowing for cost shifting in case of inaccessible data). One possible scenario to a Rule 26(f) meet and confer request to search through a billion e-mails is to allow the search, but at the expense of the searcher. In other words, "if you wish to search through my billion documents, 'Make my day'—you can pay for it and spend the time doing so." Courts already have this authority under the proportionality principle, now found in Rule 26(b)(2)(C).

paper with unusually high heat tolerances and also designs custom stationery for corporations located in fire-prone areas. The likelihood of whether an object will burn under certain circumstances is measured in terms of "ignition propensity." At approximately 3 p.m. on January 2, 2008, plaintiff was engaged in testing the ignition propensity of two particular grades of stationery. Plaintiff had recommended to the company that all debris and loose paper be removed from the surrounding areas prior to testing samples; however, no action was taken on plaintiff's requests. On that date, during a routine test, plaintiff suffered serious burns and injuries due to a machine jamming and a huge explosion of fire that ensued. She later succumbed to her injuries at a local hospital.

The Complaint alleges a cause of action for wrongful death, due to Agni Paper's failure to provide written safety instructions to its employees concerning safe operation of testing equipment, failure to provide strict supervision of dangerous testing operations, failure to follow standard practices of removing debris and loose paper from the testing area prior to starting sample testing, and failure to heed plaintiff's recommendation that debris and loose paper be removed.

Plaintiff has propounded dozens of requests for production of documents and ESI under Rule 34, one of which is the following:

REQUEST FOR PRODUCTION No. 15: Produce all reports, written memoranda, correspondence, and other documents related to any complaints, inspection reports, or warnings received from any governmental agency concerning working environment or conditions, or standards violations related to safety.

(i) Exercise: devise a proposed search protocol for the purpose of launching an automated search of defendant's database.

(ii) Consider the following proposed Boolean strings as the product of back and forth negotiations between plaintiff and defendant.

Defendant's Proposed String: (complaint! OR "inspection report!" OR warning!) AND [(working w/5 (environment OR condition*)) OR (standard* w/3 violation*)] AND safety

Plaintiff's Proposed String: (complaint! OR criticism! OR notification! OR notice) AND (inspect! OR apprais! OR exam! OR investing! OR review!) AND (warning! OR precaution! OR caution!) AND (work! OR occupation! OR industry! OR factory OR manufactur!) AND (environment! OR atmosphere! OR surrounding! OR setting!) AND (condition! OR circumstance!) AND (safety OR security! OR assurance!) AND (violation! OR infraction! OR infring! OR breach!)

Defendant's Rejoinder to Plaintiff's Proposal: (complaint! OR notification! OR notice) AND (inspect! OR apprais! OR exam! OR investing! OR review!) AND (warning! OR precaution! OR caution!) AND (work! OR occupation! OR industry! OR factory OR manufactur!) AND (environment! OR atmosphere! OR surrounding! OR setting!) AND (condition! OR circumstance!) AND safety AND (violation! OR infraction! OR infring! OR breach!) AND ((OSHA OR NIOSH OR NFPA OR CPSC) OR ("Occupational Safety & Health Administration" OR "National Institute for Occupational Safety and Health" OR "National Fire Protection Association" OR "Consumer Product Safety Commission"))

Final Agreed upon Negotiated String: (complaint! OR notification! OR notice) AND (inspect! OR apprais! OR exam! OR investing! OR review!) AND (warning! OR precaution! OR caution!) AND (work! OR occupation! OR industry! OR factory OR manufactur!) AND (environment! OR atmosphere! OR surrounding! OR setting!) AND (condition! OR circumstance!) AND (safety) AND (violation! OR infraction! OR infring! OR breach!)

NEGOTIATION COMMENTARY

At the outset of the negotiation for this string plaintiff agreed to strike the terms "security* " and "assurance* " from plaintiff's original proposal. Assume that it had been previously agreed that the term "safety* " was sufficient to locate documents responsive to workplace safety issues raised by the Complaint. At the request of defendant, plaintiff also agreed to remove the term "criticism* " from the string under the rationale that documents discussing government complaints or warnings would use more formal language. Although not in its original proposal, defendant proposed that certain government agencies (OSHA, NIOSH, NFPA, and the CPSC) concerned with workplace safety should be added to the string, to avoid retrieving documents that would involve ancillary issues related to other government agencies. Plaintiff conceded that while the four agencies suggested by defendant would be those most likely concerned with workplace safety, these agencies would not always be named in the actual documents discussing their warnings and related matters. Defendant asserted that any official communications to or from the parties would almost certainly name the agency on either the letterhead or address area. Plaintiff countered that the request appropriately asks for more than just official communications and memoranda and that internal email or more informal documents might very well assume that the reader would know the agency at issue and not name it explicitly. Defendant reluctantly conceded that such less-formal documents would be arguably responsive to the request and agreed to a string that did not include the names of the four agencies that it had proposed.

What do you see as the strengths or weaknesses of entering into negotiations on the scope of a Boolean string? What would you have done differently than the way in which the negotiations proceeded above?

C. USE OF TECHNOLOGY FOR SEARCH AND REVIEW

1. The Use of Selection Criteria and Filtering to Manage ESI

CLEARONE COMMUNICATIONS, INC. v. CHIANG

No. 07 Civ. 37, 2008 WL 920336 (D. Utah Apr. 1, 2008)

NUFFER, MAGISTRATE JUDGE

Plaintiff ClearOne Communications, Inc. (ClearOne) makes a * * * motion for entry of a search protocol order. * * * The search protocol is to be used to search the data from computers used by the WideBand Defendants (Andrew Chiang, Jun Yang, Lonny Bowers, and WideBand Solutions, Inc.) which were imaged pursuant to two orders issued last year. The first imaging order required that a third party engaged by ClearOne create and maintain custody of images of certain of WideBand Defendants' computers, while the second order provided that a third party retained by WideBand create and maintain custody of certain images of other of WideBand Defendants' computers. Neither order gave ClearOne direct access to the images or data. However, all that information is subject to existing discovery requests.

The second imaging order sought to establish "a protocol for searching the mirror images . . . to identify relevant and responsive documents." * * * The protocol as it now stands requires key word searches by technical experts; review of search result reports by Wide-Band Defendants' counsel for facial claims of privilege; delivery of the reports to ClearOne counsel for preliminary assertion of responsiveness; WideBand Defendants' counsel's review for responsiveness and privilege; and delivery of documents and privilege logs.

The issue before the court is establishment of the search terms-and the issue is greatly simplified by the parties' agreement on many search terms. ClearOne has accepted, with five additions, the search terms proposed by WideBand Defendants in September 2007. The dispute arises over the conjunctive or disjunctive use of the terms.

Conjunctive or Disjunctive Search

Essentially, there are three categories of search criteria: "Name" (searching for names of specific individuals); "Tech" (searching for a particular technological reference); and "License" terms (searching for terms relating to the licensing of certain source code). WideBand Defendants say it is "reasonable to require some connectors that would narrow the search results to subjects relevant to the issues in this lawsuit." Specifically, WideBand Defendants request "that the 'Name' and 'License' search terms be combined with the 'Tech' terms."

As to the "Name" terms, conjunctive search seems necessary. Otherwise, every occurrence of the "Name" terms will result in a positive hit, meaning that virtually every document in the electronic media will be identified as potentially responsive. In a relatively small business such as WideBand, almost every document will refer to one of the key employees in the company. Requiring a hit of one "Name" term AND one "Tech" term will ensure that more responsive documents are flagged as potentially responsive.

However, as to the "License" terms, conjunctive search could be excessively narrow. Again, because WideBand is a relatively small company, licensing activity would be relatively small. By comparison, technology is the core of its business, so disjunctive use of the "Tech" terms would probably result in an excessive number of false positives.

ClearOne * * * argues for the use of additional terms which it claims come from its Honeybee code, which it claims WideBand Defendants misappropriated. WideBand Defendants claim this code is nothing more than Texas Instrument library code which is freely available and reproducible. WideBand objects that the proposed additional search terms are "extremely broad" and are not linked "to any particular discovery responses." WideBand Defendants also say that use of these terms takes an important issue from the jury.

The newly proposed search terms are not extremely broad. In fact, they are specifically identified by ClearOne as contained within or very closely related to specific code that ClearOne uses. Without deciding whether that specific code is copyrighted or a trade secret of ClearOne, it is clear that the use of these terms, in the disjunctive, will yield evidence that is potentially very significant to this case. No ultimate facts are found or established by the use of words in a protocol, in spite of ClearOne's urgings and WideBand Defendants' protests. This is a discovery order. * * * ClearOne is free to ask the jury to draw inferences, but WideBand is also free to explain to the jury what WideBand claims actually happened.

Further, the search protocol is not the "last word" on electronic discovery in this case. The use of key word protocols is one step in the process which contemplates many more steps, including review of search result reports by WideBand Defendants' counsel for facial claims of privilege; delivery of reports to ClearOne counsel for preliminary assertion of responsiveness; WideBand Defendants' counsel's review of the reports and documents for responsiveness and privilege; and delivery of documents and privilege logs.

This order is not the last word on key words, either. If documents are discovered which suggest that other documents exist which were not identified as potentially responsive, or if a surprisingly small or unreasonably large number of documents is identified as potentially responsive, refinement may be needed. Much of the argument is now speculative, since there is no actual experience with a search. This first protocol may suffice, or it may in effect be a sampling which reveals the need for more-or less-or different-key words.

* * *

COMMENTARY

Organizations of all sizes maintain large volumes of ESI on both their active processing systems and on legacy data storage systems, such as backup tape. For any given discovery matter, however, the percentage of these large, co-mingled data sets that are likely to be considered as potentially relevant is small. How can an organization realistically, reasonably and defensibly review these large accumulations of data in order to cull out that fraction that may be responsive to the matter at hand?

Traditional models of discovery, such as printing documents to a paper or image format for review, quickly break down when applied to electronic data sets of substantial volumes. Even apart from the data loss issues associated with the conversion of electronic files to paper and/or image formats, the associated costs alone are prohibitive.

If the model of manual review does not work, can party-developed selection criteria be used as an automated methodology for identifying, locating and retrieving potentially relevant data? Selection criteria are a form of filtering. The result of performing a search using selection criteria is a subset of the original data containing matches ("hits") based on the criteria utilized. Selection criteria can include specific search terms, combinations of specific search terms with Boolean operators, date ranges, time ranges, file sizes, file types, identified data sets and any other distinctive feature or characteristic that could be used to identify the potentially relevant data.

The utility of selection criteria to filter potentially relevant data often depends upon the volume of the data maintained. The more ESI an entity manages, the more likely that it will use electronic filtering methods to identify, locate, and retrieve that targeted set of potentially relevant data. Indeed, given the costs associated with incorporating the entirety of a large set of ESI into discovery, the use of electronic searching and filtering tools may be the only realistic way that potentially relevant data can be identified and put into review in any reasonable manner.

a. Typical Positions Taken by Those Seeking ESI

* Selection criteria cannot be comprehensive enough to ensure that all potentially relevant data will be identified

* Search technologies are not reliable enough to ensure that all relevant data will be found

* If selection criteria are chosen solely by the owner of the ESI, they are going to be biased towards not finding relevant information

* We should be allowed access to all of the ESI in order to run our own selection criteria against it

b. Typical Positions Taken by Those Holding ESI

* The use of selection criteria is an accepted and widely used methodology for identifying and culling potentially responsive information from the vast amount of electronic data that exists with various formats and processing platforms

* We have taken steps to ensure that the selection criteria used are valid and reliable

* Search technology does allow the use of selection criteria to be a reliable and effective means of finding data

* We have the right to control our own data and to shield non-relevant, trade secret, privileged and other materials from the opposing party

c. A Neutral Approach

In many cases, electronic data is found in broadly categorized groupings, such as in vaguely named sub-directories within an individual's hard drive, or in generic, co-mingled folders such as an e-mail system's "inbox" or "outbox," or is otherwise not stored in a manner that can be used to efficiently identify potentially responsive information from the storage matrix alone.

The use of carefully derived and vetted selection criteria is a reasonable approach when dealing with large amounts of electronic data. Indeed, one of the key advantages of electronic data—and one of the key, underlying reasons for dealing with electronic data in electronic form—is that high-speed, efficient, automated methods exist to identify potentially relevant information, thereby allowing large, co-mingled sets of data to be defensibly and efficiently brought into the discovery process.

In projects involving large volumes of data, a defensible process would generally incorporate selection criteria and the searching of data as follows:

1. Collect data from the client

2. Sample or otherwise analyze the data set to determine the proper scope of data to be processed keeping in mind the likelihood of discovering responsive data and the corresponding cost and time burdens

3. Load the data into an electronic review platform for analysis

4. Establish and validate appropriate selection criteria

5. Filter the data using the validated selection criteria

6. Apply annotation criteria to the data

7. Perform review of the selected, annotated data in electronic form with appropriate responsiveness, privilege and production determinations

d.   A Defensible Selection Process

The steps required to develop and implement an appropriate data selection process should include the following:

i.   *Analysis of Proposed Search Terms and Selection Criteria*

Using search terms either provided by the client or created by a specialist familiar with the litigation and various data demographics, an analysis is done to determine the potential scope of search, selection and annotation processing. This analysis includes an assessment of the initial search and selection criteria to determine the best mechanisms for implementing the search and annotation process. Issues and questions regarding the criteria are developed as appropriate.

ii.   *Creation of Proposed Criteria Using Standardized Syntax*

The initial set of selection criteria are translated into a standardized syntax for expressing search and annotation criteria. This syntax combines simple structured English with notations taken from the discipline of formal linguistic analysis and specification, in addition to appropriate operators utilized by common search tools. The proposed criteria are transformed into this format to provide a compact and non-ambiguous form for subsequent reviews.

In addition to formalizing the syntax of the search criteria, groupings of the criteria are proposed. These groupings are hierarchical—usually two or three levels deep—and are considered high-level annotations. The groupings are based upon substantive, case-specific issue identification from the client, the expert's analysis of the litigation project, the particulars of the proposed criteria, and the expert's prior experience with litigation reviews. These groupings are often utilized to organize the data in ways that facilitate and expedite the downstream review of the data items.

iii.   *Validation and Update of the Proposed Search Criteria Through Client Review*

The standardized criteria are reviewed with the client and counsel to ensure correctness and completeness. Issues and questions are resolved at this time and a revised set of criteria are developed.

iv.   *Revised Criteria Are Tested Against Sample Data*

The proposed criteria are tested against the collected data. This testing involves performing searches using the proposed selection criteria and examining the results of the searches to determine if certain criteria are either over-inclusive or under-inclusive (*i.e.* returning data which is not potentially relevant or missing data that may be potentially relevant). Both "hit" and "non-hit" data is also analyzed using word-frequency and other statistical tests in an attempt to identify underlying data patterns and/or additional selection criteria.

Both client and counsel should participate in this examination to ensure that the results are appropriate for the intended final use. The results of this review may be used to further modify the selection criteria so that they better identify potentially relevant data items and to better facilitate filtering and/or annotation.

This test, review, revision cycle may be repeated as many times as necessary to ensure that the final search criteria chosen are accurate and defensible. This process may also be repeated later if additional data sets are introduced that do not have the same common source as the data previously validated.

v. Finalization of Criteria into Formats Appropriate for Expected Volumes

The finalized search criteria are converted to appropriate formats and notations for use with defensible electronic search and annotation tools. Different tools may be used depending upon the type(s) of data to be searched, the need for online reviews (as opposed to immediate electronic or paper production of matching data), and data volumes.

e. Other Issues to Consider

The holder of ESI may consider entering into discussions with the adversary regarding specific selection criteria to be used in subsequent searches of the electronic data set. While this is not always possible or advantageous, there are situations when such a dialogue can eliminate needless bottlenecks, such as disputes over the search terms used, and validate mutually agreed upon criteria and processes.

Producing parties must realize that the scope of terms employed must be broad enough to be defensible in the event of a challenge by the requesting party.[10]

2. The Use of Technology for Review

TREPPEL v. BIOVAIL CORP.
233 F.R.D. 363 (S.D.N.Y. 2006)

FRANCIS, MAGISTRATE JUDGE

* * * The plaintiff in this action, Jerry I. Treppel, alleges that the defendants engaged in a smear campaign that destroyed his career as a

---

10. *See, e.g., In re Amsted Indus., Inc. "ERISA" Litig.*, No. 01 C 2963, 2002 WL 31844956 (N.D. Ill. Dec. 18, 2002) (finding that defendants' document production efforts, which involved word searches on twenty-five backup tapes of e-mail and the questioning of selected individuals regarding e-mail on their computers, were insufficient, and that additional searches not limited by defendants' relevancy objections were required). *But see McPeek v. Ashcroft*, No. Civ. A. 00–201, 2003 WL 75780 (D.D.C. Jan. 9, 2003) (rejecting plaintiff's demands for additional searches of backup tapes based upon burden and the limited likelihood that relevant information could be retrieved from the additional searches).

securities analyst. In his initial complaint, he asserted claims of defamation, tortious interference with prospective economic advantage, prima facie tort, and civil conspiracy against the defendants, Biovail Corporation ("Biovail"); its Chairman and Chief Executive Officer, Eugene Melnyk; its General Counsel, Kenneth C. Cancellara; Sitrick and Company, Inc.; and Michael S. Sitrick. Mr. Treppel now moves pursuant to Rule 37(a) of the Federal Rules of Civil Procedure for an order compelling the defendants to * * * answer a range of questions concerning their electronic data management practices * * *.

* * *

Biovail has yet to produce any documents in response to the plaintiff's document request. When it received the request, Biovail suggested defining the scope of any review of electronic records by stipulating which files would be searched and what search terms would be utilized. The plaintiff declined, apparently believing that "the use of search terms has no application to the standard discovery process of locating and producing accessible hard copy and electronic documents." The plaintiff's assumption is flawed. Even in a case involving exclusively hard copy documents, there is no obligation on the part of a responding party to examine every scrap of paper in its potentially voluminous files in order to comply with its discovery obligations. Rather, it must conduct a diligent search, which involves developing a reasonably comprehensive search strategy. Such a strategy might, for example, include identifying key employees and reviewing any of their files that are likely to be relevant to the claims in the litigation. Defined search strategies are even more appropriate in cases involving electronic data, where the number of documents may be exponentially greater. *See* * * * *The Sedona Principles; Best Practices Recommendations & Principles for Addressing Electronic Document Production, Principle 11* (2003) ("A responding party may properly access and identify potentially responsive electronic data and documents by using reasonable selection criteria, such as search terms or samples."). Thus, the plaintiff's refusal to stipulate to a search methodology in this case was apparently based on a misconception of the scope of the responding party's obligation. At the same time, it was a missed opportunity; the plaintiff might have convinced Biovail to broaden its search in ways that would uncover more responsive documents and avoid subsequent disputes.

Yet the plaintiff's recalcitrance does not excuse Biovail's failure to produce any responsive documents whatsoever. Biovail suggested a strategy by which it would search the computer files of Mr. Melnyk, Mr. Cancellara, and Kenneth Howling, its director of investor relations, using the search terms: (i) Treppel, (ii) Jerry, (iii) Bank of America, (iv) Banc of America, (v) BAS, and (vi) BofA. (Steiner 9/1/05 Letter at 2). Absent agreement with Mr. Treppel about a search strategy, Biovail should have proceeded unilaterally, producing all responsive documents located by its search. It shall now do so promptly. In addition, Biovail shall provide the plaintiff with a detailed explanation of the search protocol it implements.

This ruling is not an endorsement of the methodology that Biovail has suggested, either in relation to the choice of files to be searched or the terms to be applied. It is, instead, an interim step that is subject to revision once Biovail has responded to the interrogatories relating to its electronic data and the plaintiff has articulated any specific concerns about the scope of the search.

Conclusion

For the reasons discussed above, the plaintiff's motion to compel is granted to the extent that Biovail and Mr. Melnyk * * * shall promptly conduct a diligent search, explain the search protocol they use, and produce the responsive documents so located * * *.

COMMENTARY

The volume of ESI within the business world requires the use of new processes and procedures for effective review during the discovery process. Traditional models of document review do not allow for the proper, economic and defensible review of the large volume of ESI.

When discoverable paper documents were created and stored, custodians managed their data sets much more stringently than the current management of electronic records. Maintaining multiple copies of drafts and final documents in paper consumed unacceptable levels of storage space and raised difficult management problems. Custodians typically maintained copies of final documents in a relatively organized system of file folders. Additionally, documents were often managed by an organization-wide document management policy, and those documents that outlived their useful business lives were destroyed.

As electronic data storage costs have decreased dramatically in the past thirty years, computer users have found it increasingly easy to save multiple drafts and copies of their documents. The constant growth of new technologies such as e-mail, results in a volume of ESI that dwarfs the volume of paper documents in earlier times.

Electronic datasets differ from collections of paper documents. Custodians generally stored and organized paper documents in files and folders. When paper documents were collected for litigation, specific files and folders likely to hold responsive documents were selected.

In comparison, electronic documents are stored more frequently in various draft and finished states, often in general storage directories. When electronic data is collected for litigation, key employee mailboxes and file storage areas are often copied in their entirety, thereby containing a mix of documents that may or may not be related to the matter at hand. Electronic document sets therefore require a more robust review methodology that provides the ability to identify relevant and/or privileged items in a timely and economical manner.

The chart below sets out the processing times associated with an electronic mail set of twenty million items. This is a rather modest email set. An organization with one hundred employees each receiving fifty email messages a day with a twenty-five percent retention rate and a thirty day backup policy with weekly tape pulls will accumulate over twenty million emails in a year. The chart demonstrates that the processing times must be less than 1/10th of a second for each email message in order to meet reasonable timelines.

Searching twenty million email messages		
Per Item Processing	Hours to Process	Calendar Time
10 seconds each	55,556 hours	6.3 years
1 second each	55,56 hours	7.7 months
1/4 second each	1,389 hours	2 months
1/10 second each	557 hours	3 weeks
1/100 second each	56 hours	2.3 days
1/1000 second each	5.6 hours	....

Using a manual review process in a discovery search will eliminate the ability to meet these processing times. Electronic processing of electronic data must be used to identify those items from the data set that are responsive to the matter at hand and that will then be subjected to review. The review of ESI using document review tools designed to search and display electronic documents in electronic form, however, offers many benefits that are not possible in a traditional paper or paper-equivalent environment.[11] A reviewer of paper documents must review documents sequentially. A reviewer using an electronic search tool may search for documents on any number of fields in order to find similar documents, revise the search as often as required, and then bulk annotate similar items, thereby dramatically speeding up the review process.

Electronic Document Review Platforms

A comprehensive electronic document review platform will provide features such as:

- Extensive pre-review analysis that identifies various attributes about the data set, including file types, file sizes, file quantities, file dates and times, file ownership, and access to any other metadata associated with both the data set and the individual files

- Group annotation capability that allows individual files to be labeled with an identifying annotation that can then be used to

---

11. Some technologies such as TIFF and PDF create electronic versions of paper. These technologies, for the most part, are static in nature and perform much like paper in search, review and other processes.

include, exclude, route, or otherwise manage the file during the review process

- Data-type specific search capabilities that provide accurate and defensible retrieval of data based on both structured and ad-hoc keywords and other criteria
- Scalability that accommodates virtually any volume of data without significantly impacting deadlines
- Ability to integrate remote reviewers over the internet or other network environment in a secure manner
- A user interface that has been designed and tested for quick, convenient review
- Centralized hosting of data files to allow effective security and data management while providing a central hub for reviewer access
- Distributed hosting of files that will not function in a central hosted environment, such as extremely large files or files that require specific hardware and/or software to function
- Seamless integration of traditional paper processes, scanned images, OCR files and coded data sets
- A multiple-litigation model that allows data to be loaded once and then used for many matters simultaneously
- Remote diagnostics, update, maintenance and support capability
- Real-time modeling and workflow management tools that allow for the effective management and oversight of simultaneous review by large, geographically dispersed teams in a controlled manner
- Structured and ad-hoc reporting and analysis of data characteristics
- Structured and ad-hoc reporting and analysis of user workflow productivity
- Flexible production options, including automated production to paper, TIFF,
- PDF, HTML, native format, export to traditional litigation support programs, virtual reading rooms, and other online repositories
- Structured review of "non-hit" data in order to validate inclusion strategies
- Ability to allocate data to reviewers by theme—such as content, custodian, hit score, or other—to optimize review efficiency and defense-of-process
- Hosting and review in native form to greatly reduce cost

- The ability to create a privilege log automatically utilizing items that have been marked with a privileged designation, including their associated data properties such as author, recipient, date, and subject line

Using the inherent attributes of electronic files, an electronically based document review environment permits a discovery process that is feasible, defensible, timely and economical.

D. METADATA

WILLIAMS v. SPRINT/UNITED MANAGEMENT CO.

230 F.R.D. 640 (D. Kan. 2005)

WAXSE, MAGISTRATE JUDGE

Plaintiff Shirley Williams filed this suit on behalf of herself and others similarly situated, asserting that her age was a determining factor in Defendant's decision to terminate her employment during a reduction-in-force (RIF). * * * The parties are presently engaged in discovery concerning the merits of Plaintiffs' pattern and practice allegations. This matter is presently before the Court on Defendant's Response to the Court's July 12, 2005 Order, which ordered Defendant to show cause why it should not produce electronic Microsoft Excel spreadsheets in the manner in which they were maintained and why it should not be sanctioned for "scrubbing" the metadata * * * prior to producing them to Plaintiffs without either the agreement of the parties or the approval of the Court.

I. Background Information

Plaintiff Williams commenced this action in April 2003, and, to date, the docket reflects that over 3300 pleadings and orders have been filed. * * * Due to the highly contentious nature of this litigation, the Magistrate Judge has conducted discovery conferences twice a month since March 2005 to resolve discovery issues identified by the parties. One of the ongoing discovery disputes has been Defendant's production of spreadsheets that relate to the RIFs at issue in this case. [After many conferences and orders of the court, the court ordered the defendant to produce the spreadsheets in the format in which they were used in the ordinary course of business. The defendant then produced the spreadsheets in Excel form.]

At the July 7, 2005 discovery conference, Plaintiffs' counsel advised the Court that Defendant, prior to producing the electronic versions of the Excel spreadsheets, had utilized software to scrub the spreadsheet files to remove the metadata. Plaintiffs claim this metadata would have contained information such as file names, dates of the file, authors of the file, recipients of the file, print-out dates, changes and modification dates, and other information. Plaintiffs' counsel stated that Defendant did not provide them with any type of log of what information was scrubbed. Plaintiffs' counsel also advised the Court that Defendant had locked certain cells and data on the Excel spreadsheets prior to producing them so that Plaintiffs could not access those cells.

Defendant admitted that it had scrubbed the metadata from and locked certain data on the spreadsheets prior to producing them. It argued that the spreadsheets' metadata is irrelevant and contains privileged information. Defendant further argued that Plaintiffs never requested the metadata be included in the electronic Excel spreadsheets it produced and that metadata was never discussed at any of the discovery conferences.

After hearing the respective arguments of counsel, the Court ordered Defendant to show cause why it should not be sanctioned for not complying with "what at least I understood my Order to be, which was that electronic data be produced in the manner in which it was maintained, and to me that did not allow for the scrubbing of metadata because when I talk about electronic data, that includes the metadata." * * * The Court advised Defendant that if it could show justification for scrubbing the metadata and locking the cells, the Court would certainly consider it, but cautioned that "it's going to take some clear showing or otherwise there are going to be appropriate sanctions, which at least will be the production of the information in the format it was maintained."

* * *

II. Discussion

* * *

Metadata

* * * Defendant claims that it scrubbed the metadata from the spreadsheets to preclude the possibility that Plaintiffs could "undelete" or recover privileged and protected information properly deleted from the spreadsheets and to limit the information in the spreadsheets to those pools from which it made the RIF decisions currently being litigated. In an attempt to justify its actions, Defendant contends that emerging standards of electronic discovery articulate a presumption against the production of metadata, which is not considered part of a document, unless it is both specifically requested and relevant. Defendant next argues that Plaintiffs never sought the production of metadata. Finally, Defendant argues that its removal of metadata was consistent with, if not compelled by, * * * prior orders. Defendant asserts that these reasons support a determination that it has shown cause for its removal of the metadata from the Excel spreadsheets prior to producing them to Plaintiffs.

1. Emerging standards of electronic discovery with regard to metadata

a. What is metadata?

Before addressing whether Defendant was justified in removing the metadata from the Excel spreadsheets prior to producing them to

Plaintiffs, a general discussion of metadata and its implications for electronic document production in discovery is instructive.

Metadata, commonly described as "data about data," is defined as "information describing the history, tracking, or management of an electronic document." Appendix F to The Sedona Guidelines: Best Practice Guidelines & Commentary for Managing Information & Records in the Electronic Age defines metadata as "information about a particular data set which describes how, when and by whom it was collected, created, accessed, or modified and how it is formatted (including data demographics such as size, location, storage requirements and media information.)" Technical Appendix E to the Sedona Guidelines provides an extended description of metadata. It further defines metadata to include "all of the contextual, processing, and use information needed to identify and certify the scope, authenticity, and integrity of active or archival electronic information or records." Some examples of metadata for electronic documents include: a file's name, a file's location (e.g., directory structure or pathname), file format or file type, file size, file dates (e.g., creation date, date of last data modification, date of last data access, and date of last metadata modification), and file permissions (e.g., who can read the data, who can write to it, who can run it). Some metadata, such as file dates and sizes, can easily be seen by users; other metadata can be hidden or embedded and unavailable to computer users who are not technically adept.

Most metadata is generally not visible when a document is printed or when the document is converted to an image file. Metadata can be altered intentionally or inadvertently and can be extracted when native files are converted to image files. Sometimes the metadata can be inaccurate, as when a form document reflects the author as the person who created the template but who did not draft the document. In addition, metadata can come from a variety of sources; it can be created automatically by a computer, supplied by a user, or inferred through a relationship to another document.

Appendix E to The Sedona Guidelines further explains the importance of metadata:

> Certain metadata is critical in information management and for ensuring effective retrieval and accountability in record-keeping. Metadata can assist in proving the authenticity of the content of electronic documents, as well as establish the context of the content. Metadata can also identify and exploit the structural relationships that exist between and within electronic documents, such as versions and drafts. Metadata allows organizations to track the many layers of rights and reproduction information that exist for records and their multiple versions. Metadata may also document other legal or security requirements that have been imposed on records; for

example, privacy concerns, privileged communications or work product, or proprietary interests.

The Microsoft Office Online website lists several examples of metadata that may be stored in Microsoft Excel spreadsheets, as well as other Microsoft applications such as Word or PowerPoint: author name or initials, company or organization name, identification of computer or network server or hard disk where document is saved, names of previous document authors, document revisions and versions, hidden text or cells, template information, other file properties and summary information, non-visible portions or embedded objects, personalized views, and comments.

It is important to note that metadata varies with different applications. As a general rule of thumb, the more interactive the application, the more important the metadata is to understanding the application's output. At one end of the spectrum is a word processing application where the metadata is usually not critical to understanding the substance of the document. The information can be conveyed without the need for the metadata. At the other end of the spectrum is a database application where the database is a completely undifferentiated mass of tables of data. The metadata is the key to showing the relationships between the data; without such metadata, the tables of data would have little meaning. A spreadsheet application lies somewhere in the middle. While metadata is not as crucial to understanding a spreadsheet as it is to a database application, a spreadsheet's metadata may be necessary to understand the spreadsheet because the cells containing formulas, which arguably are metadata themselves, often display a value rather than the formula itself. To understand the spreadsheet, the user must be able to ascertain the formula within the cell.

Due to the hidden, or not readily visible, nature of metadata, commentators note that metadata created by any software application has the potential for inadvertent disclosure of confidential or privileged information in both a litigation and non-litigation setting, which could give rise to an ethical violation. One method commonly recommended to avoid this inadvertent disclosure is to utilize software that removes metadata from electronic documents. The process of removing metadata is commonly called "scrubbing" the electronic documents. In a litigation setting, the issue arises of whether this can be done without either the agreement of the parties or the producing party providing notice through an objection or motion for protective order.

b.   Whether emerging standards of electronic discovery articulate a presumption against the production of metadata

With the increasing usage of electronic document production in discovery, metadata presents unique challenges regarding the production of documents in litigation and raises many new discovery questions. The group of judges and attorneys comprising the Sedona Conference Working Group on Best Practices for Electronic Document Retention and Production (Sedona Electronic Document Working Group) identified metadata as one of the primary ways in which producing electronic documents differs from producing paper documents. The Sedona Electronic Document Working Group also recognized that understanding when metadata should be specifically preserved and produced represents one of the biggest challenges in electronic document production.

Defendant contends that emerging standards of electronic discovery articulate a presumption against the production of metadata. To determine whether Defendant's contention is accurate, the Court must first identify the emerging standards for the production of metadata. Then the Court must determine whether these emerging standards provide any guidance on the issue before the Court, i.e., whether a court order directing a party to produce electronic documents as they are maintained in the ordinary course of business requires the producing party to produce those documents with the metadata intact. A related issue is determining which party has the initial burden with regard to the disclosure of metadata. Does the requesting party have the burden to specifically request metadata and demonstrate its relevance? Or does the party ordered to produce electronic documents have an obligation to produce the metadata unless that party timely objects to production of the metadata?

The Court starts with the current version of Federal Rule of Civil Procedure 34. This rule provides that "[a]ny party may serve on any other party a request (1) to produce and permit the party making the request, or someone acting on the requestor's behalf, to inspect and copy, any designated documents (including writings, drawings, graphs, charts, photographs, phonorecords, and other data compilations from which information can be obtained, translated, if necessary, by the respondent through detection devices into reasonably usable form)." "A party who produces documents for inspection shall produce them as they are kept in the usual course of business or shall organize and label them to correspond with the categories in the request."

Federal Rule of Civil Procedure 34 includes "data compilations" in the listing of items that constitute a "document." * * * The current version of Rule 34, however, provides limited guidance with respect to when "data compilations" or other types of electronic documents have to be produced and in what form they should be produced.

In the past year, the Civil Rules Advisory Committee has proposed to the Judicial Conference several amendments to the Federal Rules of Civil Procedure addressing the discovery of electronically stored information. [These amendments ended up taking effect on December 1, 2006]. One of the proposed amendments to Rule 34(a) adds "electronically stored information" as a separate category along with "any designated documents." In addition, the proposed amendments to Rule 34(b) add the following language about the production of electronically stored information:

Unless the parties otherwise agree, or the court otherwise orders,

* * *

(ii) if a request for electronically stored information does not specify the form or forms of production, a responding party must produce the information in a form or forms in which it is ordinarily maintained, or in a form or forms that are reasonably usable.

* * *

Although the proposed amendments to Rule 34 use the phrase "in a form or forms in which it is ordinarily maintained," they provide no further guidance as to whether a party's production of electronically stored information "in the form or forms in which it is ordinarily maintained" would encompass the electronic document's metadata.

In the few cases where discovery of metadata is mentioned, it is unclear whether metadata should ordinarily be produced as a matter of course in an electronic document production. * * *

Having concluded that neither the federal rules nor case law provides sufficient guidance on the production of metadata, the Court next turns to materials issued by the Sedona Conference Working Group on Electronic Document Production. The Court finds two of the Sedona Principles for Electronic Document Production particularly helpful in determining whether Defendant was justified in scrubbing the metadata from the electronic spreadsheets. Principle 9 states that "[a]bsent a showing of special need and relevance a responding party should not be required to preserve, review, or produce deleted, shadowed, fragmented, or residual data or documents." Principle 12 provides that "[u]nless it is material to resolving the dispute, there is no obligation to preserve and produce metadata absent agreement of the parties or order of the court."

Comment 9.a. to the Sedona Principles for Electronic Document Production * * * suggests that the best approach to understanding what constitutes a "document" is to examine what information is readily available to the computer user in the ordinary course of business. If the information is in view, it should be treated as the equivalent of a paper "document." Data that can be readily compiled into viewable information, whether presented on the screen or printed on paper, is also a "document" under Rule 34. The comment, however, cautions that data hidden and never revealed to the user in the ordinary course of business should not be presumptively treated as a part of the "document," although there are circumstances in which the data may be relevant and should be preserved and produced. The comment concludes that such data may be discoverable under Rule 34, but the evaluation of the need for and relevance of such discovery should be separately analyzed on a case-by-case basis. Comment 9.a. provides the following illustration:

A party demands that responsive documents, "whether in hard copy or electronic format," be produced. The producing party objects to producing the documents in electronic format and states that production will be made through PDF or TIF images on CD–ROMs. The producing party assembles copies of the relevant hard copy memoranda, prints out copies of relevant e-mails and electronic memoranda, and produces them in a PDF or TIF format that does not include metadata. Absent a special request for metadata (or any reasonable basis to conclude the metadata was relevant to the claims and defenses in the litigation), and a prior order of the court based on a showing of need, this production of documents complies with the ordinary meaning of Rule 34.

Metadata is specifically discussed in depth in Comment 12.a. to the Sedona Principles. The comment states that "[a]lthough there are exceptions to every rule, especially in an evolving area of the law, there should be a modest legal presumption in most cases that the producing party need not take special efforts to preserve or produce metadata." The comment further notes that it is likely to remain the exceptional situation in which metadata must be produced.

The comment lists several ways in which routine preservation and production of metadata may be beneficial. The comment balances these potential benefits against the "reality that most of the metadata has no evidentiary value, and any time (and money) spent reviewing it is a waste of resources." The comment concludes that a reasonable balance is that, unless the producing party is aware or should be reasonably aware that particular metadata is relevant, the producing party should have the option of producing all, some, or none of the metadata. The comment sets forth one important caveat to giving the option of producing metadata to the producing party: "Of course, if the producing party knows or should reasonably know that particular metadata is relevant to the dispute, it should be produced."

c. Application to this case

The narrow issue currently before the Court is whether, under emerging standards of electronic discovery, the Court's Order directing Defendant to produce electronic spreadsheets as they are kept in the ordinary course of business requires Defendant to produce those documents with the metadata intact. * * * While recognizing that the Sedona Principles and comments are only persuasive authority and are not binding, the Court finds the Sedona Principles and comments particularly instructive in how the Court should address the electronic discovery issue currently before it.

Comment 9.a. to the Sedona Principles for Electronic Document Production * * * uses viewability as the determining factor in whether something should be presumptively treated as a part of a "document." Using viewability as the standard, all metadata ordinarily visible to the user of the Excel spreadsheet application should presumptively be treated as part of the "document" and should thus be discoverable. For spreadsheet applications, the user ordinarily would be able to view the contents of the cells on the spreadsheets, and thus the contents of those cells would be discoverable.

* * * With regard to metadata in general, the Court looks to Principle 12 and Comment 12.a. to the Sedona Principles. Based upon this Principle and Comment, emerging standards of electronic discovery appear to articulate a general presumption against the production of metadata, but provide a clear caveat when the producing party is aware or should be reasonably aware that particular metadata is relevant to the dispute.

Based on these emerging standards, the Court holds that when a party is ordered to produce electronic documents as they are maintained in the ordinary course of business, the producing party should produce the electronic documents with their metadata intact, unless that party timely objects to production of metadata, the parties agree that the metadata should not be produced, or the producing party requests a protective order. The initial burden with regard to the disclosure of the metadata would therefore be placed on the party to whom the request or order to produce is directed. The burden to object to the disclosure of metadata is appropriately placed on the party ordered to produce its electronic documents as they are ordinarily maintained because that party already has access to the metadata and is in the best position to determine whether producing it is objectionable. Placing the burden on the producing party is further supported by the fact that metadata is an inherent part of an electronic document, and its removal ordinarily requires an affirmative act by the producing party that alters the electronic document.

i. Relevancy

Defendant maintains that the metadata it removed from its electronic spreadsheets has absolutely no evidentiary value and is completely irrelevant. It argues that Plaintiffs' suggestion that the metadata may identify the computers used to create or modify the spreadsheets or reveal titles of documents that may assist in efforts to piece together the facts of the RIFs at issue in this case has no relevance to Plaintiffs' claim that Defendant maintained discriminatory policies or practices used to effectuate a pattern and practice of age discrimination. Defendant likewise argues that the metadata is not necessary because the titles of documents can be gleaned from the subject spreadsheets, and these titles adequately describe the data included in such spreadsheets.

The Court agrees with Defendant that certain metadata from the spreadsheets may be irrelevant to the claims and defenses in this case. The Court, however, does not find that all of the spreadsheets' metadata is irrelevant. In light of Plaintiffs' allegations that Defendant reworked pools of employees in order to improve distribution to pass its adverse impact analysis, the Court finds that some of the metadata is relevant and likely to lead to the discovery of admissible evidence. While the Court cannot fashion an exhaustive list of the spreadsheet metadata that may be relevant, the Court does find that metadata associated with any changes to the spreadsheets, the dates of any changes, the identification of the individuals making any changes, and other metadata from which Plaintiffs could determine the final versus draft version of the spreadsheets appear relevant. Plaintiffs' allegation that Defendant reworked the pools is not a new allegation. Thus, Defendant should reasonably have known that Plaintiffs were expecting the electronic spreadsheets to contain their metadata intact. Furthermore, if Defendant believed the metadata to be irrelevant, it should have asserted a relevancy objection instead of making the unilateral decision to produce the spreadsheets with the metadata removed.

ii. Reliability

Defendant also argues that the metadata removed from the electronic spreadsheets may be inaccurate and therefore has no evidentiary value. The Court finds that this is not sufficient justification for removing the metadata absent agreement of the parties or the Court's approval. If Defendant had any concerns regarding the accuracy or reliability of the metadata, it should have communicated those concerns to the Court before it scrubbed the metadata.

iii. Privilege

Defendant also argues that production of certain metadata removed by Defendant would facilitate the revelation of information that is attorney-client privileged and/or attorney work product. Defendant claims that through the use of easily accessible technology, metadata may reveal information extracted from a document, such as * * * protected or privileged matters. It further claims that metadata may create a data trail that reveals changes to prior drafts or edits.

* * *

For any * * * metadata Defendant claims is protected by the attorney-client privilege or as attorney work product, the Court finds that Defendant should have raised this issue prior to its unilateral decision to produce the spreadsheets with the metadata removed. Fed. R. Civ. P. 26(b)(5) requires a party withholding otherwise discoverable information on the basis of privilege to make the claim expressly and to describe the nature of the documents, communications, or things not produced or disclosed in a manner that, without revealing the privileged information, will enable the other parties to assess the applicability of the privilege. Normally, this is accomplished by objecting and providing a privilege log for "documents, communications, or things" not produced.

In this case, Defendant has failed to object and has not provided a privilege log identifying the electronic documents that it claims contain privileged metadata. Defendant has not provided the Court with even a general description of the purportedly privileged metadata that was scrubbed from the spreadsheets. As Defendant has failed to provide any privilege log for the electronic documents it claims contain metadata that will reveal privileged communications or attorney work product, the Court holds that Defendant has waived any attorney-client privilege or work product protection with regard to the spreadsheets' metadata * * *.

2.   Plaintiffs never requested the production of metadata

Defendant also argues that Plaintiffs never requested the metadata and that metadata was never mentioned during any of the discovery conferences. * * * Defendant is correct in asserting that Plaintiffs never expressly requested metadata and that the Court never expressly ordered Defendant to produce the electronic spreadsheets' metadata. However, taken in the context of Plaintiffs' stated reasons for requesting the Excel spreadsheets in their native electronic format and the Court's repeated statements that the spreadsheets should be produced in the electronic form in which they are maintained, the Court finds that Defendant should have reasonably understood that the Court expected and intended for Defendant to produce the spreadsheets' metadata along with the Excel spreadsheets. If Defendant did not understand the Court's ruling, it should have requested clarification of the Court's order. As the Sedona Working Group on Electronic Document Production observed: "Of course, if the producing party knows or should reasonably know that particular metadata is relevant to the dispute, it should be produced." Here, the Court finds that Defendant should have reasonably known that the metadata was relevant to the dispute and therefore should have either been produced or an appropriate objection made or motion filed.

* * *

III.   Sanctions

The Court's Show Cause Order also required Defendant to show cause why it should not be sanctioned for its failure to comply with the Court's ruling directing Defendant to produce electronic spreadsheets in the manner in which they were maintained. Defendant states that it did not understand the Court's direction to produce electronic spreadsheets included the production of metadata and that its actions were not made in bad faith. It points out that it has already produced hundreds of documents in response to formal and informal requests for production, answered hundreds of interrogatories, and produced and scheduled scores of witnesses for deposition in support of its assertion that it has acted in good faith throughout this litigation.

The Court concludes that Defendant has shown cause why it should not be sanctioned for its actions in scrubbing the metadata * * *. Although the Court intended its ruling requiring Defendant to produce the electronic RIF-related spreadsheets in the manner in which they were ordinarily maintained to include the metadata, the Court recognizes that the production of metadata is a new and largely undeveloped area of the law. This lack of clear law on production of metadata, combined with the arguable ambiguity in the Court's prior rulings, compels the Court to conclude that sanctions are not appropriate here.

The Court, however, wants to clarify the law regarding the production of metadata in this case. When the Court orders a party to produce an electronic document in the form in which it is regularly maintained, i.e., in its native format or as an active file, that production must include all metadata unless that party timely objects to production of the metadata, the parties agree that the metadata should not be produced, or the producing party requests a protective order.

* * *

IT IS THEREFORE ORDERED that Defendant has failed to show cause why it should not produce the electronic spreadsheets in the manner in which they were maintained[,] * * * which includes the spreadsheets' metadata. * * *

WYETH v. IMPAX LABORATORIES, INC.
248 F.R.D. 169 (D. Del. 2006)

FARNAN, DISTRICT JUDGE

Pending before the Court is Defendant Impax's ("Impax") Motion To Compel Production Of Documents.

* * *

2.   *Production Of Responsive Documents In Their Native Format*

Impax contends that Wyeth should be ordered to produce electronic documents in their native format, complete with metadata, and not in the Tagged Image File Format ("TIFF") in which they were produced. Impax also contends that a document database created by Wyeth for purposes of the Teva Litigation is discoverable and should be produced. In response, Wyeth contends that Impax is not entitled to electronic copies in their natural state for two reasons: (1) Impax has not made a particularized showing of need for the metadata, and (2) collection of this data would be overly burdensome.

Metadata is defined as "information describing the history, tracking, or management of an electronic document." Removal of metadata from an electronic document usually requires an affirmative alteration of that document, through scrubbing or converting the file from its native format to an image file, for example. Most metadata is of limited evidentiary value, and reviewing it can waste litigation resources.

Emerging standards of electronic discovery appear to articulate a general presumption against the production of metadata. The Default Standard for Discovery of Electronic Documents utilized in this District follows this general presumption. Paragraph 6 directs parties to produce electronic documents as image files (e.g. PDF or TIFF) if they cannot agree on a different format for production. "Default Standard For Discovery of Electronic Documents ("E–Discovery")," Ad Hoc Committee for Electronic Discovery of the U.S. District Court for the District of Delaware, http://www.ded.uscourts.gov/Announce/Policies/Policy01.htm. [hereinafter "Default Standard"]. However, if the requesting party can demonstrate a particularized need for the native format of an electronic document, a court may order it produced. Therefore, the producing party must preserve the integrity of the electronic documents it produces. Failure to do so will not support a contention that production of documents in native format is overly burdensome.

Since the parties have never agreed that electronic documents would be produced in any particular format, Wyeth complied with its discovery obligation by producing image files. Further, neither party has argued that the need for accessing metadata was foreseeable or generally necessary. Finally, Impax has not demonstrated a particularized need for the metadata or database production it has requested. Therefore, this part of Impax's Motion is denied.

COMMENTARY

A large amount of ESI, unlike paper, is associated with or contains information that is not readily apparent on the screen view of the file. This additional information is usually known as "metadata." Metadata includes information about the document or file that is recorded by the computer to assist in storing and retrieving the document or file. The information may also be useful for system administration as it reflects data regarding the generation, handling, transfer, and storage of the document or file within the computer system. Much metadata is neither created by nor normally accessible to the computer user.

There are many examples of metadata. Such information includes file designation, create and edit dates, authorship, comments, and edit history. Indeed, electronic files may contain hundreds or even thousands of pieces of such information. For instance, e-mail has its own metadata elements that include, among about 1,200 or more properties, such information as the dates that mail was sent, received, replied to or forwarded, blind carbon copy information, and sender address book information. Typical word processing documents not only include prior changes and edits but also hidden codes that determine such features as paragraphing, font, and line spacing. The ability to recall inadvertently deleted information is another familiar function, as is tracking of creation and modification dates.

Similarly, electronically created spreadsheets may contain calculations that are not visible in a printed version or hidden columns that can only be viewed by accessing the spreadsheet in its "native" application— that is, the software application used to create or record the information.

Internet documents contain hidden data that allow for the transmission of information between an Internet user's computer and the server on which the Internet document is located. So-called "meta-tags" allow search engines to locate websites responsive to specified search criteria. "Cookies" are text files placed on a computer (sometimes without user knowledge) that can, among other things, track usage and transmit information back to the cookie's originator. Generally, the metadata associated with files used by most people today (such as Microsoft Office™ documents) is known as "application metadata." This metadata is embedded in the file it describes and moves with the file when it is moved or copied. On the other hand, "system metadata" is not embedded within the file it describes but stored externally. System metadata is used by the computer's file system to track file locations and store information about each file's name, size, creation, modification, and usage.

Understanding when metadata is relevant and subject to preservation and production represents one of the biggest challenges in electronic discovery. Sometimes metadata is needed to authenticate a disputed document or to establish facts material to a dispute, such as when a file was accessed in a suit involving theft of trade secrets. In most cases, however, the metadata will have no material evidentiary value—it does not matter when a document was printed, or who typed the revisions, or what edits were made before the document was circulated. There is also the real danger that information recorded by the computer as application metadata may be inaccurate. For example, when a new employee uses a word processing program to create a memorandum by using a memorandum template created by a former employee, the metadata for the new memorandum may incorrectly identify the former employee as the author. However, the proper use of metadata in litigation may be able to provide substantial benefit by facilitating more effective and efficient searching and retrieval of ESI.

When deciding what metadata may be relevant, consider these definitions from *The Sedona Conference Glossary of E–Discovery and Digital Information Management (Second Edition)* (December 2007 Version).

* **Application Metadata:** Data created by the application specific to the ESI being addressed, embedded in the file and moved with the file when copied; copying may alter application metadata.

* **Document Metadata:** Properties about the file stored in the file, as opposed to document content. Often this data is not immediately viewable in the software application used to create/edit the document but often can be accessed via a "Properties" view. Examples include document author and company, and create and revision dates. Contrast with File System Metadata and Email Metadata.

* **E-mail Metadata:** Data stored in the e-mail about the e-mail. Often this data is not even viewable in the e-mail client applica-

tion used to create the e-mail, e.g., blind copy addressees, received date. The amount of e-mail metadata available for a particular e-mail varies greatly depending on the e-mail system. Contrast with File System Metadata and Document Metadata.

* **Embedded Metadata:** Generally hidden, but an integral part of ESI, such as "track changes" or "comments" in a word processing file or "notes" in a presentation file. While some metadata is routinely extracted during processing and conversion for e-discovery, embedded data may not be. Therefore, it may only be available in the original, native file. *See also* Application Metadata and Metadata.

* **File System Metadata:** Metadata generated by the system to track the demographics (name, size, location, usage, etc.) of the ESI and, not embedded within, but stored externally from the ESI.

* **Metadata:** Data typically stored electronically that describes characteristics of ESI, found in different places in different forms. Can be supplied by applications, users or the file system. Metadata can describe how, when and by whom ESI was collected, created, accessed, modified and how it is formatted. Can be altered intentionally or inadvertently. Certain metadata can be extracted when native files are processed for litigation. Some metadata, such as file dates and sizes, can easily be seen by users; other metadata can be hidden or embedded and unavailable to computer users who are not technically adept. Metadata is generally not reproduced in full form when a document is printed to paper or electronic image.

* **Native Format:** Electronic documents have an associated file structure defined by the original creating application. This file structure is referred to as the "native format" of the document. Because viewing or searching documents in the native format may require the original application (for example, viewing a Microsoft Word document may require the Microsoft Word application), documents may be converted to a neutral format as part of the record acquisition or archive process. "Static" formats (often called "imaged formats"), such as TIFF or PDF, are designed to retain an image of the document as it would look viewed in the original creating application but do not allow metadata to be viewed or the document information to be manipulated. In the conversion to static format, the metadata can be processed, preserved and electronically associated with the static format file. However, with technology advancements, tools and applications are becoming increasingly available to allow viewing and searching of documents in their native format, while still preserving all metadata.

* **User-Added Metadata:** Data, possibly work product, created by a user while copying, reviewing or working with a file, including annotations and subjective coding information.

* **Vendor-Added Metadata:** Data created and maintained by the electronic discovery vendor as a result of processing the document. While some vendor-added metadata has direct value to customers, much of it is used for process reporting, chain of custody and data accountability.

2. The *Sedona Principles* and Metadata

Several excerpts from the 2007 revision of *The Sedona Principles* dealing with the issues surrounding metadata are set forth below. Can you identify similarities and differences between these sections and the court's reasoning in *Williams v. Sprint*?

a. Form of Production and Metadata

In the process of preparing the new Rules governing ESI, the Advisory Committee rejected proposals to mandate any particular form of production and did not take a position on the need to produce metadata. Rule 26(f) instead emphasizes the need to discuss this topic early to attempt to reach agreement, and Rule 34(b) provides a process for resolving disputes, while providing two alternative forms of production in the event the parties do not reach agreement or a court order is not entered: the form or forms "in which it is ordinarily maintained" or "in a form or forms that are reasonably usable."

The phrase "ordinarily maintained" is not synonymous with "native format." It is common for electronic information to be migrated to a number of different applications and formats in the ordinary course of business, particularly if the information is archived for long-term storage. Routine migration will likely result in the loss or alteration of some elements of metadata associated with the native application, and the addition of new elements.

Sedona Principle 12, in contrast, deals directly with the issue of the need to preserve and produce metadata. It has been amended in this 2007 Version to provide more explicit guidance regarding issues relating to both the relevance and usability of metadata. Previously, Principle 12 only provided guidance on a narrow aspect of the metadata issue.

Sedona Principle 12

> **12. Absent party agreement or court order specifying the form or forms of production, production should be made in the form or forms in which the information is ordinarily maintained or in a reasonably usable form, taking into account the need to produce reasonably accessible metadata that will enable the receiving party to have the same ability to access, search, and display the information as the producing party where appropriate or necessary in light of the nature of the information and the needs of the case.**

Comment 12.a. Metadata

An electronic document or file usually includes not only the visible text but also hidden text, formatting codes, formulae, and other information associated with the file. These many types of ancillary information are often lumped together as "metadata," although some distinctions between different types of metadata should be recognized.

* * *

Aside from its potential relation to the facts of the case, metadata may also play a functional role in the usability of electronically stored information. For example, system metadata may allow for the quick and efficient sorting of a multitude of files by virtue of the dates or other information captured in metadata. In addition, application metadata may be critical to allow the functioning of routines within the file, such as cell formulae in spreadsheets.

Care should be taken when using metadata, as the content of a given piece of metadata may convey information that is contextually inaccurate. For example, when a Microsoft Word™ document is created, the computer on which that document is saved may automatically assign the document an "author" based on the information available on that computer. That document may be used as a template by other persons, but the "author" information is never changed. Thus, subsequent iterations of the document may carry as an "author" a person with no knowledge of the content of the document. Accordingly, a proper and thorough analysis should be undertaken in order to properly assess how the metadata was created.

The extent to which metadata should be preserved and produced in a particular case will depend on the needs of the case. Parties and counsel should consider: (a) what metadata is ordinarily maintained; (b) the potential relevance of the metadata to the dispute (e.g., is the metadata needed to prove a claim or defense, such as the transmittal of an incriminating statement); and (c) the importance of reasonably accessible metadata to facilitating the parties' review, production, and use of the information. In assessing preservation, it should be noted that the failure to preserve and produce metadata may deprive the producing party of the opportunity later to contest the authenticity of the document if the metadata is material to that determination. Organizations should evaluate the potential benefits of retaining native files and metadata (whether or not it is produced) to ensure that documents are authentic and to preclude the fraudulent creation of evidence.

Comment 12.b. Formats used for collection and production: "ordinarily maintained" v. "reasonably usable"

* * *

[T]here should be two primary considerations in choosing the form of production: (1) the need for, or probative value of both apparent and [hidden] metadata; and (2) the extent to which the production of metadata will enhance the functional utility of the electronic information produced and allow the parties to conduct a more cost-effective and efficient review. These considerations should be weighed against the negative aspects associated with each format. For example, production in a "native" format entails both advantages and disadvantages. Native production, which generally includes the entire file and associated metadata, may afford the requesting party access to the same information and functionality available to the producing party and, from a technical perspective, usually requires minimal processing before production. However, information produced natively may be difficult or impossible to redact or Bates number, and files in their native forms must be viewed using applications capable of opening and presenting the information without alteration. Suitable applications are not always accessible to requesting parties, who may also lack the equipment or expertise required to use such applications.

A native file production that includes a substantial volume and variety of file types could become very expensive and burdensome for the requesting party. In addition, since certain metadata could contain or reveal privileged, secret, or other sensitive information, an organization may determine that it must review such metadata before producing it, which can substantially impact the speed of production.

* * *

The routine preservation of metadata pending agreements or decisions on the ultimate form of production may be beneficial in a number of ways. Preservation of metadata may provide better protection against inadvertent or deliberate modification of evidence by others and the systematic removal or deletion of certain metadata may involve significant additional costs that are not justified by any tangible benefit. Moreover, the failure to preserve and produce metadata may deprive the producing party of the opportunity later to contest the authenticity of the document if the metadata would be material to that determination.

* * *

In determining the appropriate forms of production in a case, requesting parties and counsel should consider: (a) the forms most likely to provide the information needed to establish the relevant facts of the case; (b) the need for metadata to organize and search the information produced; (c) whether the information sought is reasonably accessible in the forms requested; and (d) the requesting party's own ability to effectively manage and use the information in the forms requested.

Producing parties and counsel should consider: (a) the relative risks of inadvertent production of confidential, privileged, and work product information associated with different forms of production; (b) difficulties in redaction, tracking, and use of native files; (c) whether alternative (e.g., "nonnative") forms of production provide sufficient usability (e.g., by providing adequate accompanying information through load files) such that the producing and requesting parties have the same access to functionality; and (d) the relative costs and burdens with respect to the proposed forms of production, including the costs of preproduction review, processing, and production.

Illustration iii. Plaintiff alleges that the defendant engaged in a fraud regarding software development. The plaintiff seeks a preliminary order permitting direct access to the hard drives of the software engineers involved and demonstrates that the computer program sold by defendant appears to incorporate plaintiff's source code. In this case, production of the source code in native format may be appropriate, as well as targeted forensic examination of the hard drives concerning the development of the source code. The court should impose such conditions as it deems appropriate to protect legitimate property and privacy interests of the defendant and its employees.

* * *

PROBLEMS

1. What is relevant metadata? Consider this example. Lotus notes e-mail contains over fifteen thousand potential metadata fields. Assume that vendors in the industry have only ever encountered six thousand of them. Assume further that popular litigation support software only handle roughly one hundred metadata fields.

   a. How would you decide which metadata fields to produce?

   b. Would you/should you only produce those metadata fields that you consider "relevant?"

   b. What if the opposing party did not ask for metadata?

   d. What about attachments to e-mail? How might metadata from the attachments and the e-mail differ? What are your potential obligations regarding e-mail attachment metadata?

2. *Williams v. Sprint* teaches that it is important to preserve metadata and that it is easy to unintentionally alter metadata. What are the dangers of reviewing native files sent to you by a client before they are produced to the opposing party? What steps are necessary to ensure that the metadata is not altered before production to the opposing party? What steps do you consider reasonable?

E. ON–SITE INSPECTIONS—NEUTRAL EX-PERTS, CONFIDENTIALITY PROTEC-TION, INSPECTION PROTOCOLS

FERRON v. SEARCH CACTUS, L.L.C.

No. 2:06–CV–327, 2008 WL 1902499 (S.D. Ohio Apr. 28, 2008)

FROST, DISTRICT JUDGE

The Court held a telephone conference in this action on April 14, 2008, in which all parties were represented and this Court considered and decided the protocol for viewing and preserving information contained on Plaintiff's computer systems. This Opinion and Order memorializes that decision.

I. Background

Plaintiff is an attorney who utilizes his home and office computers for storing and working with information related to the representation of clients, the maintenance of lawsuits such as this action and other actions or potential actions similar to the subject matter of the instant action, and his personal life. Out of these three categories of information, the information related to the representation of clients in cases unrelated to email and advertising litigation has no relevance to this case and contain documents that are protected by the attorney-client privilege. The information that may be categorized as personal also has no relevance to this case and may be confidential in nature, e.g., banking and credit card information. However, the third category of information, i.e., information related to email and website advertising litigation is relevant and discoverable.

In this Court's Opinion and Order which granted in part and denied in part Defendant Search Cactus' motion for summary judgment, it held that "only the unsolicited emails Plaintiff received at jferron@ferronlaw.com after April 3, 2006 can be used to support his claim under the [Ohio Consumer Sales Practices Act] OCSPA." Thus, it is necessary for the parties to ascertain which of the emails Plaintiff received were unsolicited. As Defendants contend, Plaintiff's computer systems contain the only available documentary evidence that can show the pathways taken by Plaintiff to solicit the emails or the absence of those pathways.

II. Defendants' Discovery Requests

Defendants have requested an inspection of Plaintiff's computer systems so as to capture specific information relevant to this case that Plaintiff has not produced and, Defendants contend[,] has not been placed on a litigation hold. Specifically, Defendant wishes to inspect Plaintiff's computer systems to ascertain whether Plaintiff's efforts with respect to receiving the emails and visiting the websites (that are at the heart of this action) constituted a consumer transaction under the OCSPA, or whether Plaintiff's opening of the emails and any attempts to obtain free merchandise were part of a business designed to profit from email litigation.

The parties agree that a forensic computer expert must be utilized to obtain the information that the Court has determined Defendants are entitled to discover.[3] This is because a distinctive feature of computer operations is the routine alteration and deletion of information that attends ordinary use of the computer. Many steps essential to computer operation may alter or destroy information, for reasons that have nothing to do with how that information might relate to litigation. As a result, the ordinary operation of computer systems creates a risk that a party may lose potentially discoverable information without culpable conduct on its part. The routine operation of computer systems includes the alteration and overwriting of information, often without the operator's specific direction or awareness, a feature with no direct counterpart in hard-copy documents. Such features are essential to the operation of electronic information systems. On March 19, 2008, this Court held a telephone conference with the parties, directed that inspection of Plaintiff's computer systems' hard drives was appropriate, and instructed the parties to discuss and propose a protocol for the inspection.

III. Analysis

The parties were unable to agree on a protocol for inspection of Plaintiff's computer systems' hard drives and requested another conference with this Court to address the issue. At the April 14, 2008 telephone conference, this Court considered the parties' arguments related to the inspection of Plaintiff's computers. The issues of concern were how to protect Plaintiff's confidential personal information that is stored on the computers, e.g., personal banking and credit card information, and how to prevent Plaintiff from waiving the attorney-client privilege by allowing the information on the computers to be viewed by any third party.

Initially, the Court explains that the 2006 amendments to Rule 34 of the Federal Rules of Civil Procedure clarify "that discovery of electronically stored information stands on equal footing with discovery of paper documents." Fed. R. Civ. P. 34 Advisory Committee's Note on 2006 Amendments. Consequently, without a qualifying reason, Defendants are no more entitled to access to Plaintiff's electronic information storage systems than to Plaintiff's warehouses storing paper documents.

Here, the Court concludes that there are qualifying reasons sufficient to permit Defendants access to Plaintiff's computer systems: Plain-

---

3. The Court also notes that the parties disagree about the types of information that must be analyzed on the computers in order to reconstruct internet browser history. Plaintiff's computer consultant has attested that the internet browsing history may be re-constructed through a limited examination of certain directories on the computers' hard drive. Defendant[s'] computer consultant has attested that such an analysis can only occur by analyzing a complete mirror image of the hard drives of the computers.

tiff has apparently failed to fulfill his "duty to preserve information because of pending or reasonably anticipated litigation," Fed. R. Civ. P. 37 Advisory Committee's Note on 2006 Amendments, and Plaintiff has not otherwise produced the relevant information. Moreover, * * * Plaintiff's computers contain the only available documentary evidence of his visits to the websites in issue and such evidence has not otherwise been produced * * *.

Plaintiff takes the position that he did in fact place a proper litigation hold on electronically stored information relating to this case. Specifically, Plaintiff has represented to the Court that he has saved and preserved all of his commercial email since January 1, 2006. Plaintiff also represents to the Court that no Defendant in this case has ever requested that he place a litigation hold on any other type of electronically stored information resident on his computers. Lastly, Plaintiff represents to the Court that Plaintiff has never received any notice that Defendant[s] intended to inspect the computers he uses to retrieve this information until he received Media Breakaway, LLC's formal discovery requests on February 7, 2008. Plaintiff's arguments are not well taken.

Even if Plaintiff has preserved and saved his "commercial email," those actions do not sufficiently fulfill his duty to preserve evidence, which "arises when the party has notice that the evidence is relevant to litigation or when a party should have known that the evidence may be relevant to future litigation." *Zubulake v. UBS Warburg LLC*, 220 F.R.D. 212, 216 (S.D.N.Y.2003). Further, Plaintiff's duty to preserve this information is independent of whether Defendants requested a litigation hold. *See id.*; *see also Kemper Mortgage Inc. v. Russell*, No. 3:06–cv–042 (S.D. Ohio Apr. 18, 2006) ("While that obligation may be enforced by court order or by a later sanction for spoliation, obviously the duty arises independent of any court declaration of the duty and indeed long before a court is available to make a declaration in the particular case.").

The Court will now consider Plaintiff's concerns regarding this Court's order allowing inspection of Plaintiff's computer systems' hard drives.

A. Confidential Personal Information

The parties and this Court agree that Plaintiff's personal information is confidential in nature and is irrelevant to this lawsuit. Defendants request a current mirror image[5] of Plaintiff's computer systems' hard drives, contending that Plaintiff's removal of any information from the computer hard drives can unwittingly cause deletion of other, possibly relevant, information.

This Court attempts to strike a balance between protecting Plaintiff's personal confidential information and Defendant[s'] allegation that deletion can cause a loss of data. * * * To strike a balance between these

---

5. A mirror image copy represents a snapshot of the computer's records. It contains all the information in the computer, including embedded, residual, and deleted data.

competing interests, this Court ORDERS Plaintiff's forensic computer expert to mirror image both of Plaintiff's computer systems' hard drives and for Plaintiff to store the images safely. Plaintiff's forensic computer expert shall then remove only Plaintiff's personal confidential information that could not reasonably lead to the discovery of information relevant to this litigation. Plaintiff shall provide Defendants with the protocol his expert utilized to remove the confidential information.

B.   Attorney–Client Privileged Information

Plaintiff argues that if he is required to allow Defendants' forensic computer expert to review and copy Plaintiff's computer systems' hard drives, it will simultaneously cause the loss of the attorney-client privilege that has attached to the information related to Plaintiff's other clients because that information will be viewed by a third party. This Court disagrees.

First, the Court notes that it is Plaintiff himself that has caused this issue to become problematic because of his failure to place a sufficient litigation hold on his computer systems as of the date he anticipated this litigation. * * *

Second, Defendants have offered to have their forensic computer expert review with Plaintiff the findings and allow Plaintiff to identify the privileged documents that will then be removed before the information is forwarded to Defendants. * * *

Finally, the Court is not heedless of the intrusion copying Plaintiff's computer systems' hard drives will cause. In *Playboy Enters. v. Welles*, 60 F. Supp. 2d 1050, 1054 (S.D. Cal. 1999), a case upon which Defendants rely, the court stated that the mirror imaging process took approximately four to eight hours for each computer. This amount of time is certainly reasonable to remedy Plaintiff's failure of his duty to preserve the relevant computer-stored evidence in this action.

Accordingly, this Court ORDERS Plaintiff to permit Defendants' forensic computer expert to mirror image Plaintiff's computer systems' hard drives. Defendants' expert shall review his findings in confidence with Plaintiff prior to making any findings available to Defendants. Plaintiff shall identify for deletion any information that is irrelevant and create a specific privilege log of any relevant information for which he claims privilege. The expert shall remove the information claimed as privileged and provide all other information to Defendants.

C.   Forensic Computer Experts

It appears to the Court that both of the forensic computer experts presented to it are qualified. In certain situations, courts appoint computer forensic experts to act as officers of the court to help "reduce privacy intrusions and privilege waiver issues during forensic analysis." * * * Thus, the two identified computer forensic experts shall serve as officers of this Court.

With regard to the cost of the forensic examinations, at least initially, the parties will bear the costs associated with their chosen expert.

IV.   Conclusion

Based on the foregoing, this Court ORDERS:

1.   Within seven days of the date of this Opinion and Order, Plaintiff's forensic computer expert shall mirror image both of Plaintiff's computer systems' hard drives and Plaintiff shall preserve this mirror image.

2.   Plaintiff's forensic computer expert shall then remove only Plaintiff's confidential personal information from the mirror image of Plaintiff's computer systems' hard drives. Plaintiff's expert shall provide Defendants with the protocol he utilized to remove the confidential information.

3.   Plaintiff shall then provide Defendants' computer forensic expert access to his computer systems' hard drives.

4.   Defendants' forensic computer expert shall mirror image Plaintiff's computer systems' hard drives in approximately four to eight hours for each system. If the expert finds that this is not enough time, Plaintiff is expected to be reasonable in allowing some additional time. Defendant is expected to be considerate with regard to scheduling times that are less intrusive to Plaintiff and his business.

5.   Defendants' expert shall review his findings in confidence with Plaintiff prior to making any findings available to Defendants.

6.   Plaintiff shall identify for deletion any information that is irrelevant and create a specific privilege log of any relevant information for which he claims privilege. The computer forensic expert shall remove the information claimed as privileged and provide all other information to Defendants.

7.   Defendants' expert shall provide Plaintiff with the protocol he utilized to remove the privileged information.

8.   Forensic computer experts C. Matthew Curtin and Scott T. Simmons shall act as officers of this Court. Defendants shall be responsible for remunerating Mr. Curtin and Plaintiff shall be responsible for remunerating Mr. Simmons.

COMMENTARY

On occasion, a court will require the mirror imaging[12] of the hard drives of any computers that contain documents responsive to an opposing party's request for production. Litigants often request a court-

---

12.   A "mirror image" is generally described as "a forensic duplicate, which replicates bit for bit, sector for sector, all allocated and unallocated space, including slack space, on a computer hard drive." *Balboa Threadworks, Inc. v. Stucky*, No. 05–1157, 2006 WL 763668, at *3 (D. Kan. Mar. 24, 2006).

ordered inspection of their adversary's computer hard drives where the parties cannot agree on a protocol or there is evidence that relevant ESI will be found on a computer hard drive that the adversary has failed to produce. Such court-ordered inspections are warranted where the ESI in question goes to the heart of the action.[13]

The federal courts derive their authority to order such inspections from Rule 34(a), which allows parties to request that another party:

> produce and permit the requesting party ... to inspect, copy, test, or sample any designated documents or electronically stored information—including writings, drawings, graphs, charts, photographs, sound recordings, images, and other data or data compilations stored in any medium from which information can be obtained-translated, if necessary, by the respondent into reasonably usable form.

However, Rule 34(a) is not meant to create a routine right of direct access to the opponent's electronic information systems. Court-ordered inspections of computer hard drives usually require on-site access and can be intrusive and burdensome, causing significant inconvenience and interruption to business operations of the responding party. Furthermore, a computer hard drive is likely to contain a significant quantity of non-relevant, privileged and confidential information which raises significant privacy concerns.

Courts must therefore carefully craft inspection protocols that balance the need for discovery of relevant information against the risk of disclosure of privileged material and undue intrusiveness resulting from inspecting or testing such systems. The details of these protocols may vary depending on the unique facts and circumstances of each case, but generally comprise the following: (1) a forensic expert will obtain the images of the computer hard drives; (2) the images will be maintained by the party whose hard drives were imaged; (3) the producing party will have the opportunity to remove any non-relevant or privileged information; and (4) responsive information found on the images will be disclosed to the requesting party with a log identifying any material removed based on a claim of privilege.

1. Denying Requests for On–Site Inspections

Courts have been cautious in requiring the mirror imaging of computers where the request is extremely broad in nature and the connection between the computers and the claims in the lawsuit are vague or unsubstantiated. Mere conjecture or suspicion that an adversary has not produced discoverable information is not enough. For example, in *Hedenburg v. Aramark American Food Services*, an employment discrimination case, the defendant sought a mirror image of the plaintiff's home computer. The defendant contended that the plaintiff's personal correspondence with unnamed third parties (in the form of e-

---

13. *See Hedenburg v. Aramark Am. Food Servs.*, No. 06 Civ. 5267, 2007 WL 162716, at *1–2 (W.D. Wash. Jan. 17, 2007).

mails or Internet postings) might reveal discrepancies in her testimony about the alleged discriminatory events and the impact of certain events on her emotional state. The defendant argued that access to a plaintiff's computer was common in employment cases, and offered to have the hard drive mirror image sent to a special master in an effort to resolve the problem of disclosing privileged or other non-discoverable information. The plaintiff argued that she had already made a diligent search of her computer files. She objected to the discovery as a fishing expedition and refused to permit the defendant access to her home computer's hard drive.

The court observed that such a search is sometimes permitted where the contents of the computer go to the heart of the case. Here, the court found that the central claims in the case were wholly unrelated to the contents of plaintiff's computer, and that defendant was "hoping blindly to find something useful in its impeachment of the plaintiff."[14] In denying defendant's motion, the court stated:

> Defendant essentially seeks a search warrant to confirm that Plaintiff has not memorialized statements contrary to her testimony in this case. If the issue related instead to a lost paper diary, the court would not permit the Defendant to search the plaintiff's property to ensure that her search was complete.[15]

Similarly, in *Williams v. Massachusetts Mutual Life Insurance Co.*, a wrongful termination case, the plaintiff sought the court's help in obtaining from defendants a particular e-mail he claimed to have seen and possessed at one point, but no longer possessed. He sought an order appointing a neutral computer forensics expert to conduct the search for the e-mail, and, in the event the e-mail was discovered, to conduct an additional, more detailed electronic investigation "to locate and retrieve all electronic communications related to his employment and termination that have not as yet been produced by defendants."[16]

In denying the request, the court reasoned that the plaintiff had presented no credible evidence that the defendants were unwilling to produce computer-generated documents, whether now or in the future, or that they had withheld relevant information. "Before permitting such an intrusion into an opposing party's information system—particularly where, as here, that party has undertaken its own search and forensic analysis and has sworn to its accuracy—the inquiring party must present at least some reliable information that the opposing party's representations are misleading or substantively inaccurate."[17]

Even where there is some evidence that data on an adversary's computer systems is responsive, courts may deny a request for inspection by imaging where the burden on the responding party is too great.

---

14. *Id.* at *2.

15. *Id.*

16. *Williams v. Massachusetts Mut. Life Ins. Co.*, 226 F.R.D. 144, 145 (D. Mass. 2005).

17. *Id.* at 146.

In *Ponca Tribe of Indians of Oklahoma v. Continental Carbon*, the court rejected the plaintiffs' request that they be permitted to image or download all information stored in defendant's "data historian" program.[18] The plaintiffs initially proposed imaging or mirroring the data historian as a means of easily obtaining the requested information. However, the defendant objected and argued that such imaging would necessarily require approximately one hundred days to complete and that any such imaging would violate the licensing for the operating software used by defendant. The plaintiffs further suggested that the information be downloaded into a database using defendant's software. The defendant responded that it did not own the software modules, but that such software could be purchased for approximately $5,000 and would require another $5,000 in training/programming to make the modules useable. The court concluded that production of the data historian information was unduly burdensome, and noted that the plaintiffs had failed to present a sufficient argument demonstrating that their need for the information contained within the data historian outweighed the burden of producing it.

2. Granting Requests for On–Site Inspections

There are times, however, when a court permits an on-site inspection of an adversary's computer. In *Cenveo Corp. v. Slater*, the plaintiff sought to have its expert create a mirror image of the defendants' hard drives, which would then be searched for responsive information. Cenveo alleged that the defendants, its former employees, had used Cenveo's computers to steal its trade secrets, confidential information, and business opportunities. The court held that an on-site inspection and mirror imaging of the hard drives was warranted "[b]ecause of the close relationship between plaintiff's claims and defendants' computer equipment."[19]

Similarly, in *Ameriwood Industries v. Liberman*, another trade secrets case in which the plaintiff alleged that the defendants—its former employees—had used the plaintiff's computers and confidential files to divert its business to the defendants' new company, the court granted the plaintiff's motion to allow an independent expert to obtain and search a mirror image of the defendants' computer equipment. The court based its ruling on "the close relationship between plaintiff's claims and defendants' computer equipment, and [had] cause to question whether defendants have produced all responsive documents."[20] The court found that deleted versions of e-mails, which were not produced, might exist on the defendants' computers, along with other relevant data such as where certain files were sent and whether the defendants accessed other confidential files.

---

18. No. 05 Civ. 445, 2006 WL 2927878, at *1–2 (W.D. Okla. Oct. 11, 2006).

19. No. 06 Civ. 2632, 2007 WL 442387, at *2 (E.D. Pa. Jan. 31, 2007).

20. No. 06 Civ. 524, 2006 WL 3825291, at *1 (E.D. Mo. Dec. 27, 2006).

When courts permit inspection, they usually order measures to protect confidentiality, such as having an independent computer forensics expert conduct the imaging. In addition, the producing party is generally allowed to review the information for privilege and responsiveness before producing it to the requesting party. In *Ameriwood*, for example, the plaintiff's computer forensics expert was ordered to first provide responsive files retrieved from the defendants' hard drives to defendants' counsel, who could review the records for privilege and responsiveness before sending them to plaintiff's counsel.

3. Is a "Neutral" Computer Forensics Expert Required?

In addition to facilitating disclosure of relevant evidence, a central purpose of a court-imposed inspection is to protect the responding party's privacy and privileges in the ESI being searched. To this end, courts often require that the designated expert be made an "officer of the court" or be subject to strict confidentiality agreements or protective orders.[21]

A key issue is whether the appointed expert must be independent and neutral, or whether it is acceptable to use the forensic expert of one of the parties. While some protocols call for independent experts, often one of the litigant's experts will be appointed to the task in order to minimize costs and complexity.

For example, in *Calyon v. Mizuho Securities USA Inc.*, the plaintiff maintained that only its expert—as opposed to the defendants' expert or an independent third-party expert—would possess the requisite incentive to search exhaustively for evidence.[22] The defendants argued that granting the plaintiff's expert "unfettered access" to home computers and computer storage devices would impermissibly invade the privacy rights of the defendants and their non-party family members who also used the computers. The defendants proposed that their own expert review the mirror images by using search terms provided by the plaintiff, or, alternatively, that a search be performed by an independent expert, who would presumably be appointed by the court.

The court denied access to the plaintiff's expert to image and search the defendants' home computers and also rejected the suggestion that an independent expert be appointed to perform the work, noting that:

> [the plaintiff] does not appear to dispute that the defendants' expert has the technological capability to perform this search. Moreover, the [defendants'] counsel and expert have stated that they are willing to work cooperatively with [plaintiff]'s counsel and expert on an on-going basis to develop and refine search techniques to ensure

---

21. *See, e.g., Cenveo Corp. v. George Slater*, No. 06 Civ. 2632, 2007 WL 442387 (E.D. Pa. Jan. 31, 2007) (once expert is chosen, plaintiff shall notify defendants, and the expert shall execute a confidentiality agreement agreed to by the parties and sign a copy of the protective order); *Simon Prop. Grp. L.P. v. mySimon, Inc.*, 194 F.R.D. 639 (S.D. Ind. 2000) (because the expert served as an officer of the court, disclosure of communication to the expert not deemed a waiver of the attorney-client privilege or any other privilege.).

22. No. 07 Civ. 2241, 2007 WL 1468889, at *1 (S.D.N.Y. May 18, 2007).

that all responsive information is identified. In the end, other than arguing that only its expert has the proper incentives to conduct an exhaustive search, [plaintiff] provides no specific basis for why it believes the [defendants'] expert would not thoroughly search the hard drive images. [Plaintiff]'s argument about proper incentives is simply too generalized a basis for granting it *carte blanche* access to the [defendants'] personal hard drives, access that [plaintiff] itself acknowledges as "extraordinary." Finally, . . . the Court finds no need, at this time, to appoint [an independent expert], which would introduce yet another layer of expertise to a case where each side has already retained experts of their choice, and which would make the prosecution of this action more costly.[23]

F. DISCOVERY FROM MOST KNOWLEDGEABLE PERSON

HEARTLAND SURGICAL SPECIALTY HOSPITAL, LLC v. MIDWEST DIVISION, INC.

No. 05–2164, 2007 WL 1054279 (D. Kan. Apr. 9, 2007)

BOSTWICK, MAGISTRATE JUDGE

Before the Court is Defendants' Joint Motion to Compel Heartland Surgical Specialty Hospital LLC ("Heartland") to Produce a Rule 30(b)(6) Witness with Knowledge of Its Production of Documents and Data. In the motion, Defendants seek an order compelling Heartland to produce a witness who can testify regarding topics 8, 9, 10, 16, and 17 of Defendants' notice of 30(b)(6) deposition. * * *

FACTUAL BACKGROUND

Defendants' Rule 30(b)(6) deposition notice to Heartland on November 14, 2006 identified 55 separate topics for the deposition. The notice was discussed during the status conference held on November 16, 2006, and the Court granted Defendants' request to split the noticed deposition topics into two Rule 30(b)(6) depositions. Defendants were allowed 11 deposition hours over 2 days for topics 1 through 17 and 24 hours over 4 days for topics 18 through 55. Defendants commenced their first Rule 30(b)(6) deposition over topics 1 through 17 on November 28, 2006.

This motion concerns only whether Heartland has complied with the requirements of Rule 30(b)(6) with respect to its designated representative's responses to deposition questions on topics 8, 9, 10, 16, and 17. Those topics are described in the deposition notice as follows:

Topic 8: "The document retention policies applicable to any [Heartland] Financial Records, [Heartland] Patient Records, [Heartland] Financial Reports, or [Heartland] Plans and Forecasts."

---

23. *Id.* at *5.

Topic 9: "The destruction, alteration, or loss of any [Heartland] Financial Records, [Heartland] Patient Records, [Heartland] Financial Reports, or [Heartland] Plans and Forecasts."

Topic 10: "The capabilities of [Heartland's] AdvantX, Great Plains, and Softmed software, the data stored or used with that software, and the reports that can be generated with that software."

Topic 16: "The capabilities of the computer systems and software that [Heartland] uses or has used to create, transmit, or store e-mails and other electronic documents, and the extent to which [Heartland] can identify and produce information responsive to discovery requests in this Lawsuit that are stored in those systems."

Topic 17: "[Heartland's] search for, identification of and production of documents and information responsive to discovery requests in this Lawsuit."

DISCUSSION

* * *

Judge Rushfelt has set out the general guidelines with respect to Rule 30(b)(6) depositions:

> For a Rule 30(b)(6) deposition to operate effectively, the * * * corporation must designate and adequately prepare witnesses to address these matters. If the rule is to promote effective discovery regarding corporations the spokesperson must be informed. A notice of deposition made pursuant to Rule 30(b)(6) requires the corporation to produce one or more officers to testify with respect to matters set out in the deposition notice or subpoena. A party need only designate, with reasonable particularity, the topics for examination. The corporation then must not only produce such number of persons as will satisfy the request, but more importantly, prepare them so that they may give complete, knowledgeable and binding answers on behalf of the corporation. . . .

Rule 30(b)(6) implicitly requires the designated representative to review all matters known or reasonably available to it in preparation for the Rule 30(b)(6) deposition. This interpretation is necessary in order to make the deposition a meaningful one and to prevent the sandbagging of an opponent by conducting a half-hearted inquiry before the deposition but a thorough and vigorous one before the trial. This would totally defeat the purpose of the discovery process. The Court understands that preparing for a Rule 30(b)(6) deposition can be burdensome. However, this is merely the result of the concomitant obligation from the privilege of being able to use the corporate (or other organizational) form in order to conduct business. A party does not fulfill its obligations at the Rule 30(b)(6) deposition by stating it has no knowledge or position with respect to a set of facts or area of inquiry within its knowledge or reasonably available. . . .

Starlight Int'l Inc. v. Herlihy, 186 F.R.D. 626, 638 (D. Kan. 1999). The initial question, then, is whether Defendants' notice described with "reasonable particularity" the matters on which examination was requested. If it did, then Defendants satisfied their burden and Heartland was required to produce a knowledgeable designee.

Courts in this district have found a notice of Rule 30(b)(6) deposition topics to be overbroad when the notice lists topics, but then indicates that the listed topics are not exclusive. Here, the Court specifically limited the parties to the noticed topics 1 through 17, so there can be no argument of overbreadth on the basis that the notice was not limited to the topics designated. Likewise, a notice is not overbroad when its plain language identifies the subject matter of the testimony sought,

The Court finds that Defendants' notice as to topics 1 through 17 described matters with reasonable particularity and satisfied Rule 30(b)(6). Topics 8 and 9 identify the "document retention policies" and "destruction, alteration, or loss" of Heartland's financial records, patient records, financial reports, and plans and forecasts, as those terms are defined in the notice. The definitions of patient records and financial reports do use the phrase "including but not limited to," but are then followed by an extensive example list of the records and reports for which information is sought by Defendants. However, it is clear both from the language used in topics 8 and 9 and from the definitions provided what specific information is being sought. Topic 10 very specifically lists the information sought by Defendants (capabilities, data, and reports from three listed software programs), as does topic 16 (computer systems and software used for Heartland's email and electronic documents). The plain language of topic 17 involves Heartland's compliance with discovery requests. It is true that Defendants sought a large amount of information, but there can be no claim that Heartland could not identify the "outer limits of the areas of inquiry." Further, these topics are relevant to the discovery and documents produced to date in this litigation. *See* FED. R. CIV. P. 26(b)(1) (stating broad allowance of discovery into "any matter, not privileged," and "reasonably calculated to lead to the discovery of admissible evidence").

Having established that the notice provided to Heartland was sufficient, Heartland had a duty to adequately prepare a knowledgeable witness with respect to the noticed topics. As previously noted, Defendants' motion concerns only topics 8, 9, 10, 16, and 17, and Defendants have identified 6 specific question areas that could not be answered by Ms. Holley [the representative designated by Heartland for the Rule 30(b)(6) deposition]:

1. What computer servers does Heartland use, and what data are stored on them?

2. What computers, disk drives, and databases were searched for responsive documents?

3. What are [Heartland's] document retention policies with respect to e-mail, and what was done to prevent deletion or destruction of responsive e-mail?

4. Who is [Heartland's] e-discovery vendor, what was the vendor instructed to do, and what did it do?

5. What was done to eliminate non-responsive documents from [Heartland's] production?

6. What are the reporting capabilities of [Heartland's] Great Plains and AdvantX software, and can [Heartland] export its Great Plains and AdvantX databases to a file for production to defendants?

* * *

With regard to question 1, when asked about specific servers previously identified within Heartland documents, and the storage and retention of data items on those servers, Ms. Holley could not identify some of the servers and did not know the storage or retention policies for some identified servers. With regard to question 2, Ms. Holley did not know which network drivers were searched for responsive discovery documents, whether individual user drives for former employees were searched for responsive discovery documents, whether physician own-ers' e-mails saved to Heartland servers were searched for responsive discovery documents, whether archived e-mails were searched for re-sponsive discovery documents, whether the voice-mail server was searched for responsive discovery documents, whether the hard drives of individual computers were searched for responsive discovery docu-ments, or whether former employees Kim Krause and Jim Morse's individual computer hard drives were searched for responsive discovery documents. With regard to question 4, Ms. Holley did not know "exactly how they [the e-discovery vendor] searched" the Heartland servers, or "what all was on" the CD database that was produced to Defendants. Because Heartland's e-discovery vendor is an agent of Heartland, Ms. Holley should have been educated on this issue as it is encompassed within topic 17. With regard to question 5, Ms. Holley did not know whether Heartland's counsel did anything to determine if produced electronic documents were responsive to discovery requests. Heartland's counsel are the agents of Heartland and Ms. Holley should have been educated on this issue as it is encompassed within topic 17. With regard to question 6, Ms. Holley did not know whether Heartland's computer systems (AdvantX and Great Plains) could export data for varying means of production. This overall showing with regard to these questions establishes that Ms. Holley was unprepared to answer questions on topics 10, 16, and 17.

With regard to the question 3 identified above, however, Defendants have not shown that Ms. Holley was either unprepared or did not have the requisite knowledge to adequately answer the question. In totality regarding question 3, Defendants cite the following portions of the transcript.

Q.   I've looked through Deposition Exhibit 31 and did not see a policy about deletion or archiving of E-mail. Is there such a policy?

A.   All of the policies related to document retention have been included in this packet.

Q.   Okay. Does Heartland Surgical Specialty Hospital routinely delete E-mail?

A.   Not to my knowledge.

Q.   Are there size limitations on an individual E-mail account user's mailbox?

A.   Not that I'm aware of. . . .

Q.   Do individual E-mail account holders have the ability to save E-mail files outside their mailbox?

A.   Yes.

Q.   Where would those E-mails be-where are the potential places those E-mails could be saved?

A.   They're instructed to save those E-mail documents or attachments into their personal drive on the server.

Q.   Are you aware of any other places that E-mail account holders have saved E-mails and attachments?

A.   I wouldn't know.

Q.   Is there any policing of the policy that E-mails and attachments are to be saved to the personal drive?

MR. McGUIRE: Object to form. Vague and ambiguous.

Q.   (By Mr. Bien) Is there anyone who checks to make sure that the policy is followed?

A.   I don't know specifically.

Q.   Who would be the person who would be responsible-or withdraw that. Who would be the person with knowledge about whether the policy that E-mails and attachments are to be saved to a personal drive is followed?

A.   Mr. Coffman would have knowledge of that.

The excerpted transcript portions show only that the policies Heartland has have been given to Defendants, that Heartland does not routinely delete e-mail or limit individual user's e-mail account sizes, and that Ms. Holley did not have knowledge of whether a specific policy was regulated or enforced. The excerpted transcript portions do not show, as Defendants propound, that Ms. Holley did not know the document retention policies with respect to e-mail and what was done to prevent deletion or destruction of responsive e-mail. Defendants have not shown that Ms. Holley was unprepared to answer this question as encompassed by topics 8 and 9.

* * *

While the questions asked in the deposition, particularly about the capabilities of Heartland's computers and software, may have been detailed in nature, they clearly fall within the topics described in the notice. The fact that Ms. Holley had to state, in response to numerous questions, that the answer to the question would be known by either Mr. Coffman (Heartland's Director of Information Technology) or Mr. Van Horn (Heartland's Chief Financial Officer) clearly indicates that Plaintiff had available other persons who could have been used as additional Rule 30(b)(6) witnesses to respond to at least some of the first seventeen topics on behalf of the corporation. It also indicates that Plaintiff did not adequately prepare the tendered witness to answer the questions set out in the identified topics. The Court, therefore, finds that Heartland failed to produce a knowledgeable representative with respect to topics 10, 16, and 17.

Regarding the requested relief sought, *Starlight* instructs:

> Corporations, partnerships, and joint ventures have a duty to make a conscientious, good-faith effort to designate knowledgeable persons for Rule 30(b)(6) depositions and to prepare them to fully and unevasively answer questions about the designated subject matter. If the designated persons do not possess personal knowledge of the matters set out in the deposition notice, the entity is obligated to prepare the designees so that they may give knowledgeable and binding answers for the organization. If it becomes obvious during the course of the deposition that the designee is deficient, the organization is obligated to provide a substitute.

Heartland did not designate a knowledgeable person with regard to topics 10, 16, and 17 of the Rule 30(b)(6) deposition. Ms. Holley did not possess personal knowledge of these topics and was not prepared to give knowledgeable answers regarding the topics on behalf of the corporation. Ms. Holley's designation as the Rule 30(b)(6) designee was deficient as to these topics and Heartland must provide a substitute Rule 30(b)(6) designee.

Plaintiff argues that Defendants will have the opportunity to take fact witness depositions of other Heartland employees, including its CFO and Director of Information Technology. This, however, is not the same as a Rule 30(b)(6) deposition which presents the testimony of the corporation itself rather than just the personal knowledge of the witness.

Defendants broadly request an additional Rule 30(b)(6) deposition with respect to topics 8, 9, 10, 16, and 17, but they make their motion based on the questions discussed above. Of course, once questions 1, 2,

4, 5, and 6 are answered (the Court finds that question 3, on topics 8 and 9, has already been adequately answered), Defendants may, and probably will, have additional follow-up questions directly related to topics 10, 16, and 17. For this reason, Defendants may conduct an additional Rule 30(b)(6) deposition of Heartland, on topics 10, 16, and 17. Defendants are limited to questions 1, 2, 4, 5, and 6 and any follow-up questions that flow naturally and directly from these questions. The deposition will be limited to six (6) hours in duration.

COMMENTARY

Depositions of the "person most knowledgeable" are nothing new. There has been a long and relatively undisturbed tradition permitting the deposition of the individual in the best position to know certain information, and whose testimony speaks for and is binding on a partnership, corporation, or other non-individual legal entity. In fact, there was no change to Rule 30(b)(6) in the 2006 Rule Amendments. However, since the advent of electronic discovery, depositions noticed under Rule 30(b)(6), or its state law equivalent, have taken on additional importance in counsel's effort to understand the creation, identification, and retention of potentially relevant ESI.

Persons testifying as Rule 30(b)(6) witnesses "shall testify as to matters known or reasonably available to the organization." A witness designated as the most knowledgeable person is not simply testifying about matters within his or her own personal knowledge. Rather, this individual is speaking on behalf of the corporation about matters to which the corporation has reasonable access. It is improper for a witness to deny knowledge of facts within the knowledge of the organization as a whole or reasonably knowable by the organization. This is to avoid the gamesmanship by which various officers or managing agents of a corporation are deposed but each disclaims knowledge of facts that must be known by someone in the company. In a further effort to address this problem, many courts have held that a party cannot present evidence on a subject after its Rule 30(b)(6) witness claimed to have no knowledge about a subject that is properly described in the deposition notice.[24] When served with a "person most knowledgeable" deposition notice, an organization or corporation must therefore designate a witness who either knows the information requested in the notice, or who can reasonably obtain that knowledge.

There is some debate over whether or not the subjects outlined in a Rule 30(b)(6) notice limit the scope of the examination. The majority rule is that in the absence of an agreement, depositions are only limited by the relevance and privilege bounds described by Rule 26(b).[25] How-

---

24. *See Rainey v. American Forest & Paper Ass'n, Inc.*, 26 F. Supp. 2d 82, 94 (D.D.C. 1998); *United States v. Taylor*, 166 F.R.D. 356, 359–63 (M.D.N.C. 1996).

25. *See, e.g., Overseas Private Inv. Corp. v. Mandelbaum*, 185 F.R.D. 67 (D.D.C. 1999); *King v. Pratt & Whitney*, 161 F.R.D. 475, 476 (S.D. Fla. 1995).

ever, some courts have held that the requirement that a party noticing the Rule 30(b)(6) deposition "describe with reasonable particularity the matters on which examination is requested" limits the scope of the deposition to the contents of that notice.[26]

The topics covered in a 30(b)(6) deposition must be relevant to the claims or defenses involved, and not be redundant.[27] The topics must also be stated with "reasonable particularity," according to the Rule and its many state equivalents.[28] In order to avoid delay and objections to an overly broad deposition notice, the party requesting a 30(b)(6) deposition should carefully craft the notice to describe the topics of examination. Rather than broadly seeking information about the computer systems in general terms, the notice should specify what particular aspect of the corporate information systems (*e.g.* e-mail message creation, storage, and deletion) are to be covered.

Companies and organizations should consider e-discovery issues when selecting a "person most knowledgeable" for Rule 30(b)(6) depositions pertaining to electronic preservation and production matters. If the witness does not understand the systems and architecture involved in the request, the result could be prolonged litigation, confusion, and disputes over the costs of finding the appropriate person.[29] Depending on subjects described in the deposition notice, many organizations routinely designate an IT professional or record retention manager as the appropriate witness for "person most knowledgeable" depositions. The search for the right person for a particular system, or an outdated legacy application, can nonetheless be tedious and time consuming.

The "person most knowledgeable" may be a person or entity outside the litigation entirely, such as a storage vendor or third-party contractor responsible for system backups or archiving of electronic records. In fact, an organization cannot refuse to designate a witness on the ground that the potential deponents are beyond the control or direction of the company.[30]

What types of topics should be included in a notice for the deposition of a person most knowledgeable about a company's e-mail system? Would the IT Director be an appropriate witness for a large bank to provide in response to a deposition notice concerning the creation, storage, and retention of e-mail messages? Why or why not?

---

26. *See, e.g., Paparelli v. Prudential Ins. Co. of Am.*, 108 F.R.D. 727, 729 (D. Mass. 1985).

27. *See Cunningham v. Standard Fire Ins. Co.*, No. 07 Civ. 2538, 2008 WL 2668301, at *5 (D. Colo. July 1, 2008) (deposition on "storage, preservation and backup of emails" not relevant to claims for breach of insurance contract or bad faith in adjusting an individual claim).

28. Rule 30(b)(6). *See also* California Code of Civil Procedure § 2025.230.

29. *See Calzaturficio S.C.A.R.P.A. s.p.a. v. Fabiano Shoe Co.*, 201 F.R.D. 33, 37 (D. Mass. 2001) (party sanctioned for presenting witness with only general knowledge and insufficiently informed as to topics "that are crucial to the instant litigation").

30. *See Ecclesiastes 9:10–11–12, Inc. v. LMC Holding Co.*, 497 F.3d 1135, 1146–47 (10th Cir. 2007) (affirming district court's dismissal of the action for failure to prosecute due to plaintiffs' failure to produce 30(b)(6) witnesses on the ground that they were no longer affiliated with the plaintiff company).

Draft a sample 30(b)(6) notice seeking information about a company's IT infrastructure, storage and retention related to e-mail.

G. WHEN MUST NOT REASONABLY ACCESSIBLE DATA BE PRODUCED?

W.E. AUBUCHON CO., INC. v. BENEFIRST, LLC

245 F.R.D. 38 (D. Mass. 2007)

HILLMAN, MAGISTRATE JUDGE

INTRODUCTION

By order of this Court dated September 7, 2006, the Defendant, BeneFirst, LLC ("BeneFirst"), was ordered to produce medical claims files, including actual bills in its possession, custody, or control. On September 18, 2006, BeneFirst filed the instant Motion for Reconsideration of Court's Discovery Order Related to Medical Bills together with an accompanying memorandum and affidavit. BeneFirst claims that the documents are not reasonably accessible because the cost of their production far outweighs their value to the Plaintiffs. For the reasons set forth below, I deny the motion.

BACKGROUND

This case involves the administration of qualified benefits plans under the Employee Retirement Income Security Act of 1974 ("ERISA"). W.E. Aubuchon Co., Inc. ("Aubuchon") is the employer, sponsor and administrator of the W.E. Aubuchon Co., Inc. Employee Medical Benefit Plan ("Aubuchon Plan"). Aubuchon is the sponsor and Aubuchon Distribution, Inc. ("Aubuchon Distribution") is the employer and administrator of the W.E. Aubuchon Co., Inc. & Aubuchon Distribution, Inc. Employee Medical Benefit Plan ("Aubuchon Distribution Plan," and, together with the Aubuchon Plan, the "ERISA Plans").

BeneFirst, which is a Massachusetts limited liability company based in Marshfield, Massachusetts, entered into a contract with the Plaintiffs pursuant to which BeneFirst assumed the rights, duties and obligations to administer the ERISA Plans, as a third-party administrator. Bene-First's obligations included "investigating and determining eligibility, payments, co-pays, coinsurance and subrogation claims," for which BeneFirst allegedly "exercised discretion and control over [its] decisions [presumably with respect to payment of claims] and was paid to execute these duties properly." The Plaintiffs charge that BeneFirst failed to perform its duties in a reasonably prudent manner, thereby breaching its fiduciary duty (Counts I and II) and that it breached the underlying contract by failing to provide services accurately and completely (Counts III and IV).

In the initial motion to compel, Plaintiffs sought, among other things, to compel BeneFirst to produce all medical claims files, including the actual medical bills in BeneFirst's custody or control. This Court ruled that BeneFirst was to provide those files and bills. It is that ruling that is the subject of this motion for reconsideration.

FACTS

BeneFirst is no longer in operation. Therefore, I will set out a historical summary of the procedures utilized by BeneFirst for processing, storing and retrieving claims at the time it administered the ERISA Plans. In order to comply with this Court's initial ruling, BeneFirst would have to hire personnel to retrieve the claims sought by the Plaintiffs in accordance with the procedures described below.

BeneFirst would typically receive requests for payment from medical providers who had provided covered medical services to Aubuchon/Aubuchon Distribution personnel. These requests for payment were on claim forms. These claims would be sorted or "batched" into client groups for processing. Once processed for payment, the claim forms were retained for a 60 day period. After 60 days, the batch of claim forms would be scanned and stored as electronic images and then destroyed. These scanned forms were stored in groups according to their processing date and the person who processed the claim.

If a claim needed to be retrieved after the 60 day period, the claim number, processor, and date of processing would be needed in order to retrieve the image. If all of this information was available, then the search would take 3–4 minutes. If all of the information was not available, it could take upwards of 7 minutes. It is particularly important to the search process to have the name of the person who processed the claim because on any given day, 3–4 claims examiners would process Plaintiffs' claims and during the relevant period, 14 different examiners were employed. Furthermore, for parts of 2001, 2002 and 2003, BeneFirst utilized an outside vendor to process claims. The outside vendor would scan the claims and return them to BeneFirst on a CD–R for further processing. The images scanned by the outside vendor would then be batched in the same way as was done during in-house processing.

The search process for retrieving claims is further complicated by the fact that there is no index of images per se. The images are stored on BeneFirst's server first, according to year of processing, then by claims examiner, then by the month of processing, and finally by the actual processing date. Inexplicably, BeneFirst's system was not set up [ ] for the wholesale retrieval of claim images on a group by group basis.

During the 3.5 years at issue in this litigation, BeneFirst was administering up to 48 different plans and, by its estimation, processed between 550,000 and 600,000 claims. Of that number, 34,112 claims were submitted for processing under the ERISA Plans. Of that number, the Plaintiffs have narrowed their request, based upon a dollar value, to approximately 3,000 claims. BeneFirst estimates that it would cost approximately $80,000.00 and take almost 4,000 hours to retrieve all 34,112 claims. They have not provided a cost/time estimate for the retrieval of the 3,000 claims.

DISCUSSION

Our courts have repeatedly reiterated that "notice pleading standard relies on liberal discovery rules" and that "it is now beyond dispute that broad discovery is a cornerstone of the litigation process contemplated by the Federal Rules of Civil Procedure." *Zubulake v. UBS Warburg*, 217 F.R.D. 309, 311 (S.D.N.Y. 2003). While the principle is relatively straightforward, its application is not. This principle of liberal discovery is sorely tested when the object of the discovery is electronic data. As of December 1, 2006, the Federal Rules of Civil Procedure were amended to give greater guidance to courts and litigants in dealing with electronic discovery issues. There are four key areas of change to the Rules that address electronic discovery: early attention to e-discovery issues; the role of accessibility; the form of production; and sanctions under Rule 37. This case squarely presents the question of whether the information sought is reasonably accessible within the meaning of the Rule and if not, whether it still should be produced.

The Recent Amendments

On December 1, 2006, Rule 26 was amended, in relevant part, to provide the following limitation to the general rule that a party may obtain discovery of any matter, not privileged, that is relevant to such party's claim or defenses:

> A party need not provide discovery of electronically stored information from sources that the party identifies as not reasonably accessible because of undue burden or cost. On motion to compel discovery or for a protective order, the party from whom discovery is sought must show that the information is not reasonably accessible because of undue burden or cost. If that showing is made, the court may nonetheless order discovery from such sources if the requesting party shows good cause, considering the limitations of Rule 26(b)(2)(C). The court may specify conditions for the discovery.

F.R.C.P. 26(b)(2)(B).

* * *

Application of The Rule 26 Amendment

Under Rule 26, as revised, this Court must determine whether the information sought is reasonably accessible. If the information is not reasonably accessible, this Court may still order discovery if Aubuchon shows good cause for requesting the information, taking into consideration the limitations of Rule 26(b)(2)(C).

Is the requested information "reasonably accessible" within the meaning of FRCP 26(b)(2)?

BeneFirst asserts that the requested claims forms are not reasonably accessible within the meaning of FRCP 26(b)(2)(B) because of the high cost to retrieve such information (both in monetary terms and in terms of the man hours it would require to retrieve the information). Bene-First contends that the high cost/time to retrieve such data is necessitated by the fact that it is maintained in an inaccessible format.

* * *

In this case, the records sought by the Plaintiffs are stored on a server used by BeneFirst in Pembroke Massachusetts, which is clearly an accessible format. However, because of BeneFirst's method of storage and lack of an indexing system, it will be extremely costly to retrieve the requested data. I am hard pressed to understand the rationale behind having a system that is only searchable by year of processing, then claims examiner, then the month of processing, and finally the claims date. None of these search criteria reflect the name of the individual claimant, the date that the claimant received the medical service, who the provider was, or even the company that employed the benefit holder. It would seem that such a system would only serve to discourage audits and the type of inquiries that have led to the instant litigation Nevertheless, the retrieval of the records will be costly and for the purposes of this decision, I find that such retrieval would involve undue burden or cost. Accordingly, the images are not reasonably accessible within the meaning of Fed. R. Civ. P. 26(b)(2)(B).

Since the images are not reasonably accessible is there "good cause" to order their production?

The Plaintiffs argue that the information they have requested goes to the heart of their case and that they have established "good cause" for production of the same. In making a determination of whether the requesting party has established "good cause," this Court must consider whether: "(i) the discovery sought is unreasonably cumulative or duplicative, or is obtainable from some other source that is more convenient, less burdensome, or less expensive; (ii) the party seeking discovery has had ample opportunity by discovery in the action to obtain the information sought; or (iii) the burden or expense of the proposed discovery outweighs its likely benefit, taking into account the needs of the case, the amount in controversy, the parties' resources, the importance of the issues at stake in the litigation, and the importance of the proposed discovery in resolving the issues." Fed. R. Civ. P. 26(b)(2)(C). To the extent not covered by the aforementioned factors, the Court should also consider:

> (1) the specificity of the discovery request; (2) the quantity of information available from other and more easily accessed sources; (3) the failure to produce relevant information that seems likely to

have existed but is no longer available on more easily accessed sources; (4) the likelihood of finding relevant, responsive information that cannot be obtained from other, more easily accessed sources; (5) predictions as to the importance and usefulness of the further information; (6) the importance of the issues at stake in the litigation; and (7) the parties' resources.

Fed. R. Civ. P. 26 Advisory Committee's note, to 2006 Amendment.

The specificity of the discovery request.

BeneFirst's Motion seeks reconsideration of this Court's earlier discovery order which ordered BeneFirst to produce "all claims files, including the actual bills in BeneFirst's possession or control." The parties have responded intelligently and vigorously to this Order and there is no misunderstanding or confusion about the specificity of the information sought by the Plaintiffs.

This factor favors the Plaintiffs.

The quantity of information available from other and more easily accessed sources; The failure to produce relevant information that seems likely to have existed but is no longer available from more easily accessed sources.

The gravamen of the Plaintiffs' Amended Complaint is that Bene-First mishandled their employees' medical claims by failing to determine eligibility for payment, the availability of co-payment and co-insurance, and subrogation. The processing of the claim forms was presumably the mechanism for making these determinations. While the Amended Complaint and subsequent pleadings are silent, the relevant time period appears to be from 2001 to 2004.

According to BeneFirst, the original claim forms and medical bills were processed by hand, kept for 60 days, converted to a digital image and then destroyed. Therefore, digital images which constitute the information requested by the Plaintiffs are in the custody and control of BeneFirst and are not available through any other source.

These factors favor the Plaintiffs.

Predictions as to the importance and usefulness of the further information; the likelihood of finding relevant, responsive information that cannot be obtained from other, more easily accessed sources.

I agree with the Plaintiffs that the requested claim forms and medical bills are clearly an integral part of the litigation; the requested information goes not only to BeneFirst's culpability, but also to the amount of damages, if any, to which the Plaintiffs may be entitled. There can be no serious contention that the information is not highly relevant. In fact, it is difficult to imagine how this case could be prosecuted or defended without the claims forms and attendant bills. As previously found, they are not available from any other source (a determination which is uncontroverted).

These factors favor the Plaintiffs.

The importance of the issues at stake in the litigation.

While the importance of the claims/issues in this case are real and substantial vis a vis the parties, such claims/issues to not raise any global concerns.

This factor favors the Defendants (if it favors any party at all).

The parties' resources.

While the Defendant has understandably engaged in a lengthy discussion of the cost of production, neither party has provided the court with any information about their resources. BeneFirst does represent that they no longer have a full time staff and that in order to retrieve the images that they would have to hire temporary help. At the same time, as previously noted, the Plaintiffs have significantly narrowed the breadth of their request and therefore, the time and cost for BeneFirst to produce the requested information should be significantly reduced.

Given the lack of information available to the Court, this factor is neutral.

Other relevant considerations.

In addition to the above 7 factors, it is important to note that a provision in the Service Agreement between the parties provided that: "The Records are the property of the Plan Sponsor. The Plan Sponsor has the right of continuing access to their records...." In other words, although in the custody and control of BeneFirst, the records at issue are the property of the Plaintiffs.

The Plaintiffs Have Met Their Burden To Establish Good Cause.

On balance, I find that the Plaintiffs have clearly established good cause for requiring BeneFirst to produce the requested information. * * * [T]he Plaintiffs have significantly narrowed their original request from approximately 34,000 claims to a list of approximately 3,000. This reduction should serve to reduce the time and expense of retrieving the requested information. Under the circumstances, I find that the requested information should be produced by BeneFirst at its own expense.

ORDER

For the reasons set forth above, BeneFirst's Motion for Reconsideration of Court's Discovery Order Related to Medical Bills is denied. BeneFirst shall produce the Medical Bills and Claims Forms for the approximately 3,000 claims as specified by the Plaintiffs at their own expense.

COMMENTARY

1.   Using Sampling to Determine Accessibility

In an age where virtually every piece of data is technically accessible, a rational and defensible approach must be taken in discovery to determine what data is reasonably accessible under the undue burden or cost test. As discussed earlier, a party in litigation only needs to search for, and to produce data from, accessible sources of ESI.

The Rule gives no guidance as to how the determination of accessibility can be made using real data. A successful declaration of "non-accessibility," of course, effectively removes that particular ESI from the discovery process (absent a showing of good cause). The value associated with such a wholesale removal of data from further discovery virtually guarantees that there will be a tendency—indeed an incentive—to interpret difficulty of any kind as a sign of "non-accessibility."

Certain forms of ESI, such as backup tapes, legacy data and multi-table, enterprise databases, for example, are often quickly labeled as "not reasonably accessible" because of the inherent cost and difficulty associated with incorporating them into the discovery process. Because of the cost benefit of removing a set of ESI from discovery, battles will be waged over how accessible a particular set of ESI is from a technical point of view rather than based on whether or not responsive data is likely to be found and whether the benefit of retrieval outweighs the cost.

a.   Everything Is Accessible—For a Price

The determination of whether or not a particular source of ESI is accessible does not primarily depend upon the type of data (format) or the type of media on which it is stored (form). There are hardware and software tools that allow the restoration of virtually any type of data from virtually any type of form—for a price. Given that ability, the primary issue is not whether the data can be restored, but whether it is worth the cost to restore.

The fundamental question is:

"Will the uniqueness and/or quality of responsive data that I get from any particular set of ESI justify the cost of the acquisition of that data?"

This critical question should be addressed at every meet-and-confer and court hearing on the issue of the accessibility of ESI.

b.   Marginal Utility

In terms of discovery, the marginal utility of ESI is the probative value from one additional unit of ESI relative to the cost necessary to identify, locate, retrieve, review and produce that unit. Thus, parties engaged in discovery should be prepared to provide a comprehensive analysis as to why a particular set of ESI may or may not be reasonably accessible from a marginal utility point of view with respect to the particular litigation.

The arguments for a particular set of ESI not being reasonably accessible include:

1.   There is no responsive data on [the particular source of ESI]. If a particular source of ESI can be shown to have no responsive data, then any cost associated with identifying, locating, retrieving or reviewing it would be too much. Because there is no requirement to produce non-responsive data, there should be no requirement to deal with it in discovery, regardless of the cost. There is a tendency today to argue that if data is easily accessible—such as live (online) data—then it should be searched as a matter of course. This is no more legitimate than arguing that another set of data is not reasonably accessible just because it is on a backup tape. Both should be subjected to the marginal utility test.

2.   There is responsive data on [the particular source of ESI], but the same data is available in another, more accessible, location. If it can be shown that the same data can be retrieved from other lower-cost sources—from an online source rather than from a backup tape, for example—then the lower-cost source is preferable.

3.   There is some responsive data on [the particular source of ESI], but the cost to obtain it is not worth the value the responsive data would provide. This is the classic marginal utility argument. While there may be some data on the particular source of ESI that is arguably responsive, there is something about the data set—its volume, quality, or uniqueness—that makes retrieval unnecessary when compared with the cost to recover it. To be persuasive, this argument requires enough detail to justify the claims being made.

4.   We have no idea what is on [the particular source of ESI] but we do know that it will be difficult and expensive to deal with. This is the classic argument that is often used in an attempt to remove a set of ESI from the discovery process. It is based on a simplistic reading of the concept of accessibility, and attempts to capitalize on the "burden and cost" language of the rule without giving any consideration to the "undue" component. While it may be true that a given source of ESI will be difficult and/or expensive to deal with, such a fact alone should not be enough to remove that ESI from consideration.

The problem with arguments one, two, and three above is that in order to make them successfully, you need to have enough detailed information about the ESI in question so that you can choose which argument to make and then defend it. The problem with argument four is that it is simply inadequate.

i. Sampling

At first blush, the argument about ESI, marginal utility, and accessibility can appear circular. In order to make a defensible argument about accessibility, one must have some detailed information about the data contained within the ESI. But if one can gather such information, then how can it claim that the ESI is not reasonably accessible?

While some systemic arguments can be made (*i.e.* the underlying data processing platform had no relation to the matter at hand; or, the data set is outside the time frame at issue), the most common way to defensibly prepare an "accessible/inaccessible" argument for a particular set of ESI is to use sampling.

Sampling allows one to test the questioned ESI and to extract the metrics needed to develop a marginal utility argument in a cost-effective, timely and defensible manner. While there are different sampling models that can be applied based on the underlying data set and the nature of the matter being litigated, the theory behind sampling is consistent and parties should be prepared to present a sampling argument for including or excluding ESI. The basis of all sampling is that a subset of a population will reveal something about that population as a whole with some specified degree of certainty.

ii. Sampling Hypothetical

For the purposes of our hypothetical, we will assume that we have a single backup tape from a single computer for each day of the year. Furthermore, we will assume that it costs $1,000 to restore and retrieve all of the data from a single backup tape.

The examples below illustrate how different restored subsets of tapes can yield different percentages of the total set of data. By assessing the varying amounts of data restored vis-à-vis the associated restoration cost, one can begin to evaluate the marginal utility associated with the various restoration sets and be prepared to fully evaluate the burden and cost of retrieving a particular set of ESI. Note that the actual percentages for all subsets will vary depending upon the manner in which the backup was conducted, the nature of the data being backed up, and the underlying usage patterns of the system(s) being restored.

In order to retrieve all of the data from a set of backup tapes, every daily backup tape would have to be restored for a total cost of $365,000.

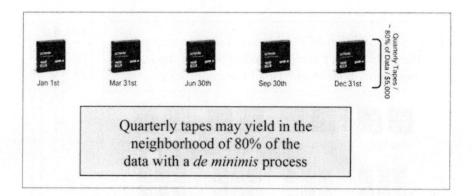

* Quarterly Tapes

Because backup tapes contain multiple copies of the same data, much of what is on any given subset of tapes is duplicative. Given this characteristic, subsets of tapes can be selected and tested to determine how much unique data they contain and what it costs to obtain that data. As can be seen in the graphic above, quarterly tapes can be selected and approximately eighty percent of the entire set of data will be recovered for a cost of only $5,000.[31]

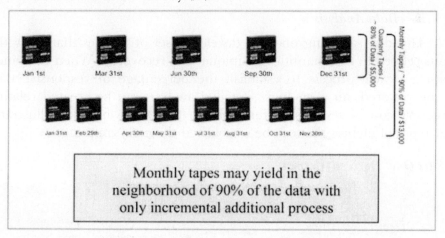

* Monthly Tapes

Selecting monthly tapes (twelve month-end tapes plus the first tape in the set as a baseline) will result in the recovery of approximately ninety percent of the entire set of data for a cost of only $13,000.

---

31. The actual percentages for all subsets will vary depending upon the manner in which the backup was conducted, the nature of the data being backed up, and the underlying usage patterns of the system(s) being restored.

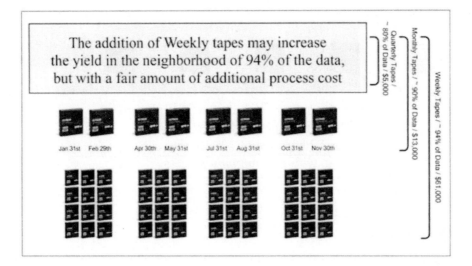

* Weekly Tapes

Choosing weekly tapes (each Friday's tape plus the first tape in the set as a baseline) recovers approximately ninety-four percent of the entire set of data for a cost of $61,000.

ii.   Data Analysis

Through sampling one can develop a set of metrics that show the costs related to the quantities of unique data recovered. When combined with a review process to establish the percentage of responsive data being restored, an even more detailed analysis can be created relating recovery cost to responsive item counts. The following chart illustrates the types of metrics that can be established through sampling.

Chart One: Derived Metrics

Tape Set	# of Tapes Restored	% of Data Set Restored	# of Data Items Restored	# of New Data Items Restored	Cost to Restore	Cost per Data Item	Cost per New Data Item	Assumed Responsive Percentage	# of New Responsive Data Items Restored	Cost per New Responsive Data Item	Total Cost for Responsive Data Items
Quarterly	5	80%	32,120,000	32,120,000	$ 5,000	$ 0.0002	$ 0.0002	1%	321,200	$ 0.02	$ 5,000
Monthly	13	90%	36,135,000	4,015,000	$ 13,000	$ 0.0004	$ 0.0032	1%	40,150	$ 0.32	$ 13,000
Weekly	61	94%	37,741,000	1,606,000	$ 61,000	$ 0.0016	$ 0.0380	1%	16,060	$ 3.80	$ 61,000
Daily	365	100%	40,150,000	2,409,000	$ 365,000	$ 0.0091	$ 0.1515	1%	24,090	$ 15.15	$ 365,000

Chart Two: Incremental Costs

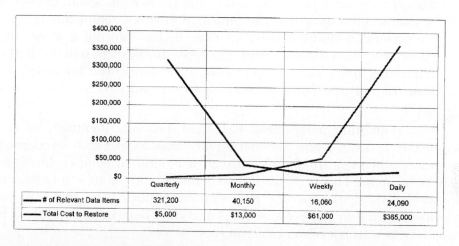

	Quarterly	Monthly	Weekly	Daily
# of Relevant Data Items	321,200	40,150	16,060	24,090
Total Cost to Restore	$5,000	$13,000	$61,000	$365,000

Chart Three: Cost per Responsive Item

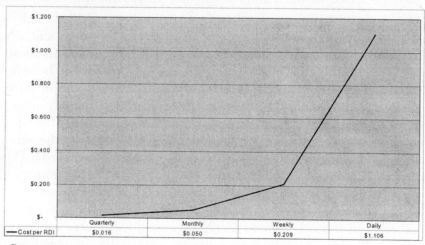

	Quarterly	Monthly	Weekly	Daily
Cost per RDI	$0.016	$0.050	$0.209	$1.106

Summary

Techniques like sampling can be used to provide a more thorough and more defensible basis for arguing that a given set of ESI is reasonably accessible or not. Only by providing metrics related to cost, volume, quality and uniqueness can a proper data discovery plan be crafted. Simplistic arguments about data being easy or hard to retrieve are meaningless without a careful analysis of marginal utility.

2. When Should a Court Permit Discovery of ESI From a Not Reasonably Accessible Source?

Rule 26(b)(2)(B) explicitly limits initial discovery of ESI to information from reasonably accessible sources. The Rule establishes a procedure for the discovery of not reasonably accessible ESI:

(B) A party need not provide discovery of electronically stored information from sources that the party identifies as not reasonably accessible because of undue burden or cost. On motion to compel discovery or for a protective order, the party from whom discovery is sought must show that the information is not reasonably accessible because of undue burden or cost. If that showing is made, the court may nonetheless order discovery from such sources if the requesting party shows good cause, considering the limitations of Rule 26(b)(2)(C). The court may specify conditions for the discovery.

If a requesting party seeks ESI from a source identified as not reasonably accessible and the parties are unable to reach agreement regarding discovery from such sources, a motion to compel discovery may be brought. This procedure is sometimes referred to as a two-tired approach, where the parties first examine information that can be provided from fully accessible sources and then determine whether it is necessary to search less-accessible sources.

The 2006 Advisory Committee Note to Rule 26(b)(2) explains the criteria to be used in determining whether to permit discovery of ESI:

> Once it is shown that a source of electronically stored information is not reasonably accessible, the requesting party may still obtain discovery by showing good cause, considering the limitations of Rule 26(b)(2)(C) that balance the costs and potential benefits of discovery. The decision whether to require a responding party to search for and produce information that is not reasonably accessible depends not only on the burdens and costs of doing so, but also on whether those burdens and costs can be justified in the circumstances of the case. Appropriate considerations may include: (1) the specificity of the discovery request; (2) the quantity of information available from other and more easily accessed sources; (3) the failure to produce relevant information that seems likely to have existed but is no longer available on more easily accessed sources; (4) the likelihood of finding relevant, responsive information that cannot be obtained from other, more easily accessed sources; (5) predictions as to the importance and usefulness of the further information; (6) the importance of the issues at stake in the litigation; and (7) the parties' resources.

3. Is ESI From a Not Reasonably Accessible Source Presumptively Not Discoverable?

The new Rule requires that the responding party bear the burden of demonstrating that data is not reasonably accessible based on the costs and burdens of recovering the data, while the requesting party must show good cause once that showing has been made. This is a change from the general presumption of the discoverability of relevant information. One commentator has criticized this change.

EXCERPT FROM Henry S. Noyes, *Good Cause Is Bad Medicine for the New E–Discovery Rules*, 21 Harv. J.L. & Tech. 49, 83–84 (2007):

First, placing the burden on the requesting party would necessarily mean that the information is presumptively not discoverable, contrary to the stated intention of the rulemakers. Second, placing the burden on the requesting party is inconsistent with the amended [Rule's] requirement that the requesting party show "good cause, considering the limitations of Rule 26(b)(2)(C)." For all other discovery scenarios in which Rule 26(b)(2)(C) applies, the party *opposing* discovery has the burden of demonstrating that the request is unduly burdensome or overbroad. Third, [Rule 26(b)(2)(B) permits the responding party to move for a protective order, but shifts the burden to show good cause for the order from the moving party, which ordinarily bears it, to the party seeking discovery].

* * *

Under the 2006 amendments, it is unclear whether ESI that is not reasonably accessible is presumptively not discoverable. On the one hand, the plain language of the amended [Rule] contemplates a presumption of nondiscoverability. Moreover, during the period of public comment, some commentators assumed that the amended rule would alter the normal presumption of discoverability. The rulemaking history ... supports a different interpretation.... The [chair of the Advisory Committee] "emphasized that the rule is not one of presumed non-discoverability, but instead makes the existing proportionality limit more effective in a novel area in which the rules can helpfully provide better guidance."[32]

If the goal of the Committee was to retain the presumption of discoverability, did it succeed?

4. How Should Counsel Address Rule 26(b)(2)(B) "Good Cause" Issues?

The Committee Note to Rule 26(b)(2)(B) provides a roadmap of the considerations associated with good cause. But one author offers additional practical guidance:

EXCERPT FROM Theodore C. Hirt, *The Two–Tier Discovery Provision of Rule 26(b)(2)(B)—A Reasonable Measure for Controlling Electronic Discovery?*, 13 Rich. J. L. & Tech. 12, 20–21 (2007)

Counsel for both parties will need to inventory what information sources were actually searched from the first tier. A court will want specifics on the "quantity of information available from other and more easily accessed sources." Counsel for the requesting party will want to be conversant with what relevant information the first tier of discovery yielded. The quality of that information will have to be assessed as well to support the requesting party's position that other information sources must be searched.

---

32. Committee on Rules of Practice & Procedure, Judicial Conference of the U.S., *Meeting of June 15–16 Minutes* 25 (statement of Judge Lee Rosenthal, Chair), *available at* http://www.uscourts. gov/rules/Minutes/ST_June_2005.pdf.

The responding party can defend its position effectively if it has been careful and comprehensive in its previous responses to the first tier of discovery. Counsel will need to document how it has provided information from the reasonably accessible sources. The more comprehensive the showing, the more reasonable a counsel's position will be that second tier sources should not be searched. Counsel for the responding party also should determine what information sources no longer exist, what kind of information was stored on them, and whether that information has migrated to other systems. That will be important because the court will evaluate the failure to produce relevant information that seems likely to have existed but is no longer available on more easily accessed sources.

Existing case law will be of considerable assistance in resolving these disputes. Courts, if given enough information about the information sources at issue, can use Rule 26(b)(2) factors to resolve these disputes. When, for example, the issue is whether relevant information might be stored on a specific information source, the court can weigh the likelihood of such information being located and contrast the expected yield of that new relevant information against the information the party already has obtained in discovery. Courts have developed experience in evaluating the burdens imposed on a producing party to locate and retrieve information from electronic sources—where the producing party can demonstrate substantial burdens in connection with such location and retrieval, the requesting party must be able to demonstrate that there will be tangible benefits from access to that information and ... how the requested information will be important to the resolution of the issues in the case.

5. Is the Rule 26(b)(2)(B) Good Cause Standard Different From the Other Good Cause Standards in Rule 26?

There are two other good cause standards in Rule 26. Rule 26(b)(1) applies a good cause standard to court ordered discovery of information relevant to the subject matter of the action. Rule 26(c) applies a good cause standard for issuance of a protective order. Should the good cause standard differ for production of ESI? Does the presumption of non-discoverability of data that is not reasonably accessible suggest there should be a lesser good cause standard than applies elsewhere in the rules? Given that Rule 26(b)(2)(B) references good cause in the context of Rule 26(b)(2)(C)'s limitations, is the good cause standard more stringent for not reasonably accessible information?

6. Should Courts Weigh the "Marginal Utility" of Allowing Discovery of Information That Is Not Reasonably Accessible?

The court in *McPeek v. Ashcroft* described the use of the marginal utility test in considering whether to allow discovery of not reasonably accessible information. In assessing burden under Rule 26(c), the court reasoned that:

> A fairer approach borrows, by analogy, from the economic principle of "marginal utility." The more likely it is that the backup tape contains information that is relevant to a claim or defense, the fairer it is that the government agency search at its own expense. The less likely it is, the more unjust it would be to make the agency search at its own expense.[33]

In *Oxford House, Inc. v. City of Topeka*, the court applied the marginal utility test and held that although the defendant could potentially access certain deleted e-mails sought by the plaintiff from the defendant's backup tapes, production of those e-mails would be unduly burdensome. The court observed that discovery should generally be allowed unless "the hardship is unreasonable in light of the benefits to be secured from the discovery."[34] In this case, however, the likelihood of retrieving the e-mails was low because the backup tapes containing the e-mails had probably been overwritten, and the cost to retrieve the data and search for the relevant e-mails was high. On this basis the court denied the plaintiff's motion to compel production.

7.   When Are Objections Waived Under the Two-Tier System?

Suppose that after discovery and production is underway, the producing party determines that some of the requested ESI is not reasonably accessible. Has the producing party waived an objection by failing to object promptly and state in its initial written responses that the ESI is not reasonably accessible?

In *Cason-Merenda v. Detroit Medical Center*, in addressing defendant's post production motion for cost-shifting, the court reasoned that the defendant could have designated the requested information as "not reasonably accessible" and refused to complete production unless ordered to do so before incurring the costs to recover the data. The court found that the defendant failed to make a timely motion for relief under Rule 26(b)(2)(B), reasoning that:

> It offends common sense . . . to read the rule in a way that requires (or permits) the producing party to suffer "undue burden or cost" *before* raising the issue with the court. Under such a reading, a court would be powerless to avoid unnecessary expense or to specify any meaningful "conditions" for the discovery other than cost sharing. Furthermore, the requesting party would be stripped of its implicit right to elect either to meet the conditions or forego the requested information. The Rule, if it is to be sensible and useful, must be read as a means of *avoiding* undue burden or cost, rather than simply distributing it.[35]

---

33.   202 F.R.D. 31, 34 (D.D.C. 2001).

34.   No. 06–4004, 2007 WL 1246200, at *4 (D. Kan. Apr. 27, 2007).

35.   No. 06–15601, 2008 WL 2714239, at *2 (E.D. Mich. July 7, 2008).

8. Is a Requesting Party Entitled to Take Discovery to Test the Assertion That the Information It Seeks Is Not Reasonably Accessible?

The Advisory Committee Note to Rule 26(b)(2)(B) explains that the requesting party may need discovery to test the assertion that certain sources are not reasonably accessible. Such discovery may include depositions, inspection of data sources, and limited data sampling, which can help refine search parameters and determine the benefits and burdens associated with a fuller search. Indeed, the concept of data sampling has been adopted by courts as a method to address accessibility issues and determine whether further discovery is appropriate. Thus, the requesting party may issue a more targeted Rule 34 request, seeking a sample of information from the sources at issue.

H.   COST SHARING/COST SHIFTING

1.   Accessible Data—Rule 26(b)(2)(B)

ZUBULAKE v. UBS WARBURG LLC
"Zubulake I"

217 F.R.D. 309 (S.D.N.Y. 2003)

SCHEINDLIN, DISTRICT JUDGE

The world was a far different place in 1849, when Henry David Thoreau opined (in an admittedly broader context) that "[t]he process of discovery is very simple." That hopeful maxim has given way to rapid technological advances, requiring new solutions to old problems. The issue presented here is one such problem, recast in light of current technology: To what extent is inaccessible electronic data discoverable, and who should pay for its production?

I.   INTRODUCTION

The Supreme Court recently reiterated that our "simplified notice pleading standard relies on liberal discovery rules and summary judgment motions to define disputed facts and issues and to dispose of unmeritorious claims." Thus, it is now beyond dispute that "[b]road discovery is a cornerstone of the litigation process contemplated by the Federal Rules of Civil Procedure." The Rules contemplate a minimal burden to bringing a claim; that claim is then fleshed out through vigorous and expansive discovery.

In one context, however, the reliance on broad discovery has hit a roadblock. As individuals and corporations increasingly do business electronically—using computers to create and store documents, make deals, and exchange e-mails—the universe of discoverable material has expanded exponentially.[6] The more information there is to discover, the more expensive it is to discover all the relevant information until, in the end, "discovery is not just about uncovering the truth, but also about how much of the truth the parties can afford to disinter."

This case provides a textbook example of the difficulty of balancing the competing needs of broad discovery and manageable costs. Laura Zubulake is suing UBS Warburg LLC, UBS Warburg, and UBS AG (collectively, "UBS" or the "Firm") under Federal, State and City law for gender discrimination and illegal retaliation. Zubulake's case is certainly not frivolous[8] and if she prevails, her damages may be substantial. She contends that key evidence is located in various e-mails exchanged among UBS employees that now exist only on backup tapes and perhaps other archived media. According to UBS, restoring those e-mails would cost approximately $175,000.00, exclusive of attorney time in reviewing the e-mails. Zubulake now moves for an order compelling UBS to produce those e-mails at its expense.

II. BACKGROUND

A. Zubulake's Lawsuit

UBS hired Zubulake on August 23, 1999, as a director and senior salesperson on its U.S. Asian Equities Sales Desk (the "Desk"), where she reported to Dominic Vail, the Desk's manager. At the time she was hired, Zubulake was told that she would be considered for Vail's position if and when it became vacant.

In December 2000, Vail indeed left his position to move to the Firm's London office. But Zubulake was not considered for his position, and the Firm instead hired Matthew Chapin as director of the Desk. Zubulake alleges that from the outset Chapin treated her differently than the other members of the Desk, all of whom were male. In particular, Chapin "undermined Ms. Zubulake's ability to perform her job by, inter alia: (a) ridiculing and belittling her in front of co-workers; (b) excluding her from work-related outings with male co-workers and clients; (c) making sexist remarks in her presence; and (d) isolating her from the other senior salespersons on the Desk by seating her apart from them." No such actions were taken against any of Zubulake's male co-workers.

Zubulake ultimately responded by filing a Charge of (gender) Discrimination with the EEOC on August 16, 2001. On October 9, 2001, Zubulake was fired with two weeks' notice. On February 15, 2002, Zubulake filed the instant action * * *. UBS timely answered on March

---

6. [See] *Rowe Entm't, Inc. v. William Morris Agency, Inc.*, 205 F.R.D. 421, 429 (S.D.N.Y.2002) (explaining that electronic data is so voluminous because, unlike paper documents, "the costs of storage are virtually nil. Information is retained not because it is expected to be used, but because there is no compelling reason to discard it"), *aff'd*, 2002 WL 975713 (S.D.N.Y. May 9, 2002).

8. Indeed, Zubulake has already produced a sort of "smoking gun": an e-mail suggesting that she be fired "ASAP" after her EEOC charge was filed, in part so that she would not be eligible for year-end bonuses. *See* 8/21/01 e-mail from Mike Davies to Rose Tong ("8/21/01 e-Mail").

12, 2002, denying the allegations. UBS's argument is, in essence, that Chapin's conduct was not unlawfully discriminatory because he treated everyone equally badly. On the one hand, UBS points to evidence that Chapin's anti-social behavior was not limited to women: a former employee made allegations of national origin discrimination against Chapin, and a number of male employees on the Desk also complained about him. On the other hand, Chapin was responsible for hiring three new female employees to the Desk.

B. The Discovery Dispute

Discovery in this action commenced on or about June 3, 2002, when Zubulake served UBS with her first document request. At issue here is request number twenty-eight, for "[a]ll documents concerning any communication by or between UBS employees concerning Plaintiff." The term document in Zubulake's request "includ[es], without limitation, electronic or computerized data compilations." On July 8, 2002, UBS responded by producing approximately 350 pages of documents, including approximately 100 pages of e-mails. UBS also objected to a substantial portion of Zubulake's requests.

On September 12, 2000—after an exchange of angry letters and a conference before United States Magistrate Judge Gabriel W. Gorenstein—the parties reached an agreement (the "9/12/02 Agreement"). With respect to document request twenty-eight, the parties reached the following agreement, in relevant part:

> Defendants will [ ] ask UBS about how to retrieve e-mails that are saved in the firm's computer system and will produce responsive e-mails if retrieval is possible and Plaintiff names a few individuals.

Pursuant to the 9/12/02 Agreement, UBS agreed unconditionally to produce responsive e-mails from the accounts of five individuals named by Zubulake: Matthew Chapin, Rose Tong (a human relations representation who was assigned to handle issues concerning Zubulake), Vinay Datta (a co-worker on the Desk), Andrew Clarke (another co-worker on the Desk), and Jeremy Hardisty (Chapin's supervisor and the individual to whom Zubulake originally complained about Chapin). UBS was to produce such e-mails sent between August 1999 (when Zubulake was hired) and December 2001 (one month after her termination), to the extent possible.

UBS, however, produced no additional e-mails and insisted that its initial production (the 100 pages of e-mails) was complete. As UBS's opposition to the instant motion makes clear * * * UBS never searched for responsive e-mails on any of its backup tapes. To the contrary, UBS informed Zubulake that the cost of producing e-mails on backup tapes would be prohibitive (estimated at the time at approximately $300,000.00).

Zubulake, believing that the 9/12/02 Agreement included production of e-mails from backup tapes, objected to UBS's nonproduction. In fact, Zubulake knew that there were additional responsive e-mails that UBS had failed to produce because she herself had produced approximately 450 pages of e-mail correspondence. Clearly, numerous responsive e-mails had been created and deleted[19] at UBS, and Zubulake wanted them.

On December 2, 2002, the parties again appeared before Judge Gorenstein, who ordered UBS to produce for deposition a person with knowledge of UBS's e-mail retention policies in an effort to determine whether the backup tapes contained the deleted e-mails and the burden of producing them. In response, UBS produced Christopher Behny, Manager of Global Messaging, who was deposed on January 14, 2003. Mr. Behny testified to UBS's e-mail backup protocol, and also to the cost of restoring the relevant data.

C. UBS's E–Mail Backup System

In the first instance, the parties agree that e-mail was an important means of communication at UBS during the relevant time period. Each salesperson, including the salespeople on the Desk, received approximately 200 e-mails each day. Given this volume, and because Securities and Exchange Commission regulations require it, UBS implemented extensive e-mail backup and preservation protocols. In particular, e-mails were backed up in two distinct ways: on backup tapes and on optical disks.

1. Backup Tape Storage

UBS employees used a program called HP OpenMail, manufactured by Hewlett–Packard, for all work-related e-mail communications. With limited exceptions, all e-mails sent or received by any UBS employee are stored onto backup tapes. To do so, UBS employs a program called Veritas NetBackup, which creates a "snapshot" of all e-mails that exist on a given server at the time the backup is taken. Except for scheduling the backups and physically inserting the tapes into the machines, the backup process is entirely automated.

UBS used the same backup protocol during the entire relevant time period, from 1999 through 2001. Using NetBackup, UBS backed up its e-mails at three intervals: (1) daily, at the end of each day, (2) weekly, on Friday nights, and (3) monthly, on the last business day of the month. Nightly backup tapes were kept for twenty working days, weekly tapes

---

19. The term "deleted" is sticky in the context of electronic data. " 'Deleting' a file does not actually erase that data from the computer's storage devices. Rather, it simply finds the data's entry in the disk directory and changes it to a 'not used' status—thus permitting the computer to write over the 'deleted' data. Until the computer writes over the 'deleted' data, however, it may be recovered by searching the disk itself rather than the disk's directory. Accordingly, many files are recoverable long after they have been deleted—even if neither the computer user nor the computer itself is aware of their existence. Such data is referred to as 'residual data.' " Shira A. Scheindlin & Jeffrey Rabkin, *Electronic Discovery in Federal Civil Litigation: Is Rule 34 Up to the Task?*, 41 B.C. L.Rev. 327, 337 (2000). Deleted data may also exist because it was backed up before it was deleted. Thus, it may reside on backup tapes or similar media. Unless otherwise noted, I will use the term "deleted" data to mean residual data, and will refer to backed-up data as "backup tapes."

for one year, and monthly tapes for three years. After the relevant time period elapsed, the tapes were recycled.

Once e-mails have been stored onto backup tapes, the restoration process is lengthy. Each backup tape routinely takes approximately five days to restore, although resort to an outside vendor would speed up the process (at greatly enhanced costs, of course). Because each tape represents a snapshot of one server's hard drive in a given month, each server/month must be restored separately onto a hard drive. Then, a program called Double Mail is used to extract a particular individual's e-mail file. That mail file is then exported into a Microsoft Outlook data file, which in turn can be opened in Microsoft Outlook, a common e-mail application. A user could then browse through the mail file and sort the mail by recipient, date or subject, or search for key words in the body of the e-mail.

Fortunately, NetBackup also created indexes of each backup tape. Thus, Behny was able to search through the tapes from the relevant time period and determine that the e-mail files responsive to Zubulake's requests are contained on a total of ninety-four backup tapes.

2. Optical Disk Storage

In addition to the e-mail backup tapes, UBS also stored certain e-mails on optical disks. For certain "registered traders," probably including the members of the Desk, a copy of all e-mails sent to or received from outside sources (i.e., e-mails from a "registered trader" at UBS to someone at another entity, or vice versa) was simultaneously written onto a series of optical disks. Internal e-mails, however, were not stored on this system.

UBS has retained each optical disk used since the system was put into place in mid–1998. Moreover, the optical disks are neither erasable nor rewritable. Thus, UBS has every e-mail sent or received by registered traders (except internal e-mails) during the period of Zubulake's employment, even if the e-mail was deleted instantaneously on that trader's system.

The optical disks are easily searchable using a program called Tumbleweed. Using Tumbleweed, a user can simply log into the system with the proper credentials and create a plain language search. Search criteria can include not just "header" information, such as the date or the name of the sender or recipient, but can also include terms within the text of the e-mail itself. For example, UBS personnel could easily run a search for e-mails containing the words "Laura" or "Zubulake" that were sent or received by Chapin, Datta, Clarke, or Hardisty.[28]

---

28. Rose Tong, the fifth person designated by Zubulake's document request, would probably not have been a "registered trader" as she was a human resources employee.

III. LEGAL STANDARD

* * *

[Judge Scheindlin sets forth the pre–2006 Rule 26(b)(1) and Rule 26(b)(2), referring to the latter as codifying a "proportionality test."]

Finally, "[u]nder [the discovery] rules, the presumption is that the responding party must bear the expense of complying with discovery requests, but [it] may invoke the district court's discretion under Rule 26(c) to grant orders protecting [it] from 'undue burden or expense' in doing so, including orders conditioning discovery on the requesting party's payment of the costs of discovery."

The application of these various discovery rules is particularly complicated where electronic data is sought because otherwise discoverable evidence is often only available from expensive-to-restore backup media. That being so, courts have devised creative solutions for balancing the broad scope of discovery prescribed in Rule 26(b)(1) with the cost-consciousness of Rule 26(b)(2). By and large, the solution has been to consider cost-shifting: forcing the requesting party, rather than the answering party, to bear the cost of discovery.

By far, the most influential response to the problem of cost-shifting relating to the discovery of electronic data was given by United States Magistrate Judge James C. Francis IV of this district in *Rowe Entertainment, Inc.[v. William Morris, Inc.]*. Judge Francis utilized an eight-factor test to determine whether discovery costs should be shifted. Those eight factors are:

> (1) the specificity of the discovery requests; (2) the likelihood of discovering critical information; (3) the availability of such information from other sources; (4) the purposes for which the responding party maintains the requested data; (5) the relative benefits to the parties of obtaining the information; (6) the total cost associated with production; (7) the relative ability of each party to control costs and its incentive to do so; and (8) the resources available to each party.[33]

Both Zubulake and UBS agree that the eight-factor *Rowe* test should be used to determine whether cost-shifting is appropriate.

IV. DISCUSSION

A. Should Discovery of UBS's Electronic Data Be Permitted?

Under Rule 34, * * * "[e]lectronic documents are no less subject to disclosure than paper records." This is true not only of electronic documents that are currently in use, but also of documents that may have been deleted and now reside only on backup disks.

That being so, Zubulake is entitled to discovery of the requested e-mails so long as they are relevant to her claims, which they clearly are. As noted, e-mail constituted a substantial means of communication among UBS employees. To that end, UBS has already produced ap-

---

33. 205 F.R.D. at 429.

proximately 100 pages of e-mails, the contents of which are unquestionably relevant.

Nonetheless, UBS argues that Zubulake is not entitled to any further discovery because it already produced all responsive documents, to wit, the 100 pages of e-mails. This argument is unpersuasive for two reasons. First, because of the way that UBS backs up its e-mail files, it clearly could not have searched all of its e-mails without restoring the ninety-four backup tapes (which UBS admits that it has not done). * * * Second, Zubulake herself has produced over 450 pages of relevant e-mails, including e-mails that would have been responsive to her discovery requests but were never produced by UBS. These two facts strongly suggest that there are e-mails that Zubulake has not received that reside on UBS's backup media.

B. Should Cost–Shifting Be Considered?

Because it apparently recognizes that Zubulake is entitled to the requested discovery, UBS expends most of its efforts urging the court to shift the cost of production to "protect [it] . . . from undue burden or expense." Faced with similar applications, courts generally engage in some sort of cost-shifting analysis, whether the refined eight-factor *Rowe* test or a cruder application of Rule 34's proportionality test, or something in between.

The first question, however, is whether cost-shifting must be considered in every case involving the discovery of electronic data, which—in today's world—includes virtually all cases. In light of the accepted principle, stated above, that electronic evidence is no less discoverable than paper evidence, the answer is, "No." The Supreme Court has instructed that "the presumption is that the responding party must bear the expense of complying with discovery requests. . . ." Any principled approach to electronic evidence must respect this presumption.

Courts must remember that cost-shifting may effectively end discovery, especially when private parties are engaged in litigation with large corporations. As large companies increasingly move to entirely paper-free environments, the frequent use of cost-shifting will have the effect of crippling discovery in discrimination and retaliation cases. This will both undermine the "strong public policy favor[ing] resolving disputes on their merits," and may ultimately deter the filing of potentially meritorious claims.

Thus, cost-shifting should be considered only when electronic discovery imposes an "undue burden or expense" on the responding party.[46] The burden or expense of discovery is, in turn, "undue" when it "outweighs its likely benefit, taking into account the needs of the case, the amount in controversy, the parties' resources, the importance of the

---

46. Fed. R. Civ. P. 26(c).

issues at stake in the litigation, and the importance of the proposed discovery in resolving the issues."[47]

Many courts have automatically assumed that an undue burden or expense may arise simply because electronic evidence is involved. This makes no sense. Electronic evidence is frequently cheaper and easier to produce than paper evidence because it can be searched automatically, key words can be run for privilege checks, and the production can be made in electronic form obviating the need for mass photocopying.

In fact, whether production of documents is unduly burdensome or expensive turns primarily on whether it is kept in an accessible or inaccessible format (a distinction that corresponds closely to the expense of production). * * * Whether electronic data is accessible or inaccessible turns largely on the media on which it is stored. Five categories of data, listed in order from most accessible to least accessible, are described in the literature on electronic data storage:

1. *Active, online data:* "On-line storage is generally provided by magnetic disk. It is used in the very active stages of an electronic record's life—when it is being created or received and processed, as well as when the access frequency is high and the required speed of access is very fast, i.e., milliseconds." Examples of online data include hard drives.

2. *Near-line data:* "This typically consists of a robotic storage device (robotic library) that houses removable media, uses robotic arms to access the media, and uses multiple read/write devices to store and retrieve records. Access speeds can range from as low as milliseconds if the media is already in a read device, up to 10–30 seconds for optical disk technology, and between 20–120 seconds for sequentially searched media, such as magnetic tape." Examples include optical disks.

3. *Offline storage/archives:* "This is removable optical disk or magnetic tape media, which can be labeled and stored in a shelf or rack. Off-line storage of electronic records is traditionally used for making disaster copies of records and also for records considered 'archival' in that their likelihood of retrieval is minimal. Accessibility to off-line media involves manual intervention and is much slower than on-line or near-line storage. Access speed may be minutes, hours, or even days, depending on the access-effectiveness of the storage facility." The principled difference between nearline data and offline data is that offline data lacks "the coordinated control of an intelligent disk subsystem," and is, in the lingo, JBOD ("Just a Bunch Of Disks").

---

47. Fed. R. Civ. P. 26(b)(2)(iii). * * * [A] court is also permitted to impose conditions on discovery when it might be duplicative, *see* Fed. R. Civ. P. 26(b)(2)(i), or when a reasonable discovery deadline has lapsed, *see id.* 26(b)(2)(ii). Neither of these concerns, however, is likely to arise solely because the discovery sought is of electronic data.

4. *Backup tapes*: "A device, like a tape recorder, that reads data from and writes it onto a tape. Tape drives have data capacities of anywhere from a few hundred kilobytes to several gigabytes. Their transfer speeds also vary considerably . . . The disadvantage of tape drives is that they are sequential-access devices, which means that to read any particular block of data, you need to read all the preceding blocks." As a result, "[t]he data on a backup tape are not organized for retrieval of individual documents or files [because] . . . the organization of the data mirrors the computer's structure, not the human records management structure." Backup tapes also typically employ some sort of data compression, permitting more data to be stored on each tape, but also making restoration more time-consuming and expensive, especially given the lack of uniform standard governing data compression.

5. *Erased, fragmented or damaged data*: "When a file is first created and saved, it is laid down on the [storage media] in contiguous clusters . . . As files are erased, their clusters are made available again as free space. Eventually, some newly created files become larger than the remaining contiguous free space. These files are then broken up and randomly placed throughout the disk." Such broken-up files are said to be "fragmented," and along with damaged and erased data can only be accessed after significant processing.

Of these, the first three categories are typically identified as accessible, and the latter two as inaccessible. The difference between the two classes is easy to appreciate. Information deemed "accessible" is stored in a readily usable format. Although the time it takes to actually access the data ranges from milliseconds to days, the data does not need to be restored or otherwise manipulated to be usable. "Inaccessible" data, on the other hand, is not readily usable. Backup tapes must be restored using a process similar to that previously described, fragmented data must be de-fragmented, and erased data must be reconstructed, all before the data is usable. That makes such data inaccessible.

The case at bar is a perfect illustration of the range of accessibility of electronic data. As explained above, UBS maintains e-mail files in three forms: (1) active user e-mail files; (2) archived e-mails on optical disks; and (3) backup data stored on tapes. The active (HP OpenMail) data is obviously the most accessible: it is online data that resides on an active server, and can be accessed immediately. The optical disk (Tumbleweed) data is only slightly less accessible, and falls into either the second or third category. The e-mails are on optical disks that need to be located and read with the correct hardware, but the system is configured to make searching the optical disks simple and automated once they are located. For these sources of e-mails—active mail files and e-mails stored on optical disks—it would be wholly inappropriate to even consider cost-shifting. UBS maintains the data in an accessible and usable format, and can respond to Zubulake's request cheaply and quickly. Like most typical discovery requests, therefore, the producing party should bear the cost of production.

E-mails stored on backup tapes (via NetBackup), however, are an entirely different matter. Although UBS has already identified the ninety-four potentially responsive backup tapes, those tapes are not currently accessible. In order to search the tapes for responsive e-mails, UBS would have to engage in the costly and time-consuming process detailed above. It is therefore appropriate to consider cost shifting.

C. What Is the Proper Cost–Shifting Analysis?

In the year since *Rowe* was decided, its eight factor test has unquestionably become the gold standard for courts resolving electronic discovery disputes. But there is little doubt that the *Rowe* factors will generally favor cost-shifting. Indeed, of the handful of reported opinions that apply *Rowe* or some modification thereof, all of them have ordered the cost of discovery to be shifted to the requesting party.

In order to maintain the presumption that the responding party pays, the cost-shifting analysis must be neutral; close calls should be resolved in favor of the presumption. The *Rowe* factors, as applied, undercut that presumption for three reasons. First, the *Rowe* test is incomplete. Second, courts have given equal weight to all of the factors, when certain factors should predominate. Third, courts applying the *Rowe* test have not always developed a full factual record.

1. The *Rowe* Test Is Incomplete

a. *A Modification of Rowe: Additional Factors*

Certain factors specifically identified in the Rules are omitted from *Rowe's* eight factors. In particular, Rule 26 requires consideration of "the amount in controversy, the parties' resources, the importance of the issues at stake in the litigation, and the importance of the proposed discovery in resolving the issues." Yet *Rowe* makes no mention of either the amount in controversy or the importance of the issues at stake in the litigation. These factors should be added. Doing so would balance the *Rowe* factor that typically weighs most heavily in favor of cost-shifting, "the total cost associated with production." The cost of production is almost always an objectively large number in cases where litigating cost-shifting is worthwhile. But the cost of production when compared to "the amount in controversy" may tell a different story. A response to a discovery request costing $100,000 sounds (and is) costly, but in a case potentially worth millions of dollars, the cost of responding may not be unduly burdensome.

Rowe also contemplates "the resources available to each party." But here too—although this consideration may be implicit in the *Rowe* test— the absolute wealth of the parties is not the relevant factor. More important than comparing the relative ability of a party to pay for discovery, the focus should be on the total cost of production as compared to the resources available to each party. Thus, discovery that would be too expensive for one defendant to bear would be a drop in the bucket for another.

Last, "the importance of the issues at stake in the litigation" is a critical consideration, even if it is one that will rarely be invoked. For example, if a case has the potential for broad public impact, then public policy weighs heavily in favor of permitting extensive discovery. Cases of this ilk might include toxic tort class actions, environmental actions, so-called "impact" or social reform litigation, cases involving criminal conduct, or cases implicating important legal or constitutional questions.

b.   A Modification of Rowe: Eliminating Two Factors

Two of the *Rowe* factors should be eliminated:

First, the *Rowe* test includes "the specificity of the discovery request." Specificity is surely the touchstone of any good discovery request, requiring a party to frame a request broadly enough to obtain relevant evidence, yet narrowly enough to control costs. But relevance and cost are already two of the *Rowe* factors (the second and sixth). Because the first and second factors are duplicative, they can be combined. Thus, the first factor should be: the extent to which the request is specifically tailored to discover relevant information.

Second, the fourth factor, "the purposes for which the responding party maintains the requested data" is typically unimportant. Whether the data is kept for a business purpose or for disaster recovery does not affect its accessibility, which is the practical basis for calculating the cost of production. Although a business purpose will often coincide with accessibility—data that is inaccessible is unlikely to be used or needed in the ordinary course of business—the concepts are not coterminous. In particular, a good deal of accessible data may be retained, though not in the ordinary course of business. For example, data that should rightly have been erased pursuant to a document retention/destruction policy may be inadvertently retained. If so, the fact that it should have been erased in no way shields that data from discovery. As long as the data is accessible, it must be produced.

* * *

c.   A New Seven–Factor Test

Set forth below is a new seven-factor test based on the modifications to *Rowe* discussed in the preceding sections.

1. The extent to which the request is specifically tailored to discover relevant information;

2. The availability of such information from other sources;

3. The total cost of production, compared to the amount in controversy;

4. The total cost of production, compared to the resources available to each party;

5. The relative ability of each party to control costs and its incentive to do so;

6. The importance of the issues at stake in the litigation; and

7. The relative benefits to the parties of obtaining the information.

2. The Seven Factors Should Not Be Weighted Equally

Whenever a court applies a multi-factor test, there is a temptation to treat the factors as a check-list, resolving the issue in favor of whichever column has the most checks. But "we do not just add up the factors." When evaluating cost-shifting, the central question must be, does the request impose an "undue burden or expense" on the responding party? Put another way, "how important is the sought-after evidence in comparison to the cost of production?" The seven-factor test articulated above provide some guidance in answering this question, but the test cannot be mechanically applied at the risk of losing sight of its purpose.

Weighting the factors in descending order of importance may solve the problem and avoid a mechanistic application of the test. The first two factors—comprising the marginal utility test—are the most important. These factors include: (1) The extent to which the request is specifically tailored to discover relevant information and (2) the availability of such information from other sources. "The more likely it is that the backup tape contains information that is relevant to a claim or defense, the fairer it is that the [responding party] search at its own expense. The less likely it is, the more unjust it would be to make the [responding party] search at its own expense. The difference is at the margin."

The second group of factors addresses cost issues: "How expensive will this production be?" and, "Who can handle that expense?" These factors include: (3) the total cost of production compared to the amount in controversy, (4) the total cost of production compared to the resources available to each party and (5) the relative ability of each party to control costs and its incentive to do so. The third "group"—(6) the importance of the litigation itself—stands alone, and as noted earlier will only rarely come into play. But where it does, this factor has the potential to predominate over the others. Collectively, the first three groups correspond to the three explicit considerations of Rule 26(b)(2)(iii). Finally, the last factor—(7) the relative benefits of production as between the requesting and producing parties—is the least important because it is fair to presume that the response to a discovery request generally benefits the requesting party. But in the unusual case where production will also provide a tangible or strategic benefit to the responding party, that fact may weigh against shifting costs.

D. A Factual Basis Is Required to Support the Analysis

Courts applying *Rowe* have uniformly favored cost-shifting largely because of assumptions made concerning the likelihood that relevant information will be found. * * * But such proof will rarely exist in advance of obtaining the requested discovery. The suggestion that a plaintiff must not only demonstrate that probative evidence exists, but also prove that electronic discovery will yield a "gold mine," is contrary to the plain language of Rule 26(b)(1), which permits discovery of "any matter" that is "relevant to [a] claim or defense."

The best solution to this problem is * * * [to require] the responding party to restore and produce responsive documents from a small sample of backup tapes * * *. When based on an actual sample, the marginal utility test will not be an exercise in speculation—there will be tangible evidence of what the backup tapes may have to offer. There will also be tangible evidence of the time and cost required to restore the backup tapes, which in turn will inform the second group of cost-shifting factors. Thus, by requiring a sample restoration of backup tapes, the entire cost-shifting analysis can be grounded in fact rather than guesswork.[77]

IV. CONCLUSION AND ORDER

In summary, deciding disputes regarding the scope and cost of discovery of electronic data requires a three-step analysis:

First, it is necessary to thoroughly understand the responding party's computer system, both with respect to active and stored data. For data that is kept in an accessible format, the usual rules of discovery apply: the responding party should pay the costs of producing responsive data. A court should consider cost-shifting only when electronic data is relatively inaccessible, such as in backup tapes.

Second, because the cost-shifting analysis is so fact-intensive, it is necessary to determine what data may be found on the inaccessible media. Requiring the responding party to restore and produce responsive documents from a small sample of the requested backup tapes is a sensible approach in most cases.

Third, and finally, in conducting the cost-shifting analysis, the following factors should be considered, weighted more-or-less in the following order:

1. The extent to which the request is specifically tailored to discover relevant information;

2. The availability of such information from other sources;

3. The total cost of production, compared to the amount in controversy;

---

77. Of course, where the cost of a sample restoration is significant compared to the value of the suit, or where the suit itself is patently frivolous, even this minor effort may be inappropriate.

4. The total cost of production, compared to the resources available to each party;

5. The relative ability of each party to control costs and its incentive to do so;

6. The importance of the issues at stake in the litigation; and

7. The relative benefits to the parties of obtaining the information.

Accordingly, UBS is ordered to produce all responsive e-mails that exist on its optical disks or on its active servers (i.e., in HP OpenMail files) at its own expense. UBS is also ordered to produce, at its expense, responsive e-mails from any five backups tapes selected by Zubulake. UBS should then prepare an affidavit detailing the results of its search, as well as the time and money spent. After reviewing the contents of the backup tapes and UBS's certification, the Court will conduct the appropriate cost-shifting analysis.

COMMENTARY

With advances in technology, written communications now take place at lightning speed. As electronic communications supplant both traditional paper correspondence and telephonic conferences, employees now find it more convenient to e-mail or text message someone sitting in the office next to them rather than pick up the phone or walk next door. This has resulted in the creation and storage of massive amounts of electronic data, much of which is of an informal or personal nature. The costs of processing such voluminous amounts of data to find the few nuggets that are relevant to a specific litigation, compounded by attorney review time, are staggering.[36]

Litigants find themselves held hostage by their data and the costs of electronic discovery may force them to settle, despite the merits of their case. As e-discovery becomes a prominent part of litigation, litigants are seeking ways to control their e-discovery related costs and more and more often ask courts to shift the burden of these expenses to the adversary.

The landmark decisions in the *Zubulake* case went a long way in setting the stage for the adoption of the amendments to the Federal Rules of Civil Procedure in 2006 that addressed these concerns regarding electronic discovery. The *Zubulake* approach towards limiting or conditioning discovery only if it is unduly burdensome has since been embraced by the 2006 amendment to Rule 26, which provides that a party need not provide discovery of ESI that is not reasonably accessible, unless good cause is found; the Rule specifically leaves the door open to cost-sharing in appropriate circumstances.

---

36. *See, e.g., Toshiba Am. Elec. Components, Inc. v. Lexar Media,* No. H027029, 2004 WL 2757873 (Cal. App. Dec. 3, 2004) (estimated cost to process some eight hundred back up tapes, including identification and restoration of the files, searching for responsive items and producing the data, was between $1.5 to $1.9 million).

Amended Rule 26 as Applied to Accessible Data

While the 2006 amendments to Rule 26(b)(2) explicitly apply to cost-shifting for data that is not reasonably accessible, do the amendments also apply to accessible data? While Rule 26(b)(2)(B) explicitly applies only to data that is not reasonably accessible, Rule 26(b)(2)(C) is applicable to both accessible data and data that is not reasonably accessible. Nonetheless, there remains a question as to whether cost-shifting is available for accessible data.

This question was considered by a Magistrate Judge in a series of opinions culminating in *Peskoff v. Faber*. In that case, the court held that "cost-shifting does not even become a possibility unless there is first a showing of inaccessibility. Thus, it cannot be argued that a party should ever be relieved of its obligation to produce accessible data merely because it may take time and effort to find what is necessary."[37] The court also noted, however, that "the search for data, even if accessible, must be justified under the relevancy standard of Rule 26(b)(1)."[38] The better rule is that cost-shifting is available even for accessible data based on the proportionality factors set forth in Rule 26(b)(2)(C). In short, the court always has the option to condition discovery on the requesting party's payment of costs for production.[39]

PROBLEM

The plaintiff has sued his former government employer, County, alleging that his employment position was eliminated as part of County's restructuring that unfairly targeted her because she provided information to federal investigating authorities regarding improper handling of tax refunds by County. The plaintiff's request for documents about the restructuring and reorganization of County produced approximately four terabytes of data extracted from various computers of County employees and supervisors. A terabyte of data is equivalent to 500 million typewritten pages. The defendant contends that the request to search this data is unduly burdensome. According to the defendant, it has already spent $25,000 in litigation costs related to discovery and would have to spend an additional $49,000 to complete the search requested by the plaintiff. The potential recovery of the lawsuit is less than $100,000. The defendant has asked that the search costs be shifted to the plaintiff. If you are the judge, how would you resolve this dispute? How would you argue this matter on behalf of the defendant and the plaintiff? Draft an argument applying the proportionality test for each side using the factors set forth in Rule 26(b)(2)(C)(iii).

---

37. *Peskoff v. Faber*, 244 F.R.D. 54, 62 (D.D.C. 2007).

38. *Id.* at 63.

39. *See Grant v. Homier Distrib. Co., Inc.*, No. 3:07–CV–116, 2007 WL 2446753 (N.D. Ind. Aug. 24, 2007) (holding that a court may order discovery subject to the requesting party's payment of production costs). *See also* 2006 Advisory Committee Note to 26(b)(2)(B) ("The limitations of Rule 26(b)(2)(C) apply to all discovery of electronically stored information.").

2. Not Reasonably Accessible Data—Rule 26(b)(2)(B)

ZUBULAKE v. UBS WARBURG LLC
"Zubulake III"

216 F.R.D. 280 (S.D.N.Y. 2003)

SCHEINDLIN, DISTRICT JUDGE

On May 13, 2003, I ordered defendants UBS Warburg LLC, UBS Warburg, and UBS AG (collectively "UBS") to restore and produce certain e-mails from a small group of backup tapes. Having reviewed the results of this sample restoration, Laura Zubulake now moves for an order compelling UBS to produce all remaining backup e-mails at its expense. UBS argues that based on the sampling, the costs should be shifted to Zubulake.

For the reasons fully explained below, Zubulake must share in the costs of restoration, although UBS must bear the bulk of that expense. In addition, UBS must pay for any costs incurred in reviewing the restored documents for privilege.

I. BACKGROUND

* * * In brief, Zubulake, an equities trader who earned approximately $650,000 a year with UBS, is now suing UBS for gender discrimination, failure to promote, and retaliation under federal, state, and city law. To support her claim, Zubulake seeks evidence stored on UBS's backup tapes that is only accessible through costly and time-consuming data retrieval. In particular, Zubulake seeks e-mails relating to her that were sent to or from five UBS employees: Matthew Chapin (Zubulake's immediate supervisor and the alleged primary discriminator), Jeremy Hardisty (Chapin's supervisor and the individual to whom Zubulake originally complained about Chapin), Rose Tong (a human relations representative who was assigned to handle issues concerning Zubulake), Vinay Datta (a co-worker), and Andrew Clarke (another co-worker). The question presented in this dispute is which party should pay for the costs incurred in restoring and producing these backup tapes.

In order to obtain a factual basis to support the cost-shifting analysis, I ordered UBS to restore and produce e-mails from five of the ninety-four backup tapes that UBS had then identified as containing responsive documents; Zubulake was permitted to select the five tapes to be restored. UBS now reports, however, that there are only seventy-seven backup tapes that contain responsive data, including the five already restored. I further ordered UBS to "prepare an affidavit detailing the results of its search, as well as the time and money spent." UBS has complied by submitting counsel's declaration.

According to the declaration, Zubulake selected the backup tapes corresponding to Matthew Chapin's e-mails from May, June, July, August, and September 2001. That period includes the time from

Zubulake's initial EEOC charge of discrimination (August 2001) until just before her termination (in the first week of October 2001).UBS hired an outside vendor, Pinkerton Consulting & Investigations, to perform the restoration.

Pinkerton was able to restore each of the backup tapes, yielding a total of 8,344 e-mails. That number is somewhat inflated, however, because it does not account for duplicates. Because each month's backup tape was a snapshot of Chapin's server for that month—and not an incremental backup reflecting only new material—an e-mail that was on the server for more than one month would appear on more than one backup tape. For example, an e-mail received in January 2001 and deleted in November 2001 would have been restored from all five backup tapes. With duplicates eliminated, the total number of unique e-mails restored was 6,203.

Pinkerton then performed a search for e-mails containing (in either the e-mail's text or its header information, such as the "subject" line) the terms "Laura", "Zubulake", or "LZ". The searches yielded 1,541 e-mails, or 1,075 if duplicates are eliminated. Of these 1,541 e-mails, UBS deemed approximately 600 to be responsive to Zubulake's document request and they were produced. UBS also produced, under the terms of the May 13 Order, fewer than twenty e-mails extracted from UBS's optical disk storage system.

Pinkerton billed UBS 31.5 hours for its restoration services at an hourly rate of $245, six hours for the development, refinement and execution of a search script at $245 an hour, and 101.5 hours of "CPU Bench Utilization" time for use of Pinkerton's computer systems at a rate of $18.50 per hour. Pinkerton also included a five percent "administrative overhead fee" of $459.38. Thus, the total cost of restoration and search was $11,524.63. In addition, UBS incurred the following costs: $4,633 in attorney time for the document review (11.3 hours at $410 per hour) and $2,845.80 in paralegal time for tasks related to document production (16.74 hours at $170 per hour). UBS also paid $432.60 in photocopying costs, which, of course, will be paid by Zubulake and is not part of this cost-shifting analysis.[24] The total cost of restoration and production from the five backup tapes was $19,003.43.

UBS now asks that the cost of any further production—estimated to be $273,649.39, based on the cost incurred in restoring five tapes and producing responsive documents from those tapes—be shifted to Zubulake. The total figure includes $165,954.67 to restore and search the tapes and $107,694.72 in attorney and paralegal review costs. These costs will be addressed separately below.

---

24. *See* Fed. R. Civ. P. 34(a) (permitting the requesting party to "inspect and copy" any documents it asks for); *see also In re Bristol–Myers Squibb Sec. Litig.*, 205 F.R.D. 437, 440 (D.N.J. 2002) (imposing cost of photocopying electronic documents on requesting party).

II. LEGAL STANDARD

* * *

Although "the presumption is that the responding party must bear the expense of complying with discovery requests," requests that run afoul of the Rule 26(b)(2) proportionality test may subject the requesting party to protective orders under Rule 26(c), "including orders conditioning discovery on the requesting party's payment of the costs of discovery." A court will order such a cost-shifting protective order only upon motion of the responding party to a discovery request, and "for good cause shown." Thus, the responding party has the burden of proof on a motion for cost-shifting.

III. DISCUSSION

A. Cost-shifting Generally

In *Zubulake I*, I considered plaintiff's request for information contained only on backup tapes and determined that cost-shifting might be appropriate. It is worth emphasizing again that cost-shifting is potentially appropriate only when inaccessible data is sought. When a discovery request seeks accessible data–for example, active on-line or near-line data–it is typically inappropriate to consider cost-shifting.

In order to determine whether cost-shifting is appropriate for the discovery of inaccessible data, [the court applied the new 7-factor test quoted in *Zubulake I*]. * * *

B. Application of the Seven Factor Test

1. Factors One and Two

As I explained in *Zubulake I*, the first two factors together comprise the "marginal utility test" * * * :

> The more likely it is that the backup tape contains information that is relevant to a claim or defense, the fairer it is that the [responding party] search at its own expense. The less likely it is, the more unjust it would be to make the [responding party] search at its own expense. The difference is "at the margin."

These two factors should be weighted the most heavily in the cost-shifting analysis.

a. The Extent to Which the Request Is Specifically Tailored to Discover Relevant Information

The document request at issue asks for "[a]ll documents concerning any communication by or between UBS employees concerning Plaintiff," and was subsequently narrowed to pertain to only five employees (Chapin, Hardisty, Tong, Datta, and Clarke) and to the period from August 1999 to December 2001. This is a relatively limited and targeted request, a fact borne out by the e-mails UBS actually produced, both initially and as a result of the sample restoration.

At oral argument, Zubulake presented the court with sixty-eight e-mails (of the 600 she received) that she claims are "highly relevant to the issues in this case" and thus require, in her view, that UBS bear the cost of production. And indeed, a review of these e-mails reveals that they are relevant. Taken together, they tell a compelling story of the dysfunctional atmosphere surrounding UBS's U.S. Asian Equities Sales Desk (the "Desk"). Presumably, these sixty-eight e-mails are reasonably representative of the seventy-seven backup tapes.

A number of the e-mails complain of Zubulake's behavior. Zubulake was described by Clarke as engaging in "bitch sessions about the horrible men on the [Desk]," and as a "conduit for a steady stream of distortions, accusations and good ole fashioned back stabbing," and Hardisty noted that Zubulake was disrespectful to Chapin and other members of the Desk. And Chapin takes frequent snipes at Zubulake. There are also complaints about Chapin's behavior. In addition, Zubulake argues that several of the e-mails contradict testimony given by UBS employees in sworn depositions.

While all of these e-mails are [relevant] none of them provide any direct evidence of discrimination. To be sure, the e-mails reveal a hostile relationship between Chapin and Zubulake—UBS does not contest this. But nowhere (in the sixty-eight e-mails produced to the Court) is there evidence that Chapin's dislike of Zubulake related to her gender.

b.   The Availability of Such Information from Other Sources

The other half of the marginal utility test is the availability of the relevant data from other sources. Neither party seemed to know how many of the 600 e-mails produced in response to the May 13 Order had been previously produced. UBS argues that "nearly all of the restored e-mails that relate to plaintiff's allegations in this matter or to the merits of her case were already produced." This statement is perhaps too careful, because UBS goes on to observe that "the vast majority of the restored e-mails that were produced do not relate at all to plaintiff's allegations in this matter or to the merits of her case." But this determination is not for UBS to make; as the saying goes, "one man's trash is another man's treasure."

It is axiomatic that a requesting party may obtain "any matter, not privileged, that is relevant to the claim or defense of any party." The simple fact is that UBS previously produced only 100 pages of e-mails, but has now produced 853 pages (comprising the 600 responsive e-mails) from the five selected backup tapes alone. UBS itself decided that it was obliged to provide these 853 pages of e-mail pursuant to the requirements of Rule 26. Having done so, these numbers lead to the unavoidable conclusion that there are a significant number of responsive e-mails that now exist only on backup tapes.

If this were not enough, there is some evidence that Chapin was concealing and deleting especially relevant e-mails. When Zubulake first filed her EEOC charge in August 2001, all UBS employees were instructed to save documents relevant to her case. In furtherance of this policy, Chapin maintained separate files on Zubulake. However, certain e-mails sent after the initial EEOC charge—and particularly relevant to

Zubulake's retaliation claim—were apparently not saved at all. For example, the e-mail from Chapin to Joy Kim instructing her on how to file a complaint against Zubulake was not saved, and it bears the subject line "UBS client attorney priviledge [sic] only," although no attorney is copied on the e-mail. This potentially useful e-mail was deleted and resided only on UBS's backup tapes.

In sum, hundreds of the e-mails produced from the five backup tapes were not previously produced, and so were only available from the tapes. The contents of these e-mails are also new. Although some of the substance is available from other sources (e.g., evidence of the sour relationship between Chapin and Zubulake), a good deal of it is only found on the backup tapes (e.g., inconsistencies with UBS's EEOC filing and Chapin's deposition testimony). Moreover, an e-mail contains the precise words used by the author. Because of that, it is a particularly powerful form of proof at trial when offered as an admission of a party opponent.

c. Weighing Factors One and Two

The sample restoration, which resulted in the production of relevant e-mail, has demonstrated that Zubulake's discovery request was narrowly tailored to discover relevant information. And while the subject matter of some of those e-mails was addressed in other documents, these particular e-mails are only available from the backup tapes. Thus, direct evidence of discrimination may only be available through restoration. As a result, the marginal utility of this additional discovery may be quite high.

While restoration may be the only means for obtaining direct evidence of discrimination, the existence of that evidence is still speculative. The best that can be said is that Zubulake has demonstrated that the marginal utility is potentially high. All-in-all, because UBS bears the burden of proving that cost-shifting is warranted, the marginal utility test tips slightly against cost-shifting.

2. Factors Three, Four and Five

"The second group of factors addresses cost issues: 'How expensive will this production be?' and, 'Who can handle that expense?' "

a. The Total Cost of Production Compared to the Amount in Controversy

UBS spent $11,524.63, or $2,304.93 per tape, to restore the five back-up tapes. Thus, the total cost of restoring the remaining seventy-two tapes extrapolates to $165,954.67.

In order to assess the amount in controversy, I posed the following question to the parties: Assuming that a jury returns a verdict in favor of plaintiff, what economic damages can the plaintiff reasonably expect to recover? Plaintiff answered that reasonable damages are between

$15,271,361 and $19,227,361, depending upon how front pay is calculated. UBS answered that damages could be as high as $1,265,000.

Obviously, this is a significant disparity. At this early stage, I cannot assess the accuracy of either estimate. Plaintiff had every incentive to high-ball the figure and UBS had every incentive to low-ball it. It is clear, however, that this case has the potential for a multi-million dollar recovery. Whatever else might be said, this is not a nuisance value case, a small case or a frivolous case. Most people do not earn $650,000 a year. If Zubulake prevails, her damages award undoubtedly will be higher than that of the vast majority of Title VII plaintiffs.

In an ordinary case, a responding party should not be required to pay for the restoration of inaccessible data if the cost of that restoration is significantly disproportionate to the value of the case. Assuming this to be a multi-million dollar case, the cost of restoration is surely not "significantly disproportionate" to the projected value of this case. This factor weighs against cost-shifting.

b. The Total Cost of Production Compared to the Resources Available to Each Party

There is no question that UBS has exponentially more resources available to it than Zubulake. While Zubulake is an accomplished equities trader, she has now been unemployed for close to two years. Given the difficulties in the equities market and the fact that she is suing her former employer, she may not be particularly marketable. On the other hand, she asserts that she has a $19 million claim against UBS. So while UBS's resources clearly dwarf Zubulake's, she may have the financial wherewithal to cover at least some of the cost of restoration. In addition, it is not unheard of for plaintiff's firms to front huge expenses when multi-million dollar recoveries are in sight. Thus, while this factor weighs against cost shifting, it does not rule it out.

c. The Relative Ability of Each Party to Control Costs and Its Incentive to Do So

Restoration of backup tapes must generally be done by an outside vendor. Here, UBS had complete control over the selection of the vendor. It is entirely possible that a less-expensive vendor could have been found. However, once that vendor is selected, costs are not within the control of either party. In addition, because these backup tapes are relatively well-organized—meaning that UBS knows what e-mails can be found on each tape—there is nothing more that Zubulake can do to focus her discovery request or reduce its cost. Zubulake has already made a targeted discovery request and the restoration of the sample tapes has not enabled her to cut back on that request. Thus, this factor is neutral.

3. Factor Six: The Importance of the Issues at Stake in the Litigation

As noted in *Zubulake I*, this factor "will only rarely come into play." Although this case revolves around a weighty issue—discrimination in the workplace—it is hardly unique. Claims of discrimination are common, and while discrimination is an important problem, this litigation does not present a particularly novel issue. If I were to consider the issues in this discrimination case sufficiently important to weigh in the cost-shifting analysis, then this factor would be virtually meaningless. Accordingly, this factor is neutral.

4. Factor Seven: The Relative Benefits to the Parties of Obtaining the Information

Although Zubulake argues that there are potential benefits to UBS in undertaking the restoration of these backup tapes—in particular, the opportunity to obtain evidence that may be useful at summary judgment or trial—there can be no question that Zubulake stands to gain far more than does UBS, as will typically be the case. Certainly, absent an order, UBS would not restore any of this data of its own volition. Accordingly, this factor weighs in favor of cost-shifting.

5. Summary and Conclusion

Factors one through four tip against cost-shifting (although factor two only slightly so). Factors five and six are neutral, and factor seven favors cost-shifting. As noted in my earlier opinion in this case, however, a list of factors is not merely a matter of counting and adding; it is only a guide. Because some of the factors cut against cost shifting, but only slightly so—in particular, the possibility that the continued production will produce valuable new information—some cost-shifting is appropriate in this case, although UBS should pay the majority of the costs. There is plainly relevant evidence that is only available on UBS's backup tapes. At the same time, Zubulake has not been able to show that there is indispensable evidence on those backup tapes (although the fact that Chapin apparently deleted certain e-mails indicates that such evidence may exist).

The next question is how much of the cost should be shifted. It is beyond cavil that the precise allocation is a matter of judgment and fairness rather than a mathematical consequence of the seven factors discussed above. Nonetheless, the analysis of those factors does inform the exercise of discretion. Because the seven factor test requires that UBS pay the lion's share, the percentage assigned to Zubulake must be less than fifty percent. A share that is too costly may chill the rights of litigants to pursue meritorious claims. However, because the success of this search is somewhat speculative, any cost that fairly can be assigned to Zubulake is appropriate and ensures that UBS's expenses will not be unduly burdensome. A twenty-five percent assignment to Zubulake meets these goals.

C. Other Costs

The final question is whether this result should apply to the entire cost of the production, or only to the cost of restoring the backup tapes.

The difference is not academic—the estimated cost of restoring and searching the remaining backup tapes is \$165,954.67, while the estimated cost of producing them (restoration and searching costs plus attorney and paralegal costs) is \$273,649.39 (\$19,003.43 for the five sample tapes, or \$3,800.69 per tape, times seventy-two unrestored tapes), a difference of \$107,694.72.

As a general rule, where cost-shifting is appropriate, only the costs of restoration and searching should be shifted. Restoration, of course, is the act of making inaccessible material accessible. That "special purpose" or "extraordinary step" should be the subject of cost-shifting. Search costs should also be shifted because they are so intertwined with the restoration process; a vendor like Pinkerton will not only develop and refine the search script, but also necessarily execute the search as it conducts the restoration. However, the responding party should always bear the cost of reviewing and producing electronic data once it has been converted to an accessible form. This is so for two reasons.

First, the producing party has the exclusive ability to control the cost of reviewing the documents. In this case, UBS decided—as is its right—to have a senior associate at a top New York City law firm conduct the privilege review at a cost of \$410 per hour. But the job could just as easily have been done (while perhaps not as well) by a first-year associate or contract attorney at a far lower rate. UBS could similarly have obtained paralegal assistance for far less than \$170 per hour.

Moreover, the producing party unilaterally decides on the review protocol. When reviewing electronic data, that review may range from reading every word of every document to conducting a series of targeted key word searches. Indeed, many parties to document-intensive litigation enter into so-called "claw-back" agreements that allow the parties to forego privilege review altogether in favor of an agreement to return inadvertently produced privileged documents. The parties here can still reach such an agreement with respect to the remaining seventy-two tapes and thereby avoid any cost of reviewing these tapes for privilege.

Second, the argument that all costs related to the production of restored data should be shifted misapprehends the nature of the cost-shifting inquiry. Recalling that cost-shifting is only appropriate for inaccessible—but otherwise discoverable—data, it necessarily follows that once the data has been restored to an accessible format and responsive documents located, cost-shifting is no longer appropriate. Had it always been accessible, there is no question that UBS would have had to produce the data at its own cost. * * *

Documents stored on backup tapes can be likened to paper records locked inside a sophisticated safe to which no one has the key or combination. The cost of accessing those documents may be onerous, and in some cases the parties should split the cost of breaking into the safe. But once the safe is opened, the production of the documents found inside is the sole responsibility of the responding party. The point is simple: technology may increasingly permit litigants to reconstruct lost or inaccessible information, but once restored to an accessible form, the usual rules of discovery apply.

IV. CONCLUSION

For the reasons set forth above, the costs of restoring any backup tapes are allocated between UBS and Zubulake seventy-five percent and twenty-five percent, respectively. All other costs are to be borne exclusively by UBS. * * *

COMMENTARY

As discussed above, litigants have been seeking means to ameliorate the related costs and burdens of processing and producing copious amounts of electronic data. One way of addressing these concerns is to shift the cost of production from the producing party to the requesting party. Under the *Zubulake* decisions, the accessibility of the data sought was a major consideration in determining whether to shift costs. However, the mere fact that data is inaccessible does not require a court to shift costs to the requesting party. The court must also analyze the utility of the data and other circumstances, such as whether the data can be found in other more accessible locations.

Ultimately the *Zubulake* court came to the conclusion that the plaintiff should pay twenty-five percent of the restoration costs. In *Zubulake III*, however, the court specifically limited the cost to be shared to search and retrieval costs—the costs associated with making inaccessible data accessible. But the court explicitly declined to shift the cost of attorney review time. However, restoration of data is only one step in the electronic discovery process that begins with data management and ends in the courtroom or hearings. As noted in *Zubulake III*, the costs to restore and search the backup tapes represented less than two-thirds of the total costs for the production of the backup tape data.[40]

Often the most significant cost driver associated with e-discovery is the human review and analysis of the culled data. The Sedona Conference estimates that the cost to review one gigabyte of text on average is $25,000. Thus, the front end work to reduce the amount of data pays significant dividends in reducing reviewing costs.

PROBLEMS

1. Would the application of *Rowe's* eight factors to the Zubulake case have changed the result? You be the judge. Write the *Zubulake* opinion using the eight factors of *Rowe*. Is the result the same? Did you shift some or all of the costs to the plaintiff Laura Zubulake?

---

40. *See Zubulake*, 216 F.R.D. at 289–90.

Questions under Zubulake's cost-shifting analysis

Zubulake's analytical framework leaves a number of questions, including the following:

    a.   Does *Zubulake III* encourage "e-discovery blackmail" where plaintiffs with small claims will propound e-discovery requests for relevant data that far exceeds the amount in controversy, essentially requiring the Defendant to settle before incurring the cost of electronic discovery?

    b.   Does *Zubulake III* encourage companies to maintain data in inaccessible locations in order to shift costs to the opponent and thus deter litigation?

    c.   Why should a party that invests in modern accessible data systems be at a cost disadvantage when litigating against a party that is an information era "dinosaur"?

2.   How would you as a judge apply the *Zubulake* seven factor test to a company that intentionally keeps information on inaccessible back-up media? Is there a *Zubulake* factor that addresses this situation?

The 2006 Federal Rules Amendment

The 2006 Advisory Committee Note to Rule 26(b)(2)(B) provides that the decision as to whether a party must search sources that are not reasonably accessible depends on whether the burden can be justified under the circumstances of the case. A court may permit discovery of such sources on a showing of "good cause." The Advisory Committee then listed a number of factors that might be considered under the "good cause" test:

> Appropriate considerations may include: (1) the specificity of the discovery request; (2) the quantity of information available from other and more easily accessed sources; (3) the failure to produce relevant information that seems likely to have existed but is no longer available on a more easily accessed sources; (4) the likelihood of finding relevant, responsive information that cannot be obtained from other, more easily accessed sources; (5) predictions as to the importance and usefulness of the further information; (6) the importance of the issues at stake in the litigation; and (7) the parties' resources.

3.   Compare the 2006 Advisory Committee Note to the *Zubulake* seven factor test. Is there a meaningful difference?

With respect to data from sources that are not reasonably accessible, how do the seven factors in the Advisory Committee Note compare to the factors articulated in Rule 26(b)(2)(C)(iii)? *Zubulake I* and *III* were written under the authority of the old Rule 26(B)(2)(b) which became Rule 26(b)(2)(C)(iii). Did the Advisory Committee merely recast *Zubulake's* seven factors into its Note? If so, does Rule 26(b)(2)(C)(iii) add anything to the mix? Must a court consider the good cause factors and then the 26(b)(2)(C) factors? Would such an effort be duplicative?

3. Additional Factors

WIGINTON v. CB RICHARD ELLIS, INC.

229 F.R.D. 568 (N.D. Ill. 2004)

ASHMAN, MAGISTRATE JUDGE

Plaintiffs have filed a Motion for Costs for Electronic Discovery. They argue that Defendant CB Richard Ellis, Inc. ("CBRE") should bear the costs of searching CBRE's e-mail backup tapes to find documents containing pornographic terms and images, as well as documents relating to CBRE's workplace environment generally, due to the large number of these types of documents that have been found in a controlled sampling. CBRE responds that only a small fraction of the e-mails that have been found contain arguably relevant material and that it should not be forced to pay for the search or production. For the following reasons the Court grants Plaintiffs' motion in part and denies it in part.

I. Background

Plaintiffs filed this class action complaint against CBRE alleging a nationwide pattern and practice of sexual harassment at the CBRE offices. As evidence of the hostile work environment prevalent at the offices of CBRE, Plaintiffs seek discovery of pornographic material that they claim was distributed electronically (i.e., via e-mail) and displayed on computers throughout the offices.

CBRE initially produced 94 monthly e-mail backup tapes from 11 offices. The backup tapes consist of the e-mails that existed on a given server at the time the backup is made. They are not a complete depiction of every e-mail that existed on the CBRE system during a month. Kroll Ontrack, an electronic discovery service, was retained by Plaintiffs to restore and extract the user e-mails from the tapes, perform searches for keywords and file attachment types, and load the results of the searches onto Kroll's ElectronicDataViewer ("EDV"), an Internet-based system, for review.

Kroll was instructed to process one monthly tape from each of three offices.[4] It correctly searched the August 1999 tape for the Chicago office, the June 1999 tape for the St. Louis office, and inadvertently searched the June 1999 tape for the Columbus office, instead of the Oak Brook office. Kroll recovered over two hundred thousand documents from the tapes, referred to as the "processing set." Next, Kroll searched the documents for a 92 pornographic term and six disciplinary term search list using a processing engine which is able to search in the text of the documents and in metadata (embedded data in an electronic document). The processing engine can find the terms at the beginning, middle or end of a word or series of symbols. Kroll searched the

---

4. If pornographic pictures or movies existed, they would likely be found in certain types of file attachments, such as GIF or JPEG files. It does not appear that such files were searched.

documents and provided the resulting review set to Plaintiffs' counsel, who noted that spam had not been removed from the review set.

* * *

Kroll processed the documents again to remove spam from the review set. It also removed documents that did not contain a search term but that would otherwise be counted as a hit due to family cascading—a phenomenon whereby a document related to a document containing a hit are counted as two separate hits even if the related document does not contain a search term. For example, an e-mail that contains a search term with an attachment that does not contain a search term was counted as two hits even if the attachment did not contain a hit. After accounting for spam and family cascading, Kroll provided the parties with the new review set which contained 17,375 documents. At this point, Kroll also gave the parties a new estimate of costs to process the tapes from the 11 offices. Although the original estimates of the project ranged from $46,000 to $61,000, due to the large number of documents containing the pornographic and disciplinary search terms, Kroll revised its cost estimate and advised the parties it could cost up to $249,000 to perform the work.

In the meantime, before the parties had the opportunity to review the most recent processing set, the Court ordered the parties to each choose four terms from the list of search terms developed by Plaintiffs. Plaintiffs instructed Kroll to search for the eight terms and produce all of the documents containing search terms.[5] Kroll was also instructed to use the process of de-duplication, the process whereby documents which appear in a user's mailbox on multiple days are not counted as multiple hits. For example, if the same e-mail appeared in an inbox over a period of several months, only one copy of the document would be produced. After de-duplication, Kroll found 8,660 documents by searching for the 8 search terms, and by accounting for spam and family-cascading.

At this point, we note that discussing documents in terms of numbers is somewhat inexact. For example, an e-mail containing a search term that exists in a user's outbox, and also exists in another user's inbox, counts as two hits, even though it is really one document. A document containing a search term that is sent from one user to another, and returned under the "reply with history" option available on CBRE's e-mail system counts as two hits. But, because of de-duplication, an e-mail that is present multiple times in one user's mailbox is not counted multiple times. So although talking about documents in terms of numbers is not entirely accurate, the search system was designed to get an idea of how frequently the documents containing search terms were being passed around by CBRE users within or between the offices. Because spam was eliminated, it means the picture does not present an entirely accurate view of any other pornographic e-mails that maybe have been available on the CBRE e-mail system, or how often users are opening such documents in view of

---

5. Plaintiffs chose "sex," "kiss," "breast," and "porn." CBRE selected "behavior," "discipline," "inappropriate," and "oral."

other people. The numbers also do not reflect e-mails that were not captured on backup tapes.

The parties are able to view the documents on Kroll's EDV, a software program designed for viewing electronic documents such as these. One problem with the EDV, however, is that the search engine is not as advanced as the initial processing search engine that was used to find the 8,660 documents. The EDV search engine can find words with root extenders (e.g. "kiss!" finds kiss, kissing, kissed), but unlike the original search engine, the EDV search engine only finds search terms located at the beginning of words (so "moral" is a hit on the original search, but not through the EDV). The parties also discovered that family cascading was still a problem. Therefore, in the end, the parties reviewed approximately 1/3 of the documents (2,667), and have agreed that the remaining documents are "non-responsive." The Court, therefore, likewise considers the remaining documents as non-responsive.

The parties have manipulated the numbers and categorized the 8,660 documents in various ways that supports their respective positions. Plaintiffs claim that 567 of the documents are responsive, i.e., are pornographic or are documents reflecting CBRE policies and procedures. Therefore they calculate that 567 of the 2,667 documents were responsive, for a 21.3% responsive rate. This is technically accurate— 21.3% of the documents that the parties reviewed were responsive. By agreeing that the remaining unreviewed documents were non-responsive, the parties effectively agreed, however, that the pertinent number for the denominator was the 8,660 documents. Therefore, (567/8,660) equals a 6.5% responsive rate. Defendants of course have calculated a much smaller responsive rate, and claim that the parties have identified only (142/8,660) documents as responsive, for a 1.64% responsive rate.

II. Discussion

A. General Principles

* * * The court may limit discovery if it determines that the burden of the discovery outweighs its likely benefit. Fed.R.Civ.P. 26(b)(2)(iii). To make this determination, the Court will consider what has been dubbed the proportionality test of Rule 26(b)(2)(iii): the needs of the case, the amount in controversy, the resources of the parties, the importance of the issues at stake in the litigation, and the importance of the proposed discovery in resolving the issues. In this way, parties are protected from unduly burdensome or expensive discovery requests. Fed.R.Civ.P. 26(c).

The Court also begins this discussion with the general presumption in discovery that the responding party must bear the expense of complying with discovery requests. However, if the responding party asks the court for an order protecting it from "undue burden or expense," the court may shift the costs to the non-producing party, rather than just disallowing the requested discovery. Fed.R.Civ.P. 26(c).

B.　Standards for Discovery of Electronic Data

* * * As contrasted with traditional paper discovery, e-discovery has the potential to be vastly more expensive due to the sheer volume of electronic information that can be easily and inexpensively stored on backup media. *Zubulake v. UBS Warburg LLC*, 217 F.R.D. 309, 316 (S.D.N.Y.2003) (*"Zubulake I"*). Depending on how the electronic data is stored, it can be difficult, and hence expensive, to retrieve the data and search it for relevant documents. Theoretically, as technology improves, retrieving and searching data will become more standard and less costly.

In the meantime, until the technology advances and e-discovery becomes less expensive, cost will continue to be an issue as parties battle over who will foot the bill. In the electronic arena, three main tests have been suggested to determine when it is appropriate to shift the costs of searching and producing inaccessible data to the requesting party in order to protect the producing party from unduly burdensome e-discovery requests.

First, under the marginal utility approach, the more likely it is that the search will discover critical information, the fairer it is to have the responding party search at its own expense. Next, the court in *Rowe* created eight factors for consideration in the cost-shifting analysis, one of which incorporated the marginal utility test. Finally, the court in *Zubulake I* modified the *Rowe* test to account for the fact that it interpreted the *Rowe* test as generally favoring cost-shifting, which had ignored the presumption that the responding party pays for discovery. We agree with both the *Rowe* court and the *Zubulake* court that the marginal utility test is the most important factor. Furthermore, while we are guided by the remainder of the *Rowe* and *Zubulake* factors, we find that the proportionality test set forth in Rule 26(b)(2)(iii) must shape the test. Thus, we modify the *Zubulake* rules by adding a factor that considers the importance of the requested discovery in resolving the issues of the litigation.

Therefore, we will consider the following factors: 1) the likelihood of discovering critical information; 2) the availability of such information from other sources; 3) the amount in controversy as compared to the total cost of production; 4) the parties' resources as compared to the total cost of production; 5) the relative ability of each party to control costs and its incentive to do so; 6) the importance of the issues at stake in the litigation; 7) the importance of the requested discovery in resolving the issues at stake in the litigation; and 8) the relative benefits to the parties of obtaining the information. At all times we keep in mind that because the presumption is that the responding party pays for discovery requests, the burden remains with CBRE to demonstrate that costs should be shifted to Plaintiffs.

C. Application of the Eight Factors

Marginal Utility

1. The likelihood of discovering critical information.

When the matter is initially brought to the court's attention, the extent to which the request appears to be specifically tailored to discover relevant information may help the court weigh this factor. If a test run is ordered, as in this case, the actual results of the test run will be indicative of how likely it is that critical information will be discovered.

The 8 term search list chosen by the parties contains five porno-graphic terms, four of which were selected by Plaintiffs, and three disciplinary terms, all three of which were chosen by CBRE. The 8 term search resulted in 8,660 hits. Whether many of the resulting documents are actually responsive is subject to debate by the parties, and they have gone to great lengths to characterize the documents in various ways that support their respective positions. Plaintiffs have identified at least 567 documents as being responsive which is a 6.5% responsive rate. These documents include graphic pornographic images, sexual correspon-dence and jokes, and CBRE policies and procedures regarding the circulation of inappropriate e-mail and the visitation of inappropriate websites, as well [as] policies relating to sexual harassment. Plaintiffs also claim they recovered documents demonstrating the demeaning attitude of CBRE towards its female employees pervading the work environ-ment. Some of these documents appeared in multiple user accounts which supports Plaintiffs' theory that these types of documents were being spread throughout the offices. On the other hand, some of these documents were sent from a single user to another single user. There is nothing to indicate that any CBRE employee indicated that these e-mails were offensive or that any employee refused any future such e-mails. Furthermore, Plaintiffs do not explain how one-to-one e-mails support their theory of a hostile work environment.

CBRE disputes these classifications, arguing that the majority of the 8,660 documents are not even relevant, extrapolating the results of the documents that were reviewed to all the documents that were found. It asserts that many of the e-mails were not considered offensive to the women who received them, or were sent from men to men.[11] CBRE's interpretation of the women's tolerance to sexually explicit e-mails, however, is necessarily slanted in its own favor, and there is no informa-tion regarding whether women routinely viewed other people's e-mails, such as secretaries who accessed their bosses' e-mails as part of their job requirements. CBRE would further decrease the number of relevant documents by excluding documents concerning CBRE's policies and procedures. It was CBRE, however, who chose the three disciplinary search terms so it cannot now complain * * * that the terms it selected

---

11. The parties spend a significant amount of time parading the other side's mistakes in front of the Court, while neglecting to provide factual support [for] their assertions that would be useful to the Court.

successfully found the documents they were intended to find. Therefore, under CBRE's analysis, even excluding what CBRE has characterized as male-to-male e-mails, there are 386 responsive documents. This is a 4.5% responsive rate.

Before determining whether this factor supports cost-shifting, we will consider whether this information is available from other sources.

2.   The availability of such information from other sources.

If the information is available from another source, the marginal utility from the e-discovery is low, and would support cost-shifting. These first two factors which comprise the marginal utility test are the most important, because the more likely it is that relevant information will be discovered, the fairer it is to make the responding party pay for the information.

Clearly, relevant information on CBRE's backup e-mail tapes is only available through restoring and searching the backup tapes unless it has been previously produced by CBRE. The test search did result in relevant documents that had not been produced by CBRE. Specifically, although CBRE argues that it has produced relevant policy documents, we note that the search did find policy documents that had not been previously produced, as well as e-mails containing pornographic material which had not been produced and are not available through any other source. In addition to confirming the existence of relevant documents on backup tapes that have not been restored, it is likely that there were relevant documents that have already been destroyed as CBRE failed in its duty to preserve relevant electronic information.

Given that the search resulted in a 4.5 to 6.5% responsive rate, and that the majority of the documents are not available from another source, we consider whether the marginal utility factors support shifting the cost to Plaintiffs. As a comparison, in *Zubulake*, the test run ordered by the court resulted in 1,075 e-mails after duplicates were eliminated, 600 of which were deemed responsive by the defendant (or 55.8%), and 68 of which were identified by the plaintiff as directly supporting her gender discrimination claim (6.3%). The court found that although all the documents had some relevancy to the claims of the case, not one e-mail provided any direct evidence of discrimination. * * *

In this case, the search has resulted in a small number of relevant documents, although substantially less than in *Zubulake*, as would be expected. In *Zubulake*, the plaintiff was able to narrow her search to five employees and used only search terms involving her name and initials. In this case, Plaintiffs are attempting to prove that discrimination existed in CBRE offices across the nation. Although CBRE argues that the number of pornographic and policy documents are only a minuscule fraction of the total documents on the backup tapes, we decline to determine at this juncture exactly what percentage of documents on the e-mail system would prove a hostile environment. But, because the test results are partially based on Plaintiffs' selection of what Plaintiffs believed are words or terms most likely to produce evidence of a sexually hostile atmosphere, the Court is of the opinion that the percentage of sexually objectionable e-mails is substantially lower than 4.5%. It will be Plaintiffs' onus to demonstrate that hostile environment existed in CBRE's offices; in the meantime they are entitled to relevant information as long as it is reasonably calculated to lead to the discovery of admissible evidence. Fed.R.Civ.P. 26(b)(1). Nevertheless, because the search also revealed a significant number of unresponsive documents, we find that the marginal utility test weighs slightly in favor of cost-shifting.

Factors 3–5: The Cost Factors

3. **The amount in controversy, as compared to the total cost of production.**

Plaintiffs' expert estimated that the total cost of the production would range from $183,500 to $249,900 for ten offices considering the initial results of the 92 term search list. The parties have not addressed whether the results of the 8 term search allowed the expert to more accurately estimate the production costs.

Plaintiffs claim that should a class be certified, their class recovery could extend into the tens of millions of dollars. While the Court cannot completely accept Plaintiffs' speculative estimate of its potential damage award, neither can it accept that their claims are worthless, especially considering that the burden of proving that cost-shifting is warranted falls on CBRE's shoulders. Furthermore, even if the class is not certified, there are still five named plaintiffs, and their recovery is potentially high enough to justify some of the costs of discovery.

CBRE would have the Court find that the total cost of production for all of its offices nationwide would stretch into the millions of dollars, ignoring the fact that discovery has been limited to only a small fraction of the 125 offices. Nevertheless, several hundred thousand dollars for one limited part of discovery is a substantial amount of actual dollars to pay for such a search. Therefore, this factor weighs in favor of cost-shifting.

4. **The parties' resources, as compared to the total cost of production.**

According to its website, CBRE is "the global leader in real estate services." As stated on its most recent from 10–K/A, CBRE had net revenues of 1.6 billion dollars for fiscal year 2003. Plaintiffs, who include former employees of CBRE, are clearly at a serious financial disadvantage. Plaintiffs' counsel, however, obviously has been willing to front substantial amounts of money, and probably could contribute to these discovery costs. CBRE is now put in the awkward position of reversing its previous argument for factor number three that this case is not worth much money, because now it must argue that the case is potentially worth millions, so that costs should be shifted to Plaintiffs. Because we found that the recovery in this case is potentially high, but we also now find that CBRE's resources are large compared to the total cost of production, we find that this factor weighs against cost-shifting.

5. The relative ability of each party to control costs and its incentive to do so.

In most cases, both parties will likely have the ability and desire to control costs. The requesting party should have an incentive for limiting its requests, and the responding party may have an incentive for using accessible searchable media, or for pressuring its software contractors to create such media or software. The responding party may also employ cost-saving measures, such as performing a key word search for a privilege review rather than examining each document.

In this case, it appears that the ability to control costs partially pivots around the selection of the vendor. Plaintiffs have agreed to work with CBRE to jointly select a new electronic discovery service and to minimize costs to the extent it is possible to do so. The costs of the search, however, are also driven to some extent by the scope of the search as selected by Plaintiffs. A smaller search term list would result in less hits, and less documents that must be transferred to an electronic viewer. For example, words that did not result in a large number of documents could be taken off the term search list. Documents that are non-responsive and appear multiple times (such as an e-mail discussing a virus with the words sexyvirgin) could easily be searched for and eliminated. However, Plaintiffs' search must necessarily be broad, due to the nature of the information for which they are searching. Therefore, we find that this factor slightly weighs in favor of cost-shifting.

Remaining Factors

6. The importance of the issues at stake in the litigation.

Plaintiffs cite *Zubulake* for the proposition that this factor "will only rarely come into play . . . [and that] discrimination in the workplace . . . is hardly unique." Because the parties agree that this factor is neutral, we find that it does not weigh in favor of or against cost-shifting.

7. The importance of the requested discovery in resolving the issues at stake in the litigation.

As this is a factor explicitly set forth in Rule 26(b)(2)(iii), we add it to the *Rowe* and *Zubulake* analysis. CBRE argues that Plaintiffs' claims are not primarily based on pornographic material that may have been circulating through its offices. Plaintiffs respond that this information supports their hostile environment claim. Plaintiffs are entitled to obtain discovery relevant to their claims, as long as the discovery is reasonably calculated to lead to the discovery of admissible evidence. If relevance is in doubt, courts should err on the side of permissive discovery. As there is reason to believe that the requested discovery would assist in resolving the issues at stake in this case, but because there is also other evidence to support Plaintiffs' claims, we find that this factor weighs slightly in favor of cost-shifting.

8. The relative benefits to the parties of obtaining the information.

This factor is the least important because in discovery the requested information is more likely to benefit the requesting party. In some cases, the information may aid the producing party, in which case it is more fair to require the producing party to pay for the discovery. In this case, the information requested will benefit Plaintiffs more than CBRE. Therefore, this factor is neutral.

D. Summary

Factors 1 and 2, the most important factors, weigh slightly in favor of cost-shifting to Plaintiffs. For the cost factors: factor 3 weighs in favor of cost-shifting; factor 4 weighs against cost-shifting; and factor 5 weighs slightly in favor of cost-shifting. Factor 6 is neutral; factor 7 weighs slightly in favor of cost-shifting; and factor 8 is neutral.

Therefore, because the factors favor cost-shifting, but the presumption is that the responding party pays for discovery costs, we find that CBRE should bear 25% and Plaintiffs 75% of the discovery costs of restoring the tapes, searching the data, and transferring it to an electronic data viewer. Each party will bear their own costs of reviewing the data and printing documents, where necessary.

COMMENTARY

This is the final case in a series of cases discussing the factors a court should consider in deciding whether to allow cost shifting or cost sharing. In *Wiginton*, the court added one more factor that is contained in the proportionality test of Rule 26(b)(2)(C)(iii).

> the needs of the case, the amount in controversy, the parties' resources, the importance of the issues at stake in the action, and ***the importance of the proposed discovery in resolving the issues.***

A comparison of the *Rowe*, *Zubulake* and *Wiginton* cost shifting factors is set forth in the matrix below:

Rowe	*Zubulake*	*Wiginton*
• The specificity of the discovery requests	• The extent to which the request is specifically tailored to discover relevant information.	• The extent to which the request is specifically tailored to discover relevant information.
• The availability of such information from other sources.	• The availability of such information from other sources.	• The availability of such information from other sources.
• The total cost associated with production.	• The total cost of production, compared to the amount in controversy.	• The total cost of production, compared to the amount in controversy.
• The purposes for which the responding	[factor not important]	[factor not important]

Rowe	Zubulake	Wiginton
party maintains the requested data.		
• The total cost associated with production. • The resources available to each party.	• The total cost of production, compared to the resources available to each party.	• The total cost of production, compared to the resources available to each party.
• The relative ability of each party to control costs and its incentive to do so.	• The relative ability of each party to control costs and its incentive to do so.	• The relative ability of each party to control costs and its incentive to do so.
	• The importance of the issues at stake in the litigation.	• The importance of the issues at stake in the litigation.
• The relative benefit to the parties of obtaining the information.	• The relative benefit to the parties of obtaining the information.	• The relative benefit to the parties of obtaining the information.
• The likelihood of discovering critical information.		• The importance of the requested discovery in resolving the issues of the litigation.

PROBLEM

Review the above matrix. Is there a substantial difference in the factors such that the result may be different if certain facts predominate? For each of the above tests, develop a set of facts which you believe would cause different cost shifting results under *Rowe*, *Zubulake* and *Wiginton*. How similar is the eighth factor in the *Wiginton* test to the second factor in the *Rowe* analysis?

The *Wiginton* court concluded that the factors weighed in favor of shifting most of the costs of discovery to the plaintiff.

Do you agree with this appraisal? By the plaintiff's calculations 6.5% of the sample produced "relevant" e-mails. If this is a low enough percentage to favor cost shifting, what percentage would not be? Or is the issue less the percentage of responsive e-mails than the quality of the e-mails? From the court's analysis it appears the court was less impressed with the recovered e-mail than the court in *Zubulake*.

Was the sampling method fair to the plaintiff? The plaintiff picked four keyword search terms. Are four words sufficient to conduct sampling? Was the plaintiff's likelihood of prevailing on the cost-shifting argument prejudiced by the limitation on the search?

The final factor considered by the court is the importance of the requested discovery in resolving the issues at stake in the litigation. The defendant argued that the plaintiff's case was not based upon pornography which may have been circulating in the office. Indeed, Wiginton's complaint contains rather graphic allegations of a hostile environment independent of whether some employees were circulating pornography. The court noted that the requested discovery from backup tapes may support Wiginton's claims but noted that "there is also other evidence to support Plaintiff's claims."[41] For this reason the court concluded that this factor weighed slightly in favor of cost-shifting.

QUESTIONS

1. Should the apparent strength of the plaintiff's case measured by the availability of other probative evidence be a factor?

2. Would Wiginton have been better off if she had amassed less information?

3. Would the result have been different if Wiginton's theory depended on the circulation of pornographic e-mails in the company?

4. To what degree is the court in a position to judge the importance of the requested discovery at the beginning of a case? What are the ways that counsel can assist the court in this process? Should the court entertain expert testimony on the importance of the requested discovery?

5. To what degree do you think the *Wiginton* court believed that the requested discovery was merely cumulative?

6. To what degree to you think courts will be open to factors other than those articulated in *Rowe*, *Zubulake*, and *Wiginton*? Can you think of any additional factors a court should consider? Consider *Quinby v. WestLB* discussed below.

In *Quinby v. WestLB AG*, the Magistrate Judge considered a request for cost-shifting in another employment discrimination case.[42] The court addressed a request to shift costs for data which had been moved to backup tapes pursuant to a company policy of moving active data to a backup media when an employee is no longer employed by the company. Such practices are called "data-downgrading" and some courts have frowned on this practice.[43] *Quinby* determined that the cost of retrieving data for six departed employees would not be shifted to the requesting plaintiff if the defendant was on reasonable notice at the time of the data transfer that the data would potentially be relevant to resolving Quinby's claims.

> I submit, however, that if a party creates its own burden or expense by converting into an inaccessible format data that it should have reasonably foreseen would be discoverable material at a time when it should have anticipated litigation, then it should not be entitled to shift the costs of restoring and searching the data.[44]

41. *Wiginton*, 229 F.R.D. at 577.

42. 245 F.R.D. 94 (S.D.N.Y. 2006).

43. *See, e.g.*, *Treppel v. Biovail Corp.*, 233 F.R.D. 363, 372 n.4 (S.D.N.Y. 2006).

44. *Quinby*, 245 F.R.D. at 104.

The court found this to be the case with some of the terminated employees.

> Because I find that, with the exception of Barron's e-mails, defendant should have reasonably anticipated having to produce all the Former Employees' e-mails, I consider the *Zubulake* cost-shifting factors with respect to the costs of restoring and searching only Barron's e-mails.[45]

The court then applied the *Zubulake* seven factor test. Ultimately the court determined that thirty percent of the cost should be shifted. Again, the court was not impressed with the marginal utility of the e-mails that were recovered from the backup tapes by using many broad search terms.

> Even though these e-mails "may be relevant, and I appreciate that discrimination is frequently subtle and often proven by circumstantial evidence, I find that merely 71 pages of relevant documents from that period of time is quite low when compared to the volume of documents produced, particularly considering that much of the alleged wrongdoing took place in 2003.... In light of the low number of relevant e-mails, and in spite of the fact that the e-mails are only on backup tapes, the marginal utility test is low and leans in favor of cost shifting.[46]

In short the court determined that the marginal relevance of Barron's e-mails was low because they lay on the fringe of relevance.

Two other factors in support of cost-shifting were advanced by the defendant. First, the defendant claimed that the additional costs (twenty-five percent) of expediting the production of backup tapes should be shifted to the plaintiff. The court denied the request. Interestingly the court did not rule out consideration of the demand for expedited discovery as a factor, but merely stated that the defendant had not met its burden.

Next, the defendant asked for the costs of complying with the plaintiff's request to produce the documents in a second format. The court denied the request as untimely. Should the costs be shifted if the requesting party seeks production in a non-native format or a second format?[47]

PROBLEM

What facts would justify a shift of the costs of expedited production? Construct a factual scenario where you believe such cost-shifting would be justified. Would this be covered by the factor as to which party is best able to control costs?

---

45. *Id.* at 106.

46. *Id.* at 109.

47. *See* Fed. R. Civ. P. 34(b)(2)(E)(iii) ("A party need not produce the same electronically stored information in more than one form.").

I. PRODUCTION FROM NON–PARTIES PURSUANT TO RULE 45

IN RE SUBPOENA DUCES TECUM TO AOL, LLC.

550 F. Supp. 2d 606 (E.D. Va. 2008)

LEE, DISTRICT JUDGE

THIS MATTER is before the Court on State Farm Fire and Casualty Co.'s Objections to Magistrate Judge Poretz's Order, entered on November 30, 2007, quashing State Farm's subpoena to AOL, LLC. This case concerns Cori and Kerri Rigsby's claims that State Farm's subpoena issued to AOL violated the Electronic Communications Privacy Act ("Privacy Act"), codified as 18 U.S.C. §§ 2701–03 (2000), [and] imposed an undue burden on the Rigsbys * * *. The issue before the Court is whether Magistrate Judge Poretz clearly erred by granting the Rigsbys' Motion to Quash, where State Farm's civil discovery subpoena requested: (1) production of the Rigsbys' e-mails from AOL; [and] (2) all of Cori Rigsby's e-mails from a six-week period * * *. The Court upholds Magistrate Judge Poretz's decision quashing State Farm's subpoena, and holds that it was not clearly erroneous for the following reasons: (1) the Privacy Act prohibits AOL from producing the Rigsbys' e-mails in response to State Farm's subpoena because a civil discovery subpoena is not a disclosure exception under the Act; [and] (2) State Farm's subpoena imposes an undue burden on the Rigsbys because the subpoena is overbroad and the documents requested are not limited to subject matter relevant to the claims or defenses in McIntosh. Thus, Magistrate Judge Poretz's Order is affirmed.

I. BACKGROUND

Cori and Kerri Rigsby are non-party witnesses in McIntosh v. State Farm Fire & Casualty Co., an action pending in the Southern District of Mississippi. The Rigsbys were employed as insurance adjusters by E.A. Renfroe and Co. ("E.A. Renfroe") and discovered what they believed to be fraud with respect to State Farm's treatment of Thomas and Pamela McIntosh's Hurricane Katrina damage claim. The Rigsbys provided supporting documents to state and federal law enforcement authorities and filed a qui tam action, United States ex rel. Rigsby v. State Farm Insurance Co., in the Southern District of Mississippi, alleging that State Farm defrauded the United States Government by improperly shifting costs from State Farm's wind damage coverage to the federal flood insurance program.

In the course of discovery litigation related to *McIntosh*, State Farm issued a subpoena through this Court to AOL, requesting production of documents from the Rigsbys' e-mail accounts pertaining to Thomas or Pamela McIntosh, State Farm Fire & Casualty Co.'s claims handling practices for Hurricane Katrina, Forensic Analysis & Engineering Corporation's documents for Hurricane Katrina, and E.A. Renfroe & Co.'s claims handling practices for Hurricane Katrina over a ten-month period.[2] State Farm's subpoena also requested any and all documents, including electronically stored information, related to Cori Rigsby's e-mail account or address from September 1, 2007, to October 12, 2007, a six-week period where Cori Rigsby and her attorneys allegedly concealed from State Farm that her computer had crashed. * * * The Rigsbys * * * moved to quash State Farm's subpoena, claiming that the subpoena violated the Privacy Act, [and] was overbroad and unduly burdensome * * *. [The magistrate judge granted the motion to quash the subpoena.]

* * *

II. DISCUSSION

* * *

B. Analysis

1. The Privacy Act

The Court upholds Magistrate Judge Poretz's Order, quashing State Farm's subpoena, because the plain language of the Privacy Act prohibits AOL from producing the Rigsbys' e-mails, and the issuance of a civil discovery subpoena is not an exception to the provisions of the Privacy Act that would allow an internet service provider to disclose the communications at issue here. * * *

The statutory language of the Privacy Act must be regarded as conclusive because it contains plain and unambiguous language and a coherent and consistent statutory scheme. Section 2701 clearly establishes a punishable offense for intentionally accessing without or exceeding authorization and obtaining electronic communications stored at an electronic communication service facility. 18 U.S.C. § 2701 (2000). Section 2702 plainly prohibits an electronic communication or remote computing service to the public from knowingly divulging to any person or entity the contents of customers' electronic communications or records pertaining to subscribing customers. Additionally, § 2702 lists unambiguous exceptions that allow an electronic communication or remote computing service to disclose the contents of an electronic communication or subscriber information. Section 2703 provides instances related to ongoing criminal investigations where a governmental entity may require an electronic communication or remote computing service to disclose the contents of customers' electronic communications

---

2. State Farm alleges that the Rigsbys admitted to: (1) stealing approximately 15,000 confidential documents from a State Farm laptop computer provided to the Rigsbys when they worked for E.A. Renfroe; (2) forwarding the stolen information via e-mail to the Rigsbys' personal AOL accounts; and (3) providing the stolen information to attorney Dickie Scruggs, who used the stolen information to file hundreds of lawsuits against State Farm, including McIntosh. In *McIntosh*, Magistrate Judge Walker ruled that "State Farm is entitled to know the basis for the Rigsbys' charges of wrongdoing," and ordered the Rigsbys "to produce the requested documents within their actual or constructive possession" to State Farm.

or subscriber information. Protecting privacy interests in personal information stored in computerized systems, while also protecting the Government's legitimate law enforcement needs, the Privacy Act creates a zone of privacy to protect internet subscribers from having their personal information wrongfully used and publicly disclosed by "unauthorized private parties," S.Rep. No. 99–541, at 3 (1986).

In * * * *Federal Trade Commission v. Netscape Communications Corp.*, the court denied the Federal Trade Commission's ("FTC") motion to compel, where an internet service provider, a non-party in the underlying action, refused to turn over documents containing subscriber identity information to the FTC. 196 F.R.D. 559 (N.D.Cal.2000). The FTC filed a civil lawsuit against the subscribers for violating the FTC unfair competition statute. During pre-trial discovery, the FTC issued a subpoena to the internet service provider pursuant to Federal Rule of Civil Procedure 45. The court distinguished discovery subpoenas from trial subpoenas based on differences in scope and operation and concluded that Congress would have specifically included discovery subpoenas in the Privacy Act if Congress meant to include this as an exception requiring an internet service provider to disclose subscriber information to a governmental entity. The court held that the statutory phrase "trial subpoena" does not apply to discovery subpoenas in civil cases and declined to allow the FTC to use Rule 45 to circumvent the protections built into the Privacy Act that protect subscriber privacy from governmental entities.

In *O'Grady v. Superior Court*, the Court of Appeal of the State of California * * * held that enforcement of a civil subpoena issued to an e-mail service provider is inconsistent with the plain terms of the Privacy Act. 139 Cal.App.4th 1423, 44 Cal.Rptr.3d 72, 76–77 (2006). Apple brought a civil action against several unknown defendants for wrongfully publishing on the World Wide Web Apple's secret plans to release a new product. To identify the unknown defendants, Apple issued civil discovery subpoenas to non-party internet service providers, requesting copies of any e-mails that contained certain keywords from the published secret plans. * * * The court * * * found that any disclosure by an internet service provider of stored e-mail violates the Privacy Act unless it falls within an enumerated exception to the general prohibition. Emphasizing the substantial burden and expense that would be imposed on internet service providers if they were required to respond to every civil discovery subpoena issued in a civil lawsuit and how such a policy may discourage users from using new media, the court refused to create an exception for civil discovery and found the subpoenas unenforceable under the Privacy Act.

* * * AOL, a corporation that provides electronic communication services to the public, may not divulge the contents of the Rigsbys' electronic communications to State Farm because the statutory language of the Privacy Act does not include an exception for the disclosure of electronic communications pursuant to civil discovery subpoenas.* * *

Because State Farm is a private party and this is a civil lawsuit, none of the exceptions for governmental entities under § 2703 apply. Furthermore, agreeing with the reasoning in *Netscape*, the Court holds that "unauthorized private parties" and governmental entities are prohibited from using Rule 45 civil discovery subpoenas to circumvent the Privacy Act's protections.

* * * [T]he Court finds that the Privacy Act protects the Rigsbys' stored e-mails because the Rigsbys have a legitimate interest in the confidentiality of their personal e-mails being stored electronically by AOL. Agreeing with the reasoning in *O'Grady*, this Court holds that State Farm's subpoena may not be enforced consistent with the plain language of the Privacy Act because the exceptions enumerated in § 2702(b) do not include civil discovery subpoenas. Furthermore, § 2702(b) does not make any references to civil litigation or the civil discovery process. For the foregoing reasons, Magistrate Judge Poretz did not clearly err when he found that the Privacy Act prohibits AOL from producing the Rigsbys' e-mails in response to State Farm's subpoena because the Privacy Act's enumerated exceptions do not authorize disclosure pursuant to a civil discovery subpoena.

2. Undue Burden

The Court upholds Magistrate Judge Poretz's Order, quashing State Farm's subpoena, because the subpoena is overbroad to the extent that it does not limit the documents requested to subject matter relevant to the claims or defenses in McIntosh and imposes an undue burden on the Rigsbys. "A party or attorney responsible for issuing and serving a subpoena must take reasonable steps to avoid imposing undue burden or expense on a person subject to the subpoena." Fed.R.Civ.P. 45(c)(1). A court must quash or modify a subpoena that subjects a person to an undue burden. Fed. R. Civ. P. 45(c)(3)(A)(iv). When a non-party claims that a subpoena is burdensome and oppressive, the non-party must support its claim by showing how production would be burdensome. A subpoena imposes an undue burden on a party when a subpoena is overbroad.

* * *

* * * State Farm's subpoena must be quashed because it imposes an undue burden on the Rigsbys by being overbroad and requesting "all" of Cori Rigsby's e-mails for a six-week period. * * * State Farm's subpoena is overbroad because it does not limit the e-mails requested to those containing subject matter relevant to the underlying action or sent to or from employees connected to the litigation, other than Cori Rigsby. Although State Farm limited the e-mails requested to an allegedly relevant six-week period, * * * State Farm's subpoena remains overbroad because the e-mails produced over a six-week period would likely include privileged and personal information unrelated to the McIntosh litigation, imposing an undue burden on Cori Rigsby. Thus, Magistrate

Judge Poretz did not clearly err when he found that State Farm's subpoena was overbroad and imposed an undue burden on Cori Rigsby because State Farm's subpoena did not limit the documents requested to subject matter relevant to *McIntosh*.

* * *

COMMENTARY

1. How Can ESI Be Obtained From Nonparties?

ESI may be obtained from nonparties by service of a subpoena. Rule 45 contains a number of provisions similar to those found in Rules 26(b) and 34(b)(2):

- Rule 26(b)(2)(B) (not reasonably accessible data) is the same as Rule 45(d)(1)(D).

- Rule 26(b)(5)(B) (inadvertent disclosure of material) is the same as Rule 45(d)(2)(B).

- Rule 34(b)(2)(E)(iii) corresponds to Rule 45(d)(1)(C).

- Rule 34(b)(2)(E)(ii) is the same as Rule 45(d)(1)(B) (form of production).

2. Is the "Undue Burden or Cost" Test In Rule 45(c)(2)(B)(ii) the Same as the Test In Rule 45(d)(1)(D)?

EXCERPT FROM *The Sedona Conference Commentary on Non–Party Production & Rule 45 Subpoenas 2 (2008):*

> Rule 45 contains a potential internal inconsistency that no court has yet addressed. Well before the 2006 amendments, Rule 45(c)(2)(B)(ii) was amended to protect a non-party under an order to compel from "significant expense" related to the production. There is a significant body of case law applying that requirement in the pre–2006 amendment context. Rule 45(d)(1)(D) now has been amended to allow a non-party to object to discovery that is "not reasonably accessible because of undue burden or cost." The interplay between those two provisions has not yet been examined. Must a non-party first object and show that the material sought by a subpoena is not reasonably accessible due to undue burden or cost, and then when opposing a motion to compel based on the same subpoena, plead "significant expense?" Are these standards the same? Will courts automatically protect a non-party from "significant expense" if, during the process, the non-party has shown "undue burden or cost?"

3. Does a Third Party Have an Obligation to Preserve Evidence Relevant to Other Litigation?

EXCERPT FROM *The Sedona Conference Commentary on Non–Party Production & Rule 45 Subpoenas 3 (2008):*

Third parties may have obligations to preserve evidence relevant to others' litigation imposed by contract or other special relationship once they have notice of the existence of the dispute. Some courts place a burden on the party to have the non-party preserve the evidence. And at least one court has ruled that the issuance of a subpoena to a third party imposes a legal obligation on the third party to preserve information relevant to the subpoena including ESI, at least through the period of time it takes to comply with the subpoena and resolve any issues before the court.[48]

Case law does not require a non-party to continue to preserve materials after [it has] taken reasonable measures to produce responsive information. In some circumstances, however, the receipt of a subpoena may serve to notify a non-party that it may become a party in the litigation or in a future litigation. In that case the non-party should take affirmative steps to preserve documents responsive to the subpoena and the potential broader scope of the proceeding. However, service of and compliance with a nonparty subpoena is not, in and of itself, sufficient to serve as a notice of future litigation.

4. Is Some Information Protected From Disclosure by Federal Law?

A number of federal laws limit disclosure of information. The Health Insurance Portability and Accountability Act ("HIPAA") was enacted in 1996 to address various issues related to health insurance and medical care. One of the purposes of HIPAA is to provide uniform privacy protection for health care records. Title II of HIPAA provides extensive rules regarding the secure storage and exchange of electronic data transactions and requirements promoting the confidentiality and privacy of individually identifiable health information.

The Federal Wiretap Act prohibits the unauthorized interception and disclosure of wire, oral or electronic communications. "Electronic communication" includes e-mail, voice mail, cellular telephones, and satellite communications. Online communications are covered by the Act. Federal courts have consistently held that, in order to be intercepted, electronic communications must be acquired contemporaneously with transmission and that electronic communications are not intercepted within the meaning of the Act if they are retrieved from storage.[49]

The Electronic Communications Privacy Act ("ECPA"), discussed in *AOL, supra,* extensively amended the Federal Wiretap Act. The ECPA prohibits the interception of wire, oral, or electronic communications, or

---

48. *See In re Napster Copyright Litig.*, Nos. C MDL–00–1369, C 04–1166, 2006 WL 3050864, at *6 (N.D. Cal. Oct. 25, 2006) (organization had legal obligation to preserve documents based on third-party subpoena).

49. *See, e.g. Theofel v. Farey–Jones*, 359 F.3d 1066, 1077 (9th Cir. 2004) (no "interception" occurred in violation of Wiretap Act when defendant allegedly gained unauthorized access to plaintiff's e-mails that were already delivered to recipients and stored electronically by plaintiff's Internet service provider).

the use of electronic means to intercept oral communications or to disclose or use any communications that were illegally intercepted. ECPA restrictions regarding disclosure of stored e-mail information facially apply only to public systems and e-mails stored within such systems.[50]

The Stored Communications and Transactional Records Act, created as part of the ECPA, prohibits certain access to electronic communications service facilities, as well as disclosure by such services of information contained on those facilities. It provides a private right of action against those who knowingly or intentionally violate the Act. The Act is sometimes useful for protecting the privacy of e-mail and other Internet communications when discovery is sought from a third-party provider.

The Act prohibits service providers from knowingly disclosing the contents of a communication to any person or entity while in electronic storage by that service. It also prohibits the service provider from knowingly disclosing to any governmental agency any record or other information pertaining to a subscriber of the service. Accordingly, most service providers will not disclose such information without a subpoena.[51]

In *Jessup-Morgan v. America Online, Inc.*, a subscriber sued AOL, alleging a violation of the Act, invasion of privacy, and other claims arising out of the provider's disclosure of her identity pursuant to a subpoena.[52] The plaintiff had posted messages inviting users to see sexual liaisons with her paramour's wife. The court held that disclosure of the subscriber's identity did not violate the Act because the Act specifically authorizes the disclosure of subscriber information to private parties.

The Computer Fraud and Abuse Act makes it illegal to access a "protected" computer under certain circumstances, including computers operated by or on behalf of financial institutions.[53] The Act also makes it a crime to intentionally access a computer without authorization or to exceed authorized access, and obtain information from any "protected computer" if the conduct involved an interstate or foreign communication. A "protected computer" is a computer: (1) used exclusively by a financial institution; or (2) used by or for a financial institution, and the conduct constituting the offense affects that use by or for the financial institution; or (3) used in interstate or foreign commerce or communication.[54]

---

50.   *See, e.g., Andersen Consulting LLP v. UOP*, 991 F. Supp. 1041 (N.D. Ill. 1998) (holding proprietary system operated by employer was not public system, although accounting firm was permitted to use system during project).

51.   *See Theofel v. Farey–Jones*, 359 F.3d 1066, 1073 (9th Cir. 2004) (disclosure by Internet service provider of customer's e-mail messages pursuant to an invalid and overly broad civil subpoena did not constitute "authorized" disclosure by the provider, as would allow the defendant to avoid liability under the Act).

52.   20 F. Supp. 2d 1105 (E.D. Mich. 1998).

53.   18 U.S.C. § 1030 *et seq.*

54.   *See, e.g., International Airport Ctrs., LLC v. Citrin*, 440 F.3d 418 (7th Cir. 2006) (former employee's installation and use of secure-erasure program to delete files on employer-issued laptop

Draft a motion to quash a subpoena using the facts in *In re Subpoena Duces Tecum to AOL.*

J. CROSS–BORDER PRODUCTION ISSUES

BACKGROUND

Societe Nationale Industrielle Aerospatiale v. U.S. District Court for the Southern District of Iowa[55]

The plaintiffs in *Aerospatiale* were U.S. citizens who filed claims for negligence and breach of warranty against a French airplane manufacturer. Initial discovery was conducted pursuant to the Federal Rules of Civil Procedure without objection. However, upon plaintiffs' second request for the production of documents and admissions, the defendants filed a motion for a protective order. Defendants alleged that the Hague Convention, which prescribes certain procedures by which a judicial authority in one contracting state may request evidence located in another contracting state, dictated the exclusive procedures that must be followed for pretrial discovery. In addition, defendants argued that under French penal law, they could not respond to discovery requests that did not comply with the Hague Convention.[56] A Magistrate Judge denied the motion, and the Court of Appeals denied defendants' mandamus petition, holding, *inter alia*, that when a district court has jurisdiction over a foreign litigant, the Hague Convention does not apply even though the information sought may be physically located within the territory of a foreign signatory to the Convention.

On appeal, the Supreme Court held that the Hague Convention does not provide exclusive or mandatory procedures for obtaining documents and information located in a foreign signatory's territory. Rather, the plain language of the Convention, as well as the history of its proposal and ratification by the U.S., "unambiguously supports the conclusion that it was intended to establish optional procedures that would facilitate the taking of evidence abroad."[57] Accordingly, the Convention does not deprive district courts of their jurisdiction to order a foreign national party to produce evidence physically located within a signatory nation. Any contrary holding, the Court reasoned, would

---

prior to leaving that job was sufficient for employer to state a claim under Computer Fraud and Abuse Act).

55. 482 U.S. 522 (1987).

56. Article 1A of the French blocking statute, French Penal Code Law No. 80–538, provides: "Subject to treaties or international agreements and applicable laws and regulations, it is prohibited for any party to request, seek or disclose, in writing, orally or otherwise, economic, commercial, industrial, financial or technical documents or information leading to the constitution of evidence with a view to foreign judicial or administrative proceedings or in connection therewith." *Aerospatiale*, 482 U.S. at 526 n.6.

57. *Id.* at 538.

effectively subject every American court hearing a case involving a national of a contracting state to the internal laws of that state. Interrogatories and document requests are staples of international commercial litigation, no less than of other suits, yet a rule of exclusivity would subordinate the court's supervision of even the most routine of these pretrial proceedings to the actions or, equally, to the inactions of foreign judicial authorities.[58]

The Court further noted that a rule of exclusivity would create three "unacceptable asymmetries."[59] *First*, within any lawsuit between a national of the U.S. and a national of another contracting party, the foreign party could obtain discovery under the Federal Rules of Civil Procedure, while the domestic party would be required to resort first to the procedures of the Hague Convention. This imbalance would run counter to the fundamental maxim of discovery that "[m]utual knowledge of all the relevant facts gathered by both parties is essential to proper litigation."[60] *Second*, a rule of exclusivity would enable a company that is a citizen of another contracting state to compete with a domestic company on uneven terms, since the foreign company would be subject to less extensive discovery procedures in the event that both companies were sued in an American court. The Court noted that the French airplane manufacturer "made a voluntary decision to market their products in the United States," and that as a result, "[t]hey are entitled to compete on equal terms with other companies operating in this market."[61] Correspondingly, the French manufacturer was subject to the same discovery burdens associated with American judicial procedures as its American competitors. The Court reasoned that "[a] general rule according foreign nationals a preferred position in pretrial proceedings in our courts would conflict with the principle of equal opportunity that governs the market they elected to enter."[62] *Third*, the Court noted that

> since a rule of first use of the Hague Convention would apply to cases in which a foreign party is a national of a contracting state, but not to cases in which a foreign party is a national of any other foreign state, the rule would confer an unwarranted advantage on some domestic litigants over others similarly situated.[63]

The Court rejected the French manufacturer's argument that a rule of first resort to the Hague Convention procedures was necessary to accord respect to the sovereignty of states in which evidence was located. Even though the Court conceded that in civil law jurisdictions such as France, the process of obtaining evidence is normally conducted by a judicial officer rather than by private attorneys, if primacy or exclusivity were required it would have been described in the text of the treaty.

---

58. *Id.* at 539.

59. *Id.* at 540 n.25.

60. *Hickman v. Taylor*, 329 U.S. 495, 507 (1947).

61. *Societe Nationale Industrielle*, 482 U.S. at 540 n.25.

62. *Id.*

63. *Id.*

The Court further reasoned that, in this context, the concept of international comity requires a particularized analysis of the respective interests of the foreign and requesting nations. Such analysis must include consideration of the particular facts of each case, the sovereign interests at issue, and the likelihood that resorting to the procedures of the Hague Convention would prove effective.

In a footnote, the Court explained that the

> French "blocking statute" . . . does not alter our conclusion. It is well settled that such statutes do not deprive an American court of the power to order a party subject to its jurisdiction to produce evidence even though the act of production may violate that statute. *See Societe Internationale Pour Participations Industrielles et Commerciales, S.A. v. Rogers*, 357 U.S. 197, 204–206 (1958). Nor can the enactment of such a statute by a foreign nation require American courts to engraft a rule of first resort onto the Hague Convention, or otherwise to provide the nationals of such a country with a preferred status in our courts.[64]

Justice Blackmun acknowledged in his concurring and dissenting opinion that "[s]ome might well regard the Court's decision in this case as an affront to the nations that have joined the United States in ratifying the Hague Convention on the Taking of Evidence."[65] The dissent observed a risk in "relegating it to an 'optional' status, without acknowledging the significant achievement in accommodating divergent interests that the Convention represents."[66] Justice Blackmun concluded as follows:

> I can only hope that courts faced with discovery requests for materials in foreign countries will avoid the parochial views that too often have characterized the decisions to date. Many of the considerations that lead me to the conclusion that there should be a general presumption favoring use of the Convention should also carry force when courts analyze particular cases. The majority fails to offer guidance in this endeavor, and thus it has missed its opportunity to provide predictable and effective procedures for international litigants in United States courts.[67]

STRAUSS v. CREDIT LYONNAIS, S.A.
242 F.R.D. 199 (E.D.N.Y. 2007)

MATSUMOTO, MAGISTRATE JUDGE

* * * [P]laintiffs, United States citizens, and several estates, survivors and heirs of United States citizens, who are victims of terrorist attacks in Israel allegedly perpetrated by the Islamic Resistance Move-

---

64. *Id.* at 544 n.29.

65. *Id.* at 547–48 (Blackmun, J. dissenting).

66. *Id.* at 548.

67. *Id.* at 568.

ment ("HAMAS"), allege that defendant Credit Lyonnais, S.A. ("Credit Lyonnais") is civilly liable for damages pursuant to 18 U.S.C. § 2333(a) for: (1) aiding and abetting the murder, attempted murder, and serious bodily injury of American nationals located outside the United States in violation of 18 U.S.C. § 2332; (2) knowingly providing material support or resources to a foreign terrorist organization in violation of 18 U.S.C. § 2339B; and (3) financing acts of terrorism, in violation of 18 U.S.C. § 2339C. On October 5, 2006, Judge Sifton granted defendant's motion to dismiss the first claim, but denied its motion as to the second and third claims.

* * *

BACKGROUND

Plaintiffs are individuals and estates, survivors and heirs of individuals who were injured or killed in thirteen separate terrorist attacks, allegedly perpetrated by HAMAS in Israel between March 28, 2002 and August 19, 2003. * * * Credit Lyonnais is a financial institution incorporated and headquartered in France * * * [and] conducts business in the United States and maintains an office at 601 Brickell Key Drive, Miami, Florida, 33131. Plaintiffs further allege that Credit Lyonnais maintains bank accounts in France for Le Comite de Bienfaisance et de Secours aux Palestinians ("CBSP"), and that although CBSP describes itself as a charitable organization, it is part of HAMAS's fundraising infrastructure and a member of the Union of Good. The Union of Good, plaintiffs maintain, is an organization established by the Muslim Brotherhood and comprised of more than fifty Islamic charitable organizations worldwide, and is a "principal fundraising mechanism for HAMAS."

* * *

Plaintiffs allege that for more than thirteen years, defendant Credit Lyonnais "maintained an account for CBSP in Paris and provided HAMAS with material support in the form of financial services." Plaintiffs further allege that, through CBSP, Credit Lyonnais "has knowingly transferred significant sums of money to HAMAS-controlled entities" and "knowingly provided material support ... to a designated FTO [Foreign Terrorist Organization], and has provided substantial assistance to HAMAS in the commission of acts of international terrorism in Israel, including the terrorist attacks that injured the plaintiffs." Accordingly, plaintiffs contend that Credit Lyonnais is civilly liable to them for damages pursuant to 18 U.S.C. § 2333(a), for providing "material support and resources" to a Specially Designated Global Terrorist ("SDGT") (in violation of § 2339B) and providing or collecting funds "with the knowledge that such funds are to be used" to support terrorism (in violation of § 2339C).

PLAINTIFFS' MOTION TO COMPEL

A. Plaintiffs' Discovery Requests.

On June 30, 2006, plaintiffs served Credit Lyonnais with their First Request for the Production of Documents. At issue are Document Requests Nos. 1–3, 11–13 and 15, in which plaintiffs request:

● No. 1: All account records maintained by, or in the custody and control of Defendant that concern CBSP, including account opening records, bank statements, wire transactions, deposit slips and all correspondence between Defendant and CBSP.

● No. 2: All documents and communications by or to Defendant concerning CBSP, including all internal reports and the contents of any internal investigations undertaken by Defendant that reference CBSP.

● No. 3: All non-privileged documents and communications by or to the Defendant from or to banking regulatory authorities in the United States, the Republic of France, or the European Union ... concerning CBSP and or accounts maintained by the Defendant on CBSP's behalf.

● No. 11: All documents concerning Defendant's decision in January 2002 to close CBSP's accounts maintained by Credit Lyonnais including any documents that were the catalyst or basis of any decision to close or freeze said accounts.

● No. 12: All documents concerning Defendant's actual closure in January 2002 of CBSP's accounts maintained by Credit Lyonnais including any documents that were the catalyst or basis of any decision to close or freeze said accounts.

● No. 13: All documents concerning Credit Lyonnais's anti-money laundering efforts, "Know Your Customer" procedures, or other measures Credit Lyonnais used to prevent the rendering of financial services to Terrorists and Terrorist Organizations.

● No. 15: Copies of all internal Credit Lyonnais documents related to the following subjects and/or departments: [enumerating departments and procedures for account opening, security, customer accounts, compliance, internal audits, bank secrecy and terror financing designations or warnings].

* * *

In response, Credit Lyonnais objected to * * * plaintiffs' Document Requests * * * on the grounds that, inter alia, the requests,

> seek the disclosure of commercial and financial information in violation of Article 1 bis of French law No. 68–678 ("Article 1 bis"), which prohibits such disclosure in connection with a foreign judicial proceeding, except pursuant to an enforceable international treaty or agreement. Under Article 1 bis, [Credit Lyonnais] would be exposed to liability under French law unless disclosure proceeds in accordance with the Convention of 18 March 1970 on the Taking of Evidence Abroad in Civil or Commercial Matters (the "Hague

Convention"), 23 U.S.T. 2555, TIAS 7444, 847 UNTS 231, to which France and the United States are parties. Such liability would be avoided by following Hague Convention procedures, which should therefore be followed here.

In addition, Credit Lyonnais also objected to all discovery requests, to the extent they seek the disclosure of information and/or production of documents in violation of applicable French laws prohibiting the disclosure of information relating to a criminal investigation. The knowing disclosure of the existence and/or substance of a criminal investigation with the objective of adversely affecting criminal proceedings constitutes a criminal offense under French law and is sanctionable by imprisonment and substantial monetary penalties under Article L 434–7–2 of the French Criminal Code.

As discussed herein, Articles 11 and L 434–7–2 of the French Criminal Code prohibit disclosure of information relating to a criminal investigation to persons "likely to be involved as perpetrators, co-perpetrators, accomplices or receivers in the commission of these infractions ... for the purpose of interfering with the progress of the investigations or the search for the truth. . . ."

Credit Lyonnais also objected to plaintiffs' discovery requests on the grounds that they "seek the disclosure of information in violation of applicable French bank customer secrecy obligations" and "applicable French anti-money laundering laws." Credit Lyonnais further noted that failure to comply with the above regulations "constitutes a criminal offense under French law and is sanctionable by imprisonment and a substantial monetary penalty under Article 226–13 of the French Criminal Code."

In order to avoid civil and criminal liability under these statutes, Credit Lyonnais twice "requested [CBSP] to release [Credit Lyonnais] from its secrecy obligations in order to permit disclosure of information in [Credit Lyonnais's] possession related to CBSP." On July 20 and September 14, 2006, the bank's French counsel sent letters to CBSP's counsel, and has yet to receive any substantive response. Instead, CBSP's counsel simply objected to disclosing correspondence between counsel for CBSP and counsel for Credit Lyonnais. Credit Lyonnais has also sought the French government's guidance regarding plaintiffs' discovery demands by sending two letters and leaving one follow-up phone message with the French Ministry of Justice, but similarly has received no response.

* * *

B.   Applicability Of French Civil And Criminal Laws.

* * *

2. French civil and criminal laws are not rendered inapplicable by plaintiffs' possession of documents and information in the United States.

* * *

Plaintiffs * * * contend that French laws do not apply to documents located in the United States. Plaintiffs cite Restatement (Third) of Foreign Relations Law of the United States § 442, which provides:

> (1)(a) A court or agency in the United States ... may order a person subject to its jurisdiction to produce documents, objects, or other information relevant to an action or investigation, even if the information or the person in possession of the information is outside the United States.

> (b) Failure to comply with an order to produce information may subject the person to whom the order is directed to sanctions....

> (c) In deciding whether to issue an order directing production of information located abroad, and in framing such an order, a court or agency in the United States should take into account the importance to the investigation or litigation of the documents or other information requested; the degree of specificity of the request; whether the information originated in the United States; the availability of alternative means of securing the information; and the extent to which noncompliance with the request would undermine the important interests of the United States, or compliance with the request would undermine the important interests of the state where the information is located.

> (2) If disclosure of information located outside the United States is prohibited by a law, regulation, or order of a court or other authority of the state in which the information or prospective witness is located,

> . . .

> (c) a court or agency may, in appropriate cases, make findings of fact adverse to a party that has failed to comply with the order for production....

Plaintiffs point to the phrases "outside the United States" (§ 442(1)(a)); "order directing production of information located abroad" (§ 442(1)(c)); and the court's power to impose sanctions for failure to comply with an order for "disclosure of information located outside the United States" even if prohibited by foreign law (§ 442(2)), as evidence that Section 442 applies only to those documents physically located abroad.

Plaintiffs further note that in *Societe Nationale Industrielle Aerospatiale v. United States District Court for the Southern District of Iowa*, 482 U.S. 522 (1987), the defendants, two French manufacturers, did not object to producing "material or information that was located in the United

States," but only to producing material or information located in France and subject to French blocking statutes. Plaintiffs here assert that because the Court in *Aerospatiale* considered "the scope of the district court's power to order foreign discovery in the face of objections by foreign states," documents located within the United States (even if they originate from foreign sources) are accorded less protection.

Plaintiffs' reasoning regarding the bank documents located in the United States is flawed. First, Restatement § 442(1)(c) identifies as a factor whether the "information originated in the United States," not whether the information currently is located in the United States. Simply because Section 442 and the Court in *Aerospatiale* address documents located outside the United States does not mean that documents, obtained involuntarily from, or without the consent of, a foreign bank or its customer, and now located in the United States, should be accorded any less protection based solely on the location of the documents. The court is unaware of any precedent which ignores the bank-customer relationship simply because the documents at issue are currently located in the United States.

* * *

C.   The [Relevant Factors] * * *.

In determining whether to compel production of documents located abroad from foreign parties, courts in the Second Circuit consider the following * * * factors elucidated by the Supreme Court in *Aerospatiale* and set forth in Restatement of Foreign Relations Law of the United States § 442(1)(c):

- the importance to the ... litigation of the documents or other information requested;
- the degree of specificity of the request;
- whether the information originated in the United States;
- the availability of alternative means of securing the information;
  * * *
- the extent to which noncompliance with the request would undermine important interests of the United States, or compliance with the request would undermine the important interests of the state where the information is located;
- the competing interests of the nations whose laws are in conflict;
- the hardship of compliance on the party or witness from whom discovery is sought.

* * *

Having already considered the third factor—noting that the information sought by plaintiffs' discovery requests did not originate in the United States–the court will consider the remaining six factors, beginning with the first.

1.   The requested information is crucial to the litigation.

* * *

* * * Given plaintiffs' allegations regarding Credit Lyonnais's provision of financial services to CBSP for more than thirteen years, including accepting deposits from and/or distributing funds to alleged terrorist organizations on behalf of CBSP the court finds that the discovery sought is both relevant and crucial to the litigation of plaintiffs' claims. Because the documents and information sought by plaintiffs are highly relevant and important to the claims and defenses in this action, the court finds that this second factor weighs heavily in plaintiffs' favor.

2.   The discovery requests are narrowly tailored.

Rst. § 442(1)(c) also provides, "[A] court or agency in the United States should take into account ... the degree of specificity of the request...." * * * Here, the court finds that the requested discovery is relevant, vital and narrowly tailored to the litigation. * * * Plaintiffs' discovery requests are sufficiently focused on the vital issues in this case: whether and to what extent Credit Lyonnais knowingly provided "material support and resources" to Specially Designated Terrorist Organizations, and/or "financial services" to a terrorist organization. Plaintiffs' discovery requests seek, inter alia, documentation of the relationship between defendant and CBSP, the nature and extent of the services that defendant provided to CBSP, the collection or distribution of funds by Credit Lyonnais that may have been used by CBSP and/or its associates to support terrorism, and Credit Lyonnais's knowledge of CBSP's alleged terrorist connections. * * * Plaintiffs have established that their discovery demands are specifically tailored to their claims.

3.   Availability of alternative methods: plaintiffs are not required to seek discovery initially or exclusively through the Hague Convention.

Section § 442(1)(c) of the Restatement also requires the court to consider the "availability of alternate means of securing the information...." The court notes that plaintiffs do not have direct or ready access to Credit Lyonnais's records through means other than discovery demands. Only Credit Lyonnais can provide plaintiffs with responses to their requested discovery.

Credit Lyonnais argues that plaintiffs "may be able to obtain the discovery they seek through letters of request pursuant to the Hague Convention...." Both France and the United States are signatories to the Hague Convention, which provides internationally agreed-upon means for conducting discovery in foreign states and which defendant here urges plaintiffs to use. As a signatory to the Hague Convention, France generally has agreed to produce documents sought by foreign courts by responding to letters rogatory from the requesting party.

The United States Supreme Court, in *Aerospatiale,* determined that parties seeking discovery need not resort to the Hague Convention as their first and exclusive means for securing foreign discovery, explaining:

> An interpretation of the Hague Convention as the exclusive means for obtaining evidence located abroad would effectively subject every American court hearing a case involving a national of a [signatory] state to the internal laws of that state. Interrogatories and document requests are staples of international ... litigation, no less than of other suits, yet a rule of exclusivity would subordinate the court's supervision of even the most routine of these pretrial proceedings to the actions or, equally, to the inactions of foreign judicial authorities.

* * *

Addressing the applicability of French blocking statutes, the Court continued,

> It is clear that American courts are not required to adhere blindly to the directives of [a foreign blocking statute]. Indeed, the language of the statute, if taken literally, would appear to represent an extraordinary exercise of legislative jurisdiction by the Republic of France over a United States district judge, forbidding him or her to order any discovery from a party of French nationality, even simple requests for admissions or interrogatories that the party could respond to on the basis of personal knowledge.... Extraterritorial assertions of jurisdiction are not one-sided.

Therefore, plaintiffs in this case need not seek discovery initially or exclusively through the Hague Convention, but, instead, may appropriately seek from this court an order compelling discovery. The court notes, however, that although plaintiffs are not required to resort to the Hague Convention, they are not discouraged from doing so.

4. The mutual interests of the United States and France in combating terrorism outweigh the French interest, if any, regarding the disputed discovery.

The comity factor-requiring analysis of the competing interests of the United States and France "is of the greatest importance in determining whether to defer to the foreign jurisdiction." The court finds that this factor weighs strongly in favor of plaintiffs. The interests of the United States and France in combating terrorist financing, as evidenced by the legislative history of the ATA, * * * Presidential Executive Orders, and both countries' participation in international treaties and task forces aimed at disrupting terrorist financing, outweigh the French interest, if any, in precluding Credit Lyonnais from responding to plaintiffs' discovery requests. Indeed, France's interest in having Credit Lyonnais respond to plaintiffs' discovery requests is evident from France's execution of international treaties facilitating international cooperation to combat terrorism, and its requirement that banks monitor and report customer ties to terrorists.

* * *

France, like the United States, also has expressed and demonstrated a profound and compelling interest in eliminating terrorist financing. That France has an interest in eradicating the financing of terrorism by imposing monitoring and reporting obligations on its banks regarding customers who finance, or may be suspected of financing, terrorist acts around the world, is established by the fact that France has signed international treaties that mandate such monitoring and disclosure and explicitly direct the member countries to cooperate in legal proceedings against suspected terrorist financing groups. Along with the United States, France is a signatory to the United Nation[s] International Convention for the Suppression of the Financing of Terrorism. Article 12 of the Convention provides,

> 1. States Parties shall afford one another the greatest measure of assistance in connection with criminal investigations or criminal or extradition proceedings in respect of the offenses set forth in article 2, including assistance in obtaining evidence in their possession necessary for the proceedings.
>
> 2. States Parties may not refuse a request for mutual legal assistance on the ground of bank secrecy.

Although Article 12 prescribes assistance and cooperation among signatory nations in connection with criminal investigations and extradition proceedings, plaintiffs' action seeking compensation for victims of international terrorist attacks and discovery from a bank alleged to be providing material support to terrorists, is not inconsistent with the French and American interests in international cooperation to detect and fight global terror.

* * *

Accordingly, ordering Credit Lyonnais to provide plaintiffs with discovery would not "undermine the important interests of the state where the information is located," but rather, enforce them.

* * *

5. Credit Lyonnais will not face substantial hardship by complying with plaintiffs' requests.

* * *

Credit Lyonnais argues that, because the "French laws prohibiting [Credit Lyonnais's] production of the discovery sought by plaintiffs are valid and enforceable," it would face substantial hardship by complying with plaintiffs' requests. The bank "and its personnel would incur substantial civil, administrative and criminal liability–including fines, imprisonment and the prospect of lawsuits–if they were to violate those laws. . . ." Credit Lyonnais also asserts that it would "suffer enormous professional and reputational hardship if it betrayed its customer's confidence by disclosing the customer's protected information in violation of French bank secrecy laws." Glaringly absent from the submission by Credit Lyonnais is any indication that civil or criminal prosecutions by the French government or civil suits by CBSP are likely, rather than mere possibilities. * * * [C]ourts have already considered and found unpersuasive the potential imposition of the same penalties Credit Lyonnais cites here. The Supreme Court examined Articles 1–3 of French Penal Code Law No. 80–538, the French blocking statute, and ordered discovery notwithstanding the penalties that could be imposed, stating, "It is clear that American courts are not required to adhere blindly to the directives of such a statute." *Aerospatiale*, 482 U.S. at 544. [The court cites other cases reviewing the French blocking statutes at issue in this case; those cases conclude that the blocking statutes would not prevent disclosure in cases similar to this one.]

Although Credit Lyonnais has demonstrated that French bank secrecy laws have been enforced, the bank has failed to demonstrate that either CBSP or the French government would likely seek to sanction the bank for complying with a United States court order compelling disclosure of documents and information regarding CBSP's accounts. CBSP has shown no interest in protecting, much less asserting, its privacy right, as established by [the fact that], the French government has failed to submit any objections to producing the requested information, in response to three inquiries by Credit Lyonnais.* * * Despite Credit Lyonnais's assertions that the "professional and reputational consequences" would be severe if it "betrayed its customer's confidence," * * * France * * * has warned financial institutions that they could be exposed "to significant reputational, operational and legal risk" if they engage in business relationships with "high risk" customers such as charities collecting funds related to terrorist activities.

Furthermore, on March 10, 2006, the court entered a confidentiality order in this case, which further lessens Credit Lyonnais's potential hardship.

Credit Lyonnais has not demonstrated any likelihood that it will be pursued civilly or criminally if it responds to plaintiffs' discovery requests, particularly where the French interest in preventing terrorist financing through monitoring and reporting is so clearly demonstrated, and neither France nor CBSP have indicated that it objects to the bank responding to plaintiffs' discovery. Thus, "the goals of the plaintiffs in this case clearly are consistent with the objectives of the French Government, as evidenced by that government's" domestic laws incorporating international recommendations to combat terrorist financing.

6. Credit Lyonnais has acted in good faith.

The last factor courts in this Circuit consider in determining whether to order production is "the good faith shown by the party resisting discovery." * * * In this case, Credit Lyonnais has made at least two efforts to contact CBSP for its consent for Credit Lyonnais to respond to plaintiffs' discovery requests, and at least three efforts to contact the French Ministry of Justice for guidance. By sending two letters each to CBSP and the French government, and leaving one telephone message with the French Ministry, the defendant has made "good faith, diligent efforts" to secure discovery.

However, "notwithstanding [a litigant's] good faith, [the court is] not precluded from issuing a production order." The court notes that the bank's second attempts to contact CBSP and the French Ministry were made following court orders to do so. Therefore, "[w]hile evincing a measure of good faith, the Court is not convinced that defendant's efforts, are sufficient to tilt the balance in its favor," and against disclosure.

CONCLUSION

* * * [T]he mutual interests of the United States and France in thwarting terrorist financing outweighs the French interest in preserving bank customer secrecy–especially where France has not expressed an interest in precluding discovery responses pursuant to its bank secrecy or other statutes, and has demonstrated its national interest in cooperating in international efforts to detect, monitor and report customer links to terrorist organizations, and freeze funds used for terrorist financing. Notably, Credit Lyonnais has shown a specific interest in CBSP, having investigated CBSP's connections to terrorism and/or money laundering, reported CBSP's activities * * * and, presumably detecting a connection with terrorism and/or money laundering, closed CBSP's accounts. In addition, the requested discovery originated outside of the United States, is crucial to this litigation and is specifically tailored to the issues in this case. Plaintiffs do not have viable alternative means of securing the discovery, as the Hague Convention can be costly, uncertain and time-consuming, and only Credit Lyonnais or CBSP have access to the requested records. Moreover, although Credit Lyonnais has made good faith efforts to provide the requested discovery, Credit Lyonnais has not demonstrated that it is likely to face substantial hardship by complying with plaintiffs' discovery requests. * * *

Accordingly, by June 25, 2007, Credit Lyonnais shall produce all documents responsive to plaintiffs' Document Requests * * *.

COMMENTARY

Cross-border electronic discovery poses a "Catch–22"[68] situation in which the need to gather relevant information from foreign jurisdictions may squarely conflict with blocking statutes and data privacy regulations that prohibit or restrict such discovery—often upon threat of severe civil

---

68. "Catch–22" describes a situation where there are only two options, and both lead to undesirable results. *See* Joseph Heller, *Catch–22* (Simon & Schuster 1955).

and criminal sanctions. Cross-border discovery has become a major source of international legal conflict,[69] and at the heart of this conflict are vastly differing notions of discovery and data privacy and protection.[70]

Federal courts in the U.S. are often skeptical of efforts to preclude the discovery of relevant information from a foreign parent or affiliate. And the frequency and intensity of these conflicts are heightened by an expanding global marketplace and the proliferation of ESI. The recent conviction of a French attorney for seeking information relating to U.S.-based litigation may cause courts in the U.S. to revisit their consistent rulings, described below, that compel cross-border discovery notwithstanding foreign blocking statutes or data protection and privacy regulations.[71]

A number of cases have addressed the conflict between the interest of a party to a U.S. litigation in obtaining discovery of foreign electronic information and the foreign entity's interest in privacy.

1. *COLUMBIA PICTURES, INC. v. BUNNELL*[72]

In *Columbia Pictures, Inc. v. Bunnell*, discussed at length in Chapter II, *supra*, the defendants had engaged a third-party web hosting service in the Netherlands just a month prior to the Magistrate Judge's evidentiary hearing on the issue of whether RAM data had to be preserved and produced. The defendants argued that they could not provide the requested discovery because to do so would violate a Dutch blocking statute, and thus subject them to civil and criminal penalties. The defendants additionally cited an opinion of the Amsterdam District Court, which held that

> [a] service provider may, in certain circumstances, be obliged to provide rights holders (or their representatives) with the information asked for. For this, the Court must first of all be satisfied that there have been (unlawful) infringement activities by the subscribers concerned and, secondly, that it is beyond reasonable doubt that those whose identifying information is made available are also actually those who have been guilty of the relevant activities.[73]

Relying upon the Supreme Court's holding in *Aerospatiale*, *supra*, the *Columbia Pictures* court emphasized that " '[foreign] statutes do not deprive an American court of the power to order a party subject to its jurisdiction to produce evidence even though the act of production may violate that statute.' "[74] Even assuming that Netherlands law prohibited

---

69. *See Restatement (Third) of Foreign Relations* § 442 Reporters' Note, n.1 (1987).

70. *See* EU Data Protection Directive 95/46/EC restricting the processing and transfer of "personal data," which is defined as any data that identifies, or can result in the identification of a person.

71. *See In re Advocat "Christopher X,"* Cour de Cassation, French Supreme Court, Dec. 12, 2007, Appeal no. 07–83228.

72. 245 F.R.D. 443 (C.D. Cal. 2007).

73. *Id.* at 453 (citing *BREIN Foundation v. UPC Nederland B.V.*, Fabrizio Decl. Ex. 28).

74. *Id.* at 452 (quoting *Aerospatiale*, 482 U.S. at 544 n.29).

the discovery at issue, the court concluded that the Magistrate Judge's decision ordering discovery was based on the proper legal standard and the applicable balancing test. Although the defendants disagreed with the discovery order, they failed to establish that the Magistrate Judge's findings were clearly erroneous, or that her legal conclusions were contrary to law.[75]

2. *LYONDELL-CITGO REFINING, LP v. PETROLEOS DE VENE-ZUELA, S.A.*[76]

In response to a discovery dispute between the plaintiff, a Texas-based owner of an oil refinery, and the defendant, the Venezuelan national oil company, the Magistrate Judge ordered the defendant to produce the requested Board of Director minutes and other documents. Because the defendant responded to the plaintiff's discovery requests, which had been pending for months, "on the 11th hour, if not the 13th hour," the court reasoned that the defendant could not be trusted to review the disputed material.[77] Accordingly, the Magistrate Judge gave the plaintiff the "unusual opportunity" to search the Board minutes directly for relevant and responsive documents.[78] The defendant objected to the discovery order, claiming that the documents contained classified information relating to national security, and that disclosure of this material would subject the defendant to criminal penalties under Venezuelan law. The district court affirmed the discovery order, but the defendant persisted in its objection based on Venezuelan law and sought reconsideration.

In again denying the defendant's request to set aside the Magistrate Judge's order, the district court explained that the defendant did not provide any additional information that might compel a different finding. The district court had previously applied a balancing test to determine the reasonableness of ordering discovery from the foreign defendant, and concluded that the possibility of criminal penalties was not sufficiently strong to impede discovery. Holding otherwise based on defendant's objection, which contained only generalized statements about the need to protect national security, would grant any government or government-related party an "unfair advantage over its adversary."[79] Because the defendant neither provided precise reasons for asserting confidentiality, nor confined the assertion of privilege to a narrow set of documents, and given the highly deferential standard of review applicable to a Magistrate's non-dispositive discovery rulings, the

---

75. *See United States v. Vetco, Inc.*, 691 F.2d 1281, 1289 (9th Cir. 1981) (the party relying on foreign law has the burden of showing that such law bars production). However, the Magistrate Judge in *Columbia Pictures* noted that even if this were the applicable standard, because the server log was anonymous, and only listed Internet Protocol (IP) addresses, the *BREIN Foundation* analysis would not apply. *See also In re Investigation of World Arrangements*, 13 F.R.D. 280, 285 (D.D.C. 1952) (holding that parent corporations generally are responsible for discovery of documents located in foreign branches or subsidiaries).

76. No. 02 Civ. 0795, 2005 WL 356808 (S.D.N.Y. Feb. 15, 2005).

77. *Id.* at *1 (quotations omitted).

78. *Id.*

79. *Id.* at *3.

district court found that the Magistrate Judge was not clearly erroneous in ordering the production of the disputed documents.

3. *UNITED STATES v. VETCO*, INC.[80]

In order to investigate possible fraudulent income reporting, the Internal Revenue Service issued summonses to Vetco, Inc., an American corporation, requesting the records of Vetco and its wholly-owned Swiss subsidiary. Upon Vetco's non-compliance, the IRS successfully moved for enforcement of the summonses in a U.S. district court. When the defendants failed to comply with the court order, the court again ordered production, and imposed sanctions for continued non-compliance.

Before the Ninth Circuit, Vetco first argued that (i) a Swiss–U.S. Tax Treaty precluded the use of IRS summonses to obtain records held in Switzerland, and (ii) IRS regulations mandated that information-exchange provisions of treaties were the exclusive means of obtaining such records. The court disagreed, finding nothing in the Tax Treaty that barred the use of IRS summonses to gather information. Moreover, after considering the pertinent IRS regulations, the court determined that treaty procedures were not the exclusive methods by which to obtain records from a foreign entity where the treaty did not so provide, or where the foreign source was a subsidiary of an American corporation. Accordingly, the court found no violation of IRS regulations.

Vetco also argued that the Supreme Court's decision in *Societe Internationale Pour Participations Industrielles et Commerciales, S.A. v. Rogers*[81] required that summonses not be enforced, and that contempt sanctions not be imposed, where compliance with the summonses would result in a violation of foreign law. Vetco claimed that any compliance with the IRS summonses would result in the violation of Article 273 of the Swiss Penal Code, which provided that

> [w]hoever makes available a manufacturing or business secret to a foreign governmental agency or a foreign organization or private enterprise or to an agent of any of them; shall be subject to imprisonment and in grave cases to imprisonment in a penitentiary. The imprisonment may be combined with a fine.[82]

The Ninth Circuit rejected this argument. *First*, the court reasoned that *Rogers* did not erect an absolute bar to summons enforcement and contempt sanctions whenever compliance was prohibited by foreign law. Rather, the Supreme Court had specifically stated that its ruling would not apply " 'to every situation where a party is restricted by law from producing documents over which it is otherwise shown to have control,' " and that the determination depended upon the circumstances of

---

80.   691 F.2d 1281 (9th Cir. 1981).

81.   357 U.S. 197 (1958) (reversing district court's dismissal of action due to Swiss plaintiff's failure to produce documents, where production of the documents violated Swiss penal law and Swiss government intervened to enjoin production).

82.   *Vetco, Inc.*, 691 F.2d at 1287 (quoting StGB Art. 273).

each case.[83] *Second*, the *Vetco* court read *Rogers* as merely standing for the proposition that a district court could not dismiss a plaintiff's complaint for failure to comply with a discovery request where the plaintiff had made extensive good faith efforts to comply. That holding afforded district courts " 'wide discretion' " to use other means of obtaining compliance, to award lesser sanctions against the plaintiff, and to draw inferences unfavorable to parties in the absence of complete disclosure.[84]

Finally, the court distinguished the *Vetco* case from *Rogers*, and concluded that the Supreme Court's decision did not control the instant matter. For example, the *Vetco* court made no finding that the defendants attempted in good faith to comply with their summonses; the Swiss government had not enjoined the defendants from complying with the American court order; and there was no finding that production would violate Swiss law—facts that were dispositive to the holding in *Rogers*. Moreover, while in *Rogers* the plaintiff's inability to produce the requested documents might have been a serious handicap to it in attempting to make its case, the reverse was true in *Vetco*: the defendants would gain by their inability to produce. Further, whereas the document request in *Rogers* was issued in a civil suit, the *Vetco* case turned on an IRS summons issued pursuant to an investigation of potentially criminal misconduct. According to the *Vetco* court, such summonses served a more pressing national function than civil discovery, and were also more widely recognized in the international community.

In rejecting the defendants' argument that Swiss law precluded the enforcement of the IRS summonses, the *Vetco* court balanced a number of factors set forth in the *Restatement (Second) of Foreign Relations Law* § 40, an earlier and slightly different version of the Restatement discussed in *Credit Lyonnais*, *supra*.

> Where two states have jurisdiction to prescribe and enforce rules of law and the rules they may prescribe require inconsistent conduct upon the part of a person, each state is required by international law to consider, in good faith, moderating the exercise of its enforcement jurisdiction, in the light of such factors as:
>
> (a) vital national interests of each of the states,
>
> (b) the extent and the nature of the hardship that inconsistent enforcement actions would impose upon the person,
>
> (c) the extent to which the required conduct is to take place in the territory of the other state,
>
> (d) the nationality of the person, and
>
> (e) the extent to which enforcement by action of either state can reasonably be expected to achieve compliance with the rule prescribed by that state.

---

83.   *Id.* (quoting *Rogers*, 357 U.S. at 205–06).

84.   *Id.* (quoting *Rogers*, 357 U.S. at 206).

Under the first prong of the balancing test, the court considered "the degree of difference in law or policy, and the nationality of the parties affected."[85] Here the court noted that the U.S. had a strong interest in collecting taxes from, and prosecuting tax fraud by, one of its nationals operating through a foreign subsidiary. Although Switzerland had a similar interest, and also demonstrated an interest in preserving the secrecy of business records, such interests were diminished due to the fact that one of the defendants was a subsidiary of an American corporation. The court next examined the extent of the hardship, and was not persuaded that Article 273 of the Swiss Penal Code posed a great danger to the defendants. The court found no evidence that unrelated third parties with an interest in the confidentiality of the summoned records would object to production. The court further emphasized that, to the extent that any hardship would result, such hardship was avoidable. The Internal Revenue Code required American corporations to maintain records pertaining to controlled foreign subsidiaries. Had Vetco kept copies of such records at its offices in the U.S., the instant discovery dispute would not have arisen, there would have been no violation of Swiss law, and no Swiss party would have had occasion to object to disclosure. The final three factors set forth in the Restatement did not alter the court's conclusion. The required conduct was to take place both in the U.S. and in Switzerland; production to the IRS would take place in the U.S.; and though two of the defendants were Swiss corporations, both were controlled subsidiaries of American firms.

The *Vetco* court also examined two additional factors. *First*, the court considered the importance of the documents to the requesting party. Because the IRS demonstrated that the summoned documents were relevant to the investigation at issue, and because the defendants made no showing that the documents were cumulative of those already produced, this factor weighed in favor of the IRS. *Second*, the court considered whether alternate means of compliance were available, and determined that none of the defendants' proposals constituted a substantially equivalent alternative.

In sum, the *Vetco* court concluded that the Swiss–U.S. tax treaty did not preclude the use of IRS summonses to obtain records of Swiss subsidiaries of American firms. Moreover, possible criminal liability in Switzerland did not preclude enforcement and sanctions. Finally, the application of the balancing approach favored enforcement and sanctions: the interest of the U.S. in enforcement of the summonses outweighed the contrary Swiss interest, and the Defendants had not shown a substantial likelihood of a successful Swiss prosecution. Query whether this analysis will need to be revisited in light of the recent French blocking statute conviction.

---

85. *Id.* at 1289.

VI

SPOLIATION AND SANCTIONS

∎ ∎ ∎

A. WHAT CONSTITUTES SPOLIATION?

1. Definition and Standard

CONNOR v. SUN TRUST BANK

546 F. Supp. 2d 1360 (N.D. Ga. 2008)

VINING, DISTRICT JUDGE

This action is brought under the Family and Medical Leave Act of 1993 ("FMLA"), 29 U.S.C. §§ 2601–19 (2000). The plaintiff alleges that her former employer, Sun Trust, violated the FMLA by interfering with her substantive rights and retaliating against her for engaging in protected activity. After conducting discovery, the plaintiff has filed a Motion for Sanctions for Destruction of Evidence * * *. For the following reasons, the motion for sanctions is granted * * *.

I. FACTUAL BACKGROUND

The plaintiff is a former vice president level employee of Sun Trust who began her employment in 2004. Throughout her employment, the plaintiff worked in Sun Trust's Business Performance Group ("BPG"), a division of the Enterprise Information Services ("EIS") department, and she reported to BPG Manager Leslie Weigel. Toward the end of her employment, the plaintiff's duties included managing internal communications for EIS and serving as communications manager for Sun Trust's Project 2010, a joint project between Sun Trust and IBM to improve the delivery of technology projects to Sun Trust; she also managed Sun Trust's Enterprise Publication Services ("EPS") group, which handled internal communications to Sun Trust employees about bank operating procedures and policies. As part of her responsibilities with the EIS communications team, Project 2010, and the EPS group, the plaintiff was given responsibility in June 2006 to manage eight employees assigned to these various groups.

* * *

In November 2006, the plaintiff adopted a child and took two months of FMLA leave starting on November 8, 2006, and ending on

362

January 2, 2007. * * * While the plaintiff was on FMLA leave, her responsibilities for the EPS group were taken away. In December 2006, one of the EPS group employees, Mr. Swanson, unexpectedly resigned. The three EPS group employees were located in Orlando (the plaintiff was located in Atlanta) and Mr. Swanson served as the on-site supervisor for the other two EPS group employees. After Mr. Swanson resigned, Ms. Weigel, the plaintiff's supervisor and business manager of BPG, approached Ms. Bitzis, the senior manager of the Banking Services department, which was another department of EIS that had a large team co-located in the same Orlando building. They discussed transferring the EPS group and its two remaining junior-level members to the Banking Services department.

The resignation of the on-site supervisor for the EPS group in Orlando created a "supervision gap" that the plaintiff contends would have been filled by her had she not been on FMLA leave. Sun Trust disputes this point and asserts that even if the plaintiff had not been on leave, Sun Trust still would have faced the "supervision gap" because the plaintiff could not have provided direct supervision over the two Orlando-based employees from her office in Atlanta. In any event, Sun Trust maintains that having Banking Services absorb the EPS group was in the best long-term interests of EPS and that it would have happened even if the plaintiff had not been on FMLA leave at the time. * * * [I]t is her loss of three out of six employees as a result of the transfer of the EPS group while she was out on leave that the plaintiff asserts substantially diminished her management position and converted it into something less than full time.

On January 2, 2007, the plaintiff returned to work. About eleven days after the plaintiff had returned, her supervisor, Ms. Weigel, decided to fire the plaintiff, and informed her of the decision two weeks later. Approximately two weeks after notifying the plaintiff, Ms. Weigel sent an email to the senior management team of EIS on February 12, 2007, informing them that the plaintiff's job had been eliminated.

The plaintiff asserts that the reason her supervisor fired her was because of the removal of all but three of the plaintiff's direct reports. According to the plaintiff, the removal of her direct reports and changes in job responsibilities substantially diminished her job and thus violated her rights under the FMLA. She further contends that this reason is confirmed in an email sent by Ms. Weigel on February 12, 2007 ("February 12 email"), in which Ms. Weigel states that the reason the plaintiff's position was eliminated was based on the changes to the plaintiff's teams and the reduction from eight to three people being managed by her. Sun Trust disputes the reasoning for the plaintiff's termination and suggests that the reduction in direct reports is only part of the justification. Another reason was, for example, that the changes in the make-up of the plaintiff's teams supported a determination that the plaintiff's functions could be absorbed by other members of BPG and no longer justified keeping the plaintiff's position. Nevertheless, Sun Trust does not dispute that Ms. Weigel told the BPG team that the reason she fired the plaintiff was because she could not justify the plaintiff's position with only three remaining direct reports. Irrespective of how Ms. Weigel justified her decision, Sun Trust asserts that the facts show plaintiff was terminated for reasons wholly unrelated to her FMLA leave and thus do not violate her rights under the FMLA.

B. Motion for Sanctions

With respect to the February 12 email, the plaintiff has put that document into the record as evidence of illegal interference with her substantive rights under the FMLA. The email from Ms. Weigel informs her team about her decision to eliminate the plaintiff's position and states.

All,

I wanted to let you know that all of my team has received the information about my decision to eliminate the [plaintiff's] Comms manager position as of the end of March. Maria has talked with her team as well. You are free to discuss it with your team as you see fit.

A couple of talking points—

1. My decision was based on the changes to the make-up of the team that resulted in a reduction from 8 to 3 people being managed, by this position[.]

2. The remaining 3 people . . . will begin reporting directly to me.

Let me know if you have other questions. Thanks, Leslie

Notably, Sun Trust did not produce this email during discovery; the plaintiff procured it through other means. It is undisputed that had the plaintiff not happened to otherwise come by the February 12 email she would not have known of its existence despite its obvious relevance to her claims and Sun Trust's duty to produce it. Sun Trust's failure to produce this relevant document is the basis for the plaintiff's motion for sanctions.

On or about February 21, 2007, approximately nine days after the February 12 email, Sun Trust received a letter from the plaintiff's attorney advising Sun Trust of her FMLA claims and the likelihood of litigation. The plaintiff's attorney also cautioned Sun Trust to identify and preserve all relevant documents relating to the plaintiff's termination. In view of the plaintiff's claims and aware of Sun Trust's obligation to take affirmative steps to preserve all relevant documents, Sun Trust's Senior Vice President and Deputy General Counsel for Regulatory Affairs, Brian Edwards, initiated an internal investigation. Within days he identified employees likely to possess relevant information and issued preservation instructions to Ms. Weigel (the plaintiff's supervisor), Ms. Drury (human resources representative to BPG), and Sue Johnson (head of human resources and Ms. Drury's supervisor), among others. Mr. Edwards' preservation instructions included express guidance to identify and preserve all documents in their possession, including email communications, that related to the plaintiff's termination.

The preservation instructions were issued and received on or about February 22, 2007, approximately ten days after the February 12 email was sent. It is undisputed that at least two employees, Ms. Weigel (the February 12 email sender) and Ms. Johnson (one of the February 12 email recipients), would have been in possession of the February 12 email at the time they received the preservation instructions absent some affirmative action on their part to delete the message prior to receiving the instructions.

The timing of the email and the preservation instructions is important because Sun Trust's email system automatically deletes all emails from the company's server that are more than thirty days old. To preserve an email and prevent it from being automatically deleted, employees must take steps to archive their messages outside of the email system. While Sun Trust does back up its email servers on a daily basis for disaster recovery purposes, the backup tapes are retained for only seven to ten days before being overwritten. Consequently, an email deleted immediately after being sent or received by an employee will survive on the server only seven to ten days; meanwhile, an email not archived and retained on an employee's server account for the maximum thirty days will survive on the server for up to thirty-seven to forty days. Thus, any inquiry into whether an employee had access to a relevant email for purposes of preservation requires determining the amount of time between when the email was first on the email server and when preservation should have commenced. It is also necessary to inquire into what, if any, steps were taken to delete a message before preservation instructions were given.

With respect to Ms. Weigel's actions concerning preservation of related documents and in particular emails, it is her failure to preserve and produce her February 12 email that is primarily the basis for the plaintiff's motion. It is undisputed that Ms. Weigel failed to preserve the February 12 email after she had been instructed to do so on or about February 22. This of course assumes that the February 12 email was still on Ms. Weigel's server account or had been archived at least ten days after it was sent. Sun Trust has stated that although she does not archive every email, Ms. Weigel does employ a general practice of archiving her email messages from her inbox and her sent mail folders weekly.

After Ms. Weigel was instructed on about February 22 to identify and preserve all documents relevant to the plaintiff's claims, including emails, she searched her email archives and provided relevant emails to Sun Trust's counsel. However, she did not provide the February 12 email. On or about September 10, 2007, when the plaintiff produced a copy of the February 12 email, Ms. Weigel again searched her email archive to determine if she had overlooked that particular message when gathering relevant documents. At that point, Ms. Weigel apparently realized that she had a gap in her sent email archive for the period of January 1, 2007, through February 18, 2007, thus indicating that she had indeed not archived the February 12 email or any others during that period.

The obvious effect of the gap in archived sent emails was that by mid-March (long before the plaintiff advised Sun Trust of the existence of the February 12 email) those emails would have been deleted for having been on the Sun Trust's email server over thirty days. Consequently, when Ms. Weigel went to redo the search of her email messages, she naturally could not locate the February 12 email if it had not been archived. * * * Sun Trust asserts that the reason for the gap in Ms. Weigel's archived sent items is because Ms. Weigel apparently did not follow her usual practice of archiving all of her sent email for the relevant time period. This apparently happens when Ms. Weigel is very busy and falls behind in her archiving routine.

With respect to Ms. Johnson, she similarly undertook a search for all relevant documents in her possession, including emails, sometime between February 22 (when she was given the preservation instruction) and March 5 (the date Sun Trust's counsel met with Ms. Weigel and Ms. Drury, and the date by which counsel had already received Ms. Johnson's documents). However, Ms. Johnson also did not produce the February 12 email though Sun Trust admits she received the message. It is apparently Ms. Johnson's usual practice to delete all incoming messages that do not require her follow-up. Based on this, Sun Trust asserts that Ms. Johnson likely deleted the email as soon as she received it because the February 12 email required no action from Ms. Johnson and because she was already aware of Ms. Weigel's decision to terminate the plaintiff. Assuming that she did delete the message soon after receipt, it would have been unavailable for her or Sun Trust to preserve. Consequently, the February 12 email allegedly no longer existed on Ms. Johnson's email profile on the server when she was given the preservation instructions and, therefore, it could not have been produced by her.

II. ANALYSIS

* * *

The plaintiff * * * moves this court for spoliation sanctions against Sun Trust for destroying the February 12 email. A court may sanction a party for spoliation of evidence by (1) dismissing the case, (2) excluding expert testimony, or (3) issuing jury instructions that raise a presumption against the spoliator. *Flury v. Daimler Chrysler Corp.*, 427 F.3d 939, 945 (11th Cir. 2005). To determine whether spoliation has occurred, a court must address five factors: (1) prejudice to the non-spoliing party as a result of the destruction of evidence, (2) whether the prejudice can be cured, (3) practical importance of the evidence, (4) whether the spoling party acted in good or bad faith, and (5) the potential for abuse of expert testimony about evidence not excluded. *Id.*

With respect to the first factor, this court concludes that the plaintiff has been prejudiced by Sun Trust's failure to produce the February 12 email during discovery. Although it is true that the plaintiff obtained the February 12 email through other means, that fact does not alleviate the damage done to the plaintiff's case when very relevant evidence, such as the February 12 email, is not produced during discovery and is subsequently destroyed by operation of Sun Trust's automatic deletion of emails that are more than thirty days old and not archived. If relevant evidence is not produced, for whatever reason, and then is destroyed before either party learns of the existence of that evidence, then the absence of the relevant evidence prejudices the party that would have relied on it to prove its case.

Here, the prejudice to the plaintiff is more attenuated than the prejudice present in *Flury.* In that case, the plaintiff brought a product liability claim against a vehicle manufacturer for injury caused by the failure of a vehicle's airbag to deploy during a collision. However, the plaintiff allowed the vehicle to be destroyed and, consequently, the defendant was prejudiced because it could not examine the vehicle's condition or airbag control unit. In this case, the prejudice resulting from Sun Trust's failure to produce an undisputedly relevant email raises a concern that * * * there were other relevant emails in existence at that time but which were also not produced, and there is no satisfactory answer because all emails not archived by the email users had since been automatically deleted from the server.

With respect to the second and third factors, this court concludes that the prejudice to the plaintiff can be cured and that the evidence is important to her case because such evidence, like the February 12 email, goes directly to Sun Trust's reasons for terminating her employment.

With respect to the fourth factor, this court concludes that Sun Trust acted in bad faith. This determination requires weighing Sun Trust's culpability against the resulting prejudice to the plaintiff, but it does not require a finding of malice. Here, the conduct of Ms. Weigel is particularly important because she sent the February 12 email and, as the plaintiff's direct supervisor, made the decision to terminate the plaintiff. However, approximately ten days after sending the February 12 email, Ms. Weigel failed to produce it in response to Sun Trust counsel's preservation instructions. Assuming, as Sun Trusts argues, that Ms. Weigel did not employ her general practice of weekly archiving her sent items, that nevertheless does not explain why she failed to preserve the document. The February 12 email still would have been in Ms. Weigel's account on Sun Trust's email server for approximately another twenty days until the system automatically deleted the email for being over thirty days old. The only way Ms. Weigel could not have preserved the February 12 email when she conducted her search of relevant emails, again assuming that she inadvertently failed to archive the message, was if she had affirmatively deleted the February 12 email from her sent items before the thirty day limit had expired. Moreover, it is doubtful that Ms. Weigel was not aware of the direct relevance of her February 12 email a mere ten days after she had sent it. In view of these facts, Ms. Weigel and, therefore, Sun Trust was at least minimally culpable for the failure to disclose the February 12 email. As discussed above, the failure to disclose the February 12 email prejudiced the plaintiff and, therefore, Sun Trust acted in bad faith.

With respect to the fifth factor, this court concludes that there is a potential for abuse. Although the leading cases on spoliation sanctions * * * involve the potential for abuse by experts, the analysis under this fifth spoliation factor is focused on whether the non-spoliating party, despite its ability to present evidence in support of its claims, has had a full opportunity to discover the most relevant and most reliable evidence. Here, the plaintiff has not had such an opportunity because Sun Trust's failure to produce what is arguably the most relevant email raises doubts about its assertions that there were never any others in existence. The absence of any other relevant emails, other than the February 12 email which Sun Trust did not produce, raises the potential for abuse by Sun Trust, albeit slight, because even the mere non-existence of emails relating to Sun Trust's reasons for terminating the plaintiff can support Sun Trust's defense that it did not interfere with the plaintiff's FMLA rights or terminate her in retaliation for exercising those rights.

Therefore, this court concludes spoliation of evidence has occurred and that sanctions are warranted against Sun Trust. This spoliation, however, can be cured by a sanction less severe than outright dismissal. In view of the minimal culpability of Sun Trust and the slight potential for abuse, the court will instruct the jury as to the appropriate inference to draw from the absence of evidence.

2. Culpability—Intentional, Bad Faith, Grossly Negligent, or Negligent Conduct

RESIDENTIAL FUNDING CORP. v. DEGEORGE FINANCIAL CORP.

306 F.3d 99 (2d Cir. 2002)

CABRANES, CIRCUIT JUDGE

We consider here the standard district courts should employ in determining whether a party's failure to comply with discovery requests warrants the imposition of sanctions.

DeGeorge Financial Corp., DeGeorge Home Alliance, Inc., and DeGeorge Capital Corp. (collectively, "DeGeorge") appeal from a final judgment in favor of Residential Funding Corporation ("RFC") entered by the United States District Court * * * after a jury trial on cross-claims for breach of contract. On appeal, DeGeorge challenges only the

District Court's denial of its motion for sanctions—in the form of an adverse inference instruction—for RFC's failure to produce certain e-mails in time for trial. The District Court denied the motion based on its finding that the delay in producing the e-mails was not caused by an action of RFC that was taken in bad faith or with gross negligence and its finding that DeGeorge had not shown that the missing e-mails would be favorable to its case.

We hold that (1) where, as here, the nature of the alleged breach of a discovery obligation is the non-production of evidence, a District Court has broad discretion in fashioning an appropriate sanction, including the discretion to delay the start of a trial (at the expense of the party that breached its obligation), to declare a mistrial if trial has already commenced, or to proceed with a trial with an adverse inference instruction; (2) discovery sanctions, including an adverse inference instruction, may be imposed where a party has breached a discovery obligation not only through bad faith or gross negligence, but also through ordinary negligence; (3) a judge's finding that a party acted with gross negligence or in bad faith with respect to discovery obligations is ordinarily sufficient to support a finding that the missing or destroyed evidence would have been harmful to that party, even if the destruction or unavailability of the evidence was not caused by the acts constituting bad faith or gross negligence; and (4) in the instant case, the District Court applied the wrong standard in deciding DeGeorge's motion for sanctions.

Accordingly, we vacate the order of the District Court denying DeGeorge's motion for sanctions and remand with instructions for a renewed hearing on discovery sanctions.

I. Background

This litigation involved cross-claims for, inter alia, breach of contract, with the parties' dispute centered principally on events in the latter part of 1998. RFC initiated the case by filing suit on January 15, 1999 * * *.

* * *

On January 4, 2001, the parties held a discovery planning conference * * *. At that meeting, the parties agreed that discovery would commence "immediately" and be completed by August 1, 2001, and that the case would be ready for trial by September 1, 2001. On January 19, 2001, the District Court entered a scheduling order reflecting the parties' agreed-upon discovery schedule.

On April 12, 2001, DeGeorge served its document discovery requests, which included a request for all documents, including electronic mail, relating to DeGeorge. RFC responded to DeGeorge's document requests on May 22, 2001, and asserted no objection to the request for e-mail.

During the first week of June 2001, the parties agreed that they would "work diligently to obtain hard copies of emails that were in computer form so that [they] could have a mutual production of emails." On June 8, 2001, RFC told DeGeorge that it was "in the process of retrieving e-mails from the back-up tapes" and that "[it] would let [DeGeorge] know when it had an estimate on a production date for the e-mails that are being retrieved off of the storage tapes."

In mid-June 2001, after RFC's in-house lawyer responsible for technology issues determined that "RFC did not have the internal resources necessary to retrieve [the e-mails from the back-up tapes] in the permitted time frame," RFC retained Electronic Evidence Discovery, Inc. ("EED") to assist RFC in the e-mail retrieval project.

In early July 2001, RFC informed DeGeorge that it had been unable to retrieve any emails from its back-up tapes. DeGeorge requested copies of the back-up tapes so that it could have its technical experts attempt to retrieve e-mails from them, and indicated its willingness to enter into any requested confidentiality agreement. RFC refused to produce the back-up tapes, prompting DeGeorge to raise the issue with the District Court.

On July 12, 2001, at a settlement conference before Magistrate Judge Joan G. Margolis, DeGeorge raised the issue of RFC's refusal to produce e-mails or back-up tapes. The parties agree that RFC told Magistrate Judge Margolis that it "was going to engage a vendor" to retrieve the emails. The parties understood at the July 12, 2001 conference that RFC would produce e-mails with the assistance of a vendor.

On or about July 25, 2001, EED apparently informed counsel for RFC that it would take "a couple of weeks" for it to print out the e-mails and transmit them to counsel for review. RFC, in turn, informed DeGeorge that day that it would begin producing responsive e-mails on a rolling basis starting on August 6, 2001. It represented that the e-mails would take "a few weeks" to produce. At this point, discovery was set to close on August 1, 2001, with jury selection to begin on September 5, 2001.

RFC did not begin producing e-mails on August 6, 2001, as it had promised. Instead, it informed DeGeorge on August 9, 2001, that it was continuing work on the production of e-mails and that "so far, most [of the e-mail printouts it had received from EED are] completely unrelated to the case."

By August 15, 2001, DeGeorge still had not received any production of e-mails from RFC. Accordingly, it raised the matter in a conference call with [trial] Judge Arterton on that date. RFC informed Judge Arterton that it had encountered technical difficulties, but that it expected to complete production "in the next couple of weeks." Judge Arterton ordered that production of the e-mails be completed by August 20, 2001.

RFC did not produce a single e-mail between August 15 and August 20, 2001. Instead, it informed DeGeorge on August 21, 2001, that EED was just beginning to print out e-mails due to additional "technical problems" and that responsive e-mails would be forthcoming "over the next couple of days."

On August 24, 2001, RFC produced 126 e-mails dating from January 1998 through early August 1998, and 2 e-mails from September 1998. There were no e-mails produced from October to December 1998—the critical factual time period.

DeGeorge immediately inquired as to the reason there were no e-mails from the end of 1998. RFC responded that "[i]f there were no responsive e-mails for 10/98–12/98 ... it was either because there were no responsive e-mails from that date or because they did not exist on the accessible back-up tapes." On August 27, 2001, RFC confirmed that it had been "unable to retrieve October [to] December 1998 e-mails for production from RFC's back-up tapes."

On August 29, 2001, RFC produced 30 additional responsive e-mails retrieved from back-up tapes, none of which were from October to December 1998.

On September 1, 2001, DeGeorge again asked RFC to produce the back-up tapes so that it could investigate why no e-mails had been produced from the critical time period. On September 3, 2001, RFC agreed to provide the back-up tapes on the condition that any e-mails DeGeorge's vendor was able to retrieve be sent to RFC for review rather than to DeGeorge. The next morning, after initially rejecting the condition, DeGeorge agreed to RFC's terms in an e-mail sent at 11:17 a.m. In that e-mail, DeGeorge requested that the tapes be made available the next morning at jury selection. RFC did not produce the tapes at jury selection; instead, it sent them by overnight courier on September 5, 2001, so that DeGeorge did not receive them until the morning of September 6, 2001—three days before trial was to begin.

Although RFC turned over the back-up tapes, it refused to answer DeGeorge's questions regarding what type of tapes had been produced and their technical characteristics—information DeGeorge sought to assist its vendor in reading the tapes. Instead, RFC took the position that it had fulfilled its discovery obligations by producing the tapes, and that DeGeorge's vendor should just try to figure it out as RFC's vendor had done. DeGeorge brought RFC's recalcitrance to the attention of the District Court in a telephone conference held that day (September 6, 2001), during which RFC agreed to answer DeGeorge's questions.

The next day—September 7, 2001—DeGeorge asked RFC to ask its vendor why it could not retrieve anything from the October [to] December 1998 tapes. RFC responded that "the reason no e-mails were produced for 10–12/98 from the back-up tapes you received was either due to the fact that some of the tapes were physically damaged or corrupted or some tapes did not have e-mail on them at all."

Within four days of obtaining the tapes, "working a normal eight hour day," DeGeorge's vendor had located 950,000 e-mails on the November and December 1998 tapes. By September 13, 2001, the vendor had begun forwarding printed e-mails to RFC's counsel for review and production. Because of time pressure, the parties agreed that RFC would produce all of the 4,000 e-mails that DeGeorge's vendor had been able to print out; RFC did so in court on September 14, 2001. Ultimately, thirty of the 4,000 e-mails were responsive, though none appear to be damaging to RFC.

On September 18, 2001, DeGeorge moved for sanctions, asking Judge Arterton to instruct the jury that "it should presume the emails from October to December of 1998, which have not been produced, would have disproved RFC's theory of the case." The next day, during oral argument on the motion, RFC's counsel described RFC's retention of EED as follows:

> I believe that as early as mid-June we began contacting Electronic Evidence Discovery, Inc., who is our vendor that helped us retrieve the e-mails. And as we represented to the magistrate on [July 12th], we were getting help doing this.

In response to Judge Arterton's question regarding why RFC had not produced the back-up tapes earlier, RFC's counsel stated:

> It was a decision that we made internally that we endeavored to work with a world class vendor to achieve this—to achieve a result that would be satisfactory both for DeGeorge and for the Court, and we have yet to see that they would have been able to do any better.

Replying to Judge Arterton's question regarding why RFC had not turned over back-up tapes created in early 1999 so as to insure that all of the December 1998 e-mails were captured, RFC's counsel told the District Court that RFC had produced back-up tapes from "as late as February of 99 and January of 99." In fact, however, RFC had not produced any 1999 back-up tapes.

In an oral ruling the next morning (September 20, 2001), Judge Arterton denied DeGeorge's motion. She held that, to obtain an adverse inference charge, a party must show that "[1] the party with control over the evidence had an obligation to preserve it at the time it was destroyed; [2] the party that destroyed the evidence had a sufficiently culpable state of mind; and [3] some evidence suggest[s] that a document or documents relevant to substantiating [the claim of the party seeking sanctions] would have been included among the destroyed files." RFC did not dispute that it had an obligation to preserve and produce the e-mails; accordingly, Judge Arterton focused on the latter two prongs of the analysis.

With respect to the second prong, Judge Arterton found * * * that DeGeorge was not entitled to an adverse inference instruction because it had not established that RFC acted with "bad faith" or "gross negligence." She gave two reasons for this conclusion. First, she found that

RFC's explanation that it decided to use an outside vendor to retrieve the e-mails rather than turn over the back-up tapes was "neither implausible nor unreasonable," and it was that decision that led to much of the delay. Second, although she recognized that

> subsequent acts by RFC, including representation that e-mails would be produced, without mentioning the absence of any from the critical time period, a missed Federal Express deadline for sending backup tapes so they could be forwarded to DeGeorge's vendors, and resistance to responding to technical questions about the tapes, suggests a somewhat purposeful sluggishness on RFC's part,

she found that these acts would not have resulted in the unavailability of the evidence absent the "compressed timeline both parties were operating under."

Judge Arterton also held that DeGeorge had failed to establish that the e-mails would be helpful to it, as it "ha[d] not identified anything, apart from the nonproduction itself, suggesting that [the unproduced e-mails] would likely have been harmful to RFC."

Mindful that the e-mails had not been destroyed but rather not timely produced, Judge Arterton noted that:

> Should material evidence surface that is adverse to RFC after trial from the eventual disclosure of these e-mails, it might be the basis for post-trial motions, since it would obviously appear to fit within the category of being newly discovered and unavailable at the time of trial.

That day (September 20, 2001) was the last day evidence was presented in the case. The following Monday, September 24, 2001, the jury heard closing arguments, received the charge, and reached a verdict in favor of RFC for $96.4 million. * * *

On appeal, DeGeorge argues that (1) the District Court erred in holding (a) that it was required to establish "bad faith" or "gross negligence" to show that RFC acted with a sufficiently culpable state of mind so as to warrant sanctions, and (b) that it was required to show that the e-mails would have been harmful to RFC; and (2) the District Court's denial of its motion for sanctions was based on a "clearly erroneous view of the evidence." DeGeorge asks us to vacate the judgment of the District Court and remand for a new trial.

II. Discussion

A. The Nature of the Alleged Breach of a Discovery Obligation

* * *

Rule 37(b)(2) of the Federal Rules of Civil Procedure provides, in relevant part, that if a party fails to obey a discovery order, the court "may make such orders in regard to the failure as are just," including, but not limited to, "[a]n order that . . . designated facts shall be taken as established for the purposes of the action in accordance with the claim of the party obtaining the order." Fed.R.Civ.P. 37(b)(2)(A). * * *

Even in the absence of a discovery order, a court may impose sanctions on a party for misconduct in discovery under its inherent power to manage its own affairs. *See generally Chambers v. NASCO, Inc.*, 501 U.S. 32, 43 (1991) ("It has long been understood that certain implied powers must necessarily result to our Courts of justice from the nature of their institution, powers which cannot be dispensed with in a Court, because they are necessary to the exercise of all others.").

Where, as here, the nature of the alleged breach of a discovery obligation is the non-production of evidence, a district court has broad discretion in fashioning an appropriate sanction, including the discretion to delay the start of a trial (at the expense of the party that breached its obligation), to declare a mistrial if trial has already commenced, or to proceed with a trial and give an adverse inference instruction. In the instant case, however, DeGeorge chose not to seek a delay of the trial or a mistrial, but rather sought only an adverse inference instruction. Accordingly, we will not disturb the District Court's denial of DeGeorge's motion unless the District Court abused its discretion in failing to give the requested instruction.

B.   The District Court's Denial of DeGeorge's Motion

We review a district court's decision on a motion for discovery sanctions for abuse of discretion. "A district court would necessarily abuse its discretion if it based its ruling on an erroneous view of the law or on a clearly erroneous assessment of the evidence." In the instant case, DeGeorge contends that, in denying its motion for sanctions, the District Court both made errors of law and based its ruling on a clearly erroneous view of the evidence.

1.   The legal standard for an adverse inference instruction

As the District Court correctly held, a party seeking an adverse inference instruction based on the destruction of evidence must establish (1) that the party having control over the evidence had an obligation to preserve it at the time it was destroyed; (2) that the records were destroyed "with a culpable state of mind"; and (3) that the destroyed evidence was "relevant" to the party's claim or defense such that a reasonable trier of fact could find that it would support that claim or defense. Similarly, where, as here, an adverse inference instruction is sought on the basis that the evidence was not produced in time for use at trial, the party seeking the instruction must show (1) that the party having control over the evidence had an obligation to timely produce it; (2) that the party that failed to timely produce the evidence had "a culpable state of mind"; and (3) that the missing evidence is "relevant" to the party's claim or defense such that a reasonable trier of fact could find that it would support that claim or defense.

RFC did not dispute in its opposition to DeGeorge's motion that it (1) had an obligation to preserve and timely produce the back-up tapes. Accordingly, the only issues before the District Court were (2) whether RFC acted "with a culpable state of mind" in failing to timely produce the e-mails and (3) whether the missing e-mails are "relevant" to DeGeorge's claim or defense such that a reasonable trier of fact could find that they would support that claim or defense.

a. The proper legal standard for determining whether RFC acted "with a culpable state of mind"

* * *

The sanction of an adverse inference may be appropriate in some cases involving the negligent destruction of evidence because each party should bear the risk of its own negligence. As Magistrate Judge James C. Francis, IV aptly put it,

> [The] sanction [of an adverse inference] should be available even for the negligent destruction of documents if that is necessary to further the remedial purpose of the inference. It makes little difference to the party victimized by the destruction of evidence whether that act was done willfully or negligently. The adverse inference provides the necessary mechanism for restoring the evidentiary balance. The inference is adverse to the destroyer not because of any finding of moral culpability, but because the risk that the evidence would have been detrimental rather than favorable should fall on the party responsible for its loss.

Turner v. Hudson Transit Lines, Inc., 142 F.R.D. 68, 75 (S.D.N.Y. 1991). *See generally Kronisch v. United States*, 150 F.3d 112, 126 (2d Cir. 1998) (stating that an adverse inference instruction serves the remedial purpose, "insofar as possible, of restoring the prejudiced party to the same position he would have been in absent the wrongful destruction of evidence by the opposing party").

* * * [T]he District Court * * * explicitly analyzed only whether RFC acted in "bad faith" or with "gross negligence." It is therefore unclear whether the District Court applied the proper legal standard. Ordinarily, we would remand for clarification of this issue, but, in view of our analysis of the remaining issues in this case, such clarification is unnecessary.

b. The proper legal standard for determining whether DeGeorge adduced sufficient evidence that the missing e-mails are "relevant"

Although we have stated that, to obtain an adverse inference instruction, a party must establish that the unavailable evidence is "relevant" to its claims or defenses, * * * our cases make clear that "relevant" in this context means something more than sufficiently probative to satisfy Rule 401 of the Federal Rules of Evidence.[3] Rather, the party seeking an adverse inference must adduce sufficient evidence from which a reasonable trier of fact could infer that "the destroyed [or unavailable] evidence would have been of the nature alleged by the party affected by its destruction." Courts must take care not to "hold the prejudiced party to too strict a standard of proof regarding the likely contents of the destroyed [or unavailable] evidence," because doing so "would subvert the purposes of the adverse inference, and would allow parties who have destroyed evidence to profit from that destruction."

Where a party destroys evidence in bad faith, that bad faith alone is sufficient circumstantial evidence from which a reasonable fact finder could conclude that the missing evidence was unfavorable to that party. Similarly, a showing of gross negligence in the destruction or untimely production of evidence will in some circumstances suffice, standing alone, to support a finding that the evidence was unfavorable to the grossly negligent party. Accordingly, where a party seeking an adverse inference adduces evidence that its opponent destroyed potential evidence (or otherwise rendered it unavailable) in bad faith or through gross negligence (satisfying the "culpable state of mind" factor), that same evidence of the opponent's state of mind will frequently also be sufficient to permit a jury to conclude that the missing evidence is favorable to the party (satisfying the "relevance" factor).[4]

A party seeking an adverse inference instruction need not, however, rely on the same evidence to establish that the missing evidence is "relevant" as it uses to establish the opponent's "culpable state of mind."
* * *
In this case, the District Court stated that the only evidence De-George had adduced "suggesting that [the unproduced e-mails] would likely have been harmful to RFC" was the nonproduction itself. It also stated, however, that RFC's actions after it retained EED, "including representation that e-mails would be produced, without mentioning the absence of any from the critical time period, a missed Federal Express deadline for sending backup tapes so they could be forwarded to DeGeorge's vendors, and resistance to responding to technical questions about the tapes, suggest a somewhat purposeful sluggishness on RFC's part."

It is unclear why the District Court did not consider RFC's acts evincing "purposeful sluggishness" as supportive of DeGeorge's claim that the e-mails were likely harmful to RFC. Just as the intentional or

---

3. Rule 401 provides:"Relevant evidence" means evidence having any tendency to make the existence of any fact that is of consequence to the determination of the action more probable or less probable than it would be without the evidence.

4. Although the issue of whether evidence was destroyed with a "culpable state of mind" is one for a court to decide in determining whether the imposition of sanctions is warranted, whether the materials were in fact unfavorable to the culpable party is an issue of fact to be determined by the jury. Accordingly, a court's role in evaluating the "relevance" factor in the adverse inference analysis is limited to insuring that the party seeking the inference had adduced enough evidence of the contents of the missing materials such that a reasonable jury could find in its favor.

grossly negligent destruction of evidence in bad faith can support an inference that the destroyed evidence was harmful to the destroying party, so, too, can intentional or grossly negligent acts that hinder discovery support such an inference, even if those acts are not ultimately responsible for the unavailability of the evidence (i.e., even if those acts do not satisfy the "culpable state of mind" factor because they did not cause the destruction or unavailability of the missing evidence). Thus, if any of RFC's acts that hindered DeGeorge's attempts to obtain the e-mails was grossly negligent or taken in bad faith,[5] then it could support an inference that the missing e-mails are harmful to RFC.

Because the District Court used the wrong legal standard in denying DeGeorge's motion, its decision was "based on an erroneous view of the law." Accordingly, the District Court abused it discretion in denying DeGeorge's motion.

2. The District Court's Factual Findings

DeGeorge also challenges the District Court's factual findings on bad faith and gross negligence. The District Court found that RFC's failure to timely produce the e-mails was neither in bad faith nor grossly negligent because (1) RFC's explanation that it decided to use an outside vendor to retrieve the e-mails rather than turn over the back-up tapes was "neither implausible nor unreasonable" and it was that decision that led to much of the delay; and (2) although RFC's subsequent actions evinced a "purposeful sluggishness," those acts would not have resulted in the unavailability of the evidence absent the "compressed timeline both parties were operating under." DeGeorge argues that these findings were clearly erroneous because (1) there was no explanation as to why e-mails from the back-up tapes were produced for January through September 1998 but not from October through December of 1998; and (2) RFC's actions amounted to more than "purposeful sluggishness."

It appears to us that, in the press of deciding this motion in the midst of trial, the District Court overlooked some evidence that could support a finding that RFC acted in bad faith or was grossly negligent. For example, the District Court did not appear to consider, in finding that RFC's explanation regarding its retention of EED was "neither implausible or unreasonable," the timing of the decision to retain EED. According to RFC's in-house counsel, "RFC retained EED in mid-June 2001," after he had determined that "RFC did not have the internal resources necessary to retrieve [the e-mails from the back-up tapes] in the permitted time frame." RFC first informed DeGeorge that it had

---

5. It appears that the District Court did not consider whether RFC's "purposefully sluggish" acts were grossly negligent or taken in bad faith, because it had already decided that those acts did not cause RFC's failure to timely produce the e-mails. Rather, the District Court found that the reason RFC did not produce the e-mails was that it hired a vendor that was unable to retrieve them.

been unable to retrieve e-mails from the back-up tapes in early July 2001—weeks after it retained EED. When DeGeorge brought the issue to the attention of Magistrate Judge Margolis at the July 12, 2001 conference, RFC told both the Magistrate Judge and DeGeorge that it would seek a vendor's assistance in retrieving the e-mails. In its September 19, 2001 brief to the District Court opposing DeGeorge's motion for sanctions, RFC stated that it "formally" retained EED on July 14, 2001, and it attached a contract between RFC and EED purportedly executed on that date as exhibit 3 to that brief.

This evidence raises a number of questions. For example, if RFC determined in mid-June that it lacked the resources to retrieve the e-mails and therefore retained EED to assist it in the task at that time, its early July 2001 statement to DeGeorge that it was unable to retrieve e-mails was presumably based not only on its own inability to retrieve the e-mails, but also on its inability to retrieve the e-mails with the assistance of EED. If so, RFC's decision to continue to use EED's services in an effort to retrieve the e-mails may not have been reasonable. If, on the other hand, RFC did not obtain EED's assistance before it told De-George in early July that it had been unable to retrieve e-mails from the back-up tapes, it should explain (1) why it delayed telling DeGeorge of its inability to retrieve messages until weeks after its in-house lawyer determined that it could not do so, and (2) why it failed to obtain outside assistance as soon as it determined it could not retrieve e-mails on its own.

In a similar vein, it is unclear whether the District Court considered the reasonableness of RFC's continued reliance on EED throughout months of apparently fruitless attempts to retrieve the critical e-mails, in light of the ability of DeGeorge's vendor to identify and begin to retrieve those e-mails in just four days. The explanation for this apparent discrepancy in competence offered by EED Project Manager Christopher Mashburn—namely, that DeGeorge's vendor had a "head start" because of technical information supplied by RFC—is thoroughly unconvincing. The "technical information" RFC supplied DeGeorge in response to DeGeorge's questions consisted merely of the identification of the software used, the identification of the type and basic parameters of the tapes, and the fact that the tapes included back-ups from both servers and workstations. This basic information should have been readily available to EED from RFC's technical personnel, and, accordingly, there is no reason to believe that DeGeorge's vendor had any more of a "head start" than EED had.

The record also contains a number of at least careless, if not intentionally misleading, statements by RFC both to DeGeorge and to the District Court regarding the effort to retrieve the e-mails, the character of which statements may not have been fully apprehended by the District Court. For example, in light of the sworn statement by RFC's in-house counsel that "RFC retained EED in mid-June," RFC's statement at the July 12, 2001 conference to the effect that it intended to hire a vendor, coupled with its failure to inform the Magistrate Judge that it had already "retained" that vendor weeks earlier and its careful use of the word "formally" to describe its purported "retention" of EED in July 2001, suggests a deliberate attempt to mislead both DeGeorge and the District Court. Similarly, RFC's counsel told the District Court during argument on DeGeorge's motion for sanctions that it had produced back-up tapes through early 1999, when in fact it had produced only back-up tapes through December 1998.

In addition to our doubts over whether the District Court fully considered all of the evidence, we are uncertain whether the District Court appreciated that as a discovery deadline or trial date draws near, discovery conduct that might have been considered "merely" discourteous at an earlier point in the litigation may well breach a party's duties to its opponent and to the court. In the circumstances presented here—i.e., trial was imminent and RFC had repeatedly missed deadlines to produce the e-mails—RFC was under an obligation to be as cooperative as possible. Viewed in that light, RFC's "purposefully sluggish" acts—particularly its as-yet-unexplained refusal to answer basic technical questions about the tape until prompted to do so by the District Court—may well have constituted sanctionable misconduct in their own right.

Despite these doubts, we need not and do not decide whether the District Court's factual findings were clearly erroneous, because the District Court will have to reevaluate those findings in the context of the proper legal standard.

C. Our Instructions on Remand

* * * DeGeorge should be given an opportunity to renew its motion for sanctions, with the benefit of discovery—including, but not necessarily limited to, reexamination of the back-up tapes and appropriate depositions of RFC's affiants—and, if appropriate, an evidentiary hearing before the District Court. Upon consideration of any such motion, the District Court should vacate the judgment and order a new trial if DeGeorge establishes that RFC acted with a sufficiently culpable state of mind (as described above) and that DeGeorge was prejudiced by the failure to produce the e-mails. Presumably, DeGeorge would attempt to establish prejudice by pointing to specific e-mails that it would have used at trial; if so, the District Court should consider the likelihood that the newly produced e-mails would have affected the jury's verdict, in light of all of the other evidence adduced at trial.

If the District Court finds that RFC acted with a culpable state of mind, but that DeGeorge was not prejudiced, it should consider whether lesser sanctions, including, but not limited to, awarding DeGeorge the costs of its motion for sanctions and this appeal, are warranted. Moreover, although it is now our holding that, absent a showing of prejudice, the jury's verdict should not be disturbed, the District Court should also consider whether, as a sanction for discovery abuse, RFC should also forfeit post-judgment interest for the time period from the date of the entry of judgment until the entry of the District Court's decision on remand. Finally, if the District Court concludes that RFC's failure to timely produce the e-mails was not caused by acts taken with "a culpable state of mind," it should separately consider whether RFC's acts of "purposeful sluggishness" nevertheless warrant the imposition of sanctions. District courts should not countenance "purposeful sluggishness" in discovery on the part of parties or attorneys and should be prepared to impose sanctions when they encounter it.

III.   Conclusion

In sum, we hold that:

(1) where, as here, the nature of the alleged breach of a discovery obligation is the non-production of evidence, a District Court has broad discretion in fashioning an appropriate sanction, including the discretion to delay the start of a trial (at the expense of the party that breached its obligation), to declare a mistrial if trial has already commenced, or to proceed with a trial with an adverse inference instruction;

(2) discovery sanctions, including an adverse inference instruction, may be imposed upon a party that has breached a discovery obligation not only through bad faith or gross negligence, but also through ordinary negligence;

(3) a judge's finding that a party acted with gross negligence or in bad faith with respect to discovery obligations is ordinarily sufficient to support a finding that the missing or destroyed evidence would have been harmful to that party, even if the destruction or unavailability of the evidence was not caused by the acts constituting bad faith or gross negligence; and

(4) in the instant case, the District Court applied the wrong standard in deciding DeGeorge's motion for sanctions.

Accordingly, we vacate the order of the District Court denying DeGeorge's motion for sanctions and remand with instructions to permit DeGeorge to renew its motion for discovery sanctions.

STEVENSON v. UNION PACIFIC RR CO.

354 F.3d 739 (8th Cir. 2004)

HANSEN, CIRCUIT JUDGE

This case arises out of a car-train grade crossing accident in which Frank Stevenson was injured and his wife was killed. In this diversity lawsuit against the Union Pacific Railroad Company ("Union Pacific" or "the Railroad"), a jury awarded damages to Mr. Stevenson and Rebecca Harshberger as Administratrix of Mary Stevenson's estate on claims of negligence. * * *

I.

On November 6, 1998, a Union Pacific train struck the Stevensons' vehicle as it crossed the tracks on Highway 364 in Vanndale, Arkansas. Mrs. Stevenson died as a result of the collision, and Mr. Stevenson suffered severe injuries and has no memory of the accident. Mr. Stevenson and the administratrix of his wife's estate filed this action alleging that the accident was caused by Union Pacific's negligence. Later, they amended their complaint to include additional negligence claims and to add Operation Lifesaver, Inc. ("Operation Lifesaver") as a defendant, asserting that it made negligent and fraudulent misrepresentations concerning the safety of the crossing. The district court granted partial summary judgment, dismissing several negligence claims, including allegations concerning the speed of the train. The district court also granted Operation Lifesaver's motion to dismiss for failure to state a claim.

The plaintiffs filed a motion for sanctions on the ground that Union Pacific had destroyed evidence, namely, a voice tape of conversations between the train crew and dispatch at the time of the accident and track maintenance records from before the accident. Union Pacific argued that sanctions were not justified because it destroyed the documents in good faith pursuant to its routine document retention policies. The district court granted the motion following a three-day evidentiary hearing. The district court imposed sanctions of an adverse inference instruction regarding the destroyed evidence and an award of costs and attorneys' fees incurred as a result of the spoliation of evidence.

Prior to trial, the plaintiffs filed a motion in limine, seeking to prohibit Union Pacific from calling witnesses to explain that it destroyed the tape and track maintenance records pursuant to its routine document retention policies. The district court granted the motion and, at the outset of trial, orally instructed the jury that the voice tape and track inspection records "were destroyed by the railroad and ... should have been preserved," and that the jurors "may, but are not required to, assume that the contents of the voice tapes and track inspection records would have been adverse, or detrimental, to the defendant." The district court thus permitted the plaintiffs to immediately reference the destroyed material and the fact that Union Pacific willfully destroyed it, but denied Union Pacific any opportunity to offer its routine document retention policy as an innocent explanation for its destruction of the evidence.

* * * At the close of trial, over Union Pacific's renewed objection, the district court repeated the spoliation instruction to the jury: "You may, but are not required to, assume that the contents of the voice tape and track inspection records would have been adverse, or detrimental, to the defendant." * * *

The jury returned a general verdict in favor of the plaintiffs, awarding Mr. Stevenson $2,000,000 in damages and awarding the estate

$10,000 for funeral and ambulance expenses. The district court entered judgment on these amounts and also awarded the plaintiffs $164,410.25 in costs and attorneys' fees on the sanctions order. Union Pacific appeals, asserting that * * * the district court abused its discretion in giving the adverse inference instruction, and that the district court abused its discretion by ordering attorneys' fees as sanctions. * * *

II

* * *

B. Sanctions

Both prior to the filing of the lawsuit and during its pendency, Union Pacific destroyed two types of evidence—the tape of any recorded voice radio communications between the train crew and dispatchers on the date of the accident and all track maintenance records close in time to the accident. The district court imposed sanctions for this conduct under its inherent power by giving an adverse inference instruction, refusing to permit testimony to rebut the adverse inference, and imposing an award of attorneys' fees.

"We review a district court's imposition of sanctions under its inherent power for an abuse of discretion." *Dillon v. Nissan Motor Co.,* 986 F.2d 263, 267 (8th Cir. 1993). A court's inherent power includes the discretionary "ability to fashion an appropriate sanction for conduct which abuses the judicial process." Our interpretation of Supreme Court authority concerning a court's inherent power to sanction counsels that a finding of bad faith is not always necessary to the court's exercise of its inherent power to impose sanctions. The Union Pacific argues that the sanctions were an abuse of discretion because it did not engage in bad faith conduct by destroying evidence pursuant to document retention policies. We will consider the extent to which a finding of bad faith is necessary separately below with regard to each type of sanction employed. * * *

1. The Adverse Inference Instruction

* * *

The district court imposed this sanction of an adverse inference instruction after concluding that Union Pacific destroyed the voice tape in bad faith, and that Union Pacific destroyed the track maintenance records in circumstances where it "knew or should have known that the documents would become material" and "should have preserved them." The district court reached these conclusions after discussing * * * (1) whether the record retention policy is reasonable considering the facts and circumstances surrounding those documents, (2) whether lawsuits or complaints have been filed frequently concerning the type of records at issue, and (3) whether the document retention policy was instituted in bad faith.

* * * We have never approved of giving an adverse inference instruction on the basis of prelitigation destruction of evidence through a routine document retention policy on the basis of negligence alone. Where a routine document retention policy has been followed in this context, we now clarify that there must be some indication of an intent to destroy the evidence for the purpose of obstructing or suppressing the truth in order to impose the sanction of an adverse inference instruction.

The facts here are as follows. The accident occurred on November 6, 1998. The Stevensons filed this lawsuit on September 20, 1999, and mailed their requests for production of the voice tape on October 25, 1999. By that time, Union Pacific had long since destroyed the voice tape from the November 6, 1998, accident by recording over it in accordance with the company's routine procedure of keeping voice tapes for 90 days and then reusing the tapes. The district court found that although Union Pacific's voice tape retention policy was not unreasonable or instituted in bad faith, it was unreasonable and amounted to bad faith conduct for Union Pacific to adhere to the principle in the circumstances of this case.

In support of its bad faith determination, the district court found that Union Pacific had been involved in many grade crossing collisions and knew that the taped conversations would be relevant in any potential litigation regarding an accident that resulted in death and serious injury. * * * The district court listened to available samples of this type of voice tape and found that they generally contain evidence that is discoverable and useful in developing a case. Additionally, the district court found that Union Pacific had preserved such tapes in cases where it was helpful to Union Pacific's position. The district court also found that the plaintiffs were prejudiced by the destruction of this tape because there are no other records of comments between the train crew and dispatch contemporaneous to the accident. The district court thus held that sanctions were justified and that an adverse inference instruction was an appropriate sanction for the destruction of the voice tape.

After considering the record and the particular circumstances of this case, we conclude that, while this case tests the limits of what we are able to uphold as a bad faith determination, the district court did not abuse its discretion by sanctioning Union Pacific's prelitigation conduct of destroying the voice tape. The district court's bad faith determination is supported by Union Pacific's act of destroying the voice tape pursuant to its routine policy in circumstances where Union Pacific had general knowledge that such tapes would be important to any litigation over an accident that resulted in serious injury or death, and its knowledge that litigation is frequent when there has been an accident involving death or serious injury. While these are quite general considerations, an important factor here is that a voice tape that is the only contemporaneous recording of conversations at the time of the accident will always be highly relevant to potential litigation over the accident. We conclude that this weighs heavier in this case than the lack of actual knowledge that litigation was imminent at the time of the destruction. Additionally, the record indicates that Union Pacific made an immediate effort to preserve other types of evidence but not the voice tape, and the district court noted that Union Pacific was careful to preserve a voice tape in other cases where the tape proved to be beneficial to Union Pacific. The prelitigation destruction of the voice tape in this combination of circumstances, though done pursuant to a routine retention policy, creates a sufficiently strong inference of an intent to destroy it for the purpose of suppressing evidence of the facts surrounding the operation of the train at the time of the accident.

There must be a finding of prejudice to the opposing party before imposing a sanction for destruction of evidence. The requisite element of prejudice is satisfied by the nature of the evidence destroyed in this case. While there is no indication that the voice tape [that was] destroyed contained evidence that could be classified as a smoking-gun, the very fact that it is the only recording of conversations between the engineer and dispatch[er] contemporaneous with the accident renders its loss prejudicial to the plaintiffs. We find no abuse of discretion in the district court's decision to sanction the Railroad through an adverse inference instruction for its prelitigation destruction of the voice tape.

As to the track maintenance inspection records, the Union Pacific demonstrated that its policy is to destroy them after one year and replace them with the new inspection records. These records generally note defects that appear at a crossing on the day of its inspection and list the name of the person who inspected the track on that particular day, but they would not show the exact condition of the tracks on the day of the accident. The Stevensons requested the production of track maintenance records for two years prior to the accident. Union Pacific made no effort to preserve these documents from its routine document destruction policy.

The district court said it was not persuaded that the document retention policy was instituted in bad faith, but "[a]s with the voice tape, however, [Union Pacific] knew or should have known that the documents would become material and should have preserved them." The "knew or should have known" language indicates a negligence standard, and as noted earlier, we have never approved of giving an adverse inference instruction on the basis of negligence alone. Even if the district court intended its findings to be the equivalent of a bad faith determination, we conclude that the findings regarding the prelitigation destruction of track maintenance records do not amount to a showing of bad faith and that the district court abused its discretion in giving the adverse inference instruction in relation to the destruction of all track maintenance records up to two years prior to the accident.

There is no showing here that Union Pacific knew that litigation was imminent when, prior to any litigation, it destroyed track maintenance records from up to two years prior to the accident pursuant to its document retention policy. Additionally, maintenance records would only be relevant to potential litigation to the extent that they were relatively close in time to the accident and defective track maintenance was alleged to be the cause of the accident. Even then, track maintenance records are of limited use. While they may reveal defects in the track that existed at the time of the last inspection, they do not show the exact condition of the track at the time of the collision. The district court weighed heavily the fact that the Union Pacific knew that litigation is possible when there has been a serious accident but did not consider whether, when the prelitigation destruction was occurring, there had been any notice in this case of potential litigation or that the track maintenance would be an issue or an alleged cause of the accident. It appears that Union Pacific was not on notice that the track maintenance records should be preserved until it received the October 1999 request for production of documents, and the condition of the track was not formally put into issue until the second amendment to the complaint in May 2000. Thus, any bad faith determination regarding the prelitigation destruction of the track maintenance records is not supported by the record, and any adverse inference instruction based on any prelitigation destruction of track maintenance records would have been given in error.

Union Pacific continued destroying track maintenance records after this lawsuit was initiated. We find no abuse of discretion in the district court's decision to impose sanctions for the destruction of track maintenance records after the commencement of litigation and the filing of the plaintiffs' request for production of documents on October 25, 1999. At the time the plaintiffs requested the production of the track maintenance records, the records from October and November 1998 (closest in time to the accident and thus most relevant) would have been available, but Union Pacific made no effort to preserve them. Although Union Pacific's counsel did not send the discovery request to the claims agent, Mr. Fuller, until November 17, 1999, even then the records from November 1998 would have been available and could have been preserved, but they were not.

At the sanctions hearing, Union Pacific claimed innocence under its routine document retention policy and a lack of knowledge because the proper agents did not know that the records were relevant or where they were kept. * * * The district court did not credit the Railroad's claimed lack of knowledge because of its specific knowledge of and participation in this litigation, the actual notice of the document request, and the relevance of track maintenance documents to the pending litigation because they could have revealed the Railroad's extent of knowledge about the track conditions at the time of the accident. After the specific document request for track maintenance records, Union Pacific cannot rely on its routine document retention policy as a shield. Sanctioning the ongoing destruction of records during litigation and discovery by imposing an adverse inference instruction is supported by either the court's inherent power or Rule 37 of the Federal Rules of Civil Procedure, even absent an explicit bad faith finding, and we conclude that the giving of an adverse inference instruction in these circumstances is not an abuse of discretion.

2. Refusal to Allow Rebuttal

Union Pacific argues that even if the district court did not abuse its discretion by giving the adverse inference instruction as a sanction for the destruction of evidence in this case, the district court abused its discretion by not permitting it to offer a reasonable rebuttal to the inference. We agree.

* * * A permissive inference is subject to reasonable rebuttal. *See Lamarca v. United States,* 31 F.Supp.2d 110, 128 (E.D.N.Y. 1999) ("An adverse inference that the missing evidence is harmful can be rebutted by an adequate explanation of the reason for non-production."). While the district court need not permit a complete retrial of the sanctions hearing during trial, unfair prejudice should be avoided by permitting the defendant to put on some evidence of its document retention policy and how it affected the destruction of the requested records as an innocent explanation for its conduct. Absent this opportunity, the jury is deprived of sufficient information on which to base a rational decision of whether to apply the adverse inference, and an otherwise permissive inference easily becomes an irrebuttable presumption.

The district court's timing of the instruction in this case also contributes to our finding of unfair prejudice by the exclusion of reasonable rebuttal testimony. At the very outset of trial, the district court informed the jury that the Railroad had destroyed evidence that should have been preserved, and the plaintiffs referred to this destruction throughout the trial. We see no need to unduly emphasize the adverse inference at the outset of trial, especially where there is no finding that the evidence destroyed was crucial to the case. No doubt the evidence destroyed was relevant and its destruction prejudiced the plaintiffs' discovery efforts, but in previous cases where we have sustained a sanction of precluding evidence completely or settling a disputed matter of fact (thus permitting no rebuttal), the offending party had destroyed the one piece of crucial physical evidence in the case. No such finding exists here.

* * *

COMMENTARY

a. What Degree of Culpable Conduct Is Required to Warrant Sanctions for Spoliation?

Culpable conduct falls along a sliding scale as follows: mere negligence, gross negligence, recklessness, bad faith, and intentional misconduct. Most courts consider two major factors when determining whether to impose sanctions and, if so, what sanctions are most appropriate. The first factor is the degree of culpability, and the second is prejudice to the innocent party.[1] Other factors include the degree of interference with the judicial process, whether a lesser sanction will remedy the harm, whether sanctions are necessary to deter similar conduct, and whether sanctions will unfairly punish an innocent party for spoliation committed by an attorney.

Just as culpable conduct is defined along a sliding scale, so is the range of sanctions that a court can impose. Those sanctions (from least to most severe) include: fines,[2] cost-shifting, burden shifting, preclusion of evidence, adverse inferences,[3] and default judgments. Most courts are careful to impose the least severe sanctions commensurate with the wrongdoing.

A sharp split of authority exists between the Eighth Circuit, which requires "a finding of intentional destruction indicating a desire to suppress the truth," and the Second Circuit, in which mere negligence will meet the culpability standard. As discussed below, courts in other circuits line up on various points on the culpability spectrum.

"Bad faith," which appears to be synonymous with intent, is uniformly required to be found before a sanction can be imposed in the Fifth, Seventh, and Tenth Circuits.[4] However, the increasing prevalence and importance of e-discovery has led to a clear trend away from the "mens rea" or "scienter" approach of these circuits.

Recent district court decisions in the Fourth, Ninth, Eleventh, and D.C. Circuits have directly followed or have leaned toward the Second Circuit's view that negligence is sufficient to establish culpability for spoliation. For example, Ninth Circuit decisions addressing dismissal as a sanction for spoliation have required a finding of "willfulness, fault, or bad faith."[5] However, at least one district court has found gross negligence to be sufficient for an adverse inference instruction.[6] More recent-

---

1. *See* Shira A. Scheindlin & Kanchana Wangkeo, *Electronic Discovery Sanctions in the Twenty–First Century*, 11 Mich. Telecomm. & Tech. L. Rev. 71, 94 (2004).

2. *See United States v. Philip Morris USA, Inc.*, 327 F. Supp. 2d 21 (D.D.C. 2004) (sanction of $2.75 million for spoliation).

3. *See MOSAID Techs. Inc. v. Samsung*, 348 F. Supp. 2d 332 (D.N.J. 2004) (imposing an adverse inference instruction and a $566,839.97 fine, *inter alia*, for failure to turn-off the auto-delete function of Samsung's e-mail system).

4. *See, e.g., Condrey v. Suntrust Bank of Georgia*, 431 F.3d 191, 203 (5th Cir. 2005) ("The Fifth Circuit permits an adverse inference against the destroyer of evidence only upon a showing of 'bad faith' or 'bad conduct.' "); *United States v. Esposito*, 771 F.2d 283, 286 (7th Cir. 1985) ("destruction must have been in bad faith"); *Aramburu v. Boeing Co.*, 112 F.3d 1398, 1407 (10th Cir. 1997) (requiring bad faith before imposing adverse inference); *Bryant v. Nicholson*, No. 07 Civ. 0183, 2008 WL 465270 at *5 (N.D. Tex. Feb. 21, 2008) (bad faith required for spoliation); *Rodgers v. Lowe's Home Ctrs., Inc.*, No. 05 Civ. 0502, 2007 WL 257714, at *5 (N.D. Ill. Jan. 30, 2007) ("mere negligence is not enough, for it does not sustain the inference of consciousness of a weak case") (quotation omitted).

5. *See Leon v. IDX Sys. Corp.*, 464 F.3d 951, 958 (9th Cir. 2006); *Anheuser-Busch, Inc. v. Natural Beverage Distribs.*, 69 F.3d 337, 348 (9th Cir. 1995).

6. *See UMG Recordings, Inc. v. Hummer Winblad Venture Partners (In re Napster, Inc. Copyright Litig.)*, 462 F. Supp. 2d 1060, 1078 (N.D. Cal. 2006).

ly, that same court expressly adopted the Second Circuit's rule that negligence is sufficient to satisfy the culpability factor for spoliation.[7]

Other district courts in the Third, Fourth, and Eleventh Circuits have held that negligence is sufficient to establish culpability.[8] The same is true of a district court for the District of Columbia, which also embraced Second Circuit precedent.[9]

Perhaps the most distinctive approach to culpability is that of the First Circuit, which leaves the entire question of a spoliation finding to the factfinder with no required finding of any particular degree of culpability. Rather, the proponent of an adverse inference need only show that its opponent "knew of (a) the claim (that is, the litigation or the potential for litigation), and (b) the document's potential relevance to that claim," and "a trier of fact may (but need not) infer from a party's obliteration of a document relevant to a litigated issue that the contents of the document were unfavorable to that party."[10]

b. WHAT STEPS MUST BE TAKEN TO AVOID A FINDING OF NEGLIGENCE?

No magic software or approved methodology exists that will be certain to eliminate any risk of the negligent loss of, or failure to produce, relevant evidence. However, attorneys and their clients must keep abreast of advances in technology affecting preservation, search, and retrieval methods.

3. Prejudice

GREYHOUND LINES, INC. v. WADE

485 F.3d 1032 (8th Cir. 2007)

Benton, Circuit Judge

Greyhound Lines, Inc. sued Robert N. Wade and Archway Cookies, LLC (collectively Archway). In August 2000, an Archway truck driven by Wade rear-ended a Greyhound bus operated by Debra Johnson on Interstate 80 in Nebraska. After a bench trial, the district court appor-

---

7. *See World Courier v. Barone*, No. 06 Civ. 3072, 2007 WL 1119196, at *2 (N.D. Cal. Apr. 16, 2007) ("[T]he 'mental culpability' factor is satisfied where the party acted 'knowingly or ... negligently.' ") (*quoting Residential Funding*, 306 F.3d at 108). *Accord Housing Rts. Ctr. v. Sterling*, No. 03 Civ. 859, 2005 WL 3320739, at *7–8 (C.D. Cal. Mar. 2, 2005) (following *Residential Funding*).

8. *See, e.g., Brown v. Chertoff*, 563 F. Supp. 2d 1372, 1381 (S.D. Ga. 2008) (negligence is enough to find spoliation); *CentiMark Corp. v. Pegnato & Pegnato Roof Mgmt.*, No. 05 Civ. 708, 2008 WL 1995305, at *10 (W.D. Pa. May 6, 2008) ("[W]hile it is not entirely clear whether the Court of Appeals for the Third Circuit ... require[s] at least some bad faith, several courts within the Third Circuit have found that it does not, and have found that even negligent destruction of evidence is sufficient to give rise to the spoliation inference."); *Samsung Elec. Co. v. Rambus Inc.*, 439 F. Supp. 2d 524, 540 (E.D. Va. 2006), *rev'd on other grounds*, 523 F.3d 1374 (Fed. Cir. 2008) ("both negligent and willful destruction can constitute spoliation"); *Teague v. Target Corp.*, No. 06 Civ. 191, 2007 WL 1041191, at *2 (W.D.N.C. Apr. 4, 2007) (" 'culpable state of mind' could include ... ordinary negligence.").

9. *See Mazloum v. D.C. Metro. Police Dep't*, 530 F. Supp. 2d 282, 293 (D.D.C. 2008) (following *Residential Funding*).

10. *Testa v. Wal–Mart Stores, Inc.*, 144 F.3d 173, 177 (1st Cir. 1998).

tioned fault at 85 percent to Archway and 15 percent to Greyhound. Archway appeals, asserting the court erred in refusing sanctions * * *.

I.

At the time of the collision, due to mechanical failure, the Greyhound bus was traveling below the posted minimum speed, in the right lane, hazard lights flashing, as the driver tried to reach the nearest off-ramp. The bus had an electronic control module (ECM) that stored information, including speed, starts, stops, and the time and type of a mechanical failure. Ten days after the accident, Greyhound removed the ECM and retrieved the information. The ECM indicated that a speed-sensor failure caused the bus's slow speed. Greyhound then sent the ECM to the engine manufacturer, who erased the information before this case was filed. Archway requested sanctions against Greyhound for spoliation of evidence, and misleading and false discovery responses. The district court denied Archway's motions.

This court reviews the imposition of sanctions for an abuse of discretion. The district court, familiar with the case and counsel, receives substantial deference in determining sanctions. If the court bases its ruling on "an erroneous view of the law or on a clearly erroneous assessment of the evidence," the court abuses its discretion.

Archway contends that Greyhound deserves sanctions for destroying the ECM data and giving evasive and misleading responses in discovery. According to Archway, Greyhound had a duty to preserve the ECM data because litigation was likely, and the ECM data detailed the bus's operation before the accident. Archway believes that by failing to retain the ECM data, Greyhound prevented identifying when and where the bus first had problems. As to the discovery responses, Archway alleges that Greyhound's initial interrogatory responses identified a "vapor lock" as the mechanical impairment, although Greyhound knew it was a speed-sensor failure. Archway claims that three months before trial, it learned about the ECM data and the speed-sensor failure.

A spoliation-of-evidence sanction requires "a finding of intentional destruction indicating a desire to suppress the truth." "Intent is rarely proved by direct evidence, and a district court has substantial leeway to determine intent through consideration of circumstantial evidence, witness credibility, motives of the witnesses in a particular case, and other factors."

Before, during and after trial, the district court reviewed Archway's spoliation claims, each time denying sanctions. Archway argues that because litigation was likely, Greyhound had a duty to preserve the ECM data. The ultimate focus for imposing sanctions for spoliation of evidence is the intentional destruction of evidence indicating a desire to suppress the truth, not the prospect of litigation. Thus, the district court did not err in finding spoliation had not occurred. Additionally, although some material was not preserved, the ECM data identified the specific mechanical defect that slowed the bus, and several bus passengers testified how the bus acted before the collision. "There must be a finding of prejudice to the opposing party before imposing a sanction for destruction of evidence"

As to the discovery responses, the district court found that Greyhound's answers were responsive and that Archway was not prejudiced by untimely disclosure. Because Archway received responsive answers months before trial, the district court properly refused discovery sanctions.

The district court did not base its determinations on an erroneous view of the law or the evidence, and did not abuse its discretion by refusing sanctions against Greyhound.

* * *

ZUBULAKE v. UBS WARBURG LLC
"ZUBULAKE V"

229 F.R.D. 422 (S.D.N.Y. 2004)

SCHEINDLIN, DISTRICT JUDGE

[The facts and background of this case are fully set forth in Chapter II.B, *supra*. Judge Scheindlin found as follows:]

Early on in this litigation, UBS's counsel—both in-house and outside—instructed UBS personnel to retain relevant electronic information. Notwithstanding these instructions, certain UBS employees deleted relevant e-mails. Other employees never produced relevant information to counsel. As a result, many discoverable e-mails were not produced to Zubulake until recently, even though they were responsive to a document request propounded on June 3, 2002. In addition, a number of e-mails responsive to that document request were deleted and have been lost altogether.

Counsel, in turn, failed to request retained information from one key employee and to give the litigation hold instructions to another. They also failed to adequately communicate with another employee about how she maintained her computer files. Counsel also failed to safeguard backup tapes that might have contained some of the deleted e-mails, and which would have mitigated the damage done by UBS's destruction of those e-mails.

* * *

Second, Zubulake argues that the e-mails that *were* produced, albeit late, "are brand new and very significant to Ms. Zubulake's retaliation claim and would have affected [her] examination of every witness . . . in this case." Likewise, Zubulake claims, with respect to the newly produced e-mails from Kim and Tong's active files, that UBS's "failure to produce these e-mails in a timely fashion precluded [her] from questioning any witness about them." These arguments stand unrebutted and are therefore adopted in full by the Court. Accordingly, UBS is ordered to pay the costs of any depositions or re-depositions required by the late production.

Third, UBS is ordered to pay the costs of this motion.[102]

[The Court concluded as follows:]

UBS failed to preserve relevant e-mails, even after receiving adequate warnings from counsel, resulting in the production of some relevant e-mails almost two years after they were initially requested, and resulting in the complete destruction of others. For that reason, Zubulake's motion is granted and sanctions are warranted. UBS is ordered to:

1. Pay for the re-deposition of relevant UBS personnel, limited to the subject of the newly-discovered e-mails;

2. Restore and produce relevant documents from Varsano's August 2001 backup tape;

3. Pay for the re-deposition of Varsano and Tong, limited to the new material produced from Varsano's August 2001 backup tape; and

4. Pay all "reasonable expenses, including attorney's fees," incurred by Zubulake in connection with the making of this motion.

In addition, I will give the following instruction to the jury that hears this case:

You have heard that UBS failed to produce some of the e-mails sent or received by UBS personnel in August and September 2001. Plaintiff has argued that this evidence was in defendants' control and would have proven facts material to the matter in controversy.

If you find that UBS could have produced this evidence, and that the evidence was within its control, and that the evidence would have been material in deciding facts in dispute in this case, you are permitted, but not required, to infer that the evidence would have been unfavorable to UBS.

In deciding whether to draw this inference, you should consider whether the evidence not produced would merely have duplicated other evidence already before you. You may also consider whether you are satisfied that UBS's failure to produce this information was reasonable. Again, any inference you decide to draw should be based on all of the facts and circumstances in this case.

* * *

---

102. Fed. R. Civ. P. 37(b)(2).

COMMENTARY

Prejudice or harm from spoliation occurs when the requesting party is unable to obtain production of relevant information that would have helped its case because the information was destroyed in violation of a legal duty to preserve. However, it is self-evident that it can be challenging at best to demonstrate the relevance of information that is no longer available to be examined because it was destroyed.

In some situations, it may be possible to demonstrate the prejudicial effect of spoliation by means of information that was preserved and produced in discovery and that in one way or another shows the likely relevance and impact of the information that was destroyed. In other cases, it may be possible to extract the lost information from other sources, albeit at great expense and with the aid of computer forensics; for example, where a witness deleted e-mails from a laptop, they may be recoverable by forensic examination of the computer's hard drive. Courts may appoint an independent expert to ensure that all steps are being taken to recover missing information. For example, in a case where the defendant failed to comply with a preservation order and overwrote certain backup tapes subject to the order, the court recognized that "[h]ow much has been lost, and the extent of prejudice to the plaintiffs from the loss cannot be determined at this time" and appointed an independent expert to determine whether appropriate efforts were underway to retrieve the e-mail lost from the destroyed backup tapes.[11]

In many situations, however, it is not possible either to determine the likely contents of the destroyed information or extract it from another source through no fault of the requesting party. Accordingly, courts will presume prejudice under certain circumstances. For example, where the culpability of the spoliator is egregious, prejudice is presumed. "Some misconduct may prove to be so 'contumacious' that the entry of a default judgment is warranted to preserve the integrity of the judicial process."[12]

Courts have recognized the inherent problem or at least the irony in requiring a party to show prejudice from spoliation when the opposing party has destroyed the means of doing so. To require too specific a showing would reward the spoliator. Thus, courts have often lowered the bar, for example, where "[t]he substantial and complete nature of the destruction of the evidence contained in the recorded telephone conversations and hard drives destroyed . . . justifies a finding of prejudice."[13]

---

   11. *Keir v. UnumProvident Corp.*, No. 02 Civ. 8781, 2003 WL 21997747, at *13 (S.D.N.Y. Aug. 22, 2003).

   12. *Danis v. USN Commc'ns, Inc.*, No. 98 C 7482, 2000 WL 1694325, at *34 (N.D. Ill. Oct. 23, 2000) (quoting *Barnhill v. United States*, 11 F.3d 1360, 1368 (7th Cir. 1993)).

   13. *E*TRADE Secs., LLC v. Deutsche Bank AG*, 230 F.R.D. 582, 592 (D. Minn. 2005).

Generally, where prejudice is demonstrated or presumed, courts will look to remedial sanctions to put the requesting party back in the position it would have been in had the spoliation not occurred. The degree of prejudice or harm will always impact the nature and degree of sanctions. The more severe the prejudice, the more likely it will be that the court will impose a severe sanction such as an adverse inference. Where the prejudice is very great, the assessment of the spoliator's culpability becomes less important. It is fair to say that the appropriate sanction turns on the facts of each case, both with respect to culpability and prejudice.

> Our case-by-case approach to the failure to produce relevant evidence seems to be working. Such failures occur along the continuum of fault ranging from innocence through the degrees of negligence to intentionality.... [I]t makes little sense to confine promotion of [the remedial purpose of spoliation sanctions] to cases involving only outrageous culpability, where the party victimized by the spoliation is prejudiced irrespective of whether the spoliator acted with intent or gross negligence.[14]

B.   RULE 37(e)—GOOD FAITH OPERATION OF AN ELECTRONIC INFORMATION SYSTEM

DOE v. NORWALK COMMUNITY COLLEGE

248 F.R.D. 372 (D.Conn. 2007)

HALL, DISTRICT JUDGE

I.   INTRODUCTION

The plaintiff, Jane Doe, brings this action against Norwalk Community College ("NCC") and the Board of Trustees, Connecticut Community Colleges ("Board") (collectively, the "defendants"), as well as against Ronald Masi in his individual capacity. In her Amended Complaint Doe alleges violations of Title IX of the Education Amendments of 1972, 20 U.S.C. §§ 1681–1688. Doe also asserts state law claims of negligent retention and supervision and negligent infliction of emotional distress.

Doe has filed a Motion for Sanctions for Discovery Misconduct and Spoliation of Evidence against the college defendants. * * *

II.   FACTS

On November 22, 2004, Doe filed her Complaint initiating this lawsuit * * *. On March 1, 2006, Doe moved to compel the inspection of certain electronic records possessed by NCC, and a hearing was held on the motion before Magistrate Judge Holly Fitzsimmons on April 26, 2006. At the hearing, Dorran Delay of DataTrack Resources, LLC, a

---

14. *Reilly v. Natwest Mkts. Group, Inc.*, 181 F.3d 253, 267–68 (2d Cir. 1999) (internal quotation marks omitted).

forensic computer firm retained by Doe to inspect NCC's computer records, testified regarding his qualifications to perform the inspection. On July 20, 2006, the court granted Doe's Motion to Compel, thereby permitting Delay to perform the inspection.

On August 15 and August 18, 2006, Delay carried out the inspection of certain NCC computers, which he memorialized in memoranda dated September 11 and October 3, 2006. Doe subsequently submitted two affidavits, written by Delay, as part of her Motion for Sanctions. In response to Delay's first affidavit, NCC's Information Technology Technician, Wyatt Bissell, submitted an affidavit as well. Their findings will be discussed below, where relevant.

This court scheduled a hearing on Doe's Motion for Sanctions, to take testimony from the computer experts regarding their results. At the hearing held on June 26, 2007 ("Hearing I"), Delay as well as Bissell were examined by counsel on both sides; additionally, the defendants presented the testimony of Mr. Olsen, the systems manager for Connecticut Community Colleges. On July 5, 2007, the court heard further testimony from Bissell and Delay ("Hearing II"), and also held Oral Argument regarding some of the remaining legal and factual issues involved in this Motion for Sanctions.

III. DISCUSSION

A. Spoliation of Evidence

Doe seeks an adverse evidentiary inference with regard to electronic files which she claims the defendants destroyed. * * * This sanction serves a threefold purpose of (1) deterring parties from destroying evidence; (2) placing the risk of an erroneous evaluation of the content of the destroyed evidence on the party responsible for its destruction; and (3) restoring the party harmed by the loss of evidence helpful to its case to where the party would have been in the absence of spoliation. * * *

A party seeking an adverse inference based on spoliation must establish "(1) that the party having control over the evidence had an obligation to preserve it at the time it was destroyed; (2) that the records were destroyed with a culpable state of mind; and (3) that the destroyed evidence was relevant to the party's claim or defense such that a reasonable trier of fact could find that it would support that claim or defense."

Doe claims that "the hard drives of key witnesses in this case were scrubbed" or "completely wiped of data." Such assertions are based on the conclusions of Delay, who inspected NCC's computer records using special forensic software. Delay explained in his affidavit and at the Hearing that Seaborn's computer had been replaced in December 2004, one month after Doe filed her lawsuit, and that Seaborn's old computer "was totally devoid of data; it appears to have had its data wiped."[3]

Additionally, Delay found the Microsoft Outlook PST files, which house electronic mailboxes, of four individuals had inconsistencies "that indicate that data has been altered, destroyed or filtered." For example, Professor Skeeter's PST file contained no Deleted Items and only one Sent Item and the Inbox and Sent Items contained data starting August 2004, "even though other activity is present starting in 2002." Doe has also presented evidence that the retention policy issued by the State Library, which provides for a two-year retention with respect to electronic correspondence, governs NCC retention, and that this policy was not followed with respect to the hard drives of the computers of faculty members who left the college.

* * *

Bissell * * * testified that, although he was familiar with the State Librarian's document retention policy, NCC did not follow it because, according to him, it did not apply to "normal computer usage" and transitory email messages did not need to be maintained. Additionally, the defendants argue that "evidence discussing Defendant Masi contained in various backup servers as well as computers from NCC faculty and staff were turned over to the plaintiff," thus presenting "powerful evidence" that the defendants did not destroy all emails or documents regarding Masi. The defendants claim that they provided Doe with "approximately six emails" referencing Masi, one of which was written by someone who claims Masi "was always touching me." Although the defendants rely on the fact that this email was written more than three months prior to Doe's filing of her lawsuit, the court finds that because this email postdates the incident with Masi by six months, it does not respond to Doe's argument that certain evidence was destroyed "that would support the plaintiff's claim that NCC had actual notice of Masi's conduct" prior to the incident of which she complained.

1. Duty to Preserve

The court finds that Doe has established the first prong of the adverse inference instruction, that the party having control over the evidence had an obligation to preserve it at the time it was destroyed. Such an obligation to preserve evidence "usually arises when a party has notice that the evidence is relevant to litigation but also on occasion in other circumstances, as for example when a party should have known that the evidence may be relevant to future litigation." In this case, the defendants argue that the duty to preserve did not arise until well after Doe filed her lawsuit in November 2004, perhaps when Doe had indicated her need for the electronic discovery in her Rule 26(f) Report, dated February 18, 2005.

---

3. According to Delay, wiping is a "process that overwrites existing data on the hard drive, making this information unrecoverable." * * *

The court strongly disagrees with the defendants. * * * [T]he court finds that the duty to preserve certainly arose no later than September 2004, when Doe's counsel sent the defendants a demand letter indicating Doe's intention to sue NCC. In fact, the court believes the duty to preserve had arisen by February 13, 2004, when a meeting was held between Dean Fisher, Professor Skeeter and Professor Seaborn regarding the Doe incident, which indicates to the court that, as of that date, NCC was aware of Doe's allegations of sexual assault by Masi. At that time, even if Doe had not yet filed her lawsuit, the defendants should have known that any documents, including e-mails and hard drives, related to Professor Masi could potentially be relevant to future litigation.* * *

"The duty to preserve attached at the time that litigation was reasonably anticipated." *Zubulake*, 220 F.R.D. at 217. At that time, the defendants "must suspend [their] routine document retention/destruction policy and put in place a 'litigation hold' to ensure the preservation of relevant documents." However, NCC did not do so. Indeed, the defendants admit that they "scrubbed" Masi's hard drive "pursuant to normal NCC practice." Even if the court assumes the duty to preserve generally arose in September 2004, it finds that the defendants should not have "scrubbed" Masi's computer after his resignation because of the state criminal investigation against him.

* * *

With respect to the destruction of electronic data, the defendants cite to newly-promulgated Rule 37(e) of the Federal Rules of Civil Procedure, which states: "Absent exceptional circumstances, a court may not impose sanctions under these rules on a party for failing to provide electronically stored information lost as a result of the routine, good-faith operation of an electronic information system." Fed.R.Civ.P. 37(e). However, the Commentary to that Rule indicates that, "[w]hen a party is under a duty to preserve information because of pending or reasonably anticipated litigation, intervention in the routine operation of an information system is one aspect of what is often called a 'litigation hold.'" *Id.* at Advisory Committee Notes to 2006 Amendment. Thus, in order to take advantage of the good faith exception, a party needs to act affirmatively to prevent the system from destroying or altering information, even if such destruction would occur in the regular course of business. Because the defendants failed to suspend it at any time, the court finds that the defendants cannot take advantage of Rule 37(e)'s good faith exception.

In addition, as the Commentary to Rule 37(e) indicates, the Rule only applies to information lost "due to the 'routine operation of an electronic information system'—the ways in which such systems are generally designed, programmed, and implemented to meet the party's technical and business needs." This Rule therefore appears to require a routine system in order to take advantage of the good faith exception, and the court cannot find that the defendants had such a system in place. Indeed, testimony at the Hearings revealed that, after NCC shifted over to the Hartford server in August 2004, emails were backed up for one year; however, emails pre-dating this transfer were only retained for six months or less. Thus, the defendants did not appear to have one consistent, "routine" system in place, and Bissell admitted at Hearing II that the State Librarian's policy was not followed. Counsel for the defendants also indicated at Oral Argument that he was not aware that the defendants did anything to stop the destruction of the backup tapes after NCC's obligation to preserve arose.[9]

* * *

2. Culpable State of Mind

As for the second prong of a spoliation of evidence claim, a culpable state of mind is established by ordinary negligence. Indeed, because this court has found that a duty to preserve exists, and that the defendants breached that duty, "[o]nce the duty to preserve attaches, any destruction of documents is, at a minimum, negligent." *Zubulake*, 220 F.R.D. at 220.

However, the court finds more: it finds the defendants' failure to place a litigation hold and to preserve emails and hard drives relevant to Doe's allegations in this case to be at least grossly negligent, if not reckless. *Chan v. Triple 8 Palace, Inc.*, 2005 WL 1925579, at *7 ("[T]he utter failure to establish any form of litigation hold at the outset of litigation is grossly negligent. That is what occurred here: the defendants systematically destroyed evidence because they had never been informed of their obligation to suspend normal document destruction policies.").

The defendants claim that everything that happened was the result of a neutral retention system with limited resources. However, as discussed above, there is no evidence that the defendants did anything to stop the routine destruction of the backup tapes after NCC's obligation to preserve arose. Moreover, with respect to Delay's findings regarding the PST files, while the defendants explain that the reason for the deleted emails was because email storage space (mailbox) was limited to only 50 megabytes maximum of space, according to Delay space was not a reason for the limited activity in Professors Schwab, Skeeter and Verna's mailboxes. Further, it is inexplicable how there could not be one mention of Masi or Doe in Schwab's PST file, when there are 500 other communications that surround the date of the incident. The court finds that this indicates selective destruction, evidencing intentional behavior.

---

9. The court finds the defendants' argument that they had no choice but to continue the routine deletion of the backup server, because the plaintiff in this case is a Jane Doe plaintiff and they would otherwise have had to reveal her identity, to be unavailing. As the court offered at Oral Argument, the defendants could at least have conferred with Doe's counsel regarding this question of how to send a systemwide communication on document retention without revealing Doe's real name. Alternatively, they could have instructed employees, most especially IT employees, to cease deletion or scrubbing of electronic data.

Delay also found what appeared to have been evidence tampering—that is, several files were accessed and deleted within minutes of Delay's investigation, and two documents were deleted from Dellamura's files about a month after the Doe incident that had "sexual harassment" in their titles. He also found significant activity on Professor's Seaborn's computer only a few days before his investigation—indeed, he found that 122 emails were sent or received at 8:43 a.m. on August 11, 2006, and that it appeared that files were copied into that computer at that time. Delay also found other activity occurred on Seaborn's computer on the morning of his investigation. Bissell testified that it was not likely another user than Seaborn had accessed her computer on those days, even if it was during summer vacation, because NCC did not know the ID's and passwords of each staff member; moreover, the defendants point to the fact that none of the 122 emails of August 11, 2006, involved Masi or the incidents in this case. While this last point may go to the third prong, the court credits the testimony of Delay, experienced in computer forensics, who concluded that Seaborn's PST file was manipulated in the time period after Doe filed her lawsuit, when the defendants were "unquestionably on notice of [their] duty to preserve." *Zubulake*, 220 F.R.D. at 221. According to Delay, the large amount of activity all at once is uncommon and when he typically examines computers, there is no activity on the day of his investigation.

Moreover, the court finds at least gross negligence, if not more, in the defendants' replacing Seaborn's computer in December 2004, one month after this lawsuit was filed. Regardless of the fact that the entire business department at NCC may have received new computers, the defendants were involved in this litigation and Seaborn was one of its key players. Thus, they had a clear obligation to preserve Seaborn's old computer rather than decommissioning it or reimaging and reissuing it, as Bissell testified at Hearing II. At the very least, they should have kept track of what was done with her old computer.

3. Relevance

Finally, to establish the third prong of a spoliation of evidence claim, that the destroyed evidence is "relevant" to a party's claims, that party "must adduce sufficient evidence from which a reasonable trier of fact could infer that the destroyed [or unavailable] evidence would have been of the nature alleged by the party affected by its destruction." However, because "holding the prejudiced party to too strict a standard of proof regarding the likely contents of the destroyed evidence would subvert the prophylactic and punitive purposes of the adverse inference, the level of proof that will suffice to support an inference in favor of the innocent party on a particular issue must be less than the amount that would suffice to survive summary judgment on that issue."

* * *

As discussed above, Doe has demonstrated that the defendants' failure to preserve hard drives and emails of certain key players in Doe's lawsuit was at a minimum grossly negligent. Therefore, no other proof of relevance is necessary, and Doe is entitled to an adverse inference instruction.

However, if the court were to only find the defendants to be negligent, Doe must demonstrate that the destroyed evidence would have been relevant and favorable to her. "In the absence of bad faith or gross negligence by the alleged spoliator, the relevance element can be established if the moving party submits extrinsic evidence tending to demonstrate that the missing evidence would have been favorable to it." "Doe has supplied some proof that the missing evidence was likely to be favorable to her: she has submitted an affidavit from R.M., in which R.M. states that she sent Seaborn an email in 2004 "complaining about what happened to Jane Doe in this case ... [and] that the college could have stopped Masi after my complaint but did nothing." That email has been destroyed. Doe also has evidence of a missing file, entitled "Masi–POL.doc," which Delay found referenced but unrecoverable on Della-mura's computer. Thus, while not required to in light of the court's finding of at least gross negligence, Doe has shown that the destroyed evidence was favorable to her allegations.

Therefore, the court finds that Doe has established the elements of an adverse inference based on spoliation: the defendants had an obligation to preserve the evidence at the time it was destroyed; the defendants' failure to preserve evidence was at a minimum grossly negligent; and even if the defendants' conduct was simple negligence, Doe has established the relevance of the missing evidence. The court thus finds that Doe is entitled to an adverse inference jury instruction with respect to the destroyed evidence.

B. Costs

Doe is entitled to an award of the costs that she incurred with this motion. See *Zubulake v. UBS Warburg LLC*, 229 F.R.D. 422, 437 (S.D.N.Y. 2004). "Such a monetary award may be appropriate to punish the offending party for its actions or to deter the litigant's conduct, sending the message that egregious conduct will not be tolerated." *Chan*, 2005 WL 1925579, at *10 (Internal quotation marks omitted). Such an award also "serves the remedial purpose of making the opposing party whole for costs incurred as a result of the spoliator's wrongful conduct." *Id.* * * * In this case, Doe expended resources to retain Mr. Delay to perform the forensic investigation of NCC's computers, and those costs are compensable.

* * *

COMMENTARY

Doe may be compared with *Escobar v. City of Houston*, where the plaintiffs alleged that the defendant City had failed to preserve the records of electronic communications by the Houston Police Department in the twenty-four hours after the shooting death of a minor, Eli Escobar.[15] The plaintiffs alleged that they had provided notice to the City of their wrongful death claim within sixty days after the shooting and that the electronic communications were likely to discuss events that occurred after the minor had been shot. Police department policy was to keep transmissions for ninety days. The plaintiffs, therefore, argued that the destruction of these communications violated the City's preservation obligation. The plaintiffs sought spoliation sanctions in the form of an adverse inference instruction.

The City argued that the plaintiffs' notice of claim did not specifically request all electronic communications, that it was unaware that the plaintiffs sought the electronic communications, and that it preserved all evidence it *believed* to be relevant. "In the Fifth Circuit, a severe sanction for spoliation, including an adverse inference instruction, requires a showing of bad faith."[16] The record did not provide a basis for an adverse inference instruction because there was no showing that relevant electronic communications were destroyed or that the destruction occurred in bad faith. Absent proof of relevance, or bad faith, the routine and automatic destruction of the police department's electronic communications was not sanctionable. Moreover,

> under Rule 37[e] of the Federal Rules of Civil Procedure, if the electronic communications were destroyed in the routine operation of the HPD's computer system, and if there is no evidence of bad faith in the operation of the system that led to the destruction of the communications, sanctions are not appropriate.[17]

Escobar demonstrates that, absent a duty to preserve and absent bad faith, Rule 37(e) offers independent protection from sanctions when ESI is destroyed in the routine operation of an electronic information system.

1. What Constitutes Bad Faith?

In re Krause provides an example of a decision in which a party's destruction of relevant ESI was found to be in bad faith.[18] Krause was an adversary proceeding instituted by the Government and joined in by a trustee to, among other things, recover assets from the debtor (Krause). Both the trustee and the Government sought sanctions against Krause for violation of a preliminary injunction and discovery orders. The court found that, after the duty to preserve had attached, Krause installed and ran a wiping software and that after Krause's computers had crashed and while the adversary proceeding was pending and document requests had been served, installed and resumed the operation of the wiping software in the restoration process. These findings led the court

---

15. *See* No. 04–1945, 2007 WL 2900581, at *17 (S.D. Tex. Sept. 29, 2007).

16. *Id.*

17. *Id.* at *18.

18. 367 B.R. 740 (D. Kan. 2007).

to the "inescapable conclusion" that Krause "willfully and intentionally destroyed" ESI.[19]

Krause also rejected any argument that the debtor could rely on Rule 37(e):

> Nor can Krause claim that his use of GhostSurf 2006 was a good faith "routine operation" of his computers. With the 2006 amendments to the Federal Rules of Civil Procedure, a party enjoys a safe harbor from sanctions where electronic evidence is "lost as a result of the routine, good-faith operation of an electronic information system."

* * *

> The undisputed evidence established that Krause's hard drives were far from being at full capacity thus making it improbable that electronic information was being overwritten or deleted by routine operation of his computers. Just as a litigant may have an obligation to suspend certain features of a "routine operation," the Court concludes that a litigant has an obligation to suspend features of a computer's operation that are not routine if those features will result in destroying evidence. Here, that obligation required Krause to disable the running of the wiping feature of GhostSurf as soon as the preservation duty attached. And it certainly obligated Krause to refrain from reinstalling GhostSurf when his computers crashed and he restored them.[20]

Evidence adduced from salvaged ESI demonstrated to the *Krause* court that the destroyed ESI would have been relevant, that the ability of the Government and the trustee to proceed had been significantly harmed, and that the court should infer that the destroyed ESI was relevant. The court entered, among other things, a partial default judgment against the debtor.

Krause adds gloss to Rule 37(e) in two respects. *First*, it suggests that automatic deletion by the "routine operation" of a computer system cannot occur unless that system is at full capacity. *Second*, it requires a litigant to suspend "nonroutine" operations—which would appear to fall outside the scope of Rule 37(e).

2. Other Decisions Citing Rule 37(e)

In *State of Texas v. City of Frisco*,[21] the plaintiff sought a declaratory judgment that it need not preserve ESI pursuant to a letter request from the defendant City. The plaintiff sought relief under the Declaratory Judgment Act. In dismissing the Complaint, the court held that the letter from the City, which requested the general preservation of ESI pertaining to a toll road project and referred only to potential litigation, was insufficient to "rise to the level of controversy sufficient to confer

---

19.   *Id.* at 767.

20.   *Id.* at 767–68.

21.   No. 07 Civ. 383, 2008 WL 828055 (E.D. Tex. Mar. 27, 2008).

jurisdiction."[22] The court did note, however, citing to Rule 37, that while they do not specifically address pre-suit litigation hold requests, the Rules contemplate that the parties will act in good faith in the preservation and production of documents, and encouraged the parties "to handle the preservation of documents in response to their respective litigation holds in such good faith."[23]

Where does *State of Texas* leave Rule 37(e)? It suggests that the Rule might be looked to as a means to determine the extent of a prelitigation duty to preserve and might be looked to as imposing a prelitigation good faith standard. However, this duty and standard already exists as a matter of common law, as demonstrated by the decisions discussed above.

Another recent decision, *John B. v. Goetz, et al.*, repeats the well-established principle that "a party to civil litigation has a duty to preserve relevant information, including ESI, when that party 'has notice that the evidence is relevant to litigation or ... should have known that the evidence may be relevant to future litigation.' "[24] When this duty to preserve the relevant data is breached, "a ... court may exercise its authority to impose appropriate discovery sanctions. *See* Fed. R. Civ. P. 37(b), (e)."[25] The court noted that sanctions should only be considered when there is a clear duty to preserve ESI, a culpable failure to preserve and produce relevant ESI, and a reasonable probability of material prejudice to the adverse party.[26]

In *John B.*, the Sixth Circuit Court of Appeals granted in part the mandamus petition of the defendants, officials of the State of Tennessee responsible for the operation of that state's managed care system. The district court below had required the forensic imaging and production of hard drives and other devices of a number of state personnel despite confidentiality and privacy concerns. The Court of Appeals held that these concerns, together with federal and comity concerns, warranted mandamus relief from the district court's order. As with *State of Texas*, the reference to Rule 37(e) in *John B.* is fleeting. The Rule is cited in reference to the duty to preserve relevant information and a court's authority to impose appropriate sanctions. Plainly, Rule 37(e) speaks to both, but there is no discussion of 37(e)'s applicability to the circumstances that were before the Court of Appeals.

3. Interpreting Terms Used in Rule 37(e)

- **"Absent exceptional circumstances ..."** Perhaps this is an attempt to restore the factor of prejudice to the requesting party's case.

---

22.   *Id.* at *3.

23.   *Id.* at *4.

24.   531 F.3d 448, 459 (6th Cir. 2008) (quoting *Fujitsu Ltd. v. Federal Express Corp.*, 247 F.3d 423, 436 (2d Cir. 2001)).

25.   *Id.*

26.   *See id.* (citing The Sedona Conference Working Group on Electronic Document Retention and Production, *The Sedona Conference Glossary: E–Discovery & Digital Information Management* (2d ed. 2007), http://www.thesedonaconference.org/dltForm?did=TSCGlossary_12_07.pdf).

- "... **a court may not impose sanctions under these rules** ..." A judge always has inherent authority or contempt powers.[27]

- "... **on a party** ..." This phrase explicitly excludes the non-party served with a *subpoena duces tecum* for ESI under Rule 45.

- "... **for failing to provide electronically stored information lost as a result of the routine, good-faith operation** ..." What is a routine, good-faith operation?

- "... **of an electronic information system.**" What is an electronic information system? Does it include the human beings who run it?

When first proposed, Rule 37(e) was looked to as a "safe harbor" from discovery sanctions that might arise from the routine deletion of information from computer systems. From the Committee Note to the case law cited and the commentaries quoted, it becomes obvious that Rule 37(e) affords no certain protection against sanctions. Indeed, it has been rarely relied on (either pro or con) and its sparse language raises serious questions about its reach and scope. The one common thread is that the Rule does not excuse a party from rule-based sanctions for a failure to comply with a preservation obligation.

In *Oklahoma ex rel. Edmondson v. Tyson Foods, Inc.,* the court addressed the adequacy of the plaintiff's privilege logs as well as the adequacy of the plaintiff's responses to interrogatories.[28] While the court did not otherwise mention Rule 37(e) in the course of its rulings, it did give this admonition:

> The Court notes that although no formal preservation order has been entered herein, the obligation of the parties to preserve evidence, including ESI, arises as soon as a party is aware the documentation may be relevant. The Court further advises the parties that they should be very cautious in relying upon any "safe harbor" doctrine as described in new Rule 37[e].[29]

C. DEFAULT JUDGMENTS, DISMISSAL, AND ADVERSE INFERENCES

METROPOLITAN OPERA ASSOCIATION, INC. v. LOCAL 100, HOTEL EMPLOYEES AND RESTAURANT EMPLOYEES INTERNATIONAL UNION

212 F.R.D. 178 (S.D.N.Y. 2003)

PRESKA, DISTRICT JUDGE

"A lawsuit is supposed to be a search for the truth," and the tools employed in that search are the rules of discovery. Our adversary

---

27. *See, e.g., Leon v. IDX Sys.,* 464 F.3d 951, 958 (9th Cir. 2006).

28. No. 05 Civ. 329, 2007 WL 1498973, at *1 (N.D. Okla. May 17, 2007).

29. *Id.* at *6.

system relies in large part on the good faith and diligence of counsel and the parties in abiding by these rules and conducting themselves and their judicial business honestly.

The judicial system prefers to resolve controversies on the merits. In the ordinary course, lawsuits should not be resolved based on who did what to whom during discovery. Indeed, a result driven by discovery abuse is justified only on the rarest of occasions and then only after the miscreant has demonstrated unquestionable bad faith and has had a last clear chance to comply with the rules.

Some judges come to the bench from academia, some from government service, some from private practice. Because I came to the bench from private civil practice, I am familiar with the hurly-burly of the discovery process in a hotly-contested civil case, with the existence of sharp elbows, speaking objections, rude responses and with the ever-popular, much-cited Rambo litigation tactics. I am certainly familiar, both from practice and from my time on the bench, with discovery disputes that devolve into arguments about which child threw the first spitball.

The discovery process in this case, however, transcended the usual clashes between adversaries, sharp elbows, spitballs and even Rambo litigation tactics. This case was qualitatively different. It presented the unfortunate combination of lawyers who completely abdicated their responsibilities under the discovery rules and as officers of the court and clients who lied and, through omission and commission, failed to search for and produce documents and, indeed, destroyed evidence—all to the ultimate prejudice of the truth-seeking process. As confirmed by discovery into the Union's and its counsel's compliance with the Met's discovery requests, both the lawyers and the clients exhibited utter and complete disregard for the rules of the truth-seeking process in civil discovery. As is set forth at length below * * *:

— in response to Met counsel's continuing assertions of lack of an adequate document search and demonstrations of non-production, the Union's counsel repeatedly represented to the Court that all documents responsive to the Met's document requests had been produced when, in fact, a thorough search had never been made and counsel had no basis for so representing;

— counsel knew the Union's files were in disarray and that it had no document retention policy but failed to cause a retention policy to be adopted to prevent destruction of responsive documents, both paper and electronic;

— counsel failed to explain to the non-lawyer in charge of document production, inter alia, that a document included a draft or other non-identical copy and included documents in electronic form;

— the non-lawyer the Union put in charge of document production failed to speak to all persons who might have relevant documents, never followed up with the people he did speak to (instead merely picked up

"Met-related" documents that some of the employees he did speak to placed in a box when they remembered to do so) and failed to contact all of the Union's internet service providers ("ISPs") to attempt to retrieve deleted e-mails as counsel represented to the Court that he would;

— no lawyer ever doubled back to inquire of the Union employee in charge of document production whether he conducted a search and what steps he took to assure complete production;

— in the face of Met counsel's constant assertions that no adequate document search had been conducted and responsive documents had not been produced, Union counsel failed to inquire of several important witnesses about documents until the night before their depositions;

— the Union's counsel lied to the Court about a witness' vacation schedule in order to delay the witness' court-ordered deposition;

— a Union officer lied in his deposition about whether Union members working on the campaign against the Met filled out reports of their activities, and, even after the lie was discovered, all such responsive documents still were not produced; and

— shortly after Met counsel announced they might seek permission to have a forensic computer expert examine the Union's computers in an attempt to retrieve deleted e-mails, the Union replaced those computers without notice.

Though perhaps technically sufficient for relief under one or the other of the rules or statutes forming the basis of the Met's motion, any one of these discovery failures, standing alone, would not ordinarily move a court to impose the most severe sanction. Here, however, the combination of outrages perpetrated by the Union and its counsel, by both omission and commission, impels the most severe sanction in order to (1) remedy the effect of the discovery abuses, viz., prejudicing the Met's ability to plan and prepare its case, (2) punish the parties responsible, and (3) deter similar conduct by others.

In so doing, I am cognizant of the relatively lengthy discussion in the Union's papers about discovery failings by the Met, the Met's motivations on this motion and the like.[1] As the referee on the ground in this engagement, however, I reject the Union's sub silentio justification that the Met and its counsel participated in the same type of conduct that is the basis of the motion. To the extent that there were failings by the Met or its counsel, they were well within the normal hurly-burly of the discovery process and, in any event, were promptly addressed. The conduct of the Union and its counsel, on the other

---

[1]. In light of the obvious seriousness of the allegations in the Met's moving papers on this motion, it is remarkable that Marianne Yen, the Herrick Feinstein associate primarily responsible for the Union's document production and the only lawyer who submitted an opposing affidavit for the time period comprising the bulk of discovery, devotes three paragraphs of her responsive declaration (¶¶ 18–20) to discovery on her watch and fifteen paragraphs to the Met's perceived failings and its motivations (¶¶ 21–35).

hand, transcended the hurly-burly into gross negligence, recklessness, willfulness and lying. * * *

I. PROCEDURAL STATUS

Plaintiff Metropolitan Opera Association (the "Met") originally commenced this action against defendants Local 100, Hotel Employees and Restaurant Employees International Union ("Local 100" or "the Union"), its President, Henry Tamarin, and Lead Organizer, Dennis Diaz, in New York State Supreme Court on May 1, 2000, claiming that Local 100 improperly involved the Met in a labor dispute between Local 100 and Restaurant Associates Corporation ("RA"), the Met's food service provider. * * * Trial initially was scheduled to commence on January 22, 2002. However, due to disputes regarding discovery and to allow the Union to file a motion for summary judgment, the trial was rescheduled for April 15, 2002.

* * *

III. THE COURSE OF DISCOVERY

A. Discovery on Joseph Lynett's Watch

1. The Met's First Document Request

The Met served its First Document Request with the Complaint on May 2, 2000, and asked for, inter alia, all documents that (a) "concern[ed] communications which concern the Met;" (b) were communicated to or intended to be communicated to the Met or any patron, donor, potential patron or donor, Board member, or agent of the foregoing (listing names); (c) concerned any of the foregoing; (d) concerned use or application of pressure on the Met or any of the foregoing persons; and (e) concern[ed] the Union "candlelight vigil" of March 30, 2000, the rally of May 11, 2000, or any other rally or similar event planned to occur through September 30, 2000 * * * Joseph Lynett, who was the Union's in-house counsel at that time and soon after became an associate at Herrick Feinstein on May 15, 2000, was counsel of record. At about that time, Lynett gave a copy of the Complaint and the First Document Request to Brooks Bitterman, Local 100's Research Director, and William Granfield, who at the time was the Union's Secretary/Treasurer and is now its President. Bitterman is not a lawyer, and there is no indication in the record that Granfield is a lawyer.

On May 23, 2000 * * * I held a teleconference with counsel and directed the parties to produce documents to each other that day. The Met received defendants' expedited production of approximately 500–600 pages, which consisted largely of leaflets that had been disseminated by the Union and form letters that the Union had sent to donors and directors of the Met. According to the Met, there were virtually no internal Local 100 documents, and Local 100 neither made objections to the First Document Request nor provided a written Rule 34 Response.

* * * Deborah Lans, counsel for the Met, told the Court, "I have a concern about the completeness of the document production that was made to us." Specifically, she noted that no letters or other communications that the Union had sent out subsequent to May 1 had been produced, even though the Met knew the Union had sent several because the Met had obtained them from third parties. When I questioned Lynett at the hearing, he said he believed that a search had been made and that all letters had been produced, adding, "The union's records aren't kept in that great of order, but I have Mr. Bitterman here and I can consult with him," to which I responded, "I presume it was not he who was going to search the files."

In his deposition testimony of March 22, 2002, Lynett recalled meeting with Bitterman, Granfield, and Diaz in May 2000 regarding the document demands and providing them with copies of the Met's First Document Request. Lynett instructed Bitterman to alert all Local 100 staff that all "Met-related documents must be retained." Passing for the moment what a "Met-related" document is, Bitterman failed to follow this instruction in that he only alerted some Union employees, certainly not all of those who were likely to have relevant documents. * * * Lynett * * * could not specifically recall discussing with Bitterman, Granfield, or Diaz what types of documents would be responsive, and there is no indication in the record that Lynett ever discussed with Bitterman or anyone else at the Union, inter alia, that a "document included all drafts and non-identical copies and electronically-stored documents." Lynett never doubled back * * * to assure the completeness of the Union's expedited document production, and had no conversations about discovery compliance with those who replaced him, Jamin Sewell and Michael Anderson.

Two days later * * * Lans again raised the issue of defendants' lack of production * * *. Lynett stated, "Your Honor, we have turned over every document that we have except for privileged documents . . . I am representing that we conducted a search, a thorough search on this matter. . . ." The colloquy continued:

MS. LANS: I think what he is saying to you, your Honor, is he may have given me—done his best to give me the things you ordered him to give me a day early, last week—I don't believe he means to say he has responded to my discovery request.

THE COURT: Counsel, have you produced ever[y] responsive document—

MR. LYNETT: *Yes, your Honor, we have produced all documents responsive to that request.*

Despite Lynett's having been presented with a last clear chance to remedy the situation by Lans' calling attention to the failures of production * * *, compliance discovery confirmed not only that these representations in open court were false but also that a thorough search, albeit on an expedited basis, had not been conducted and, therefore, that there was no basis whatsoever for the representation.

B. Discovery on Anderson's Watch

1. The Met's Duplicate Document Request to Bitterman

In early August 2000, the Met served a notice for the deposition of Brooks Bitterman and attached thereto another document request addressed solely to Bitterman, which merely repeated the requests made on May 2 * * *. On August 25, 2000, defendants produced documents that they said were, together with the production made in May, "all the non-privileged documents responsive to the requests for documents served upon Brooks Bitterman and a privilege log [which] . . . covers all documents in the union's possession." * * * Thus, Lynett's May 26 representation of full production proved to be false, and there was no explanation of why the earlier-produced documents had not been produced in a timely fashion. In any event, this August 25 representation of full production was also false and without basis.

Michael T. Anderson had assumed responsibility for supervising discovery for the defendants in August 2000. * * * At that time, Anderson instructed Bitterman to retain all documents related to the Met and to forward any responsive documents to his associate, Jennifer Matis, in Washington, D.C. According to Anderson, "Bitterman was the most logical choice to act as custodian of records because he and the researchers he supervises generated and maintained virtually all of the documents that were called for in the Met's first two sets of document requests." Anderson never visited the Union's office but contented himself with talking on the telephone to Bitterman about Met-related issues. Passing whether Bitterman was or was not a logical choice for custodian, compliance discovery confirmed that his supposed search was incomplete and haphazard and that no lawyer ever made inquiry of him about what he did.

On February 2, 2001, Met attorney Vincent Pentima wrote to Anderson * * * that, although defendants maintained that all responsive documents had been produced, the evidence showed that was not the case. He cited various types of documents which Union representatives had testified about * * * but which had never been produced. He noted specifically that, although the First Document Request was a continuing one, no documents more current than May 2000 had been produced, no notes or drafts of any kind had been produced, and no documents to, from and/or about RA which mentioned the Met (except the leaflets and letters) had been provided. He requested that defendants "conduct a thorough search and both provide written responses to our requests and a full production of documents."

Anderson responded by letter of February 6, 2001, stating that he had reviewed, with his client, Pentima's letter and the categories of documents referenced therein and that defendants would supplement their production to include "all new documents generated since our production in August." Anderson indicated that Bitterman would search the Union records for certain responsive documents. On February 16, 2001, Anderson wrote to Pentima and indicated that he would provide the Met with "new [Union] documents generated since our [last] production" and any other documents referenced on February 6.

On February 22, 2001, Anderson made a "supplemental production" which he said included "all responsive non-privileged documents generated to date since the Union's production in May 2000, as well as any further responsive documents you inquired about in your February 2, 2001 letter." He also noted that "a file drawer of publicly available documents relating to the Met and various directors and donors" would be made available at Herrick Feinstein for inspection. Compliance discovery confirmed that Anderson's February 22 representation of full production was false and was without basis.

[Another exchange resulted in production of a few more documents and another false assertion by Anderson that all responsive documents had been produced.]

2. The Met's Second Document Request

On May 25, 2001, the Met served a Second Request for Documents, which was intended to encompass all that had been covered by the First Request but to be more specific so that, to the extent defendants had been interpreting the word "responsive" in a narrow way, there could be no question of what had been requested. Also on that date, Charles Stillman, counsel for the Met, wrote to Anderson * * *. He stated, "We are troubled by Defendants' failure to produce whole categories of responsive documents," giving examples of "[a]ll internal communications concerning the Met," "[a]ll emails concerning the Met," "[t]he thousands of letters sent by defendants to Met directors, officers, employees, donors and patrons," "[t]he drafts of all documents created by defendants concerning the Met," and "[t]he responses by RA employees at the Met to the 'Survey of Working and Living Conditions.' "

According to Anderson, he reviewed Stillman's May 25 letter with Bitterman, "questioned [Bitterman] about all issues raised there, and reviewed with [Bitterman] what documents (subject to objections) were responsive to the Met's Second Request." Bitterman believed that only two flyers and "a handful of responses" had been sent or received by e-mail. Anderson "instructed the Union to search its files for any notes relating to the Met, [and] to construct a log showing what people on the Union's mail-merge list received the letters in the record . . . including any documents sent by e-mail." Passing again the meaning of "notes relating to the Met," there is no indication that Anderson (or anyone else) made inquiry to assure this instruction was carried out.

On May 30, 2001, the Union made a supplemental production of documents which consisted almost entirely of form letters sent in April and May 2001 by the Union to colleagues and fellow board members of boards other than the Met on which Met board members also sat. However, no other documents were produced, and Stillman received no response to his May 25 letter. Stillman wrote again on June 28, 2001, noting Anderson's lack of response and informing him that, unless the Met received assurance that the deficiencies in production would be corrected by July 10 (the date for response to the Met's Second Document Request), the Met would seek appropriate sanctions with the Court.

Anderson responded on July 10, 2001, enclosing defendants' Responses and Objections to the Met's Second Document Request. * * * [N]othing in Anderson's letter indicated that a thorough search had been made or that any document production had been supervised or conducted by an attorney.

* * *

When Met counsel went to inspect the items made available at the Herrick Feinstein office on July 12 and received the production to which Anderson had referred, they found that many documents were being produced that were clearly responsive to the Met's First Request served 15 months earlier. The production contained documents dating from 1999 to the then-current date, and the Met received no information as to which Union files they had come from or why they had not been produced earlier. * * *

Counsel for both sides scheduled a meeting on July 17 to discuss these matters, but as soon as the July 17 meeting began, Anderson informed Met counsel that defendants were obtaining "new" attorneys and, therefore, he would not speak about the Union's document production because that would be up to the "new" attorneys. Anderson would not discuss matters further, stating that he believed the Union's production was complete and that Met counsel could raise any problems with the Court the following day. That supposedly new counsel were to appear did not, however, prevent Anderson from discussing what he viewed as deficiencies in the Met's production of documents. * * *

At the conference with the Court the following day, the Union introduced its new attorneys at Herrick Feinstein, the firm that had been the attorneys of record for the Union before Anderson's first contact with the case in June 2000 and had continued, together with Anderson, as the attorneys of record. Met counsel began to explain the inadequacies in defendants' discovery compliance, but Anderson stated that he could no longer speak to the point, and the Herrick Feinstein lawyers stated that they were not yet familiar with the situation. While perhaps warranted in situations where genuinely new counsel are substituted, under the circumstances here where the Herrick Feinstein firm had been counsel of record throughout, such cat-and-mouse conduct is not consistent with counsel's obligation to engage in discovery in good faith.

3. Electronic Documents

During the July 18 conference, I overruled essentially all of the defendants' objections to specific document requests. Anderson stated that he had not specifically instructed the Union not to delete computer files and that no retention procedure had been put in place. Met counsel also explained that, apparently, no attorney had conducted or supervised the Union's document production and, three months before the then-fixed close of discovery, the Met was unable to take depositions and develop its case because of defendants' failure to make proper disclosure. In response to the Met's concerns about how document discovery had been conducted, defendants' counsel stated that they would look into it. I directed defendants' counsel to clarify immediately with their clients that all documents relevant to the Met's document requests must be preserved, expressly making the order applicable to all work done on computers and all information sent out or received through computers. In that conference, Union counsel undertook that all of the Union's ISPs would be contacted in an effort to retrieve deleted electronic documents. Compliance discovery later revealed that some but not all ISPs were contacted.

At that time, Anderson "mistakenly believed that e-mails are always automatically stored on the user's server" and he "had not specifically focused on e-mails in [his] original [instructions to his client]." After the July 18 conference, Anderson asked Bitterman whether e-mails were automatically stored, and Bitterman directed Anderson to check with Union staff members Dahlia Ward and Michelle Travis. On July 20, Anderson called Ward and Travis, learned that the Union's staff's servers did not store e-mail after 30 days and "instructed them and Brooks Bitterman to ensure that all staff immediately made all possible adjustments to save e-mail" or to print out hard copies of responsive e-mails and to reconstruct information about e-mails that had not been saved on a log. Between July 18 and 30, Anderson "repeatedly" asked Bitterman, Travis, and Ward whether there were responsive internal e-mails among them or to other researchers and "emphasized" that any such e-mails must be either produced or disclosed as lost. Anderson further "directed that all union staff make hard copies of all responsive incoming and outgoing e-mails, and place them in a box for production" and he "repeated the scope of discovery obligation to include all documents, drafts, e-mails and other materials defined in Plaintiff's Document Requests." Although Anderson states that he "repeated" these instructions, he nowhere states where, when and to whom he gave the initial instruction.

On July 23, Anderson wrote to Met counsel concerning these issues stating, "At my instruction, the Union staff have now gone through their computers to see if any e-mails had been overlooked, and to compare the hard copies in our production to identify any missing e-mails." Furthermore, Anderson wrote, "My clients understand that they have a duty to retain all Met-related documents. To date, my instructions have been communicated to the Union staff through Brooks Bitterman. He has asked all staff to forward copies of all Met-related documents to be placed in a box for our periodic rolling production." He additionally stated:

> Some of the union staff's servers have not been programmed to automatically retain e-mails indefinitely. All staff will now make the necessary adjustments to reprogram their servers to retain all e-mails on the server automatically.

He further explained that the Union had "retrieved" most of the deleted e-mails—that is, to the extent Union staff knew of e-mails they had sent, they contacted the recipients and asked for copies which the recipients might have retained. In other words, he explained, where mass mailings had occurred of notice of the May 11 and September 25 rallies the Union held against the Met and the Union had the "mail-merge" list of addresses, it contacted those addressees. Anderson under-stood that the Union would be contacting its ISPs to see whether e-mails could be retrieved from their servers. Although Anderson took some steps to follow up on his various instructions concerning e-mails and other electronic documents, he ended his involvement in the case in July, and the remaining follow-up fell between the cracks. For example, Bitterman contacted some but not all of the Union's ISPs.

On July 26, 2001, Stillman wrote to defendants' counsel and pointed out certain problems with the response given in the July 23 letter. Among these were the meaning of Met-related documents as opposed to documents requested and relevant to the case, the failure to address computer files other than e-mails, and the failure to explain adequately the e-mail situation and to comply with the Court's ruling. Anderson * * * did not clarify what he told his clients constituted "Met-related documents;" * * * With respect to e-mails, Anderson said that only one Union staff member, Dahlia Ward, had an internet account that retained e-mails. He further stated:

* * *

> My clients understand that their obligation extends to documents created on computer, whether at the Union office or elsewhere. The Union has provided all responsive information in its hard copy files and in its computers.

Compliance discovery confirmed that this representation was also false in that, inter alia, all ISPs had not been contacted, all Union computers had not been searched, all responsive documents had not been pro-duced, and all files had not been searched, e.g., files destined for or in the Union's document storage facility.

In late July and early August 2001, the Union produced more documents, including "retrieved" e-mails. Local 100 produced addition-al documents later in August and in September. The documents dated back to 1999 and, except for a small number of recent ones, should have been produced earlier.

C.   Discovery on Moss' and Yen's Watch

In mid-October 2001, Marianne Yen, an associate who had just joined the Herrick Feinstein firm, learned that she would be assisting James A. Moss, a partner at the firm, with completing discovery and preparing for trial. Moss' and Yen's watch extended through the present motion.

1.   The Met's Third Document Request—Benefits

The Met's Third Document Request dated October 2, 2001, requested documents "concerning the benefits which Local 100 provides or has provided to its members or their families, including but not limited to health benefits, life insurance, disability benefits, and pension and/or savings plans." In a response dated October 26, 2001, signed by Moss, the Union stated that "there are no responsive documents." In her Declaration, Yen reiterated that "this category of documents does not exist, because benefits are paid not by Local 100, but rather by the employers. . . ." Yen also stated that she "personally questioned each employee of Local 100, including the receptionist, and all have stated unequivocally that they have not seen any documents such as the Met has requested, nor have they maintained any such documents in their files. [She] searched various file drawers of Local 100's office where these documents might theoretically be kept and did not discover any."

Passing for a moment that compliance discovery demonstrated that Ms. Yen did not interview every employee of Local 100 and made only a cursory search of the Union's files, other discovery responses demonstrate that the representations that there are no responsive documents are untrue. For example, Granfield testified that he keeps files ("staff member files") in which documents concerning inquiries about hours, pay and the like from Union members are kept. He further testified that he has not provided that file to anyone in connection with document production. * * * There is no explanation by Moss of the basis for the untrue response he signed stating that there were no responsive documents.

The Met's Fourth Document Request

The Met's Fourth Document Request dated October 23, 2001 was never responded to because one associate was transitioning out of the case and another transitioning in. Moss, the partner in charge during that period, is silent.

* * *

[The Court sets forth a number of further incidents in which it became apparent that the union and its counsel either did not search for or did not produce responsive documents—and other incidents in which the union and its lawyers were not fully truthful about the state of their preservation, collection and production of electronic information.]

VI. DISCUSSION

A. Applicable Legal Standards

The Met now moves for judgment, attorneys' fees, and further relief pursuant to Rules 26 and 37 of the Federal Rules of Civil Procedure, 28 U.S.C. § 1927, and the Court's inherent power.

* * * Rule 26(g) imposes on counsel an affirmative duty to engage in pretrial discovery responsibly and "is designed to curb discovery abuse by explicitly encouraging the imposition of sanctions." Fed. R.Civ.P. 26(g) Advisory Committee Notes to 1983 Amendment. Furthermore, the Rule

> provides a deterrent to both excessive discovery and evasion by imposing a certification requirement that obliges each attorney to stop and think about the legitimacy of a discovery request, a response thereto, or an objection. The term "response" includes answers to interrogatories and to requests to admit as well as responses to production requests.

Id.

Rule 37 addresses a variety of discovery failures that are without justification and not harmless, including failure to obey a discovery order and failure to comply with Rule 26(e) obligations (supplementing responses). Like Rule 26, Rule 37 is intended to encourage and enforce strict adherence to the "responsibilities counsel owe to the Court and to their opponents," and authorizes a court to impose a variety of sanctions, including default judgment, *see* Fed.R.Civ.P. 37(c)(1) (incorporating Rule 37(b)(2)(C) which authorizes default judgment) * * *.

There are no specific requirements for the imposition of sanctions under Rule 37; rather, the decision is left to the sound discretion of the trial court. Over time, however, courts have identified relevant considerations to assist in deciding whether discovery abuse warrants the entry of judgment, including: (a) willfulness or bad faith of the noncompliant party; (b) the history, if any, of noncompliance; (c) the effectiveness of lesser sanctions; (d) whether the noncompliant party had been warned about the possibility of sanctions; (e) the client's complicity; and (f) prejudice to the moving party. *In re Sumitomo Copper Litig.*, 204 F.R.D. 58, 60 (S.D.N.Y. 2001). In addition, a court may consider the "need to deter discovery abuse and efficiently control dockets."

Pursuant to 28 U.S.C. § 1927:

> [a]ny attorney or other person admitted to conduct cases in any court of the United States . . . who so multiplies the proceedings in any case unreasonably and vexatiously may be required by the court to satisfy personally the excess costs, expenses, and attorneys' fees reasonably incurred because of such conduct.

Under that statute, a party must show bad faith, which is satisfied when "the attorney's actions are so completely without merit as to require the conclusion that they must have been undertaken for some improper purpose such as delay."

Finally * * * even in the absence of a discovery order, a court may impose sanctions on a party for misconduct in discovery under its inherent power to manage its own affairs. *See generally Chambers v. NASCO, Inc.*, 501 U.S. 32, 43 (1991) ("it has long been understood that certain implied powers must necessarily result to our Courts of justice from the nature of their institution, powers which cannot be dispensed with in a Court because they are necessary to the exercise of all others"). Like sanctions under § 1927, sanctions under the Court's inherent power require a finding of bad faith. Unlike § 1927, however, where a court may only sanction attorneys, under its inherent power, a court may impose sanctions on an attorney, a party, or both.

B. Sanctions are Warranted in This Case

* * *

[As] Judge Kugler wrote in *Tarlton v. Cumberland County Correctional Facility*, 192 F.R.D. 165 (D.N.J. 2000):

> It is not an excuse that defense counsel did not know about the retention of the cover sheets. Counsel had a duty to explain to their client what types of information would be relevant and responsive to discovery requests and ask how and where relevant documents may be maintained. The client is charged with knowledge of what documents it possesses. It was not their option to simply react to plaintiff's fortuitous discovery of the existence of relevant documents by making disjointed searches, each time coming up with a few more documents, and each time representing that that was all they had. Under the federal rules, the burden does not fall on plaintiff to learn whether, how and where defendant keeps relevant documents.

1. Rule 26

* * * Union counsel's participation in and supervision of discovery in this case was in no way "consistent with the spirit and purposes of Rules 26 through 37," and mandatory sanctions under Rule 26(g) must be imposed. Counsel had an affirmative duty under Rule 26(g) to make a reasonable inquiry into the basis of their discovery responses and to "stop and think about the legitimacy of [those responses]." Instead, as is crystal clear in hindsight, counsel's responses to the Met's discovery requests, in formal responses, in letters and to the Court—particularly counsel's repeated representations that all responsive documents had been produced—were made without any real reflection or concern for their obligations under the rules governing discovery and, in the absence of an adequate search for responsive documents, without a reason-

able basis. Especially troubling, and of great weight in my decision to impose the most severe sanction, is that counsel's conduct was not merely negligent but was aggressively willful. Union counsel's repeated representations of full production were made in response to Met counsel's continuing high-decibel allegations of failure to make adequate inquiry and repeated demonstrations of incomplete compliance and non-compliance with discovery requests. * * * Union counsel were given numerous last clear chances to comply with their discovery obligations. That, in response, Local 100's counsel continually professed full compliance—falsely and, as confirmed by compliance discovery, without making a reasonable inquiry—constitutes such gross negligence as to rise to intentional misconduct.

Counsel's primary defense to their Rule 26(g) violation is to assert that there is no requirement that counsel "personally supervise every step of the discovery process" and that "counsel is expected to rely on the client's initial document production." While, of course, it is true that counsel need not supervise every step of the document production process and may rely on their clients in some respects, the rule expressly requires counsel's responses to be made upon reasonable inquiry under the circumstances. Here, there is no doubt whatsoever that counsel failed to comply with that standard in that, among other things, counsel (1) never gave adequate instructions to their clients about the clients' overall discovery obligations, what constitutes a "document" or about what was specifically called for by the Met's document requests; (2) knew the Union to have no document retention or filing systems and yet never implemented a systematic procedure for document production or for retention of documents, including electronic documents; (3) delegated document production to a layperson who (at least until July 2001) did not even understand himself (and was not instructed by counsel) that a document included a draft or other non-identical copy, a computer file and an e-mail; (4) never went back to the layperson designated to assure that he had established a coherent and effective system to faithfully and effectively respond to discovery requests; and (5) in the face of the Met's persistent questioning and showings that the production was faulty and incomplete, ridiculed the inquiries, failed to take any action to remedy the situation or supplement the demonstrably false responses, failed to ask important witnesses for documents until the night before their depositions and, instead, made repeated, baseless representations that all documents had been produced. Indeed, given the almost complete disconnect between counsel (who had the document requests but knew nothing about the documents in the Union's possession other than that the files were in disarray and there was no retention system) and defendants (who had the documents but were entirely ignorant of the requirements of the requests), there is simply no way that any discovery response made by counsel could have been based on a reasonable inquiry under the circumstances.

Defendants' brazen assertion that looking at "comprehensive productions ... there was no reason for any of [the Union's] counsel to question the completeness of the production" betrays their willful disregard of their discovery obligations. Certainly when counsel learned that their clients, for over a year after the commencement of the litigation, had not understood that e-mails were called for and had not retained electronic documents or drafts, they should have had "reason to question" the completeness of defendants' productions (and the adequacy of their own supervision).

* * *

[I]t is plain that Union counsel failed in their duty to explain to their client what types of information would be relevant and responsive to document requests and ask how and where relevant documents may be maintained. Instead they simply reacted to Met counsel's fortuitous discovery of the existence of relevant documents by making disjointed searches, each time coming up with a few more documents, and each time representing that that was all they had. Sometimes they did not even go to the trouble of making a disjointed search but just stated that no responsive documents exist when that representation was demonstrably false.

Finally, Union counsel's attitude toward their discovery obligations is perhaps best reflected in several of their Spring 2002 responses. * * * Met counsel began questioning the adequacy of defendants' document search and document production almost from the outset of the case. By July of 2001, it was apparent that at least some electronic documents had not been preserved. * * * [B]ecause of the continuing, serious questions about defendants' compliance with their discovery obligations, I permitted the Met to propound discovery requests in early 2002 regarding defendants' compliance. It was in this context that Met counsel wrote to Union counsel yet again seeking production of long-requested, oft-promised documents. Instead of complying or taking some other action consistent with their discovery obligations, counsel demonstrated their utter contempt for their discovery obligations by mischaracterizing Met counsel's requests as new and responding that discovery had "closed" on December 31. There can be no doubt that counsel's repeated representations that all responsive documents had been produced were not the result of a reasonable inquiry, that counsel failed to stop and think about their responses, and that counsel did not engage in discovery responsibly all in violation of Rule 26. * * *

2. Rule 37

Sanctions are also appropriately imposed here under Rule 37, and the factors considered under that Rule also inform my judgment regarding sanctions under 28 U.S.C. § 1927 and the Court's inherent power.

a. Willfulness or Bad Faith

As the factual recitation above makes clear, there is ample evidence of willfulness and bad faith on the part of both counsel and the Union. First, as set out above, counsel's continuing representations of full compliance with the Met's discovery requests in the face of constant questions being raised by Met counsel about inadequate inquiries and inadequate production were so lacking in a reasonable basis as to rise to the level of bad faith.

Second, despite defendants' arguments to the contrary, defendants have failed to comply with several court orders, also constituting willfulness and bad faith. * * * As to my oral ruling at the July 18, 2001 conference regarding the retention of all documents, including electronic documents, Yen states that "defendants' counsel understood the Court to direct an investigation into the retention and production of Local 100's e-mails and to correct any deficiencies going forward." Even assuming that was the extent of the order, it was not complied with. Among other things, there is no indication that all of Local 100's computers were searched * * *. In any event, * * * all responsive e-mails have never been produced. Also, Granfield, the Union's current president, admitted that he failed to save documents and deleted documents from his diskette right up until his discovery compliance deposition. He never gave the diskette to counsel, and Yen never asked about it.

Third, the falsehoods uttered by individual defendants and by Union counsel as to simple but material factual matters also constitute willfulness and bad faith requiring severe sanctions. [The court gives examples in which union officials and lawyers made statements about the non-existence of responsive documents, when in fact they existed and were ultimately produced.]

* * *

b. The History of Non–Compliance

As is set forth at length above, the Union and its counsel have failed to comply with their discovery obligations from the very outset of this action * * *. As also set out above, defendants' non-compliance and failure to make an adequate search has continued to the present in the face of continuing complaints from Met counsel. This factor weighs heavily in favor of the most severe sanctions.

c. The Client's Complicity

[T]he discovery abuses evidenced here cannot be laid solely at counsel's door. Although the degree of the Union's complicity cannot be measured accurately on this record, that it was significant cannot be doubted. For example, the Union's failure to produce Weekly Reports proceeded initially from Granfield's false testimony that he prepared no log of his activities on behalf of the Union and that there were no documents reflecting the Union's view of the current vote tally.

The Union's failure to set up an adequate system for document production resulted primarily from the glaring omissions of Bitterman. * * * For example, Bitterman never spoke to Rimmelin, who had been at the Local since its inception in 1983 and is the office manager. Although Rimmelin knew that there was a basket somewhere that people were putting documents into for the case, she had no understanding of what documents were supposed to go into the basket and she has never put any there herself. Rimmelin keeps an inventory of documents in storage, but, as noted above, was not asked about it by Bitterman.

* * *

Perhaps most indicative of Bitterman's lack of good faith effort is that he never checked back with the few employees he did speak with to be sure they were complying with his instructions, such as they were. A review of, inter alia, the entirety of Bitterman's compliance deposition convinces me that his document production efforts were purposely scattershot, intended only to go through the motions.

Such a haphazard effort at collecting responsive documents is insufficient. More is required—even of an inadequately instructed layperson. Bitterman failed to communicate with all Union employees who were likely to have relevant documents, including such obvious persons as Rimmelin, the office manager and keeper of the storage facility inventory. * * * Even adjusting for Bitterman's lay status, he, and thus the Union, failed to establish a coherent and effective system to faithfully and effectively respond to discovery requests. Instead, the Union, through Bitterman, employed an unconscionably careless procedure to handle discovery matters, suggesting a callous disregard for its obligations as a litigant.

Finally by way of example, just after the Met informed defendants' counsel (and the Court) that it might request permission to engage a forensic computer expert to attempt to retrieve deleted material from the Union's computers, those computers were dismantled without notice to Met counsel. The Union's complicity in the discovery failures weighs in favor of sanctions against the Union itself.

d. Prejudice

First, the Union's assertion that the Met must show prejudice before a sanction may be ordered under Rule 37 is without merit. For example, in *Miller v. Time–Warner Communications, Inc.*, No. 97 Civ. 7286, 1999 WL 739528, at *3 (S.D.N.Y. Sept. 22, 1999), the court found dismissal warranted even though there was no prejudice to the moving party because the record indicated that the non-moving party and her attorney had committed perjury. Similarly, the court in *Skywark v. Isaacson* granted judgment when the plaintiff, "rather than having fully corrected his misdeeds, ... filled the record with desperate excuses and additional lies to try to cover-up earlier wrongdoings." No. 96 Civ. 2815, 1999 WL 1489038, at *16 (S.D.N.Y. Oct. 14, 1999). Thus, the Union is wrong on the law.

Second, in any event, the Met has demonstrated that it has been prejudiced by the Union's discovery failures. * * * [I]t is beyond peradventure that many documents have been destroyed that related directly to events taking place during the most critical time period in this action, that is, when the Union planned its campaign against the Met, decided what its leaflets, letters and other public statements would say and on what basis. Those documents, from that most critical period, have not been retrieved. Moreover, the documents that have been produced were often produced in an untimely, disorganized fashion, after numerous letters and telephone calls were exchanged and court conferences held and after the depositions of the relevant witnesses. The Met was not only denied the opportunity to prove its case but was denied the opportunity to plan its strategy in an organized fashion as the case proceeded. * * *

In addition, documents that were produced were not produced as required by Rule 34, that is, in the manner in which they were maintained or according to request number, see Fed.R.Civ.P. 34(b), and many important documents were produced after the depositions of key witnesses. All of these obstructions prevented the Met from adequately planning and preparing its case; it was forced to proceed with depositions before relevant documents were produced, it was no doubt hampered in opposing summary judgment and, ultimately, in preparing for trial. The Union's continued reference to the large number of pages it has produced is irrelevant in the face of conclusive evidence that at least a year's worth of electronic documents from the time period most critical to the action have been destroyed while Met counsel continually called attention to the failure. This factor weighs in favor of a severe sanction.

e. Effectiveness of Lesser Sanctions

Finally, I find that lesser sanctions, such as an adverse inference or preclusion, would not be effective in this case. I acknowledge the judicial system's preference for resolving cases on the merits. Here, however, the Union's wholesale destruction of documents, by omission or commission, has made that preferred path impossible. * * * [T]here is no indication that lesser sanctions would bring about compliance, and there is no meaningful way in which to correlate defendants' discovery failures with discrete issues in the case.

Finally, because of the egregiousness of the conduct at issue and because it continued in the face of repeated, documented examples of non-compliance and repeated inquiries by Met counsel and the Court, a lesser sanction would not be adequate to penalize the Union and its counsel here or to deter others from similar misconduct in the future. Thus, this factor also counsels the most severe sanctions. * * *

3. 28 U.S.C. § 1927

As set forth above, I have found that Union counsel's failures to comply with their discovery obligations and their unreasonable obstruction and delay of discovery to be so completely without merit as to require the conclusion that they must have been undertaken for some improper purpose such as delay. Also, the factual recitation leaves no doubt that counsel's conduct multiplied the proceedings "unreasonably and vexatiously." The time and effort spent on discovery follow-up letters and conferences with counsel and the Court was far beyond what is normal, even in a contentious, hard-fought litigation, and all of the compliance discovery well beyond normal parameters. Accordingly, sanctions are also appropriate under § 1927.

* * *

5. The Court's Inherent Power

As noted above, necessary to the Court's conducting judicial business in our adversary system is the inherent power to sanction those who deviate from the standards of good faith. Equally necessary to continuing to conduct judicial business is actually exercising that power and sanctioning counsel and parties who in bad faith fail to abide by the rules and fail to conduct themselves honestly. As has been set out at length above, defendants and their counsel are squarely in this category. To fail to use the Court's inherent power to sanction on the facts presented here would diminish the Court's authority and the adversary system and would serve as a license, encouraging similar behavior. Accordingly, the Met's motion for sanctions pursuant to the Court's inherent power is also granted.

VI. CONCLUSION

Plaintiff's motion for judgment as to liability against defendants and for additional sanctions in the form of attorneys' fees necessitated by the discovery abuse by defendants and their counsel is granted against defendants and their counsel.

COMMENTARY

1. When Is a Default Judgment or Dismissal Sanction Appropriate for Spoliation?

A district court may order a default judgment or a dismissal, either pursuant to Rule 37(b)(2), which authorizes a court to assess a sanction for violation of a discovery order, or pursuant to the court's inherent power to protect its integrity and prevent abuses of the judicial process. When evaluating the propriety of dismissal or default as a discovery sanction, a court should consider: (1) the degree of actual prejudice to the other party; (2) the amount of interference with the judicial process; (3) the culpability of the litigant; (4) whether the court warned the party in advance that default or dismissal of the action would be a likely sanction for noncompliance; and (5) the efficacy of lesser sanctions.[30]

2. When Is an Adverse Inference Jury Instruction Appropriate?

Under the "adverse inference rule," when a party has relevant evidence within its control that it fails to produce, that failure may permit a court to instruct the jury that it may infer that the missing evidence is unfavorable to the party who could have produced the evidence and did not. No inference can be drawn from the failure to produce evidence not in a party's control.

When a party has destroyed relevant evidence, a "spoliation inference" arises to the effect that the destroyed evidence would have been unfavorable to the position of the offending party. A party seeking an adverse inference based on spoliation allegations must "adduce sufficient evidence from which a reasonable trier of fact could infer that the destroyed or unavailable evidence would have been of the nature alleged by the [aggrieved] party . . . ."[31] The bottom line is that the fact-specific balancing approach provides courts with the necessary flexibility to impose whatever type of sanction the court deems appropriate.

3. What Sanctions, If Any, Should Be Awarded for the Following:

Defendant used "Window Washer" disk scrubbing software on the hard drive of his laptop the day before the hard drive was to be turned over to a forensic expert. The defendant also performed mass deletions of electronic files on his laptop. There is no other source of the information that was contained on the hard drive. What sanctions would you award? If the answer is an adverse inference instruction, draft such an instruction.

D. MONETARY SANCTIONS

DOCTOR JOHN'S, INC. v. CITY OF SIOUX CITY, IOWA

486 F. Supp. 2d 953 (N.D. Iowa 2007)

BENNETT, DISTRICT JUDGE

By order dated May 1, 2007, the court dismissed this case in its entirety, with prejudice, upon the parties' settlement and Stipulation Of Dismissal. However, the court stated in the order dismissing the case that it would retain jurisdiction over the question of whether or not sanctions should be imposed upon the City for destruction, during the pendency of litigation, of relevant records, which consisted of recordings of closed sessions of the City Council concerning the ordinances challenged in this case. Thereafter * * * the court held a conference with counsel for the parties * * * to discuss the remaining sanctions question * * * [and] also received a letter from counsel for the City clarifying

---

30. *See Procter & Gamble Co. v. Haugen*, 427 F.3d 727, 738 (10th Cir. 2005).

31. *Residential Funding Corp. v. Degeorge Financial Corp.*, 306 F.3d 99, 109 (2d Cir. 2002) (quotations omitted).

changes made to the City's policy regarding retention of recordings of closed sessions of the City Council. * * *

A first year law student should have—and most would have—known that a party must retain documents or records that are likely to be relevant in pending litigation. The City's claim that it was simply following state law in destroying key evidence is laughable and frivolous. No state or federal statute, rule, or common law allows a party to destroy critical evidence during the pendency of litigation, and the City policy that permitted destruction of certain documents after a specified period of time certainly did not require destruction of such documents.

Indeed, both state and federal law require just the opposite, retention of evidence potentially relevant to pending or reasonably anticipated litigation. *See, e.g., Dillon v. Nissan Motor Co., Ltd.*, 986 F.2d 263, 268 (8th Cir. 1993) ("[T]he destruction of evidence that a party knew or should have known was relevant to imminent litigation certainly justifies a sanction under the court's inherent power comparable to the Rule 37 sanctions."); see also *Silvestri v. Gen. Motors Corp.*, 271 F.3d 583, 591 (4th Cir. 2001) ("The duty to preserve material evidence arises not only during litigation but also extends to that period before litigation when a party reasonably should know that the evidence may be relevant to anticipated litigation.") * * * *Zubulake v. UBS Warburg LLC*, 220 F.R.D. 212, 216 (S.D.N.Y.2003) ("The duty to preserve attached at the time that litigation was reasonably anticipated.").

Thus, the City's failure to preserve the tape recordings of the City Council's closed-session meetings, and the consequential destruction of critical evidence in this case, was clearly and unquestionably improper conduct.

Moreover, the court has the inherent power to sanction such improper conduct subject to review for abuse of discretion. * * * A court's inherent power includes the discretionary "ability to fashion an appropriate sanction for conduct which abuses the judicial process." *Chambers v. NASCO, Inc.*, 501 U.S. 32, 44–45 (1991). * * * Thus, the court must determine whether and what sanctions are appropriate for the City's improper destruction of records in this case.

The Eighth Circuit Court of Appeals has recognized that, under a court's inherent power to sanction parties, "a finding of bad faith is not always necessary to the court's exercise of its inherent power to impose sanctions." * * * [H]owever, * * * a finding of "bad faith" is required to impose sanctions in the form of an adverse inference instruction or award of attorney fees to the opposing party. * * * Consequently, this court will assume that a finding of "bad faith" is required to impose other monetary sanctions.

Here, a substantial monetary sanction against the City is easily justified by the City's outrageous conduct in failing to preserve the key evidence of recordings of closed-session meetings. That conduct was of a kind that "abuses the judicial process" * * * because it went to the very heart of the plaintiff's ability to prove the City's motivation in passing the challenged ordinances. Moreover, the circumstances give rise to a powerful inference of intentional destruction indicating a desire to suppress the truth, notwithstanding the City's contention that the records were destroyed pursuant to a document retention policy.

More specifically, as noted above, the contention that the document retention policy mandated by state law excused destruction of the records in question is laughable and frivolous, because that policy plainly did not require the destruction of any documents, and certainly did not authorize the destruction of records pertinent to pending litigation. Moreover, purported adherence to the policy by destroying records that the policy did not mandate for destruction was unreasonable and amounted to bad faith conduct where litigation was pending. Indeed, this case seems to this court to fall well within, not to test the limits of, conduct that constitutes bad faith destruction of documents, where the City had not simply been made aware of the circumstances giving rise to a potential lawsuit, but was in the throes of litigating a lawsuit over the constitutionality of its sex shop ordinances at the time that it destroyed records of closed sessions in which the City Council considered those ordinances. Moreover, while the City destroyed these records, the City went out of its way to provide evidence and even to generate new evidence to try to justify the ordinances long after they were passed, enjoined, and partially struck down. Finally, the recordings of the closed sessions in question here were the only contemporaneous evidence of the motives of the decision makers at the time certain decisions were made, and as such—where the motives of the decision makers were plainly at issue—the evidence was highly relevant to pending litigation.

To the same extent and for essentially the same reasons that the court finds that the City's conduct in destroying the records in question was in "bad faith," the court also finds that such conduct was prejudicial to the plaintiff. Again, the City's motive in passing the challenged ordinances was a critical element of the plaintiff's proof, and the City's destruction of contemporaneous recordings of closed sessions of City Council meetings in which the ordinances were discussed patently prejudiced the plaintiff's ability to prove that critical element.

In this case, the court finds that a monetary sanction in the amount of $50,000 is warranted for the City's destruction of plainly relevant records.

On the other hand, because of the City's ill-conceived, illegal, and unconstitutional actions in targeting and attempting to trample the plaintiff's First Amendment rights, the taxpayers have already paid dearly, to the tune of over $600,000. No matter how you fry it, that's a ton of Sneaky's chicken. Also, notwithstanding various City Council Members' attempts to save face by claiming that the City would have ultimately prevailed in this litigation—just how those City Council

Members became such enlightened, sophisticated, and prophetic federal constitutional scholars remains a prodigious mystery—the City and Doctor John's have worked diligently to reach a settlement. In so doing, both sides engaged in substantial compromise from their equally unreasonable legal positions. Moreover, the City Council has voluntarily and wisely changed its record retention policy to prevent the destruction of such evidence in the future during pending litigation. Thus, having recognized the error of its ways, the City moved swiftly to correct its mistake.

Balancing all of these factors, the court finds that the scales of justice tip ever so slightly in favor of declining to impose sanctions against the City for destruction of relevant records. Any similar litigation misconduct in the future, however, will be dealt with severely, in light of the City's "get out of jail free" card here.

COMMENTARY

Sanctions against a spoliator may include reimbursement of attorney fees, monetary penalties against the party or attorney, and recovery of discovery costs.

Did the court's action in *Doctor John's* fail to serve the remedial purposes of discovery sanctions?

Although the defendant's bad faith destruction of documents warranted $50,000 in sanctions, the court found that countervailing factors weighed "ever so slightly" in favor of declining to impose that sanction. If, as the court determined, the defendant's bad faith conduct prejudiced the plaintiff's ability to prove its case, did the court's failure to impose sanctions effectively penalize the plaintiff?

While reimbursement of attorneys' fees and monetary penalties may constitute a sanction, pursuant to Rule 26 (g)(3), it is not entirely clear that shifting of discovery costs should be considered a sanction. A court has the power to apportion the costs of discovery pursuant to Rule 26(c)(1)(B) and Rule 26(c)(2), which provide that a court may "specify the terms" for discovery or disclosure and may "on just terms" order that "a party or person provide or permit discovery." Do you agree that the shifting of costs can be viewed as "a term" upon which discovery is permitted rather than a sanction?[32]

E. SANCTIONING A PARTY/SANCTIONING COUNSEL

QUALCOMM INC. v. BROADCOM CORP.

No. 05 Civ. 1958, 2008 WL 66932 (S.D. Cal. Jan. 7, 2008)

MAJOR, MAGISTRATE JUDGE

At the conclusion of trial, counsel for Broadcom Corporation ("Broadcom") made an oral motion for sanctions after Qualcomm

---

32. *See, e.g., Zubulake IV*, 220 F.R.D. at 222 (requiring defendant to pay costs incurred by plaintiff in taking additional discovery that resulted from defendant's failure to produce certain information in a timely manner).

Incorporated ("Qualcomm") witness Viji Raveendran testified about emails that were not produced to Broadcom during discovery. The trial judge, United States District Court Judge Rudi M. Brewster, referred the motion to this Court * * *. On May 29, 2007, Broadcom filed a written motion requesting that the Court sanction Qualcomm for its failure to produce tens of thousands of documents that Broadcom had requested in discovery. * * *

After hearing oral argument and reviewing Judge Brewster's Order on Remedy for Finding of Waiver ("Waiver Order") and Order Granting Broadcom Corporation's Motion for Exceptional Case Finding and for an Award of Attorney's Fees (35 U.S.C. § 285) ("Exceptional Case Order"), this Court issued an Order to Show Cause Why Sanctions Should Not be Imposed against Qualcomm's retained attorneys ("OSC"). Specifically, this Court ordered * * * all * * * attorneys who signed discovery responses, signed pleadings and pretrial motions, and/or appeared at trial on behalf of Qualcomm to appear and show cause why sanctions should not be imposed for their failure to comply with this Court's orders.

On October 3, 2007, nineteen attorneys filed declarations and briefs responsive to the OSC. Qualcomm filed a brief and four declarations. * * * Having considered all of the written and oral arguments presented and supporting documents submitted, and for the reasons set forth more fully below, the Court GRANTS IN PART and DENIES IN PART Broadcom's motion for sanctions against Qualcomm, REFERS TO THE STATE BAR OF CALIFORNIA six attorneys, and SANCTIONS Qualcomm and six of its retained lawyers.

BACKGROUND

A. The Patent Infringement Case

Qualcomm initiated this patent infringement action on October 14, 2005, alleging Broadcom's infringement of Qualcomm patent numbers 5,452,104 (the "104 patent") and 5,576,767 (the "767 patent") based on its manufacture, sale, and offers to sell H.264–compliant products. Qualcomm sought injunctive relief, compensatory damages, attorneys' fees and costs. On December 8, 2006, Broadcom filed a First Amended Answer and Counterclaims in which it alleged (1) a counterclaim that the 104 patent is unenforceable due to inequitable conduct, and (2) an affirmative defense that both patents are unenforceable due to waiver. Broadcom's waiver defense was predicated on Qualcomm's participation in the Joint Video Team ("JVT") in 2002 and early 2003. The JVT is the standards-setting body that created the H.264 standard, which was released in May 2003 and governs video coding.

B.   Evidence of Qualcomm's Participation in the JVT

Over the course of discovery, Broadcom sought information concerning Qualcomm's participation in and communications with the JVT through a variety of discovery devices.

* * *

In response to Broadcom's request for JVT documents, Qualcomm, in a discovery response signed by attorney Kevin Leung, stated "Qualcomm will produce non-privileged relevant and responsive documents describing QUALCOMM's participation in the JVT, if any, which can be located after a reasonable search." Similarly, Qualcomm committed to producing "responsive non-privileged documents that were given to or received from standards-setting body responsible for the ISO/IEC MPEG–4 Part 10 standard, and which concern any Qualcomm participation in setting the ISO/IEC MPEG–4 Part 10 standard." When asked for "the facts and circumstances of any and all communications between Qualcomm and any standards setting body relating to video technology, including . . . the JVT . . . ," Qualcomm responded that it first attended a JVT meeting in December 2003 and that it first submitted a JVT proposal in January 2006. In response to Interrogatory No. 13, Qualcomm stated that it submitted four proposals to the JVT in 2006 but had no earlier involvement. This response included the statement that "Qualcomm's investigation concerning this interrogatory is ongoing and Qualcomm reserves the right to supplement its response to this interrogatory as warranted by its investigation." Kevin Leung signed both of these interrogatory responses.

Qualcomm's responses to Broadcom's Rule 30(b)(6) deposition notices were more troubling. Initially, Qualcomm designated Christine Irvine as the corporation's most knowledgeable person on the issue of Qualcomm's involvement in the JVT. Although attorney Leung prepared Irvine for her deposition, Qualcomm did not search her computer for any relevant documents or emails or provide her with any information to review. Irvine testified falsely that Qualcomm had never been involved in the JVT. Broadcom impeached Irvine with documents showing that Qualcomm had participated in the JVT in late 2003. Qualcomm ultimately agreed to provide another Rule 30(b)(6) witness.

Qualcomm designated Scott Ludwin as the new representative to testify about Qualcomm's knowledge of and involvement in the JVT. Leung prepared and defended Ludwin at his deposition. Qualcomm did not search Ludwin's computer for any relevant documents nor take any other action to prepare him. Ludwin testified falsely that Qualcomm only began participating in the JVT in late 2003, after the H.264 standard had been published. In an effort to impeach him (and extract the truth), Broadcom showed Ludwin a December 2002 email reflector list from the Advanced Video Coding ("AVC") Ad Hoc Group that listed the email address viji@qualcomm.com.[2] Although Ludwin did not recognize the document, Broadcom utilized the document throughout the litigation to argue that Qualcomm had participated in the JVT during the development of the H.264 standard.

As the case progressed, Qualcomm became increasingly aggressive in its argument that it did not participate in the JVT during the time the JVT was creating the H.264 standard. This argument was vital to Qualcomm's success in this litigation because if Qualcomm had participated in the creation of the H.264 standard, it would have been required to identify its patents that reasonably may be essential to the practice of the H.264 standard, including the 104 and 767 patents, and to license them royalty-free or under non-discriminatory, reasonable terms. Thus, participation in the JVT in 2002 or early 2003 during the creation of the H.264 standard would have prohibited Qualcomm from suing companies, including Broadcom, that utilized the H.264 standard. In a nutshell, the issue of whether Qualcomm participated in the JVT in 2002 and early 2003 became crucial to the instant litigation.

C.   Trial and Decision Not to Produce avc_ce Emails

Trial commenced on January 9, 2007, and throughout trial, Qualcomm argued that it had not participated in the JVT in 2002 and early 2003 when the H.264 standard was being created. In his opening statement, Qualcomm's lead attorney, James Batchelder, stated:

> Later, in May of 03, the standard is approved and published. And then Qualcomm, in the fall of 2003, it begins to participate not in JVT because it's done. H.264 is approved and published. Qualcomm begins to participate in what are called professional extensions, things that sit on top of the standard, additional improvements.

While preparing Qualcomm witness Viji Raveendran to testify at trial, attorney Adam Bier discovered an August 6, 2002 email to viji@qualcomm.com welcoming her to the avc_ce mailing list. Several days later, on January 14, 2007, Bier and Raveendran searched her laptop computer using the search term "avc_ce" and discovered 21 separate emails, none of which Qualcomm had produced in discovery. The email chains bore several dates in November 2002 and the authors discussed various issues relating to the H.264 standard. While Raveendran was not a named author or recipient, the emails were sent to all members of two JVT email groups (jvt-experts and avc_ce) and Raveendran maintained them on her computer for more than four years. The Qualcomm trial

---

2. The document is an "Input Document to JVT" entitled "Ad Hoc Report on AVC Verification Test." The report discusses a meeting set to take place on Awaji Island. *Id.* Annex A to the document is entitled a "list of Ad Hoc Members.". It includes Raveendran's email address, viji@qualcomm.com, and identifies her as a member of list avc_ce. While the document is not an email sent to or from Raveendran, it indicates that a Qualcomm employee was receiving JVT/AVC reports in 2002. This document became critical to Broadcom as it was the only evidence in Broadcom's possession indicating the truth—that Qualcomm had been actively involved in the JVT and the development of the H.264 standard in 2002.

team decided not to produce these newly discovered emails to Broadcom, claiming they were not responsive to Broadcom's discovery requests. The attorneys ignored the fact that the presence of the emails on
Raveendran's computer undercut Qualcomm's premier argument that it
had not participated in the JVT in 2002. The Qualcomm trial team
failed to conduct any investigation to determine whether there were
more emails that also had not been produced.

Four days later, during a sidebar discussion, Stanley Young argued
against the admission of the December 2002 avc_ce email reflector list,
declaring: "Actually, there are no emails—there are no emails ...
there's no evidence that any email was actually sent to this list. This is
just a list of email ... addresses. There's no evidence of anything being
sent." None of the Qualcomm attorneys who were present during the
sidebar mentioned the 21 avc_ce emails found on Raveendran's computer a few days earlier.

During Raveendran's direct testimony on January 24th, attorney
Lee Patch pointedly did not ask her any questions that would reveal the
fact that she had received the 21 emails from the avc_ce mailing list;
instead, he asked whether she had "any knowledge of having read" any
emails from the avc_ce mailing list. But on cross-examination, Broadcom
asked the right question and Raveendran was forced to admit that she
had received emails from the avc_ce mailing list. Immediately following
this admission, in response to Broadcom's request for the emails, and
despite the fact that he had participated in the decision three days
earlier not to produce them, Patch told the Court at sidebar:

> It's not clear to me [the emails are] responsive to anything. So that's
> something that needs to be determined before they would be
> produced ... I'm talking about whether they were actually request-
> ed in discovery.... I'm simply representing that I haven't seen [the
> emails], and [whether Broadcom requested them] hasn't been deter-
> mined.

Over the lunch recess that same day, Qualcomm's counsel produced the
21 emails they previously had retrieved from Raveendran's email archive.

On January 26, 2007, the jury returned unanimous verdicts in
favor of Broadcom regarding the non-infringement of the 104 and 767
patents, and in favor of Qualcomm regarding the validity and non-
obviousness of the same. The jury also returned a unanimous advisory
verdict in favor of Broadcom that the 104 patent is unenforceable due to
inequitable conduct and the 104 and 767 patents are unenforceable due
to waiver.

On March 21, 2007, Judge Brewster found (1) in favor of Qualcomm on Broadcom's inequitable conduct counterclaim regarding the
104 patent, and (2) in favor of Broadcom on Broadcom's waiver defense
regarding the 104 and 767 patents. On August 6, 2007, Judge Brewster
issued a comprehensive order detailing the appropriate remedy for

Qualcomm's waiver. After a thorough overview of the JVT, the JVT's policies and guidelines, and Qualcomm's knowledge of the JVT and evidence of Qualcomm's involvement therein, Judge Brewster found:

> by clear and convincing evidence that Qualcomm, its employees, and its witnesses actively organized and/or participated in a plan to profit heavily by (1) wrongfully concealing the patents-in-suit while participating in the JVT and then (2) actively hiding this concealment from the Court, the jury, and opposing counsel during the present litigation.

Judge Brewster further found that Qualcomm's "counsel participated in an organized program of litigation misconduct and concealment throughout discovery, trial, and post-trial before new counsel took over lead role in the case on April 27, 2007." Based on "the totality of the evidence produced both before and after the jury verdict," and in light of these findings, Judge Brewster concluded that "Qualcomm has waived its rights to enforce the 104 and 767 patents and their continuations, continuations-in-part, divisions, reissues, or any other derivatives of either patent."

Also on August 6, 2007, Judge Brewster granted Broadcom's Motion for an Award of Attorneys' Fees pursuant to 35 U.S.C. § 285. Judge Brewster found clear and convincing evidence that Qualcomm's litigation misconduct, as set forth in his Waiver Order, justified Qualcomm's payment of all "attorneys' fees, court costs, expert witness fees, travel expenses, and any other litigation costs reasonably incurred by Broadcom" in the defense of this case. On December 11, 2007, Judge Brewster adopted this court's recommendation and ordered Qualcomm to pay Broadcom $9,259,985.09 in attorneys' fees and related costs, as well as post-judgment interest on the final fee award of $8,568,633.24 at 4.91 percent accruing from August 6, 2007.

D.   Qualcomm's Post–Trial Misconduct

Following trial, Qualcomm continued to dispute the relevancy and responsiveness of the 21 Raveendran emails. Qualcomm also resisted Broadcom's efforts to determine the scope of Qualcomm's discovery violation. By letter dated February 16, 2007, Bier told Broadcom "[w]e continue to believe that Qualcomm performed a reasonable search of Qualcomm's documents in response to Broadcom's Requests for Production and that the twenty-one unsolicited emails received by Ms. Raveendran from individuals on the avc_ce reflector are not responsive to any valid discovery obligation or commitment." In response to Broadcom's request that Qualcomm conduct additional searches to determine the scope of Qualcomm's discovery violation, Bier stated in a March 7, 2007 letter, we "believe your negative characterization of Qualcomm's compliance with its discovery obligation to be wholly without merit" but he advised that Qualcomm agreed to search the current and archived emails of five trial witnesses using the requested JVT, avc_ce and H.264 terms. Bier explained that Qualcomm has "not yet commenced these searches, and [does] not yet know the volume of results we will obtain." Throughout the remainder of March 2007, Bier repeatedly declined to update Broadcom on Qualcomm's document search.

But, on April 9, 2007, James Batchelder and Louis Lupin, Qualcomm's General Counsel, submitted correspondence to Judge Brewster in which they admitted Qualcomm had thousands of relevant unproduced documents and that their review of these documents "revealed facts that appear to be inconsistent with certain arguments that [counsel] made on Qualcomm's behalf at trial and in the equitable hearing following trial." Batchelder further apologized "for not having discovered these documents sooner and for asserting positions that [they] would not have taken had [they] known of the existence of these documents."

As of June 29, 2007, Qualcomm had searched the email archives of twenty-one employees and located more than forty-six thousand documents (totaling more than three hundred thousand pages), which had been requested but not produced in discovery. Qualcomm continued to produce additional responsive documents throughout the summer.

DISCUSSION

As summarized above, and as found by Judge Brewster, there is clear and convincing evidence that Qualcomm intentionally engaged in conduct designed to prevent Broadcom from learning that Qualcomm had participated in the JVT during the time period when the H.264 standard was being developed. To this end, Qualcomm withheld tens of thousands of emails showing that it actively participated in the JVT in 2002 and 2003 and then utilized Broadcom's lack of access to the suppressed evidence to repeatedly and falsely aver that there was "no evidence" that it had participated in the JVT prior to September 2003. Qualcomm's misconduct in hiding the emails and electronic documents prevented Broadcom from correcting the false statements and countering the misleading arguments.

A. Legal Standard

The Federal Civil Rules authorize federal courts to impose sanctions on parties and their attorneys who fail to comply with discovery obligations and court orders. Rule 37 authorizes a party to file a motion to compel an opponent to comply with a discovery request or obligation when the opponent fails to do so initially. Fed.R.Civ.P. 37(a). If such a motion is filed, the rule requires the court to award reasonable attorney's fees to the prevailing party unless the court finds the losing party's position was "substantially justified" or other circumstances make such an award unjust. Depending upon the circumstances, the court may require the attorney, the client, or both to pay the awarded fees. If the court grants a discovery motion and the losing party fails to comply with the order, the court may impose additional sanctions against the party. Fed.R.Civ.P. 37(b). There is no requirement under this rule that the failure be willful or reckless; "sanctions may be imposed even for negligent failures to provide discovery."

The Federal Rules also provide for sanctions against individual attorneys who are remiss in complying with their discovery obligations:

> Every discovery request, response or objection made by a party . . . shall be signed by at least one attorney. The signature of the attorney . . . constitutes a certification that to the best of the signer's knowledge, information, and belief, formed after a reasonable inquiry, the request, response, or objection is: consistent with the rules and law, not interposed for an improper purpose, and not unreasonable or unduly burdensome or expensive.

Fed.R.Civ.P. 26(g)(2). "[W]hat is reasonable is a matter for the court to decide on the totality of the circumstances." * * *

If an attorney makes an incorrect certification without substantial justification, the court must sanction the attorney, party, or both and the sanction may include an award of reasonable attorney's fees. Fed. R.Civ.P. 26(g)(3). If a party, without substantial justification, fails "to amend a prior response to discovery as required by Rule 26(e)(2)," the court may prevent that party from using that evidence at trial or at a hearing and impose other appropriate sanctions, including the payment of attorney's fees. Fed.R.Civ.P. 37(c)(1). * * * In addition to this rule-based authority, federal courts have the inherent power to sanction litigants to prevent abuse of the judicial process. * * * Sanctions are appropriate in response to "willful disobedience of a court order . . . or when the losing party has acted in bad faith, vexatiously, wantonly, or for oppressive reasons." When a court order is violated, a district court considering the imposition of sanctions must also examine the risk of prejudice to the complying party and the availability of less drastic sanctions.

* * *

C. Sanctions

The Court's review of Qualcomm's declarations, the attorneys' declarations, and Judge Brewster's orders leads this Court to the inevitable conclusion that Qualcomm intentionally withheld tens of thousands of decisive documents from its opponent in an effort to win this case and gain a strategic business advantage over Broadcom. Qualcomm could not have achieved this goal without some type of assistance or deliberate ignorance from its retained attorneys. Accordingly, the Court concludes it must sanction both Qualcomm and some of its retained attorneys.

1. Misconduct by Qualcomm

Qualcomm violated its discovery obligations by failing to produce more than 46,000 emails and documents that were requested in discovery and that Qualcomm agreed to produce. * * * Qualcomm has not established "substantial justification" for its failure to produce the documents. In fact, Qualcomm has not presented any evidence attempting to explain or justify its failure to produce the documents. Despite the fact that it maintains detailed records showing whose computers were searched and which search terms were used * * * Qualcomm has not presented any evidence establishing that it searched for pre-September 2003 JVT, avc_ce, or H.264 records or emails on its computer system or email databases. Qualcomm also has not established that it searched the computers or email databases of the individuals who testified on Qualcomm's behalf at trial or in depositions as Qualcomm's most knowledgeable corporate witnesses; in fact, it indicates that it did not conduct any such search. The fact that Qualcomm did not perform these basic searches at any time before the completion of trial indicates that Qualcomm intentionally withheld the documents. This conclusion is bolstered by the fact that when Qualcomm "discovered" the 21 Raveendran emails, it did not produce them and did not engage in any type of review to determine whether there were additional relevant, responsive, and unproduced documents. The conclusion is further supported by the fact that after trial Qualcomm did not conduct an internal investigation to determine if there were additional unproduced documents; but, rather, spent its time opposing Broadcom's efforts to force such a search and insisting, without any factual basis, that Qualcomm's search was reasonable.

Qualcomm's claim that it inadvertently failed to find and produce these documents also is negated by the massive volume and direct relevance of the hidden documents. As Judge Brewster noted, it is inexplicable that Qualcomm was able to locate the post-September 2003 JVT documents that either supported, or did not harm, Qualcomm's arguments but were unable to locate the pre-September 2003 JVT documents that hurt its arguments. Similarly, the inadvertence argument is undercut by Qualcomm's ability to easily locate the suppressed documents using fundamental JVT and avc search terms when forced to do so by Broadcom's threat to return to court. Finally, the inadvertence argument also is belied by the number of Qualcomm employees and consultants who received the emails, attended the JVT meetings, and otherwise knew about the information set forth in the undisclosed emails. It is inconceivable that Qualcomm was unaware of its involvement in the JVT and of the existence of these documents.

Assuming[,] *arguendo*, that Qualcomm did not know about the suppressed emails, Qualcomm failed to heed several warning signs that should have alerted it to the fact that its document search and production were inadequate. The first significant concern should have been raised in connection with the Rule 30(b)(6) depositions of Christine Irvine and Scott Ludwin. Both individuals testified as the Qualcomm employee most knowledgeable about Qualcomm's involvement in the JVT. But, Qualcomm did not search either person's computer for JVT documents, did not provide either person with relevant JVT documents to review, and did not make any other efforts to ensure each person was in fact knowledgeable about Qualcomm's JVT involvement. These omissions are especially incriminating because many of the suppressed emails were to or from Irvine. If a witness is testifying as an organization's most knowledgeable person on a specific subject, the organization has an obligation to conduct a reasonable investigation and review to ensure that the witness does possess the organization's knowledge. Fed.R.Civ.P. 30(b)(6).[6] * * * An adequate investigation should include an analysis of the sufficiency of the document search and, when electronic documents are involved, an analysis of the sufficiency of the search terms and locations. In the instant case, a reasonable inquiry should have included using the JVT, avc and H.264 search terms and searching the computers of Raveendran, Irvine, Ludwin (and other Qualcomm employees identified in the emails discovered on the computers of these witnesses). This minimal inquiry would have revealed the existence of the suppressed documents.

* * *

Qualcomm had the ability to identify its employees and consultants who were involved in the JVT, to access and review their computers, databases and emails, to talk with the involved employees and to refresh their recollections if necessary, to ensure that those testifying about the corporation's knowledge were sufficiently prepared and testified accurately, and to produce in good faith all relevant and requested discovery. * * * Qualcomm chose not to do so and therefore must be sanctioned.

2. Attorneys' Misconduct

The next question is what, if any, role did Qualcomm's retained lawyers play in withholding the documents? The Court envisions four scenarios. First, Qualcomm intentionally hid the documents from its retained lawyers and did so so effectively that the lawyers did not know or suspect that the suppressed documents existed. Second, the retained lawyers failed to discover the intentionally hidden documents or suspect their existence due to their complete ineptitude and disorganization. Third, Qualcomm shared the damaging documents with its retained lawyers (or at least some of them) and the knowledgeable lawyers worked with Qualcomm to hide the documents and all evidence of Qualcomm's early involvement in the JVT. Or, fourth, while Qualcomm did not tell the retained lawyers about the damaging documents and

---

6. Qualcomm's self-serving statements that "outside counsel selects . . . the custodians whose documents should be searched" and the paralegal does not decide "what witnesses to designate to testify on behalf of the company" (Glathe Decl. at 1) does not relieve Qualcomm of its obligations. Qualcomm has not presented any evidence establishing what actions, if any, it took to ensure it designated the correct employee, performed the correct computer searches, and presented the designated employee with sufficient information to testify as the corporation's most knowledgeable person. Qualcomm also has not presented any evidence that outside counsel knew enough about Qualcomm's organization and operation to identify all of the individuals whose computers should be searched and determine the most knowledgeable witness. And, more importantly, Qualcomm is a large corporation with an extensive legal staff; it clearly had the ability to identify the correct witnesses and determine the correct computers to search and search terms to use. Qualcomm just lacked the desire to do so.

evidence, the lawyers suspected there was additional evidence or information but chose to ignore the evidence and warning signs and accept Qualcomm's incredible assertions regarding the adequacy of the document search and witness investigation.

Given the impressive education and extensive experience of Qualcomm's retained lawyers, the Court rejects the first and second possibilities. It is inconceivable that these talented, well-educated, and experienced lawyers failed to discover through their interactions with Qualcomm any facts or issues that caused (or should have caused) them to question the sufficiency of Qualcomm's document search and production. Qualcomm did not fail to produce a document or two; it withheld over 46,000 critical documents that extinguished Qualcomm's primary argument of non-participation in the JVT. In addition, the suppressed documents did not belong to one employee, or a couple of employees who had since left the company; they belonged to (or were shared with) numerous, current Qualcomm employees, several of whom testified (falsely) at trial and in depositions. Given the volume and importance of the withheld documents, the number of involved Qualcomm employees, and the numerous warning flags, the Court finds it unbelievable that the retained attorneys did not know or suspect that Qualcomm had not conducted an adequate search for documents.

The Court finds no direct evidence establishing option three. Neither [of the parties] party nor the attorneys have presented evidence that Qualcomm told one or more of its retained attorneys about the damaging emails or that an attorney learned about the emails and that the knowledgeable attorney(s) then helped Qualcomm hide the emails. While knowledge may be inferred from the attorneys' conduct, evidence on this issue is limited due to Qualcomm's assertion of the attorney-client privilege.[8]

Thus, the Court finds it likely that some variation of option four occurred; that is, one or more of the retained lawyers chose not to look in the correct locations for the correct documents, to accept the unsubstantiated assurances of an important client that its search was sufficient, to ignore the warning signs that the document search and production were inadequate, not to press Qualcomm employees for the truth, and/or to encourage employees to provide the information (or lack of information) that Qualcomm needed to assert its non-participation argument and to succeed in this lawsuit. These choices enabled Qual-

---

8. Qualcomm asserted the attorney-client privilege and decreed that its retained attorneys could not reveal any communications protected by the privilege. Several attorneys complained that the assertion of the privilege prevented them from providing additional information regarding their conduct. This concern was heightened when Qualcomm submitted its self-serving declarations describing the failings of its retained lawyers. Recognizing that a client has a right to maintain this privilege and that no adverse inference should be made based upon the assertion, the Court accepted Qualcomm's assertion of the privilege and has not drawn any adverse inferences from it. However, the fact remains that the Court does not have access to all of the information necessary to reach an informed decision regarding the actual knowledge of the attorneys. As a result, the Court concludes for purposes of this Order that there is insufficient evidence establishing option three.

comm to withhold hundreds of thousands of pages of relevant discovery and to assert numerous false and misleading arguments to the court and jury. This conduct warrants the imposition of sanctions.

a. Identity of Sanctioned Attorneys

* * *

Attorneys Leung, Mammen and Batchelder are responsible for the initial discovery failure because they handled or supervised Qualcomm's discovery responses and production of documents. The Federal Rules impose an affirmative duty upon lawyers to engage in discovery in a responsible manner and to conduct a "reasonable inquiry" to determine whether discovery responses are sufficient and proper. In the instant case, a reasonable inquiry should have included searches using fundamental terms such as JVT, avc_ce or H.264, on the computers belonging to knowledgeable people such as Raveendran, Irvine and Ludwin. * * * Had Leung, Mammen, Batchelder, or any of the other attorneys insisted on reviewing Qualcomm's records regarding the locations searched and terms utilized, they would have discovered the inadequacy of the search and the suppressed documents. Similarly, Leung's difficulties with the Rule 30(b)(6) witnesses, Irvine and Ludwin, should have alerted him (and the supervising or senior attorneys) to the inadequacy of Qualcomm's document production and to the fact that they needed to review whose computers and databases had been searched and for what. Accordingly, the Court finds that the totality of the circumstances establish that Leung, Mammen and Batchelder did not make a reasonable inquiry into Qualcomm's discovery search and production and their conduct contributed to the discovery violation.[10]

Attorneys Bier, Mammen and Patch are responsible for the discovery violation because they also did not perform a reasonable inquiry to determine whether Qualcomm had complied with its discovery obligations. When Bier reviewed the August 6, 2002 email welcoming Raveendran to the avc_ce email group, he knew or should have known that it contradicted Qualcomm's trial arguments and he had an obligation to verify that it had been produced in discovery or to immediately produce it. If Bier, as a junior lawyer, lacked the experience to recognize the significance of the document, then a more senior or

---

10. Leung's attorney represented during the OSC hearing that Leung requested a more thorough document search but that Qualcomm refused to do so. If Leung was unable to get Qualcomm to conduct the type of search he deemed necessary to verify the adequacy of the document search and production, then he should have obtained the assistance of supervising or senior attorneys. If Mammen and Batchelder were unable to get Qualcomm to conduct a competent and thorough document search, they should have withdrawn from the case or taken other action to ensure production of the evidence. *See* The State Bar of California, Rules of Professional Conduct, Rule 5–220 (a lawyer shall not suppress evidence that the lawyer or the lawyer's client has a legal obligation to reveal); Rule 3–700 (a lawyer shall withdraw from employment if the lawyer knows or should know that continued employment will result in a violation of these rules or the client insists that the lawyer pursue a course of conduct prohibited under these rules). Attorneys' ethical obligations do not permit them to participate in an inadequate document search and then provide misleading and incomplete information to their opponents and false arguments to the court.

knowledgeable attorney should have assisted him. To the extent that Patch was supervising Bier in this endeavor, Patch certainly knew or should have recognized the importance of the document from his involvement in Qualcomm's motion practice and trial strategy sessions.

Similarly, when Bier found the 21 emails on Raveendran's computer that had not been produced in discovery, he took the appropriate action and informed his supervisors, Mammen and Patch. Patch discussed the discovery and production issue with Young and Batchelder. While all of these attorneys assert that there was a plausible argument that Broadcom did not request these documents, only Bier and Mammen actually read the emails. Moreover, all of the attorneys missed the critical inquiry: was Qualcomm's document search adequate? If these 21 emails were not discovered during Qualcomm's document search, how many more might exist? The answer, obviously, was tens of thousands. If Bier, Mammen, Patch, Young or Batchelder had conducted a reasonable inquiry after the discovery of the 21 Raveendran emails, they would have discovered the inadequacy of Qualcomm's search and the suppressed documents. And, these experienced attorneys should have realized that the presence on Raveendran's computer of 21 JVT/avc_ce emails from 2002 contradicted Qualcomm's numerous arguments that it had not participated in the JVT during that same time period. This fact, alone, should have prompted the attorneys to immediately produce the emails and to conduct a comprehensive document search.

Finally, attorneys Young, Patch, and Batchelder bear responsibility for the discovery failure because they did not conduct a reasonable inquiry into Qualcomm's discovery production before making specific factual and legal arguments to the court. Young decided that Qualcomm should file a motion for summary adjudication premised on the fact that Qualcomm had not participated in the JVT until after the H.264 standard was adopted in May 2003. Given that non-participation was vital to the motion, Young had a duty to conduct a reasonable inquiry into whether that fact was true. And, again, had Young conducted such a search, he would have discovered the inadequacy of Qualcomm's document search and production and learned that his argument was false. Similarly, Young had a duty to conduct a reasonable inquiry into the accuracy of his statement before affirmatively telling the court that no emails were sent to Raveendran from the avc_ce email group. Young also did not conduct a reasonable (or any) inquiry during the following days before he approved the factually incorrect JMOL. A reasonable investigation would have prevented the false filing.

Patch was an integral part of the trial team—familiar with Qualcomm's arguments, theories and strategies. He knew on January 14th that 21 avc_ce emails had been discovered on Raveendran's computer. Without reading or reviewing the emails, Patch participated in the decision not to produce them. Several days later, Patch carefully tailored his questions to ensure that Raveendran did not testify about the unproduced emails. And, after Broadcom stumbled into the email testimony, Patch affirmatively misled the Court by claiming that he did not know whether the emails were responsive to Broadcom's discovery requests. This conduct is unacceptable and, considering the totality of the circumstances, it is unrealistic to think that Patch did not know or believe that Qualcomm's document search was inadequate and that Qualcomm possessed numerous, similar and unproduced documents.

Batchelder also is responsible because he was the lead trial attorney and, as such, he was most familiar with Qualcomm's important arguments and witnesses. Batchelder stated in his opening statement that Qualcomm had not participated in the JVT before late 2003. Despite this statement and his complete knowledge of Qualcomm's legal theories, Batchelder did not take any action when he was informed that JVT documents that Qualcomm had not produced in discovery were found on Raveendran's computer. He did not read the emails, ask about their substance, nor inquire as to why they were not located during discovery. And, he stood mute when four days later, Young falsely stated that no emails had been sent to Raveendran from the avc_ce email group. Finally, all of the pleadings containing the lie that Qualcomm had not participated in the JVT in 2002 or early 2003 were sent to Batchelder for review and he approved or ignored all of them. The totality of the circumstances, including all of the previously-discussed warning signs, demanded that Batchelder conduct an investigation to verify the adequacy of Qualcomm's document search and production. His failure to do so enabled Qualcomm to withhold the documents.

For all of these reasons, the Court finds that these attorneys did not conduct a reasonable inquiry into the adequacy of Qualcomm's document search and production and, accordingly, they are responsible, along with Qualcomm, for the monumental discovery violation.

b. Identity of Non–Sanctioned Attorneys

* * *

The Court also declines to sanction * * * attorneys Kleinfeld and Tucker. These attorneys primarily monitored the instant case for its impact on separate Qualcomm/Broadcom litigation. However, for logistical reasons, both attorneys signed as local counsel pleadings that contained false statements relating to Qulacomm's non-participation in the JVT. Given the facts of this case as set forth above and in the declarations, the limitations provided by the referral, and the totality of the circumstances, the Court finds that it was reasonable for these attorneys to sign the pleadings, relying on the work of other attorneys more actively involved in the litigation.

* * *

3. Imposed Sanctions

As set forth above, the evidence establishes that Qualcomm intentionally withheld tens of thousands of emails and that the Sanctioned

Attorneys assisted, either intentionally or by virtue of acting with reckless disregard for their discovery obligations, in this discovery violation. The remaining issue, then, is what are the appropriate sanctions.

a. Monetary Sanctions Against Qualcomm

* * *

The suppressed emails directly rebutted Qualcomm's argument that it had not participated in the JVT during the time the H.264 standard was being developed. As such, their absence was critical to Qualcomm's hope and intent of enforcing its patents against Broadcom (as well as presumably all other cellular companies utilizing the H.264 technology in their products). Because Broadcom prevailed at trial and in the post-trial hearings despite the suppressed evidence, it is reasonable to infer that had Qualcomm intended to produce the 46,000 incriminating emails (and thereby acknowledge its early involvement in the JVT and its accompanying need to disclose its intellectual property), the instant case may never have been filed. Even if Qualcomm did file this case, the hidden evidence would have dramatically undermined Qualcomm's arguments and likely resulted in an adverse pretrial adjudication, much as it caused the adverse post-trial rulings. Accordingly, Qualcomm's failure to produce the massive number of critical documents at issue in this case significantly increased the scope, complexity and length of the litigation and justifies a significant monetary award.

The Court therefore awards Broadcom all of its attorneys' fees and costs incurred in the instant litigation. * * * Accordingly, for its monumental and intentional discovery violation, Qualcomm is ordered to pay $8,568,633.24 to Broadcom; this figure will be reduced by the amount actually paid by Qualcomm to Broadcom to satisfy the exceptional case award.

b. Referral to the California State Bar

As set forth above, the Sanctioned Attorneys assisted Qualcomm in committing this incredible discovery violation by intentionally hiding or recklessly ignoring relevant documents, ignoring or rejecting numerous warning signs that Qualcomm's document search was inadequate, and blindly accepting Qualcomm's unsupported assurances that its document search was adequate. The Sanctioned Attorneys then used the lack of evidence to repeatedly and forcefully make false statements and arguments to the court and jury. As such, the Sanctioned Attorneys violated their discovery obligations and also may have violated their ethical duties. *See e.g.*, The State Bar of California, Rules of Professional Conduct, Rule 5–200 (a lawyer shall not seek to mislead the judge or jury by a false statement of fact or law), Rule 5–220 (a lawyer shall not suppress evidence that the lawyer or the lawyer's client has a legal obligation to reveal or to produce). To address the potential ethical violations, the Court refers the Sanctioned Attorneys to The State Bar of California for an appropriate investigation and possible imposition of sanctions. Within ten days of the date of this Order, each of the Sanctioned Attorneys must forward a copy of this Order and Judge Brewster's Waiver Order to the Intake Unit, The State Bar of California, 1149 South Hill Street, Los Angeles, California 90015 for appropriate investigation.

c.   Case Review and Enforcement of Discovery Obligations

The Court also orders Qualcomm and the Sanctioned Attorneys to participate in a comprehensive Case Review and Enforcement of Discovery Obligations ("CREDO") program. This is a collaborative process to identify the failures in the case management and discovery protocol utilized by Qualcomm and its in-house and retained attorneys in this case, to craft alternatives that will prevent such failures in the future, to evaluate and test the alternatives, and ultimately, to create a case management protocol which will serve as a model for the future.

Because they reviewed and approved the false pleadings, the Court designates the following [in-house] Qualcomm attorneys to participate in this process as Qualcomm's representatives: Alex Rogers, Roger Martin, William Sailer, Byron Yafuso, and Michael Hartogs (the "Named Qualcomm Attorneys"). Qualcomm employees were integral participants in hiding documents and making false statements to the court and jury. Qualcomm's in-house lawyers were in the unique position of (a) having unlimited access to all Qualcomm employees, as well as the emails and documents maintained, possessed and used by them, (b) knowing or being able to determine all of the computers and databases that were searched and the search terms that were utilized, and (c) having the ability to review all of the pleadings filed on Qualcomm's behalf which did (or should have) alerted them to the fact that either the document search was inadequate or they were knowingly not producing tens of thousands of relevant and requested documents. Accordingly, Qualcomm's in-house lawyers need to be involved in this process.

At a minimum, the CREDO protocol must include a ***detailed analysis*** (1) identifying the factors that contributed to the discovery violation (e.g., insufficient communication (including between client and retained counsel, among retained lawyers and law firms, and between junior lawyers conducting discovery and senior lawyers asserting legal arguments); inadequate case management (within Qualcomm, between Qualcomm and the retained lawyers, and by the retained lawyers); inadequate discovery plans (within Qualcomm and between Qualcomm and its retained attorneys)); etc.), (2) creating and evaluating proposals, procedures, and processes that will correct the deficiencies identified in subsection (1), (3) developing and finalizing a comprehensive protocol that will prevent future discovery violations (e.g., determining the depth and breadth of case management and discovery plans that should be adopted; identifying by experience or authority the attorney from the retained counsel's office who should interface with the corporate counsel and on which issues; describing the frequency the attorneys should meet and whether other individuals should participate in the communications; identifying who should participate in the development of the case management and discovery plans; describing and evaluating various methods of resolving conflicts and disputes between the client and retained counsel, especially relating to the adequacy of discovery searches; describing the type, nature, frequency, and participants in case management and discovery meetings; and, suggesting required ethical and discovery training; etc.), (4) applying the protocol that was developed in subsection (3) to other factual situations, such as when the client does not have corporate counsel, when the client has a single in-house lawyer, when the client has a large legal staff, and when there are two law firms representing one client, (5) identifying and evaluating data tracking systems, software, or procedures that corporations could implement to better enable inside and outside counsel to identify potential sources of discoverable documents (e.g. the correct databases, archives, etc.), and (6) any other information or suggestions that will help prevent discovery violations.

* * *

While no one can undo the misconduct in this case, this process, hopefully, will establish a baseline for other cases. Perhaps it also will establish a turning point in what the Court perceives as a decline in and deterioration of civility, professionalism and ethical conduct in the litigation arena. To the extent it does so, everyone benefits–Broadcom, Qualcomm, and all attorneys who engage in, and judges who preside over, complex litigation. If nothing else, it will provide a road map to assist counsel and corporate clients in complying with their ethical and discovery obligations and conducting the requisite "reasonable inquiry."

Editor's Note: Qualcomm and the sanctioned lawyers appealed Judge Major's order imposing sanctions. Judge Brewster vacated the order in part. 2008 WL 638108 (S.D. Cal. Mar. 5, 2008). Judge Brewster held that the six sanctioned attorneys could not be prevented by the attorney-client privilege from using client communications to defend themselves. (*See* footnote 8 of Judge Major's opinion, *supra*, addressing the lawyers' complaint that they were limited in their defense by their inability to use privileged information.) Judge Brewster declared: "The attorneys have a due process right to defend themselves under the totality of circumstances presented in this sanctions hearing where their alleged conduct regarding discovery is in conflict with that alleged by Qualcomm concerning performance of discovery responsibilities." Judge Brewster remanded the case as to the individual attorneys for another hearing. Importantly, however, the court did not question the appropriateness of sanctions against the lawyers if the facts were as Judge Major had found them to be. And the court affirmed the sanctions against Qualcomm.

COMMENTARY

1. Should a Party Be Sanctioned Where the Fault Lies With the Party's Counsel?

A court must not sanction a party where the fault lies with inattentive, inept, or incompetent counsel. Because sanctions are based on personal responsibility, where counsel alone is responsible, counsel alone should be sanctioned.[33]

2. Can Sanctions Be Imposed on a Party and Its Counsel Jointly and Severally?

In *In re Sept. 11th Liability Insurance Coverage Cases,* the court held an insurer was subject to sanctions for not timely producing relevant documents, including an existing printed copy of a policy as it existed in electronic form on the day of the occurrence and an attached endorsement affecting the additional insured status of litigants, as well as other requested materials.[34] The court found the insurer had deleted an electronic copy of the policy as it appeared in its computer records. The court also found the insurer's attorneys did not act inadvertently in allowing a printed copy of the policy to languish in their files. The court imposed sanctions in the amount of $500,000 against the insurer and its attorneys jointly and severally, payable to the opposing party to defray the costs they unreasonably had incurred in wasted discovery proceedings. The court denied requests for more than five million dollars in sanctions because it was impossible to separate the time spent on particular issues affected by discovery abuses from other work on the same time entries.[35]

---

33. *See Exact Software N. Am., Inc. v. Infocon, Inc.*, 479 F. Supp. 2d 702, 718–19 (N.D. Ohio 2006) (ordering hearing to determine whether counsel was at fault for discovery misconduct).

34. 243 F.R.D. 114 (S.D.N.Y. 2007).

35. *See id.* at 132. *See also Phoenix Four, Inc. v. Strategic Res. Corp.*, No. 05 Civ. 4837, 2006 WL 2135798, at *2–3 (S.D.N.Y. Aug. 1, 2006) (sanctions in the amount of $45,162 to be paid equally by defendants and their law firm; defendants' share "may not be borne by their insurance carriers").

VII

ETHICAL ISSUES IN E–DISCOVERY

■ ■ ■

A. METADATA

1. Introduction

Chapter V.D discussed the issues associated with the discoverability of metadata. This chapter will address the ethical obligations imposed on lawyers when producing and reviewing metadata embedded within ESI.

2. Ethical Concerns for the Producing Attorney

The American Bar Association's Model Rules of Professional Conduct ("ABA Model Rules") are generally the starting point of any discussion involving legal ethics and the standards of professional responsibility for lawyers. A majority of the states use the ABA Model Rules as the basis for their state ethics rules; various courts rely on them in resolving cases of lawyer malpractice.[1] With regard to producing information with metadata, divergent opinions have emerged regarding the following two key issues:

1. Does a sending attorney have an affirmative duty to ensure that confidential metadata is properly protected from inadvertent or inappropriate production?

2. Is it unethical for a receiving attorney to review or "mine" the metadata?

a. Sending Attorney's Ethical Obligations

Illustration No. 1

Susie Newbie is a new associate at a large law firm. The firm is representing a hospital in a medical malpractice suit. The plaintiff in the case had been rushed to the emergency room after complaining of nausea and indigestion. The on-call doctor treated her for acid reflux. Within hours the plaintiff suffered a major heart attack, requiring invasive open heart surgery. The plaintiff claims that the doctor's

---

1. To date, California, Maine, and New York are the only states that do not have professional conduct rules that follow the format of the ABA Model Rules. New York follows the predecessor ABA Model Code of Professional Responsibility, and California and Maine developed their own rules. Also note that because these are "model" rules, the rules in states which do follow the ABA may vary from the model rules. *See* http://www.abanet.org/cpr/mrpc/model_rules.html.

negligence led to the misdiagnosis of her heart condition. In a client meeting, the doctor reveals that he had been working over seventeen hours when the plaintiff was admitted to the ER. Additionally the doctor admitted that he was overcoming depression and an addiction to alcohol.

During discovery, the partner, Joe Senior, asked Newbie to prepare the first draft of the responses to the plaintiff's interrogatories. He tells her that the client would probably be willing to settle the case before discovery is completed given the bad facts that they uncovered. Newbie prepares a draft of the responses, and she creates comments for Senior where she was unsure about content. One of the comments said, "How do we answer this question and still protect from disclosure our client's depression and alcohol problems, or the fact that he was just finishing a 17–hour shift on the day of the incident?" Senior addressed the question in the comment bubble and deleted Newbie's questions. He then saved the discovery responses as version two and served by e-mail the responses on the plaintiff's lawyer. Senior forgot to have the Word document scrubbed before sending it to the plaintiff's lawyer. After receiving the document, the plaintiff's lawyer opened the file and noticed that the document was not scrubbed and still contained metadata.

PROBLEMS

1. Did Senior owe a duty to his client to prevent the disclosure of metadata? If so, what is the duty?
2. Can the plaintiff's lawyer ethically review and use metadata embedded in electronic documents?

Attorneys routinely engage in a number of transactional activities, such as negotiating contracts or drafting agreements, where communications containing metadata are exchanged. Both the ABA and state bar association opinions agree that attorneys owe a duty to use reasonable care to guard against the disclosure of metadata containing confidential information and a duty to provide competent representation.[2] Support is found in Rules 1.1 and 1.6(a) of the ABA Model Rules.

Rule 1.1: A lawyer shall provide competent representation to a client. Competent representation requires the legal knowledge, skill, thoroughness and preparation reasonably necessary for the representation.

Rule 1.6(a): A lawyer shall not reveal information relating to the representation of a client unless the client gives informed consent,

---

2. *See* DC Ethics Op. 341 (2007), "Review and Use of Metadata in Electronic Documents," ("Lawyers sending electronic documents outside of the context of responding to discovery or subpoenas have an obligation under Rule 1.6 to take reasonable steps to maintain the confidentiality of documents in their possession."). *See also* Colorado Bar Ass'n Ethics Op. 119 (2008), "Disclosure, Review, and Use of Metadata," (same); Maryland State Bar Ass'n Formal Ethics Op. 2007–09, "Ethics of Viewing and/or Using Metadata," (same); Arizona Ethics Op. 07–03, "Confidentiality; Electronic Communications; Inadvertent Disclosure" (same); Alabama Ethics Op. RO–2007–02, "Disclosure and Mining of Metadata" (same); Florida Ethics Op. 06–2 (same); New York State Bar Ass'n Comm. on Prof'l Ethics Op. 782 (2004) (same).

the disclosure is impliedly authorized in order to carry out the representation or the disclosure is permitted by [the Rule].

Comment [16]: A lawyer must act competently to safeguard information relating to the representation of a client against inadvertent or unauthorized disclosure by the lawyer or other persons who are participating in the representation of the client or who are subject to the lawyer's supervision. See Rules 1.1, 5.1 and 5.3.

Comment [17]: When transmitting a communication that includes information relating to the representation of a client, the lawyer must take reasonable precautions to prevent the information from coming into the hands of unintended recipients. This duty, however, does not require that the lawyer use special security measures if the method of communication affords a reasonable expectation of privacy. Special circumstances, however, may warrant special precautions. Factors to be considered in determining the reasonableness of the lawyer's expectation of confidentiality include the sensitivity of the information and the extent to which the privacy of the communication is protected by law or by a confidentiality agreement. A client may require the lawyer to implement special security measures not required by this Rule or may give informed consent to the use of a means of communication that would otherwise be prohibited by this Rule.

Opinion 06–442 from the ABA's Standing Committee on Ethics and Professional Responsibility discusses steps attorneys should take when sending information containing metadata.

ABA Formal Opinion 06–442: Review and Use of Metadata

The Committee observes that counsel sending or producing electronic documents may be able to limit the likelihood of transmitting metadata in electronic documents. Computer users can avoid creating some kinds of metadata in electronic documents in the first place. For example, they often can choose not to use the redlining function of a word processing program or not to embed comments in a document. Simply deleting comments might be effective to eliminate them. Computer users also can eliminate or "scrub" some kinds of embedded information in an electronic document before sending, producing, or providing it to others.* * *

A lawyer who is concerned about the possibility of sending, producing, or providing to opposing counsel a document that contains or might contain metadata also may be able to send a different version of the document without the embedded information. For example, she might send it in hard copy, create an image of the document and send only the image (this can be done by printing and scanning), or print it out and send it via facsimile.

Finally, if a lawyer is concerned about risks relating to metadata and wishes to take some action to reduce or remove the potentially harmful consequences of its dissemination, then before sending, producing, or otherwise making available any electronic documents, she may seek to negotiate a confidentiality agreement or, if in litigation, a protective order, that will allow her or her client to "pull back," or prevent the introduction of evidence based upon, the document that contains that embedded information or the information itself. Of course, if the embedded information is on a subject such as her client's willingness to settle at a particular price, then there might be no way to "pull back" that information.

In Opinion 119, the Ethics Committee of the Colorado Bar Association examined a "sending" attorney's duties with respect to the disclosure, review, and use of metadata.

Ethics Opinion 119

Under the Colorado Rules of Professional Conduct, a Sending Lawyer has an ethical duty to take steps to reduce the likelihood that metadata containing Confidential Information would be included in an electronic document transmitted to a third party. This duty arises out of several interrelated rules.

First, Rule 1.6(a) provides that "A lawyer shall not reveal information relating to the representation of a client unless the client gives informed consent, the disclosure is impliedly authorized in order to carry out the representation, or the disclosure is [otherwise] permitted. . . ." Second, Rule 1.1 provides that "A lawyer shall provide competent representation to a client. Competent representation requires the legal knowledge, skill, thoroughness and preparation reasonably necessary for the representation." Third, Rules 5.1 and 5.3 generally require a lawyer to make reasonable efforts to ensure that the lawyer's firm, including lawyers and non-lawyers, conform to the Rules.

Under these Rules, a Sending Lawyer must act competently to avoid revealing a client's Confidential Information, and to ensure that others at the Sending Lawyer's firm similarly avoid revealing a client's Confidential Information. This requires a Sending Lawyer to use reasonable care to ensure that metadata that contain Confidential Information are not disclosed to a third party.

b.   Attorney's Duties With Respect to Discovery

Illustration No. 2

The parties in Illustration No. 1 are still in the discovery phase. The plaintiff's document requests ask the hospital to produce all of the plaintiff's medical records. The defendant hospital uses an electronic medical record system. Doctors and nurses can directly enter patient information into their tablet PC's. In response to the plaintiff's discovery request, Joe Senior printed out the plaintiff's hospital records, scanned them, and sent them to the plaintiff's lawyer as a .TIFF file (tagged image file format). In doing so all the metadata was deleted. The plaintiff's lawyer thereafter requested the actual electronic medical record file. Senior rejected this request and refused to produce the information. The plaintiff's lawyer has filed a motion to compel.

PROBLEMS

1. Does Senior have a duty to produce the electronic file in a form in which it is ordinarily maintained at the hospital? What arguments should he make to the court in requesting that the plaintiff's motion be denied?

2. What should the plaintiff's lawyer argue? How does the argument change if the plaintiff's lawyer discovers that one of the nurses changed information in the plaintiff's file retroactively, and the only proof is the underlying metadata?

Once a case enters the discovery phase, attorneys must balance the duties owed under the Model Rules with the requirements of the discovery rules. ABA Model Rule 3.4 provides that attorneys owe a duty of fairness to the opposing party and counsel.

Rule 3.4:

A lawyer shall not: (a) unlawfully obstruct another party's access to evidence or unlawfully alter, destroy or conceal a document or other material having potential evidentiary value. A lawyer shall not counsel or assist another person to do any such act.

D.C. Bar Ethics Opinion 341:

Because it is impermissible to alter electronic documents that constitute tangible evidence, the removal of metadata may, at least in some instances, be prohibited as well. In addition to issues regarding discovery sanctions, the alteration or destruction of evidence can, under some circumstances, also constitute a crime.

Federal Rule of Civil Procedure 34(b):

If a request does not specify a form for producing electronically stored information, a party must produce it in a form or forms in which it is ordinarily maintained or in a reasonably usable form or forms.

c. DOES AN ATTORNEY HAVE AN ETHICAL DUTY TO PRESERVE AND PRODUCE METADATA IN RESPONSE TO A DISCOVERY REQUEST?

Williams v. Sprint/United Management Company—set forth as a principal case in Chapter Five—was one of the first cases to discuss metadata in substantial detail, including such issues as: 1) must a party produce all electronic evidence with metadata intact; 2) what does an opposing party have to demonstrate in order to obtain metadata; 3) can an attorney be sanctioned for removing metadata?

Wyeth v. Impax, decided a year after *Williams*, announced a different standard. Unlike *Williams* which held that "when a party is ordered to produce electronic documents as they are maintained in the ordinary course of business, the producing party should produce the electronic documents with their metadata intact, unless that party timely objects to production of metadata,"[3] the *Wyeth* court supported the general presumption against the production of metadata. *See* Ch. V, *supra*.

"Sending" attorneys must exercise caution in exchanging electronic information during discovery. Inadvertent disclosure of privileged material can be detrimental to a case. Although a producing party may have a duty to produce metadata if relevant and requested, attorneys still have an obligation to protect a client's confidential information. In *Amersham Biosciences Corp. v. PerkinElmer, Inc.*, appropriate care was not taken during production.[4] The court held, *inter alia*, that by disclosing over five hundred documents that were "on their face" privileged, the plaintiff had failed to take reasonable precautions to prevent the disclosure of privileged documents. The court also found that the plaintiff's production of thirty-seven "unreadable" documents further established that the plaintiff had not taken reasonable precautions to protect the privilege. As a result, the court denied the plaintiff's motion for return of produced documents.

3. Ethics of Reviewing or "Mining" Metadata in Documents Received From Opposing Party

Mining metadata refers to the practice of deliberately searching a document's underlying metadata for hidden or embedded information. The ability to look at metadata can be hugely beneficial to the receiving party and detrimental to the producing party. For example, in the hypothetical above, if the plaintiff's lawyer was allowed to access the metadata of the draft responses to the defendant's document requests, it would provide counsel with a tremendous insight into the defendant's strategy. The plaintiff's lawyer had access to information he might not have otherwise discovered. Currently, there are conflicting answers to the question "ethically, can attorneys mine metadata?" The views range from "mining is ethical" to "it is completely unethical." Generally, the debate surrounding the answer stems from differing interpretations of ABA Model Rule 4.4(b) (or the analogous state rule).

Rule 4.4(b)

A lawyer who receives a document relating to the representation of the lawyer's client and knows or reasonably should know that the document was inadvertently sent shall promptly notify the sender.

Comment 2: Paragraph (b) recognizes that lawyers sometimes receive documents that were mistakenly sent or produced by opposing parties or their lawyers. If a lawyer knows or reasonably should know that such a document was sent inadvertently, then this Rule requires the lawyer to promptly notify the sender in order to permit

---

3. *Williams v. Sprint/United Mgmt. Co.*, 230 F.R.D. 640, 652 (D. Kan. 2005).

4. No. 03 Civ. 4901, 2007 WL 329290, at *1 (D.N.J. Jan. 31, 2007) (plaintiff "produced certain CDs allegedly containing over five hundred inadvertently produced privileged e-mails").

that person to take protective measures. Whether the lawyer is required to take additional steps, such as returning the original document, is a matter of law beyond the scope of these Rules, as is the question of whether the privileged status of a document has been waived. Similarly, this Rule does not address the legal duties of a lawyer who receives a document that the lawyer knows or reasonably should know may have been wrongfully obtained by the sending person. For purposes of this Rule, "document" includes e-mail or other electronic modes of transmission subject to being read or put into readable form.

a. Mining of Metadata Is Unethical

New York was the first jurisdiction to address the ethical obligations of attorneys in relation to metadata. The New York State Bar Association Committee on Professional Ethics recognized that "modern computer technology enables sophisticated users who receive documents by electronic transmission to 'get behind' what is visible on the computer screen" to find potentially vital information. It issued Opinion 749 stating that it is unethical for attorneys to mine metadata.

New York State Bar Association—Committee on Professional Ethics—Opinion 749—12/14/01

QUESTION

May a lawyer ethically use available technology to surreptitiously examine and trace e-mail and other electronic documents in the manner described?

OPINION

This new technology permits a user to access confidential communications relating to another lawyer's representation of a client, including "confidences" and "secrets" within the scope of DR 4–101 of the Lawyer's Code of Professional Responsibility ("Code"). For this reason, we conclude that the use of computer technology in the manner described above constitutes an impermissible intrusion on the attorney-client relationship in violation of the Code.

* * *

We believe that in light of the strong public policy in favor of preserving confidentiality as the foundation of the lawyer-client relationship, use of technology to surreptitiously obtain information that may be protected by the attorney-client privilege, the work product doctrine or that may otherwise constitute a "secret" of another lawyer's client would violate the letter and spirit of these Disciplinary Rules.

The bar associations of Florida, Alabama, and Arizona have adopted a similar view as New York about the unethical nature of mining metadata.[5]

---

5. *See* Professional Ethics of the Florida Bar Op. 06–2 (2006) ("A lawyer receiving an electronic document should not try to obtain information from metadata that the lawyer knows or should

b.   Mining Metadata Is Ethical

In August 2006, the ABA's Standing Committee on Ethics and Professional Responsibility ("Standing Committee") issued Opinion 06–442. Unlike New York, the ABA found that the Model Rules did not contain any specific provisions that would forbid attorneys from reviewing and using metadata. It held that "Rule 4.4(b) is silent as to the ethical propriety of a lawyer's review or use of such information. The Rule provides only that '[a] lawyer who receives a document relating to the representation of the lawyer's client and knows or reasonably should know that the document was inadvertently sent shall promptly notify the sender.' "

ABA—Formal Opinion 06–442: Review and Use of Metadata

The Model Rules of Professional Conduct do not contain any specific prohibition against a lawyer's reviewing and using embedded information in electronic documents, whether received from opposing counsel, an adverse party, or an agent of an adverse party. A lawyer who is concerned about the possibility of sending, producing, or providing to opposing counsel a document that contains or might contain metadata, or who wishes to take some action to reduce or remove the potentially harmful consequences of its dissemination, may be able to limit the likelihood of its transmission by "scrubbing" metadata from documents or by sending a different version of the document without the embedded information.

In 2007 the Maryland State Bar Association issued an opinion in line with the ABA.[6] It is important to note however that Maryland reached a similar conclusion using a different rationale than the ABA. The Maryland opinion addressed the following three questions:

First, whether it is ethical for the attorney recipient to view or use metadata in documents produced by another party; second, whether the attorney sender has any duty to remove metadata from the files prior to sending them; and third, whether the attorney recipient has any ethical duty not to view or otherwise use the metadata without first ascertaining whether the sender intended to include such metadata in the produced documents.

---

know is not intended for the receiving lawyer. A lawyer who inadvertently receives information via metadata in an electronic document should notify the sender of the information's receipt."); Alabama State Bar Office of the Gen. Counsel Op. No. 2007–02 (2007) ("Absent express authorization from a court, it is ethically impermissible for an attorney to mine metadata from an electronic document he or she inadvertently or improperly receives from another party."); Arizona Bar Assoc. Op. 07–03 (2007) ("[A] lawyer who receives an electronic communication may not examine it for the purpose of discovering the metadata embedded in it.... A recipient lawyer who discovers metadata embedded within an electronic communication and who knows or reasonably should know that the metadata reveals confidential or privileged information has a duty to comply with the procedures set forth in ER 4.4(b).").

6. Maryland State Bar Ass'n, Comm. on Ethics Op. 2007–092 (2006) ("[T]his Committee believes that there is no ethical violation if the recipient attorney (or those working under the attorney's direction) reviews or makes use of the metadata without first ascertaining whether the sender intended to include such metadata.").

In answering the first and third questions, the opinion stated:

> Subject to any legal standards or requirements (case law, statutes, rules of procedure, administrative rules, etc.), this Committee believes that there is no ethical violation if the recipient attorney (or those working under the attorney's direction) reviews or makes use of the metadata without first ascertaining whether the sender intended to include such metadata.

The Committee went on to highlight a major difference between the Maryland Rules of Professional Conduct and the ABA Model Rules.

> In February 2002, the ABA Model Rules of Professional Conduct were amended to add Rule 4.4(b)[.]

* * *

> The Maryland Rules of Professional Conduct, however, have not been amended to include Model Rule 4.4(b). Accordingly, the Maryland Rules of Professional Conduct do not require the receiving attorney to notify the sending attorney that there may have been an inadvertent transmittal of privileged (or, for that matter, work product) materials. Of course, the receiving lawyer can, and probably should, communicate with his or her client concerning the pros and cons of whether to notify the sending attorney and/or to take such other action which they believe is appropriate.

The question remains—would Maryland have come to the same conclusion if it had adopted ABA Model Rule 4.4(b)?

Jurisdictions that have not addressed the ethical implications of mining metadata generally use the ABA's advisory opinion as guidance in their disciplinary actions. Even though the ABA's formal opinions do not carry precedential weight, courts look to them for advice in interpreting the Model Rules that most attorneys are required to follow.

c. Hybrid Opinions

A number of states have chosen an in-between approach. Instead of placing an absolute bar on the mining of metadata, these opinions carve out situations where lawyers can ethically look at metadata.

D.C. Legal Ethics Opinion 341 (2007)

A receiving lawyer is prohibited from reviewing metadata sent by an adversary only where he has actual knowledge that the metadata was inadvertently sent. In such instances, the receiving lawyer should not review the metadata before consulting with the sending lawyer to determine whether the metadata includes work product of the sending lawyer or confidences or secrets of the sending lawyer's client.

Pennsylvania Bar Association Formal Opinion 2007–500

[I]t is the opinion of this committee that each attorney must . . . determine for himself or herself whether to utilize the metadata contained in documents and other electronic files based upon the lawyer's judgment and the particular factual situation.

* * *

[T]he decision of how or whether a lawyer may use the information contained in the metadata will depend upon many factors, including:

● The judgment of the lawyer;

● The particular facts applicable to the situation;

● The lawyer's view of his or her obligations to the client under Rule of Professional Conduct 1.3, and the relevant comments to this rule;

● The nature of the information received;

● How and from whom the information was received;

● Attorney-client privilege and work product rules; and

● Common sense, reciprocity and professional courtesy.

Colorado Bar Association Ethics Opinion 119 (2008)

[T]he Committee concludes that a Receiving Lawyer generally may ethically search for and review metadata embedded in an electronic document that the Receiving Lawyer receives from opposing counsel or other third party. This conclusion is supported by the following:

First, there is nothing inherently deceitful or surreptitious about searching for metadata.

* * *

Second, an absolute ethical bar on even reviewing metadata ignores the fact that, in many circumstances, metadata do not contain Confidential Information. To the contrary, in some circumstances metadata are intended to be searched for, reviewed, and used.

* * *

Third, metadata are often of no import. In many circumstances it is of no significance who created a document, when the document was created, or the like.

* * *

If a Receiving Lawyer knows or reasonably should know that a Sending Lawyer (or non-lawyer) has transmitted metadata that contain Confidential Information, the Receiving Lawyer should assume that the Confidential Information was transmitted inadvertently, unless the Receiving Lawyer knows that confidentiality has been waived. The Receiving Lawyer must promptly notify the Sending Lawyer (or non-lawyer sender).

4. Summary

Access to and the use of metadata pose a number of ethical concerns for attorneys. Attorneys on both sides of a matter have ethical responsibilities. Sending attorneys must take "reasonable" precautions towards the inadvertent production of information via metadata. Receiving attorneys also owe duties to the opposing counsel with regard to viewing the metadata and notifying them of inadvertent disclosure. However, the specific duty imposed varies based on jurisdiction.

PROBLEMS

1. What are "reasonable" steps a sending attorney can take to protect against inadvertent disclosure of metadata?

2. Is "scrubbing" enough protection—should the scrubbing for each document have to be verified before the document is sent to meet the reasonableness standard?

3. Can the receiving party use "all means available" to access any metadata associated with the document she or he receives?

4. How practical is a strict standard when the state of knowledge regarding metadata and software is constantly changing?

5. What if a good faith error is made in the scrubbing process? Should that be a waiver? Should there be a "safe harbor" provision similar to Rule 37(e) for the good faith operation of a software scrubbing program?

B. TRANSPARENCY IN ELECTRONIC DISCOVERY PROMOTES "JUST, SPEEDY, AND INEXPENSIVE" LITIGATION

The mandatory initial disclosure requirement of Rule 26(a) and the "meet and confer" requirement of Rule 26(f) are useful mechanisms for expediting discovery, reducing costs, and avoiding conflict. Many thoughtful lawyers—and many clients—would like to go further. Looking at the examples of arbitration and mediation, they question why discovery must be an adversarial process. If the goal of discovery is to uncover facts to be used in settlement talks or at trial, why not cooperate in the discovery process, and utilize advocacy and persuasion skills to argue the interpretation of the facts and the application of the facts to the law? Shouldn't an attorney's duty of zealous advocacy and loyalty to the client include getting the best result at a reasonable cost and within a reasonable time frame? In the summer of 2008, these questions led members of the Sedona Conference, many of whom are highly experienced lawyers and judges in the electronic discovery arena, to issue the following "Cooperation Proclamation."

THE SEDONA CONFERENCE®
COOPERATION PROCLAMATION

The costs associated with adversarial conduct in pre-trial discovery have become a serious burden to the American judicial system. This burden rises significantly in discovery of electronically stored information ("ESI"). In addition to rising monetary costs, courts have seen escalating motion practice, overreaching, obstruction, and extensive, but unproductive discovery disputes—in some cases precluding adjudication on the merits altogether—when parties treat the discovery process in an adversarial manner. Neither law nor logic compels these outcomes.

With this Proclamation, The Sedona Conference® launches a national drive to promote open and forthright information sharing, dialogue (internal and external), training, and the development of practical tools to facilitate cooperative, collaborative, transparent discovery. This Proclamation challenges the bar to achieve these goals and refocus litigation toward the substantive resolution of legal disputes.

Cooperation in Discovery Is Consistent with Zealous Advocacy

Lawyers have twin duties of loyalty: While they are retained to be zealous advocates for their clients, they bear a professional obligation to conduct discovery in a diligent and candid manner. Their combined duty is to strive in the best interests of their clients to achieve the best results at a reasonable cost, with integrity and candor as officers of the court. Cooperation does not conflict with the advancement of their clients' interests—it enhances it. Only when lawyers confuse *advocacy* with *adversarial conduct* are these twin duties in conflict.

Lawyers preparing cases for trial need to focus on the full cost of their efforts—temporal, monetary, and human. Indeed, all stakeholders in the system—judges, lawyers, clients, and the general public—have an interest in establishing a culture of cooperation in the discovery process. Over-contentious discovery is a cost that has outstripped any advantage in the face of ESI and the data deluge. It is not in anyone's interest to waste resources on unnecessary disputes, and the legal system is strained by "gamesmanship" or "hiding the ball," to no practical effect.

The effort to change the culture of discovery from adversarial conduct to cooperation is not utopian.[1] It is, instead, an exercise in economy and logic. Establishing a culture of cooperation will channel valuable advocacy skills toward interpreting the facts and arguing the appropriate application of law.

---

1. Gartner RAS Core Research Note G00148170, *Cost of eDiscovery Threatens to Skew Justice System*, 1D#G00148170 (April 20, 2007), at http://www.h5technologies.com/pdf/gartner0607.pdf (while noting that "several ... disagreed with the suggestion [to collaborate in the discovery process] ... calling it 'utopian'", one of the "take-away's" from the program identified in the Gartner Report was to "[s]trive for a collaborative environment when it comes to [e-discovery], seeking to cooperate with adversaries as effectively as possible to share the value and reduce costs.").

Cooperative Discovery Is Required by the Rules of Civil Procedure

When the first uniform civil procedure rules allowing discovery were adopted in the late 1930s,"discovery" was understood as an essentially cooperative, rule-based, party-driven process, designed to exchange relevant information. The goal was to avoid gamesmanship and surprise at trial. Over time, discovery has evolved into a complicated, lengthy procedure requiring tremendous expenditures of client funds, along with legal and judicial resources. These costs often overshadow efforts to resolve the matter itself. The 2006 amendments to the Federal Rules specifically focused on discovery of "electronically stored information" and emphasized early communication and cooperation in an effort to streamline information exchange, and avoid costly unproductive disputes.

Discovery rules frequently compel parties to meet and confer regarding data preservation, form of production, and assertions of privilege. Beyond this, parties wishing to litigate discovery disputes must certify their efforts to resolve their difficulties in good faith.

Courts see these rules as a mandate for counsel to act cooperatively.[2] Methods to accomplish this cooperation may include:

1. Utilizing internal ESI discovery "point persons" to assist counsel in preparing requests and responses;

2. Exchanging information on relevant data sources, including those not being searched, or scheduling early disclosures on the topic of Electronically Stored Information;

3. Jointly developing automated search and retrieval methodologies to cull relevant information;

4. Promoting early identification of form or forms of production;

5. Developing case-long discovery budgets based on proportionality principles; and

6. Considering court-appointed experts, volunteer mediators, or formal ADR programs to resolve discovery disputes.

The Road to Cooperation

It is unrealistic to expect a *sua sponte* outbreak of pre-trial discovery cooperation. Lawyers frequently treat discovery conferences as perfunctory obligations. They may fail to recognize or act on opportunities to make discovery easier, less costly, and more productive. New lawyers may not yet have developed cooperative advocacy skills, and senior lawyers may cling to a long-held "hide the ball" mentality. Lawyers who recognize the value of resources such as ADR and special masters may nevertheless overlook their application to discovery. And, there remain

---

2. *See, e.g. Board of Regents of Univ. of Neb. v. BASF Corp.,* No. 04 Civ. 3356, 2007 WL 3342423, at *5 (D. Neb. Nov. 5, 2007) ("The overriding theme of recent amendments to the discovery rules has been open and forthright sharing of information by all parties to a case with the aim of expediting case progress, minimizing burden and expense, and removing contentiousness as much as practicable. [citations omitted]. If counsel fail in this responsibility—willfully or not—these principles of an open discovery process are undermined, coextensively inhibiting the courts' ability to objectively resolve their clients' disputes and the credibility of its resolution.").

obstreperous counsel with no interest in cooperation, leaving even the best-intentioned to wonder if "playing fair" is worth it.

This "Cooperation Proclamation" calls for a paradigm shift for the discovery process; success will not be instant. The Sedona Conference® views this as a three-part process to be undertaken by The Sedona Conference®Working Group on Electronic Document Retention and Production (WG1):

Part I: Awareness—Promoting awareness of the need and advantages of cooperation, coupled with a call to action. This process has been initiated by The Sedona Conference® Cooperation Proclamation.

Part II: Commitment—Developing a detailed understanding and full articulation of the issues and changes needed to obtain cooperative fact-finding. This will take the form of a "Case for Cooperation" which will reflect viewpoints of all legal system stakeholders. It will incorporate disciplines outside the law, aiming to understand the separate and sometimes conflicting interests and motivations of judges, mediators and arbitrators, plaintiff and defense counsel, individual and corporate clients, technical consultants and litigation support providers, and the public at large.

Part III: Tools—Developing and distributing practical "toolkits" to train and support lawyers, judges, other professionals, and students in techniques of discovery cooperation, collaboration, and transparency. Components will include training programs tailored to each stakeholder; a clearinghouse of practical resources, including form agreements, case management orders, discovery protocols, etc.; court-annexed e-discovery ADR with qualified counselors and mediators, available to assist parties of limited means; guides for judges faced with motions for sanctions; law school programs to train students in the technical, legal, and cooperative aspects of e-discovery; and programs to assist individuals and businesses with basic e-record management, in an effort to avoid discovery problems altogether.

Conclusion

It is time to build upon modern Rules amendments, state and federal, which address e-discovery. Using this springboard, the legal profession can engage in a comprehensive effort to promote pre-trial discovery cooperation. Our "officer of the court" duties demand no less.
* * *

EXAMPLES

1. In *Williams v. Taser International, Inc.*, the court "strongly encouraged the parties to collaborate on the development of search terms and a protocol for conducting ... searches to winnow the universe of potentially responsive [electronic information]."[7] Because the parties were unable to reach an agreement, each submitted a list of search

---

7. No. 06 Civ. 51, 2007 WL 1630875, at *5 (N.D. Ga. June 4, 2007).

terms for the court's consideration. Frustrated by the parties' inability to cooperate, the court issued an order imposing on the parties its own list of broad search terms. In so ordering, the court noted:

> The Court recognizes that the production ordered above will likely impose burdens on both parties. [Defendant] will likely be required to significantly increase its privilege review capabilities; Plaintiffs will likely be required to wade through a significant number of documents. Nevertheless, this case has been ongoing for more than 18 months, and yet discovery has progressed little and we remain far from its resolution. Because that is the case, and because the parties have been unable to cooperate in the discovery process, the Court is compelled to Order the discovery procedures set forth above.[8]

The parties' refusal to cooperate resulted in an aggravated judge and an order containing broad mandatory search terms likely to retrieve large volumes of information, increasing the costs of litigation for both the defendant and the plaintiffs. Did the parties gain anything by remaining adversarial? Note that the court's order did not preclude future collaboration: "The parties may, by mutual agreement, develop and employ search protocols which vary from those set forth above. In the absence of such agreement, however, the production shall proceed in the manner described above."[9]

2.   Prior to the information age, when discovery was focused on paper records, there were no "search terms" that parties could review to cross-check each others' discovery retrieval efforts. Rather, parties had to trust that discovery obligations would be fulfilled in good faith, with attorneys using reasonable judgment in reviewing documents for relevance. Now that technology has advanced to the point where attorneys can be transparent in their discovery efforts—such as by exchanging search terms and identifying repositories of electronic information—is there any reason not to use these technological developments to advance the exchange of relevant information in discovery? If transparency improves information-sharing in litigation, doesn't that allow parties greater access to relevant evidence, thus increasing the likelihood of resolving a case on a complete and accurate record? Doesn't this improve our overall system of justice? *See* the discussion on use of search terms in Chapter V.

3.   Although transparency in electronic discovery is necessary to ensure adequate electronic discovery preservation, retrieval, and production, transparency is also necessary to support arguments that certain electronic information *not* be produced. In *Baker v. Gerould*, the plaintiff moved to compel certain e-mails from the defendant's e-mail back-up system. The defendant opposed the motion to compel on the ground that retrieval of the requested e-mails would be unduly burdensome. The court directed the defendant to submit an affidavit describing

---

8.   *Id.* at *7.

9.   *Id.*

the search undertaken to locate the e-mails. Although the defendant submitted an affidavit, the court ruled that it failed to "explain[] the steps undertaken to search for the e-mails," or "to address what efforts, if any, were employed to search for [the] e-mails from accessible sources. For example, [defendant failed to explain] whether any search was undertaken to locate archived or saved emails . . ."[10] The court held that "[i]n the absence of this information, which, despite this Court's earlier ruling, still has not been presented, this Court cannot reasonably resolve whether defendant should be put to the expense and effort of restoring deleted electronic communications spanning a multi-year period."[11] The court then ordered the defendant to produce for deposition those individuals with knowledge of the defendant's electronic discovery search and retrieval efforts, so that the parties could develop a factual record upon which the court could adjudicate the plaintiff's motion to compel.

4.   In 1969, the ABA promulgated the Model Code of Professional Responsibility, which provided, in Canon 7, that an attorney owes a duty "to represent his client zealously within the bounds of the law." In 1983, the ABA revised the model ethical rules governing attorneys with the publication of the Model Rules of Professional Conduct, now adopted in substantial part by all but three states. Unlike the 1969 Model Code, the 1983 Model Rules do not contain a provision expressly imposing on attorneys a duty of zealous advocacy. Rather, the 1983 Model Rules note that although an attorney owes his client a duty of zealous advocacy, the attorney also owes duties to the court, other litigants, herself, and the system of justice:

> A lawyer's responsibilities as a representative of clients, an officer of the legal system and a public citizen are usually harmonious. . . . In the nature of law practice, however, conflicting responsibilities are encountered. Virtually all difficult ethical problems arise from conflict between a lawyer's responsibilities to clients, to the legal system and to the lawyer's own interest in remaining an ethical person while earning a satisfactory living. The Rules of Professional Conduct often prescribe terms for resolving such conflicts. Within the framework of these Rules, however, many difficult issues of professional discretion can arise. Such issues must be resolved through the exercise of sensitive professional and moral judgment guided by the basic principles underlying the Rules. These principles include the lawyer's obligation zealously to protect and pursue a client's legitimate interests, within the bounds of the law, while maintaining a professional, courteous and civil attitude toward all persons involved in the legal system.

Preamble ¶¶ 8–9, ABA Model Rules.

---

10.   No. 03 Civ. 6558L, 2008 WL 850236, at *1 (W.D.N.Y. Mar. 27, 2008).

11.   *Id.* at *3.

Although the Federal Rules of Civil Procedure and the Sedona Principles require transparency and cooperation on matters relating to electronic discovery, an attorney must be circumspect in balancing these requirements against the attorney's obligation to zealously represent the client.

Consider whether the attorney client privilege and the work product doctrine should act as boundaries to the level of transparency and cooperation parties may achieve. In particular, consider the following scenarios:

a.   **Electronic Discovery Search Terms.** As noted above, in *Williams v. Taser International*, the parties submitted competing lists of electronic discovery search terms for the court's consideration. To effectively retrieve relevant electronic information necessary to prepare a case for trial, must an attorney's list of electronic discovery search terms necessarily reflect his or her "mental impressions, conclusions, opinions, or legal theories" regarding the case? If so, might the search terms constitute attorney work product pursuant to Rule 26(b)(3)? Could the attorneys in *Williams* have reasonably objected to the court's request that they submit lists of electronic discovery search terms on the grounds that the lists constituted attorney work product? Assuming that lists of electronic discovery search terms are indeed attorney work product, consider the circumstances under which an attorney might decide, as a matter of strategy, to waive the work product protection. Factors to consider, among others, might include the sensitivity of the information covered by the protection, whether the judge has emphasized a desire for the parties to cooperate on discovery matters, and whether all parties might waive certain protections as a matter of reciprocity.

b.   **Litigation Hold Letters.** An attorney may give written advice to his or her client regarding the implementation of a litigation hold. In a litigation hold letter, the attorney may discuss the obligation to preserve relevant information, the types of information relevant to the litigation, the client's information technology systems, potential repositories and custodians of electronic information, the client's document retention program, and the client's back-up systems. If an adversary suspects that relevant electronic information has not been preserved, the adversary might seek production of the litigation hold letter. Is a litigation hold letter protected by the attorney-client privilege or work product protection?[12] If your adversary seeks production of your litigation hold letter to your client, might you choose to waive any privilege applicable to the letter in the interest of transparency, in order to demonstrate that you and your client have taken sufficient measures to preserve relevant electronic information? If so, what precautions might you take to ensure

---

12.   *See Muro v. Target Corp.*, No. 04 C 6267, 2007 WL 3254463, at *9 (N.D. Ill. Nov. 2, 2007) ("The court has examined the litigation hold notices *in camera*. Each seem to be communications of legal advice from ... counsel to corporate employees regarding document preservation. [T]he litigation hold notices, on their face, appear to be privileged material...."); *Gibson v. Ford Motor Co.*, 510 F. Supp. 2d 1116 (N.D. Ga. 2007); *Capitano v. Ford Motor Co.*, 831 N.Y.S.2d 687 (Sup. Ct. Chautauqua Co. 2007).

that any such waiver of privilege does not constitute a subject matter waiver of all privileged communications between you and your client relating to electronic discovery? Consider whether you should condition production of your litigation hold letter upon your adversary signing a stipulation agreeing that your waiver of the attorney client privilege and work product protection is limited only to the litigation hold letter. Also consider whether such an agreement would protect against a subject matter waiver argument that could later be raised by an adversary in a different litigation.

   c. **Candor to the Court Regarding Electronic Discovery Vulnerabilities**.

   The tension between an attorney's duty to zealously represent his or her client and the obligations of cooperation and transparency in electronic discovery is particularly underscored when an attorney discovers, and must defend, vulnerabilities in the client's electronic discovery practices. In *In re Intel Corp. Microprocessor Antitrust Litigation* Intel's counsel discovered that in several instances, Intel failed to comply with its litigation hold, resulting in the destruction of numerous e-mails.[13] Intel's attorneys disclosed the destruction of the e-mails to the court and AMD, Intel's adversary. After the disclosure, the court ordered Intel to produce certain information regarding the scope and cause of the destruction, whether the destruction was deliberate, and whether back up copies of the e-mails existed.

   5. The Sedona Conference's Cooperation Proclamation calls for a "sea change" in the electronic discovery process, to be effectuated by promoting awareness, obtaining a commitment from "stakeholders" in the legal system, and developing tools to train such stakeholders on how to effectuate their obligations of cooperation and transparency. Yet, the concept of transparency is clearly a foreign one to many, if not most, lawyers who are accustomed to zealously representing their clients in an adversarial context. In order to accomplish this "sea change" as a matter of practice, consider how you might counsel a client who requests that you take an aggressively adversarial position in discovery. Suppose that during your electronic discovery retrieval efforts, you locate a non-privileged e-mail that is harmful to your client's position in the litigation, but responsive to your adversary's discovery requests. How might you advise your client that prompt disclosure of the e-mail is in its best interest?

C. DUTIES OF CANDOR, COMPETENCE AND FAIRNESS

WACHTEL v. HEALTH NET, INC.
239 F.R.D. 81 (D.N.J. 2006)

HOCHBERG, DISTRICT JUDGE

I. Introduction

   Plaintiff-beneficiaries have sued their healthcare insurance providers under ERISA, 29 U.S.C. § 1001 et seq., for breach of fiduciary duty

---

13. No. 05–441, 2008 WL 2310288, at *3 (D. Del. June 4, 2008).

and other wrongs connected to the way in which Health Net reimburses out-of-network ("ONET") claims. After a lengthy pattern of repeated and gross non-compliance with discovery emerged, exacerbated by representations to the Court that began to ring hollow, this Court granted a motion by Plaintiffs for a Hearing Under the Inherent Power of the Court to Preserve the Integrity of the Judicial Process and Under Federal Rule of Civil Procedure 37 ("Rule 37/Integrity Hearing"). This Court held eleven days of evidentiary hearings between October 2005 and March 2006 about, inter alia, whether Defendants were compliant with Court orders to retain, search, and produce e-mail and other electronic documents and candid in their representations to the Magistrate Judge and this Court about their restitution to beneficiaries. * * *

The litigation has been fierce and without respite, through several changes of defense counsel. * * * In sum, it gives new meaning to the term "scorched earth" litigation tactics. * * * This Court is extremely reluctant to sanction parties or counsel. Unfortunately, Health Net's repeated and unabated discovery abuses and lack of candor leave this Court no other choice in order to protect the integrity of the judicial process, remedy the prejudice suffered by Plaintiffs, punish the wrong-doers, and accord a measure of relief to the other parties and counsel in this case. When the abuses are as extreme as they are in this case, to refrain from sanctions is unfair to the parties who conduct themselves according to the rules.

* * *

III. Findings of Fact

A. Health Net's Lack of Candor to the Magistrate Judge and this Court concerning its Restitutions to the New Jersey Department of Banking and Insurance ("NJ–DOBI")

Health Net's strategy to limit the scope of its disclosures to NJ–DOBI about its use of outdated data to calculate the UCR[11] for medical bill reimbursements led inexorably to discovery abuses and lack of candor in this case. Health Net's small group employer plans in New Jersey are subject to state regulations requiring that Health Net must use the most recent data in calculating the UCR for certain services performed by ONET providers. Large group plans are governed by contractual language that does not expressly permit outdated data to be used for UCR. In its Northeast plans, Health Net bases its UCR determinations on a nationwide database, known as the Health Insurance Association of America ("HIAA") or Prevailing Healthcare Charges

---

11. "UCR" refers to the "usual, customary, and reasonable" charge for medical procedures.

System ("PHCS") database. The database is updated at least annually, but the insurer has the responsibility for loading the data. Health Net did not use the database in its updated form for several years at issue in this case. Thus, old costs were used to calculate current reimbursements.

* * *

B.   Discovery Violations

Throughout this litigation, Defendants have employed an obstructionist approach to discovery. A great proportion of the problem originated with the client; however, counsel in certain instances also exacerbated the problem. Despite numerous specific Court Orders, Health Net never produced thousands and thousands of pages of relevant and responsive documents within the three-year-long discovery period. Many of these documents are highly relevant to the knowledge of key personnel at Health Net about the company's use of the outdated data described above. Yet, these documents appeared for the first time more than a year after the close of discovery, and only after this Court demanded them during the Rule 37/Integrity Hearing. Others appeared as Defendants' proposed trial exhibits and as exhibits to Defendants' summary judgment motions even though they had never been produced to Plaintiffs in discovery. Health Net did not even search for many documents until it decided to look for them for its own use at trial and for its defense at the Rule 37 Hearing. Despite repeated document demands, repeated court orders to produce, and repeated assurances that all appropriate e-mails were being produced, thousands of Health Net's employees' e-mails were never searched. Many others were lost permanently due to Health Net's e-mail retention/non-retention practices, which were only disclosed to the Court after the conclusion of the Rule 37/Integrity hearing. These practices were never disclosed to the Magistrate Judge who supervised discovery for over three years.[23] These non-compliant and deceptive discovery tactics caused Plaintiffs to waste huge sums of time and money conducting numerous depositions of Health Net witnesses without the benefit of their e-mails and other documents relevant to each deponent. Such a vast amount of discovery now needs to be redone that the task is virtually impossible.

What follows is a selected summary of discovery abuses that came to light as a result of the Rule 37/Integrity hearing.

---

23. Defendants did not inform either Plaintiffs or the Magistrate Judge that e-mails were routinely sent to a back-up tape after 90 days; that employees generally could not search for their own e-mail older than 90 days; that deleted e-mails were lost forever upon transfer to the back-up tape; the numbers of e-mails that needed to be searched; the cost of such a search; or a plan for allocating the burden of e-mail production. If Defendants had candidly disclosed these issues to the Magistrate Judge, an appropriate order could have been tailored to deal with such issues and keep costs down. *See, e.g., Zubulake v. UBS Warburg LLC,* 217 F.R.D. 309 (S.D.N.Y.2003). * * * Cost-sharing options could have been considered at the outset of discovery had Health Net been candid with the Court about their e-mail policies and the expense of producing that discovery. Defendants' lack of candor, however, foreclosed such an approach. Simply put, Health Net did not even tell its outside counsel at McCarter & English about its 90–day back-up tape system for storing e-mail. Therefore, outside counsel conducting discovery did not know, when Health Net's employees were asked to search e-mail, that they could only look through the most recent 90 days.

1. Non–Production of Documents Responsive to Plaintiffs' Requests

* * *

Non-production was the rule rather than the exception in this case. As of November 17, 2003, after document requests by Plaintiffs in both the McCoy and Wachtel matters, Health Net had produced under 7,000 pages of discovery and specifically represented to the Court that it had produced all relevant documents. In fact, thousands of pages of documents were never produced during discovery. January 10, 2005 was the final deadline for document discovery (set by Magistrate Judge Shwartz after Health Net requested 15 extensions of the discovery deadline.) Over 12,000 pages of documents never produced in discovery were offered in support of Defendants' Summary Judgment Motions. These documents had been demanded by Plaintiffs but never disclosed during the discovery period. Approximately 8,000 pages of never-produced documents were designated as trial exhibits. These, too, were properly within the scope of Plaintiffs' document demands. Defendants did not alert Plaintiffs or the Court about these 20,000 pages of never-produced discovery despite Plaintiffs' repeated entreaties asking whether Defendants' production was complete and seeking a certification of completeness of production pursuant to Magistrate Judge Shwartz's December 17, 2004 Order.

* * *

Health Net's process for responding to discovery requests was utterly inadequate, relying on an in-house paralegal also responsible for approximately 60 other cases. Testimony at the Rule 37/Integrity Hearing revealed that when Health Net received document requests from Plaintiffs, it did not disseminate a comprehensive notice to employees who could reasonably be anticipated to possess responsive documents. Instead, Health Net directed its outside counsel to work with HNNE's local paralegal who would approach selected individuals about certain specific documents pursuant to instructions from Health Net's outside counsel. Once he asked these specific individuals for specified documents, the paralegal generally did not follow up with them to see if they had further responsive documents unless specifically instructed to do so by outside counsel or by the senior litigation counsel for Health Net, Inc. Nor did the paralegal attempt to identify other employees with responsive documents. Health Net relied on the specified business people within the company to search and turn over whatever documents they thought were responsive, without verifying that the searches were sufficient. The process, in sum, was one of looking for selected specific documents by a specific person rather than all responsive documents from all Health Net employees who had such documents. Many of these specific employee-conducted searches managed to exclude inculpatory documents that were highly germane to Plaintiffs' requests. * * *

Defendants' boilerplate "burdensome" objections did not excuse their obligations to produce e-mails within their possession after Plaintiffs contested the inadequate production and Magistrate Judge Shwartz ruled on them in Plaintiffs' favor. * * * [A]fter Plaintiffs served their discovery demands on Defendants, Defendants would respond with objections and a limited number of responsive documents that were by no means complete. After "meet and confer" sessions, Magistrate Judge Shwartz considered Defendants' objections based on whatever grounds they raised and entered Orders stating the discovery that Defendants had to produce. Health Net, while represented by McCarter & English, unilaterally decided that if the Magistrate Judge did not expressly state that she was ruling on their "burdensome" objections, they could continue to withhold documents. Health Net never told the Magistrate Judge that it was not complying with her discovery orders in this fashion—it just withheld documents. This Court finds that Health Net's latest argument—to wit, that their "burdensome" objections were never ruled upon by the Magistrate Judge, and that Defendants therefore could continue to rely on those objections to withhold discovery ever after Court Orders to produce—is utterly without merit. It is not made in good faith. The Magistrate Judge heard scores of oral arguments on all discovery obligations pressed by Defendants, and she ruled. Those rulings deserved compliance.

This Court also finds that the "meet and confer" process was compromised by Health Net's wilful failure to identify to the Plaintiffs the full range of documents that were responsive to Plaintiffs' document requests. As a result, the Plaintiffs could not engage in meaningful dialogue to reduce the scope of the documents requested without knowing the total number of documents that existed. * * * In sum, there was a vast failure to search for relevant documents and vast non-production as described in more detail below.

2. Failure to Preserve and Search E-mails

Although Health Net's in-house and outside counsel agree that Health Net was obligated throughout this litigation to produce e-mails in response to Plaintiffs' document demands, a vast quantity of highly relevant e-mails from Health Net employees' accounts were never searched for and never produced during the discovery period. Throughout the lengthy discovery period, Plaintiffs repeatedly expressed concern that Defendants were improperly withholding responsive documents and Health Net's outside counsel Pendleton repeatedly provided blanket assurances that Health Net was fully producing responsive documents.

* * *

As highly relevant e-mails kept appearing for the first time during the Rule 37/Integrity Hearing, this Court kept asking from October 2005 through March 2006 why they had never been produced during discovery. This Court's repeated query for an explanation was never met with a candid answer from defense counsel. On February 28, 2006, this Court learned for the first time that Health Net used an e-mail retention policy that automatically removed e-mails from employees' active files and sent them to back-up disks every 90 days. E-mails older than 90 days were not searched—ever. During the preceding four years of litigation, Health Net never told the Magistrate Judge this crucial fact, and Health Net never told the McCarter counsel tasked with discovery production this fact. Health Net did tell new outside counsel at Epstein Becker in March 2005 after discovery had ended; Epstein Becker * * * did not notify the Court or Plaintiffs of this systematic failure to search. Health Net never searched the back-up disks during the three years of open discovery and never disclosed that it did not search e-mails over 90 days old for even its most centrally involved personnel.

Further adding to spoliation, any e-mails that an employee deleted within 30 days of receipt were lost permanently upon transfer to storage at 90 days.[31] Thus, when Health Net asked its employees to search their own e-mails for documents responsive to Plaintiffs' demands, those employees could only search e-mails on their active server or those they had chosen to archive before each 90 day back-up. It was not candid of Health Net to keep this information about the 90 day back-up system from Plaintiffs, their own outside counsel at McCarter, Magistrate Judge Shwartz, and this Court throughout the entire discovery period.

Health Net did not even begin to conduct its own search of employees' backed-up e-mails until Plaintiffs moved for a Rule 37/Integrity Hearing. Throughout the several months of the Rule 37/Integrity hearing, and after warnings from the Court, Defendants found vast numbers of non-produced documents that were responsive to discovery demands and previously ordered to be produced. Rather than candidly reveal the derelictions in discovery, Defendants stated that they "elected to restore certain limited e-mail files from their legacy e-mail systems for current and former employees who appear[ed] to be central to the issues set forth in [Plaintiffs'] motion." * * * On October 18, 2005, this Court ordered that Defendants could not use such documents as evidence at the Rule 37 Hearing when they had never been produced during discovery. As a result of the October 18th Order, the Defendants made a unilateral and groundless decision to stop restoring and searching their back-up e-mails for production to Plaintiffs because they would not be able to use those emails for themselves at the Rule 37 hearing. Upon learning that Defendants had stopped reviewing restored e-mails, this Court, on November 16, 2005, referred to Magistrate Judge Shwartz the resolution of whether or not sanctions should be imposed against Herve Gouraige, Esq. of Epstein Becker.

---

31. Counsel at McCarter & English, LLP, the outside firm during the discovery period, testified that she was unaware of Health Net's practice of putting e-mails on backup tapes 90 days after creation, which made it impossible for most employees to access the e-mails through a search of their own. Nor was she told of Health Net's practice of permitting employees to delete e-mails within 30 days of creation or receipt, which could result in spoliation. Her method of "searching" e-mails was to ask certain specific employees to search their own e-mails. In most cases, this meant that employees were only "searching" the most recent 90 days of e-mails, which means the search was of a mere three month window of time often years after the events that are the subject of the litigation took place. It meant that a "search" was not a search at all.

Even more shocking, Herve Gouraige, Esq. had eight months earlier objected to searching back-up e-mails and had been overruled by the Court and ordered to produce them. Gouraige had argued in March 2005 that searching Health Net's entire e-mail system for responsive documents would be "unduly burdensome and prohibitively expensive" and concluded that Health Net's "only obligation [with regard to searching e-mails] at this point is to produce responsive e-mails from [certain West–Coast] individuals [who were recently deposed]." * * * Health Net was ordered to "provide plaintiffs with all outstanding discovery responses to all outstanding discovery demands including but not limited to those that were the subject of this Court's Order of December 17, 2004."

Despite this ruling, Health Net "interpreted" the April 5th Order to absolve them of any further discovery obligations with respect to e-mail files, with the exception of their obligation to produce "newly discovered" documents pursuant to Rule 26(c). Magistrate Judge Shwartz again soundly rejected this argument, finding that her Order unambiguously required the production of all responsive discovery. * * * Health Net's decision to ignore Magistrate Judge Shwartz's Order to produce e-mails was bold, bald, and baseless. * * *

3. Pattern of Violation and Disregard of Court Discovery Orders

Magistrate Judge Shwartz has issued dozens and dozens of orders since the summer of 2003 in furtherance of her efforts to supervise discovery and pretrial procedures in this case. The Health Net Defendants have ignored many of these Orders by "interpreting" them to avoid their discovery obligations. [Judge Hochberg lists a litany of orders to produce emails and other information that were ignored by the defendants.]

* * *[38]

IV. Conclusions of Law

* * *

This Court has considered a wide range of conduct by Defendants in this litigation and concludes that the repeated nature of that conduct and flagrant disregard of the adversary and the Magistrate Judge's Orders warrant strong sanctions.* * * The victims of Health Net's litigation tactics in this case include both Plaintiffs and the judicial process.

The Defendants have harmed the Plaintiffs in this case by: (1) deliberately failing to timely search and produce responsive documents and thereby causing Plaintiffs to take scores of depositions and prepare their lay and expert witnesses for trial without the discovery that they had properly sought; (2) willfully concealing that no effective search was

---

38. The Magistrate Judge has issued over 110 orders in this case, many ordering Defendants to produce documents they were already required to produce, and this Court has issued over 55 Orders and Opinions based on numerous hearings and appeals of the Magistrate Judge's decisions.

ever conducted for electronic documents; (3) deliberately causing Plaintiffs to conduct depositions hindered by an incomplete set of each deponents' documents, and causing Plaintiffs to prepare their case, including the summary judgment motions, without full discovery; (4) forcing Plaintiffs to seek Court intervention over and over again, wasting a huge amount of time and money in order to secure responses to their discovery requests when good faith compliance with the Federal Rules of Civil Procedure would have made such continuous costly intervention unnecessary; (5) employing a strategy of delay that has cost Plaintiffs inordinate amounts of time and money and has deprived them of the testimony of witnesses whose memories have faded in the years since this litigation began; and (6) concealing Defendants' non-compliance with discovery orders from the Plaintiffs by systematically ignoring adverse rulings.

The Health Net Defendants have violated the integrity of this Court's judicial processes by: * * * ignoring adverse orders of Magistrate Judge Shwartz and acting as if their burdensomeness objections had been granted when they had been briefed, considered, and rejected by the Magistrate Judge; * * * disingenuously claiming that they could not understand clear orders of the Magistrate Judge; * * * failing to disclose to this court or to the Magistrate Judge during three years of discovery that e-mails older than 90 days were never searched when proper discovery requests sought historic information from a period more than 90 days earlier; * * * permitting spoliation of electronic discovery by allowing employee deleted e-mails to be purged and lost, when e-mails were automatically sent to back-up tapes after 90 days, while at the same time having outside counsel inform the Magistrate Judge that a document preservation order was not needed because Health Net knew its obligations to preserve documents as evidence; * * * and * * * keeping even their own outside counsel (other than the Epstein Becker firm) unaware of their e-mail procedures that resulted in widespread dereliction of their discovery obligations.

The Court * * * has determined that each of the sanctions imposed below redresses Health Net's misconduct and is absolutely necessary to remedy the harm to Plaintiffs and the Court. * * *

1. Deeming Facts Admitted Under Rule 37(b)(2)(A)

* * *

In light of the significance of the documents withheld from Plaintiffs, the deliberate and wilful nature of the non-disclosure, and the prejudice suffered by Plaintiffs, this Court finds that aggressive sanctions are necessary to remedy the harm done to Plaintiffs, to punish Defendants for their behavior, and to make clear that such litigation tactics will not be condoned. Thus, this Court will deem established for the purposes of this litigation the facts found in this Opinion regarding Health Net's knowing and wilful use of outdated data; Health Net and its officials' actions to hide the full scope of its conduct from NJ–DOBI

* * * [and other facts pertinent to the claims]. These facts will be deemed admitted for all purposes, including equitable relief.

2. Precluding Evidence under Rule 37(c)(1) and Rule 37(b)(2)(B)

Defendants gave approximately 20,000 pages of previously unproduced discovery to Plaintiffs in the form of documents attached to certifications in support of Health Net's June 10, 2005 motion for summary judgment and as designated trial exhibits. Plaintiffs move to strike the exhibits because the vast quantity of the documents were never produced during discovery.

* * *

Plaintiffs certainly suffered surprise. Plaintiffs' counsel repeatedly asked Defendants' counsel during the several years of discovery whether Defendants had completed their production. Defendants had numerous opportunities during that time to notify the Plaintiffs about any impending document production, even as late as when they submitted their Final Pretrial Order exhibit list. However, Defendants remained silent, allowed discovery to close, and submitted their final exhibit list, which included 8,000 never-disclosed pages as trial exhibits. Additionally, for the first time in their June 10, 2005 Summary Judgment motion, Defendants decided to drop another 12,000 non-disclosed pages. There was not even the courtesy of telling Plaintiffs that the 20,000 pages were never produced in discovery.

Plaintiffs also suffered prejudice. Prejudice from an adversary's failure to file a timely or adequate discovery response may include the irretrievable loss of evidence, the inevitable dimming of witnesses' memories, or the excessive and possibly irremediable burdens or costs imposed on the opposing party. All of this prejudice occurred in this case. Prejudice need not be irremediable, even in the context of dismissal or default, and may include the burden imposed by impeding a party's ability to prepare effectively a full and complete trial strategy and the burden a party must bear when forced to file motions in response to the strategic discovery tactics of an adversary. Plaintiffs had little time to absorb the new material and no effective opportunity to depose witnesses nor to incorporate such a vast amount of material into their own motion for summary judgment. * * * Finally, Plaintiffs were forced to file a request with the Court to strike the late exhibits in response to Defendants' strategic discovery delay. This is more than ample prejudice under Third Circuit precedent to weigh in favor of precluding the never-produced exhibits.

* * * Defendants' strategic delays have disrupted this Court's and the Magistrate Judge's attempts to manage this case to trial in an efficient manner. Defendants have adopted a persistent pattern of delay and obfuscation, which has been instrumental in ensuring that this case had not reached a trial on the merits despite having been on this Court's docket for over 5 years.

Finally, this is not a case of inadvertent or negligent failure to disclose the existence of additional discovery. Defendants had the opportunity, but instead they chose not to notify Plaintiffs or the Court that they were planning to rely on documents that had never before been produced. * * * Such knowing silence constitutes sufficient evidence that Defendants chose not to produce the belated discovery until a moment when its impact would be most acute. Furthermore, Defendants' repetitive pattern of strategic delays only further supports the conclusion that this incident was, like Health Net's other discovery violations, committed in bad faith. Plaintiffs' request to strike is granted.

* * *

5. Monetary Sanctions

Rule 37(b) provides that, in addition to any of the sanctions authorized by the Rule, "the court shall require the party failing to obey the order or the attorney advising that party or both to pay the reasonable expenses, including attorney's fees, caused by the failure, unless the court finds that the failure was substantially justified or that other circumstances make an award of expenses unjust." Attorney's fees and expenses are also authorized under Rule 37(c)(1) upon a finding that a party failed to disclose information without substantial justification. Fed.R.Civ.P. 37(c)(1). This Court has found that Health Net repeatedly and systemically violated discovery orders, in violation of Rule 37(b)(2), and that they improperly withheld documents in violation of Rule 37(c)(1). This Court has considered whether Health Net or its counsel are blameworthy for each dereliction, as set forth above. * * * [P]ursuant to Rule 37(b)(2) and 37(c)(1), this Court will require Health Net forthwith to pay the Plaintiffs' reasonable attorneys' fees and expenses incurred in connection with the Rule 37/Integrity hearing and all briefing in connection therein as well as Plaintiffs' motions brought to invoke discovery compliance after an Order of the Magistrate Judge or the Court had so ordered and Health Net had still not complied, as set forth in this Opinion. Should Plaintiffs choose to re-depose any of the witnesses whose documents were not completely searched or produced prior to their depositions in violation of Court Order, Defendants shall bear all costs and attorneys fees of such renewed depositions.

This Court also has the authority, under its inherent powers, to impose a fine on parties who interfere with the efficient functioning of the Court. On December 28, 2005, Magistrate Judge Shwartz entered an Order recommending that this Court "consider, as part of the Rule 37 proceedings, whether or not sanctions should ... be imposed for: (1) the defendants failure to produce e-mails during discovery; and (2) the defendants unilateral and legally baseless decision to stop restoring and producing the e-mails." This Court has adopted Magistrate Judge Shwartz's recommendation that this Court consider Health Net's wilful actions and determine if any relief is warranted as part of the Rule 37/Integrity proceedings. * * * [T]his Court will impose a fine to be paid by Health Net to the Clerk of this Court. In order to consider the potential impact of a financial sanction on the Health Net companies, this Court will consider public filings concerning the Health Net Defendants' financial stability. Health Net shall submit public filings, including but not limited to statements submitted to the Securities and Exchange Commission, as well as a submission not longer than ten pages to help the Court assess the financial situation of Health Net * * *.

6. Discovery Monitor

In addition to the other relief considered herein, Plaintiffs move for the appointment of a discovery monitor or discovery special master to ensure that Defendants are meeting their obligations. Health Net has repeatedly violated Court orders for discovery. After the revelations at the Rule 37/Integrity Hearing about Defendants' failure to preserve and search e-mails, this Court again ordered Defendants to restore, search, and produce e-mails from their back-up files. These searches may not be complete.

* * *

Defendants' actions have led to a serious disruption in this Court's functioning, and thus this Court finds that the need is clear for help in the form of a separate Special Master to monitor discovery compliance to ensure that all documents ordered to be produced have been produced and that all of the Court's discovery Orders have been complied with. * * * Because, as described above, Defendants unreasonable behavior has occasioned the need to appoint a master to review their compliance with this Courts' Orders for production of responsive discovery, this Court will require that Health Net pay the entirety of the Special Master's fees.

V. Conclusion

This Court, the Magistrate Judge, and the parties have already devoted more than five years to this litigation. The vast majority of this time, unfortunately, has been spent dealing with Defendants' persistently obstructionist tactics in evading discovery. This Court has carefully considered the sanctions available to address Defendants' behavior and has decided to impose sanctions severe enough to reflect the harm incurred. Any lesser sanctions than those imposed herein would not be sufficient to remedy the prejudice suffered by the Plaintiffs or to punish Defendants' disrespect and abuse of this Court's procedures.

* * *

COMMENTARY

1. Introduction

Electronic discovery has significantly changed the landscape as to how counsel (in-house and outside) interact with their clients when litigation is pending or threatened. Counsel now are required to take affirmative roles in advising their clients regarding the identification, preservation, collection and production of electronic information. These lawyers also may have to confront two potentially countervailing interests—their obligations to their clients and their ethical duties as officers of the court. While this dilemma is certainly not new to attorneys, the age of electronic discovery has added a new twist to this challenging issue. This section will illustrate the ethical concerns that lawyers face regarding their duties of candor, competence, and fairness to the court and opposing counsel when confronting electronic discovery.

2. Rules of Professional Responsibility

a. Duty of Candor

i. ABA Model Rule: 3.3 Candor Toward the Tribunal

(a) A lawyer shall not knowingly:

(1) make a false statement of fact or law to a tribunal or fail to correct a false statement of material fact or law previously made to the tribunal by the lawyer;

* * *

(3) offer evidence that the lawyer knows to be false. If a lawyer, the lawyer's client, or a witness called by the lawyer, has offered material evidence and the lawyer comes to know of its falsity, the lawyer shall take reasonable remedial measures, including, if necessary, disclosure to the tribunal. A lawyer may refuse to offer evidence, other than the testimony of a defendant in a criminal matter, that the lawyer reasonably believes is false.

(b) A lawyer who represents a client in an adjudicative proceeding and who knows that a person intends to engage, is engaging or has engaged in criminal or fraudulent conduct related to the proceeding shall take reasonable remedial measures, including, if necessary, disclosure to the tribunal.

(c) The duties stated in paragraphs (a) and (b) continue to the conclusion of the proceeding, and apply even if compliance requires disclosure of information otherwise protected by Rule 1.6.

ii. State Standards

(a) New Jersey Rule (Heightened Standard): A lawyer shall not knowingly "fail to disclose to the tribunal a material fact knowing that the omission is reasonably certain to mislead the tribunal." N.J. Rule 3.3(a)(5).

(b) Maryland (Less Stringent Standard): No ethical violation when a lawyer knowingly failed to disclose to police that his client acted under a pseudonym during his arraignment. *Attorney Grievance Comm'n v. Rohrback*, 591 A.2d 488, 495 (Md. 1991).

(c) Texas (Less Stringent Standard): Defense lawyer does not have an affirmative obligation to correct a judge who misstated that the defendant did not have any prior convictions. State Bar of Tex. Prof'l Ethics Comm., Op. 504 (1995), *available at* www.txethics.org/reference_opinions.asp?opinionnum=504&searchfor=.

(d) California: Rule 5–200. Trial Conduct: In presenting a matter to a tribunal, a member:

(A) *Shall employ, for the purpose of maintaining the causes confided to the member such means only as are consistent with truth* (emphasis added to differentiate wording from ABA Model Rules);

(B) Shall not seek to mislead the judge, judicial officer, or jury by an artifice or false statement of fact or law;

* * *

(E) Shall not assert personal knowledge of the facts at issue, except when testifying as a witness.

iii. Commentary

The lawyer's duty of candor plays an extremely important role in litigation. The legal system mandates that lawyers, as officers of the court, present information in a truthful manner because judges, juries, and opposing counsel rely on this information to make legal decisions. Without the duty of candor, the integrity of the adjudicative process would be severely undermined.

With the explosion of the use of electronic information in business and in litigation, new and experienced attorneys face the challenging task of familiarizing themselves with not only the changes to federal and state rules regarding e-discovery, they must also immerse themselves in the technology in order to satisfy the required level of knowledge necessary to uphold their duty of candor. Recently, courts have levied significant sanctions against counsel for violating the duty of candor.

Violating this obligation can also pose serious danger to the attorney's client as well. Courts have issued adverse inference instructions to juries for violations by counsel of the duty of candor, in one case resulting in an award of over 1.5 billion dollars (later overturned on appeal on unrelated grounds).[14]

When litigation is pending or threatened, lawyers must be very careful in performing due diligence in the identification, preservation, review and production of electronic information to ensure that they are presenting truthful and accurate information to the court and the opposing parties. Attorneys who intentionally or unintentionally mislead a trier of fact or falsely certify compliance with a discovery order run the

---

14. *See Coleman (Parent) Holdings, Inc. v. Morgan Stanley & Co., Inc.*, No. 502003CA005045XXO-CAI, 2005 WL 679071 (Fla. Cir. Ct. Mar. 1, 2005); *Coleman (Parent) Holdings, Inc. v. Morgan Stanley & Co., Inc.*, No. CA 03–5045 AI, 2005 WL 674885 (Fla. Cir. Ct. Mar. 23, 2005).

risk of compromising not only their clients' cases but in extreme cases, their professional careers.

b.   Duty of Competence

i.   *ABA Model Rule: 1.1*

A lawyer shall provide competent representation to a client. Competent representation requires the legal knowledge, skill, thoroughness and preparation reasonably necessary for the representation.

Comment [5]: Major litigation and complex transactions ordinarily require more extensive treatment than matters of lesser complexity and consequence. See Rule 1.2(c).

ii.   *Commentary*

Lawyers have a responsibility to educate themselves and their clients about the new and pertinent legal and technical issues regarding electronic discovery. This is especially true when it comes to counsel's affirmative obligation to actively engage with his or her client in the process of identifying, preserving, reviewing, and producing electronic information. This includes an obligation to seek, as part of the lawyer's due diligence, all relevant information, positive or otherwise, which may relate to the claims at issue. To do otherwise is an ethical violation.

ABA Model Rule 8.4 notes that it is professional misconduct for a lawyer to, among other things: "(c) engage in conduct involving dishonesty, fraud, deceit or misrepresentation; or (d) engage in conduct that is prejudicial to the administration of justice." And these obligations apply to all attorneys—litigation and corporate counsel, in-house and outside counsel—alike. In the new age of electronic information and discovery, lawyers must be prepared to act with "diligence and competence" and with a sense of urgency with regard to meeting the obligations created by the recent amendments to the Federal Rules.

Moreover, lawyers cannot relieve themselves of their ethical obligations by outsourcing the work associated with electronic discovery to a more technologically-savvy organization such as a vendor, without direct supervision. Attorneys have an obligation to monitor the discovery process and ensure that relevant non-privileged information is identified, preserved, reviewed and produced. For instance, Rule 26(f) mandates that a lawyer must understand and competently investigate the electronic storage systems used by his client so that the lawyer can properly participate in the Rule 26 conference.

Ensuring that discovery procedures are properly followed involves offering adequate advice and instructions to clients regarding their obligations in discovery. Courts have not shied away from penalizing parties and their lawyers who fail to competently handle their duties of electronic discovery. In its opinion on a motion to reconsider in *Metro-*

politan Opera Association, Inc. v. Local 100, the court warned that the "defendants and their counsel may not engage in parallel know-nothing, do-nothing, head-in-the sand behavior in an effort consciously to avoid knowledge of or responsibility for their discovery obligations and to obstruct plaintiff's wholly appropriate efforts to prepare its case."[15] In another case, the court awarded defendant costs and attorneys' fees because "a reasonable inquiry by the plaintiff's counsel ... would have alerted counsel that the plaintiff possessed electronic mail that fell within the scope of [defendant's] document request."[16]

c. Duty of Fairness

i. ABA Model Rule: 3.4

> "A lawyer shall not: (a) unlawfully obstruct another party's access to evidence ..."

Comment [1]: The procedure of the adversary system contemplates that the evidence in a case is to be marshaled competitively by the contending parties. Fair competition in the adversary system is secured by prohibitions against destruction or concealment of evidence, improperly influencing witnesses, obstructive tactics in discovery procedure, and the like.

Comment [2]: Documents and other items of evidence are often essential to establish a claim or defense. Subject to evidentiary privileges, the right of an opposing party, including the government, to obtain evidence through discovery or subpoena is an important procedural right. The exercise of that right can be frustrated if relevant material is altered, concealed or destroyed.

ii. Commentary

In addition to upholding the duties of candor and competence, a lawyer must ensure that he fulfills his duty of fairness to the opposing party and counsel. As explained above, a lawyer cannot destroy or conceal evidence. This means that lawyers also have an ethical duty to produce all non-privileged ESI to opposing counsel. The duty of fairness prohibits attorneys from withholding a "smoking gun" document simply because the information is harmful to his client's position.

iii. Illustration

Plaintiff filed an employment discrimination suit against her former employer Network, a large media conglomerate. Network retained a prominent law firm, White–Shoe, to defend it in the lawsuit. Plaintiff's

---

15.   No. 00 Civ. 3613, 2004 WL 1943099, at *25 (S.D.N.Y. Aug. 27, 2004).

16.   *Invasion Media Commc'ns, Inc. v. Federal Ins. Co.,* No. 02 Civ. 5461, 2004 WL 396037, at *8 (S.D.N.Y. Mar. 2, 2004).

counsel met with representatives from White–Shoe to discuss discovery
of information relating to plaintiff's dismissal from Network. Both
parties agreed to exchange all information, paper and electronic, relating to plaintiff's employment and discharge from Network.

White–Shoe attorneys subsequently entered into discussions with
Network's in-house counsel regarding discovery in the pending matter.
Prior to the litigation, Network did not employ a data retention system
for electronic information. White–Shoe devised a document collection
plan for Network's in-house counsel, which included plans for an
electronic search engine that could find all relevant e-mails and attachments. In order to keep legal fees down, White–Shoe agreed that most
of the discovery could be handled by Network's in-house counsel.

During discovery, Network uncovered two thousand e-mails and
paper documents relating to plaintiff's employment and termination at
Network. Network produced these documents to plaintiff's counsel.
White–Shoe attorneys signed the certificate of compliance to the court
for production of the discovery requests. Network's IT executive, Te-
chie, also stated in her deposition that she felt quite positive all responsive e-mail and paper documents had been recovered and produced to
plaintiff because her staff searched all of Network's common areas of
paper and electronic storage.

Plaintiff's counsel, however, suspected that Network had not produced all relevant information, that it was withholding responsive documents, and that it did not perform a thorough search of its electronic
information systems including personal computers for relevant information. Plaintiff challenged Network's compliance and filed a motion to
compel discovery, including a request for inspection of the computers of
Network's "key players." The court granted plaintiff's request. In preparation for the inspection, defendant's counsel discovered that thousands
of documents had been recently deleted from the hard drive of a
computer used by one of defendant's "key players." However, when
confronted by plaintiff's counsel, defendant's counsel repeatedly declared that all responsive documents had been produced.

Moreover, one month before trial, Network produced an additional
three hundred e-mails with attachments. Network and its representatives explained that the reason for the supplemental production was that
there had been a "glitch" in the company's data recovery search engine.
The search engine only recovered sent and received e-mails, but not
forwarded e-mails, attachments, and carbon copies. Because discovery
had been completed, plaintiff asserted that it was extremely prejudiced
by Network's failure to produce relevant information in a timely fashion.
Plaintiff filed a motion for sanctions which included a request for an
adverse inference at trial. How should the court rule?

D. SUPERVISION, OUTSOURCING, LITIGATION SUPPORT, AND LAWYER ADJUNCTS

Editor's Note: Two cases already set forth in this book provide cautionary tales about the need for lawyer supervision of the preservation, collection, and production of ESI. *See Qualcomm, Inc. v. Broadcom Corp.* **(Chapter VI.E); and** *Wachtel v. Healthnet* **(Chapter VII.C).**

COMMENTARY

E-discovery requires a team effort. For example, litigants are well-advised to create a "preservation triage team" of insiders who are familiar with the party's systems and operations and can act quickly to preserve appropriate materials. The team should interview all key players in the litigation about their storage of information, or if this is not feasible, perhaps run a system-wide keyword search to segregate responsive documents and ensure that counsel is aware of the scope of relevant information available. These processes often require the help of outside experts and litigation support personnel.

Such measures may be necessary in order to adequately discharge a party's preservation and production obligations. But the team approach itself raises new issues. How should the e-discovery team be managed? Who is responsible for managing it? How should duties be allocated among the team members? Who has the final say between counsel and client? Who bears the ultimate responsibility for following court orders, complying with the Federal Rules of Civil Procedure, and upholding the Rules of Professional Conduct?

When there are many individuals sharing the e-discovery burden, it may be tempting to pass the buck in circles, assuming that no one person will be held responsible individually for what could be considered "team" failings. That temptation must be acknowledged—and avoided.

1. Obligations of Counsel

To ensure that litigants comply with their preservation obligations, counsel should inform their clients: (1) of the existence of the duty to preserve; (2) that the duty to preserve encompasses all "documents" potentially relevant to the dispute; and (3) that the definition of "document" encompasses hard copies and electronic documents, as well as drafts and non-identical copies. Counsel may need to periodically remind their clients of the scope of the preservation requirement over the course of any litigation, or take other affirmative steps to monitor compliance.

Counsel's obligation continues through preservation and into the production phase. In *Board of Regents of University of Nebraska v. BASF*

Corp., the court identified by name the attorney assigned to the task of managing discovery and described the lawyer's significant obligations:

> When faced with responding to a request for production of documents, counsel are required to direct the conduct of a thorough search for responsive documents.... Of course, when ordered by a court to produce documents, counsel are under an even higher obligation to affirmatively direct complete compliance with the order in ... good faith. That standard was not met in this case. There is no evidence of any specific directives from counsel to the Board regarding what was required to ensure that all documents covered by the order were produced.... There is also no evidence of any assurances requested or given, sworn or otherwise, by University personnel to counsel to the effect that all covered documents had, in fact, been produced in accordance with the order. There is also no evidence of any directives given by counsel at any time for a "litigation hold" to be placed on all relevant documents and electronically stored information....
>
> If counsel fail in this responsibility—willfully or not—[the] principles of an open discovery process are undermined, coextensively with inhibiting the courts' ability to objectively resolve their clients' disputes and the credibility of its resolution.[17]

The failure of counsel to adequately oversee the preservation and discovery process may lead to the imposition of sanctions against the client. For example, in *Metropolitan Opera Association Inc. v. Local 100, Hotel Employees & Restaurant Employees International Union*, the court awarded sanctions against the defendant where its counsel:

> (1) never gave adequate instructions to their clients about the clients' overall discovery obligations, [including a definition as to] what constitutes a "document" ...; (2) knew the [client] to have no document retention or filing systems and yet never implemented a systematic procedure for document production or for retention of documents, including electronic documents; (3) delegated document production to a layperson who (at least until July 2001) did not even understand himself (and was not instructed by counsel) that a document included a draft or other non-identical copy, a computer file and an e-mail; (4) never went back to the layperson designated to assure that he had "established[ed] a coherent and effective system to faithfully and effectively respond to discovery requests," ... and (5) in the face of the [plaintiff's] persistent questioning and showings that the production was faulty and incomplete, ridiculed the inquiries, failed to take any action to remedy the situation or supplement the demonstrably false responses, failed to ask important witnesses for documents until the night

---

17. No. 04 Civ. 3356, 2007 WL 3342423, at *5 (D. Neb. Nov. 5, 2007).

before their depositions and, instead, made repeated, baseless representations that all documents had been produced.[18]

The court awarded a default judgment in favor of the plaintiff, reasoning that "it is impossible to know what the [plaintiff] would have found if the [defendant] and its counsel had complied with their discovery obligations from the commencement of the action."[19]

A lawyer's failings may also lead to sanctions against the lawyer. The *Qualcomm* case reaffirmed that a lawyer cannot rely solely on his client's assurances, wash his hands of all e-discovery obligations, and later plead ignorance. A lawyer's seeming inaction may be deemed to actively enable the client to commit discovery violations and subject the lawyer to sanctions.

2. Responsibility of Company Management

The responsibility for preservation and production of ESI also falls on the shoulders of a company's senior management. *In re Prudential Insurance Company of America Sales Practices Litigation* was a multidistrict litigation in which a communication breakdown between upper corporate management and the company's field offices resulted in the destruction of responsive documents at various locations. The court clearly blamed the company's leadership for the "haphazard and uncoordinated approach" to document preservation. The court stated:

> [I]t became the obligation of senior management to initiate a comprehensive document preservation plan and to distribute it to all employees. Moreover, it was incumbent on senior management to advise its employees of the pending multi-district litigation . . . to provide them with a copy of the Court's Order, and to acquaint its employees with the potential sanctions, both civil and criminal, that the Court could issue for noncompliance with this Court's Order.

> When senior management fails to establish and distribute a comprehensive document retention policy, it cannot shield itself from responsibility because of field office actions. The obligation to preserve documents that are potentially discoverable materials is an affirmative one that rests squarely on the shoulders of senior corporate officers.[20]

Similarly, in *Danis v. USN Communications, Inc.*, the defendant's CEO delegated responsibility for document production to a new, in-house lawyer with no litigation experience and no experience in document preservation. The Magistrate Judge recommended that the court fine the CEO ten thousand dollars and that it additionally give a spoliation instruction.[21]

---

18. 212 F.R.D. 178, 222 (S.D.N.Y. 2003). This case can be found at Chapter VI.C, *supra.*

19. *Id.* at 230.

20. 169 F.R.D. 598, 615 (D.N.J. 1997).

21. *See* No. 98 C 7482, 2000 WL 1694325, at *6 (N.D. Ill. Oct. 23, 2000).

3. Managing the Client–Lawyer Relationship

Counsel and client may not always agree on measures necessary to discharge the party's discovery obligations. Whose position should prevail? What can a lawyer do when faced with an obstinate client? In *Qualcomm* the Magistrate Judge took a tough stance:

> Leung's attorney represented during the OSC hearing that Leung [an attorney retained by Qualcomm] requested a more thorough document search but that Qualcomm refused to do so. If Leung was unable to get Qualcomm to conduct the type of search he deemed necessary to verify the adequacy of the document search and production, then he should have obtained the assistance of supervising or senior attorneys. If Mammen and Batchelder were unable to get Qualcomm to conduct a competent and thorough document search, they should have withdrawn from the case or taken other action to ensure production of the evidence.[22]

The ABA Model Rules provide some guidelines for navigating the lawyer-client relationship. Rule 1.4 regarding Communications provides:

> (a) A lawyer shall:
>
>> (1) promptly inform the client of any decision or circumstance with respect to which the client's informed consent . . . is required by these Rules;
>>
>> (2) reasonably consult with the client about the means by which the client's objectives are to be accomplished; . . .
>
> (b) A lawyer shall explain a matter to the extent reasonably necessary to permit the client to make informed decisions regarding the representation.

Rule 1.2 regarding the Scope of Representation and Allocation of Authority Between Lawyer and Client provides:

> (a) [A] lawyer shall abide by a client's decisions concerning the objectives of representation and . . . shall consult with the client as to the means by which they are to be pursued.

4. Supervising Lawyers and Subordinates

In *Qualcomm*, the court found that each of several named attorneys "contributed to Qualcomm's monumental discovery violation and is personally responsible. . . ."[23] The sanctioned attorneys ranged from Qualcomm's lead attorney, a partner and founding member of the retained law firm, to a second-year associate who first discovered the responsive, unproduced e-mails. Regarding the responsibility of the junior associate, the court stated:

> When [Associate] reviewed the August 6, 2002 email . . . he knew or should have known that it contradicted Qualcomm's trial arguments

---

22. *Qualcomm*, 2008 WL 66932, at *13 n.10 (citation omitted).

23. *Id.* at *13.

and he had an obligation to verify that it had been produced in discovery or to immediately produce it. If [he], as a junior lawyer, lacked the experience to recognize the significance of the document, then a more senior or knowledgeable attorney should have assisted him. To the extent that [Partner] was supervising [Associate] in this endeavor, [Partner] certainly knew or should have recognized the importance of the document from his involvement in Qualcomm's motion practice and trial strategy sessions.

Similarly, when [Associate] found the 21 emails ... that had not been produced in discovery, he took the appropriate action and informed his supervisors....[24]

The following ABA Model Rules address the relationship between supervising lawyers and subordinate lawyers.

Rule 5.1 Responsibilities of Partners, Managers, and Supervisory Lawyers

(b) A lawyer having direct supervisory authority over another lawyer shall make reasonable efforts to ensure that the other lawyer conforms to the Rules of Professional Conduct.

(c) A lawyer shall be responsible for another lawyer's violation of the Rules of Professional Conduct if:

    (3) the lawyer orders or, with knowledge of the specific conduct, ratifies the conduct involved; or

    (4) the lawyer is a partner or has comparable managerial authority in the law firm in which the other lawyer practices, or has direct supervisory authority over the other lawyer, and knows of the conduct at a time when its consequences can be avoided or mitigated but fails to take reasonable remedial action.

Rule 5.2 Responsibilities of a Subordinate Lawyer

(a) A lawyer is bound by the Rules of Professional Conduct notwithstanding that the lawyer acted at the direction of another person.

(b) A subordinate lawyer does not violate the Rules of Professional Conduct if that lawyer acts in accordance with a supervisory lawyer's reasonable resolution of an arguable question of professional duty.

Rule 5.2 Responsibilities of a Subordinate Lawyer–Comment

[2] When lawyers in a supervisor-subordinate relationship encounter a matter involving professional judgment as to ethical duty, the supervisor may assume responsibility for making the judgment. Otherwise a consistent course of action or position could not be taken. If the question can reasonably be answered only one way, the duty of both lawyers is clear and they are equally responsible for

---

24. *Id.* at *14.

fulfilling it. However, if the question is reasonably arguable, someone has to decide upon the course of action. That authority
ordinarily reposes in the supervisor, and a subordinate may be
guided accordingly. For example, if a question arises whether the
interests of two clients conflict under Rule 1.7, the supervisor's
reasonable resolution of the question should protect the subordinate professionally if the resolution is subsequently challenged.

a. COMMUNICATION IS CRITICAL

Qualcomm illustrates the critical importance of communication between counsel and client and among e-discovery and litigation team
members. Knowledge may be imputed from client to counsel and from
lawyer to associated lawyer whether or not it is actually communicated.
A junior associate who is in charge of responding to discovery requests
and preparing witnesses must be able to effectively communicate with
the lead trial counsel who will be making arguments and representations
in open court and at sidebar.

b. LAWYERS AND CONSULTANTS

Litigation support personnel, technology consultants and other
outside experts play an important role on the e-discovery team. Such
consultants are often non-lawyers. A supervising lawyer must ensure
that all non-lawyers retained to assist with e-discovery conduct themselves in accordance with the Model Rules. Under some circumstances,
the lawyer may even be held responsible for a non-lawyer's conduct.
ABA Model Rule 5.3 provides:

> With respect to a non-lawyer employed or retained by or associated
> with a lawyer:
>
> (a) a partner, and a lawyer who individually or together with other
> lawyers possesses comparable managerial authority in a law firm
> shall make reasonable efforts to ensure that the firm has in
> effect measures giving reasonable assurance that the person's
> conduct is compatible with the professional obligations of the
> lawyer;
>
> (b) a lawyer having direct supervisory authority over the non-
> lawyer shall make reasonable efforts to ensure that the person's
> conduct is compatible with the professional obligations of the
> lawyer; and
>
> (c) a lawyer shall be responsible for conduct of such a person that
> would be a violation of the Rules of Professional Conduct if
> engaged in by a lawyer if:
>
>> (1) the lawyer orders or, with the knowledge of the specific
>> conduct, ratifies the conduct involved; or
>>
>> (2) the lawyer is a partner or has comparable managerial
>> authority in the law firm in which the person is employed,
>> or has direct supervisory authority over the person, and

knows of the conduct at a time when its consequences can be avoided or mitigated but fails to take reasonable remedial action.

The comments to Rule 5.3 make clear that a lawyer must give consultants appropriate instruction and supervision concerning the ethical aspects of their employment and should keep in mind that non-lawyer consultants do not have legal training and are not subject to professional discipline. The Model Rule also imposes an obligation on law firms to design internal policies and procedures to ensure that non-lawyers will conform their actions to the Model Rules.

PROBLEMS

1.   Consider how ABA Model Rule 1.2 allocates authority between attorney and client. What is the practical difference, if any, between "objectives" and "means"? How do these terms apply in the realm of e-discovery, preservation and production?

2.   ABA Model Rule 5.2 provides that a subordinate lawyer may, consistent with his professional and ethical obligations, defer to the judgment of a supervising attorney. Can the Magistrate Judge's treatment of the Associate in *Qualcomm* be reconciled with Rule 5.2? If the Associate "took the appropriate action and informed his supervisors[,]" why did the Magistrate Judge hold him personally responsible?

3.   Law Firm is representing Soft–D, the defendant in a complex patent infringement case brought by Soft–P. Law Firm has decided to retain an e-discovery vendor to provide litigation preservation, collection and production services. Law Firm is most interested in E–Vend, an electronic evidence vendor with an impressive client list and extensive experience in patent litigation discovery. E–Vend's response to Law Firm's Request for Information revealed that E–Vend had provided litigation services for Soft–P in an employment discrimination lawsuit five years ago. Consistent with the Model Rules, could Law Firm hire E–Vend in connection with *Soft-P v. Soft–D*? What ethical issues does this situation raise and how can they be addressed? *See* ABA Model Rules 1.6, 1.7, 1.8 and 1.9.

COMMENTARY

What should counsel do if she recommended to her client that it disclose certain information to the other side, and the client refuses to take counsel's advice?

An attorney is not a hired gun who must blindly follow a client's wishes. As set forth in ABA Model Rule 3.3(b), if the lawyer knows that her client is intending to engage in fraudulent conduct by failing to fulfill its discovery obligations, she must take remedial measures which could include withdrawing from a case if continued representation will result in an ethical violation.

If outside counsel asked in-house counsel to perform a more thorough document search and in-house counsel refused to do so, what should outside counsel do, if anything?

If after a reasonable inquiry into discovery procedures, outside counsel believes that in-house counsel has not and will not adequately address its discovery obligations, outside counsel might consider withdrawing from the case to avoid offering false information to the tribunal.

Can outside counsel avoid ethical problems if it is merely a scrivener for false affidavits filed by its client?

No, outside counsel would not avoid ethical problems if she aided her client in filing false statements to the court. Outside counsel has an obligation to act with good faith and make a reasonable inquiry. It is never an excuse that " 'the left hand [does not know] what the right hand is doing.' "[25]

When is reliance on information provided by in-house counsel in response to a discovery request good enough to satisfy outside counsel's ethical obligations?

The *Qualcomm* court noted that outside counsel fulfill their ethical duties if after a reasonable inquiry the certification is accurate to the best of outside counsel's knowledge. Complete dependence on representations made by in-house counsel is not sufficient for outside counsel to satisfy its ethical obligations.

Has outside counsel satisfied its duty of candor to the court when it makes statements in briefs about discovery based solely upon the client providing information to counsel?

Outside counsel must act in good faith and make a reasonable inquiry of in-house counsel regarding the discovery sought. Did outside counsel question in-house counsel about her protocol for gathering information and whether that protocol was followed? Was a record made of the results of the inquiry? Was there follow-up? Counsel is required to conduct a comprehensive search for relevant information. Qualcomm's outside counsel, for instance, failed to conduct a reasonable inquiry into Qualcomm's discovery production before making specific factual and legal arguments to the court.

What should an attorney do if she becomes aware that certain representations made to the court at a hearing are false?

The duty of candor requires the attorney to disclose to the court that certain representations were false once the attorney becomes aware that the representations were misleading.

What should local counsel do if she realizes that her pleadings contained false statements?

The duty of candor would be violated if the attorneys did not make efforts to correct the false statement. In *Qualcomm*, the court publicly

---

25. *Wachtel v. Health Net*, 239 F.R.D. 81, 87 (D.N.J. 2006).

named the local counsel who filed false pleadings but it did not sanction them. The court noted that "given the facts of this case ... the limitations provided by the referral, and the totality of the circumstances, the Court finds that it was reasonable for these attorneys [local counsel] to sign the pleadings, relying on the work of other attorneys more actively involved in the litigation."[26]

DISCUSSION

1. Role of Professionalism and Civility in Litigation

Some commentators have noted that developing and maintaining a high level of professionalism and civility among counsel and the court can be of great value in avoiding ethical dilemmas. Often contentious discovery among attorneys can be self-defeating. Therefore, a lawyer might reconsider combative discovery in favor of transparency in order to maintain his or her credibility.

2. Prepare and Follow a Discovery Protocol

Documenting discovery efforts can greatly benefit attorneys in the short and long term. The sheer volume and complexity of electronic discovery requires meticulous organization. Documenting discovery will help attorneys focus on what questions must be asked and what documents will be needed. While documenting discovery might be time consuming, it may be beneficial to an attorney not only because it can help organize the discovery process and help demonstrate to the court that proper discovery protocol has been followed, but it may also provide much needed support for evidentiary issues.

3. In–House Counsel's Role

In-house counsel plays a very important role in complex litigations, and some commentators have suggested that in-house counsel can take four steps to aid electronic discovery:

(1) Establish a document preservation plan as part of a compliance program, which stresses the importance of preservation to the company's employees.

(2) Directly involve outside counsel in the implementation of a compliance program and allow them to correct the program's deficiencies.

(3) Upon the first indication of a legal dispute, in-house counsel should issue a litigation hold on all potentially relevant electronic documents. This would entail identifying and sequestering correspondence among "key players." Furthermore, employees should be constantly reminded of the importance of litigation holds and impose penalties for employees that fail to comply.

---

26. *Qualcomm Inc. v. Broadcom Corp.*, No. 05 Civ. 1958, 2008 WL 66932, at *16 (S.D. Cal. Jan. 7, 2008).

(4) Use third-parties or outside vendors to assist in-house technical staff with the preservation of electronic documents.

While these steps are not exhaustive, they should go a long way to ensuring compliance with discovery requests.

PROBLEMS

1.   You are a Junior Associate. A Senior Partner approaches you at the end of the day and asks you to sign the affidavit certifying compliance with the court's discovery order regarding electronic discovery in a pending litigation. The certification of compliance is due by the close of that business day. You have only worked on the case peripherally and do not know if the discovery order has been fully completed. What should you do?

2.   You are a Senior Associate at a firm. You have previously certified compliance with a discovery order. A month after certifying compliance, you realize that the document production you made was incomplete and you should have produced more documents. What should you do?

3.   Your firm, Dark Suits, is trial counsel representing Record Company in an employment discrimination case. Dark Suits will coordinate the litigation with Record Company's in-house counsel. Record Company will handle all of the discovery and Dark Suits will manage the merits of the litigation. As a result, Dark Suits will have to certify compliance with discovery orders although it has not participated in much of the discovery. How should the parties divide up the work and ensure that all certifications are accurate and truthful?

4.   Your firm, Dark Suits, is hired in a pending litigation by Colonial, a Fortune 500 Company. Early in discovery, Dark Suits realizes Colonial does not have an e-mail retention system in place. Implementing a retention system and reviewing the subsequent paperwork will cost Colonial hundreds of thousands of dollars. What should Dark Suits do?

VIII

PRIVILEGE ISSUES ARISING DURING ELECTRONIC DISCOVERY

■ ■ ■

When lawyers produce information in response to a discovery demand, they must take care not to disclose the client's privileged information. Such a disclosure could constitute a waiver of the privilege and, under some circumstances, might result in a finding of subject matter waiver—meaning that the client must make a further production of all privileged communications on the same subject matter as the previously disclosed documents. Consequently, lawyers engage in pre-production review of documents to determine whether they are privileged.

While pre-production privilege review has always been necessary, the burdens of such review have skyrocketed for electronic discovery. Stories abound of teams of lawyers (junior to senior) reading e-mails for hours on end, to determine whether they contain privileged information.

The case below discusses the phenomenon of pre-production privilege review of electronic information. That case as well as the rest of the materials in this Chapter address ways in which the skyrocketing costs of pre-production privilege review can be limited.

A. THE RISKS OF WAIVER AND THE COSTS OF PRE–PRODUCTION PRIVILEGE REVIEW OF ELECTRONIC DATA

HOPSON v. THE MAYOR AND CITY COUNCIL OF BALTIMORE
232 F.R.D. 228 (D. Md. 2005)

GRIMM, MAGISTRATE JUDGE

This case has been referred to me for resolution of all discovery disputes. Pending and ripe for a decision is the Plaintiffs' motion to compel Rule 33 and 34 discovery. Plaintiffs have asserted putative class claims and individual claims against the City of Baltimore ("The City") and the Baltimore City Police Department ("BCPD") alleging that BCPD engaged in racial discrimination against African American police officers in connection with the administration of the disciplinary system for Baltimore police officers. It is alleged that the disparate impact and disparate treatment claims extend back to 1992, the commencement date for the misconduct that is the focus of the class claims.

When the court issued its scheduling order and discovery commenced, Plaintiffs promptly served interrogatories and document production requests on the Defendants. The Rule 34 requests were extensive and clearly sought both "hard copy" records as well as electronically stored records and data. Companion interrogatories included more than 15 specifically designed to discover the nature, extent, and location of electronically stored records, the Defendants' IT capabilities, the nature of archived data, e-mail, and records retention policies—in short, all of the computer generated information that is the subject of so much discussion these days.

Defendants answered, raising many objections to the discovery sought, including burdensomeness and expense. * * * One of the Defendants' concerns was the cost and burden of performing pre-production privilege review of the records sought by the Plaintiffs. * * * [T]he issues presented in this case prominently showcase challenges that recur in connection with the discovery of electronic data, * * * [and raise] significant unresolved issues relating to the nature of privilege review that must be performed by a party producing electronically stored information, whether non-waiver agreements entered into by counsel to permit post-production assertion of privilege are permissible, and effective for their intended purpose, as well as the application of principles of substantive evidence law related to the waiver of privilege by inadvertent production.

* * *

As noted in the Federal Judicial Center Manual for Complex Litigation:

> A responding party's screening of vast quantities of unorganized computer data for privilege prior to production can be particularly onerous in those jurisdictions in which inadvertent production of privileged data may constitute a waiver of privilege as to a particular item of information, items related to the relevant issue, or the entire data collection. Fear of the consequences of inadvertent waiver may add cost and delay to the discovery process for all parties. Thus, judges often encourage counsel to stipulate at the outset of discovery to a "nonwaiver" agreement, which they can adopt as a case-management order. Such agreements protect responding parties from the most dire consequences of inadvertent waiver by allowing them to "take back" inadvertently produced privileged materials if discovered within a reasonable period, perhaps thirty days from production.

Similarly, the recent report of the Judicial Conference Committee on Rules of Practice and Procedure to the Chief Justice of the United States and the Members of the Judicial Conference of the United States that forwarded proposed revisions to Federal Rules of Civil Procedure 16, 26, 33, 34, and 37, addresses this same issue:

> The problems that can result from efforts to guard against privilege waiver often become more acute when discovery of electronically stored information is sought. The volume of the information and the forms in which it is stored make privilege determinations more difficult and privilege review correspondingly more expensive and time-consuming, yet less likely to detect all privileged information. Inadvertent production is increasingly likely to occur. Because the failure to screen out even one privileged item may result in an argument that there has been a waiver as to all other privileged materials related to the same subject matter, early attention to this problem is more important as electronic discovery becomes more common. Under the proposed amendments to Rules 26(f) and 16, if the parties are able to reach an agreement to adopt protocols for asserting privilege and work-product protection claims that will facilitate discovery that is faster and at lower cost, they may ask the court to include such arrangements in a case-management or other order.

* * *

The changes recommended to Rules 16 and 26 encourage the party receiving the electronic discovery to agree not to assert waiver of privilege/work product protection against an opposing party that agrees to provide expedited production of electronically stored information without first doing a full-fledged privilege review. Similar agreements have been approved by a number of courts in the past.[10]

Although the use of "non-waiver" agreements presently may be growing * * * they certainly are not risk-free. Some commentators appear to be openly skeptical of their ability to insulate the parties from waiver, and even if they are enforceable as between the parties that enter into them, it is questionable whether they are effective against third-parties. *See Westinghouse Elec. Corp. v. Republic of the Philippines*, 951 F.2d 1414, 1426–27 (3d Cir. 1991) (agreement between litigant and DOJ that documents produced in response to investigation would not waive privilege does not preserve privilege against different entity in unrelated civil proceeding); *Bowne v. AmBase Corp.*, 150 F.R.D. 465, 478–79 (S.D.N.Y. 1993) (non-waiver agreement between producing party in one case not applicable to third party in another civil case).

* * *

---

10. Not all courts have approved non-waiver agreements between counsel. *See Koch Materials Co. v. Shore Slurry Seal, Inc.*, 208 F.R.D. 109, 118 (D.N.J. 2002) (court declined to give effect to agreement between counsel that production of certain documents would not waive privilege protection because such agreements "could lead to sloppy attorney review and improper disclosure which could jeopardize clients' cases"). * * *

* * * [T]here is a viable method of dealing with the practical challenges to privilege review of electronically stored information without running an unacceptable risk of subject-matter waiver. It lies with the courts issuing scheduling orders under Fed. R. Civ. P. 16, protective orders under Fed. R. Civ. P. 26(c), or discovery management orders under Fed. R. Civ. P. 26(b)(2) that incorporate procedures under which electronic records will be produced without waiving privilege or work product that the courts have determined to be reasonable given the nature of the case, and that have been agreed to by the parties. * * * As will be seen, it is essential to the success of this approach in avoiding waiver that the production of inadvertently produced privileged electronic data must be at the compulsion of the court, rather than solely by the voluntary act of the producing party, and that the procedures agreed to by the parties and ordered by the court demonstrate that reasonable measures were taken to protect against waiver of privilege and work product protection.

* * *

In *Transamerica Computer Co. v. IBM*, 573 F.2d 646 (9th Cir. 1978), the Ninth Circuit held that IBM had not waived its privilege claims to records that erroneously had been produced in prior litigation involving different parties, because the production was in response to an accelerated discovery schedule that the trial court had imposed, and the disclosures had been unintentional. Notably, the court observed that in the earlier litigation, IBM had produced 17 million pages of documents during a court ordered production schedule that had "dramatically accelerated the document inspection program." The court noted that during this demanding production schedule, IBM had undertaken "herculean" efforts to review documents for privilege. Therefore, it had not been guilty of any want of diligence. Of greater importance, however, was the fact that the trial judge had ruled that "the inadvertent production of allegedly privileged material by either party would not constitute a waiver of that party's right to claim the attorney-client privilege, provided only that the party disclaiming waiver had continued to employ procedures reasonably designed to screen out privileged material."

In concluding that IBM had not waived its privilege claims by producing the documents in the earlier litigation, and therefore could not be compelled by Transamerica in the subsequent litigation to produce it, the Ninth Circuit declined to view the issue solely as one of inadvertent disclosure, but rather focused on the importance of the court's compulsion of the production of the documents under conditions that unavoidably resulted in disclosure of some privileged material. * * *

Also central to the court's ruling was its recognition that the production of some privileged material by IBM had occurred as a result of the trial court's discovery order:

As the judicial officer directly in charge of supervising the discovery proceedings in that litigation ... [the trial judge] was in an ideal position to determine whether the timetable he himself had imposed was so stringent that, as a practical matter, it effectively denied IBM the opportunity to claim the attorney-client privilege for documents it was producing for inspection by CDC [in that litigation]. [Transamerica] acknowledges that waiver cannot be directly compelled, and ... [the judge's] rulings recognize and we so hold, that neither can it be indirectly compelled.

Finally, the court noted that the trial judge had further issued a ruling "explicitly protecting and preserving all claims of privilege, provided only that the parties wishing to preserve privilege had engaged in suitable screening techniques."

* * *

The *Transamerica* case and those that have followed it would allow parties that have entered into an agreement to preserve privilege claims with respect to production of electronically stored information to avoid subsequent claims by third parties that the production waived the privilege, provided: (a) the party claiming the privilege took reasonable steps given the volume of electronically stored data to be reviewed, the time permitted in the scheduling order to do so, and the resources of the producing party; (b) the producing party took reasonable steps to assert promptly the privilege once it learned that some privileged information inadvertently had been disclosed, despite the exercise of reasonable measures to screen for privilege and, importantly; (c) the production had been compelled by court order that was issued after the court's independent evaluation of the scope of electronic discovery permitted, the reasonableness of the procedures the producing party took to screen out privileged material or assert post-production claims upon discovery of inadvertent production of privileged information, and the amount of time that the court allowed the producing party to spend on the production.

* * *

In this case the BCPD did file an affidavit intended to particularize the unreasonable burden that would result from producing all of the records sought by the Plaintiffs in their Rule 34 requests. However, it was less complete than it should have been. It did identify the limited number of information technology personnel available to conduct the search for electronic records, and the competing demands on their services within the police department, but it failed to estimate the number of hours that would be required for them to conduct the requested review, or to sufficiently demonstrate how this would impact adversely the fiscal and operational capabilities of the police department. A party that seeks an order from the court that will allow it to lessen the burden of responding to allegedly burdensome electronic records discovery bears the burden of particularly demonstrating that burden and of providing suggested alternatives that reasonably accommodate the requesting party's legitimate discovery needs.

Second, as this case graphically demonstrates, it is no longer acceptable for the parties to defer good faith discussion of how to approach discovery of electronic records * * *. Rather, as the * * * changes to Rule 16(f) make clear, counsel have a duty to take the initiative in meeting and conferring to plan for appropriate discovery of electronically stored information at the commencement of any case in which electronic records will be sought. * * * At a minimum, they should discuss: the type of information technology systems in use and the persons most knowledgeable in their operation; preservation of electronically stored information that may be relevant to the litigation; the scope of the electronic records sought (i.e. e-mail, voice mail, archived data, back-up or disaster recovery data, laptops, personal computers, PDA's, deleted data) the format in which production will occur (will records be produced in "native" or searchable format, or image only; is metadata sought); whether the requesting party seeks to conduct any testing or sampling of the producing party's IT system; the burdens and expenses that the producing party will face based on the Rule 26(b)(2) factors, and how they may be reduced (i.e. limiting the time period for which discovery is sought, limiting the amount of hours the producing party must spend searching, compiling and reviewing electronic records, using sampling to search, rather than searching all records, shifting to the producing party some of the production costs); the amount of pre-production privilege review that is reasonable for the producing party to undertake, and measures to preserve post-production assertion of privilege within a reasonable time; and any protective orders or confidentiality orders that should be in place regarding who may have access to information that is produced.

It cannot be emphasized enough that the goal of the meeting to discuss discovery is to reach an agreement that then can be proposed to the court. The days when the requesting party can expect to "get it all" and the producing party to produce whatever they feel like producing are long gone. In many cases, such as employment discrimination cases or civil rights cases, electronic discovery is not played on a level field. The plaintiff typically has relatively few electronically stored records, while the defendant often has an immense volume of it. In such cases, it is incumbent upon the plaintiff to have reasonable expectations as to what should be produced by the defendant.

In this case, the Plaintiffs filed voluminous and detailed Rule 33 and 34 discovery requests that clearly identified their interest in discovering electronically stored information. The Defendants' immediate response should have been to invite the Plaintiffs to meet to discuss a reasonable discovery plan. Instead, objections first were raised, many of them boilerplate and conclusory, in the Defendants' answers to the discovery requests. The Plaintiffs responded with multiple written communications outlining their objections to the Defendants responses. When impasse was not overcome, the Plaintiffs * * * served a motion to compel. Only when that motion was fully briefed was it filed with the court. An expedited hearing was held, but even so, months had passed from the commencement of discovery while the dispute festered. Such delay is no longer acceptable, and it is the duty of the parties to initiate the negotiation process if the court has not ordered it. As I ordered during the hearing, the meeting that should have occurred months ago will be held within 30 days. A follow-up hearing with the court will be scheduled at which time a reasonable electronic discovery plan will be ordered.

One of the issues the parties were ordered to discuss was the nature of privilege review the Defendants would undertake, both pre-and post-production. The Defendants were advised that they bore the burden of demonstrating with particularity the need for less than full pre-production privilege review, as well as of proposing reasonable alternatives. I advised the parties that at the follow-up hearings, I would issue an order that compelled production of electronic records within a specific time that is reasonable. I also stated that I would independently determine, using the Rule 26(b)(2) factors, the amount of electronic discovery that would be permitted; whether less than full privilege review was reasonable given the extent of electronic discovery allowed and the time to do so and, if full privilege review was not feasible, whether the procedures agreed to by counsel are reasonable. If so, I will issue an order approving them that includes language that compliance with the approved procedures will not result in the waiver of any privilege or work product claim for any inadvertently produced privileged material. As I stated during the hearing, the issuance of such an order is essential to protecting against subject matter waiver of attorney-client privileged or work product protected information. * * *

COMMENTARY

The Magistrate Judge's solution to the risk of waiver is to have court-ordered production, and then allow the parties to argue that there was no voluntary waiver because the court ordered the production.

B. AGREEMENTS BETWEEN THE PARTIES TO CONTROL THE COST OF PRE-PRODUCTION PRIVILEGE REVIEW OF ELECTRONIC DATA

As the court noted in *Hopson*, parties often enter into arrangements to control the risks of waiver when privileged electronic data is disclosed during discovery. These arrangements can cover inadvertent disclosure, or can more broadly cover even intentional disclosures. Generally speaking there are two kinds of agreements: "claw back" and "quick peek." The 2006 Advisory Committee Note to Rule 26 discusses the costs of pre-production privilege review of electronic data, as well as the use of "claw back and quick peek" agreements:

> Parties may attempt to minimize these costs and delays by agreeing to protocols that minimize the risk of waiver. They may agree that the responding party will provide certain requested materials for initial examination without waiving any privilege or protection—sometimes known as a "quick peek." The requesting party then designates the documents it wishes to have actually produced. This designation is the Rule 34 request. The responding party then responds in the usual course, screening only those documents actually requested for formal production and asserting privilege claims as provided in Rule 26(b)(5)(A). On other occasions, parties enter agreements—sometimes called "clawback agreements"—that production without intent to waive privilege or protection should not be a waiver so long as the responding party identifies the documents mistakenly produced, and that the documents should be returned under those circumstances. Other voluntary arrangements may be appropriate depending on the circumstances of each litigation. In most circumstances, a party who receives information under such an arrangement cannot assert that production of the information waived a claim of privilege or of protection as trial-preparation material.

> Although these agreements may not be appropriate for all cases, in certain cases they can facilitate prompt and economical discovery by reducing delay before the discovering party obtains access to documents, and by reducing the cost and burden of review by the producing party.

The way these agreements often work in practice is that the disclosing party takes a "first cut" of the material and removes all the data that is clearly privileged upon a cursory review—for example, e-mails from or to counsel. The rest of the material is then produced, and if it turns out on further review that it is privileged, it is returned. Such agreements limit the multiple levels of intensive review of all the electronic data that would otherwise be required for pre-production privilege review. If a party has signed such an agreement, it waives any argument that a disclosure of privileged information by the other side is a waiver.[1]

There are a number of factors, however, that limit the utility of "claw back" and "quick peek" agreements. Most important, they provide protection only in the proceeding in which they are entered. As the *Hopson* court noted, an agreement between two parties in one litigation does not estop a third party, in a subsequent litigation, from arguing that a waiver occurred by disclosure of the privileged information in the previous matter. As the court also noted, parties have sought greater

---

1. *See, e.g., Prescient Partners, L.P. v. Fieldcrest Cannon, Inc.,* No. 96 Civ. 7590, 1997 WL 736726 (S.D.N.Y. Nov. 26, 1997) (enforcing a confidentiality agreement and refusing to find a waiver from an inadvertent disclosure of privileged information).

enforceability by asking the court to "so order" the agreement between the parties—but there was doubt under common law (before the enactment of Rule 502, *infra*) that even those orders would be binding against those who were not parties to the litigation in which the order was entered.

Another limitation on such agreements is obvious—the parties must agree. Where the discoverable electronic data on both sides is relatively equal, then all parties have an incentive to enter such an agreement. But where one side has most of the data—*e.g.*, an employment discrimination case brought by a fired employee, where all the e-mails are on the employer's server—then the party with few (if any) documents may not be inclined to limit the costs of the adversary's pre-production privilege review. (One factor that may still provide an incentive is if the party has an interest in *expedited* discovery; if there is no non-waiver agreement in effect, then the court is very likely to allow the party with custody of the data greater time to conduct a full pre-production privilege review).

Drafting Project: Draft a clawback or quick peek agreement that would be acceptable to both sides in a case in which one corporation sues another for patent infringement. Is it necessary to specify the kind of information that is covered, e.g., e-mails, spreadsheets, etc. Do you need a clause specifying how the receiving party is to act when it receives information that is apparently privileged? Do you need to specify that the receiving party is not allowed to keep a copy of the material or to use it in any way?

C. WHAT PRECAUTIONS SHOULD BE EMPLOYED?

VICTOR STANLEY, INC. v. CREATIVE PIPE, INC.

No. MJG–06–2662, 2008 WL 2221841 (D. Md. May 29, 2008)

GRIMM, MAGISTRATE JUDGE

The plaintiff, Victor Stanley, Inc. ("VSI" or "Plaintiff") filed a motion seeking a ruling that five categories of electronically stored documents produced by defendants Creative Pipe, Inc. ("CPI") and Mark and Stephanie Pappas ("M. Pappas", "S. Pappas" or "The Pappasses") (collectively, "Defendants") in October, 2007, are not exempt from discovery because they are within the protection of the attorney-client privilege and work-product doctrine, as claimed by the Defendants. VSI argues that the electronic records at issue, which total 165 documents, are not privileged because their production by Defendants occurred under circumstances that waived any privilege or protected status. * * * Defendants acknowledge that they produced all 165 electronic documents at issue to VSI during Rule 34 discovery, but argue that the production was inadvertent, and therefore that privilege/protection has not been waived. * * * For the reasons that follow, I find that all 165 electronic documents are beyond the scope of the attorney-client privilege and work-product protection because assuming, arguendo, that they qualified as privileged/protected in the first instance * * * the privilege/protection was waived by the voluntary production of the documents to VSI by Defendants.

Background Facts

The following facts are not subject to dispute. The Defendants' first Rule 34 response was a "paper production," not ESI, made in May 2007. Plaintiff objected to its sufficiency, and following a hearing, the court ordered the parties' computer forensic experts to meet and confer in an effort to identify a joint protocol to search and retrieve relevant ESI responsive to Plaintiff's Rule 34 requests. This was done and the joint protocol prepared. The protocol contained detailed search and information retrieval instructions, including nearly five pages of key-word/phrase search terms. It is noteworthy that these search terms were aimed at locating responsive ESI, rather than identifying privileged or work-product protected documents within the population of responsive ESI. After the protocol was used to retrieve responsive ESI, Defendants reviewed it to locate documents that were beyond the scope of discovery because of privilege or work-product protection. Counsel for Defendants had previously notified the court on March 29, 2007, that individualized privilege review of the responsive documents "would delay production unnecessarily and cause undue expense." To address this concern, Defendants gave their computer forensics expert a list of keywords to be used to search and retrieve privileged and protected documents from the population of documents that were to be produced to Plaintiff. However, Defendants' counsel also acknowledged the possibility of inadvertent disclosure of privileged/protected documents, given the volume of documents that were to be produced, and requested that the court approve a "clawback agreement" fashioned to address the concerns noted by this court in *Hopson v. Mayor of Baltimore*, 232 F.R.D. 228 (D. Md. 2005) [set forth at the beginning of this Chapter]. * * * However, on April 27, 2007, Defendants' counsel notified the court that because Judge Garbis recently had extended the discovery deadline by four months, Defendants would be able to conduct a document-by-document privilege review, thereby making a clawback agreement unnecessary. Accordingly, Defendants abandoned their efforts to obtain a clawback agreement and committed to undertaking an individualized document review.

* * *

After receiving Defendants' ESI production in September, 2007, Plaintiff's counsel began their review of the materials. They soon discovered documents that potentially were privileged or work-product protected and immediately segregated this information and notified counsel for Defendants of its production, following this same procedure each time they identified potentially privileged/protected information. Defendants' Counsel, Mr. Schmid, responded by asserting that the production of any privileged or protected information had been inadvertent. Defendants also belatedly provided Plaintiff with a series of privilege logs, purportedly identifying the documents that had been withheld from production pursuant to Fed. R. Civ. P. 26(b)(5).

* * *

Thus, according to the Plaintiff, the Defendants have waived any claim to attorney client privilege or work-product protection for the 165 documents at issue because they failed to take reasonable precautions by performing a faulty privilege review of the text-searchable files and by failing to detect the presence of the 165 documents, which were then given to the Plaintiff as part of Defendants' ESI production. As will be seen, under either the Plaintiff's or Defendants' version of the events, the Defendants have waived any privilege or protected status for the 165 documents in question.

Applicable Law

* * * [C]ourts have taken three different approaches when deciding whether the inadvertent production to an adversary of attorney client privileged or work-product protected materials constitutes a waiver. Under the most lenient approach there is no waiver because there has not been a knowing and intentional relinquishment of the privilege/protection; under the most strict approach, there is a waiver because once disclosed, there can no longer be any expectation of confidentiality; and under the intermediate one, the court balances a number of factors to determine whether the producing party exercised reasonable care under the circumstances to prevent against disclosure of privileged and protected information, and if so, there is no waiver. [The court rejects the most lenient approach as inconsistent with Fourth Circuit case law.] Under the strict approach, there is no legitimate doubt that Defendants' production of the 165 asserted privileged/protected documents waived the attorney-client privilege and work-product protection. Even under the intermediate test, however, the result would be the same.

The intermediate test requires the court to balance the following factors to determine whether inadvertent production of attorney-client privileged materials waives the privilege: (1) the reasonableness of the precautions taken to prevent inadvertent disclosure; (2) the number of inadvertent disclosures; (3) the extent of the disclosures; (4) any delay in measures taken to rectify the disclosure; and (5) overriding interests in justice. The first of these factors militates most strongly in favor of a finding that Defendants waived the privilege in this case.

Assuming that the Plaintiff's version of how Defendants conducted their privilege review is accurate, the Defendants obtained the results of the agreed-upon ESI search protocol and ran a keyword search on the text-searchable files using approximately seventy keywords selected by

M. Pappas and two of his attorneys. Defendants, who bear the burden of proving that their conduct was reasonable for purposes of assessing whether they waived attorney-client privilege by producing the 165 documents to the Plaintiff, have failed to provide the court with information regarding: the keywords used; the rationale for their selection; the qualifications of M. Pappas and his attorneys to design an effective and reliable search and information retrieval method; whether the search was a simple keyword search, or a more sophisticated one, such as one employing Boolean proximity operators; or whether they analyzed the results of the search to assess its reliability, appropriateness for the task, and the quality of its implementation. While keyword searches have long been recognized as appropriate and helpful for ESI search and retrieval, there are well-known limitations and risks associated with them, and proper selection and implementation obviously involves technical, if not scientific knowledge. See, e.g., *The Sedona Conference Best Practices Commentary on the Use of Search & Information Retrieval Methods in E–Discovery*, 8 Sedona Conf. J. 189, 194–95, 201–02 ("[A]lthough basic keyword searching techniques have been widely accepted both by courts and parties as sufficient to define the scope of their obligation to perform a search for responsive documents, the experience of many litigators is that simple keyword searching alone is inadequate in at least some discovery contexts. This is because simple keyword searches end up being both over-and under-inclusive in light of the inherent malleability and ambiguity of spoken and written English (as well as all other languages).").

Further, the Defendants' attempt to justify what was done, by complaining that the volume of ESI needing review and time constraints presented them with no other choice is simply unpersuasive. Defendants were aware of the danger of inadvertent production of privileged/protected information and initially sought the protections of a non-waiver agreement * * *. Had they not voluntarily abandoned their request for a court-approved non-waiver agreement, they would have been protected from waiver. Instead, they advised the court that they did not need this protection and elected to do a document-by-document privilege review. According to Defendants version of the facts, when they undertook an individualized review of the nontext-searchable ESI and determined that they could only review the title pages, they neither sought an extension of time from the court to complete an individualized review nor reinstated their request for a court-approved non-waiver agreement, despite their awareness of how it would have provided protection against waiver. In these circumstances, Defendants' protests that they did their best and that their conduct was reasonable rings particularly hollow.

The remaining factors to be assessed under the intermediate test may be quickly disposed of. The Defendants produced 165 asserted privileged/protected documents to the Plaintiff, so this case does not present an instance of a single document slipping through the cracks.

Further, the court's in camera review of the documents reflects that many of them are email and other communications between the Defendants and their various attorneys, as well as draft discovery responses, documents relating to settlements in unrelated litigation, comments from M. Pappas to counsel regarding discovery responses, and email correspondence between M. Pappas and Ms. Turner, the ESI forensic expert retained by Defendants. Thus, the disclosures were substantive—including numerous communications between defendants and their counsel. As noted by other district courts within the Fourth Circuit, any order issued now by the court to attempt to redress these disclosures would be the equivalent of closing the barn door after the animals have already run away. And, while the precise dates of the disclosures of the documents at issue are not clear from the record—since the Defendants made a series of ESI productions over a several week period—it is noteworthy that the Defendants did not discover the disclosure, but rather the Plaintiff made the discovery and notified the Defendants that potentially privileged/protected ESI had been produced. Therefore, this is not an instance in which a party inadvertently produced privileged information to an adversary, discovered the disclosure promptly, and then took immediate steps to inform the adversary that they had received the information inadvertently, thus demanding that it be returned.

While Defendants' counsel did assert privilege and inadvertent production promptly after being notified by the Plaintiff of the production of possible privileged/protected information, the more important period of delay in this case is the one-week period between production by the Defendants and the time of the discovery by the Plaintiff of the disclosures—a period during which the Defendants failed to discover the disclosure. Finally, the Defendants have pointed to no overriding interests in justice that would excuse them from the consequences of producing privileged/protected materials. The Plaintiff is blameless, but the Defendants are not, having failed to take reasonable precautions to prevent the disclosure of privileged information, including the voluntary abandonment of the non-waiver agreement that the Plaintiff was willing to sign. Every waiver of the attorney-client privilege produces unfortunate consequences for the party that disclosed the information. If that alone were sufficient to constitute an injustice, there would never be a waiver. The only "injustice" in this matter is that done by Defendants to themselves. Accordingly, even under the intermediate test, the Defendants are not insulated from waiver.

* * *

Conclusion

For the reasons stated, the court finds that the Defendants waived any privilege or work-product protection for the 165 documents at issue by disclosing them to the Plaintiff. Accordingly, the Plaintiff may use these documents as evidence in this case, provided they are otherwise admissible. In this regard, the Plaintiff has only sought use of the documents themselves, and the court has not been asked to rule, and accordingly does not, that there has been any waiver beyond the documents themselves.

COMMENTARY

Under recently-enacted Rule 502 (discussed *infra*) a court will find that a mistaken disclosure is not a waiver if the disclosing party took reasonable steps to prevent the disclosure and engaged in reasonably prompt measures to rectify the error once it was discovered. Reasonableness will of course depend on the circumstances; proper use of word searching may be a sufficient step.

Under the fault-based view of inadvertent waiver, there will be cases where the lawyer's work is so sloppy and inattentive that a mistaken disclosure will result in a forfeiture. In *S.E.C. v. Cassano*, the SEC was proceeding against investors for insider trading.[2] The case was brought in New York but was handled by the Boston office of the SEC. A discovery protocol allowed all of the unprivileged SEC electronic and hardcopy documents to be sent to New York, where defense counsel reviewed them (a process known as the "reading room"), and then an SEC paralegal on the premises would copy whatever documents defense counsel selected, and send those documents to counsel within a month. Combing through the information, defense counsel found a smoking gun document—an SEC staff memorandum, clearly privileged. He asked the paralegal if she could provide a copy of the document immediately so that he could take it with him that day. The paralegal telephoned SEC counsel in Boston, who immediately agreed to the unusual request, without checking the document number against the privilege log. A few weeks later, the SEC discovered its gaffe and sought an order requiring defense counsel to return the document. The court held that the SEC's actions in response to defense counsel's request to photocopy the memorandum were so careless as to surrender any claim that it took reasonable steps to ensure its confidentiality; hence the privilege as to the document was forfeited. The court noted that inadvertent production will constitute a forfeiture of the privilege only if the producing party's conduct was "so careless as to suggest that it was not concerned with the protection of the asserted privilege."[3] The court declared that the

> circumstances of the request clearly should have suggested to the SEC attorney that defense counsel had found what they regarded as gold at the end of the proverbial rainbow. Any attorney faced with such a request in comparable circumstances should have reviewed the document immediately, if only to find out what the other side

---

2.   189 F.R.D. 83 (S.D.N.Y. 1999).

3.   *Id.* at 85 (quotation omitted).

thought so compelling.... Yet the SEC attorney authorized production of this document, sight unseen.[4]

SEC counsel was also found delinquent in failing to promptly discover the inadvertent disclosure of the privileged memorandum.

In re Sealed Case is an example of the "strict liability" view of inadvertent disclosure.[5] There, the court held that the inadvertent disclosure of a few privileged documents in the course of a massive discovery response not only constituted a waiver of the privilege with respect to the documents, but also worked a subject matter waiver. As a result, the client was forced to make a further production of *all* previously privileged documents covering the subject matter of the inadvertently disclosed documents. The court reasoned that the privilege was costly to the search for truth, and therefore that privileged information must be guarded "like the crown jewels." The problem with this draconian rule is that it increases the costs of discovery and hence the costs of legal services; lawyers are likely to spend inordinate amounts of time ensuring that privileged material does not slip through—the cost adds up when there are seven levels of review of millions of e-mails, all to protect against a finding of waiver. This is not an efficient discovery model, in economic terms. Moreover, parties might fight tooth and nail during discovery over materials—questionably privileged, no matter how inconsequential, if a court might find it later on to be privileged, with the consequence being a subject matter waiver. Thus the D.C. Circuit view on inadvertent waiver leads to an increase in the number of privilege issues that a court will have to hear. Rule 502, discussed immediately below, explicitly rejects the strict liability view of *In re Sealed Case*.

In some state jurisdictions, there is no risk of inadvertent waiver. These jurisdictions hold that waiver of the privilege must be intentional. So it does not matter how negligent the disclosure in these jurisdictions is—the disclosing party has the right to get it back.[6]

D. LEGISLATIVE SOLUTION TO LIMIT THE COSTS OF REVIEW OF ELECTRONIC DATA FOR PRIVILEGE: FEDERAL RULE OF EVIDENCE 502

The costs of privilege review, in order to avoid the consequences of waiver, can rise to the millions of dollars. Concerned about the rising

---

4. *Id.* at 85–86.

5. 877 F.2d 976 (D.C. Cir. 1989).

6. *See, e.g.*, Rule 193.3(d) of the Texas Rules of Civil Procedure, which provides that:

A party who produces material or information without intending to waive a claim of privilege does not waive that claim under these rules or the Rules of Evidence if—within ten days or a shorter time ordered by the court, after the producing party actually discovers that such production was made—the producing party amends the response, identifying the material or information produced and stating the privilege asserted.

costs of electronic discovery and privilege review, the Judiciary Committee of the House of Representatives asked the Judicial Conference Advisory Committee on Evidence Rules ("the Advisory Committee") to prepare a rule that will provide some protection against these costs, by providing a more liberal, and a uniform, rule on waiver. That rule is discussed immediately below.

Introduction

The suggestion for the proposal of a rule dealing with waiver of attorney-client privilege and work product was presented in a January 23, 2006 letter from F. James Sensenbrenner, Jr., then-Chair of the House Committee on the Judiciary. In the letter, Congressman Sensenbrenner urged the Judicial Conference to proceed with rulemaking that would

- protect against the forfeiture of privilege where a disclosure in discovery is the result of an innocent mistake; and

- permit parties, and courts, to protect against the consequences of waiver by permitting disclosures of privileged information between the parties to a litigation.

Congressman Sensenbrenner noted the impact on litigation costs of reviewing for privilege and work product protection the enormous volume of materials in cases involving electronic discovery. He noted the concern that any disclosure could waive the privilege not only with regard to a particular document but for all other documents dealing with the same subject matter. He also observed that, while parties may make agreements limiting forfeiture of privilege, such agreements do not provide adequate assurance against waiver of the privilege in other proceedings. He added:

A federal rule protecting parties against forfeiture of privileges in these circumstances could significantly reduce litigation costs and delay and markedly improve the administration of justice for all participants.

The task of drafting a proposed rule responding to Congressman Sensenbrenner's request was referred to the Judicial Conference Advisory Committee on Evidence Rules, which prepared proposed Rule 502, recognizing that unlike other rules of evidence, privilege rules must be directly enacted by Congress.

Rule 502, set forth below, was approved by the Judicial Conference and thereafter approved by both Houses of Congress on unanimous consent. It was signed by the President on September 19, 2008.

Problems Addressed by Rule 502

Rule 502 does not attempt to deal comprehensively with either attorney-client privilege or work product protection. It also does not purport to cover all issues concerning waiver or forfeiture of either the attorney-client privilege or work product protection. The Rule covers issues of scope of waiver, inadvertent disclosure, selective waiver by disclosure to a federal office or agency, and the controlling effect of court orders and agreements.

Rule 502 provides the following protections against waiver of privilege or work product:

- *Limitations on Scope of Waiver:* Subdivision (a) provides that if a waiver is found, it applies only to the information disclosed, unless a broader waiver is made necessary by the holder's misleading use of privileged or protected communications or information.

- *Protections Against Inadvertent Disclosure:* Subdivision (b) provides that an inadvertent disclosure of privileged or protected communications or information, when made at the federal level, does not operate as a waiver if the holder took reasonable steps to prevent such a disclosure and employed reasonably prompt measures to retrieve the mistakenly disclosed communications or information.

- *Confidentiality Orders Binding on Non–Parties:* Subdivision (d) provides that if a federal court enters an order providing that a disclosure of privileged or protected communications or information does not constitute a waiver, that order is enforceable against all persons and entities in any federal or state proceeding. This provision allows parties in an action in which such an order is entered to limit the cost of preproduction privilege review.

- *Confidentiality Agreements:* Subdivision (e) provides that parties in a federal proceeding can enter into a confidentiality agreement providing for mutual protection against waiver in that proceeding. While those agreements bind the signatory parties, they are not binding on non-parties unless incorporated into a court order.

- *Disclosures Made in State Proceedings of Communications or Information Subsequently Offered in a Federal Proceeding:* Subdivision (c) provides that if privileged or protected communications or information are disclosed in a state proceeding, then admissibility in a subsequent federal proceeding is determined by the law that is most protective against waiver.

The Text of Rule 502 of the Federal Rules of Evidence

Rule 502. Attorney–Client Privilege and Work Product; Limitations on Waiver

The following provisions apply, in the circumstances set out, to disclosure of a communication or information covered by the attorney-client privilege or work-product protection.

(a) Disclosure made in a federal proceeding or to a federal office or agency; scope of a waiver.—When the disclosure is made in a federal proceeding or to a federal office or agency and waives the attorney-client privilege or work-product protection, the waiver extends to an undisclosed communication or information in a federal or state proceeding only if:

    (1) the waiver is intentional;

    (2) the disclosed and undisclosed communications or information concern the same subject matter; and

    (3) they ought in fairness to be considered together.

(b) Inadvertent disclosure.—When made in a federal proceeding or to a federal office or agency, the disclosure does not operate as a waiver in a federal or state proceeding if:

    (1) the disclosure is inadvertent;

    (2) the holder of the privilege or protection took reasonable steps to prevent disclosure; and

    (3) the holder promptly took reasonable steps to rectify the error, including (if applicable) following Fed. R. Civ. P. 26(b)(5)(B).

(c) Disclosure made in a state proceeding.— When the disclosure is made in a state proceeding and is not the subject of a state-court order concerning waiver, the disclosure does not operate as a waiver in a federal proceeding if the disclosure:

    (1) would not be a waiver under this rule if it had been made in a federal proceeding; or

    (2) is not a waiver under the law of the state where the disclosure occurred.

(d) Controlling effect of a court order.—A federal court may order that the privilege or protection is not waived by disclosure connected with the litigation pending before the court—in which event the disclosure is also not a waiver in any other federal or state proceeding.

(e) Controlling effect of a party agreement.—An agreement on the effect of disclosure in a federal proceeding is binding only on the parties to the agreement, unless it is incorporated into a court order.

(f) Controlling effect of this rule.— Notwithstanding Rules 101 and 1101, this rule applies to state proceedings and to federal court-annexed and federal court-mandated arbitration proceedings, in the circumstances set out in the rule. And notwithstanding Rule 501, this rule applies even if state law provides the rule of decision.

(g) Definitions.—In this rule:

    1) "attorney-client privilege" means the protection that applicable law provides for confidential attorney-client communications; and

    2) "work-product protection" means the protection that applicable law provides for tangible material (or its intangible equivalent) prepared in anticipation of litigation or for trial.

EXPLANATORY NOTE ON RULE 502
PREPARED BY THE JUDICIAL CONFERENCE ADVISORY COMMITTEE ON EVIDENCE RULES
(PART OF THE LEGISLATIVE HISTORY OF RULE 502)

This new rule has two major purposes:

> 1) It resolves some longstanding disputes in the courts about the effect of certain disclosures of communications or information protected by the attorney-client privilege or as work product—specifically those disputes involving inadvertent disclosure and subject matter waiver.

> 2) It responds to the widespread complaint that litigation costs necessary to protect against waiver of attorney-client privilege or work product have become prohibitive due to the concern that any disclosure (however innocent or minimal) will operate as a subject matter waiver of all protected communications or information. This concern is especially troubling in cases involving electronic discovery. *See, e.g., Hopson v. City of Baltimore*, 232 F.R.D. 228, 244 (D. Md. 2005) (electronic discovery may encompass "millions of documents" and to insist upon "record-by-record pre-production privilege review, on pain of subject matter waiver, would impose upon parties costs of production that bear no proportionality to what is at stake in the litigation").

The rule seeks to provide a predictable, uniform set of standards under which parties can determine the consequences of a disclosure of a communication or information covered by the attorney-client privilege or work product protection. Parties to litigation need to know, for example, that if they exchange privileged information pursuant to a confidentiality order, the court's order will be enforceable. Moreover, if a federal court's confidentiality order is not enforceable in a state court then the burdensome costs of privilege review and retention are unlikely to be reduced.

The rule makes no attempt to alter federal or state law on whether a communication or information is protected under the attorney-client privilege or work product immunity as an initial matter. Moreover, while establishing some exceptions to waiver, the rule does not purport to supplant applicable waiver doctrine generally.

The rule governs only certain waivers by disclosure. Other common-law waiver doctrines may result in a finding of waiver even where there is no disclosure of privileged information or work product. *See, e.g., Nguyen v. Excel Corp.*, 197 F.3d 200 (5th Cir. 1999) (reliance on an advice of counsel defense waives the privilege with respect to attorney-client communications pertinent to that defense); *Byers v. Burleson*, 100 F.R.D. 436 (D.D.C. 1983) (allegation of lawyer malpractice constituted a waiver of confidential communications under the circumstances). The rule is not intended to displace or modify federal common law concerning waiver of privilege or work product where no disclosure has been made.

Subdivision (a). The rule provides that a voluntary disclosure in a federal proceeding or to a federal office or agency, if a waiver, generally results in a waiver only of the communication or information disclosed; a subject matter waiver (of either privilege or work product) is reserved for those unusual situations in which fairness requires a further disclosure of related, protected information, in order to prevent a selective and misleading presentation of evidence to the disadvantage of the adversary. *See, e.g., In re United Mine Workers of America Employee Benefit Plans Litig.*, 159 F.R.D. 307, 312 (D.D.C. 1994) (waiver of work product limited to materials actually disclosed, because the party did not deliberately disclose documents in an attempt to gain a tactical advantage). Thus, subject matter waiver is limited to situations in which a party intentionally puts protected information into the litigation in a selective, misleading and unfair manner. It follows that an inadvertent disclosure of protected information can never result in a subject matter waiver. *See* Rule 502(b). The rule rejects the result in *In re Sealed Case*, 877 F.2d 976 (D.C.Cir. 1989), which held that inadvertent disclosure of documents during discovery automatically constituted a subject matter waiver.

The language concerning subject matter waiver—"ought in fairness"—is taken from Rule 106, because the animating principle is the same. Under both Rules, a party that makes a selective, misleading presentation that is unfair to the adversary opens itself to a more complete and accurate presentation.

To assure protection and predictability, the rule provides that if a disclosure is made at the federal level, the federal rule on subject matter waiver governs subsequent state court determinations on the scope of the waiver by that disclosure.

Subdivision (b). Courts are in conflict over whether an inadvertent disclosure of a communication or information protected as privileged or work product constitutes a waiver. A few courts find that a disclosure must be intentional to be a waiver. Most courts find a waiver only if the disclosing party acted carelessly in disclosing the communication or information and failed to request its return in a timely manner. And a few courts hold that any inadvertent disclosure of a communication or information protected under the attorney-client privilege or as work product constitutes a waiver without regard to the protections taken to avoid such a disclosure. *See generally Hopson v. City of Baltimore*, 232 F.R.D. 228 (D. Md. 2005), for a discussion of this case law.

The rule opts for the middle ground: inadvertent disclosure of protected communications or information in connection with a federal proceeding or to a federal office or agency does not constitute a waiver if the holder took reasonable steps to prevent disclosure and also promptly took reasonable steps to rectify the error. This position is in accord with the majority view on whether inadvertent disclosure is a waiver.

Cases such as *Lois Sportswear, U.S.A., Inc. v. Levi Strauss & Co.*, 104 F.R.D. 103, 105 (S.D.N.Y. 1985) and *Hartford Fire Ins. Co. v. Garvey*, 109 F.R.D. 323, 332 (N.D. Cal. 1985), set out a multi-factor test for determining whether inadvertent disclosure is a waiver. The stated factors (none of which are dispositive) are the reasonableness of precautions taken, the time taken to rectify the error, the scope of discovery, the extent of disclosure and the overriding issue of fairness. The rule does not explicitly codify that test, because it is really a set of non-determinative guidelines that vary from case to case. The rule is flexible enough to accommodate any of those listed factors. Other considerations bearing on the reasonableness of a producing party's efforts include the number of documents to be reviewed and the time constraints for production. Depending on the circumstances, a party that uses advanced analytical software applications and linguistic tools in screening for privilege and work product may be found to have taken "reasonable steps" to prevent inadvertent disclosure. The implementation of an efficient system of records management before litigation may also be relevant.

The rule does not require the producing party to engage in a post-production review to determine whether any protected communication or information has been produced by mistake. But the rule does require the producing party to follow up on any obvious indications that a protected communication or information has been produced inadvertently.

The rule applies to inadvertent disclosures made to a federal office or agency, including but not limited to an office or agency that is acting in the course of its regulatory, investigative or enforcement authority. The consequences of waiver, and the concomitant costs of pre-production privilege review, can be as great with respect to disclosures to offices and agencies as they are in litigation.

Subdivision (c). Difficult questions can arise when 1) a disclosure of a communication or information protected by the attorney-client privilege or as work product is made in a state proceeding, 2) the communication or information is offered in a subsequent federal proceeding on the ground that the disclosure waived the privilege or protection, and 3) the state and federal laws are in conflict on the question of waiver. The Committee determined that the proper solution for the federal court is to apply the law that is most protective of privilege and work product. If the state law is more protective (such as where the state law is that an inadvertent disclosure can never be a waiver), the holder of the privilege or protection may well have relied on that law when making the disclosure in the state proceeding. Moreover, applying a more restrictive federal law of waiver could impair the state objective of preserving the privilege or work-product protection for disclosures made in state proceedings. On the other hand, if the federal law is more protective, applying the state law of waiver to determine admissibility in federal court is likely to undermine the federal objective of limiting the costs of production.

The rule does not address the enforceability of a state court confidentiality order in a federal proceeding, as that question is covered both by statutory law and principles of federalism and comity. *See* 28 U.S.C. § 1738 (providing that state judicial proceedings "shall have the same full faith and credit in every court within the United States ... as they have by law or usage in the courts of such State ... from which they are taken."). *See also Tucker v. Ohtsu Tire & Rubber Co.,* 191 F.R.D. 495, 499 (D. Md. 2000) (noting that a federal court considering the enforceability of a state confidentiality order is "constrained by principles of comity, courtesy, and ... federalism"). Thus, a state court order finding no waiver in connection with a disclosure made in a state court proceeding is enforceable under existing law in subsequent federal proceedings.

Subdivision (d). Confidentiality orders are becoming increasingly important in limiting the costs of privilege review and retention, especially in cases involving electronic discovery. But the utility of a confidentiality order in reducing discovery costs is substantially diminished if it provides no protection outside the particular litigation in which the order is entered. Parties are unlikely to be able to reduce the costs of pre-production review for privilege and work product if the consequence of disclosure is that the communications or information could be used by non-parties to the litigation.

There is some dispute on whether a confidentiality order entered in one case is enforceable in other proceedings. *See generally Hopson v. City of Baltimore,* 232 F.R.D. 228 (D. Md. 2005), for a discussion of this case law. The rule provides that when a confidentiality order governing the consequences of disclosure in that case is entered in a federal proceeding, its terms are enforceable against non-parties in any federal or state proceeding. For example, the court order may provide for return of documents without waiver irrespective of the care taken by the disclosing party; the rule contemplates enforcement of "claw-back" and "quick peek" arrangements as a way to avoid the excessive costs of pre-production review for privilege and work product. *See Zubulake v. UBS Warburg LLC,* 216 F.R.D. 280, 290 (S.D.N.Y. 2003) (noting that parties may enter into "so-called 'claw-back' agreements that allow the parties to forego privilege review altogether in favor of an agreement to return inadvertently produced privilege documents"). The rule provides a party with a predictable protection from a court order—predictability that is needed to allow the party to plan in advance to limit the prohibitive costs of privilege and work product review and retention.

Under the rule, a confidentiality order is enforceable whether or not it memorializes an agreement among the parties to the litigation.

Party agreement should not be a condition of enforceability of a federal court's order.

Subdivision (e). Subdivision (e) codifies the well-established proposition that parties can enter an agreement to limit the effect of waiver by disclosure between or among them. Of course such an agreement can bind only the parties to the agreement. The rule makes clear that if parties want protection against non-parties from a finding of waiver by disclosure, the agreement must be made part of a court order.

Subdivision (f). The protections against waiver provided by Rule 502 must be applicable when protected communications or information disclosed in federal proceedings are subsequently offered in state proceedings. Otherwise the holders of protected communications and information, and their lawyers, could not rely on the protections provided by the Rule, and the goal of limiting costs in discovery would be substantially undermined. Rule 502(f) is intended to resolve any potential tension between the provisions of Rule 502 that apply to state proceedings and the possible limitations on the applicability of the Federal Rules of Evidence otherwise provided by Rules 101 and 1101.

The rule is intended to apply in all federal court proceedings, including court-annexed and court-ordered arbitrations, without regard to any possible limitations of Rules 101 and 1101. This provision is not intended to raise an inference about the applicability of any other rule of evidence in arbitration proceedings more generally.

The costs of discovery can be equally high for state and federal causes of action, and the rule seeks to limit those costs in all federal proceedings, regardless of whether the claim arises under state or federal law. Accordingly, the rule applies to state law causes of action brought in federal court.

Subdivision (g). The rule's coverage is limited to attorney-client privilege and work product. The operation of waiver by disclosure, as applied to other evidentiary privileges, remains a question of federal common law. Nor does the rule purport to apply to the Fifth Amendment privilege against compelled self-incrimination.

The definition of work product "materials" is intended to include both tangible and intangible information. *See In re Cendant Corp. Sec. Litig.*, 343 F.3d 658, 662 (3d Cir. 2003) ("work product protection extends to both tangible and intangible work product").

Drafting Choices Made by the Advisory Committee in Drafting Rule 502
Prepared by Professor Daniel Capra
Reporter to the Judicial Conference Advisory Committee on Evidence Rules

The Advisory Committee made a number of important drafting choices in Rule 502. This section explains those choices and notes the options that Congress might have in implementing those choices either in Rule 502 or in independent legislation to complement Rule 502.

1) The effect in state proceedings of disclosures initially made in state proceedings. Rule 502 does not apply to disclosures made in state proceedings when the disclosed communications or information are subsequently offered in other state proceedings. The first draft of Rule 502 provided for uniform waiver rules in federal and state proceedings, regardless of where the initial disclosure was made. This draft raised the objections of the Conference of State Chief Justices. State judges argued that the Rule as drafted offended principles of federalism and comity, by superseding state law of privilege waiver, even for disclosures that are made initially in state proceedings—and even where the disclosed material is then offered in a state proceeding (the so-called "state to state" problem). In response to these objections, the Evidence Rules Committee voted unanimously to cut back the Rule, so that it would not cover the "state-to-state" problem. While states would be bound by the Federal Rule, that would only be the case for disclosures initially made at the federal level, when the communications or information were later offered in a state proceeding (the so-called "federal to state" problem). The Conference of Chief Justices thereupon withdrew its objection to Rule 502.

During the public comment period on the scaled-back rule, the Advisory Committee received many comments from lawyers and lawyer groups suggesting that Rule 502 must be extended to provide a uniform rule of privilege waiver that would bind both state and federal courts, for disclosures made in either state or federal proceedings. These comments expressed the concern that if states were not bound by a uniform federal rule on privilege waiver, the protections afforded by Rule 502 would be undermined; parties and their lawyers might not be able to rely on the protections of the Rule, for fear that a state law would find a waiver even though the Federal Rule would not.

The Advisory Committee determined that these comments raised a legitimate concern, but decided not to extend Rule 502 to govern a state court's determination of waiver with respect to disclosures made in state proceedings. The Committee relied on the following considerations:

- Rule 502 is located in the Federal Rules of Evidence, a body of rules determining the admissibility of evidence in federal proceedings. Parties in a state proceeding determining the effect of a disclosure in those proceedings and in other state courts would be unlikely to look to the Federal Rules of Evidence for the answer.

- In the Committee's view, Rule 502, as proposed herein, does fulfill its primary goal of reducing the costs of discovery in *federal* proceedings. Rule 502 by its terms governs state courts with regard to the effect of disclosures initially made in federal proceedings. Parties and their lawyers in federal proceedings can therefore predict the consequences of disclosure of protected information by referring to Rule 502; there is no possibility that a state court could find a waiver when Rule 502 would not, when the disclosure is initially made in a federal proceeding.

While the Advisory Committee determined that Rule 502 should not be extended to disclosures initially made in state proceedings, when the protected communication or information is then offered in a state proceeding, the Judicial Conference does take this opportunity to notify Congress of the substantial public comment advocating a uniform rule of privilege waiver that would apply to all disclosures of protected information made or offered in state or federal courts. The public comment noted an alternative to extending Rule 502: separate legislation that would extend the substantive provisions of Rule 502 to state court determinations of waiver with respect to disclosures in state proceedings.

2) Other applications of Rule 502 to state court proceedings. Although disclosures made in state court proceedings later offered in state proceedings would not be covered, Rule 502 would have an effect on state court proceedings where the disclosure is initially made in a federal proceeding. State courts in such circumstances would be bound by federal confidentiality orders, and could not find a waiver after a mistaken disclosure if the holder took reasonable precautions and reasonably prompt measures to retrieve the material. The Rule, as submitted, specifically provides that it applies to state proceedings under the circumstances set out in the rule. *See* Rule 502(g).

Nevertheless, it may also be useful for Congress to consider additional legislation that would provide for the binding effect of Rule 502 in state courts for disclosures made in federal proceedings. A statute worded as follows might be appropriate: "The effect of a disclosure of privileged or protected information made in a federal proceeding is determined, in state proceedings, by Federal Rule of Evidence 502." If enacted, such legislation could serve to protect state litigants who might not look to a Federal Rule of Evidence for guidance.

3) Disclosures made in state proceedings and offered in a subsequent federal proceeding. Earlier drafts of Proposed Rule 502 did not determine the question of what rule would apply when a disclosure is made in state court and the waiver determination is made in a subsequent federal proceeding. Proposed Rule 502 as submitted herein provides that all of the provisions of Rule 502 apply unless the state law of privilege is more protective (less likely to find waiver) than the federal law. The Advisory Committee determined that this solution best preserved federal interests in protecting against waiver, and also provided appropriate respect for state attempts to protect the attorney-client privilege and work product immunity. This provision is properly placed in the rule even if Congress adopts legislation providing a uniform law of waiver. If Congress enacts independent legislation to govern state disclosures, then it is recommended that the legislation specify that the uniform rule is intended to provide a floor, not a ceiling, and that states retain the option to provide greater protection against waiver if they wish. If Congress takes that approach, then the language in Proposed Rule 502 applying state law when it is more protective will remain valid.

E.   ETHICAL QUESTIONS INVOLVED IN RECEIVING MISTAKENLY DISCLOSED PRIVILEGED INFORMATION

IN RE NITLA S.A. DE C.V.

92 S.W.3d 419 (Tex. 2002)

PER CURIAM

The issue here is whether the trial court abused its discretion when it refused to disqualify Nitla's counsel, who had reviewed privileged documents that the trial court ordered the opposing party to produce. The court of appeals issued mandamus, ordering the trial court to disqualify Nitla's counsel. However, in so doing, the court of appeals misapplied the law and thus abused its discretion. Accordingly, we granted Nitla's motion for rehearing, and we now conditionally grant a writ of mandamus and direct the court of appeals to vacate its order.

Nitla, a Mexican pharmaceutical company, sued Bank of America (BOA) in 1996. Nitla claimed that BOA misappropriated over $24 million of Nitla's funds on deposit. During discovery, Nitla asked BOA to produce certain documents. BOA resisted and asserted the attorney-client and work-product privileges. After an in camera inspection and a hearing, the trial court identified numerous documents that it determined BOA should produce. BOA asked the trial court to stay production until BOA decided whether to seek emergency relief in the court of appeals. Rather than issue an order, the trial court requested additional briefing and scheduled another hearing. The trial court also indicated it would order BOA to produce any nonprivileged documents at that time.

At the second hearing, after considering the additional briefing and oral arguments, the trial court ordered BOA to produce the previously identified documents. BOA again asked the trial court to stay production, arguing that if Nitla's counsel reviewed the documents, BOA would be irreparably harmed. Moreover, BOA argued that if Nitla's counsel reviewed the documents and the court of appeals determined them privileged, Nitla's counsel could be disqualified. Nevertheless, the trial court granted, in part, Nitla's motion to compel production. The trial court next handed the documents, which were under the trial court's control, directly to Nitla's counsel. This enabled Nitla's counsel to review the documents before BOA could seek mandamus relief.

Later that same day, BOA notified Nitla by fax that it still believed all the tendered documents were privileged. BOA also asked Nitla not to

review or distribute the documents, because BOA would seek mandamus relief. However, Nitla's counsel relied on the trial court's order and
reviewed the documents.

After BOA filed for mandamus relief, the court of appeals abated
the proceeding to allow the trial court's new judge to reconsider his
predecessor's decision. After another hearing, the trial court again
overruled BOA's objection that the documents were privileged. However, the trial court ordered Nitla to return the documents to BOA
pending appellate review. Nitla complied with this order. BOA then
reurged its mandamus petition in the court of appeals, and the court of
appeals held that most of the documents were privileged.

BOA then moved to disqualify Nitla's counsel, alleging that Nitla's
counsel "disregarded their ethical and professional obligations to gain
an unfair advantage" when they reviewed the privileged documents.
BOA also argued that the *Meador* factors support disqualification. See *In
re Meador*, 968 S.W.2d 346, 351–52 (Tex. 1998) (discussing six factors a
trial court should consider when deciding whether to disqualify an
attorney who receives privileged information outside the normal course
of discovery).

After a hearing, the trial court denied BOA's motion to disqualify.
Even though the trial court found that Nitla had extensively reviewed
the documents and that BOA had "clean hands," the trial court denied
the disqualification motion because it found: (1) Nitla's counsel did not
act unprofessionally or violate any disciplinary rules; (2) Nitla's counsel
did not obtain the documents wrongfully, but rather, after a judicial
proceeding; and (3) no competent evidence showed that Nitla's counsel
had developed its trial strategy based on the documents. Moreover, the
trial court determined that it had less severe measures available to
prevent Nitla from using the privileged information to gain unfair
advantage.

BOA sought mandamus relief from the trial court's order denying
disqualification. The court of appeals reviewed the trial court's decision
under *Meador*. The court of appeals determined that, although two
Meador factors supported the trial court's order, two other *Meador*
factors overwhelmingly supported disqualification. The court of appeals
then concluded that the trial court could have reached only one decision
under *Meador*—to disqualify Nitla's counsel. Therefore, the court of
appeals conditionally issued the writ.

* * * Nitla contends that the trial court correctly refused to disqualify Nitla's counsel, because BOA did not prove the disqualification
grounds with specificity and did not prove it would suffer actual harm.
Furthermore, Nitla argues, the court of appeals misapplied *Meador* and
improperly substituted its own judgment for the trial court's judgment.
In response, BOA claims that the court of appeals correctly applied
Meador. BOA asserts: Nitla improperly reviewed the documents when it
knew BOA intended to seek appellate relief; Nitla's actions irreparably

harmed BOA; and there is no evidence that disqualification would harm Nitla. Therefore, BOA argues, the court of appeals properly issued mandamus against the trial court. We disagree.

* * *

"Disqualification is a severe remedy." It can result in immediate and palpable harm, disrupt trial court proceedings, and deprive a party of the right to have counsel of choice. In considering a motion to disqualify, the trial court must strictly adhere to an exacting standard to discourage a party from using the motion as a dilatory trial tactic. This Court often looks to the disciplinary rules to decide disqualification issues. However, the disciplinary rules are merely guidelines—not controlling standards—for disqualification motions. Even if a lawyer violates a disciplinary rule, the party requesting disqualification must demonstrate that the opposing lawyer's conduct caused actual prejudice that requires disqualification. And, under appropriate circumstances, a trial court has the power to disqualify a lawyer even if he has not violated a specific disciplinary rule.

In *Meador*, we acknowledged that there are undoubtedly some situations when a party's lawyer who reviews another party's privileged information must be disqualified, even though the lawyer did not participate in obtaining the information. However, we did not articulate a bright-line standard for disqualification in such situations. Instead, we determined that a trial court must consider the importance of our discovery privileges along with all the facts and circumstances to decide "whether the interests of justice require disqualification." We then identified six factors a trial court should consider when a lawyer receives an opponent's privileged materials. However, we emphasized that "these factors apply only when a lawyer receives an opponent's privileged materials outside the normal course of discovery."

Here, the trial court determined that Nitla's counsel did not violate a disciplinary rule. Consequently, the disciplinary rules provide no guidance. Moreover, Nitla's counsel received the documents directly from the trial court in a discovery hearing. Thus, the six *Meador* factors do not apply. We have not defined a precise standard for disqualification in such circumstances. Nevertheless, the trial court referred to the appropriate guiding principles when it denied BOA's motion to disqualify.

In disqualification cases, our analysis begins with the premise that disqualification is a severe measure that can result in immediate harm, because it deprives a party of its chosen counsel and can disrupt court proceedings. Consequently, when a party receives documents from a trial court, and a reviewing court later deems the documents privileged, the party moving to disqualify opposing counsel must show that: (1) opposing counsel's reviewing the privileged documents caused actual harm to the moving party; and (2) disqualification is necessary, because the trial court lacks any lesser means to remedy the moving party's harm.

We conclude that the trial court correctly applied these principles. Thus, we hold that the trial court did not abuse its discretion when it denied BOA's motion to disqualify Nitla's counsel. At the disqualification hearing, the trial court focused on whether BOA proved it suffered actual prejudice. BOA argued that the mere fact that Nitla had extensively reviewed the privileged documents demonstrated prejudice to BOA. However, BOA could not show that Nitla's trial strategy had significantly changed after reviewing the documents. Indeed, BOA could only demonstrate that reviewing the documents might have enabled Nitla's counsel to identify four new witnesses to depose, and that this additional testimony could potentially harm BOA. Recognizing that disqualification is a severe measure, the trial court determined that less severe measures, such as quashing depositions, could cure BOA's alleged harm. Accordingly, the trial court concluded that disqualification was neither a necessary nor an appropriate remedy.

The court of appeals, in contrast, abused its discretion when it conditionally issued mandamus and ordered the trial court to disqualify Nitla's counsel. The court of appeals recognized that Nitla's counsel did not obtain the documents through any wrongdoing. Nonetheless, it explicitly applied the *Meador* factors and determined that some factors supported the trial court's order whereas others did not. In so doing, the court of appeals misapplied the law.

Accordingly, we grant Nitla's motion for rehearing. * * * [W]e conditionally grant a writ of mandamus and direct the court of appeals to vacate its order.

COMMENTARY

You are minding your own business and your adversary sends you a CD in response to a discovery request. You put it up on your computer, and as you toggle through, you see an email from the CEO of the adversary to litigation counsel, which reports a fact that indicates a major weakness in the adversary's case. Do you amend your pleadings? Send the information to your expert? Call the adversary? Return the information? Disqualify yourself because now you know about privileged information? Of course, if you have signed a confidentiality agreement, it will ordinarily require you, like your adversary, to return all apparently privileged information immediately. But what if there is no agreement in place?

The 2006 amendments to the Federal Rules provide some guidance for parties who receive what appears to be mistakenly disclosed privileged information. Rule 26(b)(5)(B) provides that assuming there is no confidentiality agreement in place if a receiving party is *notified* of the mistaken disclosure by the adversary, then the receiving party "must promptly return, sequester, or destroy the specified information and any copies it has; must not use or disclose the information until the claim [i.e., whether it is privileged information at all and whether the privilege has been waived] is resolved." The receiving party is allowed to go to court under seal to get a determination of whether the information is protected.

What happens if you look at the information, do not think that it is privileged, and send it to IT to be put in all the spreadsheets being prepared for the litigation or send it to your expert who plugs the information into her calculations, and then you get a call from the other side claiming privilege? In that case, Rule 26(b)(5)(B) requires the receiving party "to take reasonable steps to retrieve the information if the party disclosed it before being notified." But shouldn't the receiving party be entitled to some recompense for the cost of retrieving the information and unringing all the bells that have been rung? Rule 26 does not explicitly provide for any remedy to the receiving party—but a court would certainly have discretion to order some reimbursement as a condition of preserving the privileged information. Moreover, the burden on the receiving party can be taken into account in the fairness analysis of whether to find that the privilege has been waived. If retrieving the information would be cost-prohibitive for the receiving party, a court might be justified in finding that the party who made the mistaken disclosure has waived the privilege.

Note that Rule 26 does not require the receiving party to tell the adversary that it appears to have mistakenly disclosed privileged information. But Rule 4.4(b) of the ABA Model Rules of Professional Conduct imposes an ethical obligation on the receiving party to notify the adversary of the mistake:

> (b) A lawyer who receives a document relating to the representation of the lawyer's client and knows or reasonably should know that the document was inadvertently sent shall promptly notify the sender.

The Commentary to Model Rule 4.4(b) elaborates on the supposed need for this rule:

> [2] Paragraph (b) recognizes that lawyers sometimes receive documents that were mistakenly sent or produced by opposing parties or their lawyers. If a lawyer knows or reasonably should know that such a document was sent inadvertently, then this Rule requires the lawyer to promptly notify the sender in order to permit that person to take protective measures. Whether the lawyer is required to take additional steps, such as returning the original document, is a matter of law beyond the scope of these Rules, as is the question of whether the privileged status of a document has been waived. * * * For purposes of this Rule, document includes e-mail or other electronic modes of transmission subject to being read or put into readable form.

[3] Some lawyers may choose to return a document unread, for example, when the lawyer learns before receiving the document that it was inadvertently sent to the wrong address. Where a lawyer is not required by applicable law to do so, the decision to voluntarily return such a document is a matter of professional judgment ordinarily reserved to the lawyer.

In light of the obligations imposed on the receiving party by Rule 26 and Model Rule 4.4(b), one might wonder: What happened to the adversary system? Why can't the receiving party take full advantage of the mistakes of her adversary?

IX

ADMISSIBILITY OF DIGITAL EVIDENCE

■ ■ ■

A. INTRODUCTION

Digital evidence is now offered in virtually every trial. Examples include e-mails, spreadsheets, evidence from websites, digitally-enhanced photographs, powerpoint presentations, and computerized versions of disputed events. This Chapter addresses whether digital evidence presents any problems of admissibility that are different from those that arise in the use of traditional "hardcopy" forms of evidence.

This Chapter is not intended as a substitute for an Evidence course. Basic familiarity with the Federal Rules of Evidence is presumed.

1. How Is Digital Evidence Used in Court?

Parties most commonly use digital evidence in the following ways:

● *Electronic business records:* Most businesses now keep their records in electronic form. Even if the records are offered in hardcopy, the underlying information is almost always entered or stored electronically.

● *Computerized animation illustrating how a disputed event may have occurred:* Especially where the litigation involves an accident or injury, parties may wish to present a computerized demonstration of how the party maintains the event occurred. A simulation is based on scientific or physical principles and data entered into a computer, which is programmed to analyze the data and draw a conclusion from it.[1]

● *Digital presentation to illustrate an expert's opinion:* Expert testimony is often technical, boring, and hard to understand. The use of digital evidence—graphics, powerpoints, modeling—can help to pep up the expert's testimony and make it easier for the fact finder to follow and understand.

● *Pedagogical device:* A computerized presentation may be offered as a pedagogical device, either to summarize the trial evidence to the party's advantage, or to aid in the questioning of a witness. For example, a graphic may show how the timing of certain telephone calls or emails; or a clause of a contract may be brought out of the text and highlighted.

---

1. *See, e.g., Racz v. R.T. Merryman Trucking, Inc.*, No. 92–3404, 1994 WL 124857 (E.D. Pa. Apr. 4, 1994) (computerized accident reconstruction held inadmissible because data was presented selectively).

Such computerized presentations are not evidence. They are no different in kind from a hardcopy summary or the highlighting of trial testimony or critical language from documents. The question is whether the presentation fairly characterizes the evidence.

- *Digital enhancement:* Photos and recordings are sometimes digitally enhanced to make them easier to read, view, or hear, or to highlight some aspect that the proponent wishes to emphasize. An example is a fuzzy or poorly lighted surveillance photo, subjected to digital enhancement to make it more clear. Digital image processing can correct a blur, bring out the detail in under-or over-exposed areas of film, enlarge images without losing definition and otherwise enhance the color, brightness and definition of an image.

- *Information found on web pages, chat room conversations, etc.:* Obviously there is a lot of information on the Internet that can be relevant in a litigation. If a party makes a damaging statement on its website, or in a chat room, that information will be offered by the adversary. If a party wants to prove the price of a stock on a certain day, that information is available on the internet.

- *E-mails:* It goes without saying that e-mails can have substantial evidentiary value. The electronic discovery cases discussed in earlier chapters, *e.g., Zubulake* and *Arthur Andersen*, show that e-mails can be dispositive.

- *Other:* The above list is by no means exclusive. Other examples of the use of digital evidence include: GPS data to locate a person or car at a particular time; a Wikipedia entry used as the basis of an expert's opinion;[2] metadata found in Word documents; and information found in PDAs.

2. Which Evidentiary Rules Are Most Often Invoked When Digital Evidence Is Proffered?

Discussion of the special concerns raised by digital evidence focuses on four basic evidentiary concepts:

1. ***Relevance and Prejudice:*** Digital presentations may diminish the relevance of the underlying evidence and raise a risk of unfair prejudice, because they may present facts in a distorted or inaccurate manner. An example is *Rodd v. Raritan Radiologic Associates, P.A.*, where the plaintiff argued that a radiologist failed to detect something in a mammogram.[3] At trial, plaintiff introduced super-magnified images of portions of the decedent's mammograms. The images were created by digitally scanning the films into a computer. They were then projected onto a six-foot by eight-foot screen in the courtroom. The court found that the "digitalized, computerized images" were selectively composed

---

2. *See Alfa Corp. v. OAO Alfa Bank*, 475 F. Supp. 2d 357 (S.D.N.Y. 2007) (expert's reliance on a Wikipedia entry was acceptable because many judicial opinions have cited Wikipedia, and a study found that the number of errors in Wikipedia entries was not much higher than in the Encyclopedia Britannica).

3. 373 N.J. Super. 154 (App. Div. 2004).

by plaintiff's counsel and magnified by anywhere from 30 to 150 times the size of the original x-rays. This gave a false impression because whatever defect was shown in the blow-up, and emphasized by lighting and an electronic pointer, would not have been as visible at the time the mammogram was viewed by the radiologist.

Concerns of probative value and prejudicial effect, as raised by digital evidence, are addressed in federal courts under **Fed. R. Evid. 403:**

Rule 403. Exclusion of Relevant Evidence on Grounds of Prejudice, Confusion, or Waste of Time

Although relevant, evidence may be excluded if its probative value is substantially outweighed by the danger of unfair prejudice, confusion of the issues, or misleading the jury, or by considerations of undue delay, waste of time, or needless presentation of cumulative evidence.

2. *Authenticity:* To be admissible, evidence must be what the proponent says it is. To take a hardcopy example, the government in a criminal case wants to introduce what it argues to be the defendant's diary, because it contains incriminating admissions. But if it is not really the defendant's diary—if it's a forgery, or someone else's diary—then it should not be admitted because it is simply not relevant to the case. Thus, the question of authenticity is discussed as one of conditional relevance: proffered evidence is only relevant if it is what the proponent says it is.

Authenticity issues can arise with digital evidence. For example, if the government wants to admit the defendant's e-diary, or blog entry, it will have to show that the electronic information was entered by the defendant—not by someone else, not altered by a hacker, etc. In federal courts, most authenticity questions—for both hardcopy and digital evidence—are addressed under **Fed. R. Evid. 901:**[4]

Rule 901. Requirement of Authentication or Identification

(a) General provision.—The requirement of authentication or identification as a condition precedent to admissibility is satisfied by evidence sufficient to support a finding that the matter in question is what its proponent claims.

(b) Illustrations.—By way of illustration only, and not by way of limitation, the following are examples of authentication or identification conforming with the requirements of this rule:

(1) Testimony of witness with knowledge.—Testimony that a matter is what it is claimed to be.

* * *

---

4. The portions most pertinent to digital evidence are included here.

(4) Distinctive characteristics and the like.—Appearance, contents, substance, internal patterns, or other distinctive characteristics, taken in conjunction with circumstances.

* * *

(7) Public records or reports.—Evidence that a writing authorized by law to be recorded or filed and in fact recorded or filed in a public office, or a purported public record, report, statement, or data compilation, in any form, is from the public office where items of this nature are kept.

* * *

(9) Process or system.—Evidence describing a process or system used to produce a result and showing that the process or system produces an accurate result.

* * *

3. *Hearsay*: Like hardcopy records, digital records can present problems of hearsay. These problems arise when the record is offered to prove that the statements in the record are true. For example, in an age discrimination case, the plaintiff wants to introduce an e-mail from the CEO to the board of directors. The e-mail states: "We had to fire everyone over 40 because they are very expensive and we need to project a younger more vibrant image." Because this is an out of court statement by the CEO, it is hearsay.

Generally speaking, hearsay problems are treated the same whether they are in hardcopy or digital records. In federal courts, hearsay issues are addressed by **Fed. R. Evid. 801** (defining hearsay, and creating exemptions for, *inter alia*, admissions by a party-opponent and prior statements of testifying witnesses):

Rule 801. Definitions

The following definitions apply under this article:

(a) Statement.—A "statement" is (1) an oral or written assertion or (2) nonverbal conduct of a person, if it is intended by the person as an assertion.

(b) Declarant.—A "declarant" is a person who makes a statement.

(c) Hearsay.—"Hearsay" is a statement, other than one made by the declarant while testifying at the trial or hearing, offered in evidence to prove the truth of the matter asserted.

(d) Statements which are not hearsay.—A statement is not hearsay if—

(1) Prior statement by witness.—The declarant testifies at the trial or hearing and is subject to cross-examination concerning the statement, and the statement is (A) inconsistent with the declarant's testimony, and was given under oath subject to the

penalty of perjury at a trial, hearing, or other proceeding, or in a deposition, or (B) consistent with the declarant's testimony and is offered to rebut an express or implied charge against the declarant of recent fabrication or improper influence or motive, or (C) one of identification of a person made after perceiving the person; or

(2) Admission by party-opponent.—The statement is offered against a party and is (A) the party's own statement, in either an individual or a representative capacity or (B) a statement of which the party has manifested an adoption or belief in its truth, or (C) a statement by a person authorized by the party to make a statement concerning the subject, or (D) a statement by the party's agent or servant concerning a matter within the scope of the agency or employment, made during the existence of the relationship, or (E) a statement by a coconspirator of a party during the course and in furtherance of the conspiracy. The contents of the statement shall be considered but are not alone sufficient to establish the declarant's authority under subdivision (C), the agency or employment relationship and scope thereof under subdivision (D), or the existence of the conspiracy and the participation therein of the declarant and the party against whom the statement is offered under subdivision (E).

In addition to the exemptions to the hearsay rule set forth in Rule 801(d), the most important exception to the hearsay rule with respect to digital evidence is the business records exception. That exception is codified in **Fed. R. Evid. 803(6):**

Rule 803. Hearsay Exceptions; Availability of Declarant Immaterial

The following are not excluded by the hearsay rule, even though the declarant is available as a witness:

* * *

(6) Records of regularly conducted activity.—A memorandum, report, record, or data compilation, in any form, of acts, events, conditions, opinions, or diagnoses, made at or near the time by, or from information transmitted by, a person with knowledge, if kept in the course of a regularly conducted business activity, and if it was the regular practice of that business activity to make the memorandum, report, record or data compilation, all as shown by the testimony of the custodian or other qualified witness, or by certification that complies with Rule 902(11), Rule 902(12), or a statute permitting certification, unless the source of information or the method or circumstances of preparation indicate lack of trustworthiness. The term "business" as used in this paragraph includes business, institution, association, profession, occupation, and calling of every kind, whether or not conducted for profit.

Where the record is maintained by the government, the more likely exception to be invoked is the public records exception, codified in Fed. R. Evid. 803(8):

(8) Public records and reports.—Records, reports, statements, or data compilations, in any form, of public offices or agencies, setting forth (A) the activities of the office or agency, or (B) matters observed pursuant to duty imposed by law as to which matters there was a duty to report, excluding, however, in criminal cases matters observed by police officers and other law enforcement personnel, or (C) in civil actions and proceedings and against the Government in criminal cases, factual findings resulting from an investigation made pursuant to authority granted by law, unless the sources of information or other circumstances indicate lack of trustworthiness.

4.   *Best Evidence Rule*: The best evidence rule states that when a party is trying to prove the *contents* of a writing, recording, or photograph, the proponent must introduce the original. The best evidence rule is intended to protect against fraud and manipulation. But there is no hard and fast requirement that a proponent trying to prove a point must always choose the best available evidence. An example of a best evidence question is a copyright case in which the plaintiff alleges that the defendant stole his song. That means that the plaintiff must prove the contents of his own song. To do so, the plaintiff must produce the original recording to satisfy the best evidence rule in the first instance.

But the best evidence rule has two important exceptions: 1. Duplicates are acceptable unless the opponent raises a genuine question as to the authenticity of the original or the use of the duplicate in lieu of the original is unfair for some other reason; and 2. The proponent can forego the original—or any duplicate—if there is a good reason for not having it.

In federal courts, the best evidence rule and its exceptions are found in **Fed. R. Evid. 1001–1004** (note that the definitions are written to take account of digital evidence):

Rule 1001. Definitions

For purposes of this article the following definitions are applicable:

(1) Writings and recordings.—"Writings" and "recordings" consist of letters, words, or numbers, or their equivalent, set down by handwriting, typewriting, printing, photostating, photographing, magnetic impulse, mechanical or electronic recording, or other form of data compilation.

(2) Photographs.—"Photographs" include still photographs, Xray films, video tapes, and motion pictures.

(3) Original.—An "original" of a writing or recording is the writing or recording itself or any counterpart intended to have the same effect by a person executing or issuing it. An "original" of a photograph includes the negative or any print therefrom. If data

are stored in a computer or similar device, any printout or other output readable by sight, shown to reflect the data accurately, is an "original".

(4) Duplicate.—A "duplicate" is a counterpart produced by the same impression as the original, or from the same matrix, or by means of photography, including enlargements and miniatures, or by mechanical or electronic rerecording, or by chemical reproduction, or by other equivalent techniques which accurately reproduces the original.

Rule 1002. Requirement of Original

To prove the content of a writing, recording, or photograph, the original writing, recording, or photograph is required, except as otherwise provided in these rules or by Act of Congress.

Rule 1003. Admissibility of Duplicates

A duplicate is admissible to the same extent as an original unless (1) a genuine question is raised as to the authenticity of the original or (2) in the circumstances it would be unfair to admit the duplicate in lieu of the original.

Rule 1004. Admissibility of Other Evidence of Contents

The original is not required, and other evidence of the contents of a writing, recording, or photograph is admissible if—

(1) Originals lost or destroyed.—All originals are lost or have been destroyed, unless the proponent lost or destroyed them in bad faith; or

(2) Original not obtainable.—No original can be obtained by any available judicial process or procedure; or

(3) Original in possession of opponent.—At a time when an original was under the control of the party against whom offered, that party was put on notice, by the pleadings or otherwise, that the contents would be a subject of proof at the hearing, and that party does not produce the original at the hearing; or

(4) Collateral matters.—The writing, recording, or photograph is not closely related to a controlling issue.

5. *Requirements for Admissible Expert Testimony***:** Occasionally the presentation of digital evidence will require some foundation for expert testimony. For example, a digital manipulation of a photo, or of forensic evidence, may require a showing that it was prepared in a scientifically reliable manner. If the probative value of digital evidence is dependent on a scientific premise or procedure, then the rule on expert testimony may apply. In federal court, the basic rule on expert testimony is **Fed. R. Evid. 702,** which provides as follows:

Rule 702. Testimony by Experts

If scientific, technical, or other specialized knowledge will assist the trier of fact to understand the evidence or to determine a fact in issue, a witness qualified as an expert by knowledge, skill, experience, training, or education, may testify thereto in the form of an opinion or otherwise, if (1) the testimony is based upon sufficient facts or data, (2) the testimony is the product of reliable principles and methods, and (3) the witness has applied the principles and methods reliably to the facts of the case.

Of course, other evidence rules may have a bearing on admissibility of digital evidence in a particular case. The reader is directed to the Appendix, which sets out the Federal Rules of Evidence in their entirety.

The remainder of the Chapter discusses how these rules are applied to determine the admissibility of digital evidence.

B. GENERAL APPROACH

Generally speaking, the courts have not treated digital evidence any differently from any other kind of evidence. That is, the basic evidentiary principles apply: all evidence must be reliable, probative, and authentic. Most courts have been dismissive of arguments that the digitalization of evidence has changed the playing field or rendered basic evidentiary concepts outmoded. This is so even though in its current form, the Federal Rules of Evidence generally do not explicitly treat evidence in digital form. The following case is a good example of a court's application of basic evidentiary principles to the admissibility of electronic evidence.

COSTANTINO v. HERZOG
203 F.3d 164 (2d Cir. 2000)

McLaughlin, Circuit Judge

Dr. David Herzog was the obstetrician who delivered Amanda Costantino. During the delivery, Amanda's shoulder got trapped behind her mother's pubic bone, a condition known as "shoulder dystocia." While attempting to remedy the condition, Dr. Herzog performed: (1) the McRoberts maneuver: pulling Mrs. Costantino's legs toward her head and applying pressure to the area above her pubic bone; (2) the Woods corkscrew: reaching into the womb and rotating baby Amanda to release her trapped shoulder; and (3) the Posterior Arm Sweep: delivering Amanda's free posterior arm to create more space. Ultimately, Dr. Herzog delivered Amanda, but she was born with "Erb's Palsy," an impairment to the nerves running to the arm.

The Costantinos filed a diversity action against Dr. Herzog in the United States District Court for the Eastern District of New York

(Gleeson, J.) alleging that by pulling and rotating Amanda's head during the delivery, he had caused her Erb's Palsy. They claimed that Dr. Herzog had deviated from accepted standards of obstetrical practice, and had therefore committed malpractice under governing New York law. The defense denied any malpractice, asserting that Amanda's Erb's Palsy was caused by the normal forces of labor.

The case was tried to a jury. Plaintiffs' first witness was the defendant, Dr. Herzog. Counsel questioned him on an excerpt from a medical treatise edited by Steven G. Gabbe, entitled Obstetrics, that stated: "Once a vaginal delivery has begun, the obstetrician must resist the temptation to rotate the head to a transverse axis." Dr. Herzog acknowledged attempting to rotate Amanda's head, but disagreed with the statement read from the Gabbe treatise. Plaintiffs' medical expert was Dr. Bernard Nathanson. Among his qualifications, Dr. Nathanson testified that he was a fellow of the American College of Obstetricians and Gynecologists ("ACOG"). ACOG, according to Dr. Nathanson, "is an organization of thirty thousand obstetricians and gynecologists," that "sets up courses for doctors who are in practice so that they will continue to be current with ongoing research." Dr. Nathanson added that ACOG "publishes a great deal of material which serve[s] to contribute to setting a standard of care for obstetricians and gynecologists."

* * * Dr. Nathanson proceeded to testify that it was a departure from the standard of medical care to engage in "any manipulation of the head" during a shoulder dystocia delivery because it does nothing to relieve the trapped shoulder and greatly increases the risk of causing Erb's Palsy.

The defense sought to rebut this theory * * * by introducing a 15–minute videotape from ACOG's audiovisual library, entitled "Shoulder Dystocia." The tape was, according to the defense, "put out by [ACOG] to educate physicians" and portrayed the various techniques recommended to remedy shoulder dystocia.

Both the parties and Judge Gleeson recognized that the ACOG video was hearsay under Federal Rule of Evidence 801. The defense nevertheless sought to introduce it pursuant to the "learned treatise" exception to the hearsay rule set forth in Rule 803(18). Plaintiffs objected, arguing that Rule 803(18) enumerates only "published treatises, periodicals, or pamphlets" as learned treatises, and therefore could not encompass videotapes. * * * After an in camera review of the videotape, Judge Gleeson ruled it admissible. With respect to whether a video could qualify as a learned treatise under Rule 803(18), Judge Gleeson reasoned: "I think ... focusing on the distinction between ... something in the form of a periodical or a book, as opposed [to] a videotape is just overly artificial."

* * *

The ACOG video was played twice during trial. It was played in its entirety during the cross-examination of plaintiffs' expert, Dr. Nathanson, and portions were replayed during the direct examination of defendants' own expert Dr. James Howard.

In graphic detail the video portrays actual deliveries, complicated by shoulder dystocia, and demonstrates the recommended obstetrical responses to it. These portrayals are accompanied by a narrative given by a Dr. Young, who the video reveals is from Dartmouth College's Hitchcock Medical Center. The various procedures recommended, Dr. Young explains, were chosen "following a careful review of the available literature." Several times during its 15 minute duration, the video cautions that "unfortunately, babies cannot always be delivered without injury even when the management is optimal," and that "sometimes . . . injuries cannot be avoided."

[The tape essentially supported the defendant's claim that the defendant acted reasonably.]

* * *

After trial, the jury found for Dr. Herzog on the issue of liability. The Costantinos now appeal, arguing that Judge Gleeson erred in admitting * * * the ACOG video * * *.

DISCUSSION

I. The ACOG Video

The Costantinos argue that because videotapes are not mentioned in Rule 803(18), they can never be learned treatises. Alternatively, they maintain that even if videos can be learned treatises, reversal is still required because Judge Gleeson * * * should have excluded the video as unduly confusing and prejudicial under Rule 403. * * *

A. Rule 803(18)

The primary question presented is whether videotapes can be admitted as learned treatises pursuant to Rule 803(18). We are the first federal Court of Appeals to address this question, though various state courts have considered it under their cognate learned treatise exceptions, and have forged no consensus.

We review Judge Gleeson's legal conclusion that videos can constitute learned treatises *de novo*. In its entirety, Rule 803(18) provides:

> The following are not excluded by the hearsay rule, even though the declarant is available as a witness: * * * (18) Learned treatises. To the extent called to the attention of an expert witness upon cross-examination or relied upon by the expert witness in direct examination, statements contained in published treatises, periodicals, or pamphlets on a subject of history, medicine, or other science or art, established as a reliable authority by the testimony or admission of the witness or by other expert testimony or by judicial notice. If admitted, the statements may be read into evidence but may not be received as exhibits."

The rationale for this exception is self-evident: so long as the authority of a treatise has been sufficiently established, the factfinder should have the benefit of expert learning on a subject, even though it is hearsay.

Emphasizing plain language, the Costantinos argue that videos cannot fall within the scope of Rule 803(18) because unlike "published treatises, periodicals, or pamphlets," they are not specifically listed in the Rule. They rely on *Simmons v. Yurchak*, 28 Mass.App.Ct. 371, 551 N.E.2d 539 (1990), which accepted this contention, and affirmed a trial court's refusal to recognize videotapes as learned treatises under the Massachusetts version of Rule 803(18). According to the *Simmons* court: "adding videotapes to the list of materials in [the Massachusetts learned treatise exception] would constitute judicial legislation."

Uttering the dark incantation of "judicial legislation" is to substitute a slogan for an analysis. Indeed, we are exhorted in Rule 102 to interpret the Rules of Evidence to promote the "growth and development of the law ... to the end that the truth may be ascertained." In this endeavor a certain measure of legislative judgment is required. As Justice Holmes, in his Boston Brahmin prose conceded: "I recognize without hesitation that judges do and must legislate, but they can do so only interstitially; they are confined from molar to molecular motions." Or as a graduate of N.Y. City College, Justice Frankfurter, put it more prosaically: "legislatures make law wholesale, judges retail." Because judges "cannot escape the responsibility of filling in gaps which the finitude of even the most imaginative legislation renders inevitable," the problem is "not whether the judges make the law, but when and how much."

In this case, we are compelled to "make law." For we agree with Judge Gleeson that it is just "overly artificial" to say that information that is sufficiently trustworthy to overcome the hearsay bar when presented in a printed learned treatise loses the badge of trustworthiness when presented in a videotape. We see no reason to deprive a jury of authoritative learning simply because it is presented in a visual, rather than printed, format. In this age of visual communication a videotape may often be the most helpful way to illuminate the truth in the spirit of Rule 102.

In sum, we agree with the Texas Court of Appeals that "[v]ideotapes are nothing more than a contemporary variant of a published treatise, periodical or pamphlet." *Loven v. State*, 831 S.W.2d 387, 397 (Tex.Ct.App.1992). Accordingly, we hold that videotapes may be considered learned treatises under Rule 803(18).

* * *

C. Rule 403

Even though the ACOG video qualified as a learned treatise under Rule 803(18), Judge Gleeson retained the discretion to exclude it if its "probative value [was] substantially outweighed by the danger of unfair prejudice [or] confusion" under Rule 403. The Costantinos argue that the video should have been excluded under Rule 403. We find no basis for reversal.

There can be no doubt that much of the ACOG videotape represented highly probative evidence. * * * As Judge Gleeson explained in ruling that the video was admissible, one "dimension" of plaintiffs' malpractice claim was that "the standard of care ... prohibits a doctor from engaging in any traction" to remedy shoulder dystocia. Measured against this claim, those portions of the video portraying application of "a limited" or "appropriate" amount of traction to the baby's head were directly probative of whether such a technique is an accepted obstetrical practice. And those portions of the video portraying application of the Woods, McRoberts and Posterior Arm Sweep maneuvers were probative of whether Dr. Herzog properly used those maneuvers in delivering Amanda.

We reject the plaintiffs' claim that the ACOG video should have been excluded because of the danger of undue confusion. The Costantinos maintain that the ACOG video must have caused the jurors to confuse what they saw on the tape with what was being orally reconstructed for them throughout the trial—i.e., the birth of Amanda. They argue that because the video shows appropriate amounts of traction being applied to babies' heads, the jurors must have unfairly concluded that Dr. Herzog's management of Amanda's delivery was appropriate. This argument is pure speculation. It was obvious that Amanda's birth was not what was depicted in the video. Even if it were not obvious to the jury, any ephemeral danger of confusion was more than outweighed by the highly probative value of the video.

* * *

Because virtually all evidence is prejudicial to one party or another, to justify exclusion under Rule 403 the prejudice must be unfair. The unfairness contemplated involves some adverse effect beyond tending to prove a fact or issue that justifies admission. We fail to see how plaintiffs were unfairly prejudiced by the portrayal of the challenged procedures here. The testimony at trial established that shoulder dystocia is indeed a "complicated problem, requiring seemingly drastic" responses by the treating obstetrician.* * * [A]ny prejudice arising from the video's portrayal of the challenged procedures was not unfair within the meaning of Rule 403. To the contrary, that portrayal was probative of whether Amanda Costantino's shoulder dystocia presented an "emergency" and whether Dr. Herzog responded appropriately in attempting to remedy it.

* * *

CONCLUSION

For the reasons set forth above, the judgment of the district court is AFFIRMED.

COMMENTARY

Costantino is a typical example of a court's encounter with digital information under the Federal Rules of Evidence. While the Federal Rules were mostly not written with digital evidence in mind, the cases indicate that the courts are not having trouble accommodating and regulating electronic evidence under the existing language of the Rules. The following discussion describes the current use of electronic evidence, and the treatment of that evidence in the reported federal cases.

The following are the major questions of admissibility involving electronic evidence:

1.   A business or public record is often presented in the form of a computer print-out. Courts have had little problem in using Rules 803(6) (business records exception), 803(8) (public records exception) and 901/902 (rules on authenticity) to rule on the admissibility of computerized business records. Basically, a computerized business record is admissible whenever a comparable hardcopy record would be admissible. They are authenticated as are other records, and no special rule is required to allow the courts to rule on the admissibility or authenticity of business records.[5]

2.   A computerized presentation may be offered as proof of how an event occurred, the most prevalent example being an accident reconstruction. For this purpose, the use of a computer to recreate an event is no different in kind from videotaping a reconstruction of an accident or a product failure. Courts consistently apply Rule 403 to determine whether the reconstruction is substantially similar to the original conditions. If the conditions are substantially different, the purported reconstruction, computerized or not, is excluded as substantially more prejudicial than probative. There might also be hearsay problems in the preparation of the demonstration, and there might be problems of reliability due to the probable use of experts in the recreation process. But these problems are dealt with under standard evidentiary principles that apply to non-computerized evidence.[6]

3.   A computerized presentation may be offered to illustrate an expert's opinion or a party's version of the facts. As with any other such

---

5. *See United States v. Whitaker*, 127 F.3d 595 (7th Cir. 1997) (authenticity and admissibility of computerized business records is established by general principles applicable to non-computerized records); *Potamkin Cadillac Corp. v. B.R.I. Coverage Corp.*, 38 F.3d 627 (2d Cir. 1994) (computerized records were not admissible as business records where the underlying information was prepared in anticipation of litigation and would not itself have been admissible). *See also Monotype Corp. PLC v. International Typeface Corp.*, 43 F.3d 443 (9th Cir. 1994) (no error in excluding e-mail from employee of Microsoft to a superior, because such a communication was not regularly conducted activity within the meaning of Rule 803(6)); *DirecTV, Inc. v. Murray*, 307 F. Supp. 2d 764 (D.S.C. 2004) (e-mails admitted as business records, where they were kept in the ordinary course of business and authenticated by an affidavit from a qualified witness).

6. *See* Kristin L. Fulcher, *The Jury as Witness*, 22 U. Dayton L. Rev. 55 (1996) (noting that the admissibility of computerized re-creations can be and has been handled by standard evidentiary principles). *See also Verizon Directories Corp. v. Yellow Book USA, Inc.*, 331 F. Supp. 2d 136 (E.D.N.Y. 2004) (admitting demonstratives after conducting a Rule 403 analysis).

illustration, a computerized presentation is admissible if it helps to illustrate the expert's opinion, or a party's version of the facts, and does not purport to be a recreation of the disputed event. Again, standard evidentiary principles such as Rule 403 and Rule 702 have appeared to work well.[7]

4. A computerized presentation may be offered to illustrate or summarize the trial evidence to the party's advantage, or to aid in the questioning of a witness. Such computerized presentations are not evidence at all, but are instead pedagogical devices. They are no different in kind from a hardcopy summary or the highlighting of trial testimony or critical language from documents at issue in the case. The question is whether the presentation fairly characterizes the evidence. If the presentation is unfair, computerized or not, it will be prohibited under Rules 403 and 611.

EXCERPT FROM Mario Borelli, *The Computer as Advocate: An Approach to Computer–Generated Displays in the Courtroom*, 71 Ind. L.J. 439, 453 (1996):

> If one treats the [computerized] display as an extension of the attorney's argument, then it should be subject to the same guide-lines that govern what an attorney may say. Proper argument is supposed to be confined to facts introduced in evidence, facts of common knowledge, and logical inferences based on the evidence. Similarly, an attorney cannot argue about facts not in the record, misstate testimony, or attribute to a witness testimony not actually given. If the lawyer discloses the display to the opposing counsel and the judge beforehand, which is the recommended procedure anyway, then its basis in the evidence can be verified and the program altered, if need be. If an attorney using a computer display abides by these ground rules, then it should be allowed as a pedagogical device [without any need to change the evidence rules].

5. A computerized presentation might be offered as a summary of otherwise admissible evidence that is too voluminous to be conveniently examined in court. Such a presentation would be treated as a summary under Rule 1006. Computerized summaries are treated no differently from non-computerized summaries for purposes of Rule 1006.[8]

6. Photos, videos and other "original" documents are sometimes digitally enhanced to make them easier to read, view, or hear, or to highlight some aspect that the proponent wishes to emphasize. The courts have held that the admissibility of such enhancements is governed by Rules 403, 901 and 1002, with the basic question being whether it is a

---

7. *See, e.g., Datskow v. Teledyne Continental Motors Aircraft Products*, 826 F. Supp. 677, 685 (W.D.N.Y. 1993) (video simulation was properly admitted to illustrate the expert's opinion; jury was instructed that the electronic presentation was not to be used as proof of how the disputed event actually occurred).

8. *See, e.g., Verizon Directories Corp. v. Yellow Book USA, Inc.*, 331 F. Supp. 2d 136, 139–40 (E.D.N.Y. 2004) (finding that summaries can be admissible under Rule 1006, whether or not they are computerized).

fair and accurate depiction of the original. The language of these Rules has not proved an impediment to analyzing electronic enhancements of an original.[9]

7. Information found on web pages, and information found in e-mails, is routinely offered in a trial. As indicated later in this Chapter, the admissibility of this electronic information is evaluated under standard evidentiary concepts of hearsay, authenticity, and Rule 403.

———

Electronic evidence has been excluded in federal courts on a case-by-case basis. But the exclusions have resulted from the application of basic evidentiary principles of Rule 403, hearsay and authenticity, and not because of the paper-based language limitations in the Rules.[10]

Finally, it should be noted that the Judicial Conference Advisory Committee on the Federal Rules of Evidence is engaged in a multi-year project to update the text of the Evidence Rules to take digital evidence explicitly into account. One proposal being considered is a new definitional rule, providing as follows:

> As used in these rules, the following terms, whether singular or plural, include information in electronic form: "book," "certificate," "data compilation," "directory," "document," "entry," "list," "memorandum," "newspaper," "pamphlet," "paper," "periodical," "printed", "publication," "published", "record," "recorded", "recording," "report," "tabulation," "writing" and "written." Any "attestation," "certification," "execution" or "signature" required by these rules may be made electronically. A certificate, declaration, document, record or the like may be "filed," "recorded," "sealed" or "signed" electronically.

C. APPLICATION OF AUTHENTICITY RULES TO DIGITAL EVIDENCE

UNITED STATES v. SAFAVIAN
435 F. Supp. 2d 36 (D.D.C. 2006)

Friedman, District Judge.

[The defendant was an associate of the disgraced lobbyist Jack Abramoff. He was charged with making false statements and obstruction of justice during the investigation of Abramoff.]

———

9. *See, e.g., United States v. Seifert,* 445 F.3d 1043, 1045 (8th Cir. 2006) (noting that while the technician brightened the video, he did not brighten only the defendant but also the surrounding area, thus preserving their "relative brightness"—there was no showing that the enhancement rendered the video "inauthentic or untrustworthy"); *United States v. Luma,* 240 F. Supp. 2d 358 (D.V.I. 2002) (admitting videotapes where enhancements "did not change the substance of the videotape, but merely clarified the tapes"); *United States v. Beeler,* 62 F. Supp. 2d 136 (D. Me. 1999) (admitting videotapes over a best evidence objection, where enhancements omitted extraneous frames and made the images larger, clearer, and easier to view: "The edited and enhanced versions of the Mobil Mini–Mart surveillance videotape are admissible because they have been proven accurate and serve to present the substance of the original videotape in a more easily understood form which is in accord with the spirit of the best evidence rule.").

10. *See, e.g., Rotolo v. Digital Equip. Corp.,* 150 F.3d 223 (2d Cir. 1998) (videotape of a conversation, offered to prove that the statements therein were true, held inadmissible hearsay).

* * * These motions all make arguments regarding the admissibility of approximately 260 e-mails that the government seeks to admit in its case against the defendant.

A. Authentication of E-mails

Authentication is an aspect of relevancy. "The requirement of authentication or identification as a condition precedent to admissibility is satisfied by evidence sufficient to support a finding that the matter in question is what its proponent claims." FED. R. EVID. 901(a). See 5 SALTZBURG, MARTIN & CAPRA, FEDERAL RULES OF EVIDENCE MANUAL § 901.02[1] at 901–5 (8th ed. 2002). The threshold for the Court's determination of authenticity is not high. *See, e.g., United States v. Holmquist*, 36 F.3d 154, 168 (1st Cir. 1994) ("the standard for authentication, and hence for admissibility, is one of reasonable likelihood"); *United States v. Coohey*, 11 F.3d 97, 99 (8th Cir. 1993) ("the proponent need only demonstrate a rational basis for its claim that the evidence is what the proponent asserts it to be"). The question for the Court under Rule 901 is whether the proponent of the evidence has "offered a foundation from which the jury could reasonably find that the evidence is what the proponent says it is." 5 FEDERAL RULES OF EVIDENCE MANUAL § 901.02[1] at 901–5—901–6. The Court need not find that the evidence is necessarily what the proponent claims, but only that there is sufficient evidence that the jury ultimately might do so.

1. Rule 902(11)

Rule 902 of the Federal Rules of Evidence lists those documents that are self-authenticating—that is, those that do not require extrinsic evidence of authenticity as a condition precedent to admissibility. Rule 902(11) is intended to set forth "a procedure by which parties can authenticate certain records of regularly conducted activity, other than through the testimony of a foundation witness." Advisory Committee Note, FED. R. EVID. 902. Similarly, the Advisory Committee Notes to Rule 803 state that Rule 902(11) "provides that the foundation requirements of Rule 803(6) can be satisfied under certain circumstances without the expense and inconvenience of producing time-consuming foundation witnesses." Advisory Committee Note, FED. R. EVID. 803. These comments to each Rule make clear that they were intended to go "hand in hand." *Rambus, Inc. v. Infineon Technologies AG*, 348 F. Supp. 2d 698, 701 (E.D. Va. 2004) ("Rule 902(11) is ... the functional equivalent of testimony offered to authenticate a business record tendered under Rule 803(6)").

Pursuant to Rule 902(11), the government submitted a certification from Jay Nogle, the official custodian of records for Greenberg Traurig, LLP, the law firm that once employed Jack Abramoff. Mr. Nogle stated that in his capacity as official custodian he could certify that 467,747 e-mails had been produced by Greenberg Traurig [the law firm where Abramoff worked] to the United States and that those e-mails comport with the requirements of Rule 902(11), in part because the e-mails "would be admissible under Fed. R. Evid. 803(6) if accompanied by a written declaration of [their] custodian or other qualified person." The government does not, however, seek to admit these e-mails pursuant to the business records exception to the hearsay rule in Rule 803(6), but offers other hearsay exceptions and non-hearsay arguments as bases for admission. The defendant objects to the authentication of the Greenberg Traurig e-mails pursuant to Mr. Nogle's Rule 902(11) certification. Because Rule 902(11) was intended as a means of authenticating only that evidence which is being offered under the business records exception to the hearsay rule, the Court will not accept the proffered Rule 902(11) certification of Mr. Nogle with reference to the Greenberg Traurig e-mail exhibits.

2. Rule 901

Because it is not appropriate for these e-mails to be admitted as self-authenticating under Rule 902 of the Federal Rules of Evidence, the Court turns to the authentication requirements set forth in Rule 901. The question under Rule 901 is whether there is sufficient evidence "to support a finding that the matter in question is what its proponent claims," FED. R. EVID. 901(a)—in this case, e-mails between Mr. Safavian, Mr. Abramoff, and other individuals. * * * Rule 901(b) sets forth illustrations of how evidence may be authenticated or identified; it emphasizes, however, that these are "illustration(s) only" and are not intended to be the only methods by which the Court may determine that the e-mails are what the government says they are.[2] For the reasons that follow, the Court finds that there is ample evidence for the jury to find that these exhibits are, in fact, e-mail exchanges between Mr. Safavian, Mr. Abramoff, and other individuals.

One method of authentication identified under Rule 901 is to examine the evidence's "distinctive characteristics and the like," including "[a]ppearance, contents, substance, internal patterns, or other distinctive characteristics, taken in conjunction with circumstances." FED. R. EVID. 901(b)(4). Most of the proffered exhibits can be authenticated in this manner. The e-mails in question have many distinctive characteristics, including the actual e-mail addresses containing the "@" symbol, widely known to be part of an e-mail address, and certainly a distinctive mark that identifies the document in question as an e-mail. In addition, most of the e-mail addresses themselves contain the name of the person connected to the address, such as "abramoffj@gtlaw.com," "David. Safavian@mail.house.gov," or "david.safavian@gsa.gov." Frequently

---

2. The first method identified by the Rule is testimony of a witness with knowledge that the matter is what it is claimed to be. FED. R. EVID. 901(b)(1). Apparently, however, the government has decided not to call the one witness who could authenticate almost every one of the proffered e-mails, Jack Abramoff

these e-mails contain the name of the sender or recipient in the bodies of the e-mail, in the signature blocks at the end of the e-mail, in the "To:" and "From:" headings, and by signature of the sender. The contents of the e-mails also authenticate them as being from the purported sender and to the purported recipient, containing as they do discussions of various identifiable matters, such as Mr. Safavian's work at the General Services Administration ("GSA"), Mr. Abramoff's work as a lobbyist, Mr. Abramoff's restaurant, Signatures, and various other personal and professional matters.[3]

Those e-mails that are not clearly identifiable on their own can be authenticated under Rule 901(b)(3), which states that such evidence may be authenticated by comparison by the trier of fact (the jury) with "specimens which have been [otherwise] authenticated"—in this case, those e-mails that already have been independently authenticated under Rule 901(b)(4). For instance, certain e-mails contain the address "Merritt DC@aol.com" with no further indication of what person uses that e-mail address either through the contents or in the e-mail heading itself. This e-mail address on its own does not clearly demonstrate who was the sender or receiver using that address. When these e-mails are examined alongside Exhibit 100 (which the Court finds is authenticated under Rule 901(b)(4) by its distinctive characteristics), however, it becomes clear that MerrittDC@aol.com was an address used by the defendant. Exhibit 100 is also an e-mail sent from that address, but the signature within the e-mail gives the defendant's name and the name of his business, Janus–Merritt Strategies, L.L.C., located in Washington, D.C. (as well as other information, such as the business' address, telephone and fax numbers), thereby connecting the defendant to that e-mail address and clarifying the meaning of both "Merritt" and "DC" in it. The comparison of those e-mails containing MerrittDC@aol.com with Exhibit 100 thereby can provide the jury with a sufficient basis to find that these two exhibits are what they purport to be—that is, e-mails to or from Mr. Safavian. The Court will not perform this exercise with respect to each exhibit. Suffice it to say that the Court has examined each of these e-mails and found that all those that the Court is admitting in whole or in part meet the requirements for authentication under Rule 901.

The defendant argues that the trustworthiness of these e-mails cannot be demonstrated, particularly those e-mails that are embedded within e-mails as having been forwarded to or by others or as the previous e-mail to which a reply was sent. The Court rejects this as an argument against authentication of the e-mails. The defendant's argument is more appropriately directed to the weight the jury should give the evidence, not to its authenticity. While the defendant is correct that earlier e-mails that are included in a chain—either as ones that have been forwarded or to which another has replied—may be altered, this

---

3. Presumably, a person with personal knowledge will testify that Mr. Safavian worked at GSA, and that Mr. Abramoff worked as a lobbyist and owned a restaurant named Signatures.

trait is not specific to e-mail evidence. It can be true of any piece of documentary evidence, such as a letter, a contract or an invoice. Indeed, fraud trials frequently center on altered paper documentation, which, through the use of techniques such as photocopies, white-out, or wholesale forgery, easily can be altered. The possibility of alteration does not and cannot be the basis for excluding e-mails as unidentified or unauthenticated as a matter of course, any more than it can be the rationale for excluding paper documents (and copies of those documents). We live in an age of technology and computer use where e-mail communication now is a normal and frequent fact for the majority of this nation's population, and is of particular importance in the professional world. The defendant is free to raise this issue with the jury and put on evidence that e-mails are capable of being altered before they are passed on. Absent specific evidence showing alteration, however, the Court will not exclude any embedded e-mails because of the mere possibility that it can be done.

The defendant does raise some noteworthy points regarding the limits of what the government can show regarding these e-mails and what they purport to be. The Court notes that it is possible to authenticate these e-mails through examination of the contents, distinctive characteristics, and appearance, and others by comparison to authenticated e-mails, and the jury is free to make its own examinations and conclusions. But the Court has been aided in reaching its conclusions by the proffers of government lawyers. The government will not, of course, be permitted to make such proffers to the jury nor may government witnesses testify to facts beyond their personal knowledge concerning these e-mails. For instance, the F.B.I. agent through whom the government plans to offer these e-mails cannot testify from personal knowledge as to whether MerrittDC@aol.com is, in fact, Mr. Safavian's e-mail address. He may testify only that Exhibit 100 contains that e-mail address in the From: section of the heading, and that the Exhibit has a signature section that contains Mr. Safavian's name. Similarly, an F.B.I. agent will not be permitted to testify to the meaning of Greenberg Traurig internal e-mail codes (such as the "DIRDC–Gov" designation next to Jack Abramoff's name, which the government proffered at the May 16, 2006 hearing means that Mr. Abramoff was the Director of the Governmental Affairs Division of Greenberg Traurig's D.C. office).

Some of the e-mail addresses do not appear in full in any part of an exhibit. Rather the "To:" and "From:" parts of the heading contain full names with no e-mail address containing the @ symbol. Jay Nogle, the official custodian of records for Greenberg Traurig, explained in his Rule 902(11) certification that the "To:" and "From:" sections of these e-mails denoted that a Greenberg Traurig employee had sent or received the e-mail. Certainly, if Mr. Nogle, or another Greenberg Traurig employee with knowledge of these codes, is called to testify, he or she may testify to their meaning. An F.B.I. agent may not.

In certain e-mails, Mr. Safavian appears to have replied to Mr. Abramoff's e-mails in an atypical manner. Whereas most e-mail chains appear in reverse chronological order, the most recent of the e-mails appearing first, Mr. Safavian's responses to Mr. Abramoff's e-mails sometimes come after the e-mail from Mr. Abramoff. Further complicating the matter, this reversal of the order is not designated by the "To:" and "From:" section that normally denotes the start of a separate e-mail. The result is that the text of separate e-mails appears next to one another without a clear division between the end of one and the start of the next. Having examined these e-mails in comparison to one another, the Court has determined that it is apparent that some parts of the text are questions that lead to responses, and therefore the contents and substance serve to identify the exhibit as an exchange of e-mails. A jury, using its own knowledge of how e-mail exchanges work, and considering any testimony that may be offered by those with personal knowledge of these e-mails, may determine which persons, identified in the e-mail through their addresses and names, wrote which portions. No F.B.I. agent, however, may testify to these conclusions nor state which sections of these e-mails have been written by whom. It is beyond his or her personal knowledge and would be wholly speculative.

The jury may draw whatever reasonable conclusions and inferences it chooses to from these e-mails and determine how to consider them, but the Court will not permit any testimony beyond the bare fact of what words appear on a particular e-mail by a case agent or summary witness who neither composed nor received these e-mails. Should the government choose to call Mr. Abramoff or any other of the authors of these e-mails (other than, of course, the defendant, whom the government is not permitted to call as a witness), that witness may testify as to his or her personal knowledge of any particular e-mails he or she sent or received, and to any personal knowledge of e-mail addresses of persons with whom he or she has exchanged e-mails, even if not the specific ones in evidence.

* * *

ORDERED that defendant's motion in limine to deny the government's Rule 902(11) certifications is GRANTED with respect to Jay Nogle's certification, and DENIED with respect to all other Rule 902(11) certifications submitted by the government.

UNITED STATES v. TANK

200 F.3d 627 (9th Cir. 2000)

PREGERSON, CIRCUIT JUDGE.

Appellant David Vernon Tank appeals his conviction and sentence for conspiring to sexually exploit a child for the purpose of producing a sexually explicit visual depiction in violation of 18 U.S.C. §§ 2251(a) and (d); conspiring to engage in the receipt and distribution of sexually explicit images of children in violation of 18 U.S.C. §§ 2252(a) and (b)(1); and distributing sexually explicit images of a child to another person in violation of 18 U.S.C. § 2252(a).

Specifically, Tank appeals the district court's decisions regarding * * * the sufficiency of the foundation for admission into evidence of chat room log printouts[3] * * *.

I.

BACKGROUND

Tank belonged to a sixteen-member Internet chat room called the Orchid Club. Members of the Orchid Club discussed, traded, and produced child pornography. While online in the chat room, Orchid Club members traded digital pornographic images of children.

Ronald Riva, another member of the Orchid Club, was arrested on a child molestation charge. A search of Riva's home and computer files revealed thousands of pornographic pictures of children. The search also revealed computer text files containing "recorded" online chat room discussions that took place among members of the Orchid Club. Riva's computer was programmed to save all of the conversations among Orchid Club members as text files whenever he was online. Before any Orchid Club member was investigated or arrested, Riva had deleted from his computer nonsexual conversations and extraneous material, such as date and time stamps, to decrease the size of the text files and free space on his hard drive. These text files constitute the chat room logs at issue. The evidence seized from Riva implicated other Orchid Club members, including Tank.

Based on this evidence, U.S. Customs agents obtained and executed an arrest warrant for Tank and a search warrant for his home. [Tank was found in possession of a Zip disk.] The Zip disk was later shown to contain pornographic images of children that Tank had distributed to other Orchid Club members online.

At an evidentiary hearing, Tank argued that the district court should not admit the chat room logs into evidence because the government had laid an insufficient foundation. Tank objected that there was no foundation for admission of the chat room log printouts into evidence because: (1) they were not complete, and (2) undetectable "material alterations," such as changes in either the substance or the names appearing in the chat room logs, could have been made by Riva. The district court ruled that Tank's objection went to the evidentiary weight

---

3. The only evidentiary issue raised by Tank concerning the chat room log printouts is whether a proper foundation was laid for the district court to admit the logs into evidence. Tank did not argue on appeal that the logs were inadmissible under Fed. R. Evid. 403 (unfair prejudice or misleading to the jury), 801(d)(2) (party or co-conspirator admission), 802 (hearsay), 1002 (best evidence), or any other rule.

of the logs rather than to their admissibility, and allowed the logs into evidence.

* * *

The jury convicted Tank on all three counts, and the district court sentenced Tank to 235 months of imprisonment.

II.

CHAT ROOM LOGS

We review a district court's finding that evidence is supported by a proper foundation for an abuse of discretion. The foundational "requirement of authentication or identification as a condition precedent to admissibility is satisfied by evidence sufficient to support a finding that the matter in question is what its proponent claims." Fed.R.Evid. 901(a). The government need only make a prima facie showing of authenticity, as the rule requires only that the court admit evidence if sufficient proof has been introduced so that a reasonable juror could find in favor of authenticity or identification. The government must also establish a connection between the proffered evidence and the defendant.

The government made a prima facie showing of authenticity because it presented evidence sufficient to allow a reasonable juror to find that the chat room log printouts were authenticated. In testimony at the evidentiary hearing and at trial, Riva explained how he created the logs with his computer and stated that the printouts, which did not contain the deleted material, appeared to be an accurate representation of the chat room conversations among members of the Orchid Club. See *United States v. Catabran*, 836 F.2d 453, 458 (9th Cir. 1988) ("Any question as to the accuracy of the printouts ... would have affected only the weight of the printouts, not their admissibility."). Furthermore, the parties vigorously argued the issue of completeness of the chat room log evidence to the jury. See *United States v. Soulard*, 730 F.2d 1292, 1298 (9th Cir. 1984) ("[O]nce adequate foundational showings of authenticity and relevancy have been made, the issue of completeness then bears on the Government's burden of proof and is an issue for the jury to resolve.").

The government also established a connection between Tank and the chat room log printouts. There is no question that the chat room log printouts were relevant to prove the conspiracy charge in the indictment and Tank's participation in the conspiracy. Tank admitted that he used the screen name "Cessna" when he participated in one of the conversations recorded in the chat room log printouts. Additionally, several co-conspirators testified that Tank used the chat room screen name "Cessna" that appeared throughout the printouts. They further testified that when they arranged a meeting with the person who used the screen name "Cessna," it was Tank who showed up.

On the record before us, it is clear that the government made an adequate foundational showing of the relevance and the authenticity of the chat room log printouts. Thus, we cannot say that the district court abused its discretion by admitting the printouts into evidence and allowing the jury to decide what weight to give that evidence.[5]

COMMENTARY

In *United States v. Jackson*, the court took a harder line on authenticity.[11] The defendant was a law student charged with crimes related to sending hate mail (containing racial slurs) to a number of government offices and African–American individuals. At trial the defendant sought to introduce web site postings from web pages maintained by two white supremacist groups, the Euro–American Student Union and Storm Front. In these web postings the two groups took credit for the racist mailings and appeared to make other incriminating admissions. The trial court excluded the evidence, and the Court of Appeals found no error. The court first considered whether the web postings were properly excluded under the hearsay rule:

> The web postings were not statements made by declarants testifying at trial, and they were being offered to prove the truth of the matter asserted. That means they were hearsay. Fed. R. Evid. 801. Jackson tries to fit the web postings in as a hearsay exception under Federal Rule of Evidence 803(6) as business records of the supremacy groups' Internet service providers. Internet service providers, however, are merely conduits. The Internet service providers did not themselves post what was on Storm Front and the Euro–American Student Union's web sites. Jackson presented no evidence that the Internet service providers even monitored the contents of those web sites. The fact that the Internet service providers may be able to retrieve information that its customers posted or email that its customers sent does not turn that material into a business record of the Internet service provider.[12]

The court further held that the defendant had not shown the web postings to be authentic, because she did not establish a prima facie case that the postings were actually made by the white supremacist groups:

> Jackson needed to show that the web postings in which the white supremacist groups took responsibility for the racist mailings actually were posted by the groups, as opposed to being slipped onto the groups' web sites by Jackson herself, who was a skilled computer

---

5. * * * Tank's main argument is that the government should be required to attempt recovery of deleted data from computer disks (a technological possibility) to ensure that the files were not materially altered. But any deletions from Riva's hard drive were made by Riva himself, not by the government. Therefore, the deletions go to the weight of the evidence, not to its admissibility. Nothing prevented Tank from recovering the deleted data to show that "material alterations," if any, were made to the chat room logs. Tank cannot complain that the government offered into evidence only the relevant and not the irrelevant portions of the chat room logs. Tank had ample opportunity, before and during trial, to examine the hard drive to point out "missing" data, yet he declined to make this examination.

11. 208 F.3d 633 (7th Cir. 2000).

12. *Id.* at 637.

user. Even if these web postings did qualify for the business records hearsay exception, "the business records are inadmissible if the source of information or the method or circumstances of preparation indicate a lack of trustworthiness." Jackson was unable to show that these postings were authentic.[13]

Is the court saying that before *any* website information can be introduced, the proponent must show that nobody hacked into the website? How would that requirement mesh with Rule 901, which only requires the proponent to provide evidence sufficient to support a finding that the evidence is what the proponent says it is?

D. APPLICATION OF THE BEST EVIDENCE RULE TO DIGITAL EVIDENCE

UNITED STATES v. BENNETT

363 F.3d 947 (9th Cir. 2004)

FISHER, CIRCUIT JUDGE.

This case arises from the boarding and search of defendant-appellant Vincent Franklin Bennett's boat by members of a joint task force targeting smuggling activity from Mexico into Southern California. Coronado Police Officer Keith James initially spotted Bennett's boat near the U.S.-Mexico border on January 27, 2000, as the boat traveled north along the California coastline. Officer Sandy Joseph Sena, another task force member, boarded Bennett's boat at the entrance to San Diego Bay and eventually directed Bennett to dock his boat.

After the docking, members of the task force made multiple efforts over many hours to find drugs on Bennett's boat. When drilling three or four holes in the boat proved unproductive, they stored the boat overnight, hauled it to a Coast Guard facility the next day and x-rayed it. The x-ray revealed what turned out to be 1,541.5 pounds of marijuana. * * * [W]e conclude that improperly admitted testimony at trial requires reversal of Bennett's importation conviction. * * *

I.

Officer James was the first task force member to see Bennett's boat. James was positioned on Point Loma, which is on the far west end of Coronado, a peninsula that juts out into the Pacific Ocean from the San Diego area. From Point Loma, James trained his high grade binoculars toward the U.S.-Mexico border. He never actually saw Bennett's boat cross the border. Rather, James first spotted the boat south of the Imperial Beach pier, north of the border. The boat was heading north, traveling quickly and hugging the coastline. James notified other members of the task force when the boat reached the entrance to San Diego

---

13. *Id.* at 638.

Bay, in accordance with the task force's regular procedure for boats spotted near the border.

Officer Sena of the U.S. Coast Guard received James' call about Bennett's boat and led a team aboard at the entrance to San Diego Bay. [Bennett was convicted of illegally importing a controlled substance.]

* * *

II.

* * * Illegal importation occurs when a defendant imports a controlled substance into the United States from "any place outside thereof." 21 U.S.C. § 952(a). Here, although Bennett's boat was heading north (away from Mexico) when officers first spotted it, the boat was in U.S. waters at the time. [To prove importation, the government relied on the testimony of] U.S. Customs Officer Malcolm McCloud Chandler * * * that he discovered a global positioning system ("GPS") while searching Bennett's boat and that the GPS revealed that Bennett's boat had traveled from Mexican waters to San Diego Bay. * * * Bennett claims that the admission of Chandler's GPS-related testimony violated the rules of evidence * * *.

A.

* * * A GPS device uses global positioning satellites to track and record the location of the device and, therefore, the location of any object to which it is attached. The GPS came with a "backtrack" feature that graphed the boat's journey that day. Chandler testified that the backtrack feature mapped Bennett's journey from Mexican territorial waters off the coast of Rosarito, Mexico, to the Coronado Islands and then north to San Diego Bay. Less significantly, Chandler also retrieved "way points"—navigational points programmed into the GPS to assist the captain in navigating to a particular destination. Chandler testified that within the previous year, someone had programmed way points into the GPS that included points in Mexican waters. Chandler acknowledged on cross-examination that he had not taken possession of the GPS device itself or obtained any record of the data contained therein.

At trial, the district court overruled Bennett's foundation, best evidence rule and hearsay objections to this testimony, along with his request for a side bar conference. We review these evidentiary rulings for abuse of discretion.

The best evidence rule provides that the original of a "writing, recording, or photograph" is required to prove the contents thereof. Fed.R.Evid. 1002. A writing or recording includes a "mechanical or electronic recording" or "other form of data compilation." Fed.R.Evid. 1001(1). Photographs include "still photographs, X-ray films, video tapes, and motion pictures." Fed.R.Evid. 1001(2). An original is the writing or recording itself, a negative or print of a photograph or, "[i]f data are stored in a computer or similar device, any printout or other output readable by sight, shown to reflect the data accurately." Fed. R.Evid. 1001(3).

Where the rule applies, the proponent must produce the original (or a duplicate, see Fed.R.Evid. 1003) or explain its absence. Fed.R.Evid. 1002, 1004. The rule's application turns on "whether contents are sought to be proved." Fed.R.Evid. 1002 Advisory Committee's note. * * * Accordingly, the rule is inapplicable when a witness merely identifies a photograph or videotape "as a correct representation of events which he saw or of a scene with which he is familiar." See also *United States v. Workinger*, 90 F.3d 1409, 1415 (9th Cir. 1996) ("[A] tape recording cannot be said to be the best evidence of a conversation when a party seeks to call a participant in or observer of the conversation to testify to it. In that instance, the best evidence rule has no application at all."). However, the rule does apply when a witness seeks to testify about the contents of a writing, recording or photograph without producing the physical item itself—particularly when the witness was not privy to the events those contents describe.

That is the nature of Chandler's GPS testimony here and why his testimony violated the best evidence rule. First, the GPS display Chandler saw was a writing or recording because, according to Chandler, he saw a graphical representation of data that the GPS had compiled about the path of Bennett's boat. See Fed.R.Evid. 1001(1). Second, Chandler never actually observed Bennett's boat travel the path depicted by the GPS.[5] Thus, Chandler's testimony concerned the "content" of the GPS, which, in turn, was evidence of Bennett's travels. Fed.R.Evid. 1002. At oral argument, the government admitted that the GPS testimony was offered solely to show that Bennett had come from Mexico. Proffering testimony about Bennett's border-crossing instead of introducing the GPS data, therefore, was analogous to proffering testimony describing security camera footage of an event to prove the facts of the event instead of introducing the footage itself.

This is precisely the kind of situation in which the best evidence rule applies. *See, e.g.,* 14 Am.Jur. Proof of Facts 2d 173 § 14 (1977) ("The reported cases show that proponents of computer-produced evidence occasionally founder on the best evidence rule by presenting oral testimony based on the witness' review of computer printouts without actually introducing the printouts themselves into evidence."). Yet the government did not produce the GPS itself—or a printout or other representation of such data, see Fed.R.Evid. 1001(3)—which would have been the best evidence of the data showing Bennett's travels. Instead, the government offered only Chandler's GPS-based testimony about an event—namely, a border-crossing—that he never actually saw.

---

5. Nor did Chandler observe Bennett or anyone else enter way points into the machine. *See Pahl v. Comm'r of Internal Revenue*, 150 F.3d 1124, 1132 (9th Cir. 1998) (holding that court did not abuse its discretion in accepting duplicate over best evidence rule objection because document's signature had been witnessed).

"[O]ther evidence" of the contents of a writing, recording or photograph is admissible if the original is shown to be lost, destroyed or otherwise unobtainable. Fed.R.Evid. 1004. But the government made no such showing. When asked on cross-examination to produce the GPS or its data, Chandler simply stated that he was not the GPS's custodian. He further testified that "there was no need to" videotape or photograph the data and that he had nothing other than his testimony to support his assertions about the GPS's contents. Moreover, the government has not offered any record evidence that it would have been impossible or even difficult to download or print out the data on Bennett's GPS.[6] On the record before us, the government is not excused from the best evidence rule's preference for the original. We therefore hold that Chandler's GPS-based testimony was inadmissible under the best evidence rule.[7]

[The court reversed the conviction for importation.]

COMMENTARY

You should not take *Bennett* as an indication that the Best Evidence Rule, as applied to digital evidence, is a substantial hurdle. First, the court had to find that the GPS information was being offered to prove its contents, *i.e.*, the actual itinerary of the boat. In many cases, digital data is not offered to prove the contents. For example, if the government wanted to prove that the defendant had an operable system of radar detection (*e.g.*, as evidence that the defendant was surveilling for a police presence), that testimony would not run afoul of the Best Evidence Rule—because none of the information in the system would matter. Moreover, as the court in *Bennett* notes, the Best Evidence Rule would not have been a problem if someone could have testified that he or she saw the boat come from Mexico—because then the GPS data would have only been collateral evidence. Also, the government made no attempt to provide an acceptable duplicate, either by preserving a

---

6. Furthermore, a survey of other GPS cases (not involving the best evidence rule) suggests that outputting the data from Bennett's GPS may have been possible. *See, e.g., State v. Pirsig*, 670 N.W.2d 610, 613 (Minn. Ct. App. 2003) ("The data collected from the GPS monitor can be downloaded onto a Geographic Information System (GIS) software application. The GIS takes the location data from the GPS and overlays it onto a map. . . ."); * * *

7. We need not resolve Bennett's other objections to the admission of Chandler's GPS testimony. We do note, however, that in addition to failing to produce the GPS or its output for trial, the government did not establish that Bennett's GPS information was necessarily accurate or that the GPS itself worked properly. See 14 Am.Jur. Proof of Facts 2d 173 § 17 (1977) ("The most common reason that courts have rejected computerized evidence is that an insufficient foundation was laid to show the accuracy and trustworthiness of the evidence."); *cf. United States v. De Georgia*, 420 F.2d 889, 893 n. 11 (9th Cir. 1969) ("While . . . it is immaterial that the business record is maintained in a computer rather than in company books, this is on the assumption that: (1) the opposing party is given the same opportunity to inquire into the accuracy of the computer and the input procedures used, as he would have to inquire into the accuracy of written business records, and (2) the trial court, as in the case of challenged business records, requires the party offering the computer information to provide a foundation therefor sufficient to warrant a finding that such information is trustworthy."). Moreover, malfunctioning GPS devices are not unknown to this court. See *United States v. McIver*, 186 F.3d 1119, 1123 (9th Cir. 1999) (discussing a GPS that malfunctioned after three days of use).

printout or downloading the information from the GPS. In sum, the Best Evidence Rule is likely to be a problem only if the proponent is unprepared.

E. APPLICATION OF THE HEARSAY RULE (AND BUSINESS RECORDS EXCEPTION) TO DIGITAL EVIDENCE

UNITED STATES v. SALGADO

250 F.3d 438 (6th Cir. 2001)

GRAHAM, DISTRICT JUDGE.

Appellants Luis Salgado and Wilfredo Jambu were named along with two other defendants, Francisco Portuondo–Gonzalez and Daniel Rosalez, in a two-count indictment filed on June 1, 1998 in the Western District of Kentucky. Count 1 of the indictment alleged a conspiracy on or about May 1, 1998, to possess with the intent to distribute cocaine in violation of 21 U.S.C. § 846. Count 2 of the indictment charged the defendants with possessing with intent to distribute five kilograms of cocaine in violation of 21 U.S.C. § 841(a)(1).

* * *

[At trial, telephone records were introduced to prove that various calls among the coconspirators were made at various incriminating times.]

* * *

IV. Admissibility of Computer Records

Jambu raises as error the admission of certain telephone toll records of South Central Bell for telephone numbers subscribed to by Jambu and Portuondo–Gonzalez as business records under Rule 803(6) of the Federal Rules of Evidence. In reviewing a trial court's evidentiary determinations, this court reviews de novo the court's conclusions of law and reviews for clear error the court's factual determinations that underpin its legal conclusions.

A business record must satisfy four requirements in order to be admissible under Rule 803(6):

> (1) it must have been made in the course of a regularly conducted business activity; (2) it must have been kept in the regular course of that business; (3) the regular practice of that business must have been to have made the memorandum; and (4) the memorandum must have been made by a person with knowledge of the transaction or from information transmitted by a person with knowledge.

This information must be presented through "the testimony of the custodian or other qualified witness[.]" Fed.R.Evid. 803(6). Business records meeting these criteria are admissible "unless the source of information or the method or circumstances of preparation indicate lack of trustworthiness."

"Rule 803(6) does not require that the custodian personally gather, input, and compile the information memorialized in a business record." The custodian of the records need not be in control of or have individual knowledge of the particular corporate records, but need only be familiar with the company's recordkeeping practices. Likewise, to be an "other qualified witness," it is not necessary that the person laying the foundation for the introduction of the business record have personal knowledge of their preparation.

A computer printout is admissible under Rule 803(6) as a business record if the offer or establishes a sufficient foundation in the record for its introduction. *United States v. Cestnik*, 36 F.3d 904 (10th Cir. 1994) (holding computer-generated money transfer orders admissible); *United States v. Briscoe*, 896 F.2d 1476, 1494 (7th Cir. 1990) ("It is well established that computer data compilations are admissible as business records under Fed.R.Evid. 803(6) if a proper foundation as to the reliability of the records is established.")

In this case, William Deering, Manager of Security for Bell South, was called by the government to testify concerning South Central Bell telephone records. He indicated that he was the authorized representative to bring records to court. The records in question contained subscriber line information, including the subscriber's name, the location where the telephone was installed, the date and duration of local and long distance telephone calls, the numbers from which calls were placed and at which they were received, and billing amounts. The telephone numbers involved in the calls were recorded by computer contemporaneous to the phone call being made and received, and the information was then stored in the computer to be downloaded as needed. Mr. Deering stated that it was a regular practice of Bell South to make these reports and keep these types of records, and that the records are relied on by Bell South to ensure accuracy of billing. The above information satisfies the first three criteria for admissibility under Rule 803(6).

Jambu argues that the fourth requirement, that the memorandum must have been made by a person with knowledge of the transaction or from information transmitted by a person with knowledge, was not satisfied because the actual record was memorialized and entered into the computer's memory by the computer itself rather than being entered by a person. Similar records have been held sufficiently reliable in other cases.

In *United States v. Linn*, 880 F.2d 209, 216 (9th Cir. 1989), the court held that a computer printout showing a call placed from a hotel room was admissible as a business record where the record was generated automatically and was retained in the ordinary course of business. In *Briscoe*, 896 F.2d at 1494–95, telephone subscriber data entered into the computer contemporaneous with the placing of each telephone call and maintained in the regular course of business for billing purposes was held to be admissible. In *United States v. Miller*, 771 F.2d 1219, 1237 (9th Cir. 1985), the admission of computer-generated toll and billing records made contemporaneously by the computer itself was upheld.

Mr. Deering testified that he did not know the error rate in South Central Bell's billing system, and that he was unfamiliar with what programming was employed to ensure accuracy, although he did know that there were parameters for measurements of accuracy rates. Jambu argues that the instant case is thus distinguishable from *Briscoe*, where the evidence revealed that the computer scanned itself for error every fifteen seconds.

The government is not required to present expert testimony as to the mechanical accuracy of the computer where it presented evidence that the computer was sufficiently accurate that the company relied upon it in conducting its business. *United States v. Moore*, 923 F.2d 910, 915 (1st Cir. 1991) (not required that computers be tested for programming errors before computer records can be admitted under Rule 803(6)); *Briscoe*, 896 F.2d at 1494–95 (showing that computer was regularly tested for internal programming errors not a prerequisite to the admission of computer records). The record indicates that Mr. Deering testified that South Central Bell relied on these computer-generated records to ensure the accuracy of its billing. He was not required to testify concerning any programming features which were in place to guarantee accuracy.

Jambu also argues that Mr. Deering was not qualified to testify concerning these records because he was not sufficiently familiar with the computer system. Mr. Deering testified that he was not the individual who programmed the computer. However, it is not necessary that the computer programmer testify in order to authenticate computer-generated records. Likewise, the fact that Deering did not obtain the computer-generated records himself but rather asked someone else to provide him with the records called for in the subpoena did not mandate the exclusion of the records. Mr. Deering sufficiently demonstrated that he was familiar with the recordkeeping system employed by Bell South.

The district court properly concluded that the telephone records in question were trustworthy and that the government had established an adequate foundation for the admission of those records as business records under Rule 803(6).

COMMENTARY

Salgado, and the cases cited therein, take a permissive attitude to the admissibility of computerized business records—basically digital business records are treated no differently than hard-copy records. A few courts have taken a more rigorous approach. The court in *In re Vinhee* went so far as to require eleven foundational requirements to be met before digital business records could be admitted.[14] Under *Vinhnee* the proponent must establish the following:

1. The business uses a computer.

2. The computer is reliable.

3. The business has developed a procedure for inserting data into the computer.

4. The procedure has built-in safeguards to ensure accuracy and identify errors.

5. The business keeps the computer in a good state of repair.

6. The witness had the computer readout certain data.

7. The witness used the proper procedures to obtain the readout.

8. The computer was in working order at the time the witness obtained the readout.

9. The witness recognizes the exhibit as the readout.

10. The witness explains how he or she recognizes the readout.

11. If the readout contains strange symbols or terms, the witness explains the meaning of the symbols or terms for the trier of fact.

So far there is little indication that courts are demanding the kind of foundation articulated in *Vinhnee*.

Note that some forms of digital evidence may not be prepared or retained in the regular manner required for admissibility as business records. E-mails, for example, may be too sporadic to qualify as business records.[15]

If evidence is completely machine-generated, it is not hearsay at all, because it is not a statement from a declarant. For example, in *United States v. Washington*, the defendant was convicted of operating a motor vehicle under the influence of drugs and alcohol.[16] At trial, an expert interpreted a printout from a gas chromatograph machine. The machine issued the printout after testing the defendant's blood sample. The expert testified to his interpretation of the data issued by the machine—that the defendant's blood sample contained PCP and alcohol. The defendant argued that the testimony was hearsay, and also that his right to confrontation was violated, because the expert had no personal knowledge of whether the defendant's blood contained PCP or alcohol. He argued that the government was required to produce the lab

---

14. 336 B.R. 437, 446 (2005).

15. *See, e.g., Rambus, Inc. v. Infineon Techs. AG*, 348 F. Supp. 2d 698, 707 (E.D. Va. 2004) (" 'E-mail is far less of a systematic business activity than a monthly inventory printout. . . .' ") (quoting *Monotype Corp. PLC v. International Typeface Corp.*, 43 F.3d 443, 450 (9th Cir. 1994)); *State of N.Y. v. Microsoft Corp.*, No. 98–1233, 2002 WL 649951, at *3 (D.D.C. Apr. 12, 2002) ("While Mr. Glaser's email [recounting a meeting] may have been 'kept in the course' of RealNetworks regularly conducted business activity, Plaintiffs have not, on the present record, established that it was the 'regular practice' of RealNetworks employees to write and maintain such emails.").

16. 498 F.3d 225 (4th Cir. 2007).

personnel who conducted the test. But the court rejected this argument, finding that the machine printout was not hearsay, and admission did not violate the confrontation clause though it was prepared for use at trial, because the printout was not a statement of a witness. The court reasoned as follows:

> The technicians could neither have affirmed or denied *independently* that the blood contained PCP and alcohol, because all the technicians could do was to refer to the raw data printed out by the machine. Thus, the statements to which Dr. Levine testified in court * * * did not come from the out-of-court technicians [but rather from the machine] and so there was no violation of the Confrontation Clause * * * The raw data generated by the diagnostic machines are the "statements" *of the machines* themselves, not their operators. But "statements" made by machines are not out-of-court statements made by declarants that are subject to the hearsay rule or the Confrontation Clause.[17]

The court noted that the technicians might have been needed to provide a chain of custody, but observed that the defendant made no objection to the authenticity of the machine's report.

F.   APPLICATION OF FEDERAL RULE 403 TO DIGITAL EVIDENCE

BOWOTO v. CHEVRON CORP.

No. C99–02506, 2006 WL 1627004 (N.D. Cal. Jun. 12, 2006)

ILLSTON, DISTRICT JUDGE.

On June 9, 2006, the Court heard argument on plaintiffs' motion to exclude the expert testimony of Gary Freed and Jim Ebert. Having considered the arguments of counsel and the papers submitted, and for good cause appearing, the Court GRANTS IN PART plaintiffs' motion.

BACKGROUND

On January 9, 2006, defendants designated Freed and Ebert as expert witnesses who they expect to testify at trial. Both witnesses provided expert reports disclosing their opinions about a three-dimensional computer model of a barge, known as the "CBL–101 barge" or the "Seaway Orion," that was the location for one of the major incidents in this case. The model not only demonstrates what the barge as a whole looks like, but also allows the viewer to navigate to a specific spot on the barge to see the perspective of a person standing at that viewpoint.

Based on contemporary and historical photographs and technical drawings of the barge, Freed created the model using a program called LightWave 3D. Much of the evidence Freed used to create the model was collected by Ebert, who visited the barge at its current location in

---

17.   *Id.* at 230 (emphasis in original).

Angola in late 2005. While in Angola, Ebert obtained three technical drawings of the barge, took 472 digital photographs from the barge's deck and from a helicopter, and personally took measurements of the dimensions of features on the barge. Ebert provided these items to Freed, who created the computer model. The structure of the computer model was based entirely on the three technical drawings that Ebert obtained during his site visit, but Freed also used the photographs to include details like handrails, stairways, temporary fixtures, and colors.

Freed and Ebert now offer their opinions that the computer model accurately depicts the barge's permanent structures. Freed's report states that the model accurately depicts those structures "as well as the positions and fields of view of various witnesses." Ebert's report discloses three opinions: 1) the plan drawings correctly represent the layout of the barge; 2) the plan drawings are accurate; and 3) "perspective views made from the model correctly reflect the configuration and appearance of the CBL–101."

Plaintiffs now move to exclude Freed and Ebert from testifying at trial. Specifically, they contend that the barge model is inaccurate because it fails to reflect the configuration of the barge on May 28, 1998 [the day of the incident]. Thus, plaintiffs argue that using the model to illustrate a witness's perspective will mislead the jury into believing that the witness had an unimpeded view, when that may not have actually been the case.

LEGAL STANDARD

Federal Rule of Evidence 702 governs the admissibility of expert testimony. Under the rule, an expert may offer an opinion on an issue of "scientific, technical, or other specialized knowledge" if the knowledge "will assist the trier of fact to understand the evidence or to determine a fact in issue." * * *

Federal Rule of Evidence 403 provides that relevant evidence "may be excluded if its probative value is substantially outweighed by the danger of unfair prejudice, confusion of the issues, or misleading the jury, or by considerations of undue delay, waste of time, or needless presentation of cumulative evidence." Fed.R.Evid. 403. Even if expert testimony is admissible under Rule 702, it may still be excluded under Rule 403.

DISCUSSION

* * *

Accuracy of the Barge Model

Plaintiffs' primary argument is that the model should be excluded because it does not accurately represent the condition of the barge as of May 28, 1998. Specifically, plaintiffs argue that the model is limited to the permanent structures of the barge, and that a host of temporary fixtures were therefore left out. Plaintiffs therefore seek to exclude the model, claiming that it is irrelevant and unduly prejudicial.[1]

While the Court is unable to agree with plaintiffs' argument that the model is wholly irrelevant, it agrees with plaintiffs that the model in its current state is unduly prejudicial and misleading. As the photographs of the barge taken in 2005 clearly demonstrate, temporary fixtures on the barge can have a dramatic effect on the appearance of the barge. Indeed, the difference between aerial photographs and similar views of the model is striking; while in the former the barge's deck is cluttered with objects, the majority of which are many times larger than the workers visible in the photo, the latter exhibits an entirely clean deck, devoid of anything that might obstruct a witness's view. In the Court's opinion, this striking difference would only be magnified when the model is used to illustrate the perspective of a witness.

Although both parties agree that the current state of the barge's deck is not indicative of the deck eight years ago, plaintiffs have introduced evidence that a number of significant pieces of equipment were on the barge's deck on May 28, 1998. For example, a number of men who were working on the barge on that date testified that there was a second crane on the deck of the barge. Some of these witnesses also testified to the existence of a number of other large pieces of equipment, such as a 20–foot container, a 40–foot container, stacks of 55–gallon drums, an 8–foot by 10–foot "Conex" box, "strong boxes" that were being used as temporary living quarters for Nigerian military personnel, and scaffolding. Thus, the model's bare deck is a poor representation of the condition of the barge on May 28, 1998.

The Court believes that, because of the model's inaccurate representation of the barge's deck, the use of the model to attempt to show a witness's viewpoint should be excluded under Rule 403. As an initial matter, the probative value of the model is substantially diminished by its inaccurate depiction of the barge. While the model will allow the jury to understand where a witness was and what perspective he had on the events that transpired, the jury's understanding will be incomplete. And this incomplete understanding is likely to affirmatively mislead the jury as to what the witness could see.

While in many cases cross examination and the introduction of evidence that the barge's deck was not bare would be sufficient to remedy the risk of misleading the jury, the Court does not believe they

---

1. Although plaintiffs also purport to challenge the accuracy of the model's depiction of the barge's permanent structures, the thrust of this argument is directed at large containers that can be seen on a landing on the barge in 2005 photographs. As these containers do not appear in the technical drawings of the barge, the Court considers them temporary, not permanent, structures. Plaintiffs also point to a few structural aspects of the model that they claim are potentially inaccurate. The most significant of these is a landing extending from the first floor of the deckhouse that plaintiffs claim was extended at some point in time since the plans were made. The Court believes that these areas of uncertainty about the barge's precise layout on May 28, 1998, are relatively minor. Unlike the large obstructions that the temporary features represent, the uncertainty about the permanent features of the barge is likely to have relatively little impact on the accuracy of the model's representation of the viewpoint of a given witness.

suffice in this case. The computer model is a powerful tool, and, through its ability to place the jurors on the deck of the barge, runs a risk of making a strong impression on the mind of the jury. For this reason, the Court believes it is important to have the computer model be as accurate as possible before defendants may use it to illustrate for the jury aspects of what transpired on May 28, 1998. Accordingly, the Court finds that the model, as currently depicted, may not be used because there is a strong possibility that its probative value will be outweighed by its misleading effect on the jury.

COMMENTARY

While the *Bowoto* court excludes the digital presentation, it must be remembered that Rule 403 is a rule that is geared toward admitting evidence: under Rule 403, relevant evidence must be admitted unless its probative value is *substantially outweighed* by the risks of prejudice, confusion, and delay. This means that a digital presentation need not track the underlying facts with absolute exactitude. For example, in *Hinkle v. City of Clarksburg*, a civil rights action brought after Bea Wilson was shot and killed by police officers in an armed confrontation, the trial court directed a verdict for the police officers and plaintiffs appealed. The appellate court described the presentation of a computer animation at trial:

> At trial, Alexander Jason, a Forensic Animation Technologist, testified for the Appellees to a version of the shooting that was based on his interpretation of the evidence and was consistent with the police officers' testimony. To illustrate Jason's testimony, Appellees introduced a computer-animated videotape. The videotape depicted Wilson's apartment complex, the officers' position in relation to the open door to Wilson's apartment, and a step-by-step account of the incident. It showed an animated version of Officer Lake on the stairwell outside the apartment aiming his gun toward Wilson, who was moving toward the open door. It depicted Wilson raising his shotgun toward the doorway, Officer Lake firing the fatal shot, Wilson's body spinning around from the force of the shot, and his shotgun discharging into the stuffed chair in the back of the room. It then showed how the officers' version of the event was consistent with the physical evidence by concluding with a depiction of the trajectory of Officer Lake's bullet in-line with the wounds to Wilson's forearm, chest, back, and the bullet hole in the wall of the room.

> Appellants assign as error the district court's denial of their motion *in limine* to suppress this evidence. Appellants contend the videotape was inadmissible because it was experimental evidence that attempted to recreate the events but failed to reflect conditions substantially similar to those existing at the time of the shooting.[18]

---

18.   81 F.3d 416, 424 (4th Cir. 1996).

The *Hinkle* court recognized that Rule 403 sets forth a balancing test that is tilted in favor of admission. It then addressed the admissibility of the animation in the following passage:

> Typically, demonstrations of experiments used to illustrate principles forming an expert's opinion are not required to reflect conditions substantially similar to those at issue in the trial. *Gladhill v. General Motors Corp.*, 743 F.2d 1049, 1051 (4th Cir. 1984). We have, however, recognized the unique problems presented by the introduction of videotapes purporting to recreate events at the focus of a trial. In *Gladhill*, we noted the potential prejudicial effect of such evidence because the jury viewing a recreation might be so persuaded by its life-like nature that it becomes unable to visualize an opposing viewpoint of those events. Hence, we established a requirement that video taped evidence purporting to recreate events at issue must be substantially similar to the actual events to be admissible.

> Obviously, the requirement of similarity is moderated by the simple fact that the "actual events" are often the issue disputed by the parties. Nonetheless, to the extent the conditions are not a genuine trial issue, they should be reflected in any videotaped recreation. In *Gladhill*, for instance, the plaintiff crashed his car into a utility pole. He sued General Motors in a products liability action, contending that the brakes were faulty. The parties agreed that at the time of the accident it was night, and plaintiff was driving down a hill at a sharp curve in the road when he struck the utility pole. General Motors introduced a videotaped recreation of the accident that was conducted at a test facility on a flat, straight, asphalt surface in daylight by an experienced driver. We rejected the use of this videotape, holding that "when the demonstration is a physical representation of how an automobile behaves under given conditions, those conditions must be sufficiently close to those involved in the accident at issue to make the probative value of the demonstration outweigh its prejudicial effect."

We have not previously applied the requirement of "substantial similarity" to computer-animated videotapes that purport to recreate events at issue in trial. We fail to see a practical distinction, however, between a real-life recreation and one generated through computer animation; both can be a particularly powerful recreation of the events. * * * [W]e are satisfied the jury here fully understood this animation was designed merely to illustrate Appellees' version of the shooting and to demonstrate how that version was consistent with the physical evidence. The district court carefully instructed the jury on this point:

> [t]his animation is not meant to be a recreation of the events, but rather it consists of a computer picture to help you understand Mr. Jason's opinion which he will, I understand, be

giving later in the trial. And to reenforce the point, the video is not meant to be an exact recreation of what happened during the shooting, but rather it represents Mr. Jason's evaluation of the evidence presented.

Although there is a fine line between a recreation and an illustration, the practical distinction "is the difference between a jury believing that they are seeing a repeat of the actual event and a jury understanding that they are seeing an illustration of someone else's opinion of what happened." The jury understood that the very thing disputed in this trial was the condition under which the shooting occurred. In light of this fact and the court's cautionary instruction, there was no reason for the jury "to credit the illustration any more than they credit the underlying opinion."

We are convinced Appellants suffered no undue prejudice as a result of this computer animation, and we will not disturb the broad discretion afforded trial judges in this area. In reaching this holding, however, we are not unmindful of the dramatic power of this type of evidence; hence, we encourage trial judges to first examine proposed videotaped simulation evidence outside the presence of the jury to assess its foundation, relevance, and potential for undue prejudice.[19]

G. APPLICATION OF RULES ON EXPERT TESTIMONY TO DIGITAL EVIDENCE

IN RE THREE MILE ISLAND LITIGATION

193 F.3d 613 (3rd Cir. 1999)

McKEE, CIRCUIT JUDGE.

[An action was brought by area residents of the Three Mile Island nuclear power plant for injuries allegedly caused by a nuclear accident that released radioactive materials into the atmosphere. As part of a case management order, a group of "typical" plaintiffs was selected for trial on the issue of whether the release of radioactive materials was substantial enough to have caused them injury. One of the major disputes was whether a radioactive plume settled over the neighborhood where the plaintiffs lived. The plaintiffs proffered testimony from a number of experts, and the trial judge excluded most of that testimony as insufficiently reliable under Federal Rule of Evidence 702. In this case, the Court of Appeals, among other things, reviews the exclusions of expert testimony.]

---

19. *Id*. at 424–25.

2.   Standards Governing the Admissibility of Scientific Evidence.

* * *

In *Daubert v. Merrell Dow Pharmaceuticals, Inc.*, 509 U.S. 579 (1993), the Court set forth parameters for determining when proffered expert testimony can be admitted into evidence. The Court held

> an inference or assertion must be derived by the scientific method. Proposed testimony must be supported by appropriate validation-i.e., "good grounds," based on what is known. In short, the requirement that an expert's testimony pertaining to "scientific knowledge" establishes a standard of evidentiary reliability.

Rule 702 also requires that the evidence or testimony "assist the trier of fact to understand the evidence or to determine a fact in issue." "This condition goes primarily to relevance." This "consideration has been aptly described . . . as one of 'fit' ". Rule 702's "helpfulness standard requires a valid scientific connection to the pertinent inquiry as a precondition to admissibility."

The Court in *Daubert* concluded that Rule 702 "clearly contemplates some degree of regulation of the subjects about which an expert may testify." Thus, the Court established a "gatekeeping role for the judge." The Court wrote:

> Faced with a proffer of expert scientific testimony, . . . the trial judge must determine at the outset, pursuant to Rule 104(a), whether the expert is proposing to testify to (1) scientific knowledge that (2) will assist the trier of fact to understand or determine a fact in issue. This entails a preliminary assessment of whether the reasoning or methodology underlying the testimony is scientifically valid and of whether that reasoning or methodology properly can be applied to the facts in issue.

The Court held that these matters should be established "by a preponderance of proof" and identified some "general observations," relevant to the proponent's burden, while acknowledging that the factors it identified were not all-inclusive.

First, "a key question to be answered in determining whether a theory or technique is scientific knowledge that will assist the trier of fact will be whether it can be (and has been) tested." "Another pertinent consideration is whether the theory or technique has been subjected to peer review and publication." Publication, which is an element of peer review, "is not a sine qua non of admissibility: it does not equate with reliability."

However, submission to the scrutiny of the scientific community is a component of "good science." Accordingly, "[t]he fact of publication (or lack thereof) in a peer reviewed journal . . . will be a relevant, though not dispositive, consideration in assessing the scientific validity of a particular technique or methodology upon which an opinion is premised." Third, "in the case of a particular scientific technique, the court ordinarily should consider the known or potential rate of error, and the existence and maintenance of standards controlling the technique's operation." Fourth, and finally, "general acceptance" can have bearing on the inquiry. "Widespread acceptance can be an important factor in ruling particular evidence admissible, and a known technique which has been able to attract only minimal support with the community may properly be viewed with skepticism." However, "general acceptance" is "not a necessary precondition to the admissibility of scientific evidence." * * * Rather, general acceptance is but one factor that is considered along with all other factors relevant to the 702 inquiry.

The Court concluded by emphasizing that the "inquiry envisioned by Rule 702 is ... a flexible one" * * *. The Court also noted that the District Court should be mindful of other applicable rules in assessing a proffer of expert scientific testimony under Rule 702. Specifically, Rule 703 which provides that expert opinions based on otherwise inadmissible hearsay are to be admitted only if the facts or data relied upon are of a type reasonably relied upon by experts in the particular field in forming opinions; Rule 706 which allows the court in its discretion to procure the assistance of an expert of its own choosing; and Rule 403 which permits the exclusion of relevant evidence if its probative value is substantially outweighed by the danger of unfair prejudice, confusion of the issues, or misleading the jury.

* * *

With the parameters of our inquiry in mind, the teachings of *Daubert* and the aforementioned scientific principles as our guideposts, we can now proceed to apply the yardstick of Daubert to the expert opinions at issue here and determine if they were properly excluded under the Rules of Evidence.

3. Trial Plaintiffs' Dose Exposure Expert Witnesses.

i. Ignaz Vergeiner.

a. Qualifications.

Ignaz Vergeiner is a meteorologist with undergraduate degrees in mathematics and physics, and a Ph.D. in meteorology; all of which were earned at the University of Innsbruck in Austria. He is an Associate Professor in the Department of Meteorology and Geophysics at the University of Innsbruck and has taught graduate and undergraduate courses at that University for twenty years. He was proffered as an expert in boundary level meteorology in alpine regions. His testimony was offered to explain how the hypothesized plume containing the highly radioactive release * * * traveled and dispersed throughout the area surrounding Three Mile Island.

b. Vergeiner's Opinion.

* * *

Essentially, Vergeiner opined that a weather inversion, in combination with the alpine terrain that surrounds Three Mile Island, prevented the radioactive plume from rising high into the atmosphere, spreading out and dispersing in the expected "Gaussian" manner.[94] Instead, he believed that the radioactive plume remained narrow, concentrated and intense and moved erratically in a north, northwest direction from Three Mile Island. He believed that it frequently came in contact with hilly terrain which caused it to reconcentrate, and that after it reconcentrated, it touched down on the ground and exposed the population to high levels of radiation. To illustrate his plume dispersion theory, Vergeiner produced a water model and a "plume movie" * * * by which he illustrated the plume movement he hypothesized. The water model is a video of a large scale model he built in which colored water was injected into a tank filed with clear water that contained a model of alpine terrain.

Vergeiner's qualifications as an expert in meteorology were not in dispute. Nonetheless, the defendants moved to exclude all of his proffered testimony under Rule 702. After a hearing, the District Court subjected his proffered testimony to an exhaustive and rigorous *Daubert* * * * analysis and excluded the majority of it, including the plume movie and the water model.

c. Discussion and Conclusions.

* * * [W]e believe a few examples demonstrate that the District Court's decision to exclude the bulk of Vergeiner's proposed testimony was not an abuse of discretion.

First, in formulating his plume dispersion hypothesis, Vergeiner discarded standard and generally accepted computer models, especially the Gaussian plume model.[95] At the hearing, Vergeiner testified that the Gaussian plume model was not an adequate model to hypothesize plume dispersion given the weather conditions on the day of the accident, and considering the terrain surrounding Three Mile Island. * * * Rather than using the standard computer models, Vergeiner chose to use a "numerical model" which he initially referred to by the acronym "AMBIMET," but which he later called, in his second report, the "FITNAH model operated by AMBIMET." * * * However, Vergeiner never provided any testimony, documentation or any other evidence that the numerical models he did use are generally accepted within the meteorological or the broader scientific community. Although the "general acceptance" test of *Frye v. United States*, 293 F. 1013 (1923), was displaced by the Federal Rules of Evidence, *Daubert*, 509 U.S. at 589 "general acceptance" in the scientific community can "yet have a bearing on the inquiry," and be an "important factor in ruling particular

---

94. Under the "Gaussian plume model", dispersion is three-dimensional, i.e., dispersion will be downwind, cross-wind and vertical. See Environmental Software and Services, AirWare: Urban Air Quality Assessment and Management (visited January 4, 1999) <http://www.ess.co.at/AIRWARE/gauss.html>.

95. The Gaussian plume model was the model used by appellants' expert, Keith Woodward, to formulate his opinion as to the atmospheric dispersion of the radioactive materials released as a result of the accident. However, by referring to the Gaussian plume model, we do not mean to suggest that it is the model Vergeiner should have used. Rather, it is mentioned only as an example of a generally accepted computer model.

evidence admissible." "[A] known technique which has been able to attract only minimal support within the community may properly be viewed with skepticism." * * * Accordingly, a court may well cast a jaundiced eye upon a technique which is not supported by any evidence of general acceptance absent other indicia of reliable methodology. Here, it is impossible to know whether the disputed model's methodology can or has been tested or whether the model has been subjected to peer review or publication. Neither can we determine its known or potential rate of error. Consequently, we can hardly conclude that the plume dispersion model Vergeiner hypothesized meets the Daubert requirement of evidentiary reliability.

Second, Vergeiner's "plume movie" * * * is based on pure speculation. In his second report, Vergeiner presented his opinion as to behavior of the plume. He wrote:

> For conclusion, I present my own tentative TMI plume "movie" for the first few hours ... Its chief purpose is visualization of possible plume shifts and exposures, and realization of the kind of information we would need to be reasonably sure about transport and dispersion of TMI–2 effluents. [The plume movie] is the beginning of an investigation, not the end.

The speculative nature of the plume movie was made even more apparent during Vergeiner's deposition when he described the plume movie.

> I make it clear that the [plume movie] and following are not meant to be—I think the way I write it is that they are the beginning of a discussion and not the end of a discussion.... And I realize it's absolutely clear, and I state it, that this, this is an assumption, I think it's not an unreasonable one, it has some foundation, but at this stage it is just a, well, it's more than a provocation, but this-
>
> Q: It's the articulation of a hypothesis yet to be explored?
>
> A: Of a hypothesis, and it is an illustration, certainly an illustration of winds turning rapidly, which they did, that one is for sure, and the consequences of a plume, I wanted to illustrate how distorted a plume can become. I wanted to illustrate the effects. I just don't have enough of a database to prove details of this. This is absolutely clear and conceded. Absolutely clear.

Rule 702 not only requires that the scientific opinion proffered by the expert be supported by "good grounds," it also mandates that the challenged testimony "assist the trier of fact to understand the evidence or to determine a fact in issue." This requirement is one of relevance and expert evidence which does not relate to an issue in the case is not helpful. * * * Here, Vergeiner's report and testimony make clear that his plume movie was merely an assumption visualizing possible plume movements. Given its speculative character, the plume movie was properly excluded under Daubert.

We note that in order for expert testimony to be reliable, and therefore admissible, it must be based on the methods and procedures of science rather than subjective belief or speculation. Consequently, Vergeiner's plume movie, and, (as will be discussed), his water model, are also lacking in scientific reliability and are inadmissible because of their speculative character. Nevertheless, we believe that the plume movie and the water model are more appropriately inadmissible because they lack fit.

The water model does not "fit." The water model is a video of a large scale model tank, the bottom of which is a topographical map of alpine terrain. The tank is filled with water, a dye is injected into the water and a current is run through the water to simulate air flow. Its intended purpose is to demonstrate how a material will disperse in the atmosphere in relation to terrain and air patterns. However, the water model is just as speculative as the plume movie. In his deposition, Vergeiner testified that the water model was a demonstration and a "tool for visualization," but was not intended "to exactly simulate flows at the time of the TMI accident." In fact, Vergeiner testified that "[t]here's no way to [simulate the complete atmospheric structure] in a simple shallow water model." Simply put, the water model does not assist the finder of fact and is, therefore, not admissible under Rule 702.

* * *

UNITED STATES v. QUINN
18 F.3d 1461 (9th Cir. 1994)

SCHROEDER, CIRCUIT JUDGE.

On September 5, 1991, a lone robber, wearing a dark mask and armed with a silver handgun, entered a bank in Berkeley, California, and took $24,625 from the bank's teller drawers. The robbery was styled a "takeover" robbery by the police because the robber went behind the teller counter and removed the money himself. Two weeks later, on September 19, 1991, at 10:30 a.m., two men entered a San Leandro, California bank dressed in dark clothing and wearing face masks. One of these men was armed with a silver handgun. As in the Berkeley robbery, the man with the gun went behind the teller counter and removed cash—$17,842—from the teller drawers.

During interviews by the police after the Berkeley robbery, four of the tellers described the robber as being 5′ 6″ to 5′ 8″ tall and weighing 140 to 165 pounds. After the San Leandro robbery, witnesses described the robber with the gun as being 5′ 3″ to 6 feet tall and weighing 160 to 180 pounds. The San Leandro bank's customer service manager described the robber as being 5′ 9″ tall, and weighing 170–175 pounds.

A witness on the street outside the San Leandro bank saw the robbers rolling up ski masks as they left the bank. The witness was interviewed by the police immediately after the robbery, and he told them that he saw the robbers drive away in a light blue Ford or Mercury. The witness also reported that he had seen the vehicle's license plate, and he told the police the tag number he had seen. The license number quickly was traced to a California woman who, within hours of the robbery, told the police that she had sold the car to appellant Keith Wayne Quinn and produced a bill of sale bearing Quinn's signature. The police recognized the name immediately, as Quinn was suspected of being connected to other "takeover" robberies in the area. [A search uncovered incriminating evidence against Quinn.]

Quinn was charged with two counts of armed bank robbery and two counts of using a firearm during a crime of violence. This case was first tried in February 1992, resulting in a hung jury. The retrial, which is the subject of this appeal, began March 10, 1992. Quinn was convicted on all four counts.

* * *

The Admission of Photogrammetry Evidence

Quinn * * * contends that the district court erred in permitting the government's expert to testify to his use of "photogrammetry" to render an opinion as to the height of the individual in surveillance photographs from the Berkeley robbery. By analyzing two photographs, FBI Agent Douglas Goodin concluded and testified that the Berkeley robber was between 5′ 3″ tall and 5′ 6″ tall. Quinn is 5′ 5″ tall. To determine the Berkeley robber's height, Agent Goodin used a process in which a formula is derived by measuring the change in the dimensions of objects in a photograph as they move away from the camera. After testing the formula against objects of known dimensions in the photograph, Goodin was able to make an estimate of the robber's height.

Fed.R.Evid. 702 provides the appropriate standard for determining the admissibility of expert scientific testimony. See *Daubert v. Merrell Dow Pharmaceuticals, Inc.*, 509 U.S. 579 (1993). Rule 702 embodies two primary criteria: a district court must determine whether proffered expert scientific testimony is relevant and reliable. There is no dispute in this case as to relevance. The only issue is whether the district court erred in concluding that the process used by Goodin was scientifically valid and sufficiently reliable to be placed before the jury.

The court permitted Goodin to testify after a proffer from the government as to the basics of the photogrammetry process. During this proffer, counsel for the government explained that by using vanishing points, an analyst is able to measure the rate of change in the size of objects as they move away from a camera. Counsel explained that by referring to objects of known dimension in the photograph, an analyst can judge the size of other objects in the photograph. After hearing the government's proffer, the court concluded that the process used by Goodin was nothing more than a series of computer-assisted calculations that did not involve any novel or questionable scientific technique.

Quinn contends that he was entitled to a full evidentiary hearing on the reliability of the process used by Agent Goodin. We cannot conclude that the court abused the discretion trial courts must exercise in choosing the best manner in which to determine whether scientific evidence will assist a jury. Quinn points to nothing in the record calling the reliability of the photogrammetry process into question. Moreover, he was permitted to cross-examine the government's expert as to the specifics of the process, the techniques he used, and the witness's qualifications to give his findings. The court gave Quinn the opportunity to call his own photogrammetry expert, which he did not do—although he had an expert in the courtroom during the government expert's testimony. The district court did not err in admitting this evidence.

* * *

COMMENTARY

The two cases above show that experts may present digital information, but only if they provide a sufficient foundation that they are using a reliable process. If the expert in *Three Mile Island* had used the computer models that all the other scientists were using, he would have had no problem. When he strayed from the norm, the fact that he was using computers and "modeling" could not save the opinion.

Even if an expert uses a reliable computer program to reach an opinion, the opinion may still be inadmissible if the expert did not employ it properly. In *Smith v. BMW North America, Inc.*, the plaintiff alleged that her air bag did not properly deploy during an accident.[20] She proffered an accident reconstructionist to testify that the car's velocity was great enough that a properly functioning air bag would have deployed upon impact. At the *Daubert* hearing, the expert testified regarding his calculations of the principal direction of force and measurements of vehicle deformation, or crush, which he entered into the EDCrash computer program to calculate the barrier equivalent velocity of Smith's vehicle when it crashed. The EDCrash computer program takes as input the principal direction of force, measurements of displacement in the car's structure (deformation or crush), and known data regarding the car's structure and materials from which it is manufactured. The program then outputs the barrier equivalent velocity for a given vehicle accident. The court found that the expert's opinion was properly excluded as unreliable, because the figures he plugged into the program were completely speculative. Therefore, the opinion was the product of an unreliable application of a reliable computer program. Because the end result of that process is unreliable, the court concluded that the expert's testimony was properly excluded under *Daubert* and Rule 702.

---

20.   308 F.3d 913, 915 (8th Cir. 2002).

Note that presentation of digital evidence may raise reliability issues even when it is not presented as part of an expert's testimony. For example, if the opponent of digital evidence raises a legitimate question about the operation of a software program, the proponent may be required to show that the program reaches reliable results.

H. SUMMARY ON ADMISSIBILITY OF DIGITAL EVIDENCE

EXCERPT FROM Gregory P. Joseph, *Internet and Email Evidence*

Editors' Note: Mr. Joseph is the former chair of the ABA Section of Litigation, a former member of the Judicial Conference Advisory Committee on Evidence Rules, and one of the country's foremost experts in digital evidence. We are grateful for his contribution to this book.

The explosive growth of the Internet and burgeoning use of electronic mail are raising a series of novel evidentiary issues. The applicable legal principles are familiar—this evidence must be authenticated and, to the extent offered for its truth, it must satisfy hearsay concerns. The novelty of the evidentiary issues arises out of the novelty of the media—thus, it is essentially factual. These issues can be resolved by relatively straightforward application of existing principles in a fashion very similar to the way they are applied to other computer-generated evidence and to more traditional exhibits.

I. Internet Evidence

There are primarily three forms of Internet data that are offered into evidence—(1) data posted on the website by the owner of the site ("website data"); (2) data posted by others with the owner's consent (a chat room is a convenient example); and (3) data posted by others without the owner's consent ("hacker" material). The wrinkle for authenticity purposes is that, because Internet data is electronic, it can be manipulated and offered into evidence in a distorted form. Additionally, various hearsay concerns are implicated, depending on the purpose for which the proffer is made.

A. Authentication

Website Data. Corporations, government offices, individuals, educational institutions and innumerable other entities post information on their websites that may be relevant to matters in litigation. Alternatively, the fact that the information appears on the website may be the relevant point. Accordingly, courts routinely face proffers of data (text or images) allegedly drawn from websites. The proffered evidence must be authenticated in all cases, and, depending on the use for which the offer is made, hearsay concerns may be implicated.

The authentication standard is no different for website data or chat room evidence than for any other. Under Rule 901(a), "The requirement of authentication . . . is satisfied by evidence sufficient to support a finding that the matter in question is what its proponent claims."

In applying this rule to website evidence, there are three questions that must be answered, explicitly or implicitly:

1.   What was actually on the website?

2.   Does the exhibit or testimony accurately reflect it?

3.   If so, is it attributable to the owner of the site?

In the first instance, authenticity can be established by the testimony of any witness that the witness typed in the URL associated with the website (usually prefaced with www); that he or she logged on to the site and reviewed what was there; and that a printout or other exhibit fairly and accurately reflects what the witness saw. This last testimony is no different than that required to authenticate a photograph, other replica or demonstrative exhibit. The witness may be lying or mistaken, but that is true of all testimony and a principal reason for cross-examination. Unless the opponent of the evidence raises a genuine issue as to trustworthiness, testimony of this sort is sufficient to satisfy Rule 901(a), presumptively authenticating the website data and shifting the burden of coming forward to the opponent of the evidence. It is reasonable to indulge a presumption that material on a web site (other than chat room conversations) was placed there by the owner of the site.

The opponent of the evidence must, in fairness, be free to challenge that presumption by adducing facts showing that proffered exhibit does not accurately reflect the contents of a website, or that those contents are not attributable to the owner of the site. First, even if the proffer fairly reflects what was on the site, the data proffered may have been the product of manipulation by hackers (uninvited third parties). Second, the proffer may not fairly reflect what was on the site due to modification—intentional or unintentional, material or immaterial—in the proffered exhibit or testimony.

Detecting modifications of electronic evidence can be very difficult, if not impossible. That does not mean, however, that nothing is admissible because everything is subject to distortion. The same is true of many kinds of evidence, from testimony to photographs to digital images, but that does not render everything inadmissible. It merely accentuates the need for the judge to focus on all relevant circumstances in assessing admissibility under Fed.R.Evid. 104(a)—and to leave the rest to the jury, under Rule 104(b).

In considering whether the opponent has raised a genuine issue as to trustworthiness, and whether the proponent has satisfied it, the court will look at the totality of the circumstances, including, for example:

● The length of time the data was posted on the site.

● Whether others report having seen it.

- Whether it remains on the website for the court to verify.

- Whether the data is of a type ordinarily posted on that website or websites of similar entities (e.g., financial information from corporations).

- Whether the owner of the site has elsewhere published the same data, in whole or in part.

- Whether others have published the same data, in whole or in part.

- Whether the data has been republished by others who identify the source of the data as the website in question.

A genuine question as to trustworthiness may be established circumstantially. For example, more by way of authentication may be reasonably required of a proponent of Internet evidence who is known to be a skilled computer user and who is suspected of possibly having modified the proffered website data for purposes of creating false evidence.

In assessing the authenticity of website data, important evidence is normally available from the personnel managing the website ("webmaster" personnel). A webmaster can establish that a particular file, of identifiable content, was placed on the website at a specific time. This may be done through direct testimony or through documentation, which may be generated automatically by the software of the web server. It is possible that the content provider—the author of the material appearing on the site that is in issue—will be someone other than the person who installed the file on the web. In that event, this second witness (or set of documentation) may be necessary to reasonably ensure that the content which appeared on the site is the same as that proffered.

Self-Authentication. Government offices publish an abundance of reports, press releases and other information on their official web sites. Internet publication of a governmental document on an official website constitutes an "official publication" within Federal Rule of Evidence 902(5). Under Rule 902(5), official publications of government offices are self-authenticating.

Judicial Notice. Under Federal Rule of Evidence 201(b) and (d), when requested, a court must take judicial notice of facts that are "not subject to reasonable dispute in that it is ... capable of accurate and ready determination by resort to sources whose accuracy cannot reasonably be questioned." Government website data—particularly data that may be confirmed by the court's accessing the site—are subject to mandatory judicial notice under Rule 201. *See, e.g., Denius v. Dunlap*, 330 F.3d 919 (7th Cir. 2003) (district court abused its discretion in withdrawing its judicial notice of information from National Personnel Records Center's official website).

A court may take judicial notice of information publicly announced on a party's website, as long as the website's authenticity is not in dispute and it is capable of accurate and ready determination, within Fed. R.Evid. 201.

Chat Room Evidence. A proffer of chat room postings generally implicates the same authenticity issues discussed above in connection with web site data, but with a twist. While it is reasonable to indulge a presumption that the contents of a website are fairly attributable to the site's owner, that does not apply to chat room evidence. By definition, chat room postings are made by third parties, not the owner of the site. Further, chat room participants usually use screen names (pseudonyms) rather than their real names.

Since chat room evidence is often of interest only to the extent that the third party who left a salient posting can be identified, the unique evidentiary issue concerns the type and quantum of evidence necessary to make that identification—or to permit the finder of fact to do so. Evidence sufficient to attribute a chat room posting to a particular individual may include, for example:

- Evidence that the individual used the screen name in question when participating in chat room conversations (either generally or at the site in question).

- Evidence that, when a meeting with the person using the screen name was arranged, the individual in question showed up.

- Evidence that the person using the screen name identified him-or herself as the individual (in chat room conversations or otherwise), especially if that identification is coupled with particularized information unique to the individual, such as a street address or email address.

- Evidence that the individual had in his or her possession information given to the person using the screen name (such as contact information provided by the police in a sting operation).

- Evidence from the hard drive of the individual's computer reflecting that a user of the computer used the screen name in question.

With respect to the dialog itself, a participant in the chat room conversation may authenticate a transcript with testimony based on firsthand knowledge that the transcript fairly and accurately captures the chat. *Ford v. State,* 274 Ga. App. 695, 697–98, 617 S.E.2d 262, 265–66 (2005) ("we find this situation analogous to the admission of a videotape, which is admissible where the operator of the machine which produced it, or one who personally witnessed the events recorded, testifies that the videotape accurately portrayed what the witness saw take place at the time the events occurred. Here, [the witness] personally witnessed the real-time chat recorded in Transcript B as it was taking place, and he testified that the transcript accurately represented the on-line conversation. Under these circumstances, [his] testimony was tantamount to that of a witness to an event and was sufficient to authenticate the transcript").

Internet Archives. Websites change over time. Lawsuits focus on particular points in time. The relevant web page may be changed or deleted before litigation begins. Various internet archive services exist that provide snapshots of web pages at various points in time. To the extent that those services, in the ordinary course of their business, accurately retrieve and store copies of the website as it appeared at specified points in time, the stored webpages are admissible. The certification should contain the same elements as set forth in § I(A) (Website Data), with necessary modifications (e.g., the retrieval process may be automated, requiring authentication the automated function, such as that it is used and relied on in the ordinary course of business and produces reliable results).

Evidence that an internet archive reflects that a site carried certain content may be corroborative of other evidence, such as a download from the site by a witness or testimony from a witness. Under Federal Rule of Evidence 104(a) and similar state provisions, in making its determination as to the admissibility of evidence, the court "is not bound by the rules of evidence except those with respect to privileges." With a proper foundation, internet archive evidence may also form part of the basis of a forensic IT expert's testimony, in accordance with the strictures of Federal Rule of Evidence 703 and similar state rules.

Temporary Internet Files. When a computer user accesses the Internet, web browsers like Microsoft Explorer temporarily store all accessed images in a Temporary Internet Files folder so that, if the computer user attempts to view the same web page again, the computer is able to retrieve the page much more quickly. Even deleted images in the Temporary Internet Files folder may be retrieved and viewed by an expert using an appropriate program, and expert testimony about this process is sufficient to authenticate the images.

Search Engines. The results generated by widely recognized search engines, like Google or Yahoo!, may be pertinent in litigation—e.g., a trademark action to show dilution of a mark or a privacy/right of publicity action to show appropriation of a likeness. Proper authentication would consist of testimony—or, under Federal Rule of Evidence 902(11) or (12), a certification—from a witness that the witness typed in the website address of the search engine; that he or she logged on to the site; the precise search run by the witness; that the witness reviewed the results of the search; and that a printout or other exhibit fairly and accurately reflects those results. The witness should be someone capable of further averring that he or she, or the witness's employer, uses the search engine in the ordinary course of business and that it produces accurate results. Further, the testimony or certification should reflect that the witness logged onto some of the websites identified by the search engine to demonstrate, as a circumstantial matter, that the particular search generated accurate results.

B. Hearsay

Authenticity aside, every extrajudicial statement drawn from a website must satisfy a hearsay exception or exemption if the statement is offered for its truth. *See United States v. Jackson*, 208 F.3d 633, 637 (7th Cir.) ("The web postings were not statements made by declarants testifying at trial, and they were being offered to prove the truth of the matter asserted. That means they were hearsay."); *Monotype Imaging, Inc. v. Bitstream Inc.*, 376 F. Supp. 2d 877, 884–85 (N.D. Ill 2005) ("The Court refused to admit Exhibits 15 and 17 for the truth of the matter asserted in them because these exhibits are inadmissible hearsay. The Court admitted Exhibits 15 and 17 only for the limited purpose of proving that the diagrams in those exhibits were displayed on the respective websites on the dates indicated on the exhibits").

To establish that material appeared on a website, it is sufficient for a witness with knowledge to attest to the fact that the witness logged onto the site and to describe what he or she saw. That obviates any hearsay issue as to the contents of the site.

Data Entry. Some website data is entered into Internet-readable format in the same way that a bookkeeper may enter numbers into a computer. This act of data entry is an extrajudicial statement—i.e., assertive nonverbal conduct within Rule 801(a)—which means that the product is hearsay, within Rule 801(c). Since each level of hearsay must satisfy the hearsay rule, under Rule 805 (Hearsay within Hearsay), the act of data entry must be addressed separately from the content of the posted declaration.

Data entry is usually a regularly-conducted activity within Rule 803(6) (or, in the context of a government office, falls within Rule 803(8) (public records exception)). It also often falls within Rule 803(1) (present sense impression exception).

The real question about the data entry function is its accuracy. This is, in substance, an issue of authenticity and should be addressed as part of the requisite authentication foundation whenever a genuine doubt as to trustworthiness has been raised. If the foundational evidence establishes that the data have been entered accurately, the hearsay objection to the data entry function should ordinarily be overruled. See also Rule 807 (residual exception).

Much Internet evidence does not involve data entry, in the sense described above. If the webmaster is simply transferring an image or digitally converting an electronic file into web format, that is a technical process that does not involve assertive non-verbal conduct within Rule 801(a) and is best judged as purely an authentication issue. The difference, analytically, is between the grocery store clerk who punches the price into the check-out computer (this is assertive non-verbal conduct), and the clerk who simply scans the price into the computer (non-assertive behavior). Only assertive non-verbal conduct raises hearsay issues and requires an applicable hearsay exception or exemption.

Business and Public Records. Businesses and government offices publish countless documents on their websites in ordinary course. Provided that all of the traditional criteria are met, these documents will satisfy the hearsay exception for "records" of the business or public office involved, under Rules 803(6) or (8). Reliability and trustworthiness are said to be presumptively established by the fact of actual reliance in the regular course of an enterprise's activities. (Recall that public records which satisfy Rule 803(8) are presumptively authentic under Rule 901(b)(7) (if they derive from a "public office where items of this nature are kept") and even self-authenticating under Rule 902(5).)

As long as the website data constitute business or public records, this quality is not lost simply because the printout or other image that is proffered into evidence was generated for litigation purposes. Each digital data entry contained on the website is itself a Rule 803(6) or (8) "record" because it is a "data compilation, in any form." Consequently, if each entry has been made in conformance with Rule 803(6) or Rule 803(8), the proffered output satisfies the hearsay exception even if it: (a) was not printed out at or near the time of the events recorded (as long as the entries were timely made), (b) was not prepared in ordinary course (but, e.g., for trial), and (c) is not in the usual form (but, e.g., has been converted into graphic form). If the data are simply downloaded into a printout, they do not lose their business-record character. To the extent that significant selection, correction and interpretation are involved, their reliability and authenticity may be questioned.

* * *

Rules 803(6) and (8) effectively incorporate an authentication requirement. Rule 803(6) contemplates the admission of hearsay, if its criteria are satisfied, "unless the source of information or the method or circumstances of preparation indicate lack of trustworthiness." Rule 803(8) contains substantially identical language. This trustworthiness criterion parallels the Rule 901(a) requirement of "evidence sufficient to support a finding that the matter in question is what its proponent claims." As a result, untrustworthy proffers of business or public records may be excluded on hearsay as well as authenticity grounds.

Market Reports & Tables. Rule 803(17) excepts from the hearsay rule "Market quotations, tabulations, lists, directories, or other published compilations, generally used and relied upon by the public or by persons in particular occupations." A number of cases have applied this rule to commercial websites furnishing such data as interest rates and blue-book prices of used cars. This rationale plainly extends to the other sorts of traditional information admitted under Rule 803(17), such as tables reflecting the prices of such items as stock, bonds and currency; real estate listings; and telephone books.

Admissions. Website data published by a litigant comprise admissions of that litigant when offered by an opponent. Accordingly, even if the owner of a website may not offer data from the site into evidence, because the proffer is hearsay when the owner attempts to do so, an opposing party is authorized to offer it as an admission of the owner.

Non-Hearsay Proffers. Not uncommonly, website data is not offered for the truth of the matters asserted but rather solely to show the fact that they were published on the web, either by one of the litigants or by unaffiliated third parties. For example, in a punitive damages proceeding, the fact of Internet publication may be relevant to show that the defendant published untruths for the public to rely on. Or, in a trademark action, Internet listings or advertisements may be relevant on the issue of consumer confusion or purchaser understanding. In neither of these circumstances is the website data offered for its truth. Accordingly, no hearsay issues arise.

Judicial Skepticism. As they were with computerized evidence prior to the mid–1990s, some judges remain skeptical of the reliability of anything derived from the Internet. *See, e.g., St. Clair v. Johnny's Oyster & Shrimp, Inc.,* 76 F.Supp.2d 773, 774–75 (S.D. Tex. 1999):

> While some look to the Internet as an innovative vehicle for communication, the Court continues to warily and wearily view it largely as one large catalyst for rumor, innuendo, and misinformation. . . . Anyone can put anything on the Internet. No web-site is monitored for accuracy and nothing contained therein is under oath or even subject to independent verification absent underlying documentation. Moreover, the Court holds no illusions that hackers can adulterate the content on any web-site from any location at any time. For these reasons, any evidence procured off the Internet is adequate for almost nothing, even under the most liberal interpretations of the hearsay exception rules found in Fed.R.Evid. 807.

While there is no gainsaying a healthy judicial skepticism of any evidence that is subject to ready, and potentially undetectable, manipulation, there is much on the web which is not subject to serious dispute and which may be highly probative. To keep matters in perspective, there is very little in the way of traditional documentary or visual evidence that is not subject to manipulation and distortion. As with so many of the trial judge's duties, this is a matter that can only be resolved on a case-by-case basis.

II.   Email Evidence

Like Internet evidence, email evidence raises both authentication and hearsay issues. The general principles of admissibility are essentially the same since email is simply a distinctive type of Internet evidence—namely, the use of the Internet to send personalized communications.

Authentication. The authenticity of email evidence is governed by Federal Rule of Evidence 901(a), which requires only "evidence sufficient to support a finding that the matter in question is what its proponent claims." Under Fed.R.Evid. 901(b)(4), email may be authenticated by reference to its "appearance, contents, substance, internal patterns, or other distinctive characteristics, taken in conjunction with circumstances."

If email is produced by a party from the party's files and on its face purports to have been sent by that party, these circumstances alone may suffice to establish authenticity. Further, a party's failure to challenge as inauthentic emails sent by it or its counsel may be deemed sufficient evidence of the emails' authenticity. Authenticity may also be established by testimony of a witness who sent or received the emails—in essence, that the emails are the personal correspondence of the witness.

It is important, for authentication purposes, that email generated by a business or other entity on its face generally reflects the identity of the organization. The name of the organization, usually in some abbreviated form, ordinarily appears in the email address of the sender (after the @ symbol). This mark of origin has been held to self-authenticate the email as having been sent by the organization, under Fed.R.Evid. 902(7), which provides for self-authentication of: "Trade inscriptions and the like.—Inscriptions, signs, tags, or labels purporting to have been affixed in the course of business and indicating ownership, control, or origin." Where the email reflects the entire email name of a party (and not just the mark of origin), it has been held to comprise a party admission of origin.

Independently, circumstantial indicia that may suffice to establish that proffered email were sent, or were sent by a specific person, including evidence that:

● A witness or entity received the email.

● The email bore the customary format of an email, including the addresses of the sender and recipient.

● The address of the recipient is consistent with the email address on other emails sent by the same sender.

● This email contained the typewritten name or nickname of the recipient (and, perhaps, the sender) in the body of the email.[1]

● The email recited matters that would normally be known only to the individual who is alleged to have sent it (or to a discrete number of persons including this individual).

● Following receipt of the email, the recipient witness had a discussion with the individual who purportedly sent it, and the conversa-

---

1. *Interest of F.P.*, 878 A.2d 91 (Pa. Super. 2005) ("He referred to himself by his first name"). Thus, too, courts have looked at the "electronic 'signature'" at the end of the email message identifying the name and business affiliation of the sender. *See, e.g., Sea–Land Serv., Inc. v. Lozen Int'l, LLC,* 285 F.3d 808, 821 (9th Cir. 2002) (held, email by one employee forwarded to party opponent by a fellow employee—containing the electronic signature of the latter—constitutes an admission of a party opponent and thus is not hearsay).

tion reflected this individual's knowledge of the contents of the email.

As with all other forms of authentication, the testimony of a witness with knowledge is prerequisite to authenticate email. It is insufficient to proffer email through a witness with no knowledge of the transmissions at issue, unless the witness has sufficient technical knowledge of the process to be in a position to authenticate the email through expert testimony.

Transcriptions of email or text message exchanges, the originals of which have been lost through no fault of the proponent, may be authenticated by testimony of a witness with knowledge that he or she transcribed them and that they accurately reflect the contents of the email or text message exchange.

There are a variety of technical means by which email transmissions may be traced. Therefore, if serious authentication issues arise, a technical witness may be of assistance. This may become important, for example, in circumstances where a person or entity denies sending an email, or denies receipt of an email and has not engaged in conduct that furnishes circumstantial evidence of receipt (such as a subsequent communication reflecting knowledge of the contents of the email). See, e.g., *Carafano v. Metrosplash.com, Inc.*, 207 F.Supp.2d 1055, 1072 (C.D. Cal. 2002) ("Plaintiff provides no evidence that [defendant Internet service] ever received the reply email in response to its welcome confirmation email").

* * *

While it is true that an email may be sent by anyone who, with a password, gains access to another's email account, similar uncertainties exist with traditional documents. Therefore, there is no need for separate rules of admissibility. See, e.g., *Interest of F.P.*, 878 A.2d 91 (Pa. Super. 2005) (just as an email can be faked, a "signature can be forged; a letter can be typed on another's typewriter; distinct letterhead stationary can be copied or stolen. We believe that e-mail messages and similar forms of electronic communication can be properly authenticated within the existing framework of Pa. R.E. 901 and Pennsylvania case law.").

Hearsay. The hearsay issues associated with email are largely the same as those associated with conventional correspondence. An email offered for the truth of its contents is hearsay and must satisfy an applicable hearsay exception. The prevalence and ease of use of email, particularly in the business setting, makes it attractive simply to assume that all email generated at or by a business falls under the business-records exception to the hearsay rule. That assumption would be incorrect.

What Is a Business Record? Or a Present Sense Impression? In *United States v. Ferber*, 966 F.Supp. 90 (D. Mass. 1997), the government offered into evidence a multi-paragraph email from a subordinate to his superior describing a telephone conversation with the defendant (not a fellow employee). In that conversation, the defendant inculpated himself, and the email so reflected. Chief Judge Young rejected the proffer under Fed.R.Evid. 803(6) because, "while it may have been [the employee's] routine business practice to make such records, there was not sufficient evidence that [his employer] required such records to be maintained. . . . [I]n order for a document to be admitted as a business record, there must be some evidence of a business duty to make and regularly maintain records of this type." The *Ferber* Court nonetheless admitted the email, but under 803(1), the hearsay exception for present sense impressions. *See also Rambus, Inc. v. Infineon Techs. AG*, 348 F. Supp. 2d 698, 707 (E.D. Va. 2004) ("Email is far less of a systematic business activity than a monthly inventory printout").

Hearsay within Hearsay. Because business records are written without regard for the rules of evidence, they commonly contain multiple layers of hearsay. Under Federal Rule of Evidence 805, each layer of hearsay must independently satisfy an exception to the hearsay rule. Absent that, any hearsay portion of an email that is offered for the truth will be excluded. See, e.g., State of New York v. Microsoft Corp., 2002 WL 650047 (D.D.C. April 12, 2002) (" 'If both the source and the recorder of the information, as well as every other participant in the chain producing the record, are acting in the regular course of business, the multiple hearsay is excused by Rule 803(6). If the source of the information is an outsider, Rule 803(6) does not, by itself, permit the admission of the business record. The outsider's statement must fall within another hearsay exception to be admissible because it does not have the presumption of accuracy that statements made during the regular course of business have' ").

Admission of Party Opponent. Under Fed.R.Evid. 801(d)(2), emails sent by party opponents constitute admissions and are not hearsay. The email address itself, which reflects that it originates from a party, may be admissible as a party admission. Further, an email from a party opponent that forwards another email may comprise an adoptive admission of the original message, depending on the text of the forwarding email. *Sea-Land Serv., Inc. v. Lozen Int'l, LLC*, 285 F.3d 808, 821 (9th Cir. 2002) (one of plaintiff's employees "incorporated and adopted the contents" of an email message from a second of plaintiff's employees when she forwarded it to the defendant with a cover note that "manifested an adoption or belief in [the] truth" of the information contained in the original email, within Fed.R.Evid. 801(d)(2)(B)). If there is not an adoptive admission, however, the forwarded email chain may comprise hearsay-within-hearsay.

Excited Utterance. In dicta, the Oregon Court of Appeals has indicated that, in appropriate circumstances, an email message might fall within the excited utterance exception to the hearsay rule. *State v. Cunningham*, 40 P.3d 1065, 1076 n.8 (2002). (The federal excited utterance exception, contained in Fed.R.Evid. 803(2), is identical to the Oregon exception, Oregon Rule 803(2).)

State of Mind. Email may be admissible to demonstrate a party's then-existing state of mind, within Fed.R.Evid. 803(3). * * *

Other Non–Hearsay Uses. Not all extrajudicial statements are hearsay or, more precisely, need not be offered for hearsay purposes. The contents of an authenticated email may, for example, constitute a verbal act—e.g., constitute defamation or the offer or acceptance of a contract.

An email may itself reflect the conduct at issue. See *United States v. Safavian*, 435 F. Supp. 2d 36, 44 (D.D.C. 2006) (certain emails themselves comprised "lobbying work" of defendant Jack Abramoff).

* * *

Email may be admitted to reflect the fact of third party statements. *Damon's Restaurants, Inc. v. Eileen K Inc.*, 2006 WL 3290891 (S.D. Ohio Nov. 13, 2006) (consumer complaints in a franchise dispute); United States v. Dupre, 462 F.3d 131 (2d Cir. 2006) (non-testifying investors emails admitted in fraud prosecution to provide context for emails sent by defendant, which were admissions pursuant to Rule 801(d)(2)).

Email Address. A party's chosen email address may itself be admissible as evidence of the party's state of mind. See, e.g. Illinois v. Mertz, 218 Ill.2d 1, 842 N.E.2d 618 (2005) (murder prosecution; proper for trial court to admit evidence that defendant's email address was "Cereal Kilr 2000" because it provided insight into his frame of mind).

EXCERPT FROM Gregory P. Joseph, *A Simplified Approach to Computer–Generated Evidence and Animations*

* * *

Charts, graphs and diagrams are admissible if they are fairly accurate, are judged helpful in understanding the matters at issue, and any deficiencies are made known to the factfinder. Exhibits of this sort today are commonly computer-generated rather than drawn by hand. The test of admissibility, however, remains the same.[2] Once a knowledgeable witness testifies that a graph, chart, diagram, or other demonstrative exhibit generated by a computer fairly and accurately portrays a relevant subject matter, the exhibit has been authenticated and may be received, without more, subject to Rule 403 (prejudice, confusion, waste

---

2. *See, e.g.*, People v. Hood, 53 Cal. App. 4th 965, 969–70, 62 Cal. Rptr. 2d 137 (4th Dist.), *review denied*, 1997 Cal. Lexis 4499 (Sup. Ct. July 16, 1997) ("The prosecution and defense computer animations were tantamount to drawings by the experts from both sides to illustrate their testimony. We view them as a mechanized version of what a human animator does when he or she draws each frame of activities"); *Ladeburg v. Ray*, 508 N.W.2d 694, 695–6 (S.D. 1993) (affirming admission of "diagrams drawn by a computer" where "[t]he expert testified that he used the computer as a drafting tool" on the theory that "[t]he diagrams were merely mechanical drawings made by a computer and the expert who prepared them was available for cross-examination").

of time, cumulativeness), Rule 611(a) (vesting in the trial judge discretion over the mode and order of the presentation of evidence), and, where applicable, Rule 1006 (charts, calculations and summaries permissible to present the contents of voluminous data that are independently admissible and have previously been made available to adversaries). Unless the opponent raises a genuine issue as to trustworthiness—calling into question the computerized genesis of the exhibit—no additional authentication is generally requisite.

* * *

The South Carolina Supreme Court has articulated a sound four-part test for the admission of computer-generated animations: "We hold that a computer-generated video animation is admissible as demonstrative evidence when the proponent shows that the animation is (1) authentic under Rule 901 ...; (2) relevant under Rules 401 and 402 ...; (3) a fair and accurate representation of the evidence to which it relates, and (4) its probative value substantially outweighs the danger of unfair prejudice, confusing the issues or misleading the jury under Rule 403." *Clark v. Cantrell*, 339 S.C. 369, 384, 529 S.E.2d 528, 536 (2000) (citing Gregory P. Joseph, *A Simplified Approach to Computer–Generated Evidence and Animations*, 156 F.R.D. 327 (1994) (an earlier version of this article)).

The Connecticut Supreme Court has adopted a six-part test for the admission of all computer-generated evidence of all sorts—from the simplest output to the most complicated animation or simulation. Under this test, the standard for the admission of computer-generated evidence will "generally be satisfied by evidence that (1) the computer equipment is accepted in the field as standard and competent and was in good working order, (2) qualified computer operators were employed, (3) proper procedures were followed in connection with the input and output of information, (4) a reliable software program was utilized, (5) the equipment was programmed and operated correctly, and (6) the exhibit is properly identified as the output in question." *State v. Swinton*, 268 Conn. 781, 811–12, 847 A.2d 921, 945 (Conn. Sup. Ct. 2004).

The general concern that has motivated some courts to require more detailed authentication—often when the exhibit is of critical importance to proving the claim or defense—is summarized in the Federal Judicial Center's MANUAL FOR COMPLEX LITIGATION (Fourth) as follows:

> In general, the Federal Rules of Evidence apply to computerized data as they do to other types of evidence. Computerized data, however, raise unique issues concerning accuracy and authenticity. Accuracy may be impaired by incomplete data entry, mistakes in output instructions, programming errors, damage and contamination of storage media, power outages, and equipment malfunctions. The integrity of data may also be compromised in the course of discovery by improper search and retrieval techniques, data conversion, or mishandling.

Use of an authentic computer program, however, will not necessarily result in the creation of admissible evidence. The program must be used properly. In the construct of Federal Rule of Evidence 702(2)-(3) (because this will often be an area requiring expert testimony), reliable principles and methods are essential, but they must also be applied reliably to the facts of the case.

IV. SPECIAL AUTHENTICATION ISSUES FOR COMPUTER-GENERATED ANIMATIONS AND SIMULATIONS

A. Animations

Computer-generated animations and simulations raise some unique issues. At its simplest, an animation is merely a sequence of illustrations that, when filmed, video-recorded or computer-generated, creates the illusion that the illustrated objects are in motion. Traditionally—because they are drawings—animations have been subjected to the fair-and-accurate-portrayal test and have been admitted, within the trial judge's discretion, generally for illustrative purposes.

B. Simulations (Reconstructions, Re-creations)

Computer-generated simulations are based on mathematical models, and particular attention must be paid to the reliability and trustworthiness of the model. A model is a set of operating assumptions—a mathematical representation of a defined set of facts, or system. To be accurate, it must produce results that are identical or very similar to those produced by the physical facts (or system) being modeled. In order to do that, the model must contain all relevant elements—and reflect all relevant interactions—that occur in the real world.

The model must be based on material factual assumptions substantially the same as those reflected in the record to be admissible.[3] To the extent that there is a dispute over the facts, that is an issue for the jury under Federal Rule of Evidence 104(b) and analogous state provisions.

A simulation model, in particular, is a computer program that consists of a set of assumptions about precisely what would transpire under certain clearly defined circumstances. If the simulation model works well, the result is to show the probable consequences that are predicted by the theory that underlies the equations.

Because of the difficulty of reflecting all of the complexities of any real world system in a computer program, various simplification techniques are used. The danger is that the introduction of simplification creates the risk of invalidating the simulation that is produced.

As observed above, a key test of admissibility is reliability, and a strong indicator of reliability is the extent to which a computer program that has been used to create evidence is accepted in the world of commerce and affairs—the relevant business, governmental, academic

---

3. *Dunkle v. Oklahoma*, 139 P.3d 228, 250–51 (Okla. Crim. App. 2006) (prosecution-proffered computer-generated animations improperly admitted as at odds with the "physical evidence, analysis of evidence at the crime scene, and statements from" the defendant).

or other apt community. This reflects the practical test that the rules of evidence commonly employ—is the evidence sufficiently reliable that people rely on it to conduct their affairs outside of litigation? That entails the requirement that the model is used in a manner consistent with its use by others in the field.[4]

---

4. *Compare Liquid Dynamics Corp. v. Vaughan Co.*, 449 F.3d 1209 (Fed. Cir. 2006) (affirming admission of widely used analysis applied to reliable computer model; "[t]he identification of . . . flaws in generally reliable scientific research is precisely the role of cross-examination") *with Aurora ex rel. Utility Enterprise v. Simpson*, 105 P.3d 595, 612–13 (Colo. Sup. Ct. 2005) (affirming exclusion because, although the computer model used was widely accepted, it was not used in a manner that was consistent with accepted modeling techniques).

*

APPENDICES

■ ■ ■

APPENDIX I

2006 ADVISORY COMMITTEE NOTES TO ELECTRONIC DISCOVERY AMENDMENTS

■ ■ ■

RULE 16

2006 Amendment

The amendment to Rule 16(b) is designed to alert the court to the possible need to address the handling of discovery of electronically stored information early in the litigation if such discovery is expected to occur. Rule 26(f) is amended to direct the parties to discuss discovery of electronically stored information if such discovery is contemplated in the action. Form 35 is amended to call for a report to the court about the results of this discussion. In many instances, the court's involvement early in the litigation will help avoid difficulties that might otherwise arise.

Rule 16(b) is also amended to include among the topics that may be addressed in the scheduling order any agreements that the parties reach to facilitate discovery by minimizing the risk of waiver of privilege or work-product protection. Rule 26(f) is amended to add to the discovery plan the parties' proposal for the court to enter a case-management or other order adopting such an agreement. The parties may agree to various arrangements. For example, they may agree to initial provision of requested materials without waiver of privilege or protection to enable the party seeking production to designate the materials desired or protection for actual production, with the privilege review of only those materials to follow. Alternatively, they may agree that if privileged or protected information is inadvertently produced, the producing party may by timely notice assert the privilege or protection and obtain return of the materials without waiver. Other arrangements are possible. In most circumstances, a party who receives information under such an arrangement cannot assert that production of the information waived a claim of privilege or of protection as trial-preparation material.

An order that includes the parties' agreement may be helpful in avoiding delay and excessive cost in discovery. *See Manual for Complex Litigation* (4th) § 11.446. Rule 16(b)(6) recognizes the propriety of including such agreements in the court's order. The rule does not provide the court with authority to enter such a case-management or other order without party agreement, or limit the court's authority to act on motion.

RULE 26

2006 Amendment

Subdivision (a). Rule 26(a)(1)(B) is amended to parallel Rule 34(a) by recognizing that a party must disclose electronically stored information as well as documents that it may use to support its claims or defenses. The term "electronically stored information" has the same broad meaning in Rule 26(a)(1) as in Rule 34(a). This amendment is consistent with the 1993 addition of Rule 26(a)(1)(B). The term "data compilations" is deleted as unnecessary because it is a subset of both documents and electronically stored information.

[Subdivision (a)(1)(E).] Civil forfeiture actions are added to the list of exemptions from Rule 26(a)(1) disclosure requirements. These actions are governed by new Supplemental Rule G. Disclosure is not likely to be useful.

Subdivision (b)(2). The amendment to Rule 26(b)(2) is designed to address issues raised by difficulties in locating, retrieving, and providing discovery of some electronically stored information. Electronic storage systems often make it easier to locate and retrieve information. These advantages are properly taken into account in determining the reasonable scope of discovery in a particular case. But some sources of electronically stored information can be accessed only with substantial burden and cost. In a particular case, these burdens and costs may make the information on such sources not reasonably accessible.

It is not possible to define in a rule the different types of technological features that may affect the burdens and costs of accessing electronically stored information. Information systems are designed to provide ready access to information used in regular ongoing activities. They also may be designed so as to provide ready access to information that is not regularly used. But a system may retain information on sources that are accessible only by incurring substantial burdens or costs. Subparagraph (B) is added to regulate discovery from such sources.

Under this rule, a responding party should produce electronically stored information that is relevant, not privileged, and reasonably accessible, subject to the (b)(2)(C) limitations that apply to all discovery. The responding party must also identify, by category or type, the sources containing potentially responsive information that it is neither searching nor producing. The identification should, to the extent possible, provide enough detail to enable the requesting party to evaluate the burdens and costs of providing the discovery and the likelihood of finding responsive information on the identified sources.

A party's identification of sources of electronically stored information as not reasonably accessible does not relieve the party of its common-law or statutory duties to preserve evidence. Whether a responding party is required to preserve unsearched sources of potentially responsive information that it believes are not reasonably accessible depends on the circumstances of each case. It is often useful for the parties to discuss this issue early in discovery.

The volume of—and the ability to search—much electronically stored information means that in many cases the responding party will be able to produce information from reasonably accessible sources that will fully satisfy the parties' discovery needs. In many circumstances the requesting party should obtain and evaluate the information from such sources before insisting that the responding party search and produce information contained on sources that are not reasonably accessible. If the requesting party continues to seek discovery of information from sources identified as not reasonably accessible, the parties should discuss the burdens and costs of accessing and retrieving the information, the needs that may establish good cause for requiring all or part of the requested discovery even if the information sought is not reasonably accessible, and conditions on obtaining and producing the information that may be appropriate.

If the parties cannot agree whether, or on what terms, sources identified as not reasonably accessible should be searched and discoverable information produced, the issue may be raised either by a motion to compel discovery or by a motion for a protective order. The parties must confer before bringing either motion. If the parties do not resolve the issue and the court must decide, the responding party must show that the identified sources of information are not reasonably accessible because of undue burden or cost. The requesting party may need discovery to test this assertion. Such discovery might take the form of requiring the responding party to conduct a sampling of information contained on the sources identified as not reasonably accessible; allowing some form of inspection of such sources; or taking depositions of witnesses knowledgeable about the responding party's information systems.

Once it is shown that a source of electronically stored information is not reasonably accessible, the requesting party may still obtain discovery by showing good cause, considering the limitations of Rule 26(b)(2)(C) that balance the costs and potential benefits of discovery. The decision whether to require a responding party to search for and produce information that is not reasonably accessible depends not only on the burdens and costs of doing so, but also on whether those burdens and costs can be justified in the circumstances of the case. Appropriate considerations may include: (1) the specificity of the discovery request; (2) the quantity of information available from other and more easily accessed sources; (3) the failure to produce relevant information that seems likely to have existed but is no longer available on more easily accessed sources; (4) the likelihood of finding relevant, responsive information that cannot be obtained from other, more easily accessed sources; (5) predictions as to the importance and usefulness of the further information; (6) the importance of the issues at stake in the litigation; and (7) the parties' resources.

The responding party has the burden as to one aspect of the inquiry—whether the identified sources are not reasonably accessible in light of the burdens and costs required to search for, retrieve, and produce whatever responsive information may be found. The requesting party has the burden of showing that its need for the discovery outweighs the burdens and costs of locating, retrieving, and producing the information. In some cases, the court will be able to determine whether the identified sources are not reasonably accessible and whether the requesting party has shown good cause for some or all of the discovery, consistent with the limitations of Rule 26(b)(2)(C), through a single proceeding or presentation. The good-cause determination, however, may be complicated because the court and parties may know little about what information the sources identified as not reasonably accessible might contain, whether it is relevant, or how valuable it may be to the litigation. In such cases, the parties may need some focused discovery, which may include sampling of the sources, to learn more about what burdens and costs are involved in accessing the information, what the information consists of, and how valuable it is for the litigation in light of information that can be obtained by exhausting other opportunities for discovery.

The good-cause inquiry and consideration of the Rule 26(b)(2)(C) limitations are coupled with the authority to set conditions for discovery. The conditions may take the form of limits on the amount, type, or sources of information required to be accessed and produced. The conditions may also include payment by the requesting party of part or all of the reasonable costs of obtaining information from sources that are not reasonably accessible. A requesting party's willingness to share or bear the access costs may be weighed by the court in determining whether there is good cause. But the producing party's burdens in reviewing the information for relevance and privilege may weigh against permitting the requested discovery.

The limitations of Rule 26(b)(2)(C) continue to apply to all discovery of electronically stored information, including that stored on reasonably accessible electronic sources.

Subdivision (b)(5). The Committee has repeatedly been advised that the risk of privilege waiver, and the work necessary to avoid it, add to the costs and delay of discovery. When the review is of electronically stored information, the risk of waiver, and the time and effort required to avoid it, can increase substantially because of the volume of electronically stored information and the difficulty in ensuring that all information to be produced has in fact been reviewed. Rule 26(b)(5)(A) provides a procedure for a party that has withheld information on the basis of privilege or protection as trial-preparation material to make the claim so that the requesting party can decide whether to contest the claim and the court can resolve the dispute. Rule 26(b)(5)(B) is added to provide a procedure for a party to assert a claim of privilege or trial-preparation material protection after information is produced in discovery in the action and, if the claim is contested, permit any party that received the information to present the matter to the court for resolution.

Rule 26(b)(5)(B) does not address whether the privilege or protection that is asserted after production was waived by the production. The courts have developed principles to determine whether, and under what circumstances, waiver results from inadvertent production of privileged or protected information. Rule 26(b)(5)(B) provides a procedure for presenting and addressing these issues. Rule 26(b)(5)(B) works in tandem with Rule 26(f), which is amended to direct the parties to discuss privilege issues in preparing their discovery plan, and which, with amended Rule 16(b), allows the parties to ask the court to include in an order any agreements the parties reach regarding issues of privilege or trial-preparation material protection. Agreements reached under Rule 26(f)(4) and orders including such agreements entered under Rule 16(b)(6) may be considered when a court determines whether a waiver has occurred. Such agreements and orders ordinarily control if they adopt procedures different from those in Rule 26(b)(5)(B).

A party asserting a claim of privilege or protection after production must give notice to the receiving party. That notice should be in writing unless the circumstances preclude it. Such circumstances could include the assertion of the claim during a deposition. The notice should be as specific as possible in identifying the information and stating the basis for the claim. Because the receiving party must decide whether to challenge the claim and may sequester the information and submit it to the court for a ruling on whether the claimed privilege or protection applies and whether it has been waived, the notice should be sufficiently detailed so as to enable the receiving party and the court to understand the basis for the claim and to determine whether waiver has occurred. Courts will continue to examine whether a claim of privilege or protection was made at a reasonable time when delay is part of the waiver determination under the governing law.

After receiving notice, each party that received the information must promptly return, sequester, or destroy the information and any copies it has. The option of sequestering or destroying the information is included in part because the receiving party may have incorporated the information in protected trial-preparation materials. No receiving party may use or disclose the information pending resolution of the privilege claim. The receiving party may present to the court the questions whether the information is privileged or protected as trial-preparation material, and whether the privilege or protection has been waived. If it does so, it must provide the court with the grounds for the privilege or protection specified in the producing party's notice, and serve all parties. In presenting the question, the party may use the content of the information only to the extent permitted by the applicable law of privilege, protection for trial-preparation material, and professional responsibility.

If a party disclosed the information to nonparties before receiving notice of a claim of privilege or protection as trial-preparation material, it must take reasonable steps to retrieve the information and to return it, sequester it until the claim is resolved, or destroy it.

Whether the information is returned or not, the producing party must preserve the information pending the court's ruling on whether the claim of privilege or of protection is properly asserted and whether it was waived. As with claims made under Rule 26(b)(5)(A), there may be no ruling if the other parties do not contest the claim.

Subdivision (f). Rule 26(f) is amended to direct the parties to discuss discovery of electronically stored information during their discovery-planning conference. The rule focuses on "issues relating to disclosure or discovery of electronically stored information"; the discussion is not required in cases not involving electronic discovery, and the amendment imposes no additional requirements in those cases. When the parties do anticipate disclosure or discovery of electronically stored information, discussion at the outset may avoid later difficulties or ease their resolution.

When a case involves discovery of electronically stored information, the issues to be addressed during the Rule 26(f) conference depend on the nature and extent of the contemplated discovery and of the parties' information systems. It may be important for the parties to discuss those systems, and accordingly important for counsel to become familiar with those systems before the conference. With that information, the parties can develop a discovery plan that takes into account the capabilities of their computer systems. In appropriate cases identification of, and early discovery from, individuals with special knowledge of a party's computer systems may be helpful.

The particular issues regarding electronically stored information that deserve attention during the discovery planning stage depend on the specifics of the given case. *See Manual for Complex Litigation* (4th) § 40.25(2) (listing topics for discussion in a proposed order regarding meet-and-confer sessions). For example, the parties may specify the topics for such discovery and the time period for which discovery will be sought. They may identify the various sources of such information within a party's control that should be searched for electronically stored information. They may discuss whether the information is reasonably accessible to the party that has it, including the burden or cost of retrieving and reviewing the information. *See* Rule 26(b)(2)(B). Rule 26(f)(3) explicitly directs the parties to discuss the form or forms in which electronically stored information might be produced. The parties may be able to reach agreement on the forms of production, making discovery more efficient. Rule 34(b) is amended to permit a requesting party to specify the form or forms in which it wants electronically stored information produced. If the requesting party does not specify a form, Rule 34(b) directs the responding party to state the forms it intends to use in the production. Early discussion of the forms of production may facilitate the application of Rule 34(b) by allowing the parties to determine what forms of production will meet both parties' needs. Early identification of disputes over the forms of production may help avoid the expense and delay of searches or productions using inappropriate forms.

Rule 26(f) is also amended to direct the parties to discuss any issues regarding preservation of discoverable information during their conference as they develop a discovery plan. This provision applies to all sorts of discoverable information, but can be particularly important with regard to electronically stored information. The volume and dynamic nature of electronically stored information may complicate preservation obligations. The ordinary operation of computers involves both the automatic creation and the automatic deletion or overwriting of certain information. Failure to address preservation issues early in the litigation increases uncertainty and raises a risk of disputes.

The parties' discussion should pay particular attention to the balance between the competing needs to preserve relevant evidence and to continue routine operations critical to ongoing activities. Complete or broad cessation of a party's routine computer operations could paralyze the party's activities. *Cf. Manual for Complex Litigation* (4th) § 11.422 ("A blanket preservation order may be prohibitively expensive and unduly burdensome for parties dependent on computer systems for their day-to-day operations.") The parties should take account of these considerations in their discussions, with the goal of agreeing on reasonable preservation steps.

The requirement that the parties discuss preservation does not imply that courts should routinely enter preservation orders. A preservation order entered over objections should be narrowly tailored. Ex parte preservation orders should issue only in exceptional circumstances.

Rule 26(f) is also amended to provide that the parties should discuss any issues relating to assertions of privilege or of protection as trial-preparation materials, including whether the parties can facilitate discovery by agreeing on procedures for asserting claims of privilege or protection after production and whether to ask the court to enter an order that includes any agreement the parties reach. The Committee has repeatedly been advised about the discovery difficulties that can result from efforts to guard against waiver of privilege and work-product protection. Frequently parties find it necessary to spend large amounts of time reviewing materials requested through discovery to avoid waiving privilege. These efforts are necessary because materials subject to a claim of privilege or protection are often difficult to identify. A failure to withhold even one such item may result in an argument that there has been a waiver of privilege as to all other privileged materials on that subject matter. Efforts to avoid the risk of waiver can impose substantial costs on the party producing the material and the time required for the privilege review can substantially delay access for the party seeking discovery.

These problems often become more acute when discovery of electronically stored information is sought. The volume of such data, and the informality that attends use of e-mail and some other types of electronically stored information, may make privilege determinations more difficult, and privilege review correspondingly more expensive and time consuming. Other aspects of electronically stored information pose particular difficulties for privilege review. For example, production may be sought of information automatically included in electronic files but not apparent to the creator or to readers. Computer programs may retain draft language, editorial comments, and other deleted matter (sometimes referred to as "embedded data" or "embedded edits") in an electronic file but not make them apparent to the reader. Information describing the history, tracking, or management of an electronic file (sometimes called "metadata") is usually not apparent to the reader viewing a hard copy or a screen image. Whether this information should be produced may be among the topics discussed in the Rule 26(f) conference. If it is, it may need to be reviewed to ensure that no privileged information is included, further complicating the task of privilege review.

Parties may attempt to minimize these costs and delays by agreeing to protocols that minimize the risk of waiver. They may agree that the responding party will provide certain requested materials for initial examination without waiving any privilege or protection—sometimes known as a "quick peek." The requesting party then designates the documents it wishes to have actually produced. This designation is the Rule 34 request. The responding party then responds in the usual course, screening only those documents actually requested for formal production and asserting privilege claims as provided in Rule 26(b)(5)(A). On other occasions, parties enter agreements—sometimes called "clawback agreements"—that production without intent to waive privilege or protection should not be a waiver so long as the responding party identifies the documents mistakenly produced, and that the documents should be returned under those circumstances. Other voluntary arrangements may be appropriate depending on the circumstances of each litigation. In most circumstances, a party who receives information under such an arrangement cannot assert that production of the information waived a claim of privilege or of protection as trial-preparation material.

Although these agreements may not be appropriate for all cases, in certain cases they can facilitate prompt and economical discovery by reducing delay before the discovering party obtains access to documents, and by reducing the cost and burden of review by the producing party. A case-management or other order including such agreements may further facilitate the discovery process. Form 35 is amended to include a report to the court about any agreement regarding protections against inadvertent forfeiture or waiver of privilege or protection that the parties have reached, and Rule 16(b) is amended to recognize that the court may include such an agreement in a case-management or other order. If the parties agree to entry of such an order, their proposal should be included in the report to the court.

Rule 26(b)(5)(B) is added to establish a parallel procedure to assert privilege or protection as trial-preparation material after production, leaving the question of waiver to later determination by the court.

RULE 27 [no 2006 amendment]

RULE 28 [no 2006 amendment]

RULE 29 [no 2006 amendment]

RULE 30 [no 2006 amendment]

RULE 31 [no 2006 amendment]

RULE 32 [no 2006 amendment]

RULE 33

2006 Amendment

Rule 33(d) is amended to parallel Rule 34(a) by recognizing the importance of electronically stored information. The term "electronically stored information" has the same broad meaning in Rule 33(d) as in Rule 34(a). Much business information is stored only in electronic form; the Rule 33(d) option should be available with respect to such records as well.

Special difficulties may arise in using electronically stored information, either due to its form or because it is dependent on a particular computer system. Rule 33(d) allows a responding party to substitute access to documents or electronically stored information for an answer only if the burden of deriving the answer will be substantially the same for either party. Rule 33(d) states that a party electing to respond to an interrogatory by providing electronically stored information must ensure that the interrogating party can locate and identify it "as readily as can the party served," and that the responding party must give the interrogating party a "reasonable opportunity to examine, audit, or inspect" the information. Depending on the circumstances, satisfying these provisions with regard to electronically stored information may require the responding party to provide some combination of technical support, information on application software, or other assistance. The key question is whether such support enables the interrogating party to derive or ascertain the answer from the electronically stored information as readily as the responding party. A party that wishes to invoke Rule 33(d) by specifying electronically stored information may be required to provide direct access to its electronic information system, but only if that is necessary to afford the requesting party an adequate opportunity to derive or ascertain the answer to the interrogatory. In that situation, the responding party's need to protect sensitive interests of confidentiality or privacy may mean that it must derive or ascertain and provide the answer itself rather than invoke Rule 33(d).

RULE 34

2006 Amendment

Subdivision (a). As originally adopted, Rule 34 focused on discovery of "documents" and "things." In 1970, Rule 34(a) was amended to include discovery of data compilations, anticipating that the use of computerized information would increase. Since then, the growth in electronically stored information and in the variety of systems for creating and storing such information has been dramatic. Lawyers and judges interpreted the term "documents" to include electronically stored information because it was obviously improper to allow a party to evade discovery obligations on the basis that the label had not kept pace with changes in information technology. But it has become increasingly difficult to say that all forms of electronically stored information, many dynamic in nature, fit within the traditional concept of a "document." Electronically stored information may exist in dynamic databases and other forms far different from fixed expression on paper. Rule 34(a) is amended to confirm that discovery of electronically stored information stands on equal footing with discovery of paper documents. The change clarifies that Rule 34 applies to information that is fixed in a tangible form and to information that is stored in a medium from which it can be retrieved and examined. At the same time, a Rule 34 request for production of "documents" should be understood to encompass, and the response should include, electronically stored information unless discovery in the action has clearly distinguished between electronically stored information and "documents."

Discoverable information often exists in both paper and electronic form, and the same or similar information might exist in both. The items listed in Rule 34(a) show different ways in which information may be recorded or stored. Images, for example, might be hard-copy documents or electronically stored information. The wide variety of computer systems currently in use, and the rapidity of technological change, counsel against a limiting or precise definition of electronically stored information. Rule 34(a)(1) is expansive and includes any type of information that is stored electronically. A common example often sought in discovery is electronic communications, such as e-mail. The rule covers—either as documents or as electronically stored information—information "stored in any medium," to encompass future developments in computer technology. Rule 34(a)(1) is intended to be broad enough to cover all current types of computer-based information, and flexible enough to encompass future changes and developments.

References elsewhere in the rules to "electronically stored information" should be understood to invoke this expansive approach. A companion change is made to Rule 33(d), making it explicit that parties choosing to respond to an interrogatory by permitting access to responsive records may do so by providing access to electronically stored information. More generally, the term used in Rule 34(a)(1) appears in a number of other amendments, such as those to Rules 26(a)(1), 26(b)(2), 26(b)(5)(B), 26(f), 34(b), 37(f), and 45. In each of these rules, electronically stored information has the same broad meaning it has under Rule 34(a)(1). References to "documents" appear in discovery rules that are not amended, including Rules 30(f), 36(a), and 37(c)(2). These references should be interpreted to include electronically stored information as circumstances warrant.

The term "electronically stored information" is broad, but whether material that falls within this term should be produced, and in what form, are separate questions that must be addressed under Rules 26(b), 26(c), and 34(b).

The Rule 34(a) requirement that, if necessary, a party producing electronically stored information translate it into reasonably usable form does not address the issue of translating from one human language to another. *See In re Puerto Rico Elect. Power Auth.*, 687 F.2d 501, 504–510 (1st Cir. 1989).

Rule 34(a)(1) is also amended to make clear that parties may request an opportunity to test or sample materials sought under the rule in addition to inspecting and copying them. That opportunity may be important for both electronically stored information and hard-copy materials. The current rule is not clear that such testing or sampling is authorized; the amendment expressly permits it. As with any other form of discovery, issues of burden and intrusiveness raised by requests to test or sample can be addressed under Rules 26(b)(2) and 26(c). Inspection or testing of certain types of electronically stored information or of a responding party's electronic information system may raise issues of confidentiality or privacy. The addition of testing and sampling to Rule 34(a) with regard to documents and electronically stored information is not meant to create a routine right of direct access to a party's electronic information system, although such access might be justified in some circumstances. Courts should guard against undue intrusiveness resulting from inspecting or testing such systems.

Rule 34(a)(1) is further amended to make clear that tangible things must—like documents and land sought to be examined—be designated in the request.

Subdivision (b). Rule 34(b) provides that a party must produce documents as they are kept in the usual course of business or must organize and label them to correspond with the categories in the discovery request. The production of electronically stored information should be subject to comparable requirements to protect against deliberate or inadvertent production in ways that raise unnecessary obstacles for the requesting party. Rule 34(b) is amended to ensure similar protection for electronically stored information.

The amendment to Rule 34(b) permits the requesting party to designate the form or forms in which it wants electronically stored information produced. The form of production is more important to the exchange of electronically stored information than of hard-copy materials, although a party might specify hard copy as the requested form. Specification of the desired form or forms may facilitate the orderly, efficient, and cost-effective discovery of electronically stored information. The rule recognizes that different forms of production may be appropriate for different types of electronically stored information. Using current technology, for example, a party might be called upon to produce word processing documents, e-mail messages, electronic spreadsheets, different image or sound files, and material from databases. Requiring that such diverse types of electronically stored information all be produced in the same form could prove impossible, and even if possible could increase the cost and burdens of producing and using the information. The rule therefore provides that the requesting party may ask for different forms of production for different types of electronically stored information.

The rule does not require that the requesting party choose a form or forms of production. The requesting party may not have a preference. In some cases, the requesting party may not know what form the producing party uses to maintain its electronically stored information, although Rule 26(f)(3) is amended to call for discussion of the form of production in the parties' prediscovery conference.

The responding party also is involved in determining the form of production. In the written response to the production request that Rule 34 requires, the responding party must state the form it intends to use for producing electronically stored information if the requesting party does not specify a form or if the responding party objects to a form that the requesting party specifies. Stating the intended form before the production occurs may permit the parties to identify and seek to resolve disputes before the expense and work of the production occurs. A party that responds to a discovery request by simply producing electronically stored information in a form of its choice, without identifying that form in advance of the production in the response required by Rule 34(b), runs a risk that the requesting party can show that the produced form is not reasonably usable and that it is entitled to production of some or all of the information in an additional form. Additional time might be required to permit a responding party to assess the appropriate form or forms of production.

If the requesting party is not satisfied with the form stated by the responding party, or if the responding party has objected to the form specified by the requesting party, the parties must meet and confer under Rule 37(a)(2)(B) in an effort to resolve the matter before the requesting party can file a motion to compel. If they cannot agree and the court resolves the dispute, the court is not limited to the forms initially chosen by the requesting party, stated by the responding party, or specified in this rule for situations in which there is no court order or party agreement.

If the form of production is not specified by party agreement or court order, the responding party must produce electronically stored information either in a form or forms in which it is ordinarily maintained or in a form or forms that are reasonably usable. Rule 34(a) requires that, if necessary, a responding party "translate" information it produces into a "reasonably usable" form. Under some circumstances, the responding party may need to provide some reasonable amount of technical support, information on application software, or other reasonable assistance to enable the requesting party to use the information. The rule does not require a party to produce electronically stored information in the form it which it is ordinarily maintained, as long as it is produced in a reasonably usable form. But the option to produce in a reasonably usable form does not mean that a responding party is free to convert electronically stored information from the form in which it is ordinarily maintained to a different form that makes it more difficult or burdensome for the requesting party to use the information efficiently in the litigation. If the responding party ordinarily maintains the information it is producing in a way that makes it searchable by electronic means, the information should not be produced in a form that removes or significantly degrades this feature.

Some electronically stored information may be ordinarily maintained in a form that is not reasonably usable by any party. One example is "legacy" data that can be used only by superseded systems. The questions whether a producing party should be required to convert such information to a more usable form, or should be required to produce it at all, should be addressed under Rule 26(b)(2)(B).

Whether or not the requesting party specified the form of production, Rule 34(b) provides that the same electronically stored information ordinarily need be produced in only one form.

RULE 35 [no 2006 amendment]

RULE 36 [no 2006 amendment]

RULE 37

2006 Amendment

Subdivision (f). Subdivision (f) is new. It focuses on a distinctive feature of computer operations, the routine alteration and deletion of information that attends ordinary use. Many steps essential to computer operation may alter or destroy information, for reasons that have nothing to do with how that information might relate to litigation. As a result, the ordinary operation of computer systems creates a risk that a party may lose potentially discoverable information without culpable conduct on its part. Under Rule 37(f), absent exceptional circumstances, sanctions cannot be imposed for loss of electronically stored information resulting from the routine, good-faith operation of an electronic information system.

Rule 37(f) applies only to information lost due to the "routine operation of an electronic information system"—the ways in which such systems are generally designed, programmed, and implemented to meet the party's technical and business needs. The "routine operation" of computer systems includes the alteration and overwriting of information, often without the operator's specific direction or awareness, a feature with no direct counterpart in hard-copy documents. Such features are essential to the operation of electronic information systems.

Rule 37(f) applies to information lost due to the routine operation of an information system only if the operation was in good faith. Good faith in the routine operation of an information system may involve a party's intervention to modify or suspend certain features of that routine operation to prevent the loss of information, if that information is subject to a preservation obligation. A preservation obligation may arise from many sources, including common law, statutes, regulations, or a court order in the case. The good faith requirement of Rule 37(f) means that a party is not permitted to exploit the routine operation of an information system to thwart discovery obligations by allowing that operation to continue in order to destroy specific stored information that it is required to preserve. When a party is under a duty to preserve information because of pending or reasonably anticipated litigation, intervention in the routine operation of an information system is one aspect of what is often called a "litigation hold." Among the factors that bear on a party's good faith in the routine operation of an information system are the steps the party took to comply with a court order in the case or party agreement requiring preservation of specific electronically stored information.

Whether good faith would call for steps to prevent the loss of information on sources that the party believes are not reasonably accessible under Rule 26(b)(2) depends on the circumstances of each case. One factor is whether the party reasonably believes that the information on such sources is likely to be discoverable and not available from reasonably accessible sources.

The protection provided by Rule 37(f) applies only to sanctions "under these rules." It does not affect other sources of authority to impose sanctions or rules of professional responsibility.

This rule restricts the imposition of "sanctions." It does not prevent a court from making the kinds of adjustments frequently used in managing discovery if a party is unable to provide relevant responsive information. For example, a court could order the responding party to produce an additional witness for deposition, respond to additional interrogatories, or make similar attempts to provide substitutes or alternatives for some or all of the lost information.

RULE 45

2006 Amendments

Rule 45 is amended to conform the provisions for subpoenas to changes in other discovery rules, largely related to discovery of electronically stored information.

Rule 34 is amended to provide in greater detail for the production of electronically stored information. Rule 45(a)(1)(C) is amended to recognize that electronically stored information, as defined in Rule 34(a), can also be sought by subpoena. Like Rule 34(b), Rule 45(a)(1) is amended to provide that the subpoena can designate a form or forms for production of electronic data. Rule 45(c)(2) is amended, like Rule 34(b), to authorize the person served with a subpoena to object to the requested form or forms. In addition, as under Rule 34(b), Rule 45(d)(1)(B) is amended to provide that if the subpoena does not specify the form or forms for electronically stored information, the person served with the subpoena must produce electronically stored information in a form or forms in which it is usually maintained or in a form or forms that are reasonably usable. Rule 45(d)(1)(C) is added to provide that the person producing electronically stored information should not have to produce the same information in more than one form unless so ordered by the court for good cause.

As with discovery of electronically stored information from parties, complying with a subpoena for such information may impose burdens on the responding person. Rule 45(c) provides protection against undue impositions on nonparties. For example, Rule 45(c)(1) directs that a party serving a subpoena "shall take reasonable steps to avoid imposing undue burden or expense on a person subject to the subpoena," and Rule 45(c)(2)(B) permits the person served with the subpoena to object to it and directs that an order requiring compliance "shall protect a person who is neither a party nor a party's officer from significant expense resulting from" compliance. Rule 45(d)(1)(D) is added to provide that the responding person need not provide discovery of electronically stored information from sources the party identifies as not reasonably accessible, unless the court orders such discovery for good cause, considering the limitations of Rule 26(b)(2)(C), on terms that protect a nonparty against significant expense. A parallel provision is added to Rule 26(b)(2).

Rule 45(a)(1)(B) is also amended, as is Rule 34(a), to provide that a subpoena is available to permit testing and sampling as well as inspection and copying. As in Rule 34, this change recognizes that on occasion the opportunity to perform testing or sampling may be important, both for documents and for electronically stored information. Because testing or sampling may present particular issues of burden or intrusion for the person served with the subpoena, however, the protective provisions of Rule 45(c) should be enforced with vigilance when such demands are made. Inspection or testing of certain types of electronically stored information or of a person's electronic information system may raise issues of confidentiality or privacy. The addition of sampling and testing to Rule 45(a) with regard to documents and electronically stored information is not meant to create a routine right of direct access to a person's electronic information system, although such access might be justified in some circumstances. Courts should guard against undue intrusiveness resulting from inspecting or testing such systems.

Rule 45(d)(2) is amended, as is Rule 26(b)(5), to add a procedure for assertion of privilege or of protection as trial-preparation materials after production. The receiving party may submit the information to the court for resolution of the privilege claim, as under Rule 26(b)(5)(B).

Other minor amendments are made to conform the rule to the changes described above.

APPENDIX II

UNIFORM RULES RELATING TO THE DISCOVERY OF ELECTRONICALLY STORED INFORMATION*

■ ■ ■

drafted by the

NATIONAL CONFERENCE OF COMMISSIONERS
ON UNIFORM STATE LAWS

October 10, 2007

**Uniform Rules Relating to the Discovery
of Electronically Stored Information**

Drafted by:

Uniform Law Commission (ULC), 211 E. Ontario Street, Suite 1300, Chicago, IL 60611

312–915–0195, www.nccusl.org

Brief description of act:

The Uniform Rules Relating to the Discovery of Electronically Stored Information provides states with up-to-date rules for the discovery of electronic documents in civil cases. The Uniform Rules provide procedures for parties in a civil case to jointly follow relating to a number of issues, including the preservation of the electronic information; the form in which the information will be produced; and the period of time in which the information must be produced. The Uniform Rules limit the sanctions which may be imposed on a party

---

* Reprinted with permission of the National Conference of Commissioners on Uniform State Laws.

for failure to provide electronic information that has been lost as the result of routine operation of an electronic information system, only if the system was operated in good faith. The Uniform Rules address the unique difficulties in accessing some electronic information by providing certain restrictions on its discovery. For instance, a party may object to discovery of electronically stored information on the grounds that the information is not reasonably accessible because of undue burden or expense. However, the court may order discovery of such information if it is shown that the likely benefit of the proposed discovery outweighs the likely burden or expense, and may allocate between the parties the expense of conducting the discovery.

* * *

UNIFORM RULES RELATING TO THE DISCOVERY OF ELECTRONICALLY STORED INFORMATION

RULE 1. DEFINITIONS. In these rules:

(1) "Discovery" means the process of providing information in a civil proceeding in the courts of this state pursuant to [insert reference to state rules of civil procedure] or these rules.

(2) "Electronic" means relating to technology having electrical, digital, magnetic, wireless, optical, electromagnetic, or similar capabilities.

(3) "Electronically stored information" means information that is stored in an electronic medium and is retrievable in perceivable form.

(4) "Person" means an individual, corporation, business trust, estate, trust, partnership, limited liability company, association, joint venture, public corporation, government or governmental subdivision, agency, or instrumentality, or any other legal or commercial entity.

Judicial Note: The term "civil proceeding" as used in the definition of "discovery" may need to be modified in certain states to specify that it includes civil courts with differing or limited jurisdiction within the same state. As the term is used in paragraph (1), it is intended to encompass not only civil courts of general jurisdiction, but also courts of limited jurisdiction such as domestic relations and probate courts. The term is used in various rules, including Rules 3, 4, and 7.

RULE 2. SUPPLEMENTAL RULES OF DISCOVERY. Unless displaced by particular provisions of these rules, [insert reference to state rules of civil procedure] supplement these rules.

RULE 3. CONFERENCE, PLAN, AND REPORT TO COURT.

(a) Unless the parties otherwise agree or the court otherwise orders, not later than [21] days after each responding party first appears in a civil proceeding, all parties that have appeared in the proceeding shall confer concerning whether discovery of electronically stored information is reasonably likely to be sought in the proceeding. If discovery of electronically stored information is reasonably likely to be sought, the parties at the conference shall discuss:

(1) any issues relating to preservation of the information;

(2) the form in which each type of the information will be produced;

(3) the period within which the information will be produced;

(4) the method for asserting or preserving claims of privilege or of protection of the information as trial-preparation materials, including whether such claims may be asserted after production;

(5) the method for asserting or preserving confidentiality and proprietary status of information relating to a party or a person not a party to the proceeding;

(6) whether allocation among the parties of the expense of production is appropriate; and

(7) any other issue relating to discovery of the information.

(b) If discovery of electronically stored information is reasonably likely to be sought in a civil proceeding, the parties shall:

(1) develop a proposed plan relating to discovery of the information; and

(2) not later than [14] days after the conference under subsection (a), submit to the court a written report that summarizes the plan and states the position of each party as to any issue about which they are unable to agree.

RULE 4. ORDER GOVERNING DISCOVERY.

(a) In a civil proceeding, the court may issue an order governing the discovery of electronically stored information pursuant to:

(1) a motion by a party seeking discovery of the information or by a party or person from which discovery of the information is sought;

(2) a stipulation of the parties and of any person not a party from which discovery of the information is sought; or

(3) the court's own motion, after reasonable notice to, and an opportunity to be heard from, the parties and any person not a party from which discovery of the information is sought.

(b) An order governing discovery of electronically stored information may address:

(1) whether discovery of the information is reasonably likely to be sought in the proceeding;

(2) preservation of the information;

(3) the form in which each type of the information is to be produced;

(4) the time within which the information is to be produced;

(5) the permissible scope of discovery of the information;

(6) the method for asserting or preserving claims of privilege or of protection of the information as trial-preparation material after production;

(7) the method for asserting or preserving confidentiality and the proprietary status of information relating to a party or a person not a party to the proceeding;

(8) allocation of the expense of production; and

(9) any other issue relating to discovery of the information.

RULE 5. LIMITATION ON SANCTIONS. Absent exceptional circumstances, the court may not impose sanctions on a party under these rules for failure to provide electronically stored information lost as the result of the routine, good-faith operation of an electronic information system.

RULE 6. REQUEST FOR PRODUCTION.

(a) In a civil proceeding, a party may serve on any other party a request for production of electronically stored information and for permission to inspect, copy, test, or sample the information.

(b) A party on which a request to produce electronically stored information is served shall serve a response on the requesting party in a timely manner. The response must state, with respect to each item or category in the request:

(1) that inspection, copying, testing, or sampling of the information will be permitted as requested; or

(2) any objection to the request and the reasons for the objection.

RULE 7. FORM OF PRODUCTION.

(a) A party requesting production of electronically stored information may specify the form in which each type of electronically stored information is to be produced.

(b) If a party responding to a request for production of electronically stored information objects to a specified form for producing the information, or if a form is not specified in the request, the responding party shall state in its response the form in which it intends to produce each type of the information.

(c) Unless the parties otherwise agree or the court otherwise orders:

(1) if a request for production does not specify a form for producing a type of electronically stored information, the re-

sponding party shall produce the information in a form in which it is ordinarily maintained or in a form that is reasonably usable; and

(2) a party need not produce the same electronically stored information in more than one form.

RULE 8. LIMITATIONS ON DISCOVERY.

(a) A party may object to discovery of electronically stored information from sources that the party identifies as not reasonably accessible because of undue burden or expense. In its objection the party shall identify the reason for the undue burden or expense.

(b) On motion to compel discovery or for a protective order relating to the discovery of electronically stored information, a party objecting to discovery under subsection (a) bears the burden of showing that the information is from a source that is not reasonably accessible because of undue burden or expense.

(c) The court may order discovery of electronically stored information that is from a source that is not reasonably accessible because of undue burden or expense if the party requesting discovery shows that the likely benefit of the proposed discovery outweighs the likely burden or expense, taking into account the amount in controversy, the resources of the parties, the importance of the issues, and the importance of the requested discovery in resolving the issues.

(d) If the court orders discovery of electronically stored information under subsection (c) it may set conditions for discovery of the information, including allocation of the expense of discovery.

(e) The court shall limit the frequency or extent of discovery of electronically stored information, even from a source that is reasonably accessible, if the court determines that:

(1) it is possible to obtain the information from some other source that is more convenient, less burdensome, or less expensive;

(2) the discovery sought is unreasonably cumulative or duplicative;

(3) the party seeking discovery has had ample opportunity by discovery in the proceeding to obtain the information sought; or

(4) the likely burden or expense of the proposed discovery outweighs the likely benefit, taking into account the amount in controversy, the resources of the parties, the importance of the issues, and the importance of the requested discovery in resolving the issues.

RULE 9. CLAIM OF PRIVILEGE OR PROTECTION AFTER PRODUCTION.

(a) If electronically stored information produced in discovery is subject to a claim of privilege or of protection as trial-preparation material, the party making the claim may notify any party that received the information of the claim and the basis for the claim.

(b) After being notified of a claim of privilege or of protection under subsection (a), a party shall immediately sequester the specified information and any copies it has and:

(1) return or destroy the information and all copies and not use or disclose the information until the claim is resolved; or

(2) present the information to the court under seal for a determination of the claim and not otherwise use or disclose the information until the claim is resolved.

(c) If a party that received notice under subsection (b) disclosed the information subject to the notice before being notified, the party shall take reasonable steps to retrieve the information.

RULE 10. SUBPOENA FOR PRODUCTION.

(a) A subpoena in a civil proceeding may require that electronically stored information be produced and that the party serving the subpoena or a person acting on the party's request be permitted to inspect, copy, test, or sample the information.

(b) Subject to subsections (c) and (d), Rules 7, 8, and 9 apply to a person responding to a subpoena under subsection (a) as if that person were a party.

(c) A party serving a subpoena requiring production of electronically stored information shall take reasonable steps to avoid imposing undue burden or expense on a person subject to the subpoena.

(d) An order of the court requiring compliance with a subpoena issued under this rule must provide protection to a person that is not a party from undue burden or expense resulting from compliance.

Appendix III

Guidelines for State Trial Courts Regarding Discovery of Electronically-Stored Information

■ ■ ■

CONFERENCE OF CHIEF JUSTICES

Guidelines For
State Trial Courts Regarding Discovery
Of Electronically-Stored Information

Approved August 2006

Richard Van Duizend, Reporter

Table Of Contents

Introduction[1]

Overview of Electronic Discovery

Most documents today are in digital form. "Electronic (or digital) documents" refers to any information created, stored, or best utilized with computer technology of any sort, including business applications, such as word processing, databases, and spreadsheets; Internet applications, such as e-mail and the World Wide Web; devices attached to or peripheral to computers, such as printers, fax machines, pagers; web-enabled portable devices and cell phones; and media used to store computer data, such as disks, tapes, removable drives, CDs, and the like.

There are significant differences, however, between conventional documents and electronic documents—differences in degree, kind, and costs.

Differences in degree. The volume, number of locations, and data volatility of electronic documents are significantly greater than those of conventional documents.

> A floppy disk, with 1.44 megabytes, is the equivalent of 720 typewritten pages of plain text. A CD-ROM, with 650 megabytes, can hold up to 325,000 typewritten pages. One gigabyte is the equivalent of 500,000 typewritten pages. Large corporate computer networks create backup data measured in terabytes, or 1,000,000 megabytes: each terabyte represents the equivalent of 500 [m]illion typewritten pages of plain text.[2]

One paper document originating from a corporate computer network and shared with other employees who commented on it may result in well over 1,000 copies or versions of that document in the system. A company with 100 employees sending or receiving the industry average 25 e-mail messages a day produces 625,000 e-mail messages a year, generally unorganized and full of potentially embarrassing or inappropriate comments. Document search locations not only include computer hard drives, but also network servers, backup tapes, e-mail servers; outside computers, servers, and back up tapes; laptop and home computers; and personal digital assistants or other portable devices. Electronic documents are easily damaged or altered – e.g., by simply opening the file. Computer systems automatically recycle and reuse memory space, overwrite backups, change file locations, and otherwise maintain themselves automatically—with the effect of altering or destroying computer data without any human intent, intervention, or even knowledge. And, every electronic document can look like an original.

---

[1]   Much of the material in this introduction is condensed directly from a presentation on electronic discovery by Ken Withers, former Senior Judicial Education Attorney at the Federal Judicial Center, to the National Workshop for United States Magistrate Judges on June 12, 2002.

[2]   Committee on Rules of Practice and Procedures of the Judicial Conference of the United States, *Report of the Civil Rules Advisory Committee*, p.3 (Washington, DC: August 3, 2004).

Conference Of Chief Justices Working Group On Electronic Discovery

Differences in kind. One difference in kind between digital discovery and conventional paper discovery is that digital transactions (creation of an electronic airline ticket, for example) often create no permanent document in electronic or any other form. There are only integrated databases containing bits and pieces of millions of transactions. After a customer has printed out an e-ticket and moved to a different screen, the e-ticket "disappears." In addition, unlike conventional documents, electronic documents contain non-traditional types of data including metadata, system data, and "deleted" data. Metadata refers to the information embedded in an electronic file about that file, such as the date of creation, author, source, history, etc. System data refers to computer records regarding the computer's use, such as when a user logged on or off, the websites visited, passwords used, and documents printed or faxed. "Deleted" data is not really deleted at all. The computer has merely been told to ignore the "deleted" information and that the physical space that the data takes up on the hard drive is available for overwriting when the space is needed. The possibility that a deleted file can be restored or retrieved presents a temptation to engage in electronic discovery on a much broader scale than is usually contemplated in conventional paper discovery.

Differences in costs. Cost differences are often thought to include differences in the allocation of costs as well as the amount of costs. In conventional "big document" cases, for example, when responding parties simply make boxes of documents available for the requesting party to review, the costs of searching through the boxes typically fall on the requesting parties. On the other hand, the cost to the responding parties of locating, reviewing, and preparing vast digital files for production is perceived to be much greater than in conventional discovery proceedings. One reported case, for example, involved the restoration of 93 backup tapes. The process was estimated to cost $6.2 million before attorney review of the resulting files for relevance or privilege objections. Complete restoration of 200 backup tapes of one of the defendants in another prominent reported decision was estimated to cost $9.75 million, while restoration of eight randomly selected tapes to see if any relevant evidence appeared on them, could be done for $400,000.

The high costs of electronic discovery frequently include the costs of experts. Systems experts know the computers, software, and files at issue in the case. Outside experts are often brought in to conduct electronic discovery. Their role is to take the data collections, convert them into indexed and reviewable files, and ready them for production. Forensic examiners, the most expensive of all, may be brought in to search for deleted documents, missing e-mail, and system data.

On the other hand, electronic discovery can also greatly reduce the costs of discovery and facilitate the pretrial preparation process. When properly managed, electronic discovery allows a party to organize, identify, index, and even authenticate documents in a fraction of the time and at a fraction of the cost of paper discovery while virtually eliminating costs of copying and transport.

Purpose and Role of the Guidelines

Until recently, electronic discovery disputes have not been a standard feature of state court litigation in most jurisdictions. However, because of the near universal reliance on electronic records both by businesses and individuals, the frequency with which electronic discovery-related ques-

Guidelines For State Trial Courts Regarding Discovery Of Electronically-Stored Information

tions arise in state courts is increasing rapidly, in all manner of cases. Uncertainty about how to address the differences between electronic and traditional discovery under current discovery rules and standards "exacerbates the problems. Case law is emerging, but it is not consistent and discovery disputes are rarely the subject of appellate review."[3]

Accordingly, the Conference of Chief Justices established a Working Group at its 2004 Annual Meeting to develop a reference document to assist state courts in considering issues related to electronic discovery. The initial draft of the first four Guidelines was sent to each state's chief justice in March, 2005. A Review Draft was circulated for comment in October 2005 to each Chief Justice and to a wide array of lawyer organizations and e-discovery experts. Seventeen sets of comments were received[4] and were reviewed by the Working Group in preparing the March 2006 version of the Guidelines. The Working Group wishes to express its deep appreciation to all those who took the time to share their experience, insights, and concerns.

These Guidelines are intended to help reduce this uncertainty in state court litigation by assisting trial judges faced by a dispute over e-discovery in identifying the issues and determining the decision-making factors to be applied. The Guidelines should not be treated as model rules that can simply be plugged into a state's procedural scheme. They have been crafted only to offer guidance to those faced with addressing the practical problems that the digital age has created and should be considered along with the other resources cited in the attached bibliography including the newly revised provisions on discovery in the Federal Rules of Civil Procedure[5] and the most recent edition of the American Bar Association Standards Relating to Discovery.[6]

---

[3]   *Id.* at 3.

[4]   From: The American College of Trial Lawyers (ACTL); The Association of Trial Lawyers of America (ATLA); Courtney Ingraffia Barton, Esq., LexisNexis® Applied Discovery; Gary M. Berne, Esq., Stoll Stoll Berne Lokting & Shlachter PC, Portland, OR; Richard C. Broussard, Esq., Broussard & David, Lafayette, LA; David Dukes, Esq., President, The Defense Research Institute (DRI); Walter L. Floyd, Esq., The Floyd Law Firm, PC, St. Louis, MO; Thomas A. Gottschalk, Executive Vice President – Law & Public Policy and General Counsel, General Motors; Robert T. Hall, Esq., Hall, Sickells, Frei and Kattenberg, PC Reston, VA; Justice Nathan L. Hecht, Supreme Court of Texas; Andrea Morano Quercia, Eastman Kodak Company; Prof. Glenn Koppel, Western State University Law School; Michelle C. S. Lange, Esq., & Charity J. Delich, Kroll Ontrack Inc.; Lawyers for Civil Justice (LCJ), U.S. Chamber Institute for Legal Reform, DRI, the Federation of Defense and Corporate Counsel, & the International Association of Defense Counsel; Charles W. Matthews, Vice President and General Counsel, Exxon Mobil; Harry Ng, American Petroleum Institute; Clifford A. Rieders, Esq., Riders, Travis, Humphrey, Harris, Waters & Waffenschmidt, Williamsport, PA.

[5]   The revised rules were approved by the United States Supreme Court on April 12, 2006, and will take effect on December 1, 2006, unless Congress enacts legislation to reject, modify, or defer the amendments."

[6]   American Bar Association Standards Relating to Civil Discovery, (Chicago, IL: August 2004).

Preface

Recognizing that:

- there are significant differences in the discovery of conventional paper documents and electronically stored information in terms of volume, volatility, and cost;

- until recently, electronic discovery disputes have not been a standard feature of state court litigation in most jurisdictions;

- the frequency with which electronic discovery-related questions arise in state courts is increasing rapidly, because of the near universal reliance on electronic records both by businesses and individuals; and

- uncertainty about how to address the differences between discovery of conventional and electronically-stored information under current discovery rules and standards exacerbates the length and costs of litigation; and

- discovery disputes are rarely the subject of appellate review;

the Conference of Chief Justices (CCJ) established a Working Group at its 2004 Annual Meeting to develop a reference document to assist state courts in considering issues related to electronic discovery.

A review draft of proposed Guidelines was widely circulated for comment in October, 2005. Many sets of thorough and thoughtful comments were received and discussed by the Working Group in preparing a final draft for consideration by the members of CCJ at its 2006 Annual Meeting. At its business meeting on August 2, 2006, CCJ approved the *Guidelines for State Trial Courts Regarding Discovery of Electronically-Stored Information* as a reference tool for state trial court judges faced by a dispute over e-discovery.

These *Guidelines* are intended to help in identifying the issues and determining the decision-making factors to be applied in the circumstances presented in a specific case. They should not be treated as model rules or universally applicable standards. They have been crafted only to offer guidance to those faced with addressing the practical problems that the digital age has created. The Conference of Chief Justices recognizes that the *Guidelines* will become part of the continuing dialogue concerning how best to ensure the fair, efficient, and effective administration of justice as technology changes. They should be considered along with the other resources such as the newly revised provisions on discovery in the Federal Rules of Civil Procedure and the most recent edition of the American Bar Association Standards Relating to Discovery. Although the *Guidelines* acknowledge the benefits of uniformity and are largely consistent with the revised Federal Rules, they also recognize that the final determination of what procedural and

Conference Of Chief Justices Working Group On Electronic Discovery

evidentiary rules should govern questions in state court proceedings (such as when inadvertent disclosures waive the attorney-client privilege) are the responsibility of each state, based upon its legal tradition, experience, and process.

The *Guidelines* are being sent you to because of your interest in the civil justice process generally and electronic discovery issues in particular. Additional copies can be downloaded from the National Center for State Courts' website – www.ncsconline.org.

Conference of Chief Justices

Guidelines For State Trial Courts Regarding Discovery Of Electronically-Stored Information

1. Definitions

A. Electronically-stored information is any information created, stored, or best utilized with computer technology of any type. It includes but is not limited to data; word-processing documents; spreadsheets; presentation documents; graphics; animations; images; e-mail and instant messages (including attachments); audio, video, and audiovisual recordings; voicemail stored on databases; networks; computers and computer systems; servers; archives; back-up or disaster recovery systems; discs, CD's, diskettes, drives, tapes, cartridges and other storage media; printers; the Internet; personal digital assistants; handheld wireless devices; cellular telephones; pagers; fax machines; and voicemail systems.

B. Accessible information is electronically-stored information that is easily retrievable in the ordinary course of business without undue cost and burden.

COMMENT: The definition of electronically-stored information is based on newly revised section 29 of the American Bar Association *Standards Relating to Civil Discovery* (August 2004). It is intended to include both on-screen information and system data and metadata that may not be readily viewable. The list included in the Guideline should be considered as illustrative rather than limiting, given the rapid changes in formats, media, devices, and systems.

The definition of accessible information is drawn pending Federal Rule 26(b)(2)(B) (2006). *See also Zubulake v. UBS Warburg LLC*, 217 F.R.D. 390 (S.D.N.Y. 2003) (*Zubulake* III). What constitutes an undue cost or burden will need to be determined on a case by case basis. However, examples of information that may not be reasonably accessible in all instances include data stored on back-up tapes or legacy systems; material that has been deleted; and residual data.

2. Responsibility Of Counsel To Be Informed About Client's Electronically-Stored Information

In any case in which an issue regarding the discovery of electronically-stored information is raised or is likely to be raised, a judge should, when appropriate, encourage counsel to become familiar with the operation of the party's relevant information management systems, including how information is stored and retrieved. If a party intends to seek the production of electronically-stored information in a specific case, that fact should be communicated to opposing counsel as soon as possible and the categories or types of information to be sought should be clearly identified.

COMMENT: This provision is drawn from the Electronic Discovery Guidelines issued by the U.S. District Court for the District of Kansas (para. 1) and is consistent with other rules and proposed rules that place a responsibility on counsel, when appropriate and reasonable, to learn about their client's data storage and management systems and policies at the earliest stages of litigation in order to facilitate the smooth operation of the discovery process. [See e.g., pending Federal Rules of Civil Procedure 26(f) (2006)]. While the manner in which this encouragement should be given will, of necessity, depend on the procedures and practices of a particular jurisdiction and the needs of the case before the court, the court should establish the expectation early that counsel must be well informed about their clients' electronic records. Voluntary resolution of issues involving electronically-stored information by counsel for the parties should be encouraged. Such agreements can be facilitated if the party seeking discovery clearly indicates the categories of information to be sought so that counsel for the producing party may confer with its clients about the sources of such information and render advice regarding preservation obligations.

3. Agreements By Counsel; Pre-Conference Orders

A.   In any case in which an issue regarding the discovery of electronically-stored information is raised or is likely to be raised, a judge should encourage counsel to meet and confer in order to voluntarily come to agreement on the electronically-stored information to be disclosed, the manner of its disclosure, and a schedule that will enable discovery to be completed within the time period specified by [the Rules of Procedure or the scheduling order].

B.   In any case in which an issue regarding the discovery of electronically-stored information is raised or is likely to be raised, and in which counsel have not reached agreement regarding the following matters, a judge should direct counsel to exchange information that will enable the discovery process to move forward expeditiously. The list of information subject to discovery should be tailored to the case at issue. Among the items that a judge should consider are:

(1)   A list of the person(s) most knowledgeable about the relevant computer system(s) or network(s), the storage and retrieval of electronically-stored information, and the backup, archiving, retention, and routine destruction of electronically stored information, together with pertinent contact information and a brief description of each person's responsibilities;

(2)   A list of the most likely custodian(s), other than the party, of relevant electronic data, together with pertinent contact information, a brief description of each custodian's responsibilities, and a description of the electronically-stored information in each custodian's possession, custody, or control;

(3)   A list of each electronic system that may contain relevant electronically-stored information and each potentially relevant electronic system that was operating during the time periods relevant to the matters in dispute, together with a general description of each system;

Guidelines For State Trial Courts Regarding Discovery Of Electronically-Stored Information

(4) An indication whether relevant electronically-stored information may be of limited accessibility or duration of existence (e.g., because they are stored on media, systems, or formats no longer in use, because it is subject to destruction in the routine course of business, or because retrieval may be very costly);

(5) A list of relevant electronically-stored information that has been stored off-site or off-system;

(6) A description of any efforts undertaken, to date, to preserve relevant electronically-stored information, including any suspension of regular document destruction, removal of computer media with relevant information from its operational environment and placing it in secure storage for access during litigation, or the making of forensic image back-ups of such computer media;

(7) The form of production preferred by the party; and

(8) Notice of any known problems reasonably anticipated to arise in connection with compliance with e-discovery requests, including any limitations on search efforts considered to be burdensome or oppressive or unreasonably expensive, the need for any shifting or allocation of costs, the identification of potentially relevant data that is likely to be destroyed or altered in the normal course of operations or pursuant to the party's document retention policy.

COMMENT: This Guideline combines the approaches of the pending Federal Rules of Procedure 26(f)(3) (2006) and the rule proposed by Richard Best that relies heavily on the Default Standard for Discovery of Electronic Documents promulgated by the U.S. District Court for the District of Delaware. The Guideline expresses a clear preference for counsel to reach an agreement on these matters. Because not all states follow the three-step process contemplated by the Federal Rules[7] or require initial party conferences, paragraph 3(A) recommends that trial judges "encourage" counsel to meet in any case in which e-discovery is or is likely to be an issue.

When counsel fail to reach an agreement, the Guideline recommends that judges issue an order requiring the exchange of the basic informational foundation that will assist in tailoring e-discovery requests and moving the discovery process forward. While not all of these items may be needed in every case, the list provides the elements from which a state judge can select to craft an appropriate order.

In order to address concerns regarding the Delaware Default Order expressed by defense counsel, the Guideline inserts a standard of relevance.[8] For example, unlike the proposed California rule and the Delaware Default Standard, it requires a list of only those electronic systems

---

[7]   Step 1: Counsel exchange basic information and become familiar with their client's information systems; Step 2: Counsel confer to attempt to resolve key discovery issues and develop a discovery plan; and Step 3: A hearing and order to memorialize the plan and determine unsettled issues.

[8]   Relevance in this context refers to a state's standard of relevance for discovery purposes, not the standard used to determine admissibility at trial.

on which relevant electronically-stored information may be stored or that were operating during the time periods relevant to the matters in dispute, rather than the broader "each relevant electronic system that has been in place at all relevant times." It is hoped that in this way, the burden on the responding party may be reduced by being able to focus solely on the systems housing the actual electronically-stored information or data that is or will be requested. Of course, the best way of limiting the burden is for counsel to agree in advance, thus obviating the need to issue a pre-conference order.

Subparagraph 2(B)(3) suggests that the parties be required to provide a general description of each electronic system that may contain relevant electronically-stored information. Ordinarily, such descriptions should include the hardware and software used by each system, and the scope, character, organization, and formats each system employs.

Subparagraph 2(B)(7) of the Guideline includes one issue not covered in the proposed California rule or Delaware Default Standard -- the form of production preferred by the party. [See the pending *Federal Rules of Civil Procedure* 26(f)(3) (2006).] Including an exchange of the format preferences early will help to reduce subsequent disputes over this thorny issue.

4. *Initial Discovery Hearing Or Conference*

Following the exchange of the information specified in Guideline 3, or a specially set hearing, or a mandatory conference early in the discovery period, a judge should inquire whether counsel have reached agreement on any of the following matters and address any disputes regarding these or other electronic discovery issues:

A.   The electronically-stored information to be exchanged including information that is not readily accessible;

B.   The form of production;

C.   The steps the parties will take to segregate and preserve relevant electronically stored information;

D.   The procedures to be used if privileged electronically-stored information is inadvertently disclosed; and

E.   The allocation of costs.

COMMENT: This Guideline is derived from Electronic Discovery Guidelines issued by the U.S. District Court for the District of Kansas. It addresses the next stage of the process, and lists for the trial judge some of the key issues regarding electronic discovery that the judge may be called upon to address. The intent is to identify early the discovery issues that are in dispute so that they can be addressed promptly.

5. *The Scope Of Electronic Discovery*

In deciding a motion to protect electronically-stored information or to compel discovery of such information, a judge should first determine whether the material sought is subject to production under the applicable standard for discovery. If the requested information is subject to production, a judge should then weigh the benefits to the requesting party against the burden and expense of the discovery for the responding party, considering such factors as:

A.   The ease of accessing the requested information;

B.   The total cost of production compared to the amount in controversy;

C.   The materiality of the information to the requesting party;

D.   The availability of the information from other sources;

E.   The complexity of the case and the importance of the issues addressed;

F.   The need to protect privileged, proprietary, or confidential information, including trade secrets;

G.   Whether the information or software needed to access the requested information is proprietary or constitutes confidential business information;

H.   The breadth of the request, including whether a subset (e.g., by date, author, recipient, or through use of a key-term search or other selection criteria) or representative sample of the contested electronically stored information can be provided initially to determine whether production of additional such information is warranted;

I.   The relative ability of each party to control costs and its incentive to do so;

J.   The resources of each party compared to the total cost of production;

K.   Whether the requesting party has offered to pay some or all of the costs of identifying, reviewing, and producing the information;

L.   Whether the electronically-stored information is stored in a way that makes it more costly or burdensome to access than is reasonably warranted by legitimate personal, business, or other non-litigation-related reasons; and

M.   Whether the responding party has deleted, discarded, or erased electronic information after litigation was commenced or after the responding party was aware that litigation was probable.

Conference Of Chief Justices Working Group On Electronic Discovery

COMMENT: This Guideline recommends that when a request to discover electronically-stored information is contested, judges should first assess whether the information being sought is subject to discovery under the applicable state code, rules, and decisions (e.g., whether the material sought is relevant to the claims and defenses of the party, or relevant to the subject matter under dispute, or could lead to admissible evidence). Once this question has been answered, the Guideline suggests that judges balance the benefits and burdens of requiring discovery, offering a set of factors to consider derived from the revised American Bar Association *Standards Relating to Civil Discovery*, Standard 29.b.iv. (August 2004). In so doing, it sets out a framework for decision-making rather than specific presumptions regarding "reasonably accessible" vs. "not reasonably accessible" data; active data vs. "deleted" information; information visible on-screen vs. meta-data; or forensic vs. standard data collection. *But see e.g.*, Pending Federal Rule of Civil Procedure 26(b)(2)(2006); The Sedona Conference Working Group on Best Practices for Electronic Document Retention and Production, *The Sedona Principles*, Principles 8, 9, and 12 (Silver Spring, MD: The Sedona Conference 2004). It is unlikely that all of the factors will apply in a particular case, though the first six will arise in most disputes over the scope of electronically stored information. *See e.g.*, *Public Relations Society of America, Inc. v. Road Runner High Speed Online*, 2005 WL 1330514 (N.Y. May 27, 2005).

Depending on the circumstances and the decision regarding the scope of discovery, the judge may wish to consider shifting some or all of the costs of production and review in accordance with the factors cited in Guideline 7, *infra*.

6. *Form Of Production*

In the absence of agreement among the parties, a judge should ordinarily require electronically-stored information to be produced in no more than one format and should select the form of production in which the information is ordinarily maintained or in a form that is reasonably usable.

COMMENT: In conventional discovery, the form of production was seldom disputed. In electronic discovery, there are many choices besides paper. While a party could produce hard-copy printouts of all electronic files, doing so would likely hide metadata, embedded edits, and other non-screen information. It also would be voluminous and cumbersome to store, and costly to produce and search. On the other hand, producing all data in "native format" (i.e. streams of electrons on disks or tapes exactly as they might be found on the producing party's computer) would provide all the "hidden" data and be more easily stored, but would be just as difficult to search without the word-processing, e-mail, or database software needed to organize and present the information in a coherent form.

This Guideline is based on pending Federal Rule of Civil Procedure 34(b)(ii) and (iii) (2006). It recommends that parties should not be required to produce electronically-stored information in multiple formats absent a good reason for doing so. See also comment 12.c of *The Sedona Principles*. [The Sedona Conference Working Group on Best Practices for Electronic Document Retention and Production, *The Sedona Principles* (Silver Spring, MD: The Sedona Conference 2004).] Requests for multiple formats should be subject to the same cost-benefit analysis as suggested in Guideline 5.

The Guideline, like the pending Federal Rule, suggests rendition in the form in which the information is ordinarily maintained or in another form that is reasonably useable. The Guideline, thus, assumes that the information's standard format is reasonably usable or it would be of no benefit to the party who has produced it, but allows substitution of another format that may still be helpful to the requesting party. Whether the production of metadata and other forms of hidden information, are discoverable should be determined based upon the particular circumstances of the case.

7. *Reallocation of Discovery Costs*

Ordinarily, the shifting of the costs of discovery to the requesting party or the sharing of those costs between the requesting and responding party should be considered only when the electronically-stored information sought is not accessible information and when restoration and production of responsive electronically-stored information from a small sample of the requested electronically-stored information would not be sufficient. When these conditions are present, the judge should consider the following factors in determining whether any or all discovery costs should be borne by the requesting party:

A. The extent to which the request is specifically tailored to discover relevant information;

B. The availability of such information from other sources;

C. The total cost of production compared to the amount in controversy;

D. The total cost of production compared to the resources available to each party;

E. The relative ability of each party to control costs and its incentive to do so;

F. The importance of the issues at stake in the litigation; and

G. The relative benefits of obtaining the information.

COMMENT: This Guideline reflects the analysis conducted in *Zubulake v. UBS Warburg LLC, 216 F.R.D. 280 (S.D.N.Y. 2003)(Zubulake* III), the leading federal case on the issue. The Court in *Zubulake* established a three-tiered test for determining when it is appropriate to require a requesting party to pay or contribute to the cost of producing discoverable material. The first tier is a determination of whether the electronically-stored information is accessible. The second tier is a determination that a less-costly method of obtaining the needed information such as restoration of a representative sample of the tapes, disks, or other storage media would not be feasible. The final step is a cost-benefit analysis similar to that recommended in Guideline 5 for determining the appropriate scope of discovery.

The *Zubulake* litigation involved a sex discrimination complaint in which the plaintiff requested e-mail messages beyond the approximately 100 pages produced by the defendants.

Conference Of Chief Justices Working Group On Electronic Discovery

> "She presented substantial evidence that more responsive e-mail existed, most likely on backup tapes and optical storage media created and maintained to meet SEC records retention requirements. The defendants objected to producing e-mail from these sources, which they estimated would cost $175,000 exclusive of attorney review time." Withers, K.J., *Annotated Case Law and Further Reading on Electronic Discovery* 17 (June 16, 2004).

The Court found the requested material to be relevant and ordered restoration of 5 of the total of 77 back-up tapes at a cost of approximately $19,000. After determining that 600 of the restored messages were responsive to the plaintiff's discovery request, the Court ordered restoration of the remaining tapes at an estimated cost of $165,954.67 for restoration and another $107,695 for review, requiring the plaintiff to bear 25% and the defendants 75% of the costs of restoration and the defendants to pay 100% of the costs of reviewing the material for privileged information. *Id.*, 30.

Like Zubulake, the Guideline treats cost-shifting as a matter for the judge's discretion. (*But see* Texas Rule of Civil Procedure 196.4 which requires that whenever a court orders a responding party to produce information that is not 'reasonably available," the court must require the requesting party to pay "the reasonable expenses of any extraordinary steps required to retrieve and produce the information.") It anticipates that the proposed cost/benefit analysis will both encourage requesting parties to carefully assess whether all the information sought is worth paying for, while discouraging the producing party from storing the information in such a way as to make it extraordinarily costly to retrieve.

8. *Inadvertent Disclosure of Privileged Information*

In determining whether a party has waived the attorney-client privilege because of an inadvertent disclosure of attorney work-product or other privileged electronically stored information, a judge should consider:

A.   The total volume of information produced by the responding party;

B.   The amount of privileged information disclosed;

C.   The reasonableness of the precautions taken to prevent inadvertent disclosure of privileged information;

D.   The promptness of the actions taken to notify the receiving party and otherwise remedy the error; and

E.   The reasonable expectations and agreements of counsel.

COMMENT: Inadvertent disclosure of privileged information is sometimes unavoidable because of the large amounts of information that are often involved in electronic discovery, and the time and cost required to screen this voluminous material for attorney work product and other privileged materials. As indicated in Guideline 4, the best practice is for the parties to agree on the process to use if privileged information is inadvertently disclosed and that such a disclosure shall not be considered a waiver of attorney-client privilege. While "claw-back" or "quick peek" agreements[9] are not perfect protections against use of privileged information by third parties not subject to the agreement or by the receiving party in another jurisdiction, they do allow the litigation to move forward and offer significant protection in many cases, especially when coupled with a court order recognizing the agreement and declaring that inadvertent production of privileged information does not create an express or implied waiver. [*See* The Sedona Conference Working Group on Best Practices for Electronic Document Retention and Production, *The Sedona Principles*, Comment 10.d (Silver Spring, MD: The Sedona Conference 2004); and Report of the Judicial Conference Committee on Practice and Procedure, pp 33-34 (September 2005).]

This Guideline applies when the parties have not reached an agreement regarding the inadvertent disclosure of electronically stored information subject to the attorney-client privilege. The first four factors are based on *Alldread v. City of Grenada*, 988 F.2d, 1425, 1433, 1434 (5th Cir. 1993). [*See also United States v. Rigas*, 281 F. Supp. 2d 733 (S.D.N.Y. 2003). The fifth factor listed by the Court in *Alldread* – "the overriding issue of fairness" – is omitted, since the four factors listed help to define what is fair in the circumstances surrounding a disclosure in a particular case, but the reasonable expectations and agreements of counsel has been added to reinforce the importance of attorneys discussing and reaching at least an informal understanding on how to handle inadvertent disclosures of privileged information.

Unlike Texas Rule of Civil Procedure 193.3(d) and the most recent revisions to Federal Rule of Civil Procedure 26(b)(5)(B), the Guideline does not create a presumption against a waiver when, within 10 days after discovering that privileged material has been disclosed, "the producing party amends the response, identifying the material or information produced and stating the privilege asserted." While the Texas rule has apparently worked well, creation of a presumption is a matter for state rules committees or legislatures and goes beyond the scope of these Guidelines.

9. *Preservation Orders*

A. When an order to preserve electronically-stored information is sought, a judge should require a threshold showing that the continuing existence and integrity of the information is threatened. Following such a showing, the judge should consider the following factors in determining the nature and scope of any order:

(1) The nature of the threat to the continuing existence or integrity of the electronically-stored information;

(2) The potential for irreparable harm to the requesting party absent a preservation order;

---

[9]   Claw-back agreements are a formal understanding between the parties that production of privileged information is presumed to be inadvertent and does not waive the privilege and the receiving party must return the privileged material until the question is resolved. Under "quick peek" agreements, counsel are allowed to see each other's entire data collection before production and designate those items which they believe are responsive to the discovery requests. The producing party then reviews the presumably much smaller universe of files for privilege, and produces those that are responsive and not privileged, along with a privilege log. K.J., Withers, "Discovery Disputes: Decisional Guidance," 3 Civil Action No. 2, 4,5 (2004).

(3) The capability of the responding party to maintain the information sought in its original form, condition, and content; and

(4) The physical, technological, and financial burdens created by ordering preservation of the information.

B. When issuing an order to preserve electronically stored information, a judge should carefully tailor the order so that it is no broader than necessary to safeguard the information in question.

COMMENT: One consequence of the expansion in the volume of electronically-stored information resulting from the use of computer systems, is the reliance on automated data retention programs and protocols that result in the periodic destruction of defined types of files, data, and back-up tapes. These programs and protocols are essential for smooth operation, effectively managing record storage, and controlling costs. The factors for determining when to issue a preservation order apply after existence of a threat to the sought information has been demonstrated. They are drawn from the decision in *Capricorn Power Co. v. Siemens Westinghouse Power Corp.*, 220 F.R.D. 429 (W.D. Pa. 2004). They require balancing the danger to the electronically stored information against its materiality, the ability to maintain it, and the costs and burdens of doing so.

Because electronically-stored information, files, and records are seldom created and stored with future litigation in mind, they cannot always be easily segregated. An order directing a business to "halt all operations that can result in the destruction or alteration of computer data, including e-mail, word-processing, databases, and financial information . . . can effectively unplug a computer network and put a computer dependent company out of business." K.J. Withers, "Electronic Discovery Disputes: Decisional Guidance," 3 *Civil Action* No. 2, p.4 (NCSC 2004). Thus, the Guideline urges that when a preservation order is called for, it should be drawn as narrowly as possible to accomplish its purpose so as to limit the impact on the responding party's operations.

10. *Sanctions*

Absent exceptional circumstances, a judge should impose sanctions because of the destruction of electronically-stored information only if:

A. There was a legal obligation to preserve the information at the time it was destroyed;

B. The destruction of the material was not the result of the routine, good faith operation of an electronic information system; and

C. The destroyed information was subject to production under the applicable state standard for discovery.

COMMENT: This Guideline closely tracks pending Federal Rule of Civil Procedure 37(f) (2006), but provides greater guidance to courts and litigants without setting forth the stringent standards suggested in the *Sedona Principles* ["a clear duty to preserve," "intentional or reckless failure to preserve and produce," and a "reasonable probability" of material prejudice]. [The Sedona Conference Working Group on Best Practices for Electronic Document Retention and Production, *The Sedona Principles*, Principle 14 (Silver Spring, MD: The Sedona Conference 2004).]

Selected Bibliography On Discovery Of Electronically-Stored Information

RULES AND STANDARDS[10]

ABA Section of Litigation. *ABA Civil Discovery Standards*. Revised August 2004.

Ad Hoc Committee for Electronic Discovery of the U.S. District Court for the District of Delaware. *Default Standard for Discovery of Electronic Documents "E-Discovery"* (May 2004).

Committee on Rules of Practice and Procedures of the Judicial Conference of the United States. Report (September 2005).

District of Delaware. *Default Standard for Discovery of Electronic Documents* (May 2004).

U.S. District Court for the District of Kansas. *Electronic Discovery Guidelines* (March 2004).

Local and Civil Rules of the U.S. District Court for the District of New Jersey, R. 26.1(d), Discovery of Digital Information Including Computer-Based Information.

Mississippi Rules of Civil Procedure, Rule 26(b)(5), 2003.

Sedona Conference Working Group on Best Practices for Electronic Document Retention and Production. *The Sedona Principles: Best Practices Recommendations and Principles for Addressing Electronic Document Production*. Sedona, AZ: Sedona Conference Working Group Series, January 2004. Updated version.

Texas Rules of Civil Procedure. 193.3(d) and 196.4 (1999).

ARTICLES

Allman, Thomas Y. "A Proposed Model for State Rules re: Electronic Discovery." National Center for State Courts, November 15, 2001.

Best, Richard E. "Taming the Discovery Monster." *California Litigation: The Journal of the Litigation Section, State Bar of California* (November, 2005).

Best, Richard E. "E-Discovery Basics." *California Litigation: The Journal of the Litigation Section, State Bar of California* (August 2005).

Best, Richard E. "The Need for Electronic Discovery Rules." *Modern Practice* (August 2002).

---

[10]   The following additional federal jurisdictions have codified the practice of electronic discovery: Eastern and Western Districts of Arkansas [Rule 26.1(4) (2000)]; Middle District of Pennsylvania [Rule 26.1 (2005)]; Wyoming [Rule 26.1(d)(3)(B).

Conference Of Chief Justices Working Group On Electronic Discovery

Bobelian, Michael. "N.Y. Judge Charts a Course on Electronic Discovery; Finding No Exact Precedent, Nassau Justice Applies Rule that Requesting Side Pays." *New York Law Journal* (August 24, 2004).

Carroll, John L. and Withers, Kenneth J. Observations on "The Sedona Principles," 2003 (www.kenwithers.com).

Hedges, Ronald J. Discovery of Digital Information, 2004 (www.kenwithers.com).

Johnson, Molly Treadway, Kenneth J. Withers, and Meghan A. Dunn, "A Qualitative Study of Issues Raised by the Discovery of Computer-Based Information in Civil Litigation." Submitted to the Judicial Conference Advisory Committee on Civil Rules for its October 2002 meeting, Federal Judicial Center, Washington, D.C., September 13, 2002 (www.kenwithers.com).

Joseph, Gregory P. "Electronic Discovery Standards". November 2003 (www.kenwithers.com).

Joseph, Gregory P. "Electronic Discovery." *National Law Journal* (October 4, 2004): 12.

Redgrave, Jonathan M., and Erica J. Bachmann. "Ripples on the Shores of Zubulake: Practice Considerations from Recent Electronic Discovery Decisions." *Federal Lawyer* (November/December 2003): 31.

Solovy, Jerold S., and Robert L. Byman. "Cost-Shifting." *National Law Journal* (November 10, 2003): 23.

Van Duizend, Richard. "Electronic Discovery: Questions and Answers." *Civil Action* 3, no. 2 (2004): 4.

Withers, Kenneth J. "Electronic Discovery Disputes: Decisional Guidance", *Civil Action* 3 no. 2, (2004): 4.

Withers, Kenneth J. Annotated Case Law and Further Reading on Electronic Discovery, June 16, 2004 (www.kenwithers.com).

Withers, Kenneth J. "Two Tiers and a Safe Harbor: Federal Rulemakers Grapple with E-Discovery," August 23, 2004 (www.kenwithers.com).

Withers, Kenneth J. Is *Digital Different? Electronic Disclosure and Discovery in Civil Litigation.* Washington, DC: Federal Judicial Center, 2001.

THE SEDONA CONFERENCE® WORKING GROUP SERIES

THE SEDONA PRINCIPLES:
SECOND EDITION

*Best Practices Recommendations
& Principles for Addressing
Electronic Document Production*

A Project of The Sedona Conference®
Working Group on Electronic Document
Retention & Production (WG1)

JUNE 2007

The Sedona Principles for Electronic Document Production
Second Edition

1. Electronically stored information is potentially discoverable under Fed. R. Civ. P. 34 or its state equivalents. Organizations must properly preserve electronically stored information that can reasonably be anticipated to be relevant to litigation.

2. When balancing the cost, burden, and need for electronically stored information, courts and parties should apply the proportionality standard embodied in Fed. R. Civ. P. 26(b)(2)(C) and its state equivalents, which require consideration of the technological feasibility and realistic costs of preserving, retrieving, reviewing, and producing electronically stored information, as well as the nature of the litigation and the amount in controversy.

3. Parties should confer early in discovery regarding the preservation and production of electronically stored information when these matters are at issue in the litigation and seek to agree on the scope of each party's rights and responsibilities.

4. Discovery requests for electronically stored information should be as clear as possible, while responses and objections to discovery should disclose the scope and limits of the production.

5. The obligation to preserve electronically stored information requires reasonable and good faith efforts to retain information that may be relevant to pending or threatened litigation. However, it is unreasonable to expect parties to take every conceivable step to preserve all potentially relevant electronically stored information.

6. Responding parties are best situated to evaluate the procedures, methodologies, and technologies appropriate for preserving and producing their own electronically stored information.

7. The requesting party has the burden on a motion to compel to show that the responding party's steps to preserve and produce relevant electronically stored information were inadequate.

8. The primary source of electronically stored information for production should be active data and information. Resort to disaster recovery backup tapes and other sources of electronically stored information that are not reasonably accessible requires the requesting party to demonstrate need and relevance that outweigh the costs and burdens of retrieving and processing the electronically stored information from such sources, including the disruption of business and information management activities.

9. Absent a showing of special need and relevance, a responding party should not be required to preserve, review, or produce deleted, shadowed, fragmented, or residual electronically stored information.

10. A responding party should follow reasonable procedures to protect privileges and objections in connection with the production of electronically stored information.

11. A responding party may satisfy its good faith obligation to preserve and produce relevant electronically stored information by using electronic tools and processes, such as data sampling, searching, or the use of selection criteria, to identify data reasonably likely to contain relevant information.

12. Absent party agreement or court order specifying the form or forms of production, production should be made in the form or forms in which the information is ordinarily maintained or in a reasonably usable form, taking into account the need to produce reasonably accessible metadata that will enable the receiving party to have the same ability to access, search, and display the information as the producing party where appropriate or necessary in light of the nature of the information and the needs of the case.

13. Absent a specific objection, party agreement or court order, the reasonable costs of retrieving and reviewing electronically stored information should be borne by the responding party, unless the information sought is not reasonably available to the responding party in the ordinary course of business. If the information sought is not reasonably available to the responding party in the ordinary course of business, then, absent special circumstances, the costs of retrieving and reviewing such electronic information may be shared by or shifted to the requesting party.

14. Sanctions, including spoliation findings, should be considered by the court only if it finds that there was a clear duty to preserve, a culpable failure to preserve and produce relevant electronically stored information, and a reasonable probability that the loss of the evidence has materially prejudiced the adverse party.

APPENDIX V

FEDERAL RULES OF EVIDENCE

■ ■ ■

ARTICLE I. GENERAL PROVISIONS

Rule 101. Scope

These rules govern proceedings in the courts of the United States and before United States bankruptcy judges and United States magistrate judges, to the extent and with the exceptions stated in rule 1101.

Rule 102. Purpose and Construction

These rules shall be construed to secure fairness in administration, elimination of unjustifiable expense and delay, and promotion of growth and development of the law of evidence to the end that the truth may be ascertained and proceedings justly determined.

Rule 103. Rulings on Evidence

(a) Effect of erroneous ruling.

Error may not be predicated upon a ruling which admits or excludes evidence unless a substantial right of the party is affected, and

(1) Objection.—In case the ruling is one admitting evidence, a timely objection or motion to strike appears of record, stating the specific ground of objection, if the specific ground was not apparent from the context; or

(2) Offer of proof.—In case the ruling is one excluding evidence, the substance of the evidence was made known to the court by offer or was apparent from the context within which questions were asked.

Once the court makes a definitive ruling on the record admitting or excluding evidence, either at or before trial, a party need not renew an objection or offer of proof to preserve a claim of error for appeal.

(b) Record of offer and ruling.

The court may add any other or further statement which shows the character of the evidence, the form in which it was offered, the objection made, and the ruling thereon. It may direct the making of an offer in question and answer form.

(c) Hearing of jury.

In jury cases, proceedings shall be conducted, to the extent practicable, so as to prevent inadmissible evidence from being suggested to the jury by any means, such as making statements or offers of proof or asking questions in the hearing of the jury.

(d) Plain error.

Nothing in this rule precludes taking notice of plain errors affecting substantial rights although they were not brought to the attention of the court.

Rule 104.　Preliminary Questions

(a) Questions of admissibility generally.

Preliminary questions concerning the qualification of a person to be a witness, the existence of a privilege, or the admissibility of evidence shall be determined by the court, subject to the provisions of subdivision (b). In making its determination it is not bound by the rules of evidence except those with respect to privileges.

(b) Relevancy conditioned on fact.

When the relevancy of evidence depends upon the fulfillment of a condition of fact, the court shall admit it upon, or subject to, the introduction of evidence sufficient to support a finding of the fulfillment of the condition.

(c) Hearing of jury.

Hearings on the admissibility of confessions shall in all cases be conducted out of the hearing of the jury. Hearings on other preliminary matters shall be so conducted when the interests of justice require, or when an accused is a witness and so requests.

(d) Testimony by accused.

The accused does not, by testifying upon a preliminary matter, become subject to cross-examination as to other issues in the case.

(e) Weight and credibility.

This rule does not limit the right of a party to introduce before the jury evidence relevant to weight or credibility.

Rule 105.　Limited Admissibility

When evidence which is admissible as to one party or for one purpose but not admissible as to another party or for another purpose is admitted, the court, upon request, shall restrict the evidence to its proper scope and instruct the jury accordingly.

Rule 106.　Remainder of or Related Writings or Recorded Statements

When a writing or recorded statement or part thereof is introduced by a party, an adverse party may require the introduction at that time of any other part or any other writing or recorded statement which ought in fairness to be considered contemporaneously with it.

ARTICLE II.   JUDICIAL NOTICE

Rule 201.   Judicial Notice of Adjudicative Facts

(a) Scope of rule.

This rule governs only judicial notice of adjudicative facts.

(b) Kinds of facts.

A judicially noticed fact must be one not subject to reasonable dispute in that it is either (1) generally known within the territorial jurisdiction of the trial court or (2) capable of accurate and ready determination by resort to sources whose accuracy cannot reasonably be questioned.

(c) When discretionary.

A court may take judicial notice, whether requested or not.

(d) When mandatory.

A court shall take judicial notice if requested by a party and supplied with the necessary information.

(e) Opportunity to be heard.

A party is entitled upon timely request to an opportunity to be heard as to the propriety of taking judicial notice and the tenor of the matter noticed. In the absence of prior notification, the request may be made after judicial notice has been taken.

(f) Time of taking notice.

Judicial notice may be taken at any stage of the proceeding.

(g) Instructing jury.

In a civil action or proceeding, the court shall instruct the jury to accept as conclusive any fact judicially noticed. In a criminal case, the court shall instruct the jury that it may, but is not required to, accept as conclusive any fact judicially noticed.

ARTICLE III.   PRESUMPTIONS IN CIVIL ACTIONS AND PROCEEDINGS

Rule 301.   Presumptions in General Civil Actions and Proceedings

In all civil actions and proceedings not otherwise provided for by Act of Congress or by these rules, a presumption imposes on the party against whom it is directed the burden of going forward with evidence to rebut or meet the presumption, but does not shift to such party the burden of proof in the sense of the risk of nonpersuasion, which remains throughout the trial upon the party on whom it was originally cast.

Rule 302.   Applicability of State Law in Civil Actions and Proceedings

In civil actions and proceedings, the effect of a presumption respecting a fact which is an element of a claim or defense as to which State law supplies the rule of decision is determined in accordance with State law.

ARTICLE IV. RELEVANCY AND ITS LIMITS

Rule 401. Definition of "Relevant Evidence"

"Relevant evidence" means evidence having any tendency to make the existence of any fact that is of consequence to the determination of the action more probable or less probable than it would be without the evidence.

Rule 402. Relevant Evidence Generally Admissible; Irrelevant Evidence Inadmissible

All relevant evidence is admissible, except as otherwise provided by the Constitution of the United States, by Act of Congress, by these rules, or by other rules prescribed by the Supreme Court pursuant to statutory authority. Evidence which is not relevant is not admissible.

Rule 403. Exclusion of Relevant Evidence on Grounds of Prejudice, Confusion, or Waste of Time

Although relevant, evidence may be excluded if its probative value is substantially outweighed by the danger of unfair prejudice, confusion of the issues, or misleading the jury, or by considerations of undue delay, waste of time, or needless presentation of cumulative evidence.

Rule 404. Character Evidence Not Admissible To Prove Conduct; Exceptions; Other Crimes

(a) Character evidence generally.

Evidence of a person's character or a trait of character is not admissible for the purpose of proving action in conformity therewith on a particular occasion, except:

(1) Character of accused—In a criminal case, evidence of a pertinent trait of character offered by an accused, or by the prosecution to rebut the same, or if evidence of a trait of character of the alleged victim of the crime is offered by an accused and admitted under Rule 404 (a)(2), evidence of the same trait of character of the accused offered by the prosecution;

(2) Character of alleged victim—In a criminal case, and subject to the limitations imposed by Rule 412, evidence of a pertinent trait of character of the alleged victim of the crime offered by an accused, or by the prosecution to rebut the same, or evidence of a character trait of peacefulness of the alleged victim offered by the prosecution in a homicide case to rebut evidence that the alleged victim was the first aggressor;

(3) Character of witness—Evidence of the character of a witness, as provided in rules 607, 608, and 609.

(b) Other crimes, wrongs, or acts.

Evidence of other crimes, wrongs, or acts is not admissible to prove the character of a person in order to show action in conformity therewith. It may, however, be admissible for other purposes, such as proof of motive, opportunity, intent, preparation, plan, knowledge, identity, or absence of mistake or accident, provided that upon request by the accused, the prosecution in a criminal case shall provide reasonable notice in advance of trial, or during trial if the court excuses pretrial notice on good cause shown, of the general nature of any such evidence it intends to introduce at trial.

Rule 405.   Methods of Proving Character

(a) Reputation or opinion.

In all cases in which evidence of character or a trait of character of a person is admissible, proof may be made by testimony as to reputation or by testimony in the form of an opinion. On cross-examination, inquiry is allowable into relevant specific instances of conduct.

(b) Specific instances of conduct.

In cases in which character or a trait of character of a person is an essential element of a charge, claim, or defense, proof may also be made of specific instances of that person's conduct.

Rule 406.   Habit; Routine Practice

Evidence of the habit of a person or of the routine practice of an organization, whether corroborated or not and regardless of the presence of eyewitnesses, is relevant to prove that the conduct of the person or organization on a particular occasion was in conformity with the habit or routine practice.

Rule 407.   Subsequent Remedial Measures

When, after an injury or harm allegedly caused by an event, measures are taken that, if taken previously, would have made the injury or harm less likely to occur, evidence of the subsequent measures is not admissible to prove negligence, culpable conduct, a defect in a product, a defect in a product's design, or a need for a warning or instruction. This rule does not require the exclusion of evidence of subsequent measures when offered for another purpose, such as proving ownership, control, or feasibility of precautionary measures, if controverted, or impeachment.

Rule 408.   Compromise and Offers to Compromise

(a) Prohibited uses.—Evidence of the following is not admissible on behalf of any party, when offered to prove liability for, invalidity of, or amount of a claim that was disputed as to validity or amount, or to impeach through a prior inconsistent statement or contradiction:

(1) furnishing or offering or promising to furnish or accepting or offering or promising to accept a valuable consideration in compromising or attempting to compromise the claim; and

(2) conduct or statements made in compromise negotiations regarding the claim, except when offered in a criminal case and the negotiations related to a claim by a public office or agency in the exercise of regulatory, investigative, or enforcement authority.

(b) Permitted uses. This rule does not require exclusion if the evidence is offered for purposes not prohibited by subdivision (a). Examples of permissible purposes include proving a witness's bias or prejudice; negating a contention of undue delay; and proving an effort to obstruct a criminal investigation or prosecution.

Rule 409.   Payment of Medical and Similar Expenses

Evidence of furnishing or offering or promising to pay medical, hospital, or similar expenses occasioned by an injury is not admissible to prove liability for the injury.

Rule 410.   Inadmissibility of Pleas, Plea Discussions, and Related Statements

Except as otherwise provided in this rule, evidence of the following is not, in any civil or criminal proceeding, admissible against the defendant who made the plea or was a participant in the plea discussions:

(1) a plea of guilty which was later withdrawn;

(2) a plea of nolo contendere;

(3) any statement made in the course of any proceedings under Rule 11 of the Federal Rules of Criminal Procedure or comparable state procedure regarding either of the foregoing pleas; or

(4) any statement made in the course of plea discussions with an attorney for the prosecuting authority which do not result in a plea of guilty or which result in a plea of guilty later withdrawn.

However, such a statement is admissible (i) in any proceeding wherein another statement made in the course of the same plea or plea discussions has been introduced and the statement ought in fairness be considered contemporaneously with it, or (ii) in a criminal proceeding for perjury or false statement if the statement was made by the defendant under oath, on the record and in the presence of counsel.

Rule 411.   Liability Insurance

Evidence that a person was or was not insured against liability is not admissible upon the issue whether the person acted negligently or otherwise wrongfully. This rule does not require the exclusion of evidence of insurance against liability when offered for another purpose, such as proof of agency, ownership, or control, or bias or prejudice of a witness.

Rule 412. Sex Offense Cases; Relevance of Alleged Victim's Past Sexual Behavior or Alleged Sexual Predisposition

(a) Evidence generally inadmissible.

The following evidence is not admissible in any civil or criminal proceeding involving alleged sexual misconduct except as provided in subdivisions (b) and (c):

(1) Evidence offered to prove that any alleged victim engaged in other sexual behavior.

(2) Evidence offered to prove any alleged victim's sexual predisposition.

(b) Exceptions.

(1) In a criminal case, the following evidence is admissible, if otherwise admissible under these rules:

(A) evidence of specific instances of sexual behavior by the alleged victim offered to prove that a person other than the accused was the source of semen, injury, or other physical evidence;

(B) evidence of specific instances of sexual behavior by the alleged victim with respect to the person accused of the sexual misconduct offered by the accused to prove consent or by the prosecution; and

(C) evidence the exclusion of which would violate the constitutional rights of the defendant.

(2) In a civil case, evidence offered to prove the sexual behavior or sexual predisposition of any alleged victim is admissible if it is otherwise admissible under these rules and its probative value substantially outweighs the danger of harm to any victim and of unfair prejudice to any party. Evidence of an alleged victim's reputation is admissible only if it has been placed in controversy by the alleged victim.

(c) Procedure to determine admissibility.

(1) A party intending to offer evidence under subdivision (b) must—

(A) file a written motion at least 14 days before trial specifically describing the evidence and stating the purpose for which it is offered unless the court, for good cause requires a different time for filing or permits filing during trial; and

(B) serve the motion on all parties and notify the alleged victim or, when appropriate, the alleged victim's guardian or representative.

(2) Before admitting evidence under this rule the court must conduct a hearing in camera and afford the victim and parties a right to attend and be heard. The motion, related papers, and the record of

the hearing must be sealed and remain under seal unless the court orders otherwise.

Rule 413.   Evidence of Similar Crimes in Sexual Assault Cases

(a) In a criminal case in which the defendant is accused of an offense of sexual assault, evidence of the defendant's commission of another offense or offenses of sexual assault is admissible, and may be considered for its bearing on any matter to which it is relevant.

(b) In a case in which the Government intends to offer evidence under this rule, the attorney for the Government shall disclose the evidence to the defendant, including statements of witnesses or a summary of the substance of any testimony that is expected to be offered, at least fifteen days before the scheduled date of trial or at such later time as the court may allow for good cause.

(c) This rule shall not be construed to limit the admission or consideration of evidence under any other rule.

(d) For purposes of this rule and Rule 415, "offense of sexual assault" means a crime under Federal law or the law of a State (as defined in section 513 of title 18, United States Code) that involved—

(1) any conduct proscribed by chapter 109A of title 18, United States Code;

(2) contact, without consent, between any part of the defendant's body or an object and the genitals or anus of another person;

(3) contact, without consent, between the genitals or anus of the defendant and any part of another person's body;

(4) deriving sexual pleasure or gratification from the infliction of death, bodily injury, or physical pain on another person; or

(5) an attempt or conspiracy to engage in conduct described in paragraphs (1)-(4).

Rule 414.   Evidence of Similar Crimes in Child Molestation Cases

(a) In a criminal case in which the defendant is accused of an offense of child molestation, evidence of the defendant's commission of another offense or offenses of child molestation is admissible, and may be considered for its bearing on any matter to which it is relevant.

(b) In a case in which the Government intends to offer evidence under this rule, the attorney for the Government shall disclose the evidence to the defendant, including statements of witnesses or a summary of the substance of any testimony that is expected to be offered, at least fifteen days before the scheduled date of trial or at such later time as the court may allow for good cause.

(c) This rule shall not be construed to limit the admission or consideration of evidence under any other rule.

(d) For purposes of this rule and Rule 415, "child" means a person below the age of fourteen, and "offense of child molestation" means a crime under Federal law or the law of a State (as defined in section 513 of title 18, United States Code) that involved—

(1) any conduct proscribed by chapter 109A of title 18, United States Code, that was committed in relation to a child;

(2) any conduct proscribed by chapter 110 of title 18, United States Code;

(3) contact between any part of the defendant's body or an object and the genitals or anus of a child;

(4) contact between the genitals or anus of the defendant and any part of the body of a child;

(5) deriving sexual pleasure or gratification from the infliction of death, bodily injury, or physical pain on a child; or

(6) an attempt or conspiracy to engage in conduct described in paragraphs (1)–(5).

Rule 415. Evidence of Similar Acts in Civil Cases Concerning Sexual Assault or Child Molestation

(a) In a civil case in which a claim for damages or other relief is predicated on a party's alleged commission of conduct constituting an offense of sexual assault or child molestation, evidence of that party's commission of another offense or offenses of sexual assault or child molestation is admissible and may be considered as provided in Rule 413 and Rule 414 of these rules.

(b) A party who intends to offer evidence under this Rule shall disclose the evidence to the party against whom it will be offered, including statements of witnesses or a summary of the substance of any testimony that is expected to be offered, at least fifteen days before the scheduled date of trial or at such later time as the court may allow for good cause.

(c) This rule shall not be construed to limit the admission or consideration of evidence under any other rule.

ARTICLE V. PRIVILEGES

Rule 501. General Rule

Except as otherwise required by the Constitution of the United States or provided by Act of Congress or in rules prescribed by the Supreme Court pursuant to statutory authority, the privilege of a witness, person, government, State, or political subdivision thereof shall be governed by the principles of the common law as they may be interpreted by the courts of the United States in the light of reason and experience. However, in civil actions and proceedings, with respect to an element of a claim or defense as to which State law supplies the rule of decision, the privilege of a witness, person, government, State, or political subdivision thereof shall be determined in accordance with State law.

Rule 502—Enacted September 19, 2008—Is Fully Set Forth in Chapter VIII

ARTICLE VI. WITNESSES

Rule 601. General Rule of Competency

Every person is competent to be a witness except as otherwise provided in these rules. However, in civil actions and proceedings, with respect to an element of a claim or defense as to which State law supplies the rule of decision, the competency of a witness shall be determined in accordance with State law.

Rule 602. Lack of Personal Knowledge

A witness may not testify to a matter unless evidence is introduced sufficient to support a finding that the witness has personal knowledge of the matter. Evidence to prove personal knowledge may, but need not, consist of the witness' own testimony. This rule is subject to the provisions of rule 703, relating to opinion testimony by expert witnesses.

Rule 603. Oath or Affirmation

Before testifying, every witness shall be required to declare that the witness will testify truthfully, by oath or affirmation administered in a form calculated to awaken the witness' conscience and impress the witness' mind with the duty to do so.

Rule 604. Interpreters

An interpreter is subject to the provisions of these rules relating to qualification as an expert and the administration of an oath or affirmation to make a true translation.

Rule 605. Competency of Judge as Witness

The judge presiding at the trial may not testify in that trial as a witness. No objection need be made in order to preserve the point.

Rule 606. Competency of Juror as Witness

(a) At the trial.

A member of the jury may not testify as a witness before that jury in the trial of the case in which the juror is sitting. If the juror is called so to testify, the opposing party shall be afforded an opportunity to object out of the presence of the jury.

(b) Inquiry into validity of verdict or indictment.

Upon an inquiry into the validity of a verdict or indictment, a juror may not testify as to any matter or statement occurring during the course of the jury's deliberations or to the effect of anything upon that or any other juror's mind or emotions as influencing the juror to assent to or dissent from the verdict or indictment or concerning the juror's mental processes in connection therewith. But a juror may testify about (1) whether extraneous prejudicial information was improperly brought to the jury's attention, (2) whether any outside influence was improperly brought to bear upon any juror, or (3) whether there was a mistake in entering the verdict onto the verdict form. A juror's affidavit or evidence of any statement by the juror may not be received on a matter about which the juror would be precluded from testifying.

Rule 607.   Who May Impeach

The credibility of a witness may be attacked by any party, including the party calling the witness.

Rule 608.   Evidence of Character and Conduct of Witness

(a) Opinion and reputation evidence of character.

The credibility of a witness may be attacked or supported by evidence in the form of opinion or reputation, but subject to these limitations: (1) the evidence may refer only to character for truthfulness or untruthfulness, and (2) evidence of truthful character is admissible only after the character of the witness for truthfulness has been attacked by opinion or reputation evidence or otherwise.

(b) Specific instances of conduct.

Specific instances of the conduct of a witness, for the purpose of attacking or supporting the witness' character for truthfulness, other than conviction of crime as provided in rule 609, may not be proved by extrinsic evidence. They may, however, in the discretion of the court, if probative of truthfulness or untruthfulness, be inquired into on cross-examination of the witness (1) concerning the witness' character for truthfulness or untruthfulness, or (2) concerning the character for truthfulness or untruthfulness of another witness as to which character the witness being cross-examined has testified.

The giving of testimony, whether by an accused or by any other witness, does not operate as a waiver of the accused's or the witness' privilege against self-incrimination when examined with respect to matters that relate only to character for truthfulness.

Rule 609.   Impeachment by Evidence of Conviction of Crime

(a) General rule.

For the purpose of attacking the character for truthfulness of a witness,

(1) evidence that a witness other than an accused has been convicted of a crime shall be admitted, subject to Rule 403, if the crime was punishable by death or imprisonment in excess of one year under the law under which the witness was convicted, and evidence that an accused has been convicted of such a crime shall be admitted if the court determines that the probative value of admitting this evidence outweighs its prejudicial effect to the accused; and

(2) evidence that any witness has been convicted of a crime shall be admitted regardless of the punishment, if it readily can be determined that establishing the elements of the crime required proof or admission of an act of dishonesty or false statement by the witness.

(b) Time limit.

Evidence of a conviction under this rule is not admissible if a period of more than ten years has elapsed since the date of the conviction or of the release of the witness from the confinement imposed for that conviction, whichever is the later date, unless the court determines, in the interests of justice, that the probative value of the conviction supported by specific facts and circumstances substantially outweighs its prejudicial effect. However, evidence of a conviction more than 10 years old as calculated herein, is not admissible unless the proponent gives to the adverse party sufficient advance written notice of intent to use such evidence to provide the adverse party with a fair opportunity to contest the use of such evidence.

(c) Effect of pardon, annulment, or certificate of rehabilitation.

Evidence of a conviction is not admissible under this rule if (1) the conviction has been the subject of a pardon, annulment, certificate of rehabilitation, or other equivalent procedure based on a finding of the rehabilitation of the person convicted, and that person has not been convicted of a subsequent crime which was punishable by death or imprisonment in excess of one year, or (2) the conviction has been the subject of a pardon, annulment, or other equivalent procedure based on a finding of innocence.

(d) Juvenile adjudications.

Evidence of juvenile adjudications is generally not admissible under this rule. The court may, however, in a criminal case allow evidence of a juvenile adjudication of a witness other than the accused if conviction of the offense would be admissible to attack the credibility of an adult and the court is satisfied that admission in evidence is necessary for a fair determination of the issue of guilt or innocence.

(e) Pendency of appeal.

The pendency of an appeal therefrom does not render evidence of a conviction inadmissible. Evidence of the pendency of an appeal is admissible.

Rule 610.   Religious Beliefs or Opinions

Evidence of the beliefs or opinions of a witness on matters of religion is not admissible for the purpose of showing that by reason of their nature the witness' credibility is impaired or enhanced.

Rule 611.   Mode and Order of Interrogation and Presentation

(a) Control by court.

The court shall exercise reasonable control over the mode and order of interrogating witnesses and presenting evidence so as to (1) make the interrogation and presentation effective for the ascertainment of the truth, (2) avoid needless consumption of time, and (3) protect witnesses from harassment or undue embarrassment.

(b) Scope of cross-examination.

Cross-examination should be limited to the subject matter of the direct examination and matters affecting the credibility of the witness. The court may, in the exercise of discretion, permit inquiry into additional matters as if on direct examination.

(c) Leading questions.

Leading questions should not be used on the direct examination of a witness except as may be necessary to develop the witness' testimony. Ordinarily leading questions should be permitted on cross-examination. When a party calls a hostile witness, an adverse party, or a witness identified with an adverse party, interrogation may be by leading questions.

Rule 612.   Writing Used to Refresh Memory

Except as otherwise provided in criminal proceedings by section 3500 of title 18, United States Code, if a witness uses a writing to refresh memory for the purpose of testifying, either—

(1) while testifying, or

(2) before testifying, if the court in its discretion determines it is necessary in the interests of justice,

an adverse party is entitled to have the writing produced at the hearing, to inspect it, to cross-examine the witness thereon, and to introduce in evidence those portions which relate to the testimony of the witness. If it is claimed that the writing contains matters not related to the subject matter of the testimony the court shall examine the writing in camera, excise any portions not so related, and order delivery of the remainder to the party entitled thereto. Any portion withheld over objections shall be preserved and made available to the appellate court in the event of an appeal. If a writing is not produced or delivered pursuant to order under this rule, the court shall make any order justice requires, except that in criminal cases when the prosecution elects not to comply, the order shall be one striking the testimony or, if the court in its discretion determines that the interests of justice so require, declaring a mistrial.

Rule 613.   Prior Statements of Witnesses

(a)   Examining witness concerning prior statement.

In examining a witness concerning a prior statement made by the witness, whether written or not, the statement need not be shown nor its contents disclosed to the witness at that time, but on request the same shall be shown or disclosed to opposing counsel.

(b)   Extrinsic evidence of prior inconsistent statement of witness.

Extrinsic evidence of a prior inconsistent statement by a witness is not admissible unless the witness is afforded an opportunity to explain or deny the same and the opposite party is afforded an opportunity to interrogate the witness thereon, or the interests of justice otherwise require. This provision does not apply to admissions of a party-opponent as defined in rule 801(d)(2).

Rule 614.   Calling and Interrogation of Witnesses by Court

(a)   Calling by court.

The court may, on its own motion or at the suggestion of a party, call witnesses, and all parties are entitled to cross-examine witnesses thus called.

(b)   Interrogation by court.

The court may interrogate witnesses, whether called by itself or by a party.

(c)   Objections.

Objections to the calling of witnesses by the court or to interrogation by it may be made at the time or at the next available opportunity when the jury is not present.

Rule 615.   Exclusion of Witnesses

At the request of a party the court shall order witnesses excluded so that they cannot hear the testimony of other witnesses, and it may make the order of its own motion. This rule does not authorize exclusion of (1) a party who is a natural person, or (2) an officer or employee of a party which is not a natural person designated as its representative by its attorney, or (3) a person whose presence is shown by a party to be essential to the presentation of the party's cause, or (4) a person authorized by statute to be present.

ARTICLE VII.   OPINIONS AND EXPERT TESTIMONY

Rule 701.   Opinion Testimony by Lay Witnesses

If the witness is not testifying as an expert, the witness' testimony in the form of opinions or inferences is limited to those opinions or inferences which are (a) rationally based on the perception of the witness, and (b) helpful to a clear understanding of the witness' testimony or the determination of a fact in issue, and (c) not based on scientific, technical, or other specialized knowledge within the scope of Rule 702.

Rule 702.   Testimony by Experts

If scientific, technical, or other specialized knowledge will assist the trier of fact to understand the evidence or to determine a fact in issue, a witness qualified as an expert by knowledge, skill, experience, training, or education, may testify thereto in the form of an opinion or otherwise, if (1) the testimony is based upon sufficient facts or data, (2) the testimony is the product of reliable principles and methods, and (3) the witness has applied the principles and methods reliably to the facts of the case.

Rule 703.   Bases of Opinion Testimony by Experts

The facts or data in the particular case upon which an expert bases an opinion or inference may be those perceived by or made known to the expert at or before the hearing. If of a type reasonably relied upon by experts in the particular field in forming opinions or inferences upon the subject, the facts or data need not be admissible in evidence in order for the opinion or inference to be admitted. Facts or data that are otherwise inadmissible shall not be disclosed to the jury by the proponent of the opinion or inference unless the court determines that their probative value in assisting the jury to evaluate the expert's opinion substantially outweighs their prejudicial effect.

Rule 704.   Opinion on Ultimate Issue

(a) Except as provided in subdivision (b), testimony in the form of an opinion or inference otherwise admissible is not objectionable because it embraces an ultimate issue to be decided by the trier of fact.

(b) No expert witness testifying with respect to the mental state or condition of a defendant in a criminal case may state an opinion or inference as to whether the defendant did or did not have the mental state or condition constituting an element of the crime charged or of a defense thereto. Such ultimate issues are matters for the trier of fact alone.

Rule 705.   Disclosure of Facts or Data Underlying Expert Opinion

The expert may testify in terms of opinion or inference and give reasons therefor without first testifying to the underlying facts or data, unless the court requires otherwise. The expert may in any event be required to disclose the underlying facts or data on cross-examination.

Rule 706.   Court Appointed Experts

(a) Appointment.

The court may on its own motion or on the motion of any party enter an order to show cause why expert witnesses should not be appointed, and may request the parties to submit nominations. The court may appoint any expert witnesses agreed upon by the parties, and may appoint expert witnesses of its own selection. An expert witness shall not be appointed by the court unless the witness consents to act. A witness so appointed shall be informed of the witness' duties by the court in writing, a copy of which shall be filed with the clerk, or at a conference in which the parties shall have opportunity to participate. A witness so appointed shall advise the parties of the witness' findings, if any; the witness' deposition may be taken by any party; and the witness may be called to testify by the court or any party. The witness shall be subject to cross-examination by each party, including a party calling the witness.

(b) Compensation.

Expert witnesses so appointed are entitled to reasonable compensation in whatever sum the court may allow. The compensation thus fixed is payable from funds which may be provided by law in criminal cases and civil actions and proceedings involving just compensation under the fifth amendment. In other civil actions and proceedings the compensation shall be paid by the parties in such proportion and at such time as the court directs, and thereafter charged in like manner as other costs.

(c) Disclosure of appointment.

In the exercise of its discretion, the court may authorize disclosure to the jury of the fact that the court appointed the expert witness.

(d) Parties' experts of own selection.

Nothing in this rule limits the parties in calling expert witnesses of their own selection.

ARTICLE VIII.   HEARSAY

Rule 801.   Definitions

The following definitions apply under this article:

(a) Statement.

A "statement" is (1) an oral or written assertion or (2) nonverbal conduct of a person, if it is intended by the person as an assertion.

(b) Declarant.

A "declarant" is a person who makes a statement.

(c) Hearsay.

"Hearsay" is a statement, other than one made by the declarant while testifying at the trial or hearing, offered in evidence to prove the truth of the matter asserted.

(d) Statements which are not hearsay.

A statement is not hearsay if—

(1) Prior statement by witness. The declarant testifies at the trial or hearing and is subject to cross-examination concerning the statement, and the statement is (A) inconsistent with the declarant's testimony, and was given under oath subject to the penalty of perjury at a trial, hearing, or other proceeding, or in a deposition, or (B) consistent with the declarant's testimony and is offered to rebut an express or implied charge against the declarant of recent fabrication or improper influence or motive, or (C) one of identification of a person made after perceiving the person; or

(2) Admission by party-opponent. The statement is offered against a party and is

(A) the party's own statement, in either an individual or a representative capacity or

(B) a statement of which the party has manifested an adoption or belief in its truth, or

(C) a statement by a person authorized by the party to make a statement concerning the subject, or

(D) a statement by the party's agent or servant concerning a matter within the scope of the agency or employment, made during the existence of the relationship, or

(E) a statement by a coconspirator of a party during the course and in furtherance of the conspiracy.

The contents of the statement shall be considered but are not alone sufficient to establish the declarant's authority under subdivision (C), the agency or employment relationship and scope thereof under subdivision (D), or the existence of the conspiracy and the participation therein of the declarant and the party against whom the statement is offered under subdivision (E).

Rule 802. Hearsay Rule

Hearsay is not admissible except as provided by these rules or by other rules prescribed by the Supreme Court pursuant to statutory authority or by Act of Congress.

Rule 803. Hearsay Exceptions; Availability of Declarant Immaterial

The following are not excluded by the hearsay rule, even though the declarant is available as a witness:

(1) Present sense impression. A statement describing or explaining an event or condition made while the declarant was perceiving the event or condition, or immediately thereafter.

(2) Excited utterance. A statement relating to a startling event or condition made while the declarant was under the stress of excitement caused by the event or condition.

(3) Then existing mental, emotional, or physical condition. A statement of the declarant's then existing state of mind, emotion, sensation, or physical condition (such as intent, plan, motive, design, mental feeling, pain, and bodily health), but not including a statement of memory or belief to prove the fact remembered or believed unless it relates to the execution, revocation, identification, or terms of declarant's will.

(4) Statements for purposes of medical diagnosis or treatment. Statements made for purposes of medical diagnosis or treatment and describing medical history, or past or present symptoms, pain, or sensations, or the inception or general character of the cause or external source thereof insofar as reasonably pertinent to diagnosis or treatment.

(5) Recorded recollection. A memorandum or record concerning a matter about which a witness once had knowledge but now has insufficient recollection to enable the witness to testify fully and accurately, shown to have been made or adopted by the witness when the matter was fresh in the witness' memory and to reflect that knowledge correctly. If admitted, the memorandum or record may be read into evidence but may not itself be received as an exhibit unless offered by an adverse party.

(6) Records of regularly conducted activity. A memorandum, report, record, or data compilation, in any form, of acts, events, conditions, opinions, or diagnoses, made at or near the time by, or from information transmitted by, a person with knowledge, if kept in the course of a regularly conducted business activity, and if it was the regular practice of that business activity to make the memorandum, report, record or data compilation, all as shown by the testimony of the custodian or other qualified witness, or by certification that complies with Rule 902(11), Rule 902(12), or a statute permitting certification, unless the source of information or the method or circumstances of preparation indicate lack of trustworthiness. The term "business" as used in this paragraph includes business, institution, association, profession, occupation, and calling of every kind, whether or not conducted for profit.

(7) Absence of entry in records kept in accordance with the provisions of paragraph (6). Evidence that a matter is not included in the memoranda reports, records, or data compilations, in any form, kept in accordance with the provisions of paragraph (6), to prove the nonoccurrence or nonexistence of the matter, if the matter was of a kind of which a memorandum, report, record, or data compilation was regularly made and preserved, unless the sources of information or other circumstances indicate lack of trustworthiness.

(8) Public records and reports. Records, reports, statements, or data compilations, in any form, of public offices or agencies, setting forth (A) the activities of the office or agency, or (B) matters observed pursuant to duty imposed by law as to which matters there was a duty to report, excluding, however, in criminal cases matters observed by police officers and other law enforcement personnel, or (C) in civil actions and proceedings and against the Government in criminal cases, factual findings resulting from an investigation made pursuant to authority granted by law, unless the sources of information or other circumstances indicate lack of trustworthiness.

(9) Records of vital statistics. Records or data compilations, in any form, of births, fetal deaths, deaths, or marriages, if the report thereof was made to a public office pursuant to requirements of law.

(10) Absence of public record or entry. To prove the absence of a record, report, statement, or data compilation, in any form, or the nonoccurrence or nonexistence of a matter of which a record, report, statement, or data compilation, in any form, was regularly made and preserved by a public office or agency, evidence in the form of a certification in accordance with rule 902, or testimony, that diligent search failed to disclose the record, report, statement, or data compilation, or entry.

(11) Records of religious organizations. Statements of births, marriages, divorces, deaths, legitimacy, ancestry, relationship by blood or marriage, or other similar facts of personal or family history, contained in a regularly kept record of a religious organization.

(12) Marriage, baptismal, and similar certificates. Statements of fact contained in a certificate that the maker performed a marriage or other ceremony or administered a sacrament, made by a clergyman, public official, or other person authorized by the rules or practices of a religious organization or by law to perform the act certified, and purporting to have been issued at the time of the act or within a reasonable time thereafter.

(13) Family records. Statements of fact concerning personal or family history contained in family Bibles, genealogies, charts, engravings on rings, inscriptions on family portraits, engravings on urns, crypts, or tombstones, or the like.

(14) Records of documents affecting an interest in property. The record of a document purporting to establish or affect an interest in property, as proof of the content of the original recorded document and its execution and delivery by each person by whom it purports to have been executed, if the record is a record of a public office and an applicable statute authorizes the recording of documents of that kind in that office.

(15) Statements in documents affecting an interest in property. A statement contained in a document purporting to establish or affect an interest in property if the matter stated was relevant to the purpose of the document, unless dealings with the property since the document was made have been inconsistent with the truth of the statement or the purport of the document.

(16) Statements in ancient documents. Statements in a document in existence twenty years or more the authenticity of which is established.

(17) Market reports, commercial publications. Market quotations, tabulations, lists, directories, or other published compilations, generally used and relied upon by the public or by persons in particular occupations.

(18) Learned treatises. To the extent called to the attention of an expert witness upon cross-examination or relied upon by the expert witness in direct examination, statements contained in published treatises, periodicals, or pamphlets on a subject of history, medicine, or other science or art, established as a reliable authority by the testimony or admission of the witness or by other expert testimony or by judicial notice. If admitted, the statements may be read into evidence but may not be received as exhibits.

(19) Reputation concerning personal or family history. Reputation among members of a person's family by blood, adoption, or marriage, or among a person's associates, or in the community, concerning a person's birth, adoption, marriage, divorce, death, legitimacy, relationship by blood, adoption, or marriage, ancestry, or other similar fact of personal or family history.

(20) Reputation concerning boundaries or general history. Reputation in a community, arising before the controversy, as to boundaries of or customs affecting lands in the community, and reputation as to events of general history important to the community or State or nation in which located.

(21) Reputation as to character. Reputation of a person's character among associates or in the community.

(22) Judgment of previous conviction. Evidence of a final judgment, entered after a trial or upon a plea of guilty (but not upon a plea of nolo contendere), adjudging a person guilty of a crime punishable by death or imprisonment in excess of one year, to prove any fact essential to sustain the judgment, but not including, when offered by the Government in a criminal prosecution for purposes other than impeachment, judgments against persons other than the accused. The pendency of an appeal may be shown but does not affect admissibility.

(23) Judgment as to personal, family or general history, or boundaries. Judgments as proof of matters of personal, family or general history, or boundaries, essential to the judgment, if the same would be provable by evidence of reputation.

(24) [Other exceptions.] [Transferred to Rule 807]

Rule 804. Hearsay Exceptions; Declarant Unavailable

(a) Definition of unavailability.

"Unavailability as a witness" includes situations in which the declarant—

(1) is exempted by ruling of the court on the ground of privilege from testifying concerning the subject matter of the declarant's statement; or

(2) persists in refusing to testify concerning the subject matter of the declarant's statement despite an order of the court to do so; or

(3) testifies to a lack of memory of the subject matter of the declarant's statement; or

(4) is unable to be present or to testify at the hearing because of death or then existing physical or mental illness or infirmity; or

(5) is absent from the hearing and the proponent of a statement has been unable to procure the declarant's attendance (or in the case of a hearsay exception under subdivision (b)(2), (3), or (4), the declarant's attendance or testimony) by process or other reasonable means.

A declarant is not unavailable as a witness if exemption, refusal, claim of lack of memory, inability, or absence is due to the procurement or wrongdoing of the proponent of a statement for the purpose of preventing the witness from attending or testifying.

(b) Hearsay exceptions.

The following are not excluded by the hearsay rule if the declarant is unavailable as a witness:

(1) Former testimony. Testimony given as a witness at another hearing of the same or a different proceeding, or in a deposition taken in compliance with law in the course of the same or another proceeding, if the party against whom the testimony is now offered, or, in a civil action or proceeding, a predecessor in interest, had an opportunity and similar motive to develop the testimony by direct, cross, or redirect examination.

(2) Statement under belief of impending death. In a prosecution for homicide or in a civil action or proceeding, a statement made by a declarant while believing that the declarant's death was imminent, concerning the cause or circumstances of what the declarant believed to be impending death.

(3) Statement against interest. A statement which was at the time of its making so far contrary to the declarant's pecuniary or proprietary interest, or so far tended to subject the declarant to civil or criminal liability, or to render invalid a claim by the declarant against another, that a reasonable person in the declarant's position would not have made the statement unless believing it to be true. A statement tending to expose the declarant to criminal liability and offered to exculpate the accused is not admissible unless corroborating circumstances clearly indicate the trustworthiness of the statement.

(4) Statement of personal or family history. (A) A statement concerning the declarant's own birth, adoption, marriage, divorce, legitimacy, relationship by blood, adoption, or marriage, ancestry, or other similar fact of personal or family history, even though declarant had no means of acquiring personal knowledge of the matter stated; or (B) a statement concerning the foregoing matters, and death also, of another person, if the declarant was related to the other by blood, adoption, or marriage or was so intimately associated with the other's family as to be likely to have accurate information concerning the matter declared.

(5) [Other exceptions.] [Transferred to Rule 807]

(6) Forfeiture by wrongdoing. A statement offered against a party that has engaged or acquiesced in wrongdoing that was intended to, and did, procure the unavailability of the declarant as a witness.

Rule 805.   Hearsay Within Hearsay

Hearsay included within hearsay is not excluded under the hearsay rule if each part of the combined statements conforms with an exception to the hearsay rule provided in these rules.

Rule 806.   Attacking and Supporting Credibility of Declarant

When a hearsay statement, or a statement defined in Rule 801(d)(2)(C), (D), or (E), has been admitted in evidence, the credibility of the declarant may be attacked, and if attacked may be supported, by any evidence which would be admissible for those purposes if declarant had testified as a witness. Evidence of a statement or conduct by the declarant at any time, inconsistent with the declarant's hearsay statement, is not subject to any requirement that the declarant may have been afforded an opportunity to deny or explain. If the party against whom a hearsay statement has been admitted calls the declarant as a witness, the party is entitled to examine the declarant on the statement as if under cross-examination.

Rule 807. Residual Exception

A statement not specifically covered by Rule 803 or 804 but having equivalent circumstantial guarantees of trustworthiness, is not excluded by the hearsay rule, if the court determines that (A) the statement is offered as evidence of a material fact; (B) the statement is more probative on the point for which it is offered than any other evidence which the proponent can procure through reasonable efforts; and (C) the general purposes of these rules and the interests of justice will best be served by admission of the statement into evidence. However, a statement may not be admitted under this exception unless the proponent of it makes known to the adverse party sufficiently in advance of the trial or hearing to provide the adverse party with a fair opportunity to prepare to meet it, the proponent's intention to offer the statement and the particulars of it, including the name and address of the declarant.

ARTICLE IX. AUTHENTICATION AND IDENTIFICATION

Rule 901. Requirement of Authentication or Identification

(a) General provision.

The requirement of authentication or identification as a condition precedent to admissibility is satisfied by evidence sufficient to support a finding that the matter in question is what its proponent claims.

(b) Illustrations.

By way of illustration only, and not by way of limitation, the following are examples of authentication or identification conforming with the requirements of this rule:

(1) Testimony of witness with knowledge. Testimony that a matter is what it is claimed to be.

(2) Nonexpert opinion on handwriting. Nonexpert opinion as to the genuineness of handwriting, based upon familiarity not acquired for purposes of the litigation.

(3) Comparison by trier or expert witness. Comparison by the trier of fact or by expert witnesses with specimens which have been authenticated.

(4) Distinctive characteristics and the like. Appearance, contents, substance, internal patterns, or other distinctive characteristics, taken in conjunction with circumstances.

(5) Voice identification. Identification of a voice, whether heard firsthand or through mechanical or electronic transmission or recording, by opinion based upon hearing the voice at any time under circumstances connecting it with the alleged speaker.

(6) Telephone conversations. Telephone conversations, by evidence that a call was made to the number assigned at the time by the telephone company to a particular person or business, if (A) in the case of a person, circumstances, including self-identification, show the person answering to be the one called, or (B) in the case of a business, the call was made to a place of business and the conversation related to business reasonably transacted over the telephone.

(7) Public records or reports. Evidence that a writing authorized by law to be recorded or filed and in fact recorded or filed in a public office, or a purported public record, report, statement, or data compilation, in any form, is from the public office where items of this nature are kept.

(8) Ancient documents or data compilation. Evidence that a document or data compilation, in any form, (A) is in such condition as to create no suspicion concerning its authenticity, (B) was in a place where it, if authentic, would likely be, and (C) has been in existence 20 years or more at the time it is offered.

(9) Process or system. Evidence describing a process or system used to produce a result and showing that the process or system produces an accurate result.

(10) Methods provided by statute or rule. Any method of authentication or identification provided by Act of Congress or by other rules prescribed by the Supreme Court pursuant to statutory authority.

Rule 902.   Self-authentication

Extrinsic evidence of authenticity as a condition precedent to admissibility is not required with respect to the following:

(1) Domestic public documents under seal. A document bearing a seal purporting to be that of the United States, or of any State, district, Commonwealth, territory, or insular possession thereof, or the Panama Canal Zone, or the Trust Territory of the Pacific Islands, or of a political subdivision, department, officer, or agency thereof, and a signature purporting to be an attestation or execution.

(2) Domestic public documents not under seal. A document purporting to bear the signature in the official capacity of an officer or employee of any entity included in paragraph (1) hereof, having no seal, if a public officer having a seal and having official duties in the district or political subdivision of the officer or employee certifies under seal that the signer has the official capacity and that the signature is genuine.

(3) Foreign public documents. A document purporting to be executed or attested in an official capacity by a person authorized by the laws of a foreign country to make the execution or attestation, and accompanied by a final certification as to the genuineness of the signature and official position (A) of the executing or attesting person, or (B) of any foreign official whose certificate of genuineness of signature and official position relates to the execution or attestation or is in a chain of certificates of genuineness of signature and official position relating to the execution or attestation. A final certification may be made by a secretary of an embassy or legation, consul general, consul, vice consul, or consular agent of the United States, or a diplomatic or consular official of the foreign country assigned or accredited to the United States. If reasonable opportunity has been given to all parties to investigate the authenticity and accuracy of official documents, the court may, for good cause shown, order that they be treated as presumptively authentic without final certification or permit them to be evidenced by an attested summary with or without final certification.

(4) Certified copies of public records. A copy of an official record or report or entry therein, or of a document authorized by law to be recorded or filed and actually recorded or filed in a public office, including data compilations in any form, certified as correct by the custodian or other person authorized to make the certification, by certificate complying with paragraph (1), (2), or (3) of this rule or complying with any Act of Congress or rule prescribed by the Supreme Court pursuant to statutory authority.

(5) Official publications. Books, pamphlets, or other publications purporting to be issued by public authority.

(6) Newspapers and periodicals. Printed materials purporting to be newspapers or periodicals.

(7) Trade inscriptions and the like. Inscriptions, signs, tags, or labels purporting to have been affixed in the course of business and indicating ownership, control, or origin.

(8) Acknowledged documents. Documents accompanied by a certificate of acknowledgment executed in the manner provided by law by a notary public or other officer authorized by law to take acknowledgments.

(9) Commercial paper and related documents. Commercial paper, signatures thereon, and documents relating thereto to the extent provided by general commercial law.

(10) Presumptions under Acts of Congress. Any signature, document, or other matter declared by Act of Congress to be presumptively or prima facie genuine or authentic.

(11) Certified domestic records of regularly conducted activity. The original or a duplicate of a domestic record of regularly conducted activity that would be admissible under Rule 803(6) if accompanied by a written declaration of its custodian or other qualified person, in a manner complying with any Act of Congress or rule prescribed by the Supreme Court pursuant to statutory authority, certifying that the record:

(A) was made at or near the time of the occurrence of the matters set forth by, or from information transmitted by, a person with knowledge of those matters;

(B) was kept in the course of the regularly conducted activity; and

(C) was made by the regularly conducted activity as a regular practice.

A party intending to offer a record into evidence under this paragraph must provide written notice of that intention to all adverse parties, and must make the record and declaration available for inspection sufficiently in advance of their offer into evidence to provide an adverse party with a fair opportunity to challenge them.

(12) Certified foreign records of regularly conducted activity. In a civil case, the original or a duplicate of a foreign record of regularly conducted activity that would be admissible under Rule 803(6) if accompanied by a written declaration by its custodian or other qualified person certifying that the record:

(A) was made at or near the time of the occurrence of the matters set forth by, or from information transmitted by, a person with knowledge of those matters;

(B) was kept in the course of the regularly conducted activity; and

(C) was made by the regularly conducted activity as a regular practice.

The declaration must be signed in a manner that, if falsely made, would subject the maker to criminal penalty under the laws of the country where the declaration is signed. A party intending to offer a record into evidence under this paragraph must provide written notice of that intention to all adverse parties, and must make the record and declaration available for inspection sufficiently in advance of their offer into evidence to provide an adverse party with a fair opportunity to challenge them.

Rule 903. Subscribing Witness' Testimony Unnecessary

The testimony of a subscribing witness is not necessary to authenticate a writing unless required by the laws of the jurisdiction whose laws govern the validity of the writing.

ARTICLE X. CONTENTS OF WRITINGS, RECORDINGS, AND PHOTOGRAPHS

Rule 1001. Definitions

For purposes of this article the following definitions are applicable:

(1) **Writings and recordings.** "Writings" and "recordings" consist of letters, words, or numbers, or their equivalent, set down by handwriting, typewriting, printing, photostating, photographing, magnetic impulse, mechanical or electronic recording, or other form of data compilation.

(2) **Photographs.** "Photographs" include still photographs, X-ray films, video tapes, and motion pictures.

(3) **Original.** An "original" of a writing or recording is the writing or recording itself or any counterpart intended to have the same effect by a person executing or issuing it. An "original" of a photograph includes the negative or any print therefrom. If data are stored in a computer or similar device, any printout or other output readable by sight, shown to reflect the data accurately, is an "original".

(4) **Duplicate.** A "duplicate" is a counterpart produced by the same impression as the original, or from the same matrix, or by means of photography, including enlargements and miniatures, or by mechanical or electronic re-recording, or by chemical reproduction, or by other equivalent techniques which accurately reproduces the original.

Rule 1002. Requirement of Original

To prove the content of a writing, recording, or photograph, the original writing, recording, or photograph is required, except as otherwise provided in these rules or by Act of Congress.

Rule 1003. Admissibility of Duplicates

A duplicate is admissible to the same extent as an original unless (1) a genuine question is raised as to the authenticity of the original or (2) in the circumstances it would be unfair to admit the duplicate in lieu of the original.

Rule 1004. Admissibility of Other Evidence of Contents

The original is not required, and other evidence of the contents of a writing, recording, or photograph is admissible if—

(1) **Originals lost or destroyed.** All originals are lost or have been destroyed, unless the proponent lost or destroyed them in bad faith; or

(2) **Original not obtainable.** No original can be obtained by any available judicial process or procedure; or

(3) **Original in possession of opponent.** At a time when an original was under the control of the party against whom offered, that party was put on notice, by the pleadings or otherwise, that the contents would be a subject of proof at the hearing, and that party does not produce the original at the hearing; or

(4) Collateral matters. The writing, recording, or photograph is not closely related to a controlling issue.

Rule 1005.   Public Records

The contents of an official record, or of a document authorized to be recorded or filed and actually recorded or filed, including data compilations in any form, if otherwise admissible, may be proved by copy, certified as correct in accordance with rule 902 or testified to be correct by a witness who has compared it with the original. If a copy which complies with the foregoing cannot be obtained by the exercise of reasonable diligence, then other evidence of the contents may be given.

Rule 1006.   Summaries

The contents of voluminous writings, recordings, or photographs which cannot conveniently be examined in court may be presented in the form of a chart, summary, or calculation. The originals, or duplicates, shall be made available for examination or copying, or both, by other parties at reasonable time and place. The court may order that they be produced in court.

Rule 1007.   Testimony or Written Admission of Party

Contents of writings, recordings, or photographs may be proved by the testimony or deposition of the party against whom offered or by that party's written admission, without accounting for the nonproduction of the original.

Rule 1008.   Functions of Court and Jury

When the admissibility of other evidence of contents of writings, recordings, or photographs under these rules depends upon the fulfillment of a condition of fact, the question whether the condition has been fulfilled is ordinarily for the court to determine in accordance with the provisions of rule 104. However, when an issue is raised (a) whether the asserted writing ever existed, or (b) whether another writing, recording, or photograph produced at the trial is the original, or (c) whether other evidence of contents correctly reflects the contents, the issue is for the trier of fact to determine as in the case of other issues of fact.

ARTICLE XI.   MISCELLANEOUS RULES

Rule 1101.   Applicability of Rules

(a) Courts and judges.

These rules apply to the United States district courts, the District Court of Guam, the District Court of the Virgin Islands, the District Court for the Northern Mariana Islands, the United States courts of appeals, the United States Claims Court, and to the United States bankruptcy judges and United States magistrate judges, in the actions, cases, and proceedings and to the extent hereinafter set forth. The terms "judge" and "court" in these rules include United States bankruptcy judges and United States magistrate judges.

(b) Proceedings generally.

These rules apply generally to civil actions and proceedings, including admiralty and maritime cases, to criminal cases and proceedings, to contempt proceedings except those in which the court may act summarily, and to proceedings and cases under title 11, United States Code.

(c) Rule of privilege.

The rule with respect to privileges applies at all stages of all actions, cases, and proceedings.

(d) Rules inapplicable.

The rules (other than with respect to privileges) do not apply in the following situations:

(1) Preliminary questions of fact. The determination of questions of fact preliminary to admissibility of evidence when the issue is to be determined by the court under rule 104.

(2) Grand jury. Proceedings before grand juries.

(3) Miscellaneous proceedings. Proceedings for extradition or rendition; preliminary examinations in criminal cases; sentencing, or granting or revoking probation; issuance of warrants for arrest, criminal summonses, and search warrants; and proceedings with respect to release on bail or otherwise.

* * *

Rule 1102.   Amendments

Amendments to the Federal Rules of Evidence may be made as provided in section 2072 of title 28 of the United States Code.

Rule 1103. Title

These rules may be known and cited as the Federal Rules of Evidence.

*

APPENDIX VI

SEDONA CONFERENCE® GLOSSARY: COMMONLY USED TERMS FOR E–DISCOVERY AND DIGITAL INFORMATION MANAGEMENT

・・・

THE SEDONA CONFERENCE® WORKING GROUP SERIES

THE SEDONA CONFERENCE® GLOSSARY:

E-Discovery & Digital Information Management (SECOND EDITION)

A Project of The Sedona Conference®
Working Group on On Electronic Document
Retention & Production (WG1) RFP+ Group

DECEMBER 2007 VERSION

The Sedona Conference®

The Sedona Conference® Glossary is published as a tool to assist in the understanding and discussion of electronic discovery and electronic information management issues; it is not intended to be an all-encompassing replacement of existing technical glossaries published by ARMA International (www.arma.org), American National Standards Institute (www.ansi.org), International Organization for Standardization (www.iso.org), U.S. National Archives & Records Administration (www.archives.gov) and other professional organizations. As with all of our publications, your comments are welcome. Please forward them to us at tsc@sedona.net.

Richard G. Braman
Executive Director
The Second Conference®
Sedona, AZ
USA
November, 2007

The Sedona Conference® Glossary

Commonly Used Terms
for E–Discovery and
Digital Information Management

30(b)(6): Under Federal Rule of Civil Procedure 30(b)(6), a corporation, partnership, association, or governmental agency is subject to the deposition process, and to provide one or more witnesses to "testify as to matters known or reasonably available to the organization" on the topics requested by the notice without compromising attorney-client privilege communications or work product. It is not unusual for the 30(b)(6) topics to be directed toward the discovery process, including procedures for preservation, collection, chain of custody, processing, review, and production. Early in the litigation, when developing a discovery plan, particularly with regard to electronic discovery, a party should be mindful of the obligation to provide one or more 30(b)(6) witnesses should the request be made by another party to the litigation, and include this contingency in the discovery plan.

Ablate: Describes the process by which laser-readable "pits" are burned into the recorded layer of optical discs, DVD–ROMs and CD–ROMs.

Ablative: Unalterable data. *See Ablate.*

Acetate-base film: A safety film (ANSI Standard) substrate used to produce microfilm.

ACL (Access Control List): A security method used by Lotus Notes developers to grant varying levels of access and user privileges within Lotus Notes databases.

ACM (Association for Computing Machinery): Professional association for computer professionals with a number of resources, including a special interest group on search and retrieval. See http://www.acm.org.

Active Data: Information residing on the direct access storage media (disc drives or servers) that is readily visible to the operating system and/or application software with which it was created. It is immediately accessible to users without restoration or reconstruction.

Active Records: Records related to current, ongoing or in-process activities referred to on a regular basis to respond to day-to-day operational requirements. *See* Inactive Records.

ADC: Analog to Digital Converter. Converts analog data to a digital format.

Address: Addresses using a number of different protocols are commonly used on the Internet. These addresses include email addresses (Simple Mail Transfer Protocol or SMTP), IP (Internet Protocol) addresses and URLs (Uniform Resource Locators), commonly known as Web addresses.

ADF: Automatic Document Feeder. This is the means by which a scanner feeds the paper document.

Adware: *See* Spyware.

Agent: A program running on a computer that performs as instructed by a central control point to track file and operating system events, and take directed actions, such as transferring a file or deleting a local copy of a file, in response to such events.

AIIM: The Association for Information and Image Management, www.aiim.org–focused on ECM (enterprise content management).

Algorithm: A detailed formula or set of steps for solving a particular problem. To be an algorithm, a set of rules must be unambiguous and have a clear stopping point.

Aliasing: When computer graphics output has jagged edges or a stair-stepped, rather than a smooth, appearance when magnified. The graphics output can be smoothed using anti-aliasing algorithms.

Alphanumeric: Characters composed of letters, numbers (and sometimes non-control characters, such as @, #, $). Excludes control characters.

Ambient Data: *See* Residual Data.

Analog: Data in an analog format is represented by continuously variable, measurable, physical quantities such as voltage, amplitude or frequency. Analog is the opposite of digital.

Annotation: The changes, additions, or editorial comments made or applicable to a document—usually an electronic image file—using electronic sticky notes, highlighter, or other electronic tools. Annotations should be overlaid and not change the original document.

ANSI: American National Standards Institute, www.ansi.org—a private, non-profit organization that administers and coordinates the U.S. voluntary standardization and conformity assessment system.

Aperture Card: An IBM punch card with a window that holds a 35mm frame of microfilm. Indexing information is punched in the card.

Application: A collection of one or more related software programs that enable an end-user to enter, store, view, modify, or extract information from files or databases. The term is commonly used in place of "program" or "software." Applications may include word processors, Internet browsing tools, spreadsheets, email clients, personal information managers (contact information and calendars), and other databases.

Application Metadata: Data created by the application specific to the ESI being addressed, embedded in the file and moved with the file when copied; copying may alter application metadata. *See also* Metadata.

Application Service Provider (ASP): An Internet-based organization hosting software applications on its own servers within its own facilities. Customers rent the use of the application and access it over the Internet or via a private line connection. *See* SaaS.

Architecture: The term architecture refers to the hardware, software or combination of hardware and software comprising a computer system or network. The term "open architecture" is used to describe computer and network components that are more readily interconnected and interoperable. Conversely, the term "closed architecture" describes components that are less readily interconnected and interoperable.

Archival Data: Archival Data is information an organization maintains for long-term storage and record keeping purposes, but which is not immediately accessible to the user of a computer system. Archival data may be written to removable media such as a CD, magneto-optical media, tape or other electronic storage device, or may be maintained on system hard drives. Some systems allow users to retrieve archival data directly while other systems require the intervention of an IT professional.

Archive, Electronic Archive: Long-term repositories for the storage of records. Electronic archives preserve the content, prevent or track alterations, and control access to electronic records.

ARMA International: A not-for-profit association and recognized authority on managing records and information, both paper and electronic, www.arma.org.

Artificial Intelligence (AI): The subfield of computer science concerned with the concepts and methods of symbolic inference by computer and symbolic knowledge representation for use in making inferences—an attempt to model aspects of human thought process with computers. It is also sometimes defined as trying to solve by computer any problem once believed to be solvable only by humans. AI is the capability of a device to perform functions that are normally associated with human intelligence, such as reasoning and optimization through experience. It attempts to approximate the results of human reasoning by organizing and manipulating factual and heuristic knowledge. Areas of AI activity include expert systems, natural language understanding, speech recognition, vision, and robotics.

ASCII (American Standard Code for Information Interchange): Pronounced "ask-ee," A non-proprietary text format built on a set of 128 (or 255 for *extended* ASCII) alphanumeric and control characters. Documents in ASCII format consist of only text with no formatting and can be read by most computer systems.

Aspect Ratio: The relationship of the height to the width of any image. The aspect ratio of an image must be maintained to prevent distortion.

Attachment: A record or file associated with another record for the purpose of retention, transfer, processing, review, production and routine records management. There may be multiple attachments associated with a single "parent" or "master" record. In many records and information management programs, or in a litigation context, the attachments and associated record(s) may be managed and processed as a single unit. In common use, this term often refers to a file (or files) associated with an email for retention and storage as a single Message Unit. *See* Document Family and Message Unit.

Attribute: A characteristic of data that sets it apart from other data, such as location, length, or type. The term attribute is sometimes used synonymously with "data element" or "property."

Audit Log or Audit Trail: In computer security systems, a chronological record of when users logged in, how long they were engaged in various activities, what they were doing, and whether any actual or attempted security violations occurred. An audit trail is an automated or manual set of chronological records of system activities that may enable the reconstruction and examination of a sequence of events and/or changes in an event.

Author or Originator: The person, office or designated position responsible for an item's creation or issuance. In the case of a document in the form of a letter, the author or originator is usually indicated on the letterhead or by signature. In some cases, the software application producing the document may capture the author's identity and associate it with the document. For records management purposes, the author or originator may be designated as a person, official title, office symbol, or code.

Avatar: A graphical representation of a user in a shared virtual reality, such as web forums or chat rooms.

AVI (Audio–Video Interleave): A Microsoft standard for Windows animation files that interleaves audio and video to provide medium quality multimedia.

Backbone: The top level of a hierarchical network. It is the main channel along which data is transferred.

Backfiles: Existing paper or microfilm files.

Backup: To create a copy of data as a precaution against the loss or damage of the original data. Many users backup their files, and most computer networks utilize automatic backup software to make regular copies of some or all of the data on the network.

Backup Data: An exact copy of ESI that serves as a source for recovery in the event of a system problem or disaster. Backup Data is generally stored separately from Active Data on portable media. Backup Data is distinct from Archival Data in that Backup Data may be a copy of Active Data, but the more meaningful difference is the method and structure of storage that impacts its suitability for certain purposes.

Backup Tape: Magnetic tape used to store copies of ESI, for use when restoration or recovery is required. ESI on backup tape is generally recorded and stored sequentially, rather than randomly, meaning in order to locate and access a specific file or data set, all ESI on the tape preceding the target must first be read, a time-consuming and inefficient process. Backup tapes typically use data compression, which increases restoration time and expense, given the lack of uniform standards governing data compression.

Backup Tape Recycling: Describes the process whereby an organization's backup tapes are overwritten with new data, usually on a fixed schedule determined jointly by records management, legal, and IT sources. For example, the use of nightly backup tapes for each day of the week with the daily backup tape for a particular day being overwritten on the same day the following week; weekly and monthly backups being stored offsite for a specific period of time before being placed back in the rotation.

Bandwidth: The amount of ESI that a network connection can accommodate in a given period of time. Bandwidth is usually stated in kilobits per second (kbps) or megabits per second (mps).

Bar Code: A small pattern of vertical lines that can be read by a laser or an optical scanner. In records management and electronic discovery, bar codes may be affixed to specific records for indexing, tracking and retrieval purposes.

Batch File: A batch file is a set of one or more instructions that are created in a computer program to perform a particular type of computer system function (.BAT is the DOS batch file extension).

Batch Processing: The processing of a large amount of ESI in a single step.

Bates Number: Sequential numbering used to track documents and images in production data sets, where each page is assigned a unique production number. Often used in conjunction with a suffix or prefix to identify the producing party, the litigation, or other relevant information. *See also* Production Number.

Baud Rate: The number of times per second a communications channel changes the carrier signal it sends on a phone line. A 2400–baud modem changes the signal 2400 times a second.

Bayesian: Refers to the statistical approach of Thomas Bayes, an 18th C. mathematician and clergyman. Bayes published a theorem which shows how to calculate conditional probabilities from the combinations of observed events and prior probabilities. Many information retrieval systems implicitly or explicitly use Bayes' probability rules to compute the likelihood that a document is relevant to a query.

BBS (Bulletin Board System): A computer system or service that users access to participate in electronic discussion groups, post messages and/or download files.

BCS: Boston Computer Society, one of the first associations of PC/Apple users (one of the largest and most active).

Beginning Document Number or BegDoc#: The Bates Number identifying the first page of a document or record.

Bibliographical/Objective Coding: Recording objective information from electronic documents such as date created, author/recipient/copies, and associating the information with a specific electronic document.

Binary: The Base 2 numbering system used in digital computing that represents all numbers using combinations of zero and one.

BIOS (Basic Input Output System): The set of user-independent computer instructions stored in a computer's ROM, immediately available to the computer when the computer is turned on. BIOS information provides the code necessary to control the keyboard, display screen, disc drives and communication ports in addition to handling certain miscellaneous functions.

Bit: A bit (**b**inary dig**it**) is the smallest unit of computer data. A bit consists of either 0 or 1. There are eight bits in a byte.

Bitmap: A Bitmap provides information on the placement and color of individual bits, as well as allows the creation of characters or images by creating a picture composed of individual bits (pixels).

Bit Stream Back-up: A Bit Stream Back-up is a sector-by-sector/bit-by-bit copy of a hard drive. A Bit Stream Back-up is an exact copy of a hard drive, preserving all latent data in addition to the files and directory structures. Bit Stream Back-up may be created using applications such as Encase, SnapBack and Ghost. *See* Forensic Copy.

Bitonal: A bitonal image uses only black and white.

BMP: A Windows file format for storing bitmap images.

Bookmark: A stored link to a Web site or page previously visited.

Boolean Search: Boolean Searches use the logical operators "and", "or" and "not" to include or exclude terms from a search. Opposite of natural language search. *See* Natural Language Search.

Boot: To start up or reset a computer.

Boot Sector/Record: *See* Master Boot Sector/Record and Volumn Boot Sector/Record.

BPI (Bits Per Inch): BPI measures data densities in disc and magnetic tape systems.

Bps: Bits per second.

Broadband: Communications of high capacity and usually of multimedia content.

Browser: An application, such as Internet Explorer or Netscape Navigator, used to view and navigate the World Wide Web and other Internet resources.

Burn: The process of creating a copy of information onto a CD, DVD or other storage media.

Bus: A parallel circuit that connects the major components of a computer, allowing the transfer of electric impulses from one connected component to any other.

Business Process Outsourcing: Business process outsourcing occurs when an organization turns over the management of a business function, such as accounts payable, purchasing, payroll or information technology, to a third party.

Byte (Binary Term): A Byte is the basic measurement of most computer data and consists of 8 bits. Computer storage capacity is generally measured in bytes. Although characters are stored in bytes, a few bytes are of little use for storing a large amount of data.

Therefore, storage is measured in larger increments of bytes. *See* Kilobyte, Megabyte, Gigabyte, Terabyte, Petabyte, Exabyte, Zettabyte and Yottabyte (listed here in order of increasing volume).

Cache: A dedicated, high speed storage location that can be used for the temporary storage of frequently used data. As data may be retrieved more quickly from cache than the original storage location, cache allows applications to run more quickly. Web site contents often reside in cached storage locations on a hard drive.

Caching: The temporary storage of frequently-used data to speed access. *See also* Cache.

CAD (Computer Aided Design): The use of a wide range of computer-based tools that assist engineers, architects and other design professionals in their design activities

Case De–Duplication: Eliminates duplicates to retain only one copy of each document per case. For example, if an identical document resides with three custodians, only the first custodian's copy will be saved. *See* De–Duplication.

Catalog: *See* Index.

CCD (Charge Coupled Device): A computer chip the output of which correlates with the light or color passed by it. Individual CCDs or arrays of these are used in scanners as a high-resolution, digital camera to read documents.

CCITT Group 4: A lossless compression technique/format that reduces the size of a file, generally about 5:1 over RLE and 40:1 over bitmap. CCITT Group 4 compression may only be used for bi-tonal images.

CCITT: Consultative Committee for International Telephone & Telegraphy. Sets standards for phones, faxes, modems, etc. The standard exists primarily for fax documents.

CDPD (Cellular Digital Packet Data): A data communication standard utilizing the unused capacity of cellular voice providers to transfer data.

CD-R (Compact Disc Recordable): A CD–ROM on which a user may permanently record data once using a CD Burner.

CD-RW (Compact Disc Re–Writable): A CD–ROM on which a user may record data multiple times.

CD-ROM: *See* Compact Disc.

Certificate: An electronic affidavit vouching for the identity of the transmitter. *See* Digital Signature, PKI Digital Signature.

CGA (Color Graphics Adapter): *See Video Graphics Adapter (VGA).*

Chaff/winnowing: Advanced encryption technique involving data dispersal and mixing.

Chain of Custody: Documentation and testimony regarding the possession, movement, handling and location of evidence from the time it is obtained to the time it is presented in court; used to prove that evidence has not been altered or tampered with in any way; necessary both to assure admissibility and probative value.

Character Treatment: The use of all caps or another standard form of treating letters in a coding project.

Checksum: A value used to ensure data is stored or transmitted without error. It is created by calculating the binary values in a block of data using some algorithm and storing the results with the data. When the data is retrieved from memory or received at the other end of a network, a new checksum is computed and matched against the existing checksum. A non-match indicates an error.

Child: *See* Document.

CIE (Commission International de l'Eclairage): The international commission on color matching and illumination systems.

CIFS (Common Internet File System): Used for client/server communication within Microsoft® operating systems. With CIFS, users with different platforms and computers can share files without having to install new software.

Cine-Mode: Data recorded on a film strip such that it can be read by a human when held vertically.

Cinepak: A compression algorithm; *see* MPEG.

CITIS (Contractor Integrated Technical Information Service): The Department of Defense now requires contractors to have an integrated electronic document image and management system.

Clawback Agreement: An agreement outlining procedures to be followed to protect against waiver of privilege or work product protection due to inadvertent production of documents or data.

Client/Server: An architecture whereby a computer system consists of one or more server computers and numerous client computers (workstations). The system is functionally distributed across several nodes on a network and is typified by a high degree of parallel processing across distributed nodes. With client-server architecture, CPU intensive processes (such as searching and indexing) are completed on the server, while image viewing and OCR occur on the client. This dramatically reduces network data traffic and insulates the database from workstation interruptions.

Client: Any computer system that requests a service of another computer system. A workstation requesting the contents of a file from a file server is a client of the file server. *See* Thin Client.

Clipboard: A holding area that temporarily stores information copied or cut from a document.

Cluster (File): The smallest unit of storage space that can be allocated to store a file on operating systems. Windows and DOS organize hard discs based on Clusters (also known as allocation units), which consist of one or more contiguous sectors. Discs using smaller cluster sizes waste less space and store information more efficiently.

Cluster (System): A collection of individual computers that appear as a single logical unit. Also referred to as matrix or grid systems.

Cluster bitmaps: Used in NTFS (New Technology File System) to keep track of the status (free or used) of clusters on the hard drive. *See* NTFS.

Clustering: *See* Data Categorization.

CMYK: Cyan, Magenta, Yellow and Black. A subtractive method used in four color printing and Desktop Publishing.

Coding: Automated or human process by which documents are examined and evaluated using pre-determined codes, and the results recorded. Coding usually identifies names, dates, and relevant terms or phrases. Coding may be structured (limited to the selection of one of a finite number of choices), or unstructured (a narrative comment about a document). Coding may be objective, *i.e.*, the name of the sender or the date, or subjective, *i.e.*, evaluation as to the relevancy or probative value of documents. *See* Bibliographical/Objective Coding and Subjective Coding.

COLD (Computer Output to Laser Disc): A computer programming process that outputs electronic records and printed reports to laser disc instead of a printer.

COM (Computer Output to Microfilm): A process that outputs electronic records and computer generated reports to microfilm.

Comb: A series of boxes with their top missing. Tick marks guide text entry and separate characters. Used in forms processing rather than boxes.

Comic Mode: Human-readable data, recorded on a strip of film that can be read when the film is moved horizontally to the reader.

Comma Separated Value (CSV): A record layout that separates data fields/values with a comma and typically encloses data in quotation marks.

Compact Disc (CD): A type of optical disc storage media, compact discs come in a variety of formats. These formats include CD–ROMs ("CD Read–Only Memory") that are read-only; CD–Rs ("CD Recordable") that are written to once and are then read-only; and CD–RWs ("CD Re–Writable") that can be written to multiple times.

Compliance Search: The identification of and search for relevant terms and/or parties in response to a discovery request.

Component Video: Separates video into luminosity and color signals that provide the highest possible signal quality.

Composite Video: Combines red, green, blue and synchronization signals into one video signal so that only one connector is required; used by most TVs and VCRs.

Compound Document: A file that collects or combines more than one document into one, often from different applications, by embedding objects or linked data; multiple elements may be included, such as images, text, animation or hypertext. *See also* OLE.

Compression: Compression algorithms such as Zip and RLE reduce the size of files saving both storage space and reducing bandwidth required for access and transmission. Data compression is widely used in backup utilities, spreadsheet applications and database management systems. Compression generally eliminates redundant information and/or predicts where changes will occur. "Lossless" compression techniques such as Zip and RLE preserve the integrity of the input. Coding standards such as JPEG and MPEG employ "lossy" methods that do not preserve all of the original information, and are most commonly used for photographs, audio, and video. *See* Container File, Decompression, Lossless Compression and Lossy Compression.

Compression Ratio: The ratio of the size of an uncompressed file to a compressed file, *e.g.*, with a 10:1 compression ratio, a 1 MB file can be compressed to 100 KB.

Computer Forensics: Computer Forensics is the use of specialized techniques for recovery, authentication and analysis of electronic data when an investigation or litigation involves issues relating to reconstruction of computer usage, examination of residual data, authentication of data by technical analysis or explanation of technical features of data and computer usage. Computer forensics requires specialized expertise that goes beyond normal data collection and preservation techniques available to end-users or system support personnel, and generally requires strict adherence to chain-of-custody protocols. *See also* Forensics *and* Forensic Copy.

Computer: Includes but is not limited to network servers, desktops, laptops, notebook computers, mainframes and PDAs (personal digital assistants).

Concatenate: Generally, to add by linking or joining so as to form a chain or series; two or more databases of similar structure can be concatenated to enable referencing as one.

Concept Search: Searching electronic documents to determine relevance by analyzing the words and putting search requests in conceptual groupings so the true meaning of the request is considered. Concept searching considers both the word and the context in which it appears to differentiate between concepts such as diamond (baseball) and diamond (jewelry).

Container File: A single file containing multiple documents and/or files, *e.g.* .pst, .nsf and .zip files. The file must be ripped or decompressed to determine volume, size, record count, etc., and to be processed for litigation review and production. *See* Decompression *and* Rip.

Content Comparison: A method of de-duplication that compares file content or output (to image or paper) and ignores metadata. *See also* De–Duplication.

Contextual Search: Searching electronic documents where the surrounding text is analyzed to determine relevancy.

Continuous Tone: An image (*e.g.* a photograph) that has all the values of gray from white to black.

Convergence: Integration of computing, communications and broadcasting systems.

Cookie: A message given to a Web browser by a Web server. The browser stores the message in a text file. The message is then sent back to the server each time the browser requests a page from the server. The main purpose of cookies is to identify users and possibly prepare customized Web pages for them.

Coordinated Universal Time (UTC): a high precision atomic time standard with uniform seconds defined by International Time and leap seconds announced at regular internals to compensate for the earth's slowing rotation and other discrepancies. Leap seconds allow UTC to closely track Universal Time, a time standard based not on the uniform passage of seconds, but on the Earth's angular rotation. Time zones around the world are expressed as positive or negative offsets from UTC. Local time is UTC plus the time zone offset for that location, plus an offset (typically $+1$) for daylight savings, if in effect. As the zero point reference, UTC is also referred to as Zulu time (Z). *See also* Normalization.

Corrupted File: A file damaged in some way, such as by a virus, or by software or hardware failure, so that it is partially or completely unreadable by a computer.

COTS (Commercial Off-the-Shelf): Hardware or software products that are commercially manufactured, ready-made and available for use by the general public without the need for customization.

CPI: Characters Per Inch.

CPU (Central Processing Unit): The primary silicon chip that runs a computer's operating system and application software. It performs a computer's essential mathematical functions and controls essential operations.

CRC (Cyclical Redundancy Checking): Used in data communications to create a checksum character at the end of a data block to ensure integrity of data transmission and receipt. *See* Checksum.

CRM (Customer Relationship Management): Applications that help manage clients and contacts. Used in larger companies. Often a significant repository of sales, customer, and sometimes marketing data.

Cross-Custodian De–Duplication: Culls a document to the extent multiple copies of that document reside within different custodians' data sets. *See* De–Duplication.

CRT (Cathode Ray Tube): The picture tube of older computer monitors or televisions, to be distinguished from newer "flat" LCD or plasma screens.

Cryptography: Technique to scramble data to preserve confidentiality or authenticity.

Cull (verb): To remove a document from the collection to be produced or reviewed. *See* Data Filtering, Harvesting.

Custodian: Person having control of a network, computer or specific electronic files.

Custodian De–Duplication: Culls a document to the extent multiple copies of that document reside within the same custodian's data set. *See* De–Duplication.

Customer-Added metadata: *See* User–Added Metadata.

CYAN: Cyan-colored ink reflects blue and green and absorbs red.

Cylinder: The set of tracks on both sides of each platter in the hard drive that is located at the same head position. *See* Platter.

DAC (Digital to Analog Converter): Converts digital data to analog data.

DAD (Digital Audio Disc): Another term for compact disc.

DAT (Digital Audio Tape): A magnetic tape generally used to record audio but can hold up to 40 gigabytes (or 60 CDs) of data if used for data storage. Has the disadvantage of being a serial access device. Often used for backup.

Data: Any information stored on a computer. All software is divided into two general categories: data and programs. Programs are collections of instructions for manipulating data. In database management systems, data files are the files that store the database information. Other files, such as index files and data dictionaries, store administrative information, known as metadata.

Data Categorization: The categorization and sorting of ESI—such as foldering by "concept", content, subject, taxonomy, etc.—through the use of technology—such as search and retrieval software or artificial intelligence—to facilitate review and analysis.

Data Collection: See Harvesting.

Data Controller (as used with regard to the EU Data Protection Act): The natural or legal person who alone or jointly with others determines the purposes for which and the manner in which any Personal Data are to be processed.

Data Element: A combination of characters or bytes referring to one separate piece of information, such as name, address, or age.

Data Encryption Standard (DES): A form of private key encryption developed by IBM in the late 1970's.

Data Extraction: The process of retrieving data from documents (hard copy or electronic). The process may be manual or electronic.

Data Field: *See* Field.

Data Filtering: The process of identifying for extraction specific data based on specified parameters.

Data Formats: The organization of information for display, storage or printing. Data is sometimes maintained in certain common formats so that it can be used by various programs, which may only work with data in a particular format, *e.g.* PDF, html.

Data Harvesting: *See* Harvesting.

Data Mining: Data mining generally refers to knowledge discovery in databases (structured data); often techniques for extracting summaries and reports from databases and data sets. In the context of electronic discovery, this term often refers to the processes used to cull through a collection of ESI to extract evidence for production or presentation in an investigation or in litigation. *See also* Text Mining.

Data Processor (as used with regard to the EU Data Protection Act): A natural or legal person (other than an employee of the Data Controller) who processes Personal Data on behalf of the Data Controller.

Data Set: A named or defined collection of data. *See also* Production Data Set and Privilege Data Set.

Data Subject (as used with regard to the EU Data Protection Act): An individual who is the subject of Personal Data.

Data Verification: Assessment of data to ensure it has not been modified. The most common method of verification is hash coding by some method such as MD5. *See also* Digital Fingerprint *and* File Level Binary Comparison *and* Hash Coding.

Database Management System (DBMS): A software system used to access and retrieve data stored in a database.

Database: In electronic records, a database is a set of data elements consisting of at least one file, or of a group of integrated files, usually stored in one location and made available to several users. Databases are sometimes classified according to their organizational approach, with the most prevalent approach being the relational database—a tabular database in which data is defined so that it can be reorganized and accessed in a number of different ways. Another popular organizational structure is the distributed database, which can be dispersed or replicated among different points in a network. Computer databases typically contain aggregations of data records or files, such as sales transactions, product catalogs and inventories, and customer profiles. SQL (Structured Query Language) is a standard computer language for making interactive queries from and updates to a database.

Date/Time Normalization: *See* Normalization.

Daubert (challenge): *Daubert v. Merrell Dow Pharmaceuticals*, 509 U.S. 579 (1993), addresses the admission of scientific expert testimony to ensure that the testimony is reliable before considered for admission pursuant to Rule 702. The court assesses the testimony by analyzing the methodology and applicability of the expert's approach. Faced with a proffer of expert scientific testimony, the trial judge must determine first, pursuant to Rule 104(a), whether the expert is proposing to testify to (1) scientific knowledge that (2) will assist the trier of fact to understand or determine a fact at issue. This involves preliminary assessment of whether the reasoning or methodology is scientifically valid and whether it can be applied to the facts at issue. *Daubert* suggests an open approach and provides a list of four potential factors: (1) whether the theory can be or has been tested; (2) whether the theory has been subjected to peer review or publication; (3) known or potential rate of error of that particular technique and the existence and maintenance of standards controlling the technique's operation; and (4) consideration of general acceptance within the scientific community. 509 U.S. at 593–94.

DDE (Dynamic Data Exchange): A form of interprocess communications used by Microsoft Windows to support the exchange of commands and data between two simultaneously running applications.

DEB (Digital Evidence Bag): a standardized electronic "wrapper" or "container" for electronic evidence to preserve and transfer evidence in an encrypted or protected form that prevents deliberate or accidental alteration. The secure "wrapper" provides metadata concerning the collection process and context for the contained data.

Decompression: To expand or restore compressed data back to its original size and format. *See* Compression.

Decryption: Transformation of encrypted (or scrambled) data back to original form.

De-Duplication: De–Duplication ("De–Duping") is the process of comparing electronic records based on their characteristics and removing or marking duplicate records within the data set. The definition of "duplicate records" should be agreed upon, *i.e.*, whether an exact copy from a different location (such as a different mailbox, server tapes, etc.) is considered to be a duplicate. De-duplication can be selective, depending on the agreed-upon criteria. *See also* Case De–Duplication, Content Comparison, Cross–Custodian De–Duplication, Custodian De–Duplication, Data Verification, Digital Fingerprint, File Level Binary Comparison, Hash Coding, Horizontal De–Duplication, Metadata Comparison, Near De–Duplication, and Production De–Duplication.

De-Fragment ("de-frag"): Use of a computer utility to reorganize files so they are more contiguous on a hard drive or other storage medium, if the files or parts thereof have become fragmented and scattered in various locations within the storage medium in the course of normal computer operations. Used to optimize the operation of the computer, it will overwrite information in unallocated space. *See* Fragmented.

Deleted Data: Deleted Data is data that existed on the computer as live data and which have been deleted by the computer system or end-user activity. Deleted data may remain on storage media in whole or in part until they are overwritten or "wiped." Even after the data itself has been wiped, directory entries, pointers or other information relating to the deleted data may remain on the computer. "Soft deletions" are data marked as deleted (and not generally available to the end-user after such marking), but not yet physically removed or overwritten. Soft-deleted data can be restored with complete integrity.

Deleted File: A file with disc space that has been designated as available for reuse; the deleted file remains intact until it is overwritten.

Deletion: Deletion is the process whereby data is removed from active files and other data storage structures on computers and rendered inaccessible except through the use of special data recovery tools designed to recover deleted data. Deletion occurs on several levels in modern computer systems: (a) *File level deletion* renders the file inaccessible to the operating system and normal application programs and marks the storage space occupied by the file's directory entry and contents as free and available to re-use for data storage, (b) *Record level deletion* occurs when a record is rendered inaccessible to a database management system (DBMS) (usually marking the record storage space as available for re-use by the DBMS, although in some cases the space is never reused until the database is compacted) and is also characteristic of many email systems (c) *Byte level deletion* occurs when text or other information is deleted from the file content (such as the deletion of text from a word processing file); such deletion may render the deleted data inaccessible to the application intended to be used in processing the file, but may not actually remove the data from the file's content until a process such as compaction or rewriting of the file causes the deleted data to be overwritten.

De-NIST: The use of an automated filter program that screens files against the NIST list of computer file types to separate those generated by a system and those generated by a user. *See* NIST List.

Descenders: The portion of a character that falls below the main part of the letter (*e.g.* g, p, q)

De-shading: Removing shaded areas to render images more easily recognizable by OCR. De-shading software typically searches for areas with a regular pattern of tiny dots.

De-skewing: The process of straightening skewed (tilted) images. De-skewing is one of the image enhancements that can improve OCR accuracy. Documents often become skewed when scanned or faxed.

Desktop: Generally refers to the working area of the display on an individual PC.

De-speckling: Removing isolated speckles from an image file. Speckles often develop when a document is scanned or faxed. *See* Speckle.

DIA/DCA (Document Interchange Architecture): An IBM standard for transmission and storage of voice, text or video over networks.

Digital: Information stored as a string of ones and zeros. Opposite of analog.

Digital Certificate: Electronic records that contain keys used to decrypt information, especially information sent over a public network like the Internet.

Digital Fingerprint: A fixed-length hash code that uniquely represents the binary content of a file. *See also* Data Verification *and* File Level Binary Comparison *and* Hash Coding.

Digital Signature: A way to ensure the identity of the sender, utilizing public key cryptography and working in conjunction with certificates. *See* Certificate and PKI Digital Signature.

Digitize: The process of converting an analog value into a digital (numeric) representation.

Directory: A simulated file folder or container used to organize files and directories in a hierarchical or tree-like structure. UNIX and DOS use the term "directory," while Mac and Windows use the term "folder."

Dirty Text: OCR output reflecting text as read by the OCR engine(s) with no clean up.

Disaster Recovery Tapes: Portable media used to store data for backup purposes. *See* Backup Data/Backup Tapes.

Disc mirroring: A method of protecting data from a catastrophic hard disc failure or for long term data storage. As each file is stored on the hard disc, a "mirror" copy is made on a second hard disc or on a different part of the same disc. *See also* Mirroring and Mirror Image.

Disc Partition: A hard drive containing a set of consecutive cylinders.

Disc/Disk: Round, flat storage media with layers of material that enable the recording of data.

Discovery: Discovery is the process of identifying, locating, securing and producing information and materials for the purpose of obtaining evidence for utilization in the legal process. The term is also used to describe the process of reviewing all materials that may be potentially relevant to the issues at hand and/or that may need to be disclosed to other parties, and of evaluating evidence to prove or disprove facts, theories or allegations. There are several ways to conduct discovery, the most common of which are interrogatories, requests for production of documents and depositions.

Discwipe: Utility that overwrites existing data. Various utilities exist with varying degrees of efficiency—some wipe only named files or unallocated space of residual data, thus unsophisticated users who try to wipe evidence may leave behind files of which they are unaware.

Disposition: The final business action carried out on a record. This action generally is to destroy or archive the record. Electronic record disposition can include "soft deletions" (*see* Deletion), "hard deletions," "hard deletions with overwrites," "archive to long-term store," "forward to organization," and "copy to another media or format and delete (hard or soft)."

Distributed Data: Distributed Data is that information belonging to an organization that resides on portable media and non-local devices such as remote offices, home computers, laptop computers, personal digital assistants ("PDAs"), wireless communication devices (*e.g.*, Blackberry) and Internet repositories (including email hosted by Internet service providers or portals and web sites). Distributed data also includes data held by third parties such as application service providers and business partners. *Note*: Information Technology organizations may define distributed data differently (for example, in some organizations distributed data includes any non-server-based data, including workstation disc drives).

Dithering: In printing, dithering is usually called *halftoning*, and shades of gray are called *halftones*. The more dither patterns that a device or program supports, the more shades of gray it can represent. Dithering is the process of converting grays to different densities of black dots, usually for the purposes of printing or storing color or grayscale images as black and white images.

DLT (Digital Linear Tape): A type of backup tape that can hold up to 80 GB depending on the data file format.

Document (or Document Family): A collection of pages or files produced manually or by a software application, constituting a logical single communication of information, but consisting of more than a single stand-alone record. Examples include a fax cover, the faxed letter, and an attachment to the letter—the fax cover being the "Parent," and the letter and attachment being a "Child." *See also* Attachment, Load File, Message Unit, and Unitization—Physical and Logical.

Document Date: The original creation date of a document. For an email, the document date is indicated by the date-stamp of the email.

Document Imaging Programs: Software used to store, manage, retrieve and distribute documents quickly and easily on the computer.

Document Metadata: Properties about the file stored in the file, as opposed to document content. Often this data is not immediately viewable in the software application used to create/edit the document but often can be accessed via a "Properties" view. Examples include document author and company, and create and revision dates. Contrast with File System Metadata and Email Metadata. *See also* Metadata.

Document Type or Doc Type: A typical field used in bibliographical coding. Typical doc type examples include correspondence, memo, report, article and others.

DoD 5015: Department of Defense standard addressing records management.

Domain: A sub-network of servers and computers within a LAN. Domain information is useful when restoring backup tapes, particularly of email.

Domino Database: Another name for Lotus Notes Databases versions 5.0 or higher. *See* NSF.

DOS: *See* MS–DOS.

Dot Pitch: Distance of one pixel in a CRT to the next pixel on the vertical plane. The smaller the number, the higher quality display.

Double Byte Language: *See* Unicode.

Download: To copy data from another computer to one's own, usually over a network or the Internet.

DPI (Dots Per Inch): The measurement of the resolution of display in printing systems. A typical CRT screen provides 96 dpi, which provides 9,216 dots per square inch (96x96). When a paper document is scanned, the resolution, or level of detail, at which the scanning was performed is expressed in DPI. Typically, documents are scanned at 200 or 300 DPI.

Draft Record: A draft record is a preliminary version of a record before it has been completed, finalized, accepted, validated or filed. Such records include working files and notes. Records and information management policies may provide for the destruction of draft records upon finalization, acceptance, validation or filing of the final or official version of the record. However, draft records generally must be retained if (1) they are deemed to be subject to a legal hold; or (2) a specific law or regulation mandates their retention and policies should recognize such exceptions.

Drag-and-Drop: The movement of on-screen objects by dragging them with the mouse, and dropping them in another place.

DRAM: Dynamic Random Access Memory, a memory technology that is periodically "refreshed" or updated—as opposed to "static" RAM chips that do not require refreshing. The term is often used to refer to the memory chips themselves.

Drive Geometry: A computer hard drive is made up of a number of rapidly rotating platters that have a set of read/write heads on both sides of each platter. Each platter is divided into a series of concentric rings called tracks. Each track is further divided into sections called sectors, and each sector is sub-divided into bytes. Drive geometry refers to the number and positions of each of these structures.

Driver: A driver is a computer program that controls various devices such as the keyboard, mouse, monitor, etc.

Drop-Down Menu: A menu window that opens on-screen to display context-related options. Also called pop-up menu or pull-down menu.

DSP (Digital Signal Processor/Processing): A special purpose computer (or technique) which digitally processes signals and electrical/analog waveforms.

DTP (Desktop Publishing): PC applications used to prepare direct print output or output suitable for printing presses.

Duplex Scanners vs. Double–Sided Scanning: Duplex scanners automatically scan both sides of a double-sided page, producing two images at once. Double-sided scanning uses a single-sided scanner to scan double-sided pages, scanning one collated stack of paper, then flipping it over and scanning the other side.

Duplex: Two-sided page(s).

DVD (Digital Video Disc or Digital Versatile Disc): A plastic disc, like a CD, on which data can be written and read. DVDs are faster, can hold more information, and can support more data formats than CDs.

ECM: Enterprise content management.

EDB: Microsoft Exchange Server email container file.

EDI (Electronic Data Interchange): Eliminating forms altogether by encoding the data as close as possible to the point of the transaction; automated business information exchange.

EDMS (Electronic Document Management System): A system to electronically manage documents during all life cycles. *See* Electronic Document Management.

EGA (Extended Graphics Adapter): *See* VGA.

EIA: Electronic Industries Association

EIM: Electronic Image Management.

EISA (Extended Industry Standard Architecture): One of the standard buses used for PCs.

Electronic Discovery ("E–Discovery"): The process of collecting, preparing, reviewing, and producing electronically stored information ("ESI") in the context of the legal process. *See* Discovery.

Electronic Document Management: For paper documents, involves imaging, indexing/coding and archiving of scanned documents/images, and thereafter electronically managing them during all life cycle phases. Electronic documents are likewise electronically managed from creation to archiving and all stages in between. Often referred to as ILM (information lifecycle management).

Electronic File Processing: Generally includes extraction of certain metadata and text from files, identification of duplicates/de-duplication and rendering of data into delimited format.

Electronic Image: An electronic or digital picture of a document (*e.g.* TIFF, PDF, etc.).

Electronic Record: Information recorded in a form that requires a computer or other machine to process it and that otherwise satisfies the definition of a record.

Electrostatic Printing: A process in which paper is exposed to electron charge, causing toner to stick to the charged pixels.

Em: In any print, font or size is equal to the width of the letter "M" in that font and size.

Email (Electronic Mail): An electronic means for communicating information under specified conditions, generally in the form of text messages, through systems that will send, store, process, and receive information and in which messages are held in storage until the addressee accesses them.

Email address: An electronic mail address. Internet email addresses follow the formula: user-ID@domain-name; other email protocols may use different address formats. In some email systems, a user's email address is "aliased" or represented by his or her natural name rather than a fully qualified email address. For example, john.doe@ abc.com might appear simply as John Doe.

Email Message: A document created or received via an electronic mail system, including brief notes, formal or substantive narrative documents. Any attachments that may be transmitted with the email message, such as word processing and other electronic documents, are not part of the email message, but are part of the "Message Unit."

Email Metadata: Data stored in the email about the email. Often this data is not even viewable in the email client application used to create the email, *e.g.*, blind copy addressees, received date. The amount of email metadata available for a particular email varies greatly depending on the email system. Contrast with File System Metadata and Document Metadata.

Email String: A series of emails linked together by email responses or forwards. The series of email messages created through multiple responses and answers to an originating message. Also referred to as an email "thread." Comments, revisions, and attachments are all part of an email string. *See* Thread.

Email Store: Files containing message units. *See* Container Files, Message Unit, EDB, OST, PST, *and* NSF.

Embedded Metadata: Generally hidden, but an integral part of ESI, such as "track changes" or "comments" in a word processing file or "notes" in a presentation file. While some metadata is routinely extracted during processing and conversion for e-discovery, embedded data may not be. Therefore, it may only available in the original, native file. *See also* Application Metadata and Metadata.

Embedded Object: An object embedded within another object, often appearing as an icon or hyperlink. *See also* Compound Document.

EML: Generic email format.

Encoding: To change or translate into code; to convert information into digital format. For software, encoding is used for video and audio references, like encoding analogue format into digital or raw digital data into compressed format.

Encryption: A procedure that renders the contents of a message or file scrambled or unintelligible to anyone not authorized to read it. Encryption is used to protect information as it moves from one computer to another and is an increasingly common way of sending credit card numbers and other personal information over the Internet.

Encryption Key: A data value that is used to encrypt and decrypt data. The number of bits in the encryption key is a rough measure of the encryption strength; generally, the more bits in the encryption key, the more difficult it is to break.

End Document Number or End Doc#: The last single page image of a document.

Endorser: A small printer in a scanner that adds a document-control number or other endorsement to each scanned sheet.

Enhanced Titles: A meaningful/descriptive title for a document. The opposite of Verbatim Titles.

Enterprise Architecture: Framework for how software, computing, storage and networking systems should integrate and operate to meet the changing needs across an entire business

EOF (End of File): A distinctive code that uniquely marks the end of a data file.

EPP (Enhanced Parallel Port): *See* Port.

EPS (Encapsulated PostScript): Uncompressed files for images, text and objects. Only print on PostScript printers.

Erasable Optical Drive: A type of optical drive that uses erasable optical discs.

ESDI (Enhanced Small Device Interface): A defined, common electronic interface for transferring data between computers and peripherals, particularly disc drives.

ESI: Electronically stored information, regardless of the media or whether it is in the original format in which it was created, as opposed to stored in hard copy (i.e. on paper).

Ethernet: A common way of networking PCs to create a Local Area Network (LAN).

Evidentiary Image or Copy: *See* Forensic Copy.

Exabyte: 1,152,921,504,606,846,976 bytes—1024^6 (a quintillion bytes). *See* Byte.

Exchange Server: A server running Microsoft Exchange messaging and collaboration software. It is widely used by enterprises using Microsoft infrastructure solutions. Among other things, Microsoft Exchange manages email, shared calendars and tasks.

Expanded Data: *See* Decompression.

Export: Data extracted or taken out of one environment or application usually in a prescribed format, and usually for import into another environment or application.

Extended Partitions: If a computer hard drive has been divided into more than four partitions, extended partitions are created. Under such circumstances each extended partition contains a partition table in the first sector that describes how it is further subdivided.

Extensible Markup Language (XML): A specification developed by the W3C (World Wide Web Consortium—the Web development standards board). XML is a pared-down version of SGML, designed especially for Web documents. It allows designers to create their own customized tag, enabling the definition, transmission, validation, and interpretation of data between applications and between organizations.

Extranet: An Internet based access method to a corporate intranet site by limited or total access through a security firewall. This type of access is often utilized in cases of joint defense, joint venture and vendor client relationships.

False Negative: A result that is not correct because it fails to indicate a match where one exists.

False Positive: A result that is not correct because it indicates a match where there is none.

Fast Mode Parallel Port: *See* Port.

FAT (File Allocation Table): An internal data table on hard drives that keeps track of where the files are stored. If a FAT is corrupt, a drive may be unusable, yet the data may be retrievable with forensics. *See* Cluster.

FAX: Short for facsimile. A process of transmitting documents by scanning them to digital, converting to analog, transmitting over phone lines and reversing the process at the other end and printing.

Fiber Optics: Transmitting information by sending light pulses over cables made from thin strands of glass.

Field (or Data Field): A name for an individual piece of standardized data, such as the author of a document, a recipient, the date of a document or any other piece of data common to most documents in an image collection, to be extracted from the collection.

Field Separator: A code that separates the fields in a record. For example, the CSV format uses a comma as the field separator.

File: A collection of data or information stored under a specified name on a disc.

File Compression: *See* Compression.

File Extension: Many systems, including DOS and UNIX, allow a filename extension that consists of one or more characters following the proper filename. For example, image files are usually stored as .bmp, .gif, .jpg or .tiff. Audio files are often stored as .aud or .wav. There are a multitude of file extensions identifying file formats. The filename extension should indicate what type of file it is; however, users may change filename extensions to evade firewall restrictions or for other reasons. Therefore, file types should be identified at a binary level rather than relying on file extensions. To research file types, see (http://www.filext.com). Different applications can often recognize only a predetermined selection of file types. *See also* Format.

File Format: The organization or characteristics of a file that determine with which software programs it can be used. *See also* Format.

File Header: *See* Header.

File Level Binary Comparison: Method of de-duplication using the digital fingerprint (hash) of a file. File Level Binary comparison ignores metadata, and can determine that "SHOPPING LIST.DOC" and "TOP SECRET.DOC" are actually the same document. *See also* Data Verification, De–Duplication, Digital Fingerprint, and Hash coding.

File Plan: A document containing the identifying number, title, description, and disposition authority of files held or used in an office.

File Server: When several or many computers are networked together in a LAN situation, one computer may be utilized as a storage location for files for the group. File servers may be employed to store email, financial data, word processing information or to back-up the network. *See* Server.

File Sharing: Sharing files stored on the server among several users on a network.

File Signature: *See* Digital Signature.

File Slack: The unused space on a cluster that exists when the logical file space is less than the physical file space. *See* Cluster.

File System: The engine that an operating system or program uses to organize and keep track of ESI. More specifically, the logical structures and software routines used to control access to the storage on a hard disc system and the overall structure in which the files are named, stored, and organized. The file system plays a critical role in computer forensics because the file system determines the logical structure of the hard drive, including its cluster size. The file system also determines what happens to data when the user deletes a file or subdirectory.

File System Metadata: Metadata generated by the system to track the demographics (name, size, location, usage, etc.) of the ESI and, not embedded within, but stored externally from the ESI. *See also* Metadata.

File Table: *See* MFT.

File Transfer: The process of moving or transmitting a file from one location to another, as between two programs or from one computer to another.

Filename: The name of a file, excluding root drive and directory path information. Different operating systems may impose different restrictions on filenames, for example, by prohibiting use of certain characters in a filename or imposing a limit on the length of a filename. The filename extension should indicate what type of file it is. However, users often change filename extensions to evade firewall restrictions or for other reasons. Therefore, file types must be identified at a binary level rather than relying on file extensions. *See also* File Extension *and* Full Path.

FIPS: Federal Information Processing Standards issued by the National Institute of Standards and Technology after approval by the Secretary of Commerce pursuant to Section 111(d) of the Federal Property and Administrative Services Act of 1949, as amended by the Computer Security Act of 1987, Public Law 100–235.

Firewall: A set of related programs, or hardware, that protect the resources of a private network from users from other networks. A firewall filters information to determine whether to forward the information toward its destination.

Filter (verb): See Data Filtering.

Flash Drive: *See* Key Drive.

Flash Memory: The ability to retain data even when power is removed; the equivalent to film for digital cameras.

Flat File: Flat file is a non-relational text based file (ie: a word processing document).

Flatbed Scanner: A flat-surface scanner that allows users to create a digital image of books and other hard copy documents or objects. *See* Scanner.

Floppy Disc: A thin magnetic film disc housed in a protective sleeve used to copy and transport relatively small amounts of data.

Folder: *See* Directory.

Forensic Copy: A forensic copy is an exact copy of an entire physical storage media (hard drive, CD–ROM, DVD–ROM, tape, etc.), including all active and residual data and unallocated or slack space on the media. Compresses and encrypts to ensure authentication and protect chain of custody. Forensic copies are often called "image" or "imaged copies." *See* Bit Stream Back-up and Mirror Image.

Forensics: The scientific examination and analysis of data held on, or retrieved from, ESI in such a way that the information can be used as evidence in a court of law. It may include the secure collection of computer data; the examination of suspect data to determine details such as origin and content; the presentation of computer based information to courts of law; and the application of a country's laws to computer practice. Forensics may involve recreating "deleted" or missing files from hard drives, validating dates and logged in authors/editors of documents, and certifying key elements of documents and/or hardware for legal purposes.

Form of Production: The manner in which requested documents are produced. Used to refer both to file format (*e.g.,* native vs. imaged format) and the media on which the documents are produced (paper vs. electronic).

Format (noun): The internal structure of a file, which defines the way it is stored and used. Specific applications may define unique formats for their data (*e.g.*, "MS Word document file format"). Many files may only be viewed or printed using their originating application or an application designed to work with compatible formats. There are several common email formats, such as Outlook and Lotus Notes. Computer storage systems commonly identify files by a naming convention that denotes the format (and therefore the probable originating application). For example, "DOC" for Microsoft Word document files; "XLS" for Microsoft Excel spreadsheet files; "TXT" for text files; "HTM" for Hypertext Markup Language (HTML) files such as web pages; "PPT" for Microsoft Powerpoint files; "TIF" for tiff images; "PDF" for Adobe images; etc. Users may choose alternate naming conventions, but this will likely affect how the files are treated by applications.

Format (verb): To make a drive ready for first use. Erroneously thought to "wipe" drive. Typically, only overwrites FAT, but not files on the drive.

Forms Processing: A specialized imaging application designed for handling pre-printed forms. Forms processing systems often use high-end (or multiple) OCR engines and elaborate data validation routines to extract hand-written or poor quality print from forms that go into a database.

Fragmented: In the course of normal computer operations when files are saved, deleted or moved, the files or parts thereof may be broken into pieces, or fragmented, and scattered in various locations on the computer's hard drive or other storage medium, such as removable discs. Data saved in contiguous clusters may be larger than contiguous free space, and it is broken up and randomly placed throughout the available storage space. *See* De–Fragment.

FTP (File Transfer Protocol): An Internet protocol that enables the transfer of files between computers over a network or the Internet.

Full Duplex: Data communications devices that allow full speed transmission in both directions at the same time.

Full Path: A path name description that includes the drive, starting or root directory, all attached subdirectories and ending with the file or object name.

Full-Text Indexing: Every word in the ESI is indexed into a master word list with pointers to the location within the ESI where each occurrence of the word appears.

Full-Text Search: The ability to search ESI for specific words, numbers and/or combinations or patterns thereof.

Fuzzy Search: Subjective content searching (as compared to word searching of objective data). Fuzzy Searching lets the user find documents where word matching does not have to be exact, even if the words searched are misspelled due to optical character recognition (OCR) errors. This search locates all occurrences of the search term, as well as words that are "close" in spelling to the search term.

GAL: A Microsoft Outlook global address list—directory of all Microsoft Exchange users and distribution lists to whom messages can be addressed. The administrator creates and maintains this list. The global address list may also contain public folder names. Entries from this list can be added to a user's personal address book (PAB).

Ghost: See Bit Stream Back-up.

GIF(Graphics Interchange Format): CompuServe's native file format for storing images. Limited to 256 colors.

Gigabyte (GB): 1,073,741,824 bytes—1,024³ (a billion bytes). *See* Byte.

GMT Timestamp: Identification of a file using Greenwich Mean Time as the central time authentication method. *See also* Normalization.

GPS Generated Timestamp: Timestamp identifying time as a function of its relationship to Greenwich Mean Time.

Gray Scale: The use of many shades of gray to represent an image. *Continuous-tone* images, such as black-and-white photographs, use an almost unlimited number of shades of gray. Conventional computer hardware and software, however, can only represent a limited number of shades of gray (typically 16 or 256).

Groupware: Software designed to operate on a network and allow several people to work together on the same documents and files.

GUI (Graphical User Interface, pronounced "gooey"): Presenting an interface to the computer user comprised of pictures and icons, rather than words and numbers.

Hacker: Someone who breaks into computer systems in order to steal, change or destroy information.

Half Duplex: Transmission systems that can send and receive, but not at the same time.

Halftone: *See* Dithering.

Handshake: A transmission that occurs at the beginning of a communications session between computers to ensure they agree on how the communication will proceed.

Hard Drive: The primary storage unit on PCs, consisting of one or more magnetic media platters on which digital data can be written and erased magnetically. *See* Platter.

Harvesting: The process of retrieving or collecting ESI from storage media or devices; an e-discovery vendor or specialist "harvests" ESI from computer hard drives, file servers, CDs, and backup tapes for processing and load to storage media or a database management system.

Hash: A mathematical algorithm that represents a unique value for a given set of data, similar to a digital fingerprint. Common hash algorithms include MD5 and SHA.

Hash Coding: To create a digital fingerprint that represents the binary content of a file unique to every electronically-generated document; assists in subsequently ensuring that data has not been modified. *See also* Data Verification, Digital Fingerprint *and* File Level Binary Comparison.

Hash Function: A function used to create a hash value from binary input. The hash is substantially smaller than the text itself, and is generated by the hash function in such a way that it is extremely unlikely that some other input will produce the same hash value.

HD (High Density): A 5.25" HD Floppy Disc holds 1.2 MB and a 3.5" holds 1.4 MB.

Head: Each platter on a hard drive contains a head for each side of the platter. The heads are devices which ride very closely to the surface of the platter and allow information to be read from and written to the platter.

Header: In information technology, a header is, in general, something that goes in front of something else and is usually repeated as a standard part of the units of something else. A header can consist of multiple fields, each containing its own value. In email it is the part of the message containing information about the message, such as the sender, date sent and other brief details.

Hexadecimal: A number system with a base of 16. The digits are 0–9 and A–F, where F equals the decimal value of 15.

Hidden Files or Data: Files or data not visible in the file directory; cannot be accessed by unauthorized or unsophisticated users. Some operating system files are hidden, to prevent inexperienced users from inadvertently deleting or changing these essential files. *See also* Steganography.

Hierarchical Storage Management (HSM): Software that automatically migrates files from on-line to near-line storage media, usually on the basis of the age or frequency of use of the files.

Hold: *See* Legal Hold.

Holorith: Encoded data on aperture cards *or* old-style punch cards that contained encoded data.

Horizontal De-duplication: A way to identify ESI duplicated across multiple custodians or other production data sets. *See* De–Duplication.

Host: In a network, the central computer that controls the remote computers and holds the central databases.

HP-PCL & HPGL: Hewlett–Packard graphics file formats.

HRS: Handwriting recognition software for interpreting handwriting into machine readable form.

HTCIA (High Technology Crime Investigation Association): Computer forensics non-profit association; resources include educational programs and list servs.

HTML: HyperText Markup Language, developed by CERN of Geneva, Switzerland. The document format used on the Internet. (HTML+ adds support for multi-media.) The tag-based ASCII language used to create pages on the World Wide Web—uses tags to tell a web browser to display text and images. HTML is a markup or "presentation" language, not a programming language. Programming code can be imbedded in an HTML page to make it interactive. *See* Java.

HTTP (HyperText Transfer Protocol): The underlying protocol used by the World Wide Web. HTTP defines how messages are formatted and transmitted, and what actions Web servers and browsers should take in response to various commands. For example, when you enter a URL in your browser, this actually sends an HTTP command to the Web server directing it to fetch and transmit the requested Web page.

Hub: A network device that connects multiple computers/peripherals together and allows them to share ESI. A central unit that repeats and/or amplifies data signals being sent across a network.

Hyperlink: A link—usually appearing as an underlined or highlighted word or picture within a hypertext document—that when clicked changes the active view, possibly to another place within the same document or view, or to another document altogether, usually regardless of the application or environment in which the other document or view exists.

HyperText: Text that includes links or shortcuts to other documents or views, allowing the reader to easily jump from one view to a related view in a non-linear fashion.

Icon: In a GUI, a picture or drawing that is activated by "clicking" a mouse to command the computer program to perform a predefined series of events.

ICR (Intelligent Character Recognition): The conversion of scanned images (bar codes or patterns of bits) to computer recognizable codes (ASCII characters and files) by means of software/programs that define the rules of and algorithms for conversion, helpful for interpreting handwritten text. *See* HRS and OCR.

IDE (Integrated Drive Electronics): An engineering standard for interfacing PCs and hard discs.

IEEE (Institute of Electrical and Electronic Engineers): An international association that sponsors meetings, publishes a number of journals and establishes standards.

ILM: Information lifecycle management.

Image: (1) To image a hard drive is to make an identical copy of the hard drive, including empty sectors. Also known as creating a "mirror image" or "mirroring" the drive. *See* Bit Stream Backup. (2) An electronic or digital picture of a document (*e.g.* TIFF, PDF, etc.).

Image Copy, Imaged Copy: *See* Forensic Copy.

Image Enabling: A software function that creates links between existing applications and stored images.

Image File Format: *See* File Format and Format.

Image Key: The name of a file created when a page is scanned in a collection.

Image Processing Card (IPC): A board mounted in the computer, scanner or printer that facilitates the acquisition and display of images. The primary function of most IPCs is the rapid compression and decompression of image files.

Image Processing: To capture an image or representation, usually from electronic data in native format, enter it in a computer system, and process and manipulate it. *See also* Native Format.

Import: Data brought into an environment or application that has been exported from another environment or application.

Inactive Record: Inactive records are those Records related to closed, completed, or concluded activities. Inactive Records are no longer routinely referenced, but must be retained in order to fulfill reporting requirements or for purposes of audit or analysis. Inactive records generally reside in a long-term storage format remaining accessible for purposes of business processing only with restrictions on alteration. In some business circumstances inactive records may be re-activated.

Index/Coding Fields: Database fields used to categorize and organize documents. Often user-defined, these fields can be used for searches.

Index: The searchable catalog of documents created by search engine software. Also called "catalog." Index is often used as a synonym for search engine.

Indexing: Universal term for Coding and Data Entry.

Information: For the purposes of this document, information is used to mean both documents and data.

Input device: Any peripheral that allows a user to communicate with a computer by entering information or issuing commands (*e.g.*, keyboard).

Instant Messaging ("IM"): A form of electronic communication involving immediate correspondence between two or more online users. Peer-to-peer IM communications may not be stored on servers after receipt; logging of peer-to-peer IM messages is typically done on the client computer, if at all, and may be optionally enabled or disabled on each client.

Interlaced: TV & CRT pictures must constantly be "refreshed." Interlace is to refresh *every other* line once/refresh cycle. Since only half the information displayed is updated each cycle, interlaced displays are less expensive than "non-interlaced." However, interlaced displays are subject to jitters. The human eye/brain can usually detect displayed images that are completely refreshed less than 30 times per second.

Interleave: To arrange data in a noncontiguous way to increase performance. When used to describe disc drives, it refers to the way sectors on a disc are organized. In one-to-one interleaving, the sectors are placed sequentially around each track. In two-to-one interleaving, sectors are staggered so that consecutively numbered sectors are separated by an intervening sector. The purpose of interleaving is to make the disc drive more efficient. The disc drive can access only one sector at a time, and the disc is constantly spinning beneath.

International Telecommunication Union (ITU): An international organization under the UN, headquartered in Geneva, concerned with telecommunications that develops international data communications standards; known as CCITT prior to March 1, 1993. *See http://www.itu.int*.

Internet: A worldwide network of networks that all use the TCP/IP communications protocol and share a common address space. It supports services such as email, the World Wide Web, file transfer (FTP), and Internet Relay Chat (IRC). Also known as "the net," "the information superhighway," and "cyberspace."

Internet Publishing Software: Specialized software that allows materials to be published on the Internet. The term Internet Publishing is sometimes used to refer to the industry of online digital publication as a whole.

Inter-Partition Space: Unused sectors on a track located between the start of the partition and the partition boot record. This space is important because it is possible for a user to hide information here. *See* Track and Partition.

Intranet: A private network that uses Internet-related technologies to provide services within an organization or defined infrastructure.

IP address (Internet Protocol address): A string of four numbers separated by periods used to represent a computer on the Internet—a unique identifier for the physical location of the server containing the data. *See* TCP/IP (*e.g.*, 128.24.62.1).

IPX/SPX: Communications protocol used by Novell networks.

IRC (Internet Relay Chat): System allowing internet users to chat in real time.

IS/IT Information Systems or Information Technology: Usually refers to the people who make computers and computer systems run.

ISA: Industry Standard Architecture.

ISDN (Integrated Services Digital Network): An all digital network that can carry data, video and voice.

ISIS and TWAIN Scanner Drivers: Specialized applications used for communication between scanners and computers.

ISO (International Organization for Standards): A worldwide federation of national standards bodies, www.iso.org.

ISO 9660 CD Format: The ISO format for creating CD–ROMs that can be read worldwide.

ISO 15489–1: The ISO standard addressing standardization of international best practices in records management.

ISP (Internet Service Provider): A business that provides access to the Internet, usually for a monthly fee. ISPs may be a source of evidence through files (such as ISP email) stored on ISP servers.

IT (Information Technology) Infrastructure: The overall makeup of business-wide technology operations, including mainframe operations, standalone systems, email, networks (WAN and LAN), Internet access, customer databases, enterprise systems, application support, regardless of whether managed, utilized or provided locally, regionally, globally, etc., or whether performed or located internally or by outside providers (outsourced to vendors). The IT Infrastructure also includes applicable standard practices and procedures, such as backup procedures, versioning, resource sharing, retention practices, janitor program utilization, and the like.

Janitor Program: An application that runs at scheduled intervals to manage business information by deleting, transferring, or archiving on-line data (such as email) that is at or past its scheduled active life. Janitor programs are sometimes referred to as "agents"—software that runs autonomously "behind the scenes" on user systems and servers to carry out business processes according to pre-defined rules. Janitor programs must include a facility to support disposition and process holds.

Java: Sun Microsystems' Java is a platform-independent, programming language for adding animation and other actions to websites.

Jaz (or Jazz) Drive: A removable disc drive. A Jaz drive holds up to 2 GB of data. Commonly used for backup storage as well as everyday use.

JMS: Jukebox Management Software. *See* Jukebox.

Journal: A chronological record of data processing operations that may be used to reconstruct a previous or an updated version of a file. In database management systems, it is the record of all stored data items that have values changed as a result of processing and manipulation of the data.

Journaling: A function of e-mail systems (such as Microsoft Exchange and Lotus Notes) that copies sent and received items into a second information store for retention or preservation. Because Journaling takes place at the information store (server) level when the items are sent or received, rather than at the mailbox (client) level, some message-related metadata, such as user foldering (what folder the item is stored in within the recipient's mailbox) and the status of the "read" flag, is not retained in the journaled copy. The Journaling function stores items in the system's native format, unlike e-mail archiving solutions, that use proprietary storage formats designed to reduce the amount of storage space required. Journaling systems may also lack the sophisticated search and retrieval capabilities available with many e-mail archiving solutions.

JPEG (Joint Photographic Experts Group): A compression algorithm for still images that is commonly used on the web.

Jukebox: A mass storage device that holds optical discs and loads them into a drive.

Jump Drive: *See* Key Drive.

Kerning: Adjusting the spacing between two letters.

Key Drive: A small removable data storage device that uses flash memory and connects via a USB port. Key drives are also known as keychain drive, thumb drive, jump drive, and/or USB flash drive. Can be imaged and may contain residual data. Metadata detail may not be the equivalent of ESI maintained in more robust storage media.

Key Field: Database fields used for document searches and retrieval.

Keyword: Any specified word, or combination of words, used in a search, with the intent of locating certain results.

Kilobyte (KB): A unit of 1,024 bytes. *See* Byte.

Kofax Board: The generic term for a series of image processing boards manufactured by Kofax Imaging Processing. These are used between the scanner and the computer, and perform real-time image compression and decompression for faster image viewing, image enhancement, and corrections to the input to account for conditions such as document misalignment.

LAN (Local Area Network): A group of computers at a single location (usually an office or home) that are connected by phone lines, coaxial cable or wireless transmission. *See* Network.

Landscape Mode: The image is represented on the page or monitor such that the width is greater than the height.

Laser Disc: Same as an optical CD, except 12″ in diameter.

Laser Printing: A beam of light hits an electrically charged drum and causes a discharge at that point. Toner is then applied, which sticks to the non-charged areas. Paper is pressed against the drum to form the image and is then heated to dry the toner. Used in laser printers and copying machines.

Latency: The time it takes to read a disc (or jukebox), including the time to physically position the media under the read/write head, seek the correct address and transfer it.

Latent Data: Latent or ambient data are deleted files and other ESI that are inaccessible without specialized forensic tools and techniques. Until overwritten, these data reside on media such as a hard drive in unused space and other areas available for data storage.

Latent Semantic Indexing and Analysis: A statistical method for finding the underlying dimensions of correlated terms. For example, words like law, lawyer, attorney, lawsuit, etc., all share some meaning. The presence of any one of them in a document could be recognized as indicating something consistent about the topic of the document. Latent Semantic Analysis uses statistics to allow the system to exploit these correlations for concept searching and clustering.

LCD (Liquid Crystal Display): Two polarizing transparent panels with a liquid crystal surface between; application of voltage to certain areas causes the crystal to turn dark, and a light source behind the panel transmits though crystals not darkened.

Leading/Ledding: The amount of space between lines of printed text.

Legacy Data, Legacy System: Legacy Data is ESI in which an organization may have invested significant resources, but has been created or stored by the use of software and/or hardware that has become obsolete or replaced ("legacy systems"). Legacy data may be costly to restore or reconstruct when required for investigation or litigation analysis or discovery.

Legal Hold: A legal hold is a communication issued as a result of current or reasonably anticipated litigation, audit, government investigation or other such matter that suspends the normal disposition or processing of records. Legal holds may encompass procedures affecting data that is accessible as well as data that is not reasonably accessible. The specific communication to business or IT organizations may also be called a "hold," "preservation order," "suspension order," "freeze notice," "hold order," or "hold notice." *See, The Sedona*

Conference® Commentary on Legal Holds, August 2007 Public Comment Version, available for download at http://www.thesedonaconference. org.

Level Coding: Used in Bibliographical coding to facilitate different treatment, such as prioritization or more thorough extraction of data, for different categories of documents, such as by type or source.

LFP: IPRO Tech's image cross reference file; an ASCII delimited text file required for cross-reference of images to data.

Lifecycle: The records lifecycle is the life span of a record from its creation or receipt to its final disposition. It is usually described in three stages: creation, maintenance and use, and archive to final disposition.

Line Screen: The number of half-tone dots that can be printed per inch. As a general rule, newspapers print at 65 to 85 lpi.

Link: *See* Hyperlink.

Load file: A file that relates to a set of scanned images or electronically processed files, and indicates where individual pages or files belong together as documents, to include attachments, and where each document begins and ends. A load file may also contain data relevant to the individual documents, such as metadata, coded data, text, and the like. Load files must be obtained and provided in prearranged formats to ensure transfer of accurate and usable images and data.

Local Area Network (LAN): *See* Network.

Locale: A set of parameters that define language, country and any special system configurations that correspond to the language and country. For example, locale typically determines the date format (month first in the US, day first in the UK), the time format (12–hour clock in the US, 24–hour clock in some European countries), the keyboard layout, and so forth. These settings can be overridden, but the locale sets the default.

Logical File Space: The actual amount of space occupied by a file on a hard drive. The amount of logical file space differs from the physical file space because when a file is created on a computer, a sufficient number of clusters (physical file space) are assigned to contain the file. If the file (logical file space) is not large enough to completely fill the assigned clusters (physical file space) then some unused space will exist within the physical file space.

Logical Unitization: *See* Unitization—Physical and Logical.

Logical Volume: An area on the hard drive that has been formatted for files storage. A hard drive may contain a single or multiple volumes.

Lossless Compression: Exact construction of image, bit-by-bit, with no loss of information.

Lossy Compression: Reduces storage size of image by reducing the resolution and color fidelity while maintaining minimum acceptable standard for general use. A lossy image is one where the image after compression is different from the original image due to lost information. The differences may or may not be noticeable, but a lossy conversion process does not retain all the original information. JPEG is an example of a lossy compression method.

Lotus Domino: An IBM server product providing enterprise-level email, collaboration capabilities, and custom application platform; began life as Lotus Notes Server, the server component of Lotus Development Corporation's client-server messaging technology. Can be used as an application server for Lotus Notes applications and/or as a web server. Has a built-in database system in the format of .NSF.

Lotus Notes: *See* Lotus Domino.

Lumen: Measure of brightness often associated with the amount of light output of a projector.

LTO (Linear Tape–Open): A type of backup tape that can hold as much as 800 GB of data, or 1200 CDs depending on the data file format.

LZW (Lempel–Ziv & Welch): A common, lossless compression standard for computer graphics, used for most TIFF files. Typical compression ratios are 4/1.

Magenta: Used in four color printing. Reflects blue & red and absorbs green.

Magnetic/Optical Storage Media: Includes, but is not limited to, hard drives, backup tapes, CD–ROMs, DVD–ROMs, Jaz and Zip drives.

Magneto-Optical Drive: A drive that combines laser and magnetic technology to create high-capacity erasable storage.

Mailbox: An area on a storage device where email is placed. In email systems, each user has a private mailbox. When the server receives email, the mail system automatically puts it in the appropriate mailbox.

Make-Available Production: A process whereby what is usually a large universe of potentially responsive documents are made available to the requestor; from which universe, the requestor then reviews and selects or tags the documents they wish to obtain, and the producing party produces to the requestor only the selected documents. This is sometimes done under an agreement protecting against privilege and confidentiality waiver during the initial make available production; and the producing party, after the requestor has selected the documents they wish to obtain, reviews only the selected documents for privilege and confidentiality before the selected documents are physically produced to the requestor.

Malware: Any type of malicious software program, typically installed illicitly, including viruses, Trojans, worms, key loggers, spyware, adware and others.

MAPI (Mail Application Program Interface): A Windows software standard that has become a popular email interface used by MS Exchange, GroupWise, and other email packages.

MAPI Mail Near–Line: Documents stored on optical discs or compact discs that are housed in the jukebox or CD changer and can be retrieved without human intervention.

Marginalia: Handwritten notes in the margin of the page in documents.

Master Boot Sector/Record: The sector on a hard drive which contains the computer code (boot strap loader) necessary for the computer to start up and the partition table describing the organization of the hard drive.

Mastering: Making many copies of a disc from a single master disc.

MBOX: The format in which email is stored on traditional UNIX email systems.

MCA (Micro Channel Architecture): IBM bus standard rendered obsolete by the PCI bus.

MDE (Magnetic Disc Emulation): Software that makes a jukebox look and operate like a hard-drive such that it will respond to all the I/O commands ordinarily sent to a hard drive.

MD5: Message-digest algorithm meant for digital signature applications where a large message has to be "compressed" in a secure manner before being signed with the private key. *See* Hash.

Media: An object or device, such as a disc, tape, or other device, on which data is stored.

Megabyte (M or MB): 1,048,576 bytes—$1,024^2$ (a million bytes). *See* Byte.

Memory: Data storage in the form of chips, or the actual chips used to hold data; "storage" is used to describe memory that exists on tapes, discs, CDs, DVDs, key drives and hard drives. See RAM and ROM.

Menu: A list of options, each of which performs a desired action such as choosing a command or applying a particular format to a part of a document.

Message Header: Message headers generally contain the identities of the author and recipients, the subject of the message, and the date the message was sent.

Message Unit: An email and any attachments that are associated with the email.

Metadata: Data typically stored electronically that describes characteristics of ESI, found in different places in different forms. Can be supplied by applications, users or the file system. Metadata can describe how, when and by whom ESI was collected, created, accessed, modified and how it is formatted. Can be altered intentionally or inadvertently. Certain metadata can be extracted when native files are processed for litigation. Some metadata, such as file dates and sizes, can easily be seen by users; other metadata can be hidden or embedded and unavailable to computer users who are not technically adept. Metadata is generally not reproduced in full form when a document is printed to paper or electronic image. *See also* Application Metadata, Document Metadata, Email Metadata, Embedded Metadata, File System Metadata, User–Added Metadata and Vendor–Added Metadata. For a more thorough discussion, *see The Sedona Guidelines: Best Practice Guidelines & Commentary for Managing Information & Records in the Electronic Age (Second Edition).*

Metadata Comparison: A comparison of specified metadata as the basis for de-duplication without regard to content. *See* De–Duplication.

MFT (Master File Table): Index to files on a computer. If corrupt, a drive may be unusable, yet ESI may be retrievable using forensic methods.

MICR (Magnetic Ink Character Recognition): The process used by banks to encode checks.

Microfiche: Sheet microfilm (4" by 6") containing reduced images of 270 pages or more in a grid pattern.

Microsoft Outlook: A personal information manager from Microsoft, part of the Microsoft Office suite. Although often used mainly as an email application, it also provides calendar, task and contact management, note taking, a journal and web browsing. Can be used as a stand-alone application, or operate in conjunction with Microsoft Exchange Server to provide enhanced functions for multiple users in an organization, such as shared mailboxes and calendars, public folders, and meeting time allocation.

Microsoft Outlook Express: A scaled down version of Microsoft Outlook.

Migrated Data: ESI that has been moved from one database or format to another.

Migration: Moving ESI to another computer application or platform; may require conversion to a different format.

Mirror Image: A bit by bit copy of the device that ensures it is not altered during the imaging process. *See* Forensic Copy.

Mirroring: The duplication of ESI for purposes of backup or to distribute Internet or network traffic among several servers with identical ESI. *See also* Disc Mirroring and Bit Stream Backup

MIS: Management Information Systems.

MODEM: Modulator/Demodulator. A device that translates digital data from a computer into analog signals (modulates) and transmits the information over telephones lines. Another modem at the receiving computer will receive the information, translate it back from analog to digital (demodulate) and store it.

Monochrome: Displays capable of only two colors, usually black and white, or black and green.

Mosaic: A web browser popular before the introduction of Netscape and Internet Explorer.

Mount, Mounting: The process of making off-line ESI available for on-line processing. For example, placing a magnetic tape in a drive and setting up the software to recognize or read that tape. The terms "load" and "loading" are often used in conjunction with, or synonymously with, "mount" and "mounting" (as in "mount and load a tape"). "Load" may also refer to the process of transferring ESI from mounted media to another media or to an on-line system.

MPEG–1, –2, –3, and –4: Different standards for full motion video to digital compression/decompression techniques advanced by the Moving Pictures Experts Group. MPEG–1 compresses 30 frames/second of full-motion video down to about 1.5 Mbits/sec from several hundred megabytes. MPEG–2 compresses the same files down to about 3.0 Mbits/sec and provides better image quality. MPEG–3 refers to the playing of CD clips.

MS-DOS: Microsoft (MS)-Disc Operating System. Used in PCs as the control system prior to the introduction of 32–bit operating systems.

MSG: Generic format in which emails can be saved.

MTBF (Mean Time Between Failure): Average time between failures. Used to compute the reliability of devices/equipment.

MTTR (Mean Time To Repair): Average time to repair. The higher the number, the more costly and difficult to fix.

Multimedia: The combined use of different media; integrated video, audio, text and data graphics in digital form.

Multisynch: Analog video monitors that can receive a wide range of display resolutions, usually including TV (NTSC). Color analog monitors accept separate red, green & blue (RGB) signals.

Native Format: Electronic documents have an associated file structure defined by the original creating application. This file structure is referred to as the "native format" of the document. Because viewing or searching documents in the native format may require the original application (for example, viewing a Microsoft Word document may require the Microsoft Word application), documents may be converted to a neutral format as part of the record acquisition or archive process. "Static" formats (often called "imaged formats"), such as TIFF or PDF, are designed to retain an image of the document as it would look viewed in the original creating application but do not allow metadata to be viewed or the document information to be manipulated. In the conversion to static format, the metadata can be processed, preserved and electronically associated with the static format file. However, with technology advancements, tools and applications are becoming increasingly available to allow viewing and searching of documents in their native format, while still preserving all metadata.

Native Format Review: Review of ESI in its current "native" format using either an application capable of supporting native format review or the original application in which the ESI was created.

Natural Language Search: A manner of searching that permits the use of plain language without special connectors or precise terminology, such as "Where can I find information on William Shakespeare?" as opposed to formulating a search statement (such as "information" **and** "William Shakespeare"). Opposite of boolean search. *See* Boolean Search.

Near De-duplication: Identification and grouping or tagging of electronic files with "near duplicate" similarities, yet some differences in terms of content or metadata, or both—for example, document versions, emails sent to multiple custodians, different parts of email chains, or similar proposals sent to several clients.

Near-Line Data: A term used to refer to ESI or a robotic storage device (robotic library) that houses removable media, uses robotic arms to access the media, and uses multiple read/write devices to store and retrieve records. Examples include optical discs.

Near-Line Data Storage: Storage in a system that is not a direct part of the network in daily use, but that can be accessed through the network. There is usually a small time lag between the request for ESI stored in near-line media and its being made available to an application or end-user. Making near-line data available will not require human intervention (as opposed to "off-line" data which can only be made available through human actions).

Network: A group of two or more computers and other devices connected together ("networked") for the exchange and sharing of ESI and resources. A local-area network (LAN) refers to connected computers and devices geographically close together (*i.e.* in the same building). A wide-area network (WAN) refers generally to a network of PCs or other devices, remote to each other, connected by telecommunications lines. Typically, a WAN may connect two or more LANs together.

Network Gear: Refers to the actual hardware used in the operation of networks—for example routers, switches and hubs.

Neural Network: Neural networks are made up of interconnected processing elements called units, which respond in parallel to a set of input signals given to each

NIST—National Institute of Standards and Technology: a federal technology agency that works with industry to develop and apply technology measurements and standards.

NIST List: A hash database of computer file types developed by NIST to identify those generated by a system and those generated by a user.

Node: Any device connected to a network. PCs, servers, and printers are all nodes on the network.

Non-Apparent Data: Data not normally seen on a printed version of ESI—whether "printed" to paper or image, such as tiff or pdf, *e.g.* spreadsheet formulas. *See* Embedded Metadata and Metadata.

Non-Interlace: When each line of a video image is scanned separately. Older CRT computer monitors use non-interlaced video.

NOS (Network Operating System): *See* Operating System.

Normalization: The process the process of reformatting data so that it is stored in a standardized form, such as setting the date and time stamp of a specific volume of ESI to a specific zone, often GMT, to permit advanced processing of the ESI, such as de-duplication. *See also* Coordinated Universal Time.

Notes Server: *See* Lotus Domino.

NSF: Lotus Notes container file (*i.e.* database.nsf); can be either an email database or the *traditional* type of fielded database. *See* Lotus Domino.

NTFS (New Technology File System): A high-performance and self-healing file system proprietary to Microsoft, used in Windows NT, Windows 2000, Windows XP, and Windows Vista Operating Systems, that supports file-level security, compression and auditing. It also supports large volumes and powerful storage solution such as RAID. An important feature of NTFS is the ability to encrypt files and folders to protect sensitive data.

Object: In personal computing, an object is a representation of something that a user can work with to perform a task and can appear as text or an icon. In a high-level method of programming called object-oriented programming (OOP), an object is a freestanding block of code that defines the properties of some thing.

OCR (Optical Character Recognition): A technology process that translates and converts printed matter on an image into a format that a computer can manipulate (ASCII codes, for example) and, therefore, renders that matter text searchable. OCR software evaluates scanned data for shapes it recognizes as letters or numerals. All OCR systems include an optical scanner for reading text, and software for analyzing images. Most OCR systems use a combination of hardware (specialized circuit boards) and software to recognize characters, although some inexpensive systems operate entirely through software. Advanced OCR systems can read text in a large variety of fonts, but still have difficulty with handwritten text. OCR technology relies upon the quality of the imaged material, the conversion accuracy of the software, and the quality control process of the provider. The process is generally acknowledged to be between 80 and 99 percent accurate. *See* HRS and ICR.

Official Record Owner: *See* Record Owner.

Off-Line Data: The storage of ESI outside the network in daily use (*e.g.*, on backup tapes) that is only accessible through the off-line storage system, not the network.

Off-Line Storage: ESI maintained or archived on removable disc (optical, compact, etc.) or magnetic tape used for making disaster-recovery copies of records for which retrieval is unlikely. Accessibility to off-line media usually requires manual intervention and is much slower than on-line or near-line storage depending on the storage facility. The major difference between near-line data and offline data is that offline data lacks an intelligent disc subsystem, and is not connected to a computer, network, or any other readily-accessible system.

OLE (Object Linking and Embedding): A feature in Microsoft's Windows that allows each section of a compound document to call up its own editing tools or special display features. This allows for combining diverse elements in compound documents. *See also* Compound Document.

On-Line Review: The culling process produces a dataset of potentially responsive documents that are then reviewed for a final selection of relevant or responsive documents and assertion of privilege exception as appropriate. On-line Review enables the culled dataset to be accessed via PC or other terminal device via a local network or remotely via the Internet. Often, the On–Line Review process is facilitated by specialized software that provides additional features and functions which may include: collaborative access of multiple reviewers, security, user logging, search and retrieval, document coding, redaction, and privilege logging.

On-Line Storage: The storage of ESI as fully accessible information in daily use on the network or elsewhere.

Online/On–Line: Connected (to a network).

Ontology: A collection of categories and their relationships to other categories and to words. An ontology is one of the methods used to find related documents when given a specific query.

Operating System (OS): An Operating system provides the software platform that directs the overall activity of a computer, network or system, and on which all other software programs and applications can run. In many ways, choice of an operating system will effect which applications can be run. Operating systems perform basic tasks, such as recognizing input from the keyboard, sending output to the display screen, keeping track of files and directories on the disc and controlling peripheral devices such as disc drives and printers. For large systems, the operating system has even greater responsibilities and powers—becoming a traffic cop to makes sure different programs and users running at the same time do not interfere with each other. The operating system is also responsible for security, ensuring that unauthorized users do not access the system. Examples of operating systems are UNIX, DOS, Windows, LINUX, Macintosh, and IBM's VM. Operating systems can be classified in a number of ways, including: multi-user (allows two or more users to run programs at the same time—some operating systems permit hundreds or even thousands of concurrent users); multiprocessing (supports running a program on more than one CPU); multitasking (allows more than one program to run concurrently); multithreading (allows different parts of a single program to run concurrently); and real time (instantly responds to input—general-purpose operating systems, such as DOS and UNIX, are not real-time).

Optical Discs: Computer media similar to a compact disc that cannot be rewritten. An optical drive uses a laser to read the ESI.

Optical Jukebox: See "Jukebox."

OST: A Microsoft Outlook information store that is used to save folder information that can be accessed offline.

Outlook: See Microsoft Outlook.

Over-inclusive: When referring to data sets returned by some method of query, search, filter or cull, results that are returned overly broad.

Overwrite: To record or copy new data over existing data, as in when a file or directory is updated. Data that is overwritten cannot be retrieved.

PAB (Personal Address Book): A Microsoft Outlook list of recipients created and maintained by an individual user for personal use. The personal address book is a subset of the global address list (GAL).

PackBits: A compression scheme that originated with the Macintosh. Suitable only for black & white.

Packet: A unit of data sent across a network that may contain identity and routing information. When a large block of data is to be sent over a network, it is broken up into several packets, sent, and then reassembled at the other end. The exact layout of an individual packet is determined by the protocol being used.

Page: A single image of the equivalent of "one piece of paper." One or several pages make up a "Document."

Page File/Paging File: A file used to temporarily store code and data for programs that are currently running. This information is left in the swap file after the programs are terminated, and may be retrieved using forensic techniques. Also referred to as a swap file.

Parallel Port: *See* Port.

Parent: See Document.

Parsing: Transforms input text into a data structure suitable for later processing, while capturing the implied hierarchy of the input. Data may be parsed from one source of ESI to another.

Partition: A partition is an individual section of computer storage media such as a hard drive. For example, a single hard drive may be divided into several partitions. When a hard drive is divided into partitions, each partition is designated by a separate drive letter, i.e., C, D, etc.

Partition Table: The partition table indicates each logical volume contained on a disc and its location.

Partition Waste Space: After the boot sector of each volume or partition is written to a track, it is customary for the system to skip the rest of that track and begin the actual useable area of the volume on the next track. This results in unused or "wasted" space on that track where information can be hidden. This "wasted space" can only be viewed with a low level disc viewer. However, forensic techniques can be used to search these "wasted space" areas for hidden information.

Password: A secret code utilized, usually along with a user ID, in order to log on or gain access to a PC, network or other secure system, site or application.

Path: The hierarchical description of where a directory, folder, or file is located on a computer or network. In DOS and Windows systems, a path is a list of directories where the operating system looks for executable files if it is unable to find the file in the working directory. The list of directories can be specified with the PATH command. Path is also used to refer to a transmission channel, the path between two nodes of a network that a data communication follows, and the physical cabling that connects the nodes on a network.

Pattern Matching: A generic term that describes any process that compares one file's content with another file's content.

Pattern Recognition: Technology that searches ESI for like patterns and flags, and extracts the pertinent data, usually utilizing an algorithm. For instance, in looking for addresses, alpha characters followed by a comma and a space, followed by two capital alpha characters, followed by a space, followed by five or more digits, are usually the city, state and zip code. By programming the application to look for a pattern, the information can be electronically identified, extracted, or otherwise utilized or manipulated.

PCI: Peripheral Component Interconnect (Interface). A high-speed interconnect local bus used to support multimedia devices.

PCMCIA: Personal Computer Memory Card International Association. Plug-in cards for computers (usually portables) that extend the storage and/or functionality.

PDA (Personal Digital Assistant): A small, usually hand-held, computer that "assists" business tasks, *e.g.* Blackberry, Palm Pilot Treo.

PDF (Portable Document Format): An imaging file format technology developed by Adobe Systems. PDF captures formatting information from a variety of applications in such a way that they can be viewed and printed as they were intended in their original application by practically any computer, on multiple platforms, regardless of the specific application in which the original was created. PDF files may be text-searchable or image-only. Adobe® Reader, a free application distributed by Adobe Systems, is required to view a file in PDF format. Adobe® Acrobat, an application marketed by Adobe Systems, is required to edit, capture text, or otherwise manipulate a file in PDF format.

Peripheral: Any accessory device attached to a computer, such as a disk drive, printer, modem or joystick.

Personal Computer (PC): Computer based on a microprocessor and designed to be used by one person at a time

Personal Data (as used with regard to the EU Data Protection Act): Data which relate to a natural person who can be identified from those Data, directly or indirectly, in particular by reference to an identification number or to one or more factors specific to his or her physical, physiological, mental, economic, cultural or social identity.

Petabyte (PB): 1,125,899,906,824,624 bytes—10245 (a quadrillion bytes). See Byte.

Phase Change: A method of storing information on rewritable optical discs.

Physical Disc: An actual piece of computer media, such as the hard disc or drive, floppy discs, CD–ROM discs, Zip discs, etc.

Physical File Space: When a file is created on a computer, a sufficient number of clusters (physical file space) are assigned to contain the file.

If the file (logical file space) is not large enough to completely fill the assigned clusters (physical file space) then some unused space will exist within the physical file space. This unused space is referred to as file slack and can contain unused space, previously deleted/overwritten files or fragments thereof.

Physical Unitization: See Unitization—Physical and Logical.

PICA: One sixth (⅙) of an inch. Used to measure graphics/fonts. There are 12 points per pica; 6 picas per inch; 72 points per inch.

Picture Element: The smallest addressable unit on a display screen. The higher the resolution (the more rows of columns), the more information can be displayed.

Ping: Executable command, used as a test for checking network connectivity.

Pitch: Characters (or dots) per inch, measured horizontally.

PKI (Public Key Infrastructure) Digital Signature: A document or file may be digitally signed using a party's private signature key, creating a "digital signature" that is stored with the document. Anyone can validate the signature on the document using the public key from the digital certificate issued to the signer. Validating the digital signature confirms who signed it, and ensures that no alterations have been made to the document since it was signed. Similarly, an email message may be digitally signed using commonly available client software that implements an open standard for this purpose, such as Secure Multipurpose Internet Mail Extensions (S/MIME). Validating the signature on the email can help the recipient know with confidence who sent it, and that it was not altered during transmission. See Certificate.

Plaintext: The least formatted and therefore most portable form of text for computerized documents.

Plasma: A type of flat panel display commonly use for large televisions, although quickly being replaced by LCD due to advances in technology; many tiny cells are located between two panels of glass holding an inert mixture of gases.

Platter: One of several components that make up a computer hard drive. Platters are thin, rapidly rotating discs that have a set of read/write heads on both sides of each platter. Each platter is divided into a series of concentric rings called tracks. Each track is further divided into sections called sectors, and each sector is sub-divided into bytes.

PMS (Pantone Matching System): A color standard in printing.

POD (Print On Demand): Document images are stored in electronic format and are available to be quickly printed and in the exact quantity required, long or short runs.

Pointer: A pointer is an index entry in the directory of a disc (or other storage medium) that identifies the space on the disc in which an electronic document or piece of electronic data resides, thereby preventing that space from being overwritten by other data. In most cases, when an electronic document is "deleted," the pointer is deleted, that allows the document to be overwritten, but the document is not actually erased.

Port: Hardware ports are an interface between a computer and other computers or devices, and can be divided into two primary groups based on signal transfer: serial ports send and receive one bit at a time via a single wire pair, while parallel ports send multiple bits at the same time over several sets of wires. Software ports are virtual data connections used by programs to exchange data directly instead of going through a file or other temporary storage locations; the most common types are TCP and UDP.

Portable Volumes: A feature that facilitates the moving of large volumes of documents without requiring copying multiple files. Portable volumes enable individual CDs to be easily regrouped, detached and reattached to different databases for a broader information exchange.

Portrait Mode: A display where the height exceeds the width.

Preservation: The process of ensuring retention and protection from destruction or deletion all potentially relevant evidence, including electronic metadata. See also Spoliation.

Preservation Notice, Preservation Order: See Legal Hold.

Printout: A printed version of text of data, another term for which is hard copy.

Private Network: A network that is connected to the Internet but is isolated from the Internet with security measures allowing use of the network only by persons within the private network.

Privilege Data Set: The universe of documents identified as responsive and/or relevant, but withheld from production on the grounds of privilege, a log of which is usually required to notify of withheld documents and the grounds on which they were withheld (e.g., work product, attorney-client privilege).

Process/processing (as used with regard to the EU Data Protection Act): Any operation or set of operations which is performed upon Personal Data, whether or not by automatic means, such as collection, recording, organisation, storage, adaptation or alteration, retrieval, consultation, use, disclosure by transmission, dissemination or otherwise making available, alignment or combination, blocking, erasure or destruction.

Processing Data: In the context of this document, synonymous with Image Processing.

Production: The process of delivering to another party, or making available for that party's review, documents and/or ESI deemed responsive to a discovery request.

Production Data Set: The universe of documents and/or ESI identified as responsive to document requests and not withheld on the grounds of attorney-client, work product, or other privilege.

Production De–Duplication: Removal of a document if multiple copies of that document reside within the same production set. For example, if two identical documents are both marked responsive, non-privileged, production de-duplication ensures that only one of those documents is produced. See De–Duplication.

Production Number: Often referred to as the "bates" number. A sequential number assigned to every page of a production for tracking and reference purposes. Often used in conjunction with a suffix or prefix to identify the producing party, the litigation, or other relevant information. See also Bates Number.

Program: See Application and Software.

Properties: Fields of electronic information, or certain "metadata," associated with a record or document such as creation date, author, date modified, blind copy recipients and date received. See Metadata.

Protocol: Defines a common series of rules, signals and conventions that allow different kinds of computers and applications to communicate over a network. One of the most common protocols for networks is called TCP/IP.

Protodigital: Primitive or first-generation digital. Applied as an adjective to systems, software, "documents," or ways of thinking. The term was first used in music to refer to early computer synthesizers that attempted to mimic the sound of traditional musical instruments, and to early jazz compositions written on computers with that instrumentation in mind. In electronic discovery, this term is most often applied to systems or ways of thinking that—on the surface—appear to embrace digital technology, but attempt to equate ESI to paper records, ignoring the unique attributes of ESI. When someone says, "What's the big deal with e-discovery? Sure we have a lot of email. You just print it all out and produce it like you used to," that is an example of protodigital thinking. When someone says, "We embrace electronic discovery. We scan everything to .PDF before we produce it," that person is engaged in protodigital thinking—attempting to fit ESI into the paper discovery pardigm.

Proximity Search: For text searches, the ability to look for words or phrases within a prescribed distance of another word or phrase, such as "accident" within 5 words of "tire."

PST: A Microsoft Outlook email store. Multiple .pst files may exist in different locations (hard drive, network shares, backup tapes or discs, etc.) and contain archived email.

Public Key: *See* PKI Digital Signature.

Public Network: A network that is part of the public Internet.

QBIC (Query By Image Content): An IBM search system for stored images that allows the user to sketch an image, and then search the image files to find those which most closely match. The user can specify color and texture–such as "sandy beaches" or "clouds."

Quality Control (QC): Steps taken to ensure that results of a given task, product or service are of sufficiently high quality; the operational techniques and activities that are used to fulfill requirements for quality. In document handling and management processes, this includes image quality (resolution, skew, speckle, legibility, etc.), and data quality (correct information in appropriate fields, validated data for dates, addresses, names/issues lists, etc.).

Quarter Inch Cartridge (QIC): Digital recording tape, 2000 feet long, with an uncompressed capacity of 5 GB.

Query: A request for specific information from a database or other ESI.

Queue: A sequence of items such as packets or print jobs waiting to be processed. For example, a print queue holds files that are waiting to be printed.

Quick Peek: A production whereby documents and/or ESI are made available to the opposing party before being reviewed for privilege, confidentiality or privacy, requiring stringent guidelines and restrictions to prevent waiver.

RAID (Redundant Array of Independent Discs): A method of storing data on servers that usually combines multiple hard drives into one logical unit thereby increasing capacity, reliability and backup capability. RAID systems may vary in levels of redundancy, with no redundancy being a single, non-mirrored disc as level 0, two discs that mirror each other as level 1, on up, with level 5 being one of the most common. RAID systems are more complicated to copy and restore.

RAM (Random Access Memory): Hardware inside a computer that retains memory on a short-term basis and stores information while the computer is in use. It is the "working memory" of the computer into which the operating system, startup applications and drivers are loaded when a computer is turned on, or where a program subsequently started up is loaded, and where thereafter, these applications are executed. RAM can be read or written in any section with one instruction sequence. It helps to have more of this "working space" installed when running advanced operating systems and applications.

RAM content is erased each time a computer is turned off. *See* Dynamic Random Access Memory—DRAM.

Raster/Rasterized (Raster or Bitmap Drawing): A method of representing an image with a grid (or "map") of dots. Typical raster file formats are GIF, JPEG, TIFF, PCX, BMP, etc.

Record: Information, regardless of medium or format that has value to an organization.

Record Custodian: A record custodian is an individual responsible for the physical storage and protection of records throughout their retention period. In the context of electronic records, custodianship may not be a direct part of the records management function in all organizations. For example, some organizations may place this responsibility within their Information Technology Department, or they may assign responsibility for retaining and preserving records with individual employees.

Record Lifecycle: The time period from which a record is created until it is disposed.

Record Owner: The record owner is the subject matter expert on the contents of the record and is responsible for the lifecycle management of the record. This may be, but is not necessarily, the author of the record.

Record Series: A description of a particular set of records within a file plan. Each category has retention and disposition data associated with it, applied to all record folders and records within the category. (DOD 5015)

Record Submitter: The Record Submitter is the person who enters a record in an application or system. This may be, but is not necessarily, the author or the record owner.

Records Archive: *See* Repository for Electronic Records.

Records Hold: *See* Legal Hold.

Records Management: Records Management is the planning, controlling, directing, organizing, training, promoting, and other managerial activities involving the life-cycle of information, including creation, maintenance (use, storage, retrieval), and disposition, regardless of media.

Records Manager: The records manager is responsible for the implementation of a records management program in keeping with the policies and procedures that govern that program, including the identification, classification, handling and disposition of the organization's records throughout their retention life. The physical storage and protection of records may be a component of this individual's functions, but it may also be delegated to someone else. *See* Records Custodian.

Records Retention Period, Retention Period: The length of time a given records series must be kept, expressed as either a time period (*e.g.*, four years), an event or action (*e.g.*, audit), or a combination (*e.g.*, six months after audit).

Records Retention Schedule: A plan for the management of records listing types of records and how long they should be kept; the purpose is to provide continuing authority to dispose of or transfer records to historical archives.

Records Store: *See* Repository for Electronic Records.

Recover, Recovery: *See* Restore.

Redaction: A portion of an image or document is intentionally concealed to prevent disclosure of specific portions. Often done to conceal and protect privileged portions or avoid production of irrelevant portions that may contain highly confidential, sensitive or proprietary information.

Refresh Rate: The number of times per second a display (such as on a CRT or TV) is updated.

Region (of an image): An area of an image file that is selected for specialized processing. Also called a "zone."

Registration: Lining up a forms image to determine which fields are where. Also, entering pages into a scanner such that they are correctly read.

Relative Path: An implied path.

Remote Access: The ability to access and use digital information from a location off-site from where the information is physically located. For example, to use a computer, modem, and some remote access software to connect to a network from a distant location.

Render Images: To take a native format electronic file and convert it to an image that appears as the original format file as if printed to paper.

Report: Formatted output of a system providing specific information.

Repository for Electronic Records: Repository for Electronic Records is a direct access device on which the electronic records and associated metadata are stored. (DoD 5015) Sometimes called a "records store" or "records archive."

Residual Data: Residual Data (sometimes referred to as "Ambient Data") refers to data that is not active on a computer system. Residual data includes (1) data found on media free space; (2) data found in file slack space; and (3) data within files that has functionally been deleted in that it is not visible using the application with which the file was created, without use of undelete or special data recovery techniques. May contain copies of deleted files, Internet files and file fragments.

Resolution: Refers to the sharpness and clarity of an image. The term is most often used to describe monitors, printers, and graphic images. *See* DPI.

Restore: To transfer data from a backup medium (such as tapes) to an on-line system, often for the purpose of recovery from a problem, failure, or disaster. Restoration of archival media is the transfer of data from an archival store to an on-line system for the purposes of processing (such as query, analysis, extraction, or disposition of that data). Archival restoration of systems may require not only data restoration but also replication of the original hardware and software operating environment. Restoration of systems is often called "recovery."

Retention Schedule: *See* Records Retention Schedule.

Reverse Engineering: The process of analyzing a system to identify its intricacies and their interrelationships, and create depictions of the system in another form or at a higher level. Reverse engineering is usually undertaken in order to redesign the system for better maintainability or to produce a copy of a system without utilizing the design from which it was originally produced. For example, one might take the executable code of a computer program, run it to study how it behaved with different input, and then attempt to write a program that behaved the same or better.

Review: The culling process produces a dataset of potentially responsive documents that are then examined and evaluated for a final selection of relevant and/or responsive documents and assertion of privilege, confidentiality, etc., as appropriate. *Also see* On–Line Review.

Rewriteable Technology: Storage devices where the data may be written more than once–typically hard drives, floppies and optical discs.

RFC822: Standard that specifies a syntax for text messages that are sent among computer users, within the framework of email.

RGB (Red, Green and Blue): The three primary colors in the additive color family which create all the computer color video signals for a computer's color terminal.

Rip: The procedure used to extract ESI files from container files, such as to unbundle email collections into individual emails, during the e-discovery process while preserving metadata, authenticity and ownership.

RIM: Records and information management.

RLE (Run Length Encoded): Compressed image format; supports only 256 colors; most effective on images with large areas of black or white.

ROM (Read Only Memory): Random memory that can be read but not written or changed. Also, hardware, usually a chip, within a computer containing programming necessary for starting up the computer, and essential system programs that neither the user nor the computer can alter or erase. Information in the computer's ROM is permanently maintained even when the computer is turned off.

Root Directory: The top level in a hierarchical file system. For example on a PC, the root directory of your hard drive, usually C:, contains all the second-level subdirectories on that drive.

Rotary Camera: In microfilming, the papers are read "on the fly" with a camera that is synchronized to the motion.

Router: A device that forwards data packets along networks. A router is connected to at least two networks, commonly two LANs or WANs or a LAN and its ISPs network. Routers are located at gateways, the places where two or more networks connect.

RTF (Rich Text Format): A file format that allows exchange of text files between different word processors in different operating systems.

SaaS (Software as a Service): Software application delivery model where a software vendor develops a web-native software application and hosts and operates (either independently or through a third-party) the application for use by its customers over the Internet. Customers pay not for owning the software itself but for using it. *See* Application Service Provider.

Sampling: Sampling usually (but not always) refers to the process of testing a database or a large volume of ESI for the existence or frequency of relevant information. It can be a useful technique in addressing a number of issues relating to litigation, including decisions about what repositories of data are appropriate to search in a particular litigation, and determinations of the validity and effectiveness of searches or other data extraction procedures.

Sampling Rate: The frequency at which analog signals are converted to digital values during digitization. The higher the rate, the more accurate the process.

SAN (Storage Area Network): A high-speed subnetwork of shared storage devices. A storage device is a machine that contains nothing but a disc or discs for storing data. A SAN's architecture works in a way that makes all storage devices available to all servers on a LAN or WAN. As more storage devices are added to a SAN, they too will be accessible from any server in the larger network. In this case, the server merely acts as a pathway between the end user and the stored data. Because stored data does not reside directly on any of a network's servers, server power is utilized for business applications, and network capacity is released to the end user. *Also see* Network.

SAS–70: Statement on Auditing Standards (SAS) No. 70, Service Organizations—an auditing standard developed by the American Institute of Certified Public Accountants (AICPA), which includes and examination of an entity's "controls" over information technology and related processes.

SAS–70 Assessment: Application of the standards of SAS–70 to demonstrate adequate controls and safeguards are in place for hosted or processed data.

Scalability: The capacity of a system to expand without requiring major reconfiguration or re-entry of data. For example, multiple servers or additional storage can be easily added.

Scale-to-Gray: An option to display a black and white image file in an enhanced mode, making it easier to view. A scale-to-gray display uses gray shading to fill in gaps or jumps (known as aliasing) that occur when displaying an image file on a computer screen. Also known as grayscale.

Scanner: An input device commonly used to convert paper documents into images. Scanner devices are also available to scan microfilm and microfiche. *See* Flatbed Scanner.

Scanning Software: Software that enables a scanner to deliver industry standard formats for images in a collection. Enables the use of OCR and coding of the images.

Schema: A set of rules or conceptual model for data structure and content, such as a description of the data content and relationships in a database.

Scroll Bar: The bar on the side or bottom of a window that allows the user to scroll up and down through the window's contents. Scroll bars have scroll arrows at both ends, and a scroll box, all of which can be used to scroll around the window.

SCSI (Small Computer System Interface): Pronounced "skuzzy." A common, industry standard, electronic interface (highway) between computers and peripherals, such as hard discs, CD–ROM drives and scanners. SCSI allows for up to 7 devices to be attached in a chain via cables. As of this writing, the current SCSI standard is "SCSI II," also known as "Fast SCSI."

SDLT (Super DLT): A type of backup tape that can hold up to 300 GB or 450 CDs, depending on the data file format. *See* DLT.

Search: *See* Compliance Search, Concept Search, Contextual Search, Boolean Search, Full–Text Search, Fuzzy Search, Index, Keyword Search, Pattern Recognition, Proximity Search, QBIC, Sampling, *and* Search Engine.

Search Engine: A program that enables search for keywords or phrases, such as on web pages throughout the World Wide Web, *e.g.* Google, Lycos, etc.

Sector: A sector is normally the smallest individually addressable unit of information stored on a hard drive platter, and usually holds 512 bytes of information. Sectors are numbered sequentially starting with 1 on each individual track. Thus, Track 0, Sector 1 and Track 5, Sector 1 refer to different sectors on the same hard drive. The first PC Hard discs typically held 17 sectors per track. Today, they can hold thousands of sectors per track.

Serial Line Internet Protocol (SLIP): A connection to the Internet in which the interface software runs in the local computer, rather than the Internet's.

Serial Port: *See* Port.

Serif: The little cross bars or curls at the end of strokes on certain type fonts.

Server: Any central computer on a network that contains ESI or applications shared by multiple users of the network on their client PCs. A computer that provides information to client machines. For example, there are web servers that send out web pages, mail servers that deliver email, list servers that administer mailing lists, FTP servers that hold FTP sites and deliver ESI to requesting users, and name servers that provide information about Internet host names. *See* File Server.

Service-Level Agreement: A service-level agreement is a contract that defines the technical support or business parameters that a service provider or outsourcing firm will provide its clients. The agreement typically spells out measures for performance and consequences for failure.

Session: A lasting connection, usually involving the exchange of many packets between a user or host and a server, typically implemented as a layer in a network protocol, such as telnet or FTP.

SGML/HyTime: A multimedia extension to SGML, sponsored by DoD.

SHA–1: Secure Hash Algorithm, for computing a condensed representation of a message or a data file specified by FIPS PUB 180–1. *See* Hash.

Signature: *See* Certificate.

SIMM (Single, In–Line Memory Module): A mechanical package (with "legs") used to attach memory chips to printed circuit boards.

Simplex: One-sided page(s)

Single Instance Storage: When several files in a computer filesystem contain exactly the same data, single instance storage can replace the references to these identical files by references to a single stored copy of the file. This can potentially save large amounts of disk space in systems with many copies of the same file. Microsoft Exchange can use single instance storage to eliminate redundant copies of a message. The reduction occurs at the Microsoft Exchange Store level, so when mailboxes that receive a given message exist across Exchange Stores, each store will have one copy of the message.

Skewed: Tilted images. *See* De-skewing.

Slack/Slack Space: The unused space on a cluster that exists when the logical file space is less than the physical file space. Also known as file slack. A form of residual data, the amount of on-disc file space from the end of the logical record information to the end of the physical disc record. Slack space can contain information soft-deleted from the record, information from prior records stored at the same physical location as current records, metadata fragments, and other information useful for forensic analysis of computer systems. *See* Cluster.

Smart Card: A credit card size device that contains a microprocessor, memory and a battery.

SMTP (Simple Mail Transfer Protocol): The protocol widely implemented on the Internet for exchanging email messages.

Snapshot: *See* Bit Stream Backup.

Software application: *See* Application and Software.

Software: Any set of coded instructions (programs) stored on computer-readable media that tells a computer what to do. Includes operating systems and software applications.

Speckle: Imperfections in an image as a result of scanning paper documents that do not appear on the original. *See* De-speckling.

Splatter: ESI that should be kept on one disc of a jukebox goes instead to multiple platters.

Spoliation: Spoliation is the destruction of records or properties, such as metadata, that may be relevant to ongoing or anticipated litigation, government investigation or audit. Courts differ in their interpretation of the level of intent required before sanctions may be warranted.

SPP (Standard Parallel Port): *See* Port.

Spyware: A data collection program that secretly gathers information about the user and relays it to advertisers or other interested parties. Adware usually displays banners or unwanted pop-up windows, but often includes spyware as well. *See* Malware.

SQL (Structured Query Language): A standard fourth generation programming language (4GL—a programming language that is closer to natural language and easier to work with than a high-level language). The popular standard for running database searches (queries) and reports.

Stand-Alone Computer: A personal computer that is not connected to any other computer or network, except possibly through a modem.

Standard Generalized Markup Language (SGML): An informal industry standard for open systems document management that specifies the data encoding of a document's format and content. Has been virtually replaced by XML.

Status Bar: A bar at the bottom of a window that is used to indicate the status of a task. For example, when an email message is sent, the status bar will fill with dots indicating that a message is being sent.

Steganography: The hiding of information within a more obvious kind of communication. Although not widely used, digital steganography involves the hiding of data inside a sound or image file. Steganalysis is the process of detecting steganography by looking at variances between bit patterns and unusually large file sizes.

Storage Device: A device capable of storing ESI. The term usually refers to mass storage devices, such as disc and tape drives.

Storage Media: *See* Magnetic or Optical Storage Media.

Streaming Indexing: Real-time or near real-time, indexing of data as it being moved from one storage medium to another.

Structured Data: Data stored in a structured format, such as databases or data sets. *Contrast to* Unstructured Data.

Subjective Coding: The coding of a document using legal interpretation as the data that fills a field, versus objective data that is readily apparent from the face of the document, such as date, type, author, addresses, recipients and names mentioned. Usually performed by paralegals or other trained legal personnel.

Subtractive Colors: Since the colors of objects are white light *minus* the color absorbed by the object, they are called subtractive. This is how ink on paper works. The subtractive colors of process ink are CMYK (Cyan, Magenta, Yellow and Black) and are specifically balanced to match additive colors (RGB).

Suspension Notice, Suspension Order: *See* Legal Hold.

SVGA (Super Video Graphics Adapter): A graphics adapter one that exceeds the minimum VGA standard of 640 by 480 by 16 colors. Can reach 1600 by 1280 by 256 colors.

Swap File: A file used to temporarily store code and data for programs that are currently running. This information is left in the swap file after the programs are terminated, and may be retrieved using forensic techniques. Also referred to as a page file or paging file.

System: A system is: (1) a collection of people, machines, and methods organized to perform specific functions; (2) an integrated whole composed of diverse, interacting, specialized structures and sub-functions; and/or (3) a group of sub-systems united by some interaction or interdependence, performing many duties, but functioning as a single unit.

System Administrator ("sysadmin," or "sysop"): The person in charge of keeping a network working.

System Files: Files allowing computer systems to run; non-user-created files.

System Metadata: *See* File System Metadata.

T1: A high speed, high bandwidth leased line connection to the Internet. T1 connections deliver information at 1.544 megabits per second.

T3: A high speed, high bandwidth leased line connection to the Internet. T3 connections deliver information at 44.746 megabits per second.

Tape Drive: A hardware device used to store or backup ESI on a magnetic tape. Tape drives are usually used to back up large quantities of ESI due to their large capacity and cheap cost relative to other storage options.

Taxonomy: The science of categorization, or classification, of things based on a predetermined system. In reference to Web sites and portals, a site's taxonomy is the way it organizes its ESI into categories and subcategories, sometimes displayed in a site map. Used in information retrieval to find documents that are related to a query by identifying other documents in the same category.

TCP/IP (Transmission Control Protocol/Internet Protocol): The first two networking protocols defined; enable the transfer of data upon which the basic workings of the features of the Internet operate. *See* Port.

Telnet (Telecommunications Network): A protocol for logging onto remote computers from anywhere on the Internet.

Telephony: Converting sounds into electronic signals for transmission.

Templates, Document: Sets of index fields for documents, providing framework for preparation.

Temporary ("Temp") File: files stored on a computer for temporary use only, often created by Internet browsers. These temp files store information about Web sites that a user has visited, and allow for more rapid display of the Web page when the user revisits the site. Forensic techniques can be used to track the history of a computer's Internet usage through the examination of these files. Temp files are also created by common office applications, such as word process or spreadsheet applications.

Terabyte: 1,099,511,627,776 bytes—1024^4 (a trillion bytes). *See* Byte.

Text Mining: The application of data mining (knowledge discovery in databases) to unstructured textual data. Text mining usually involves structuring the input text (often parsing, along with application of some derived linguistic features and removal of others, and ultimate insertion into a database), deriving patterns within the data, and evaluating and interpreting the output, providing such ranking results as relevance, novelty, and interestingness. Also referred to as "Text Data Mining." *See* Data Mining.

TGA: Targa format. This is a "scanned format"–widely used for color-scanned materials (24–bit) as well as by various "paint" and desktop publishing packages.

Thin Client: A networked user computer that acts only as a terminal and stores no applications or user files. May have little or no hard drive space. *See* Client.

Thread: A series of communications, usually on a particular topic. Threads can be a series of bulletin board messages (for example, when someone posts a question and others reply with answers or additional queries on the same topic). A thread can also apply to emails or chats, where multiple conversation threads may exist simultaneously. *See* Email String.

Thumb Drive: *See* Key Drive.

Thumbnail: A miniature representation of a page or item for quick overviews to provide a general idea of the structure, content and appearance of a document. A thumbnail program may be a standalone or part of a desktop publishing or graphics program. Thumbnails provide a convenient way to browse through multiple images before retrieving the one needed. Programs often allow clicking on the thumbnail to retrieve it.

TIFF (Tagged Image File Format): A widely used and supported graphic file formats for storing bit-mapped images, with many different compression formats and resolutions. File name has .TIF extension. Can be black and white, gray-scaled, or color. Images are stored in tagged fields, and programs use the tags to accept or ignore fields, depending on the application. The format originated in the early 1980s.

TIFF Group III (compression): A one-dimensional compression format for storing black and white images that is utilized by many fax machines. *See* TIFF.

TIFF Group IV (compression): A two-dimensional compression format for storing black and white images. Typically compresses at a 20–to–1 ratio for standard business documents. *See* TIFF.

Time Zone Normalization: *See* Nomalization.

Toggle: A switch that is either on or off, and reverses to the opposite when selected.

Tone Arm: A device in a computer that reads to/from a hard drive.

Tool Kit Without An Interesting Name (TWAIN): A universal toolkit with standard hardware/software drivers for multi-media peripheral devices.

Toolbar: The row of graphical or text buttons that perform special functions quickly and easily.

Topology: The geometric arrangement of a computer system. Common topologies include a bus (network topology in which nodes are connected to a single cable with terminators at each end), star (local area network designed in the shape of a star, where all end points are connected to one central switching device, or hub), and ring (network topology in which nodes are connected in a closed loop; no terminators are required because there are no unconnected ends). Star networks are easier to manage than ring topology.

Track: Each of the series of concentric rings contained on a hard drive platter.

TREC (Text Retrieval Conference): An on-going series of workshops co-sponsored by NIST and the U. S. Department of Defense.

Trojan: A program that does something undocumented which the programmer intended, but that the user would not approve of if known to the user. Sometimes referred to as a "Trojan horse." *See* Malware.

True Resolution: The "true" optical resolution of a scanner is the number of pixels per inch (without any software enhancements).

Twiki: A "WikiWiki"—enables simple form-based web applications without programming, and granular access control (thought it can also operate in the classic 'no authentication' mode). Other enhancements include configuration variables, embedded searches, server-side includes, file attachments, and a plug-in API that has spawned over 150 plug-ins to link into databases, create charts, sort tables, write spreadsheets, make drawings, track Extreme Programming projects, and so on.

Typeface: There are over 10,000 typefaces available for computers. The general categories are: oldstyle (faces have slanted serifs, gradual thick to thin strokes and a slanted stress—the "O" appears slanted), modern (faces have thin, horizontal serifs, radical thick to thin strokes and a vertical street—the "O" does not appear to slant); slab serif (faces have thick, horizontal serifs, little or no thick-to-thin in the strokes and a vertical stress—the "O" appears vertical); sans serif (faces have no serifs), script (from elaborate handwriting styles to casual, freeform, unconnected letter forms), decorative unusual fonts (designed to be very different and attention getting).

UDP: A protocol allowing computers to send short messages to one another. *See* Port.

Ultrafiche: Microfiche that can hold 1,000 documents/sheet as opposed to the normal 270.

UMS: Universal messaging system.

Unicode: A 16–bit ISO 10646 character set accommodating many more characters than ASCII for uniform representation of character sets from all languages, thus allowing for easier internationalization. Unicode supports characters 2 bytes wide rather than 1 byte currently supported by most systems. Sometimes referred to as "double byte language." *See* www.unicode.org for more information. *See* Double Byte.

Unallocated Space: The area of computer media, such as a hard drive, that does not contain normally *accessible* data. Unallocated space is usually the result of a file being deleted. When a file is deleted, it is not actually erased, but is simply no longer accessible through normal means. The space that it occupied becomes unallocated space, *i.e.*, space on the drive that can be reused to store new information. Until portions of the unallocated space are used for new data storage, in most instances, the old data remains and can be retrieved using forensic techniques.

Under-inclusive: When referring to data sets returned by some method of query, search, filter or cull, results that are returned incomplete or too narrowly. *See* False Negative.

Unitization—Physical and Logical: The assembly of individually scanned pages into documents. Physical Unitization utilizes actual objects such as staples, paper clips and folders to determine pages that belong together as documents for archival and retrieval purposes. Logical unitization is the process of human review of each individual page in an image collection using logical cues to determine pages that belong together as documents. Such cues can be consecutive page numbering, report titles, similar headers and footers and other logical indicators. This process should also capture document relationships, such as parent and child attachments. *See also* Attachment, Load File and Message Unit.

UNIX: A software operating system designed to be used by many people at the same time (multi-user) capable of performing multiple tasks or operations at the same time (multi-tasking); common operating system for Internet servers.

Unstructured Data: Refers to masses of data which either do not have a data structure or have a data structure not easily readable by machine. Examples of unstructured data may include audio, video and unstructured text such as the body of an email or word processing document. Data with some form of structure may also be referred to as unstructured if the structure is not helpful for the processing task at hand. For example, an HTML webpage is highly structured, but is often oriented towards formatting, rather than performing complex tasks with the content of the page.

Upgrade: New or better version of some hardware, software or application

Upload: To send a file from one computer to another via modem, network, or serial cable. With a modem-based communications link, the process generally involves the requesting computer instructing the remote computer to prepare to receive the file on its disc and wait for the transmission to begin.

URI (Uniform Resource Indicators): *See* URL.

URL (Uniform Resource Locators): The addressing system used in the World Wide Web and other Internet resources. The URL contains information about the method of access, the server to be accessed and the path of any file to be accessed. Although there are many different formats, a URL might look like this: http://thesedona conference.org/publications_html. *See* Address.

User-Added Metadata: Data, possibly work product, created by a user while copying, reviewing or writing with a file, including annotations and subjective coding information.

UTC: *See* Coordinated Universal Time.

Validate: In the context of this document, to confirm or ensure well grounded logic, and true and accurate determinations.

VAR/VAD/VASD: Value–Added Reseller/Value–Added Dealer/Value–Added Specialty Distributor. Companies or people who sell computer hardware or software *and* "add-value" in the process. Usually, the value added is specific technical or marketing knowledge and/or experience.

VDT (Video Display Terminal): generic name for all display terminals.

Vector: Representation of graphic images by mathematical formulas. For instance, a circle is defined by a specific position and radius.

Vendor-Added Metadata: Data created and maintained by the electronic discovery vendor as a result of processing the document. While some vendor-added metadata has direct value to customers, much of it is used for process reporting, chain of custody and data accountability. Contrast with User–Added Metadata. *See also* Metadata.

Verbatim Coding: Extracting data from documents in a collection in a way that matches exactly as the information appears in the documents.

Version, Record Version: A particular form or variation of an earlier or original record. For electronic records the variations may include changes to file format, metadata or content.

Vertical De–Duplication: A process through which duplicate documents/data are eliminated within a single custodial or production data set. *See also* Content Comparison, File level Binary Comparison Horizontal De-duplication, Metadata Comparison, and Near De–Duplication.

VGA (Video Graphics Adapter): A PC industry standard, first introduced by IBM in 1987, for color video displays. The *minimum* dot (pixel) display is 640 by 480 by 16 colors. Then "Super VGA" was introduced at 800 x 600 x 16, then 256 colors. VGA can extend to 1024 by 768 by 256 colors. Replaces EGA, an earlier standard and the even older CGA. Newer standard displays can range up to 1600 by 1280.

Video Electronics Standards Association (VESA): Concentrates on computer video standards.

Video Scanner Interface: A type of device used to connect scanners with computers. Scanners with this interface require a scanner control board designed by Kofax, Xionics or Dunord.

Virus: A self-replicating program that spreads by inserting copies of itself into other executable code or documents. A program into which a virus has inserted itself is said to be infected, and the infected file (or executable code that is not part of a file) is a host. Viruses are a kind of malware (malicious software). Viruses can be intentionally destructive, for example by destroying ESI, but many viruses are merely annoying. Some viruses have a delayed payload, sometimes referred to a bomb. The primary downside of viruses is uncontrolled self-reproduction, which desecrates or engulfs computer resources.

Vital Record: A record that is essential to the organization's operation or to the reestablishment of the organization after a disaster.

VoIP (Voice over Internet Protocol): Telephonic capability across an IP connection; increasingly used in place of standard telephone systems.

Volume: A volume is a specific amount of storage space on computer storage media such as hard drives, floppy discs, CD–ROM discs, etc. In some instances, computer media may contain more than one volume, while in others, one volume may be contained on more than one disc.

Volume Boot Sector/Record: When a partition is formatted to create a volume, a volume boot sector is created to store information about the volume. One volume contains the operating system and its volume boot sector contains code used to load the operating system when the computer is booted up. *See* Partition.

VPN (Virtual Private Network): A secure network that is constructed by using public wires to connect nodes. For example, there are a number of systems that enable creation of networks using the Internet as the medium for transporting data. These systems use encryption and other security mechanisms to ensure that only authorized users can access the network and that the data cannot be intercepted.

WAV: File extension name for Windows sound files. ".WAV" files can reach 5 Megabytes for one minute of audio.

Web Site: A collection of Uniform Resource Indicators (URIs), including Uniform Resource Locators (URLs), in the control of one administrative entity. May include different types of URIs (*e.g.*, FTP, telnet, or Internet sites). *See* URI and URL.

Wiki: A collaborative website that allows visitors to add, remove, and edit content.

Wildcard Operator: A character used in keyword searching that assumes the value of any alphanumeric character and permits more options, such as alternative spellings, to be identified quickly.

Workflow: The automation of a business process, in whole or part, during which ESI or tasks are passed from one participant to another for action according to a set of procedural rules.

Workflow, Ad Hoc: A simple manual process by which documents can be moved around a multi-user review system on an "as-needed" basis.

Workflow, Rule–Based: A programmed series of automated steps that route documents to various users on a multi-user review system.

Workgroup: A group of computer users connected to share individual talents and resources as well as computer hardware and software–often to accomplish a team goal.

Worm: A self-replicating computer program, sending copies of itself, possibly without any user intervention. *See* Malware.

WORM Discs: Write Once Read Many Discs. A popular archival storage media during the 1980s. Acknowledged as the first optical discs, they are primarily used to store archives of data that cannot be altered. WORM discs are created by standalone PCs and cannot be used on the network, unlike CD–ROM discs.

WWW (World Wide Web): All of the computers on the Internet which use HTML-capable software (Netscape, Explorer, etc.) to exchange data. Data exchange on the WWW is characterized by easy-to-use graphical interfaces, hypertext links, images, and sound. Today the WWW has become synonymous with the Internet, although technically it is really just one component.

WYSIWYG: "What You See Is What You Get"–Display and software technology that shows on the computer screen exactly what will print. Often requires a large, high-density monitor.

X.25: A Standard Protocol for Data Communications.

XML: *See* Extensible Markup Language.

Yottabyte: 1,208,925,819,614,629,174,706,176 bytes—1024^8 (a septillion bytes). *See* Byte.

Zettabyte: 1,180,591,620,717,411,303,424 bytes—1024^7 (a sextillion bytes). *See* Byte.

Zip Drive: A floppy disc drive that can usually hold as much as 750 megabytes or more. When first available, was often used for backing up hard discs.

ZIP: A common file compression format that allows quick and easy storage for transport.

Zone OCR: An add-on feature of the imaging software that populates document templates by reading certain regions or zones of a document, and then placing the text into a document index.

†